revising, **5c**
mm	Misplaced modifier: **13a–13d**
ms	Incorrect manuscript form: *preparing a paper,* **B1–B5**
mix	Mixed construction: **15b**
num	Incorrect use of numbers: **35a–35e**
p	Punctuation: *typing punctuation,* **B6**
par/¶	New paragraph
no ¶	No paragraph
¶ coh	Paragraph not coherent: **4c**
¶ dev	Paragraph not developed: **4d;** *patterns of development,* **4e**
¶ un	Paragraph not unified: **4b**
plan	Planning: **1a–1b**
purp	Purpose not clear: *determining purpose,* **1a.1;** *selecting diction,* **16a.2**
ref	Incorrect pronoun reference: **21e–21f**
rep	Needless repetition: *eliminating,* **9b;** *for emphasis,* **3d**
rev	Revise: *revision strategies,* **3c;** *revising drafts,* **3d**
run-on	Run-on sentence: **12f–12i** (See also *fused sentence.*)
shap	Shaping: **2a–2d**
shft	Inappropriate shift: **15a**
sl	Inappropriate use of slang: *fresh language,* **16c**
sp	Error in spelling: **19a–19c;** *commonly misspelled words,* **19c.1**
thesis	Thesis unclear or unstated: **2b;** *thesis and support,* **3a**
var	Lack of variety: **10a–10f**
w	Wordiness: *eliminating,* **9a**
//	Faulty parallelism; *using parallelism,* **14a;** *revising,* **14b**
,	Comma: **26a–26f;** *editing misuse/ overuse,* **26g**
;	Semicolon: **27a–27d,** *editing misuse/ overuse,* **27e–27f**
./?/!	Period: **25a;** Question mark: **25b;** Exclamation point: **25c**
'/" "	Apostrophe: **28a–28d;** Quotation marks: **29a–29e;** *with other punctuation marks,* **29f**
:	Colon: **30a–30b;** *editing misuse/ overuse,* **30c**
–	Dash: **30d–30f;** *editing misuse/ overuse,* **30g**
( )/[ ]	Parentheses: **30h–30i;** Brackets: **30j–30k**
/	Slash: **30l–30n**
. . .	Ellipsis mark: **30o–30q**

The Holt Handbook

Laurie G. Kirszner
Philadelphia College of Pharmacy and Science

Stephen R. Mandell
Drexel University

Holt, Rinehart and Winston
New York Chicago San Francisco Philadelphia
Montreal Toronto London Sydney Tokyo Mexico
City Rio de Janeiro Madrid

Publisher Susan Katz
Acquisitions Editor Charlyce Jones Owen
Development Editor Cheryl Kupper
Senior Project Editor Françoise Bartlett
Senior Production Manager Nancy Myers
Art Director Gloria Gentile
Design Caliber Design Planning
Cover Design Gloria Gentile

Library of Congress Cataloging-in-Publication Data

Kirszner, Laurie G.
  The Holt handbook.

  Includes index.
  1. English language—Rhetoric. 2. English language—Grammar—
1950–   I. Mandell, Stephen R.
II. Title.
PE1408.K675 1986   808'.042   85-17537

ISBN 0-03-062762-1

Holt, Rinehart and Winston
The Dryden Press
Saunders College Publishing

Acknowledgments follow the Glossary of Grammatical Terms.

Preface
to the Instructor

In planning the *The Holt Handbook*, our aim was to create a true writer's handbook, one that would serve not only as a text and a reference guide but also as a writer's companion that would be useful in the many writing situations in which students must function. In preparing this book we concentrated on making it inviting, accessible, useful, and interesting to both students and teachers. Throughout, we have relied extensively on much of the exciting research that is taking place in composition today, being especially careful to apply the results of this research in a practical and straightforward manner. We believe that its organization, its process approach, its emphasis on revision, and its focus on student writing make *The Holt Handbook* truly a writing-centered text. In addition, its descriptive approach to grammar and its nonthreatening tone make it particularly appealing to students.

The Holt Handbook is divided into eight sections and two appendices. Section I, "Composing an Essay," discusses the writing process, moving from planning, shaping, and writing and revising an essay to writing paragraphs and constructing a logical argument. Section II, "Composing Sentences," concentrates on crafting sentences, paying particular attention to the rhetorical choices that writers can make as they build and combine sentences. Section III, "Solving Common Sentence Problems," focuses on correcting the most common sentence problems students encounter when they write. Throughout this section, the emphasis is on revision and experimentation, not on error. Section IV, "Using Words Effectively," examines word use and contains detailed chapters on using the dictionary, building a vocabulary, and improving spelling. Sections V and VI together comprise an editor's handbook. Section V, "Understanding Grammar," is a survey of grammar, and Section VI, "Understanding Punctuation and Mechanics," is a guide to punctuation and mechanics. Section VII, "Writing with Sources," is a comprehensive four-chapter unit that places emphasis on nonlibrary research (observation, interviews, field trips, and other nonprint sources) as well as print sources. After surveying how professionals conduct research, this section devotes separate chapters to working with source material, documentation (MLA, APA, number-reference, and endnote formats), and writing a research paper. The process approach follows a student's research through planning, shaping, and writing and revising and culminates with an annotated student paper that illustrates the current MLA documentation. Section VIII, "Writing Special Assignments," includes detailed chapters on writing essay examinations, writing about literature, and writing business letters and memos. Following these sections are informative and timely appendices on composing on a word processor and manuscript preparation; the book ends with glossaries of usage and grammatical terms.

In addition to treating grammar, mechanics, and style, *The Holt Handbook* gives detailed coverage to many subjects usually treated fully only in a rhetoric—for instance, writing short essays, research papers, examinations, and critical papers about literature. Unlike other handbooks, *The Holt Handbook* follows the development of a single student essay—from choice of topic to completion of a final draft—through three chapters. The four-chapter section devoted to research, paying particular attention to nonlibrary research, also deserves special attention. Throughout *The Holt Handbook* we include abundant practice exercises, including sentence combining and imitation exercises. Most exercises and examples represent a wide variety of disciplines and subject matter. At the end of many chapters is the "Student Writer at Work" feature, a complete student essay that students are asked to revise. These essays provide a context in which students can identify and correct key problems associated with chapters or chapter clusters.

The Holt Handbook approaches writing as a recursive process, giving students the opportunity to practice planning, shaping, and writing and revising. This approach, consistent with current research, encourages students to become involved with every stage of the process and to view revision as a natural and ongoing part of their writing. The style, grammar, and mechanics and punctuation chapters present clear, concise definitions of key concepts followed by examples and exercises that gradually increase in difficulty and sophistication. Whenever possible, sentence-level skills are taught in groups of related sentences that focus on a single high-interest topic instead of in isolated sentences. This pedagogically sound methodology allows students to learn incrementally, practicing each skill as it is introduced. In this way students learn to recognize and revise sentence-level problems within longer units of discourse, duplicating the way that they must actually interact with their own writing.

The Holt Handbook is a classroom text, a reference guide, and above all, a writing companion that students can turn to for advice and guidance as they write in college and beyond. Our goal throughout has been to translate the best of current research in composition theory into the most useful terms. In writing this book, we have taken pains to avoid lists of rules or pages of do's and don't's. Instead, we have chosen to explain the principles that writers must understand to make informed choices about grammar, usage, rhetoric, and style. The result is a book that students and instructors can use with ease, confidence, and, we hope, pleasure.

A comprehensive ancillary package is available: an *Instructor's Handbook* on teaching composition, with answers to the exercises in the text; *The Holt Workbook;* an *Instructor's Edition* of the workbook; *Supplementary Exercises; Diagnostic Tests;* and *The Holt Writing Tutor,* an interactive software program for the Apple and IBM computers. For complimentary copies of these teaching and learning aids, write to: English Editor, Holt, Rinehart and Winston, 383 Madison Avenue, New York, NY 10017.

We wish to thank the following colleagues for their comments and sound advice: Virginia Allen, Iowa State University; Stanley Archer, Texas A & M University; Rance G. Baker, Alamo Community College; John G. Bayer, St. Louis Community College/Meramec; Margaret A. Bretschneider, Lakeland Community College; Alma Bryant, University of South Florida; Patricia Carter, George Washington University; Peggy Cole, Arapahoe Community College; Sarah H. Collins, Rochester Institute of Technology; Charles Dodson, University of North Carolina/Wilmington; Margaret Gage, Northern Illinois University; George Haich, Georgia State University; Robert E. Haines, Hillsborough Community College; Ruth Hamilton, Northern Illinois University; John Harwood, Penn State University; Keith N. Hull, University of Wyoming/Laramie; Zena Jacobs, Polytechnic Institute of New York; D. G. Kehl, Arizona State University; Philip Keith, St. Cloud State University; Edward Kline, University of Notre Dame; Susan Landstrom, University of North Carolina/Chapel Hill; Marie Logye, Rutgers University; Helen Marlborough, DePaul University; Nancy Martinez, University of New Mexico/Valencia; Richard N. Ramsey, Indiana University/Purdue University; Emily Seelbinder, Wake Forest University; Charles Staats, Broward Community College/North; Frank Steele, Western Kentucky University; Josephine K. Tarvers, Rutgers University; Daryl Troyer, El Paso Community College; Ben Vasta, Camden County Community College; and Joyce Williams, Jefferson State Junior College.

We owe a special debt to the late Arthur Liebman, Professor of Sociology at SUNY/Binghamton, who was so generous in sharing with us his knowledge of research in the social sciences. He will be missed.

We would also like to thank the following people at Holt: Nedah Abbott, who offered us the chance to write this book; Susan Katz, who supported the project each step of the way; Fran Bartlett, whose care and concern are reflected on every page; Nancy Myers and Gloria Gentile, who contributed so much to the book's design and production; and Cheryl Kupper, a first-class editor. Most of all we are indebted to Charlyce Jones Owen, friend and editor, who is, quite simply, the best there is.

Finally, we would like to thank our families—Mark, Adam, and Rebecca Kirszner and Demi, David, and Sarah Mandell—who gave us no editorial assistance, did not type the manuscript, and offered no helpful suggestions, but whose love and understanding helped make it all possible.

Philadelphia
September 1985

L.G.K.
S.R.M.

Preface
to the Student

The Holt Handbook is a comprehensive guide that you should consult whenever you have a question about grammar, usage, style, or rhetoric. We suggest that you read Section I of the book to become acquainted with the stages of the writing process and the techniques that good writers use when they write. Only after you are familiar with the choices that you have as a writer will you be able to place information about grammar, usage, sentence structure, and the like into perspective. As you use *The Holt Handbook*, you will notice that whenever possible we give advice, not rules. We believe that student writers do best when they have the freedom to make informed choices about their writing and are able to take into consideration the demands of varying audiences, purposes, and writing situations.

You can find material in *The Holt Handbook* in a number of ways. Individual chapters offer in-depth discussions of a wide variety of topics, and, outside of the chapter clusters on the writing process and on research, you can read them without referring to other chapters. Cross references in the text point you to definitions and discussions of unfamiliar terms. As you write, however, you will often need a quick answer to questions that arise. *The Holt Handbook* has a number of features that will help you locate specific information quickly and efficiently.

The **inside front cover** contains a list of Correction Symbols that your instructor may use to help you edit and revise your papers. These symbols consist of an abbreviation (*agr* for agreement, for example) and a combination of numbers and letters (such as 23a) that refer you to a specific section of the text (section twenty-three, subsection a). You can locate the section of the book that you need by looking at the red tabs in the margin of each page.

The **detailed table of contents** on the inside back cover highlights key elements of the table of contents on pages ix to xix and gives an overview of the entire book. Use these guides when you are looking for a specific subject or a discussion that you know is part of a specific chapter. On page viii is an alphabetical list of topics for quick reference and review.

The **index** presents a detailed alphabetical listing of all subjects covered in the book. Because it lists all major topics, subtopics, and cross references, the index offers you the most comprehensive way of researching a topic.

The **glossary of usage** gives you an alphabetical listing of commonly confused words (*continually/continuously*, for example) and other problems in usage (*data/datum*, for instance). Although this section does not eliminate the need to consult a dictionary, it enables you to solve many problems that regularly occur in your writing.

The **glossary of grammatical terms** lists definitions of the grammatical and rhetorical terms that appear throughout *The Holt Handbook*. When you encounter a term with which you are unfamiliar, consult this glossary for a definition. Here you will find the definition of a term as well as a cross reference to the section of the book that contains a more detailed discussion of it.

When you use *The Holt Handbook* keep in mind that at best it is a guide, not a final authority. To determine what is appropriate for a specific writing situation you must ultimately rely on your own sense of the language and your own assessment of your purpose and audience. Used with this principle in mind, *The Holt Handbook* should serve you well for the writing that you will do both in and out of college.

Philadelphia   L.G.K.
September 1985   S.R.M.

For Quick Reference and Review

Contents

SECTION II   Composing Sentences   129

SECTION III   Solving Common Sentence Problems   211

SECTION IV   Using Words Effectively   279

SECTION V   Understanding Grammar   361

SECTION VI   Understanding Punctuation and Mechanics   429

SECTION VII   Writing with Sources   541

SECTION VIII   Writing Special Assignments   681

Composing an Essay

Planning an Essay

Writing is a constant process of decision-making, of selecting, deleting, and rearranging material. This process can be said to have three stages: *planning an essay, shaping your material,* and *writing and revising.*

When planning an essay, you consider your audience, your purpose, and the possibilities suggested by the assignment. When shaping your material, you decide how to organize your essay. When writing and revising, you write a first draft; then you "re-see" what you have written and, reworking content, organization, and style, take your essay through one or more additional drafts.

But these neatly defined stages really do not communicate either the complexity or the flexibility of the writing process. Although we will examine these stages separately, they actually overlap: at any point in the process you may engage in any one of them. As you seek ideas you begin to shape your material; as you shape your material you begin to write; as you write a first draft you change your organization; as you revise you come up with more material.

During your college years, and in the years that follow, you will develop your own version of the writing process and use it whenever you write.

1a Thinking About Writing

Planning your essay—thinking about what you want to say and how you want to say it—begins well before you actually put pen to paper. In fact, this planning is as important a part of the writing process as writing itself. Two factors—your purpose and your audience—influence your planning, and both factors continue to guide you as you shape, write, and revise your material. As you work through the process, you develop a clearer idea of what material to include, how to organize it, and how to express it.

(1) Determining your purpose

We write for a number of purposes. One purpose in composing a particular piece of writing might be simply to *express feelings or attitudes,* as when writing a diary, an autobiography, a personal letter, even a humor column. Another might be to *persuade.* In this case you would try to convince your audience to agree with certain ideas and, often, to take some action, as when writing advertisements, proposals, editorials, and sermons. Another purpose might be to *convey information,* as when writing reports, news articles, textbooks, and encyclopedia entries. Still another could be to *give pleasure,* as we do when writing short stories, plays, novels, poems, and so on. The aim might also be to evaluate, discover, analyze, debunk, criticize, satirize, speculate, warn, reassure, or amuse, among many other specific approaches or combinations of approaches.

The material you choose and the way you arrange and express it are determined by your primary purpose. For instance, a paper on summer camps could *inform*—explain how camping has changed in the last twenty years, for example. Such a paper would present pertinent facts and statistics straightforwardly. An advertisement designed to recruit potential campers would *persuade* by enumerating the benefits of the camping experience. Such an advertisement would stress positive details—the opportunity to meet new friends, for example—and play down the possibilities of homesickness and rainy weather. A letter from a camper to a friend might try to *amuse,* describing all the things that would not appear in the promotional literature—mosquitoes, poison ivy, institutional food, shaving cream fights, and so on. To *evaluate* the camping experience a writer would aim for a balanced discussion of such things as recreational programs and sports facilities. In each case, your purpose determines what material you choose and how you present it.

College writing may call for any of a wide variety of approaches, but your primary purpose is usually to convey information: to show your audience that you understand your subject, can make valid points about it, and may sometimes even ask provocative questions.

► EXERCISE 1

plan
1a

What is the primary purpose of each of these paragraphs? To express feelings? To convey information? To persuade? To give pleasure? Is there more than one purpose? More specifically, what did each writer intend?

1. Incidentally, early computer-science history is also a key to current computer slang. One day the ENIAC failed without warning, and it took two hours to find the problem. As it turned out, nothing was really wrong with the computer, but a moth had been caught and killed in one of the relays. That dead moth was the first "bug" ever found in a computer, and the word passed into technical jargon as programmers started speaking of "debugging" their systems. (Jacques Valee, *Popular Computing*)

2. Like a basketball team that wins by dominating the boards, John McEnroe controlled the net yesterday and ended a seven-match, 28-month drought against Ivan Lendl to capture the U.S. Pro Indoor tennis championship for the second straight year. (Steve Goldstein, *Philadelphia Inquirer*)

3. The Jaguar XJ-S is a car built in the belief that performance need not suffer at the expense of luxury. Beneath its sweeping exterior is an awesome 12 cylinder fuel injected aluminum engine, making the XJ-S the most powerful and sophisticated motorcar Jaguar has ever built. (Advertisement, *Money*)

4. The dawn is dirty, yellowish, menacing. In the coconut-palm plantations, just now barely, grayly visible, the heavy fronds are too still, and the ocean, glimpsed at intervals, is flat and black, dangerous-looking. (Alice Adams, *New Yorker*)

5. The average American consumes a little more than 150 pounds of food additives a year. About 98 percent of this is sugars and salt (the dangers of which we have often heard about), plus other substances like citric acid from oranges and lemons, baking soda, vegetable colors, mustard and pepper. The other 2 percent are some 2800 other substances *intentionally* added to what we eat, and as many as 10,000 more than that *unintentionally* find their way into food in the course of growing, processing, packaging and storing. (Virginia DeMoss, *Runner's World*)

► EXERCISE 2

This brief article presents information in an entertaining manner. How would you change it to convince readers that the federal government is needlessly extravagant in a time of high unemployment and that it should focus on more critical issues? Would you omit any details? Would you rearrange any information? Would you add anything? Explain.

Squirrel Census

The Government put out a call for volunteers last November to help with its newest census: a study of squirrels in Lafayette Park, across the street from the White House.

The National Park Service wanted the volunteers to count the squirrels, observe their habits and take photos.

"They had lots of volunteers and finally settled on 35," reports Duncan Morrow, a spokesman for the park agency. The group has "wrapped up the training phase," he says, and for the next few months will be in the "serious data collection phase."

"They have nice little forms to fill out," Mr. Morrow notes, including one that "calls for them to pick an individual squirrel and follow it for five minutes, recording exactly what it's doing each minute." Another duty is to keep track of squirrel traffic into and out of the 8.2 acre park. It goes without saying that a computer will be used to help analyze the data.

Why is the department doing it?

"What they're focusing on is why there is such a concentration of squirrels there," Mr. Morrow says, adding that there never has been any "really good study" on how city squirrels live.

Some residents suspect the squirrels have become hardcore welfare cases, subsidized not only by kind taxpayers but even the White House.

"There are a number of White House staff people," Mr. Morrow notes, "who show up pretty regularly with stuff they feed the squirrels." *(New York Times)*

(2)   Identifying your audience

Writing is often such a solitary activity that you can forget about your audience. But except for diaries, journals, letters written to let off steam (but not to mail), and drafts you will discard, everything you write addresses an audience—a particular set of readers.

When writing, you will be addressing many different kinds of audiences. As a citizen, consumer, and member of a community or civic, political, or religious group, you may respond to society's most pressing issues by writing letters to a newspaper editor; public official; representative of a special interest group, business, or corporation; or other recipient you do not know well or at all. In your personal life you write notes and letters to friends and family and perhaps diary or journal entries to your-self. As an employee, you may write letters, memos, and reports to your superiors, to workers you supervise, or to workers on your level; you may also be called on to address customers or critics, board members or stockholders, funding agencies or the general public. As a student, you write essays, reports, and other papers addressed to one or more instructors and sometimes to other students or outside evaluators.

plan
1a

As you work through the writing process, you shape your paper increasingly in terms of what you believe your audience needs and expects. Your decisions about your readers' interests, educational level, biases, and expectations determine not only what information you include but also what emphasis, arrange-ment of material, and style or tone you choose.

A student very often writes for an audience of one: the in-structor who assigns the paper. But instructors differ regarding interests and expertise, concerns and standards. How, then, do you identify your audience? You generalize. When addressing an instructor, you address a representative of a class of readers who apply accepted standards of academic writing.

What are these standards? Basically, instructors expect cor-rect information, acceptable grammar and spelling, logical orga-nization, and some stylistic fluency. Instructors further ask that you define your terms and support your generalizations with specifics. In general, they want to know what you know and whether you can express what you know clearly, precisely, and accurately. Your instructors assign written work to see how well you can think, so the way you organize and present your ideas is as important as the ideas themselves.

Of course, as already stated, each of your instructors is also a unique person with special knowledge and interests. Even though instructors generally have similar overall requirements concerning the quality of your work, many will look for a particu-lar emphasis or approach. Your assessment of these special re-quirements also influences what and how you write. You can assume that all your instructors are specialists in their fields, so you can safely omit long overviews and basic definitions unless you are specifically asked to include them. But outside their areas of expertise, most instructors are simply general readers. If you think you may know more about a subject than your instruc-tor does, be sure to provide ample background and definitions, examples, and analogies to make your ideas clear. Considering these factors is vital to helping you make the best possible writing choices.

What course you are writing for will also influence your choices. Let's say you have decided to write about the underground mine fires that for years have been burning out of control near your hometown of Centralia, Pennsylvania. For different courses you would focus on different aspects of the topic. For chemistry, you might consider the origins of the fires; for sociology, you could examine what kind of people have left the area and what kind plan to remain; for economics, you could consider how local business and real estate have been affected; for psychology, you could center on the emotional impact of the spreading fires on the town's children; for political science, you could recommend what role the federal government should take in relocating people or putting out the fires. In each case your subject would be the same, but you would choose which details and points to stress according to your audience's interest in and knowledge of the subject.

EXERCISE 3

How would you develop each topic below for the different audiences listed? For each topic list three points you would include and specify which you would emphasize.

1. The advantages of vegetable gardens. Audience: the rural poor, vegetarians, retired people, nutrition majors.
2. The dangers of teenage alcoholism. Audience: junior high school students, parents, law-enforcement personnel, tavern owners.
3. Why it makes sense to develop a fitness regimen. Audience: office workers, cardiac patients, the overweight, professional football players.
4. The value of soap operas. Audience: television programmers, sociologists, actors, advertisers.
5. The pros and cons of adult orthodontia. Audience: dentists, insurance companies, adolescents, movie stars.

EXERCISE 4

Different audiences call for differences in the content and emphasis of your writing.

1. Think for a moment about the best—or worst—teacher you ever had. What made this teacher so perfect or so dreadful?

   a. Explore this question in a one-page diary entry written for your eyes only.
   b. In a few paragraphs, tell your composition instructor about this teacher's strengths or weaknesses.
   c. Reread the two pieces of writing. List the most obvious differences in content and emphasis between the two.
2. Be prepared to discuss how you might revise the material you have presented when writing
   a. A letter to the school board, which is considering whether or not to renew the teacher's contract
   b. A short paper for a course in educational methods
   c. Notes for a speech at the teacher's retirement dinner

(3) Setting your tone

Your purpose and your audience dictate the attitude you adopt as you write. This attitude, or mood—serious or frivolous, respectful or condescending, intimate or detached—sets the tone of your piece. This tone usually emerges during the planning stage and should remain consistent with your purpose and your audience as you shape, write, and revise your material. It gives your readers clues about your feelings toward your material, and this in turn helps them understand what you have to say.

How you feel about your readers—sympathetic or superior, concerned or indifferent, friendly or critical—is also revealed by your tone. For instance, if you identify with your readers or feel close to them, you use a personal and conversational tone. When, however, you address a generalized, distant reader indirectly or anonymously, you use a more formal, impersonal tone.

When your audience is an instructor and your purpose is to inform, you should strive for an objective tone, neither too personal and informal nor too elevated and formal (unless you are directed otherwise). This paragraph from a student paper on the resistance to various drugs of a specific group of microorganisms achieves an appropriate tone for its audience (students in a medical technology lab) and purpose (to present information).

One of the major characteristics of streptococci is that they are gram-positive. This means that after a series of dyes and rinses they take on a violet color. (Gram-negative organisms take on a red color.) Streptococci are also non-spore forming and non-motile. Most strains produce a protective shield called a capsule. They use organic substances instead of oxygen for their metabolism. This process is called fermentation.

This student conveys her facts objectively. She expresses no personal feelings about her subject, makes no judgments, and carefully maintains her distance from her audience.

An English composition assignment asking students to write a short essay expressing their feelings about the worst job they had ever had calls for an entirely different tone. Here is how a student chose to write about his work during cucumber season.

> Every day I followed the same boring, monotonous routine. After clocking in like a good little laborer, I proceeded over to a grey file cabinet, forced open the half-caved-in doors, and removed a staple gun, various packs of size cards, and a blue ballpoint pen. Now here comes the excitement! Each farmer had a specific number assigned to his name. As his cucumbers were being sorted into their particular size, they were loaded into two-hundred-pound bins which I had to label with a stapled size card with the farmer's number on it. I had to complete a specific size card for every bin containing that size cucumber. Doesn't it sound wonderful? Any second grader could have handled it. And all the time I worked the machinery moaned and rattled and the odor of cucumbers filled the air.

This student's sarcastic tone effectively conveys his attitude toward his job, and his use of the first person encourages audience identification. Ironic comments ("good little laborer," "Now here comes the excitement") further involve the reader.

In a letter applying for another job, however, both his distance from his audience and his purpose (to impress readers with his qualifications) demanded a much more objective and formal tone.

> My primary duty at Germaine Produce was to label cucumbers as they were sorted into bins. I was responsible for making sure each 200-pound bin bore the name of the farmer who had grown those cucumbers and also for keeping track of the cucumbers' sizes. Accuracy was extremely important in this task.

▶
EXERCISE 5

Use the list that follows to write two paragraphs: one informing curious readers of the nature of the Domestic Abuse Project's services and clientele and one convincing a skeptical audience that the project deserves continued funding.

Before you write, consider how these different purposes dictate different organizations. You may add brief remarks as you write, but in each paragraph be sure to use *all* the information provided below and *only* this information. Your choice of language (*not* your choice of content) will help you achieve the desired effect.

The Domestic Abuse Project
Agency's purpose: to aid the victims of mental and physical abuse
Located in small room in Chester Police Department
Offers support groups and advice hotlines
Started when police began receiving excessive number of reports of abuse
Most clients from low-income families
Staff of two professionals and eight volunteers
Funded by State Civil Service Welfare Program
Future plans include new programs (especially counseling) and hiring of more workers

▶
EXERCISE 6

Take as your general subject a book that you liked or disliked very much. How would each writing situation listed below affect the content, style, organization, tone, and emphasis of an essay on this book? Jot down your responses.

A journal entry recording your informal impressions of the book
An examination question that asks you to summarize the book
A book report for a composition class in which you evaluate both the book's strengths and its weaknesses
An editorial in which you try to convince your readers that, regardless of the book's style or content, it should not be banned from the local public library
A letter to your school newspaper in which you try to persuade other students that the book is not worth reading

1b Getting Started

Before you begin any writing task, it is extremely important to understand the exact requirements of your assignment and to keep them in mind as you write and revise. What is the word, paragraph, or page limit? How much time do you have to complete your assignment? Is the assignment to be done in class or at home? Can you make notes or do research? If the assignment requires a specific format, do you know what its conventions are? Don't make any guesses—and don't assume anything. Ask questions and make sure you understand the answers.

Sometimes an assignment allows you to choose your own topic. If so, consider your audience and purpose carefully in light of what you know about the assignment—length, format, and so on. Then choose a topic you know something about or want to learn about. Perhaps you have seen a movie or television special or had a provocative conversation about an interesting subject. You may know where to find helpful material on this subject. If you do, this is a good beginning. If not, your instructor can help you develop an unfocused idea into a workable topic.

(1) Choosing a topic

Though you are sometimes able to choose your topic, your instructor's assignment generally limits your options. Sometimes it asks a specific question for you to answer: "How did the boundaries of Europe change following World War I?" "What are the advantages and disadvantages of the Federal Guaranteed Student Loan Program?" More often, it specifies a length, format, and particular subject area or list of subjects to choose from.

> Write a short essay about a place that you know well. (Specifies subject area)
>
> Write a two-page critical analysis of a film. (Specifies subject area)
>
> Write a three-to-five-page essay on some aspect of either *The Scarlet Letter, The House of the Seven Gables,* or *The Blithedale Romance.* (Gives list of specific subjects to choose from)
>
> Write an essay explaining the significance of *one* of these court decisions: *Marbury* v. *Madison, Baker* v. *Carr, Brown* v. *Board of Education, Roe* v. *Wade.* (Gives list of specific subjects to choose from)

Even here you cannot start to write immediately. You must narrow down the assignment to a workable topic that suits your purpose and audience. What examples will you choose? What aspects will you include? What will you emphasize? How much detail should you go into? Given the assigned time and length, how will you limit your topic?

For example, look at these typical broad assignments:

Course	Assignment
Biology	Examine some aspect of AIDS (Acquired Immune Deficiency Syndrome).

Sociology	Consider the plight of the homeless in Chicago.
Freshman Composition	Discuss an activity that monopolizes your time.
Psychology	Write a three-to-five-page paper on treating depression.

How could you hope to cover all AIDS research, all the problems of the homeless, all time-consuming activities, or all treatments for depression in one short paper? Clearly you must make some choices. You must choose an area that fits within the limits of the assignment while meeting the demands of your audience and suiting your purpose. Ask yourself some questions: Are you writing solely for an audience familiar with the subject or for those who may know less? Are you writing to set forth factual information or to convince your audience to support your views?

Here are some narrower topics that could emerge from the assignments listed above.

Subject	*Topic*
AIDS	What effects has the discovery of AIDS had on metropolitan-area blood banks?
The homeless	The Salvation Army Shelter's role in providing for the area's homeless
Video games	Star Raiders vs. Centipede: too close to call
Treating depression	How dogs are trained to work with severely depressed patients

When Lisa Owen, a freshman in a composition class, was assigned an essay, she had some decisions to make. The assignment was "Write a 500-word essay about a place that you know well." The class had one week to complete the essay, and the instructor did not want students to do library research. The instructor explained that he would be encouraging peer criticism, so students knew that their classmates would read their papers. The purpose of the essay was to help readers see the place described and to understand its importance to the writer.

Lisa began to think about the subject right away but initially rejected each place she considered. Her ideas about her room at home seemed too personal, even sentimental. She considered writing about her dorm room, but she saw at once that it was still unfamiliar to her. She could not remember much about the house she had lived in as a child. The ice-skating rink she used to go to while in junior high would limit her essay to a relatively short (and distant) period in her life. What she needed, she realized, was a place that had been important to her for a long time, for many different reasons, and that still remained important. Only one place really qualified: The West End Mall.

In one way or another the Mall had been part of her life ever since she could remember. Even now it was important— partly because of memories and partly because she still went there from time to time. The Mall's size and diverse population provided a lot of material. Finally, Lisa had read an article on the general subject of shopping malls. She knew that research was not expected, but she thought that the few details she could recall from this article might add a nice bit of background.

Whatever your assignment, review your options just as Lisa did. Consider your assignment, your audience, and your purpose; also consider the things you know best and like best. Do not write on your dorm room because it is the first thing you think of or on the treasures of the Metropolitan Museum of Art because you think it sounds important. But if your dorm room represents your first taste of independence and your essay is about making a new start, it could be an ideal topic. If you know the collections at the Metropolitan well and plan to study art, you may legitimately use this knowledge in a paper about how your career goals developed. Still, do not automatically settle for a routine glance at the Mississippi River when you can describe Catfish Creek vividly.

You must always consider both what you *can* write about and what you *want* to write about. You may be very much interested in the Yukon but have nothing interesting to say about it;

you may know more than you care to admit about Staten Island but not have the faintest desire to write about it. The trick is to fill both requirements.

plan
1b

▶
EXERCISE 7

Which of these topics are suitable for an essay of about 500 words, and which need to be narrowed further? Explain.

1. How college students budget their time
2. Cars of the future
3. English: the ideal preprofessional major
4. How to make pizza
5. New trends in advertising
6. Cigarette advertising: 1945–1985
7. Three advertisements that insult senior citizens
8. Why grades should be abolished
9. Anorexia: Is there a cure?
10. A comparison of John D. Rockefeller and Andrew Carnegie

▶
EXERCISE 8

Narrow each of these broad subject areas to three topics suitable for short essays.

1. Gun control
2. Television sitcoms
3. Saturday night
4. The Cowboy
5. Pornography
6. Grandparents
7. Athletic scholarships
8. Little League baseball
9. The Miss America pageant
10. Health foods

▶
EXERCISE 9

Read the following excerpt from Ron Kovic's autobiographical *Born on the Fourth of July.* Then list ten possible essay topics about your own childhood suggested by Kovic's memories of his. Each topic should be suitable for a 500-word essay directed to your composition instructor. Your purpose is to give your audience a sense of what some aspect of your childhood was like. Finally, choose the one topic you feel best qualified to write about and explain the reasons for your choice.

> When we weren't down at the field or watching the Yankees on TV, we were playing whiffle ball and climbing trees checking out birds' nests, going down to Fly Beach in Mrs. Zimmer's old car that honked the horn every time it turned the corner, diving un-

derwater with our masks, kicking with our rubber frog's feet, then running in and out of our sprinklers when we got home, waiting for our turn in the shower. And during the summer nights we were all over the neighborhood, from Bobby's house to Kenny's, throwing gliders, doing handstands and backflips off fences, riding to the woods at the end of the block on our bikes, making rafts, building tree forts, jumping across the streams with tree branches, walking and balancing along the back fence like Houdini, hopping along the slate path all around the back yard seeing how far we could go on one foot.

And I ran wherever I went. Down to school, to the candy store, to the deli, buying baseball cards and Bazooka bubblegum that had the little fortunes at the bottom of the cartoons.

When the Fourth of July came, there were fireworks going off all over the neighborhood. It was the most exciting time of year for me next to Christmas. Being born on the exact same day as my country I thought was really great. I was so proud. And every Fourth of July, I had a birthday party and all my friends would come over with birthday presents and we'd put on silly hats and blow these horns my Dad brought home from the A&P. We'd eat lots of ice cream and watermelon and I'd open up all the presents and blow out the candles on the big red, white, and blue birthday cake and then we'd all sing "Happy Birthday" and "I'm a Yankee Doodle Dandy." At night everyone would pile into Bobby's mother's old car and we'd go down to the drive-in, where we'd watch the fireworks display. Before the movie started, we'd all get out and sit up on the roof of the car with our blankets wrapped around us watching the rockets and Roman candles going up and exploding into fountains of rainbow colors, and later after Mrs. Zimmer dropped me off, I'd lie on my bed feeling a little sad that it all had to end so soon. As I closed my eyes I could still hear strings of firecrackers and cherry bombs going off all over the neighborhood. . . .

The whole block grew up watching television. There was Howdy Doody and Rootie Kazootie, Cisco Kid and Gabby Hayes, Roy Rogers and Dale Evans. The Lone Ranger was on Channel 7. We watched cartoons for hours on Saturdays—Beanie and Cecil, Crusader Rabbit, Woody Woodpecker—and a show with puppets called Kukla, Fran, and Ollie. I sat on the rug in the living room watching Captain Video take off in his space-ship and saw thousands of savages killed by Ramar of the Jungle.

I remember Elvis Presley on the Ed Sullivan Show and my sister Sue going crazy in the living room jumping up and down. He kept twanging this big guitar and wiggling his hips, but for some reason they were mostly showing just the top of him. My mother was sitting on the couch with her hands folded in her lap like she was praying, and my dad was in the other room talking about how the Church had advised us all that Sunday that watching Elvis Presley could lead to sin.

(2) Finding something to say

Once you have a topic, you can assemble ideas for your paper. Ideas seldom spring magically from your pen, so you will usually have to rely on more systematic ways of finding them. One or several of the following strategies should help you in your college writing; be ready to modify your strategy, however, as the writing situation demands.

Brainstorming

One of the most useful ways to accumulate ideas is **brainstorming**. This strategy jogs your memory, encouraging you to recall pieces of information you have stored away and to see connections among the pieces.

You brainstorm by listing all the points you can think of that seem pertinent to your topic. Keeping your topic in mind, write down all the ideas that surface—words, phrases, occasionally complete sentences—as quickly as you can, without pausing to consider their relevance or their importance (you do this later). At this stage, crossing out ideas or rearranging them only slows you down.

For her essay on the West End Mall Lisa Owen made the brainstorming list illustrated in Figure 1.

Looking at the list, Lisa saw that she had plenty of material to work with. She already saw some links between items on her list ("things to do," for instance) and had discovered a few interesting ideas: that the mall is both like and unlike home, both appealingly safe and unpleasantly artificial, and representative of both freedom—even irresponsibility—and security. Not every item would appear in her essay, but the list did uncover a lot of ideas, and it suggested some promising directions to explore.

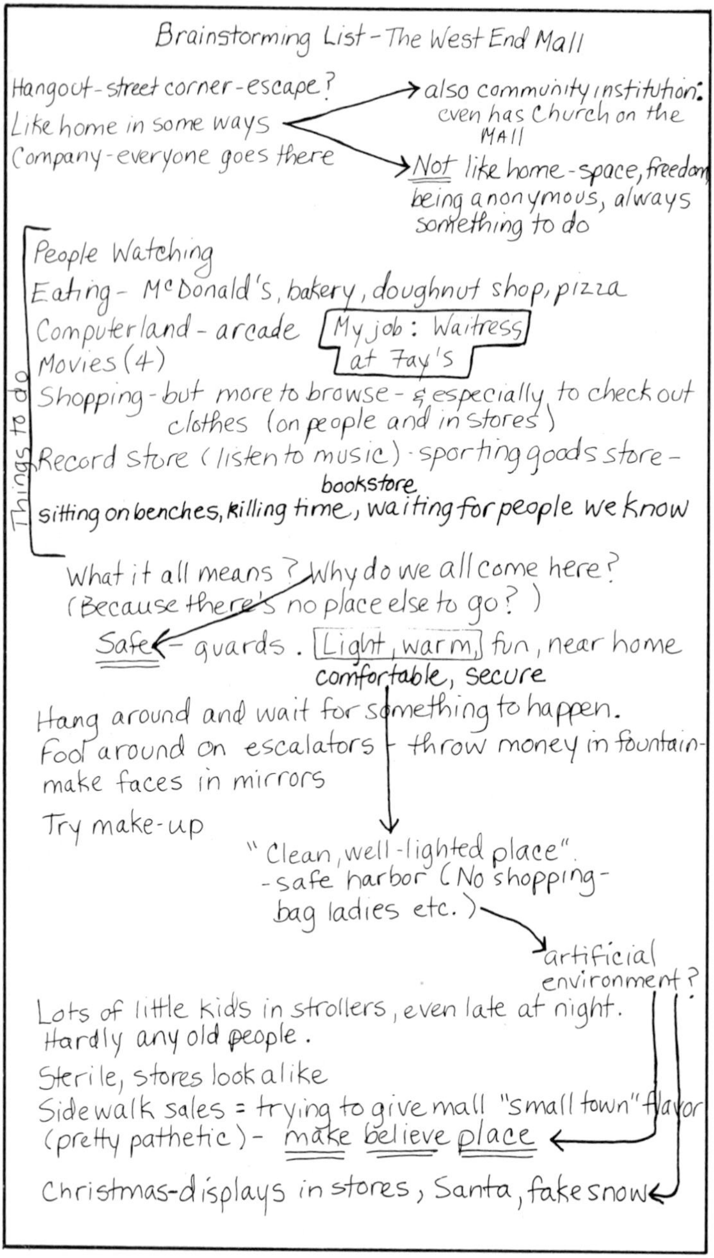

**plan
1b**

Brainstorming List – The West End Mall

Hangout – street corner – escape?
Like home in some ways
Company – everyone goes there

→ also community institution:
even has Church on the MALL

→ Not like home – space, freedom, being anonymous, always something to do

Things to do

People Watching
Eating – McDonald's, bakery, doughnut shop, pizza
Computerland – arcade | My job: Waitress at Fay's |
Movies (4)
Shopping – but more to browse – & especially to check out clothes (on people and in stores)
Record store (listen to music) – sporting goods store – bookstore
sitting on benches, killing time, waiting for people we know

What it all means? Why do we all come here?
(Because there's no place else to go?)
Safe ← guards. | Light, warm, | fun, near home
comfortable, secure

Hang around and wait for something to happen.
Fool around on escalators + throw money in fountain –
make faces in mirrors

Try make-up

"Clean, well-lighted place".
– safe harbor (No shopping-
bag ladies etc.)
artificial environment?

Lots of little kids in strollers, even late at night.
Hardly any old people.
Sterile, stores look alike
Sidewalk sales = trying to give mall "small town" flavor
(pretty pathetic) – make believe place ←

Christmas – displays in stores, Santa, fake snow ←

FIGURE 1

▶
EXERCISE 10

Make a brainstorming list on the topic "The Trouble with Television."

▶
EXERCISE 11

Brainstorm on the topic you selected in Exercise 9.

Freewriting

Freewriting can be an especially helpful strategy for dealing with writer's block (see 3b). When you freewrite, you fix your mind on your topic and write nonstop, as quickly as you can, for a certain period of time—say, five minutes—without worrying about punctuation, spelling, or grammar, or about whether your mind is wandering. The momentum generated by this strategy encourages your mind to make connections and frees ideas that you may not be aware you have. If you run out of things to say about your topic, write about *anything*—the weather, the spot on the wall—until you pick up your subject again. When your time is up, look over what you have written and see if you have anything you can use. Sometimes you have nothing at all, but sometimes you will see new details, a new approach to your topic, or even a new topic.

▶
EXERCISE 12

Freewrite for five minutes on one of these topics.

> Ice cream
> Drunk drivers
> Superheroes
> October
> My dream house
> If I won the lottery

▶
EXERCISE 13

Freewrite for five minutes on the topic you chose in Exercise 9.

Keeping a Journal

Professional writers sometimes keep **journals,** writing in them regularly whether or not they have a specific project in mind. Such a record of your own thoughts and reactions is a storehouse of information when you run short of ideas. Journals, unlike diaries, do more than record personal experiences and reactions. In a journal you explore ideas as well as events and emotions, thinking on paper and drawing conclusions. You might, for example, explore the evolution of your position on a political issue or solve on paper a problem you find difficult to work through in your mind. You might also record quotations that mean something special to you or summarize important news events, films, or conversations. A good journal is a scrapbook of ideas that you can leaf through in search of new material and new ways of looking at old material.

When Lisa Owen began planning an essay on the West End Mall, one of the first things she did was look at her journal. Here she found one brief entry she thought she might be able to use: a fragment describing her reactions to a robbery attempt at Fay's Fine Foods, where she had worked as a waitress.

It's been a week, and I still can't settle down. My mind tells me that I couldn't have done anything, that just keeping quiet was right, but I still feel terrified, and also guilty and angry. I'm furious at myself because I can't remember what they looked like, what they wore—I was useless when the detectives came around. I always thought a big experience like this would be great material, but I just can't call anything up to write about. All the clichés are real—it all happened so fast, my mind went blank, time stood still.

▶
EXERCISE 14

Write a journal entry on *one* of these subjects. You are your own audience; your purpose is to explore ideas.

A party (or job interview) I should not have gone to
The most frightening experience I ever had
A time my friends (or family) and I disagreed

Bracket any details you might use for an English composition essay on the same topic and cross out details you would not use. Your audience for this essay is your instructor; your purpose here is to convey your emotional reactions to the experience.

(3) Reading and observing

Keep your eyes and ears open from the time you receive your assignment until you turn it in. As you read textbooks in various subjects or look through magazines and newspapers, be on the lookout for new ideas that pertain to your topic. Also make a point of talking with friends or family about your topic. Focused observation and discussion can be surprisingly useful.

For her shopping-mall paper, Lisa Owen had a week to talk with the friends she used to meet at the Mall and to talk with her parents about where people shopped before the Mall was built. She could even have met with her boss and other Mall employees or visited the Mall and observed the goings-on. But since her instructor had discouraged research and since her time was short, Lisa decided against such strategies. Instead, she spent her time talking informally with her friends at school, using their experiences at malls to help her to better understand her own.

If your instructor encourages you to do formal research, you can use material from nonprint sources such as films and television programs as well as material from books and articles. Interviews, telephone calls, letters, and questionnaires can be as fruitful as library research. But remember to document ideas that are not your own. (See Section VII for detailed information on doing research.)

▶
EXERCISE 15

For an essay entitled "Why Computers Are So Popular," list the sources you encounter in one day—people, books, magazines, observations, and so on—that could provide you with relevant information.

(4) Asking questions

Another way to uncover information about your topic is to ask questions. Your answers to these questions will enable you to explore your topic in an orderly and systematic fashion.

Journalistic Questions

One strategy involves asking six simple questions: Who? What? Why? Where? When? How? Journalists often use these questions to assure themselves that they have touched on all angles of a story. You can use them to see whether you have considered all sides of your topic too.

Lisa Owen asked these questions, with the following results.

Who goes to the Mall? Everybody—lots of teenagers hanging out, serious shoppers, children with parents, people going to work.

Who was responsible for building the Mall? Any state or federal funding? *Who* doesn't go to the Mall? Very old and very poor people.

What is the Mall? Circus? Town square? Park bench? Nightclub? Home? Just a mall? Land of make-believe?

Why do people go there? To shop? To keep moving? To keep busy? To have something to do? Because everyone else comes? To pretend? *Why* was the Mall located here? Lots of people live nearby.

Where do most people go? To department stores, restaurants, specialty stores, movies, other activities, nowhere in particular.

When do different people come to the Mall? Little kids and mothers in morning, few people in late afternoon, couples in evening, whole families on Saturdays and Sundays, high school and college kids on Friday and Saturday nights. *When* is the Mall busiest? Weekends—and between Thanksgiving and New Year's Day.

How do people feel about the Mall? Is it just a convenience or a special place? *How* did it get to be so popular? Word of mouth? Supply and demand? *How* do people move around? Aimlessly—stop-and-go traffic. Not orderly.

As you can see, Lisa's questions quickly suggested both possible answers and additional questions, which in turn suggested material for her essay.

In-Depth Questions

If you have time, and if you still need more material, you can explore your topic in greater detail by asking questions that suggest familiar ways of organizing material. These questions not only give you a great deal of information about your topic but also help you shape your ideas into paragraphs and whole essays. (As you review these questions, keep in mind that not every question will apply to every topic.)

What happened? When did it happen? Where did it happen?	Suggests <u>narration</u> EXAMPLES: account of your first day of school a summary of Emily Dickinson's life
What does it look like? What are its characteristics?	Suggests <u>description</u> EXAMPLES: of the Louvre of the electron microscope
What are some typical cases or examples of it?	Suggests <u>exemplification</u> EXAMPLES: three infant day-care settings four popular fad diets
How did it happen? What makes it work? How is it made?	Suggests <u>process</u> EXAMPLES: how to apply for financial aid how a bill becomes a law
Why did it happen? What caused it? What does it cause? What are its effects?	Suggests <u>cause and effect</u> EXAMPLES: events leading to the Korean War the results of Prohibition the impact of a new math curriculum on slow learners
How is it like other things? How is it different from other things?	Suggests <u>comparison and contrast</u> EXAMPLES: compare the music of the 1950's and the 1960's compare two paintings
What are its parts or types? Can they be separated or grouped? Do they fall into a logical order? Can they be categorized?	Suggests <u>division and classification</u> EXAMPLES: components of the catalytic converter kinds of occupational therapy kinds of dietary supplements

| What is it?
How does it resemble other members of its class? How does it differ from other members of its class? | Suggests <u>definition</u>
EXAMPLES: What is Marxism?
What is photosynthesis?
What is schizophrenia? |

When you are almost ready to sort through the material you have collected, the answers to these questions can suggest ways of shaping your material. If the questions that suggest *process* seem most productive, consider organizing your essay as a step-by-step explanation of a procedure; if the questions that suggest *cause and effect* yield the most material, perhaps you should devote your essay to tracing causes or predicting effects (see 4e).

Lisa knew that her audience—her instructor and fellow students—would know nothing about the Mall and that one of her purposes was to help them visualize it; she also had to explain why she considered it so special. After she had assembled most of her ideas, she reviewed these questions and saw many possibilities for shaping her essay. She could *narrate* the events of a typical day or evening at the Mall. She could *describe* a particular store and the people who go there. She could give *examples* of the Mall's most interesting features or explain the *process* by which it was built. She could analyze the *causes* of its popularity or its *effects* on local businesses. She could *compare* and *contrast* suburban with downtown shopping or *classify* the Mall's services. She could *define* the Mall, trying to pin down its unique role in the community. Or she could combine these patterns.

Lisa felt that she would best be able to *describe* and *define* the Mall. She really wanted to pin down what it actually was. This decision jarred loose some additional ideas. When she asked the questions relevant to *description* and *definition,* she added her responses to her brainstorming list.

What does it look like? What are its characteristics?

| *Suggests description* | Glittery—distracts from outside problems. Falseness is its main characteristic—maybe appeals to people because they can dream and pretend. |

<u>What is it?</u> <u>How does it resemble other members of its class?</u> <u>How does</u> <u>it differ from other members of its class?</u>

Suggests *definition*	Mall is American phenomenon—symbol of society that likes to spend money.

Mall is a conveyor belt, a people mover. Crowds hurry and sweep you along before you can think— Momentum.

Pressure—to keep moving, keep spending, keep looking for people, even to keep eating.

Now Lisa felt ready to put her notes into a tentative order and start to shape her material.

▶
EXERCISE 16

Choose one of the following subjects and narrow it to a topic suitable for a short in-class essay. (Your audience is your instructor; your purpose is to communicate factual information.) Then review the questions in 1b.4, using those that seem most helpful.

1. Hockey
2. Science fiction
3. Child care centers
4. Paper dolls
5. Crime

6. Silent films
7. Fast food
8. Kites
9. The funnies
10. The American West

▶
EXERCISE 17

Using a journal entry, reading and observation, and question strategies as necessary to supplement the work you did in Exercises 11 and 13, generate enough information for a short essay on your topic from Exercise 9.

2

Shaping Your Material

2a Grouping Ideas

When you begin to see the direction your ideas are taking, it is time to sort your notes, to sift through your ideas and choose those you can use to build the most effective essay. One way to do this is to make a **topic tree** that will help you to see which ideas are general or specific, alike or different. This device enables you to group ideas logically, develop an overview of your topic, and see relationships among ideas.

Begin by reviewing all your notes and writing down the three or four basic ideas that seem most pertinent to your essay. Write these concepts across the top of a piece of paper. Then go through your notes again, select points that are related to these concepts, and write each point under the relevant concept, thereby filling in your tree. Continue going through your notes and adding related points. You will find as you move down the page that you are dealing with increasingly specific information.

Of course you will add to, delete from, rearrange, and rewrite the points on your topic tree as you review your brainstorming list and other notes. You will have skipped over points that seem irrelevant. When you finish, you will see how your ideas are related and which are subordinate and which dominant.

Lisa Owen's topic tree (see Figure 2) contained four main categories that she could treat individually in an essay. She considered eliminating one category, "employment," because it did not seem consistent with her purpose, which was to explain the true nature of the Mall. But her job had been a big part of her life at the Mall, so she decided to keep this category for the time being.

Now Lisa felt well on her way toward writing an effective

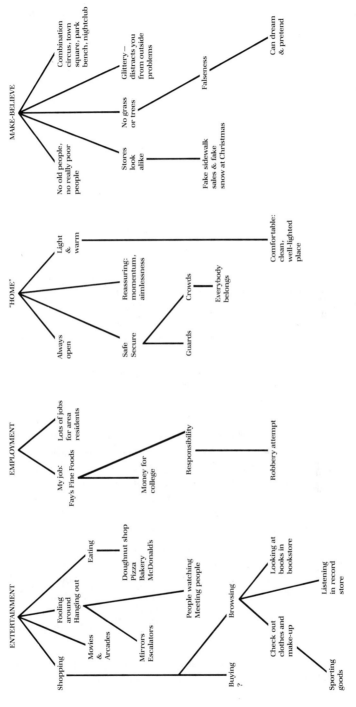

shap 2a

FIGURE 2

essay. But before she could begin drafting her paper, she
needed to bring her ideas into sharper focus: to find a thesis
or central idea for her essay.

▶

EXERCISE 1

Construct a topic tree from the work you did for Exercises 11, 13, and 17
in Chapter 1.

2b Developing a Tentative Thesis

A **thesis** is a clear, succinct statement of the main idea of an
essay. Almost every piece of college writing includes such a statement, and you should include yours in your first paragraph to
alert your readers to the essay's direction.

The thesis you develop as you plan your essay is only tentative. It gives you sufficient focus to guide you through your first
draft, but you should expect to modify it in subsequent drafts. As
you write and revise, you constantly change and sharpen your
thesis to make it increasingly consistent with your purpose, audience, and assignment.

Your thesis should be specific: it should accurately portray
what your essay covers and how it is organized. Your thesis
should be so clearly worded that your readers immediately understand the scope of your essay. The statement "Computers
offer people many advantages" does not give your essay much
focus. What advantages? For whom? You cannot enumerate
every point of the essay in your thesis, but you can set forth a
specific view. Furthermore, your thesis should not make promises that your essay does not fulfill. If your paper covers *only* the
benefits of computer education for young children, do not promise to discuss the benefits for adults—or anything else.

A good thesis is more than a statement of fact, a title, or an
announcement of your subject. A thesis takes a stand: it reflects
your attitude toward your material. These are *not* thesis statements.

More and more children are being introduced to computers.
(statement of fact)

Children and Computers (title)

In this paper I will consider the impact of computers on young children. (announcement of your paper's subject)

This statement, however, *is* a possible thesis.

Access to microcomputers gives children more than game-playing opportunities: computers can improve hand-eye coordination and problem-solving skills.

This statement not only states a position but also shows how you could organize your essay. First you could *briefly* discuss computer games, and then you could talk about the importance of computers in improving hand–eye coordination and problem-solving skills.

Thus, a specifically worded thesis takes a firm stand, communicates your purpose, and gives readers a guide to follow.

As Lisa mulled over her topic tree and notes and analyzed her thoughts concerning the Mall, several thesis statements came to mind. She discarded "The West End Mall is a place that is extremely important to many people" as far too general. It said nothing about why the Mall was so important. Next she tried "The West End Mall is important because of its many sources of entertainment and employment and because it represents escape to so many people." This statement said nothing about the relative importance of the three reasons it offered, and Lisa certainly did not consider them equally important. Besides, to communicate the true nature of the Mall as she saw it, the thesis would need to suggest a definition.

Lisa found herself struggling to develop the idea that the Mall was not what most people consider it to be. She tried "Most people probably think the West End Mall is a place to have fun or to work, but it is really a place where people can find escape." This statement got the emphasis right and presented a definition, but it still was not specific enough. Lisa's notes covered other aspects of the Mall: its glittery surface, its warm atmosphere, and its falseness. Lisa kept trying to convey these ideas in one clearly worded sentence.

The sentence "People come to the West End Mall because they think it can be whatever they want it to be" seemed too vague and abstract to serve as a guide. It did, however, make Lisa's point that the Mall represented something different to her from what it meant to most people. She tried once more and came up with this tentative thesis:

People think the West End Mall is just a place to shop or have fun or work, but it is really a unique combination of home and make-believe.

This was specific enough to give Lisa some direction and general enough to give her readers an overview. And it presented a definition, which was consistent with her purpose. Now she could get ready to write and revise her essay.

▶
EXERCISE 2

Analyze the following statements or topics, and determine why none of them qualifies as a good thesis. Be prepared to explain your criticisms and to discuss how each could be improved.

1. In the pages that follow, I will examine the use of pesticides in the Great Plains states.
2. The development of the nuclear freeze movement
3. How to apply for a civil service position
4. ROTC: Pro and Con
5. Medicare benefits many senior citizens, but it has some drawbacks.
6. The feminist position on pornography
7. Unemployment is rising steadily in the auto industry.
8. Welfare reform is sorely needed.
9. Benjamin Franklin was a statesman and scientist.
10. Most of my friends like running or skiing, but I prefer tennis.

▶
EXERCISE 3

Narrow the following topics to thesis statements.

1. An embarrassing moment
2. The appeal of Elvis Presley
3. How to use the library
4. Is corporal punishment ever justified?
5. The role of women in the military
6. Why the drinking age should be lowered/raised
7. Does vitamin C affect the common cold?
8. The rise of Japanese industry
9. The perfect vacation spot
10. Private vs. public education

▶
EXERCISE 4

Review the topic tree you made in Exercise 1. Use it to help formulate a thesis for an essay on the topic you chose in Exercise 9 in Chapter 1.

2c Preparing a Working Plan

A **working plan** is a blueprint for an essay, an informal outline that gives you more detailed, specific guidance than a thesis statement. You need not always prepare such a plan; a short essay on a topic with which you are familiar may require nothing beyond a thesis and a mental outline of supporting points. More often, however, you need additional help. A working plan arranges your main ideas and supporting points in an informal but orderly way to guide you as you write.

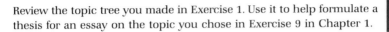

Reviewing her notes carefully, Lisa selected material she could use and prepared this working plan.

Working Plan: What the West End Mall Is Really Like

Thesis Statement: People think the West End Mall is just a place to shop or have fun or work, but it is really a unique combination of home and make-believe

Entertainment
    Shopping
        Buying?
        Browsing:
            Checking out clothes, make-up, etc.
            Sporting goods
            Listening to records
            Books
    Movies
    Arcades
    Food
        McDonald's
        Pizza
        Bakery, Doughnut Shop

Fooling Around/Hanging Out
   Mirrors, Escalators
   People Watching
     Meeting new people
     People we know
Employment
   Jobs for area residents
   Fay's
     Money for college
     Teaches responsibility
       (mention robbery attempt?)
Home
   Safe—guards, crowds
   Everybody comes here; everybody belongs—reassuring
    [Aimless wandering—but carried by momentum]
   Light, warm
   <u>Always</u> <u>open</u> when you need it
Make-believe
   No old or poor people
   Stores look alike
    "Sidewalk sales" ⎫
    Xmas snow   ⎬ <u>fake</u>
   No grass or trees
   [Circus, town square, park bench, nightclub—parts of all of
   these but really none of them]

Lisa referred to this working plan as she wrote her first draft.

▶
EXERCISE 5

The following are additional details about the West End Mall. Read the points carefully and mark those that do *not* fit logically into Lisa Owen's working plan. Be ready to explain in class where you think each of the useful points could be added.

   —Greeting card store
   —Hiring Christmas help
   —Celebrity appearances at the Mall
   —Fire last year damaged three stores
   —Nearest competing shopping mall 15 miles away
   —Two recent muggings in parking lot
   —Mall offers courses taught by local community college faculty
   —Ample parking

—Church on the Mall
—Health spa
—The local unemployment rate
—Pet store; cute puppies
—Running into a former teacher
—Free blood pressure screening available

2d Preparing an Outline

Many writers find that they do not need to prepare a formal outline for a short essay, but others prefer to have one and some instructors require outlines regardless of the essay's length.

A **formal outline** is more polished than a working plan. It is more strictly parallel and more precise; more attention is paid to form; and the points are presented in the exact order in which they will appear in the paper. A working plan is not inaccurate or illogical, but it is informal; neither the order of ideas nor their exact relationship is firmly fixed. Because your paper's logic depends on it, a formal outline requires more thought and care than does a working plan.

A formal outline indicates two things: the order in which you will present your ideas and the relationship of main ideas to supporting details. The outline format uses indentation and a specified system of symbols: Roman numerals, Arabic numerals, and upper-case and lower-case letters—to indicate subordination. Roman numerals indicate major divisions and are flush with the left margin of the page. Upper-case letters precede divisions of secondary importance and are indented slightly. Arabic numerals, which signal major supporting examples, are indented further. Lower-case letters announce specific supporting details and are indented still further. For example:

I. First major division of your paper
   A. First secondary division
   B. Next secondary division
      1. First supporting example
      2. Next supporting example
         a. First specific detail
         b. Second specific detail
II. Second major division

This prescribed structure tells you at a glance what ideas are of equal importance, for they occupy the same level. All ideas on a given level have the same level of specificity—a heading preceded by an Arabic numeral, for example, is more specific than a heading preceded by an upper-case letter. Thus, a formal outline helps you to see that you have covered all relevant topics in an effective order, with the correct emphasis, within a logical system of subordination.

You should express all topics on the same level of the outline in *grammatically parallel terms*. For instance, on each level use all single words (all nouns, all verbs), all noun phrases, all gerund phrases, or all prepositional phrases—or, in the case of a sentence outline, use complete sentences throughout. Parallel phrasing ensures that ideas of equal weight are presented similarly and gives balance and logic to your outline—and to your essay.

Keep one final rule in mind. No heading can contain only one subheading. If heading A has a subheading 1, then it must have a subheading 2; if heading 1 has a subheading a, it must also have a subheading b. You cannot subdivide a heading into one part. If you find a heading with a single subdivision, either delete the subdivision (perhaps revising the larger category to include it) or add another one.

A formal outline of Lisa's paper would look like this.

I. Introduction
   Thesis: People think the West End Mall is just a place to
           shop or have fun or work, but it is really a
           unique combination of home and make-believe.

II. Entertainment
   A. Shopping
      1. Buying
      2. Browsing
         a. clothing
         b. make-up
         c. sporting goods
         d. records
         e. books

B. Going to movies
C. Going to arcades
D. Eating
    1. McDonald's
    2. Fiesta Pizza
    3. Bakery
    4. Doughnut Shop
E. Fooling around
    1. Mirrors
    2. Escalators
F. People watching
    1. New people
    2. People we know

III. Employment
    A. Jobs for area residents
    B. My job
        1. Money for college
        2. Responsibility
        3. Robbery attempt

IV. Home
    A. Safety
        1. Guards
        2. Crowds
    B. Sense of belonging
    C. Light and warmth

V. Make-believe
    A. No old or poor people
    B. No individuality
    C. Sense of falseness
        1. "Sidewalk Sales"
        2. Christmas "snow"
        3. No trees or grass

VI. Conclusion

For examples of detailed topic and sentence outlines, see 39e and 39h.

EXERCISE 6

Review your notes and prepare a working plan for a paper on the thesis you worked up in Exercise 4. Then prepare a formal outline.

3

Writing and Revising

3a Using Thesis and Support

With a tentative thesis and an appropriate outline as a guide you are ready to write a first (or rough) draft. Although you will arrive at new insights about your material as you write, this draft will have a focus that freewriting does not have.

Most of your college papers require you to support a thesis with specific examples or evidence. As you write your rough draft, then, you should be familiar with one of the most common methods of presenting information: **thesis and support.** Knowing this method helps you as you begin to write and simplifies later revision.

A thesis-and-support paper begins with an **introduction.** One- or two-page essays usually have single introductory paragraphs. Your audience needs to know the direction of your essay at the outset, so include your thesis in this introductory paragraph.

In the **body** of a thesis-and-support paper you present evidence—facts, reasons, arguments, or examples—that support your thesis. By providing clear answers to the questions you anticipate from your readers, you convince them that what you are saying is valid. Usually you summarize the unifying idea of each paragraph in the body of your paper in a topic sentence. (For a full treatment of topic sentences, see 4b).

In the **conclusion** of your thesis-and-support paper, you review your major points, sum up your evidence, and restate your thesis.

When you write a thesis-and-support paper, regard your readers as skeptical. Put yourself in their place and ask "Why should I accept this statement?" "What evidence supports this point?" Remember, your examples are your evidence. A sufficient number and variety of good examples make your case. Empty generalizations and unsupported opinions detract from it.

Thesis and support is simply a general type of essay structure. How you present your support—how you arrange the reasons, examples, and arguments offered in your body paragraphs—can vary. (See 4e for a discussion of narration, description, exemplification, process, cause and effect, comparison and contrast, division and classification, and definition.) Your thesis helps you visualize the appropriate way to structure your essay. It suggests how your points are related, in what order your major points should be introduced, and where you should place your emphasis.

The following thesis statement conveys a good deal of information.

> Widely ridiculed as escape reading, romance novels are becoming increasingly important as a proving-ground for many never-before-published writers and, most significantly, as a showcase for strong heroines.

First, this thesis tells you that this essay focuses primarily on what the writer considers to be the two major new roles of the romance novel: providing markets for new writers and (most importantly) presenting strong female characters. To a lesser extent, the role of the romance as escapist fiction may also be treated. The thesis statement even suggests a possible order for the various ideas discussed.

Paragraph 1 Introduction: Romance formulas; general settings, plots and characters; thesis

Paragraph 2 Romance novels as escapist reading

Paragraph 3 Romance novels as an outlet for unpublished writers

Paragraph 4 Romance novels as a showcase for strong heroines

Paragraph 5 Conclusion: Review of major points; significance of recent developments; restatement of thesis

In an essay written according to this plan, the body paragraphs would provide the evidence necessary to support the thesis.

In the following example the thesis suggests not only the order of the ideas but also a specific way of arranging them.

> Romance novels may be extremely popular, but science fiction contributes more to the art of popular fiction.

The phrasing of the thesis clearly indicates that the essay *compares and contrasts* two kinds of popular fiction and concludes something about their relative merits.

What did Lisa Owen's tentative thesis predict about the structure of her essay? Let us look at it again.

People think the West End Mall is just a place to shop or have
fun or work, but it is really a unique combination of home and
make-believe.

This tentative thesis gave Lisa a good sense of direction and a
possible order in which to present her ideas: she could proceed from the least important characteristics of the Mall to
the most important. That is, she could first treat shopping,
entertainment, and work briefly; then she could move on to
consider the concepts of "home" and "make-believe" in more
depth.

Usually, however, you cannot plot the structure of your
whole essay using your thesis alone, particularly when you
work with a complex topic or one that forces you to juggle
many different ideas. In such cases, you have to do more
planning before you begin your first draft, just as Lisa did.

3b Writing a Rough Draft

The purpose of a rough draft is to get your thoughts down on
paper so you can react to them. Often you draft only the body
paragraphs (the section outlined in your working plan). The introduction and conclusion may be weak or nonexistent. This is
not a problem. In fact, students who struggle to write the perfect
opening and closing paragraphs are usually wasting their time:
the effort slows them down, and these paragraphs are likely to
change substantially in subsequent drafts.

A rough draft is often messy and full of false starts. Experienced writers know that they will generally rewrite a paper several times. They expect to cross out words and sentences and to
have choppy, disconnected paragraphs. They realize that they
will correct these problems when they revise.

The following suggestions should make writing rough
drafts easier.

Prepare your work area. Once you begin to write, you

should not have to stop because you need a sharp pencil, important notes, or anything else. Unscheduled breaks can ruin your concentration.

Get your ideas down on paper as quickly as you can. Don't worry about sentence structure, spelling, or finding exactly the right word. Concentrate on getting down your points. Writing quickly helps you uncover new ideas or new connections between ideas.

Take regular breaks as you write. Write one section of your essay at a time. When you have completed a section, take a break. Your unconscious mind may continue to focus on your assignment while you do other things. When you return to your essay, writing may very well be easier.

Fight writer's block. Writer's block—being unable to start (or continue) writing—is generally caused by fear that you will not write well or that you have nothing to say. If you really do not feel ready to write, spend a little time doing something else— listening to music, jogging, baking cookies. A short break may give your mind a chance to relax, which in turn may inspire new ideas. But remember: the least productive response to writer's block is procrastination—doing anything and everything except writing.

When you get stuck, try freewriting. Your rough draft provides raw material for future drafts, and new ideas are always welcome. At this stage you are talking to *yourself,* so you can put down thoughts freely without worrying about what the reader thinks.

Leave yourself enough time to revise. A single draft does not make an essay. All writing benefits from revision, so be sure you have time to reconsider your work and to write as many drafts as necessary.

Prepare to revise extensively. You will probably be revising much of what you write, but careful preparation of your first draft will make these revisions less painful.

1. Write on every other line. (If you type, triple space.) This makes seeing errors easier. It also gives you plenty of room to add new material or to try out new versions of sentences.

2. Develop a system of symbols, each indicating a different type of revision. For instance, you can circle individual words or box longer groups of words (or even entire paragraphs) that you want to relocate. You can use an arrow to indicate the new loca-

tion, or you can use asterisks or matching numbers or letters to indicate how you want to rearrange ideas. When you want to add words, use a caret like ᴧthis.

3. Write on only one side of a sheet of paper. This lets you reread your pages side by side. Writing on one side only also allows you to cut and paste without destroying material on the other side of the page. And, incidentally, you should keep rearranging the sections or paragraphs of your paper until you find their most effective arrangement.

If you are composing on a **word processor,** revision is easier. You can delete words and sentences or rearrange paragraphs just by touching a few keys. But be careful not to discard information that you may need later: writers often decide later that an earlier version is best. If you have stored all the versions of your draft in the computer's memory, you can recall whatever you need. If you have not, your ideas will have disappeared without a trace. (For detailed information on composing and revising on a word processor, see Appendix A.)

Notice that in this typed version of her first draft, Lisa Owen set up four body paragraphs to correspond to the four major headings in her working plan.

The West End Mall

The West End Mall opened eight years ago, when I was ten, and it's been a big part of my life ever since. It's a place my friends and I, and thousands of other people, can't seem to stay away from. We're attracted by the lights and glitter, the hustle and bustle, and the things for sale. But sometimes I wonder if that's really why we come. People think the West End Mall is just a place to shop or have fun or work, but it is really a unique combination of home and make-believe.

The Mall is a terrific place to hang out. We never seem to buy much, but we do a lot of browsing. My friends and I usually start with the two department stores, where we check out the make-up and clothes. Then we wander around and see what's

going on in the other stores. We check out sporting goods, looking at running shoes and other gear, and we spend lots of time
in the two record stores. There's usually some good music playing, so it's a good place to hang around. If we have time, we
like to look through the books and magazines in B. Dalton.
Then we hit the arcades, trying to find a time when they're not
too crowded. If there's a good movie playing, we might see it.
And we spend a lot of time eating—fries at McDonald's, pizza,
eclairs at the bakery, warm doughnuts at Mr. Donut. Mostly,
though, we just hang out. We fool around on the escalators,
watch people, watch ourselves in the big mirrors. Sometimes
we meet new people, but most of the time we just keep running
into people we know.

The Mall is important to a lot of people because it's where
they work, and this is true for me, too. For the last two years
I've worked weekends and summers as a waitress at Fay's Fine
Foods, a dinerlike restaurant. I was able to save a lot of money
for college from my tips, and I developed a sense of responsibility at Fay's—I was responsible for keeping track of my tables,
budgeting my money, even making sure I got to work on time
and had a clean uniform ready. And I think I grew up a little
when a robbery attempt took place while I was on my shift, and
I learned not to panic.

The Mall is more than a place to work or have fun, though.
In a lot of ways, the Mall is home. Like home, the Mall is a
safe place. There are guards posted inconspicuously around, and
crowds are everywhere. There's supposed to be safety in numbers, and here it's true. Everybody comes to the Mall, and everybody belongs. It's very reassuring to let yourself wander aimlessly, knowing you'll be swept along in the momentum of the
crowds. It's light and warm in the Mall. And it's comforting to
know it's always open when you need it, and your friends are
always there, and there's always a store to welcome you with
doors always open.

At the same time, the Mall isn't home; it's a make-believe

**rev
3c**

environment which is completely unlike "real life." There are no really old or poor people at the Mall; this is a prettied-up, picture-book setting. All the stores look alike—it's like a cardboard movie set, or Disneyland. They even have fake "sidewalk sales," and fake snow at Christmas. Unlike a real neighborhood shopping street, there are no trees here, and no grass (except at Easter). There is a lot of glitter, though, but the lights that sparkle aren't stars but electric lights. Sometimes it seems like a circus, with all the noise and music. But circuses don't have piped-in Muzak. Sometimes it seems like a town square, but not for long. Real town squares are never so crowded, and real town squares have trees. Sometimes it seems like a nightclub, all glitter and dazzle. But no one is dressed in elegant nightclub clothes. In a way, then, the Mall is all of these things but none of them.

People come to the Mall for entertainment, but they're also looking for something—for home, or maybe for escape.

▶
EXERCISE 1

Consult your working plan and write a rough draft of the essay you began.

3c Understanding Revision

Revision makes your writing conform with your goals as defined by your purpose, audience, and assignment. In your rough draft you write for yourself. In your next draft, you begin to shape your writing for others. Now you "re-see" what you have written and make the changes necessary to your readers' understanding and appreciation of your ideas. This difference in approach is basic to revision.

Revision does not simply follow planning, shaping, and writing as the next step in a sequence. Rather, it is a process you engage in from the moment you begin to discover ideas for your essay. As you work you are constantly rethinking your topic or thesis and reconsidering your ideas, their order, and the pattern in which you arrange them. Revision is a creative and individual aspect of the writing process, and everyone does it somewhat differently. You will have to do a lot of experimenting before you find the particular techniques that work best for you.

Inexperienced writers sometimes believe they have failed if their first drafts are not perfect, but more experienced writers expect to revise. They also differ from inexperienced writers in *how* they revise. Inexperienced writers tend to concentrate on words, spelling, and grammar. They might refine word choices, proofread, and recopy their papers to make them neater. Experienced writers, however, see revision as a series of internal upheavals. They are willing to rethink a thesis and to disassemble and reassemble an entire essay. Only by doing so can they find a voice and a shape for their writing.

Revision reflects not just your private criticism of your first draft but also your response to outside influences—peer reaction, teachers' comments, new observations and experiences. You revise to satisfy yourself, of course, but also to accommodate your readers. Revision, in fact, should bring you closer and closer to your readers.

One of your goals is to write in a readable fashion. All your changes should make what you say clearer and more interesting and keep readers moving forward. Certain strategies help make your ideas more accessible.

Present one idea at a time and sum up regularly. When you overload your paper with more information than readers can take in, you lose them. Readers should not have to backtrack constantly to understand your message.

Fulfill your readers' expectations. Readers expect your paper to do what your thesis says it will do, with major points introduced in an understandable order and appropriate support cited in your body paragraphs. They also expect style, grammar, and mechanics to be correct: parallel elements must appear in parallel terms; subjects must agree with verbs, and pronouns with antecedents; person, voice, tense, and mood must be logical and appropriate.

Accommodate your readers by frequently placing your ideas in context. Repeating key points regularly, constructing clear topic sentences, using transitional words and phrases to link ideas logically, and identifying major and subordinate ideas accurately all help provide continuity.

Finally, pay close attention to editing and proofreading. When you edit and proofread, approach your work as a critical reader would. Check spelling and punctuation, mechanics, manuscript conventions, and the like.

3d Applying Strategies for Revision

Everyone revises differently, and every writing task demands a slightly different kind of revision. Three strategies, however, can help you revise.

(1) Outlining

Outlining your draft helps you to check the structure of your paper. (For specific instructions on outlining, see 2d.) An outline reveals at once whether points are irrelevant or poorly placed—or, worse, missing. It also reveals the hierarchy of your ideas—which points are dominant and which subordinate. This strategy is especially helpful early in revision, when you are reworking the larger structural elements of your essay.

(2) Peer criticism

Instead of trying to imagine your audience, you can address a real audience by asking a friend, classmate, or parent to read your draft and comment on it (with your instructor's permission, of course). The response should tell you whether or not your essay has the effect you intended and perhaps why it succeeds or fails. **Peer criticism** can also be more formal. Your instructor may ask you to exchange essays with another student and may even require you both to write an evaluation.

In either case, take the analysis of your essay seriously. Peer criticism is a kind of test marketing: you know what you want to say; now you have to find out whether you have said it. If your writing fails to communicate your ideas, it hardly matters how sharp your observations are.

Suggested Questions for Peer Criticism
1. What is the main point of the essay? Is the thesis stated? If so, is it clearly worded? If not, how can the wording be improved? Is the thesis stated soon enough?

2. How is the essay arranged? Do the body paragraphs appear in an appropriate order?

3. What ideas support the thesis? Does each body paragraph develop one of these ideas?

4. Does each body paragraph have a topic sentence? Do the topic sentences summarize the information in the paragraph? Are the topic sentences related clearly to the thesis?

5. Is any additional supporting information needed? List any missing points. Is any information irrelevant? If so, indicate possible deletions.

6. Are all the necessary transitions provided? Or would additional links between sentences or paragraphs help? If so, where are such links needed?

7. Does the introductory paragraph attract your attention? Would another introduction work better?

8. Does the conclusion add interest to the essay and reinforce the thesis? Would another conclusion be more appropriate?

9. Consider the sentences and words used in this paper. Without correcting them, point out errors in sentence structure, phrasing or word choice, spelling, and punctuation.

10. Is anything unclear or confusing?

11. What is the essay's greatest strength?

12. What is the essay's greatest weakness?

(3) Checklists

Using a **revision checklist**—either one your instructor prepares or one you devise yourself—is a systematic way of examining your writing. A checklist helps you focus on revising one element at a time: the whole essay; paragraphs; individual sentences, phrases, and words; tone and style; and spelling, punctuation, mechanics, and the like. Depending upon the problems you have and the time you have to deal with them, you can survey your paper using all the questions on the checklist or only some of them.

Following is a comprehensive checklist that parallels the normal revision process, moving in four stages from largest to smallest elements and then considering the issues of tone and style. This checklist may be more helpful when you have become familiar with concepts discussed later in the book. For now, you can certainly use the questions listed under "The Whole Essay."

You may also know from experience which questions apply to your current writing problems. As your understanding of the writing process increases and you are better able to identify the strengths and weaknesses of your writing, you can widen the scope of your revision. Perhaps you will even add points to the checklist. You can also use your teachers' comments to tailor this checklist to your own needs.

Revision Checklist

The Whole Essay

Does your essay have an overall organizational pattern? Is it appropriate to your topic, purpose, and audience? Consider alternative ways of arranging your ideas. (See Chapter 2, 3e.1.)

Do all body paragraphs support your thesis? Revise paragraphs or thesis to make them consistent. (See 2b, 3a, 3e.1.)

Are your thesis and supporting points easily understood? Make sure they are correctly placed and worded. (See 2b, 3a, 3e.1.)

Have you drawn explicit connections between your thesis and your supporting information? Make sure your support is clearly related to your thesis. (See 2b, 3a, 3e.1.)

Did you present your ideas in a logical sequence? If not, reorder them so that they make sense. (See 2d, 3e.1.)

Have you discussed everything promised in your thesis? Develop additional points if necessary. (See 2b, 3a, 3e.1.)

Have you included any irrelevant points? If so, delete. (See 3e.1.)

Did you present enough information—reasons, examples, arguments—to make your point? Add support if necessary. (See 3a, 3e.1.)

Do clear transitions between paragraphs allow your readers to follow your essay's structure? If not, add transitions or modify existing ones. (See 4c.5.)

Have you stressed your key points through judicious use of repetition? Underscore major concepts as necessary. (See 3c.)

Did you sum up your progress as you went along? Be sure to take stock of your ideas at regular intervals. (See 3c.)

Paragraphs

Does each body paragraph have one unifying idea? Delete or relocate extraneous information, and make sure topic sentences identify the unifying idea of each paragraph. (See 4b.1.)

Are topic sentences clearly recognizable and linked to the thesis? Make a brief outline to check. (See 4b.2.)

Do your body paragraphs contain enough detail—reasons, facts, examples—to support your ideas? Add more information if necessary. (See 4d.)

Are your paragraphs constructed according to familiar patterns?

Be sure to use patterns your readers will recognize and understand. (See 4e.)

Are the relationships of sentences within paragraphs clear? If not, add the linking words or phrases your audience needs to follow your ideas. (See 4c.)

Do your introductory paragraphs arouse reader interest and prepare them for what is to come? Consider other introductory strategies. (See 4f.1.)

Do your concluding paragraphs sum up your main points? Be sure that they provide a sense of completion. (See 4f.2.)

Sentences

Are sentences overloaded with too many clauses? Break long, hard-to-follow sentences into simpler, more comprehensive units. (See 9c.)

Have you used correct sentence structure? Revise to eliminate sentence fragments, comma splices, and fused sentences. (See Chapters 11 and 12.)

Have you placed modifiers clearly and logically? Make sure each modifier is clearly related to the word or word group it modifies. (See Chapter 13.)

Have you made potentially confusing shifts in tense, voice, or person? Proofread to eliminate them. (See 15a.)

Have you strengthened sentences through repetition, balance, and parallelism? Reconsider ways to use these strategies. (See 8c, 8d, 14a.)

Have you used emphatic word order? Revise sentences to place stress where you want it. (See 8a.)

Have you used the passive voice appropriately? Eliminate it wherever it may be confusing and wherever the active voice will work more effectively. (See 8e.)

Does careful subordination signal the relative importance of clauses in a sentence and their logical relationship to one another? Combine or revise sentences when necessary. (See 8b.)

Can you find nonessential words and needless repetition? Delete empty expressions that may obscure your meaning and distract or annoy your readers. (See 9a, 9b.)

Have you varied your sentence structure? Experiment with different structures to make your presentation interesting. (See Chapter 10.)

Have you combined sentences where necessary? Link sentences to clarify relationships between ideas and to avoid monotony. (See 10b.)

Words

Have you selected words that accurately reflect your intentions? Consider both the denotations and connotations of your words and make sure you are saying what you want to say. (See 16b.1).

rev
3d

Is your level of diction appropriate for your audience and your purpose? If not, revise to make it suitable and consistent. (See 16a.)

Have you chosen words that are specific, concrete, and unambiguous? Replace any words that are not precise. (See 16b.4, 16b.5.)

Have you enriched your writing with figurative language? Add figurative language where appropriate. (See 16d.)

Have you eliminated jargon, neologisms, pretentious diction, and ineffective figures of speech from your writing? Delete all such verbal clutter from your writing. (See 16c, 16e.)

Tone and Style

Is your tone consistent with your primary purpose? If your purpose is to inform, use a balanced, objective tone. If you are writing to influence your readers, consider ways in which to appeal to their emotions without alienating them. (See 1a.)

Have you maintained the proper distance from your readers? Reconsider your purpose and audience when assessing this point. (See 1a.)

Is your style appropriate for your subject, purpose, and audience? Decide whether a formal or informal style is most appropriate, and make sure to use that style consistently throughout. (See 16a.)

3e Revising Your Drafts

(1) Revising the first draft

Set your rough draft aside for a day, if possible. When you look back over it, you will probably spot dozens of areas that need attention. You cannot solve every problem at once, however. You must focus on only a few areas at a time and rework your essay in several drafts. As you review your first draft, look primarily for content and organization, carefully checking your thesis and support. Once you have fixed problems in these areas, you can attend to other problems more easily.

Lisa Owen revised her first draft with an emphasis on content and organization. Here is her first try at a revised and edited manuscript.

The West End Mall

The West End Mall opened eight years ago, ~~when I was ten,~~ *at the junction of* *routes 202 and 378 about five miles from Clarion, N.Y.* ~~and it's been a big part of my life every since.~~ It's a place ~~my~~ ~~friends and I, and~~ thousands of ~~other~~ people *visit every week,* ~~can't seem to stay~~ ~~away from. We're~~ attracted by the lights and *the* ~~,~~ glitter, ~~the hustle~~ ~~and bustle,~~ and the things ~~for sale.~~ *to buy.* ~~But sometimes I wonder if~~ *They spend endless hours wandering around the mall's two levels, stopping to browse* ~~that's really why we come.~~ *or to buy or to have a snack.* People think the West End Mall is

just a place to shop or have fun or work, but it is really a

unique combination of home and make-believe.

~~The Mall is a terrific place to hang out.~~ ~~We never seem~~ to

buy much, but we do a lot of browsing. My friends and I usually

start with the two department stores, where we check out the

make-up and clothes. Then we wander around and see what's

going on in the other stores. We check out sporting goods, look-

ing at running shoes and other gear, and we spend lots of time

in the two record stores. There's usually some good music playing, so it's a good place to hang around. If we have time, we

like to look through the books and magazines in B. Dalton.

Then we hit the arcades, trying to find a time when they're not

cu

too crowded. If there's a good movie playing, we might see it.

And we spend a <u>lot</u> of time eating—fries at McDonald's, pizza,

eclairs at the bakery, warm doughnuts at Mr. Donut. Mostly,

though, we just hang out. [We fool around on the escalators,

— save for later?

watch people, watch ourselves in the big mirrors.] ~~Sometimes~~

~~we meet new people, but most of the time we just keep running~~

~~into people we know.~~

The ~~Mall is important to a lot of people because~~ it's where

they work, and this is true for me too. For the last two years

I've worked weekends and summers as a waitress at Fay's Fine

Foods, a dinerlike restaurant. I was able to save a lot of money

ut

for college from my tips, and I really developed a sense of re-

sponsibility at Fay's—I was responsible for keeping track of my

tables, budgeting my money, even making sure I got to work on time and had a clean uniform ready. And I think I grew up a

little when a robbery attempt took place while I was on my

shift, and I learned not to panic.

The Mall is ~~more than a place to work or have fun, though.~~ *a lot of things to a lot of people,*

~~In a lot of ways, the Mall is home.~~ Like home, the Mall is a

safe place. ~~There are~~ guards *are* posted inconspicuously around, and

crowds are everywhere. There's supposed to be safety in num-

bers, and here it's true. Everybody comes to the Mall, and every-

body belongs. It's very reassuring to ~~let yourself~~ wander aim-

lessly, knowing you'll be swept along in the momentum of the

crowds. ~~It's~~ *The mall is clean and* light and warm, ~~in the Mall.~~ ~~A~~nd it's comforting to

-just like home-

know it's always open when you need it, and your friends ~~are~~

always *seem to be* there, and ~~there's always~~ a store *is always* to welcome you with *open ing* *open*

doors. ~~always open.~~ *The mall is comfortable and comforting.*

insert new (below)

¶ ~~At the same time, the Mall isn't home; it's~~ a make-believe *¶ The mall is*

environment which is ~~completely~~ *perfect for this kind of play-acting.* Unlike "real life," There are

no really old or poor people at the Mall; this is a prettied-up,

**rev
3e**

picture-book setting. *Because* All the stores look alike, it's like a card-

board movie set, or Disneyland. They even have fake "sidewalk

sales," and fake snow at Christmas. Unlike a real neighborhood

shopping street, there are no trees here, and no grass (except at *the fake grass*

Easter). There is a lot of glitter, though, but the lights that

Still, the sparkle and glitter distract you from outside problems

sparkle aren't stars but electric lights. Sometimes ~~it~~ seems like

the mall

because of   *have animals an*

a circus, ~~with~~ all the noise and music. But circuses don't have

acrobats and t...

and Washington's Birthday sales.

~~piped-in~~ Muzak Sometimes it seems like a town square, but not

for long. Real town squares are never so crowded, and real

town squares have trees. Sometimes it seems like a nightclub,

gowns

all glitter and dazzle. But no one is dressed in elegant ~~nightclub~~

or suits. The mall seems to be all these things,

~~clothes. In a way, then, the Mall is all of these things but none~~

but although it has elements of each, it is really a unique entity.

~~of them.~~

While the mall is more than just a place to shop, then, it is not a movie set, not Disneyland

~~People come to the Mall for entertainment, but they're also~~

not a circus or a town square or a nightclub. What is it? It is a unique blend of home and

~~looking for something~~ for home, or maybe for escape. *make-belie...*

Add after A
about home

At the same time it's a symbol of security,
the mall is also a symbol of freedom, even
irresponsibility. You can be anyone you
want to be at the mall. You can buy
things on impulse, try on crazy clothes
and wild punk make-up, run haphazardly up and down the escalators or
toss pennies into the fountain, or
see yourself from all different angles
in the dozens of mirrors. You can lose
yourself at the mall, or just temporarily trade your old image in for
a new one.

No matter what specific revision strategies you decide to
apply, you should focus on your paper's content, organization,
and thesis as you revise your first draft.

Reconsider your paper's content. Keeping audience, purpose, and assignment in mind, decide whether you ought to add
or delete any information. Should you discuss additional ideas?
Does all the material you included seem relevant?

When Lisa reread her draft, she noticed that she had not
identified the Mall or said where it was. Because her audience
would not know this information, Lisa added it to her essay's
first paragraph.

When she looked at her paper for the relevance of ideas, however, she saw that she had a more serious problem. The content seemed to fall into two categories: the first two body paragraphs were a chatty inventory of the Mall's attractions and an account of how Lisa and her friends spend their time there, but the two succeeding paragraphs were much more analytical. Before she could proceed any further, Lisa had to decide which approach she wanted to take.

When she considered her audience and purpose, the nature of her assignment, and the notes she had not yet used, she decided on the second approach. Her assignment had asked her to treat a place she knew *well* and to demonstrate the depth of her knowledge; a superficial overview of the Mall would not do. So Lisa reevaluated the content of body paragraphs 2 and 3. She decided to delete the entire paragraph (paragraph 3) about her job because it seemed irrelevant to her thesis. She also decided to drop paragraph 2, perhaps using one or two of its best points elsewhere. Much of its detail was unenlightening, and Lisa wanted to shift her emphasis from her activities with her friends. With these cuts the essay would stress the real nature of the Mall and so would be more in line with her purpose: to communicate to her readers why she thought the Mall was so important.

When she took the time to review and reevaluate her notes in light of her narrowed focus, Lisa came up with a good idea for her new draft. Incorporating a few points on entertainment from paragraph 3 and some unused material from her brainstorming list, Lisa worked on a new paragraph to follow what was currently paragraph 4. Devoted to a discussion of how people play-act at the Mall, the new paragraph tied in nicely with the idea of the Mall as a setting for make-believe. Subsequent paragraphs, then, could develop this idea.

Reconsider your paper's organization. Do you want to reorder your paragraphs or rearrange the information within paragraphs? Does your essay follow your working plan? Do you need to shape your material further to bring it into line with a particular organizational pattern? An after-the-fact outline can help here. Do your paragraphs present information clearly? Are they effective? (See Chapter 4.)

Lisa looked at the rest of her essay carefully and decided that its organization was logical enough. The draft seemed consistent with her working plan. It made sense to discuss the homelike aspects of the Mall before its make-believe aspects. She had more to say about the latter point and felt it to be more important. She did see, however, that paragraph 5 was far too long, so she divided it into two paragraphs. She also saw a definition pattern emerging in the essay, so she knew she was on the right track.

Reconsider your paper's thesis. This is a good time to make sure that your thesis is specific and that it says what you intend. Check to make sure that it appears in one sentence, preferably at the end of your first paragraph. Do the body paragraphs support the thesis? If not, revise your thesis or change your supporting material. Are your thesis and support consistent with your audience, purpose, and assignment?

In checking her thesis, Lisa saw further evidence of the problem that she had already noted. Her first draft had followed her working plan closely, putting too much emphasis on entertainment (paragraph 2) and employment (paragraph 3). But the wording of her thesis should have led her to place less stress on what "people think" the Mall is and more on what it "really" is, on its elements of home and make-believe. This confirmed Lisa's decision to cut paragraphs 2 and 3 and develop her paper in the direction of her thesis.

▶
EXERCISE 2

Consulting 2d, make a formal outline of the points in the essay you have been working on and check the logic of your organization.

▶
EXERCISE 3

Revise the large structure—content, organization, and thesis—of your essay, following the guidelines just listed, and write a second draft reflecting your changes.

(2)   Revising the second draft

Lisa's second draft, recopied from the edited first draft on pages 49–53, appears below. Notice that in preparing this draft she has paid most attention to the larger elements of the paper: its content, its organization, and its thesis.

The West End Mall

The West End Mall opened eight years ago at the junction of routes 202 and 378 about five miles from Clarion, N.Y.   It's a place thousands of people visit every week, attracted by the lights and the glitter and the things to buy.   They spend endless hours wandering around the Mall's two levels, stopping to browse or to buy or to have a snack.   People think the West End Mall is just a place to shop or have fun or work, but it is also a unique combination of home and make-believe.

The Mall is a lot of things to a lot of people.   Like home, the Mall is a safe place.   Guards are posted inconspicuously around, and crowds are everywhere. There's supposed to be safety in numbers, and here it's true.   Everybody comes to the Mall, and everybody belongs.   It's very reassuring to wander aimlessly, knowing you'll be swept along in the momentum of the crowds.   The Mall is clean and light and warm, and it's comforting to know it's always open when you need it—just like home—and your friends always seem to be there, and a store is always welcoming you with open doors.   The Mall is comfortable and comforting.

At the same time it's a symbol of security, the Mall is also a symbol of freedom, even irresponsibility. You can be anyone you want to be at the Mall. You can buy things on impulse, try on crazy clothes and wild punk make-up, run haphazardly up and down the escalators or toss pennies into the fountain, or see yourself from all different angles in the dozens of mirrors. You can lose yourself at the Mall, or just temporarily trade your old image in for a new one.

The Mall is a make-believe environment which is perfect for this kind of play-acting. Unlike "real life," there are no really old or poor people at the Mall; this is a prettied-up, picture-book setting. Because all the stores look alike, it's like a cardboard movie set, or Disneyland. They even have fake "sidewalk sales" and fake snow at Christmas. Unlike a real neighborhood shopping street, there are no trees here, and there is no grass (except the fake grass at Easter). There is a lot of glitter, though, but the lights that sparkle aren't stars but electric lights. Still, the sparkle and glitter distract you from outside problems.

Sometimes the Mall seems like a circus, because of all the noise and music. But circuses have animals and acrobats, and they don't have Muzak and Washington's Birthday sales. Sometimes it seems like a town square, but not for long. Real town squares are never so crowded, and real town squares have trees. Sometimes it seems like a nightclub, all glitter and dazzle. But no one is dressed in elegant gowns or suits. The Mall seems to be all these things, but although it has elements of each, it is really a unique entity.

While the Mall is more than just a place to shop, then, it is not a movie set, not Disneyland, not a circus or a town square or a nightclub. What is it? It is a unique blend of home and make-believe.

In this draft Lisa corrected many of her first draft's most obvious shortcomings in content and organization. She now felt confident that her body paragraphs provided sufficient support for her thesis by developing points she believed could prove it. She therefore moved on to consider more refined elements of her second draft: sentence structure and word choice, topic sentences and transitions, style and tone. At this stage, she had the benefit of an evaluation provided by one of her classmates.

Although Lisa had added new material, occasionally changing word and sentence construction, the style and tone in her second draft remained much the same as in her first draft. The first thing she and her student critic noticed about her essay was that this tone and style were too informal for her college audience. Lisa decided to eliminate her habit of using the informal (and vague) *you*—as in "You can be anyone you want to be"—and her use of contractions.

Once again considering her reader's needs and expectations, Lisa saw that her topic sentences were weak. She strengthened the vague topic sentence of paragraph 2, which did nothing to signal the subject. She kept the topic sentences of paragraphs 3 and 4, which she felt were strong and clear. Each of these topic sentences would give her readers a good sense of what its paragraph's content would be. The newly created paragraph 5 had no topic sentence, so she added "At first glance the Mall seems easy to characterize, but this first impression is deceptive." She also planned to add a sentence to her conclusion, which did not seem finished. Then she turned to the sentences and words of her essay.

▶
EXERCISE 4

Review the second draft of your paper, paying particular attention to topic sentences and transitions and to the way you structure your sentences and select your words.

▶
EXERCISE 5

Ask a friend to read your second draft and respond to the peer criticism questions in 3d.2. Then revise your draft, incorporating any suggestions you find helpful.

(3) Writing the final draft

Having revised her second draft, Lisa recopied her essay, adding an occasional supporting detail and rephrasing some
ideas as she went along.

The West End Mall

Located just outside of Clarion, New York, the West End
Mall is a place thousands of people visit each week, attracted by
the lights and the glitter and the things to buy. They spend
endless hours wandering around the Mall's two levels, stopping
only to browse, buy, or snack. As a result, most people think of
the Mall as a place they go to out of necessity or convenience.
People think the West End Mall is a place to shop or have fun or
work, but it is more: a unique combination of home and make-
believe.

The Mall is more than a place for employment or entertainment; in a lot of ways, the Mall is home. Like home, the
Mall is safe and secure. Guards are posted inconspicuously
around, and crowds are everywhere. Everybody comes to the
Mall, and everybody belongs. It is very reassuring for shoppers
to wander aimlessly, knowing they will be swept along in the
momentum of the crowds. In fact, so dense are the Mall's
"streets" that they resemble a conveyor belt, a people mover.
Like home, the Mall is clean and light and warm, and people
find it comforting to know it is always open when they need it—
just like home. Regular visitors to the Mall always seem to find
their friends there, and stores always seem to be welcoming
them with open doors. The Mall is comfortable and comforting.

At the same time it is a symbol of security, the Mall is also
a symbol of freedom, even irresponsibility. People can be anyone they want to be at the Mall. Normally careful shoppers can
buy things on impulse, conservative dressers can try on wild

**rev
3e**

clothes and punk make-up, well-behaved teenagers can run up and down the escalators or toss pennies in the fountains or make crazy faces in the dozens of mirrors. People can lose themselves at the Mall, or just temporarily trade their old images in for new ones.

The Mall's make-believe environment is a perfect setting for this kind of play-acting. Unlike "real life," there are no really old or poor people at the Mall, and certainly no shopping-bag ladies. This is a picture-book setting, and it is picture-perfect. Because the facades of all the stores look alike, the total effect is like a prefabricated movie set, or Disneyland. The Mall even boasts fake "sidewalk sales" (there are no sidewalks) and fake snow at Christmas. Unlike a real neighborhood shopping street, there are no trees at the Mall, and no grass (except the fake grass at Easter). There is a lot of glitter sprinkled around, though, and this sparkle enhances the make-believe setting and distracts shoppers from any problems they may have.

At first glance, the Mall seems easy to characterize, but this first impression is deceptive. Sometimes the Mall seems like a three-ring circus, because of all the noise and excitement. But circuses have animals and clowns and acrobats, and they don't have Muzak or Washington's Birthday sales. Sometimes it seems like an old-fashioned town square, but not for long. Real old-time town squares have courthouses and churches and trees. Sometimes it seems like a roaring twenties nightclub, all glitter and dazzle. But no one is dressed in elegant gowns and tuxedos. The Mall seems at various times to be all these things, but although it has elements of each, it is really a unique entity.

The Mall is more than just a place to shop, then, but it is not a movie set, not Disneyland, not a circus or a town square or a nightclub. What is it? It is a unique blend of home and make-believe. The West End Mall is a place to escape to, a place where a person can find a comforting home away from home or a whole new identity.

With this draft, Lisa felt her paper was essentially complete. Before she handed it in, though, she had some editing and proofreading to do. She needed to check spelling, punctuation, and mechanics carefully and to prepare the manuscript according to the conventions specified by her instructor.

rev

3e

▶

EXERCISE 6

What exactly has Lisa changed between her second and third drafts? List each of these changes and evaluate them as any careful reader would. Are all her changes for the better? Are any other changes called for?

▶

EXERCISE 7

Using the revision checklist in 3d.3 as a guide, create a checklist that reflects the specific concerns you need to consider to revise your essay. Then revise your essay according to this checklist.

4 Writing Paragraphs

A **paragraph** is a group of related sentences that usually develop a single idea. Paragraphs serve three important functions in an essay. First, they group sentences into units of thought. Second, they provide breaks between thoughts, giving readers a chance to pause and assimilate each thought. Finally, they call attention to the way you are developing an idea. In most essays each paragraph presents a specific point contributing to a more general thesis. By fitting in with your overall purpose, paragraphs help you control the organization of your paper and convey your ideas clearly to your readers.

How long a paragraph should be depends on its subject and its function within a piece of writing. In a chemistry lab manual you may write short paragraphs, running one or two sentences, that outline each stage of an experiment. In discussing a complex sociological theory you may use longer paragraphs running possibly three-quarters of a typed page or more. Typically, however, your paragraphs will run five to ten sentences, with transition paragraphs running shorter.

4a Charting Paragraph Structure

Charting the ideas in a paragraph helps you recognize its underlying structure. You begin by assigning the sentence that expresses the main or **unifying idea** of the paragraph to level 1. Then, read each sentence of the paragraph. Assign to level 1 sentences as important as that containing the unifying idea. Indent and assign to level 2 more specific sentences. Indent again and assign to level 3 more specific sentences that support level-2 sentences. Do this for every sentence in the paragraph. For example:

1 My grandmother told me that fifty years ago life was not easy for a girl in rural Italy.
  2 At the age of six a girl was expected to help her mother with household chores.

    3 Girls of this age were no longer permitted to play games or to indulge in childish activities.

  2 At the age of twelve, a girl assumed most of the responsibilities of an adult.

    3 She worked in the fields, prepared meals, carried water, and took care of the younger children.

    3 Education was usually out of the question; it was an unusual family that allowed a girl to enroll in one of the few convent schools that took peasant children.

The first sentence (level 1) of this paragraph introduces the unifying idea, and each level-2 sentence gives a specific, equally weighted illustration of that idea. The level-3 sentences support these examples with specifics. Note that in a properly constructed paragraph you will probably have only one level-1 sentence.

By charting the pattern of sentences you can make certain your paragraphs are *unified, coherent,* and *well developed.* These three principles, which we will examine in this chapter, govern the construction of paragraphs.

▶
EXERCISE 1

A. Paragraph indentations have been intentionally deleted from the following essay. Divide it into paragraphs. Notice how paragraphs emphasize ideas and make the essay easier to understand.

Frankly Speaking
Book banning destroys our freedom to learn

Recently, in a small farming town near my home, the parents of an eleventh-grade student decided that an assigned book, John Steinbeck's *Of Mice and Men,* was unfit for their son to read. Their attempts to have it banned caused a bitter split in the community. Protests were filed. More books joined the "unfit" list, including *The Learning Tree,* by Gordon Parks, and John Hersey's *Hiroshima.* Local newspapers ran comments from angry parents, and community meetings degenerated into shouting matches. When the smoke finally cleared, the censors had lost the battle, and the books were not banned. But the effects of the fray will be long-lasting. One teacher confided that as a result of the dispute, she will no longer assign even slightly controversial books. Despite the bucolic setting, this incident wasn't a statistical surprise. The American Library Association reports that the number of similar episodes is the highest in twenty-five years, shaking up communities from Pennsylvania to California—in all, over 148 titles have been challenged, in thirty-four states. Among the banned books are *The Catcher in the Rye*, by J. D. Salinger; *Slaughterhouse-Five*, by Kurt Vonnegut; *The Fixer*, by Bernard Malamud; and even *The American Heritage Dictionary*. What is at stake here is the basis of education. The intellectual exercise that results from the discussion of new and controversial ideas is what keeps our educational system healthy and vigorous. Book banning nudges us toward an institutional hardening of the arteries. The goal of education should not be to tell us *what* to think but to teach us *how* to think. Thinking is a skill, and it has to be practiced. Instead of being told whether or not a book has merit, students should be taught to decide for themselves. Censors claim they are attempting to promote community values in community schools. But values must evolve; they can't be dictated. Moreover, I think that book banners view literature in far too narrow a fashion. Instead of singling out isolated paragraphs containing four-letter words, they should consider each book as a whole. The quality of the entire work is much more important than a few four-letter words. A good example of this is J. D. Salinger's *The Catcher in the Rye*. The novel is filled with swear words, and censors usually have a field day with it. Examined as a whole, though, it becomes apparent that the book has real value. The main character's constant use of four-letter words in a transparently unnatural tough-guy style reveals the vulnerable, frightened boy hiding beneath a veneer of manhood. The vulgar language serves a purpose, but this is something the book banners usually overlook. Ironically, banning a book may actually backfire. Curiosity about the contents of a so-called unfit book may make more people in a community desire to read it. When James Joyce's novel *Ulysses* was banned in the United States many years ago, for example, it instantly became *the* book to read. Instead of restricting the books students read, more positive methods of maintaining good values should be used. A solid education, which includes learning to tell the difference between what's worthwhile and what's trash, does more to improve literary tastes and overall morality than censorship could ever do. *(Seventeen)*

B. Chart the underlying structure of the following paragraphs.

   Two kinds of movies are characteristic of the 1930's. The first, and most popular, are escapist movies. This includes big-budget musicals, and to some extent gangster and horror films. *The Wizard of Oz* falls into this category and so do *Frankenstein* and *Dracula*. The second, and certainly less popular, are movies that focus on the Depression. These include limited-distribution documentaries and a small number of films made by major studios. *Power and the Land* and *The Plow That Broke the Plains* fall into this category. (Film midterm)

¶ *un*
4b

Antipathy to the city goes back a long way. When industrialization drove the European workingman into the major cities of that continent, books and pamphlets appeared attacking the city as a source of crime, corruption, filth, disease, vice, licentiousness, subversion and high prices. The theme of some of the earliest English novels—*Moll Flanders* abounds in it—is that of the innocent country youth coming to the big city and being subjected to all forms of horror until justice—and a return to the pastoral life—follows. (John V. Lindsay, *The City*)

Ursula K. LeGuin grew up in a stimulating environment. Her father, Alfred Kroeber, was a distinguished anthropologist and her mother was a successful author. Her parents' interests included history and biology as well as art and literature. Her father could speak several languages. The family lived in Berkeley during the school year, but every summer they went to the forty acres they owned in the hills of the Napa Valley. For the Kroebers summer was a time for exploring, working, and creating in an environment where a variety of intellectuals gathered. (Student)

4b Writing Unified Paragraphs

Readers expect a paragraph to focus on a single idea and to develop it. Without this **unifying idea** readers become frustrated and confused.

Focusing on a single unifying idea helps readers understand what your paragraph is about. Often you tell your readers what your unifying idea is in a **topic sentence.** The sentences in the following paragraph focus on the unifying idea stated in the topic sentence.

1   <u>Bananas, like many other kinds of fruit, are always picked in</u>
2 <u>their green, or unripened, state.</u> This is not, however, for reasons of marketing convenience, as is the case with most other fruits and
3 vegetables. Gourmet hearsay to the contrary, a banana is not at its
4 best when freshly picked from the tree. A tree-ripened banana lacks the melting sweetness and velvety texture for which the store-
5 bought banana is relished. Bananas ripen properly only after pick-
6 ing. They must, moreover, be picked at a certain stage of maturity.

7   There is a period, usually set at about three weeks, during which
8   they must be cut in order to ripen satisfactorily. The distance the
banana must travel to market determines the moment of cutting.
9   Bananas consigned to the most distant markets are cut on the earliest possible days, for a day, even a few hours, can be important in
10 their fragile market life. Few fruits (the strawberry, perhaps, and the
raspberry) are more sensitive than the banana to the destructive-
ness of time. (Berton Roueché, *The River World and Other Explorations*)

The writer of this paragraph stays with his purpose. The topic
sentence states the unifying idea of the paragraph: that bananas
are always picked in their green, or unripened, state. Sentence 2
clarifies the topic sentence. The rest of the paragraph tells why
bananas are not best when picked fresh from the tree. None of
the sentences in this paragraph distracts readers with irrelevant
information. The tight connection of each subsequent sentence
to the topic sentence gives the paragraph its unity.

    You achieve paragraph unity in two ways: by using a topic
sentence carefully and by making sure that all the sentences in
your paragraph relate to this topic sentence.

(1) Using topic sentences to achieve unity

Placement and direct or indirect use of a topic sentence will vary
according to your purpose. A topic sentence at the beginning of a
paragraph immediately establishes the shape of the paragraph. A
topic sentence at the end of a paragraph draws information together. An implied topic sentence enables readers to infer the
point of a paragraph when a direct statement would be awkward
or out of place.

    TOPIC SENTENCE AT THE BEGINNING.   When you use this op-
tion, you begin with a topic sentence and follow with support.
The following paragraph illustrates this format.

Topic
sentence

Supporting
examples

    A Hindoo temple is a conglomeration of adornment.
The lines of the building are completely hidden by the deco-
rations. Sculptured figures and ornaments crowd its surface,
stand out from it in thick masses, break it up into a bewilder-
ing series of irregular tiers. It is not a unity but a collection,
rich, confused. It looks like something not planned but built
this way and that as the ornament required. The convictions
underlying it can be perceived: each bit of exquisitely
wrought detail had a mystical meaning and the temple's ex-

terior was important only as a means for the artist to ascribe thereon the symbols of truth. It is decoration, not architecture. (Edith Hamilton, *The Greek Way*)

Using a topic sentence at the beginning of each paragraph is effective when you want your readers to grasp your meaning immediately. This technique is especially appropriate when you are writing essay- or paragraph-length answers on examinations and in short essays, lab reports, technical reports, and memos.

Beginning with topic sentences also helps you stay focused on your subject. This technique helps you hold to a line of thought without trailing off in irrelevant discussions.

Topic sentences at the beginning also make your readers' job easier. Each topic sentence refers back to your thesis, reminding readers what your paper is about. Notice that we use this technique in the three-paragraph cluster above to help you follow our discussion.

¶1. Using a topic sentence at the beginning of each paragraph is effective when you want your readers to grasp your meaning immediately.
¶2. Beginning with topic sentences also helps you stay focused on your subject.
¶3. Topic sentences at the beginning also make your readers' job easier.

When revising your essay, you should make sure that your body paragraphs accurately reflect your thesis and that they form a clear, well-marked path for your readers to follow.

TOPIC SENTENCE AT THE END. Using topic sentences at the end of paragraphs enables you to present controversial issues effectively. If you lead your readers through a logical and carefully thought out argument and *then* present your conclusion, you are more likely to convince them that your conclusion is reasonable. Leading off with a controversial statement can alienate an audience.

Notice how Rachel Carson maintains interest by placing her topic sentence at the end of the following paragraph. By doing so, she effectively introduces an idea that not all of her audience would readily accept.

These sprays, dusts and aerosols are now applied almost universally to farms, gardens, forests, and homes—nonselective chemicals that have the power to kill every insect, the "good" and the "bad," to still the song of birds and the leaping of fish in the streams, to coat the leaves with a deadly film, and to linger on in soil—all this though the intended target may be only a few weeds or insects. Can anyone believe it is possible to lay down such a barrage of poisons on the surface without making it unfit for life? They should not be called "insecticides," but "biocides." ("The Obligation to Endure," *Silent Spring*)

In the following paragraph from a short report, a work-study student summarizes the results of a survey of fifty-nine identified weaknesses in the accounting department of her firm. Notice that she prepares her audience by presenting her facts first and then states her conclusion.

The managers of the ten concerned departments were interviewed to determine the status of the comments and recommendations. Of the 41 internal accounting control weaknesses, 26 have been corrected, nine changes are being developed for implementation, and two have been included in the 1986 Proposed Department Objectives. The remaining four are not considered by management to be worthy of additional control—that is, existing controls are believed to provide reasonable assurance that records accurately reflect transactions. Thus, of the 41 identified control weaknesses, most are being taken care of and should present no future difficulties. (Student)

TOPIC SENTENCE IMPLIED.   At times you will want to avoid a direct statement of your unifying idea. In some situations— especially narrative or descriptive ones—a topic sentence can seem forced or artificial. The natural flow of the material best conveys your meaning. The following paragraph describes how immigrants felt as their ship steamed into New York's harbor. Because the author wants each detail of the paragraph to speak for itself, he does not include a summary topic sentence.

They stood on the deck as the ancient, rusty ship that had been their home and ark for seventeen days wore into Ellis Island— shoulder to shoulder, cheek to jowl. Everyone was on deck, the old and the young, screaming children, weeping babies, the silent, the terrified, the sick, the hopeful, nationalities and tongues in a flux of tears and laughter. The great lady of hope welcomed them, and this they had been waiting to see. The Eighth Wonder of the World. "Give me your tired, your poor, your huddled masses yearning to breathe free." In five tongues the statistics floated over the babble of sound. She is a hundred and fifty-two feet high and she weighs two hundred and twenty-five tons. Yes, you can stand up there in the torch at the very end of her arm. Across the water, there was the mass of buildings on the battery, but the lady of liberty was something else. (Howard Fast, *The Immigrants*)

¶ *un*
4b

Although professional writers use this technique often, as a beginning writer you should use it sparingly and then only when you are certain that your readers can infer your unifying idea.

(2) Relating sentences to the unifying idea

When you revise your paragraphs, look for sentences that do not support the topic sentence or contribute to the overall effect of the paragraph. Bring your paragraph into focus by rewriting these sentences or, in some cases, deleting them. The following paragraph contains sentences that wander from the subject.

1   One of the first problems that freshmen have is learning to use a
2   microcomputer. All freshmen were required to buy a computer before
3   school started. Throughout the first semester we took a special course
4   to teach us to use a computer. The Apple IIe has a large memory and
5   can function as a word processor as well as a calculator. It has an
6   eighty-character screen and a disk drive. My parents were happy that
7   I had a computer, but they were concerned about the price. Tuition
    was high, and when they added in the price of the computer it was
8   almost out of reach. To offset expenses, I arranged for a part-time job
9   in the school library. Even so, I am determined to overcome my "com-
    puter anxiety" and to master my Apple IIe by the end of the semester.
    (Student)

The opening statement that freshmen have problems learning to use a microcomputer is the topic sentence, so readers expect the rest of the paragraph to develop this idea. Sentences 2 and 3 seem to do so. But sentence 4 shifts to a description of the Apple IIe computer, and this digression continues in sentence 5. Sentence 6 introduces a new subject—the parents' problem of paying tuition, an idea further developed in sentences 7 and 8. Sentence 9 returns to the idea introduced in sentence 1, but by this time the subject has shifted so often that readers cannot be sure what the paragraph is about.

This lack of unity becomes obvious when you chart the paragraph.

1 One of the first problems that freshmen have is learning how to use a microcomputer.

    2 All freshmen were required to buy a computer before school started.

       3 Throughout the first semester we took a special course to teach us to use a computer.

1 The Apple IIe has a large memory and can function as a word processor as well as a calculator.

    2 It has an eighty-character screen and a disk drive.

1 My parents were happy that I had a computer, but they were concerned about the price.

    2 Tuition was high, and when they added in the price of the computer it was almost out of reach.

       3 To offset expenses, I arranged for a part-time job in the school library.

1 Even so, I am determined to overcome my "computer anxiety" and to master my Apple IIe by the end of the semester.

If each level-1 sentence represents a topic that should be developed in its own paragraph, this paragraph has not one but four topics. The writer simply made a series of false starts.

To unify this paragraph around the subject of overcoming his computer anxiety, the writer must take out the sentences about his parents' financial situation and the computer's characteristics. Only details that relate to the unifying idea should stay in. Here is his revision.

> One of the first problems I had as a freshman was overcoming "computer anxiety." All freshmen were required to buy a computer before school started. Throughout the first semester, we took a special course to teach us to use the computer. In theory this system sounded fine, but in my case it was a disaster. In the first place, the closest I had ever come to a computer was the hand-held calculator I used in math class. In the second place, I could not type. And to make matters worse, many of the people in my computer orientation course already knew how to operate a computer. By the end of the first week I was convinced that I would never be able to work with my Apple IIe.

Now the topic is clear, and each sentence is related to the unifying idea.

▶
EXERCISE 2

A. Identify the unifying idea in each of the following paragraphs. If there is a topic sentence, underline it. If the unifying idea is not stated, write your own topic sentence.

1.   From the very beginning of school we make books and reading a constant source of possible failure and public humiliation. When children are little we make them read aloud, before the teacher and other children, so that we can be sure they "know" all the words they are reading. This means that when they don't know a word, they are going to make a mistake, right in front of everyone. Instantly they are made to realize that they have done something wrong. Perhaps some of the other children will begin to wave their hands and say "Ooooh! O-o-o-oh!" Perhaps they will just giggle, or nudge each other, or make a face. Perhaps the teacher will say, "Are you sure" or ask someone else what he thinks. Or perhaps, if the teacher is kindly, she will just smile a sweet, sad smile—often one of the most painful punishments a child can suffer in school. In any case, the child who has made the mistake knows he has made it, and feels foolish, stupid, and ashamed, just as any of us would in his shoes. (John Holt, *Redbook*)

2.   "Sesame Street" is produced and distributed by Children's Television Workshop (CTW), which also franchises the sale of Sesame Street products. The first cycle of "Sesame Street" programs made its debut in November 1969 in this country and the series has been going strong ever since. Nineteen seventy-six marked the eighth cycle in the domestic series: which means that hundreds of these charming programs will have been broadcast and repeated, broadcast and repeated, coast to coast. At least fifteen million U.S. children have seen numerous episodes of "Sesame Street" during their preschool years. The few who may not have seen the shows know about them anyway, having picked up the information from their peers and their general surroundings. One result is that "Sesame Street" characters and the "Sesame Street" slant on learning and on childhood are now entrenched in this country's thought-environment. The program has penetrated the culture of childhood so that three-year-olds who may never have heard of Paul Bunyan, Johnny Appleseed, or Brer Rabbit are almost certain to know Big Bird, Kermit the Frog, and the Cookie Monster. (Rose Goldsen, *The Show and Tell Machine: How Television Works and Works You Over*)

3.   The vulture sails in silence, for no vocal signals could serve him at such a distance from his fellows. He croaks, growls, whistles only in his family circle, and at its feasts. He circles by almost imperceptible adjustments of his wing planes, aided by slight twists of his tail. But his head is in constant and active movement. He swivels it from one side to the other, bringing each eye in turn to bear on the earth. Then he bends his neck to right or left to check on one of his neighbors to north, south, east or west. (John D. Stewart, "Vulture Country")

4.   The *shinkansen* or "bullet train" speeds across the rural areas of Japan giving a quick view of cluster after cluster of farmhouses surrounded by rice paddies. This particular pattern did not develop purely by chance, but as a consequence of the technology peculiar to the growing of rice, the staple of the Japanese diet. The growing of rice requires the construction and maintenance of an irrigation system, something

that takes many hands to build. More importantly, the planting and the harvesting of rice can only be done efficiently with the cooperation of twenty or more people. The "bottom line" is that a single family working alone cannot produce enough rice to survive, but a dozen families working together can produce a surplus. Thus the Japanese have had to develop the capacity to work together in harmony, no matter what the forces of disagreement or social disintegration, in order to survive. (William Ouchi, *Theory "Z": How American Business Can Meet the Japanese Challenge*)

B. Read the following paragraphs and choose the best topic sentence from the list after each paragraph.

>   For one thing the cost of paper has gone up dramatically. The shortage of wood and increased labor costs have contributed to this increase. Another problem is the high cost of upgrading equipment. The expense of complex computer-assisted systems has put many publishers on the brink of bankruptcy. Finally, publishers work on very small profit margins. With competition from nonprint sources most publishers feel that they cannot set prices of books at a level that makes them profitable. As one publisher said, "People are just not ready for the thirty-five-dollar bestseller."

1. Books are expensive.
2. Publishers are having a difficult time.
3. Why are most publishers working on a very small profit margin?
4. There are several different reasons why most publishers are having a difficult time.

>   The Department of Transportation did a lot to clarify federal regulations. The DOT is concerned with safety and realized the need for clear and coherent regulations. The Coast Guard also tried to recodify and rewrite regulations. Although not as successful as the DOT, it made inroads, considering the task. The largest agency to attempt to clarify its regulations using plain English was the Social Security Administration. Because their regulations have a great impact on the public, their task was especially important. The SSA program was carried out by in-house writers who were told to cut out the government gobbledygook.

1. The Social Security Administration has done a lot to eliminate confusion concerning federal regulations.
2. Government regulations should be put in plain English.
3. Several government agencies have done much to clarify federal regulations by using plain English.
4. Executive agencies have a responsibility to clarify federal regulations.

C. The following paragraphs do not have topic sentences. Read them and supply the missing topic sentence.

¶ coh
4c

_____ . Spray the hinges with a silicone lubricating compound or a light oil. You can buy these products in any hardware store. Be sure the spray soaks into the hinges and work the door back and forth as you spray. If this does not stop the squeak you will have to remove the hinges and clean them of rust and dirt. You can do this by soaking them in oil for several hours and then scouring them with fine steel wool.

The sun came up early. Both of us got up, washed, and walked to the stream. We fished for several hours and then returned to camp to cook our catch. After breakfast we swam and then hiked through the woods that began about a hundred yards from our camp. That evening we drank beer and ate the cheese we had brought from home. We went to bed early and slept until it was time to leave for home the next morning. _____

4c Writing Coherent Paragraphs

A paragraph is unified if all its sentences express parts of a single idea. A paragraph is coherent if all its sentences are related to one another logically and grammatically. Consider this paragraph—which, although it is unified, lacks coherence.

People who have never taken a film course don't know the amount of planning that goes into making a movie. Communications 101 requires a movie as a final project. First, you have to get an idea. You write a treatment, and after the instructor approves it, you write a script. You decide on actors, equipment, and locations. Deciding in advance on camera placement and shooting angles can save a lot of time. You are actually ready to shoot your movie when you have taken care of all the preliminaries. I had to shoot one scene three times before I got it right. (Student)

Incoherent paragraph

1
2
3–4

5
6
7

8

On first reading, this paragraph seems to make sense. It has a topic sentence to which its sentences refer. Even so, it is difficult

¶ coh

4c

to read because its ideas are not clearly connected. The writer never indicates what sentence 2 has to do with sentence 1. Sentence 3 begins explaining the steps involved in making a movie, but without words to cue us, we cannot be certain that this discussion continues in sentences 4 and 5. Sentence 6 may amplify sentence 5, or it may be another step in the process. Sentence 7 attempts to draw these steps together, but the whole idea is still vague. Finally, sentence 8 is simply an afterthought.

A revision of this paragraph eliminates these problems and results in a coherent paragraph.

> 1   People who have never taken a film course don't know the
> 2   amount of planning that goes into making a movie. I found out when
>   I took Communications 101, a course that requires students
> 3   to make a film as a final project. Before you actually begin shooting
> 4   there are a number of things you have to do. First, you have to get an
> 5   idea. Next, you have to write a treatment, and after the instructor
> 6   approves it, you write a script. Finally, you have to decide on actors,
> 7   equipment, and locations. These steps, along with deciding in ad-
>   vance on camera placement and shooting angles, can save a lot of
> 8   time. For example, I had to shoot one scene three times before I got it
> 9   right. With some advance planning I could have gotten it right
> 10 the first time. When you have taken care of these preliminaries, you
>   are actually ready to shoot your movie.

This paragraph contains the same information as the first one but is easier for readers to understand. The writer now clearly connects one sentence with another. The opening topic sentence still broadly states the unifying idea. The revised sentence 2 restricts the discussion to one experience the writer had. A new sentence (sentence 3) now introduces the process discussed in sentences 4, 5, and 6, telling readers in advance what to expect. Sentence 7 sums up the steps and adds two more points. Sentences 8 and 9 illustrate sentence 7 by giving an example. Sentence 10 draws the paragraph to an end and sets up the topic of the next paragraph: shooting a film.

Notice the connecting words and phrases: *before* (3), *first* (4), *next* (5), and *finally* (6). *These steps* (7) reviews the preceding three sentences. *For example* (8) clearly says that this sentence illustrates the sentence before. Repetition of the pronoun *these* also draws the sentences together. And repetition of verb forms (*have to* in sentences 3, 4, 5, and 6) sets up a parallel structure.

You can use a number of strategies to achieve coherence in

your paragraphs. You can signal relationships with pronoun reference, parallel structures, repeated key words, and transitional words and phrases.

¶ *coh*
4c

(1) Using pronouns to achieve coherence

Because **pronouns** refer to nouns or pronouns, they establish connections among sentences. Precise, well-placed pronoun references can lead readers through a paragraph. Inexact pronoun references, however, can ruin an otherwise well-planned paragraph.

> Both Martin Luther and John Calvin wanted to return 1
> to principles of early Christianity described in the New Testament. Martin Luther founded the evangelical churches in 2
> Germany and Scandinavia and he founded a number of reformed churches in other countries. A third Protestant 3
> branch, episcopacy, developed in England. They rejected 4
> the word *Protestant* because they agreed with Roman Catholicism on most points. They rejected the primacy of the 5
> Pope. They accepted the Bible as the only source of revealed truth and they held that faith, not good works, de- 6
> fined a person's relationship to God. (Student)

Inexact pronoun reference

This paragraph moves by a series of bumps and jolts. Inexact pronoun references make the ideas difficult to follow. Does *he* in sentence 2 refer to Luther or Calvin? Does *they* in sentence 4 refer to the episcopacy, the evangelical churches, or the reformed churches?

In this revised version, exact pronoun references draw ideas together and establish coherence.

1   Both Martin Luther and John Calvin wanted to return to the principles of early Christianity described in the New Testament.
2   Martin Luther founded the evangelical churches in Germany, and John Calvin founded a number of reformed churches in other
3   countries. A third Protestant branch, episcopacy, developed in England. It rejected the word *Protestant* because it agreed with Roman
4
5   Catholicism on most points. All these sects rejected the primacy of
6   the Pope. They accepted the Bible as the only source of revealed truth, and they held that faith, not good works, defined a person's relationship to God. (Student)

The writer has replaced *he* in sentence 2 with *John Calvin*, and changed *they* in sentence 4 to *it*, which refers to "A third Protestant branch." By adding the phrase *all these sects,* the writer makes clear that *they* in sentence 6 refers to sects, not the episcopacy. Correct pronoun usage has pulled the paragraph together. Correctly used, pronouns connect ideas. Wrongly used, they confuse readers and destroy coherence. Make certain that your pronouns refer directly to a noun or another pronoun. As a good rule of thumb, do not separate a pronoun from the word it refers to by more than a single sentence. (See 21f.)

(2)   Using parallel structure to achieve coherence

Carefully repeated words and phrases also establish coherence. Readers expect related events to be discussed with similar (or at least related) grammatical structures and words. We call this device **parallelism** (see 8c). Consider the following paragraph.

*Without
parallel
structure*
    Thomas Jefferson was born in 1743 and died at Monticello, Virginia, on July 4, 1826. During his eighty-four years he accomplished a number of things. Although best known for his draft of the Declaration of Independence, Jefferson was a delegate to the Continental Congress. Not only was Jefferson a patriot, he was also a profound thinker. During the Revolution he drafted the Statute for Religious Freedom. In 1784 he drafted an ordinance for governing the West and he formulated the first decimal monetary system. After being elected president, he abolished internal taxes, reduced the national debt, and made the Louisiana Purchase. Jefferson also designed Monticello and the University of Virginia. (Student)

There is nothing wrong with this paragraph. It is unified and fairly coherent. It presents information straightforwardly if not memorably. But this revision shows how parallel structure can strengthen the paragraph.

1   Thomas Jefferson was born in 1743 and died at Monticello, Vir-
2 ginia, on July 4, 1826. During his eighty-four years he accomplished a
3 number of things. Although best known for his draft of the Declaration of Independence, Jefferson was a man of many talents who had a
4 wide intellectual range. He was a patriot who was one of the revolu-
5 tionary founders of the United States. He was a reformer who, when
he was governor of Virginia, drafted the Statute for Religious Freedom.
6 He was an innovator who devised the first decimal monetary system.

7 He was a president who abolished internal taxes, reduced the na-
8 tional debt, and made the Louisiana Purchase. And finally he was an
architect who designed Monticello and the University of Virginia.

¶ coh
4c

The first three general sentences still introduce the discussion, but sentence 3 now limits the subject and establishes categories for sentences 4 through 8. Examples are now grouped, not sequentially but in categories: *patriot, reformer, innovator, president,* and *architect.* The same basic sentence structure introduces each category: *He was a patriot who . . . ; He was an innovator who . . . ; And finally he was an architect who . . . .* This display of Jefferson's accomplishments in parallel form helps the reader comprehend the material and adds emphasis (see 8c).

Whether subtle or dramatic, parallelism helps link sentences and gives coherence to a paragraph. But repetition for its own sake does not always aid coherence. It is effective only when it makes the readers' job easier by highlighting your main ideas.

(3) Repeating key words to achieve coherence

Repeating key words or phrases throughout a paragraph reminds readers how the sentences relate to one another and to the topic sentence. Such reinforcement emphasizes the sequence of your ideas and keeps your discussion tied together.

You should not repeat words and phrases monotonously—a well-written paragraph must have variety. But you have to balance this need to vary your vocabulary against your audience's need to understand what you have written. Whenever your readers may be in danger of losing sight of your topic, you can repeat the key words referring to it. In the following paragraph, the absence of repeated key words or phrases makes the discussion difficult to follow.

Without repeated key words or phrases

Mercury poisoning is a problem that has long been 1
recognized. "Mad as a hatter" refers to the malady preva- 2
lent among nineteenth-century workers who manufactured felt hats. Workers in many other industries such as 3
mining, chemicals, and dentistry were also affected. In the 4
1950's and 1960's there were cases of poisoning in Mina-
mata, Japan. Research showed that there were high levels 5
of pollution in streams and lakes. In the United States this 6
condition came to light in 1969 when a New Mexico family

¶ coh

4c

got sick from eating tainted food. Since then certain pesti-   7
cides have been withdrawn from the market and chemical
wastes can no longer be dumped into the ocean. (Student)

This paragraph demands a lot from readers. Sentence 1 introduces mercury poisoning as the topic of the paragraph. Sentences 2 through 7 may concern this subject, but they never
mention it. This forces readers to decide for themselves how the
examples relate to the topic sentence. This revision shows how
repetition can help readers focus on the subject.

1   Mercury poisoning is a problem that has long been recognized.
2   "Mad as a hatter" refers to the condition prevalent among nineteenth-
    century workers who were exposed to mercury during the manufac-
3   turing of felt hats. Workers in many other industries, such as mining,
4   chemicals, and dentistry, were similarly affected. In the 1950's and
    1960's there were cases of mercury poisoning in Minamata, Japan.
5   Research showed that there were high levels of mercury pollution in
6   streams and lakes surrounding the village. In the United States this
    problem came to light in 1969 when a New Mexico family got sick
7   from eating food tainted with mercury. Since then pesticides contain-
    ing mercury have been withdrawn from the market and chemical
    wastes can no longer be dumped into the ocean.

The words *mercury* and *mercury poisoning* throughout the paragraph now remind readers of the subject. Notice that to avoid
monotony the writer sometimes refers indirectly to this subject
with phrases such as *similarly affected* (sentence 3) and *this
problem* (sentence 6).

(4)   Using transitional words and phrases to achieve coherence

Transitional words and phrases—*but, similarly, also, on the
other hand, moreover, in contrast, the same as, therefore, however,* and so on—indicate the relationship among elements of
the sentence. These words not only limit the meaning of a clause,
they also connect that clause in some specific way to what has
gone before. By establishing these connections, transitional
words and phrases tie together ideas in a paragraph before readers have a chance to forget them. Thus, transitional elements
establish coherence and speed the reader's understanding.

You should use transitional words or phrases unless the

relationship between elements in a sentence is obvious. The following paragraph shows how the omission of these words and phrases can make a passage difficult to understand.

¶ coh 4c

Without transitional words and phrases

> Napoleon certainly made a change for the worse by leaving his small kingdom of Elba. He went to Paris and he abdicated for a second time. He fled to Rochfort in hope of escaping to America. He gave himself up to the English captain of the ship *Bellerophon*. He suggested that the Prince Regent should grant him asylum and he was refused. All he saw of England was the Devon coast and Plymouth Sound as he passed on to the remote island of St. Helena. He died on May 5, 1821, at the age of fifty-two.

Although the unifying idea of this paragraph is clear—Napoleon made a change for the worse—the exact chronological relationships among events is not. With no transitional words or phrases, the paragraph reads like a list of unconnected events. Readers can, with difficulty, guess at some of the connections. But when did Napoleon go to Paris? What does fleeing to America have to do with surrendering to the captain? Effective writing must anticipate readers' needs and address them. This revision contains transitions that emphasize the sequence of events.

> Napoleon certainly made a change for the worse by leaving his small kingdom of Elba. <u>After Waterloo</u>, he went back to Paris and he abdicated for a second time. <u>A hundred days after</u> his return from Elba, he fled to Rochfort in hope of escaping to America. <u>Finally</u>, he gave himself up to the English captain on the ship *Bellerophon*. <u>Once again</u>, he suggested that the Prince Regent grant him asylum, and <u>once again</u>, he was refused. <u>In the end</u>, all he saw of England was the Devon coast and Plymouth Sound as he passed on to the remote island of St. Helena. <u>After six years of exile</u>, he died on May 5, 1821, at the age of fifty-two. (Norman Mackenzie, *The Escape from Elba*)

In this revised paragraph, words and phrases like *after, finally, once again,* and *in the end* provide the links that clarify the chronological order of the events in the passage.

Here are some of the more commonly used transitional expressions.

Words that signal sequence

and	besides
again	finally
also	furthermore

Words that signal sequence (cont.)

moreover	in addition
next	one . . . another
lastly	first . . . second . . . third

Words that signal time

at first, second (etc.)	former . . . latter
soon	afterward
before	at length
after	meanwhile
finally	in the meantime
then	until
later	
next	

Words that signal comparison

however	nevertheless
but	instead
yet	on the one hand . . .
still	on the other hand
nonetheless	in contrast
on the contrary	although
	meanwhile

Words that signal examples

for example
for instance
to illustrate
the following example . . .

Words that signal conclusions or summaries

in summary	consequently
in conclusion	in other words
to conclude	thus
therefore	as a result

Words that signal concession

although it is true that . . .
granted
naturally
although you could say that . . .
of course

Words that signal causes or effects

because	consequently
hence	then
since	thus
therefore	as a result

(5)   Achieving coherence among paragraphs

**¶ coh
4c**

The same methods you use to establish coherence within paragraphs—pronoun reference, parallel structures, repeated key words, and transitional words and phrases—may also be used to link paragraphs. The following three paragraphs show how some of these strategies work.

A language may borrow a word directly or indirectly. A direct borrowing means that the borrowed item is a native word in the language it is borrowed from. The native Middle French word *festa* (Modern French *fête;* the Old French was *feste* from Latin *festa*) was directly borrowed by Middle English, and has become Modern English *feast.* On the other hand, the word *algebra* was borrowed from Spanish, which in turn was borrowed from Arabic. English borrowed *algebra* indirectly from Arabic, with Spanish as an intermediary.

Some languages are heavy borrowers. Albanian has borrowed so heavily that few native words are retained. On the other hand, many American Indian languages have borrowed but lightly from their neighbors.

English has borrowed extensively. Of the 20,000 or so words in common use, about three-fifths are borrowed. However, the figure is misleading. Of the 500 most frequently used words, only two-sevenths are borrowed, and since these "common" words are used over and over again in sentences, the actual frequency of appearance of native words is much higher than the statistics on borrowing would lead one to believe. "Little" words such as *and, be, have, it, of, the, to, will, you, on, that,* and *is* are all native to English, and constitute about one-fourth of the words regularly used. Thus it is not unreasonable to suppose that more than four-fifths of the words commonly used in speaking English are native to the language. (Victoria Fromkin and Robert Rodman, *An Introduction to Language,* 3d ed.)

These three paragraphs make a tightly knit unit. The first paragraph introduces the idea that a language may borrow a word directly or indirectly. The second paragraph narrows the discussion to languages that are heavy borrowers, and the third focuses on English, a language that has borrowed extensively.

The topic sentences of this three-paragraph sequence reinforce the structure. Each establishes coherence by repeating a variation of *A language may borrow,* which appears in paragraph 1. In addition, the narrowing of focus from *some languages* to *English* reinforces the structure. Finally, some form of the key words *language* and *borrow* appears in almost every sentence.

▶ EXERCISE 3

A. Read the following paragraphs and determine how the authors achieve coherence. Note patterns or parallel structures and underline pronouns, repeated words, and transitional words and phrases that link sentences.

1 1. Life for the young doctors and nurses was not easy at the
2   Schweitzer Hospital. Dr. Schweitzer knew it and gave himself
3   the task of supplying nutrients for their spirits. At mealtimes,
       when the staff came together, Schweitzer always had an amus-
4   ing story or two to go with the meal. Laughter at the dinner
5   hour was probably the most important course. It was fascinat-
       ing to see the way the staff members seemed to be rejuvenated
6   by the wryness of his humor. At one meal, for example, Dr.
       Schweitzer reported to the staff that, "as everyone knows, there
       are only two automobiles within seventy-five miles of the hos-
7   pital. This afternoon, the inevitable happened; the cars col-
8   lided. We have treated the drivers for their superficial wounds.
9   Anyone who has reverence for machines may treat the cars."
       (Norman Cousins, *Anatomy of an Illness*)

1 2. Some years ago the old elevated railway in Philadelphia was
2   torn down and replaced by the subway system. This ancient El
       with its barnlike stations containing nut-vending machines and
       scattered food scraps had, for generations, been the favorite
       feeding ground of flocks of pigeons, generally one flock to a
3   station along the route of the El. Hundreds of pigeons were
4   dependent upon the system. They flapped in and out of its
       stanchions and steel work or gathered in watchful little audi-
       ences about the feet of anyone who rattled the peanut-vending
5   machines. They even watched people who jingled change in
       their hands, and prospected for food under the feet of the
6   crowds who gathered between trains. Probably very few among
       the waiting people who tossed a crumb to an eager pigeon
       realized that this El was like a food-bearing river, and that the
       life which haunted its banks was dependent upon the running
       of the trains with their human freight. (Loren Eiseley, *The Night
       Country*)

B. Reorder the sentences in the following scrambled paragraph. After doing so, determine how certain words and phrases help the paragraph achieve coherence.

1. He empathized with the plight of persecuted religious sects, especially those in Germany and England.
2. These ideas again caused him problems.

3. William Penn was not unfamiliar with persecution.
4. Because of a pamphlet he wrote, Penn was imprisoned in the Tower of London from December 1668 through August 1669.
5. This persecution caused Penn to consider the idea of establishing a religious refuge in America.
6. He was imprisoned in 1671 for preaching at a Quaker meeting.
7. When he was released, Penn continued to follow Quaker ideas.

¶ *dev*
4d

C. Supplying the missing transitional words and phrases, revise the following paragraph to make it coherent.

> The theory of continental drift was first put forward by Alfred Wegener in 1912. The continents fit together like a gigantic jigsaw puzzle. The opposing Atlantic coasts, especially South America and Africa, seem to have been attached. He believed that at one time, probably 225 million years ago, there was one supercontinent. This continent broke into parts that eventually drifted into their present positions. The theory stirred controversy during the 1920's and eventually was ridiculed by the scientific community. In 1954 the theory was revived. The theory of continental drift is accepted as a reasonable geologic explanation of the continental system.

D. Write coherent paragraphs for any two of the following topic sentences.

1. Communicating is something we do a lot of at my house.
2. When I came to college, I had a big problem to solve.
3. This season television programs seem to be getting better/worse.
4. Why do some athletes get such high salaries?
5. In times of crisis, Americans can be the most generous people in the world.

4d   Writing Well-Developed Paragraphs

A paragraph is well developed when it contains the examples, details, or evidence readers need to understand the unifying idea. Without adequate **development** a paragraph gives readers only a partial picture.

Unfortunately, no rule exists to define *adequate*. The amount of detail you need in a paragraph depends on your purpose, your audience, and how much or how little your topic sentence claims. You can, however, examine your topic sentence to see that you have supplied all of the information it promises.

Consider this paragraph.

**¶ dev
4d**

*Inadequate
detail*
  From Thanksgiving until Christmas, children are saturated with ads for violent toys. Advertisers persist in thinking
that only toys that appeal to children's aggressiveness will
sell. Far from improving the situation, video games have escalated the arms race. The real question is why toy manufacturers continue to pour millions of dollars into violent toys,
especially in light of the success of toys that promote learning and cooperation. (Student)

The writer of this paragraph does not provide enough specific
information. Just as charting structure can help you see whether
a paragraph is unified, it can also help you determine if it is
well developed. Looking at the underlying structure of the paragraph above, we get a better idea of the problem.

1 From Thanksgiving until Christmas, children are saturated
 with ads for violent toys.
 2 Advertisers persist in thinking that only toys that appeal to
  children's aggressiveness will sell.
 2 Far from improving the situation, video games have escalated the arms race.
 2 The real question is why toy manufacturers continue to
  pour millions of dollars into violent toys, especially in light
  of the success of toys that promote learning and cooperation.

The level-1 sentence of this paragraph is the topic sentence. The
level-2 sentences expand the discussion, but the paragraph offers no level-3 examples. What kinds of toys appeal to a child's
aggressive tendencies? Exactly what video games does the writer
object to? Notice how the writer adds this information in the
revision.

  From Thanksgiving until Christmas, children are saturated
with ads for violent toys. Advertisers persist in thinking that only
toys that appeal to children's aggressiveness will sell. <u>One television commercial praises the merits of an Eagle Force commando
team that attacks and captures a miniature enemy base. Toy soldiers wear realistic uniforms and carry automatic rifles, pistols,
knives, grenades, and ammunition. Another commercial shows
laughing children shooting one another with plastic rocket fighters and tanklike "walkers."</u> Far from improving the situation, video
games have escalated the arms race. <u>The most popular video</u>

games involve children in realistic combat situations. One game, Star Raiders, lets children search out and destroy enemy rocket fighters in outer space. Other best-selling games simulate attacks on enemy fortresses or fight off an array of hostile creatures. The real question is why toy manufacturers continue to pour millions of dollars into violent toys, especially in light of the success of toys that promote learning and cooperation.

¶ *dev*
4e

This paragraph develops by means of examples; by providing examples the writer now convincingly supports his topic sentence.

4e Using Patterns of Development

The pattern of a paragraph, like the pattern of an entire essay, reflects the way the writer thinks. Such patterns suggest the in-depth questions used to develop a topic (see 1b.4). Most writers do not consciously decide in advance on a particular method of development and then write their paragraphs accordingly. Only in revision do they see the patterns their thoughts fall into. When you see the direction a paragraph is taking, you can rework the topic sentence and rearrange information to support the unifying idea more effectively.

Of course, some paragraphs, like some essays, have more than one pattern of development. As a beginning writer, however, you should learn to use each pattern separately. After you have developed good paragraph skills, you can combine strategies to express your ideas.

(1) What happened? (Narration)

Narrative paragraphs present events in chronological order. They tell a story. Often they do not have topic sentences, but even so they do have unifying ideas. The following narrative paragraph has no topic sentence. The order of events and the transitions that signal that sequence give it all the unity it needs.

About midnight, having fallen asleep, I was awakened and greatly surprised at finding the most of my companions up in arms, and furiously engaged with a large alligator but a few yards from me. One of our company, it seems, awoke in the night, and perceived the monster within a few paces of the camp; when giving the alarm to the rest, they readily came to his assistance, for it was a rare piece of sport. Some took fire-brands and cast them at his head, whilst others formed javelins of saplings, pointed and hardened with fire; these they thrust down his throat . . . which caused the monster to roar and bellow hideously; but his strength and fury were so great, that he easily wrenched or twisted them out of their hands, and wielding and brandishing them about, kept his enemies at a distance for a time. Some were for putting an end to his life and sufferings with a rifle ball, but the majority thought this would too soon deprive them of the diversion and pleasure of exercising their various inventions of torture: they at length grew tired, and agreed in one opinion, that he had suffered sufficiently; and put an end to his existence. (William Bartram, *Travels of William Bartram*)

Topic sentences can sometimes put the incidents of a narrative into very clear focus. The topic sentence of this paragraph performs such a function.

My academic career almost ended as soon as it began. Three weeks after I arrived at college I decided to pledge a fraternity. By midterms I was wearing a straw hat and saying "Yes sir" to every fraternity brother I met. I ate lunch at the fraternity house, and when classes were over I ran errands for the fraternity members. After dinner I socialized and worked on projects with the other people in my pledge class. In between these activities I tried to study. Somehow I managed to write reports, take tests, and attend lectures. By the end of the semester, though, my grades had slipped and I was exhausted. It was then that I began to ask myself some important questions. Why was I putting myself through this? Why did I want to join a fraternity? I realized that I wanted to be popular, but not at the expense of my grades and my future career. At the beginning of my second semester I dropped out of the fraternity and volunteered to work in the biology lab. Looking back, I realize that it was then that I actually began to grow up. (Student)

Details are vital to a narrative paragraph. They re-create the scene and supply the information that readers must have to understand what you are talking about. Here details enrich this account of a student's family history.

My mother's family settled in Washington, D.C., in the Irish neighborhoods of Swamp Poodle, Georgetown, and Watergate. My great-grandfather, John Howard, owned a livery stable near Ford's Theatre in Washington. Several hours before John Wilkes Booth assassinated President Lincoln, Booth came to Howard's livery stable to rent a horse. Since Howard didn't know him, he refused. In anger Booth threw down his riding boots and stormed out of the stable. That night in Ford's Theatre, after Booth shot Lincoln, he jumped from the president's box to the stage and broke his ankle. My great-grandfather claimed that if Booth had not thrown down his favorite riding boots in the livery stable, he might have escaped uninjured and never been caught. (Student)

¶ *dev*
4e

(2) What does it look like? (Description)

To **describe** something you must first see it, and to see it, you must first look at it part by part. You then present your perception of these separate parts in such a way that they form a pattern for your audience. The sequential arrangement you use in your essay follows the sequence in which you would look at a scene or an object: near to far, top to bottom, side to side, or front to back.

The following descriptive paragraph begins with a far view of the Great Beach on Cape Cod and then moves closer. This organization makes it easy for readers to see the details.

> The sand bar of Eastham is the sea wall of the inlet. Its crest overhangs the beach, and from the high, wind-trampled rim, a long slope well overgrown with dune grass descends to the meadows on the west. Seen from the tower at Nauset, the land has an air of geological simplicity; as a matter of fact, it is full of hollows, blind passages and amphitheatres in which the roaring of the sea changes into the far roar of a cataract. I often wander into these curious pits. On their floors of sand, on their slopes, I find patterns made of the feet of visiting birds. Here, in a little disturbed and claw-marked space of sand, a flock of larks has alighted; here one of the birds has wandered off by himself; here are the deeper tracks of hungry crows; here the webbed impressions of a gull. There is always something poetic and mysterious to me about these tracks in the pits of the dunes; they begin at nowhere, sometimes with the faint impression of an alighting wing, and vanish as suddenly into the trackless nowhere of the sky. (Henry Breston, *The Outmost House*)

In the next paragraph, the author describes the things she sees as she approaches William Randolph Hearst's California estate. She arranges details spatially, beginning with a view of the castle sitting on a mountaintop and ending with a description of the tiles lining the interior pool.

"La Casa Grande," William Randolph Hearst's estate in California, was to be the centerpiece of his empire. The castle sits on top of the San Lucia Mountains above San Simeon. The structure can be seen for miles down the highway. At the front of the estate is a ticket office that stands beside a five-mile private road that leads to the castle. On the way to the castle are orchards, horse trails, pastures, and the world's largest private zoo. Surrounding the main house are three guest houses. Hearst had them built for his children when they visited. Each guest house contains ten rooms, including marble baths, a formal dining room, and servants' quarters. The castle itself was begun in 1922 and was still not finished in 1951, the year of Hearst's death. It has over one hundred rooms that contain priceless works of art. The dining room is lined with silk banners from Italy and the long oak table can seat fifty. The billiard room contains three tables. All four walls are covered with tapestries and the floors are covered with antique rugs. The indoor Roman pool is as large as two tennis courts and is lined with gold inlaid tiles. (Student)

(3)   What are some typical cases or examples of it? (Exemplification)

One of the basic ways we explain something or prove a point is with **examples,** specific illustrations that clarify a general statement. Often several well-chosen examples are all you need to develop a paragraph. The author of this paragraph illustrates the general statement "Summer was a great time" with a number of examples that enable his audience to experience the color and sound of life in New York during the 1920's.

> *Topic*   <u>Summer was a great time.</u> I think now with a special joy
> *sentence* of the long afternoons of mildew and quietness in the school
>   courtyard, now a lazy playground, and the cool stored-up bas-
> *Examples* ketball sweat along the silence of the main hall, where the
>   dust rose up brown as we played quoits against the principal's
>   door. Then of those holidays even on week days when my
>   mother would cry out as she suddenly wiped the sweat off her
>   neck, "Oh, how hot it is today! Too hot! Too hot!" and decide
>   on a day at Coney Island. (Alfred Kazin, *A Walker in the City*)

Examples also persuade readers that what you are saying is accurate and worth listening to. Carefully chosen examples often can be much more convincing than pages of your own analysis. And they certainly give your writing the edge it needs to be effective and easily understood. For instance,

¶ *dev*
4e

> From an engineering standpoint alcohol could supplement oil as a fuel source. Alcohol could easily be substituted for diesel fuel if engineers implemented simple engine modifications and made ignition timing and fuel tank capacity changes. In addition, alcohol in anything down to a seventy percent alcohol/thirty percent water mixture could burn in a home furnace. A farmer could use animal and plant waste to make enough fuel for his own consumption or could use the dried distiller's grain as a feed supplement. Finally, studies have shown that industrial consumers of fuel oil could, with little or no trouble, adapt their furnaces to use alcohol. (Student)

Each example in this paragraph specifically illustrates the topic sentence. By discussing several major areas of fuel use, the writer supplies readers with needed information.

In the following paragraph a single extended example gives readers enough detail to help them accept the author's point about hormone secretion and aggressiveness.

> The influence of aggressiveness and dominance on hormones and sex reaches its peak in the case of small tropical fish called "cleaners," which feed off parasites that they remove from the skin of other fish. One species, studied on the Australian Great Barrier Reef, lives in groups of one male with a harem of three to six females; the male dominates the females and the larger, older females dominate the smaller, younger ones. If the male dies or is removed from the group, the largest of the females almost immediately begins to act like a male, carrying out typical male aggressive displays toward the other females. And within a couple of weeks *she actually turns into a male*, producing sperm instead of eggs! I am not suggesting, of course, that anything of the sort could occur in primates or other mammals; for one thing, most or all cleaner-fish females possess rudimentary testes, as mammalian females do not. Nonetheless, I find rather mind-blowing the fact that a female can change into a male simply by acting like one. (Robert Claiborne, *God or Beast*)

Whether you need one example or many depends on your point. Some specific assertions require only an example or two. Others call for many examples.

(4)   How did—or does—it happen? (Process)

Process paragraphs describe how something works, usually in chronological order. The topic sentence (when there is one) identifies the process, and the rest of the paragraph itemizes the steps involved. Throughout the paragraph, transitional terms like *first, next, then,* and *finally* signal the organizational pattern and hold the paragraph together. Here, for example, is how members of the Supreme Court decide whether or not to grant an appeal.

> Members of the court have disclosed, however, the general way the conference is conducted. It begins at ten A.M. and usually runs on until late afternoon. At the start each justice, when he enters the room, shakes hands with all others there (thirty-six handshakes altogether). The custom, dating back generations, is evidently designed to begin the meeting at a friendly level, no matter how heated the intellectual differences may be. The conference takes up, first, the applications for review—a few appeals, many more petitions for certiorari. Those on the Appellate Docket, the regular paid cases, are considered first, then the pauper's applications on the Miscellaneous Docket. (If any of these are granted, they are then transferred to the Appellate Docket.) After this the justices consider, and vote on, all the cases argued during the preceding Monday through Thursday. These are tentative votes, which may be and quite often are changed as the opinion is written and the problem thought through more deeply. There may be further discussion at later conferences before the opinion is handed down. (Anthony Lewis, *Gideon's Trumpet*)

Sometimes a process paragraph *instructs*, telling readers how to do something or how to perform an activity. Instructions are written in the present tense and, like commands, in the imperative mood: "Remove the cover . . . and check the valve." This directness of both tense and mood helps readers follow the directions more easily. This set of instructions tells how to treat a photograph that has curled around the edges.

> If you have a photograph that hasn't been framed or mounted, sooner or later it will ripple or curl up at the corners. But you *can* treat the malady. Put the picture in a pan of room-temperature water. Take the photograph out after a few minutes. Shake the water droplets off it, then gently insert it in a folded paper towel. Put this flat packet on your ironing board. Cover the picture-side with more clean, white paper toweling. *Note:* Do not use a decorated towel! If you do, you'll transfer the design to your

photograph. Set your *dry* iron on a low temperature, then iron across the towel. Now take the towel off. Lo and behold! A flat, ready-to-frame photograph! (Marcia D. Liles and Robert M. Liles, *Good Housekeeping Guide to Fixing Things Around the House*)

¶ dev 4e

(5)   What caused it? What are its effects? (Cause and effect)

Like narrative and process, **cause and effect** is concerned with events in time. But instead of focusing on the order in which events occur, cause-and-effect paragraphs explore why they occur and what happens because of them. Cause-and-effect relationships are often complicated, so you must take care to distinguish cause from effect. Topic sentences and transitional words and phrases *(one cause, another cause, a more important result, because, as a result)* help to mark these relationships.

Often a paragraph focuses on either causes or effects. In the following paragraph, the writer suggests a *cause* of thumb-sucking and then summarizes a study to support his assertion.

> The main reason that a young baby sucks his thumb seems to be that he hasn't had enough sucking at the breast or bottle to satisfy his sucking needs. Dr. David Levy pointed out that babies who are fed every 3 hours don't suck their thumbs as much as babies fed every 4 hours, and that babies who have cut down on nursing time from 20 minutes to 10 minutes . . . are more likely to suck their thumbs than babies who still have to work for 20 minutes. Dr. Levy fed a litter of puppies with a medicine dropper so that they had no chance to suck during their feedings. They acted just the same as babies who don't get enough chance to suck at feeding time. They sucked their own and each other's paws and skin so hard that the fur came off. (Benjamin Spock, *Baby and Child Care*)

In the next paragraph, a student identifies the *effects* of Saturday cartoon-watching on her younger brother. She begins by identifying the effects she will examine and then gives her examples and draws her conclusions.

> Although I have not carried out a scientific study, I have noticed the effects of television violence on my younger brother. Every Saturday he goes on a four-hour television cartoon binge. His diet includes *The Hulk, Superfriends, Spider Man*, and occasionally *The Smurfs*. (He sneaks this one because he thinks he is too old for it.) As my brother watches the cartoons, he gets more

and more excited. He runs and jumps around the room and has mock battles with furniture and imaginary enemies. Later, after he has finished watching, he and his friends act out things they have seen in the cartoons. Their games always involve fighting, shooting, stabbing, and killing. Even though some people might say that this aggressive behavior is normal for a nine-year-old boy, I feel that television cartoons cause his play to be excessively violent. (Student)

(6) How is it like other things? How is it different? (Comparison and contrast)

Comparison-and-contrast paragraphs look at the similarities and differences between two subjects. Comparison usually emphasizes similarities, while contrast always deals with differences. When using this pattern of development, be sure that the subjects you compare have things in common and that you compare the same or similar qualities of both. Do not forget to use transitional words and phrases *(however, but, on the contrary, although, nevertheless)* to signal comparison and to indicate movement from one subject to another.

Comparison and contrast is organized in one of two ways. First, you can compare and contrast each subject point by point. This organization is especially useful in a complex paragraph in which your readers may have trouble keeping track of your points. To compare and contrast two automobiles, for example, your paragraph pattern might look like this.

Mileage
 Automobile A
 Automobile B

Safety
 Automobile A
 Automobile B

Warranty
 Automobile A
 Automobile B

A second way to organize a comparison-and-contrast paragraph is to treat one subject in its entirety in the beginning of your paragraph and the other subject in its entirety at the end.

This organization works well when you know that your readers can remember what you have said about the first subject while they read about the second. The pattern might look like this.

¶ dev
4e

Automobile A
  Mileage
  Safety
  Warranty

Automobile B
  Mileage
  Safety
  Warranty

The following paragraph uses point-by-point comparison. Notice how the author handles his complex subjects as he compares them.

> There are two Americas. One is the America of Lincoln and Adlai Stevenson; the other is the America of Teddy Roosevelt and the modern superpatriots. One is generous and humane, the other narrowly egotistical; one is self-critical, the other self-righteous; one is sensible, the other romantic; one is good-humored, the other solemn; one is inquiring, the other pontificating; one is moderate, the other filled with passionate intensity; one is judicious and the other arrogant in the use of great power. (J. William Fulbright, *The Arrogance of Power*)

By repeating *one* and *the other* the writer sets up a parallel structure. Not only does this technique establish coherence, it also emphasizes the ideas the writer wants to convey.

In the next paragraph, the writer treats all of one subject before going on to the next. He signals the shift from one subject to the other with the transitional word *now*.

> This seems to be an era of gratuitous inventions and negative improvements. Consider the beer can. It was beautiful—as beautiful as the clothespin, as inevitable as the wine bottle, as dignified and reassuring as the fire hydrant. A tranquil cylinder of delightfully resonant metal, it could be opened in an instant, requiring only the application of a handy gadget freely dispensed by every grocer. Who can forget the small, symmetrical thrill of those two triangular punctures, the dainty *pfff*, the little crest of suds that foamed eagerly in the exultation of release? Now we are given, instead, a top beetling with an ugly, shmoo-shaped "tab," which,

after fiercely resisting the tugging, bleeding fingers of the thirsty man, threatens his lips with a dangerous and hideous hole. However, we have discovered a way to thwart Progress, usually so unthwartable. *Turn the beer can upside down and open the bottom.* The bottom is still the way the top used to be. True, this operation gives the beer an unsettling jolt, and the sight of a consistently inverted beer can might make people edgy, not to say queasy. But the latter difficulty could be eliminated if manufacturers would design cans that looked the same whichever end was up, like playing cards. What we need is Progress with an escape hatch. (John Updike, *Assorted Prose*)

(7) What are its parts? (Division) Into what categories can its parts be arranged? (Classification)

In **division,** you take a single item and break it into its components. You could, for instance, divide blood into its various parts: plasma, white cells, red cells, and so on. In **classification,** you take many separate items and group them according to qualities or characteristics they have in common. You could, for instance, group books according to subject, author, or size.

In the following paragraph from a lab manual, a student divides blood into several components.

> The blood can be divided into several distinct components. There is plasma, and the formed elements consisting of red cells, white cells, and platelets. Plasma is 90 percent water and holds a great number of things in suspension. It contains proteins, sugars, fat, and inorganic salts. Plasma also contains urea and other by-products from the breaking down of proteins, hormones, enzymes, and dissolved gasses. In addition, plasma contains the red blood cells that give it color, the white cells, and the platelets. The red cells are most numerous; they get oxygen from the lungs and release it in the tissues. The less numerous white cells are part of the body's defense against invading organisms. The platelets occur in almost the same number as white cells and are responsible for clotting. (Student)

First the student identifies the subject that she will analyze. Then she identifies the components of blood and their characteristics, moving from the most frequently to the least frequently found.

The paragraph below establishes the subject, scientific frauds, and then goes on to classify frauds into three categories.

Charles Babbage, an English mathematician, reflecting in 1830 on what he saw as the decline of science at the time, distinguished among three major kinds of scientific fraud. He called the first "forging," by which he meant complete fabrication—the recording of observations that were never made. The second category he called "trimming"; this consists of manipulating the data to make them look better, or, as Babbage wrote, "in clipping off little bits here and there from those observations which differ most in *excess* from the mean and in sticking them on to those which are too small." His third category was data selection, which he called "cooking"—the choosing of those data that fitted the researcher's hypothesis and the discarding of those that did not. To this day, the serious discussion of scientific fraud has not improved on Babbage's typology. (Morton Hunt, *New York Times Magazine*)

Unlike division, which breaks down a single subject (blood), classification focuses on a subject with many parts (scientific frauds) and groups them into categories of like things. Such groups are mutually exclusive; that is, items in one category (forging) do not also fit in another category (trimming or cooking).

(8) What is it? (Definition)

A **formal definition** includes the term you are defining, the class to which it belongs, and its attributes—the things that distinguish it from other members of its class.

Carbon is a nonmetallic element
(term)   *(class to which it belongs)*
occurring as diamond, graphite, and charcoal.
                (distinguishing details)

A puck is a rubber disk
(term)   *(class to which it belongs)*
used in ice hockey.
(distinguishing details)

An **extended definition** builds on this format and can be a paragraph or more in length. Such paragraphs may combine the pattern of definition with other patterns of development. You can define *happiness*, for instance, by telling a story (narration). You can define a diesel engine by telling how it works (process). Extended definitions may also include the background or origins of a term. Terms can also be defined by telling what they are like (using synonyms) or what they are not (using negation).

The following paragraph illustrates extended definition by example. It begins with a straightforward definition of *gadget* and then cites an example.

> A gadget is nearly always novel in design or concept and it often has no proper name. For example, the semaphore which signals the arrival of the mail in our rural mailbox certainly has no proper name. It is a contrivance consisting of a piece of shingle. Call it what you like, it saves us frequent frustrating trips to the mailbox in winter when you have to dress up and wade through snow to get there. That's a gadget! (*Smithsonian*)

The next paragraph uses narration to define. The writer tells a story to convey a clear idea of what *fear* means to him.

> I never knew what fear meant until the day I went on my first cave descent. Because I was a novice, I entered last. For the first hour things went smoothly; then, as I squeezed through a narrow passageway, I got stuck. I had always thought of myself as being calm in emergencies, but when I realized I couldn't move, I panicked. I forgot everything I had been taught during my orientation. All I could think of was that I was wedged in so tightly that I couldn't move forward or backward. I must have been screaming, even though I didn't realize it, because almost at once the leader of the descent crawled up to me. It took him about ten minutes to calm me down and to convince me to let out a deep breath. As soon as I exhaled, he was able to pull me free. (Student)

▶

EXERCISE 4

A. Chart the following paragraphs to determine why they are adequately developed. Supply any further information needed to support each paragraph's unifying idea.

1. With some advance planning you can make sure that a job interview goes well. You should know about the job you are trying to get and you should know about your qualifications. You should also make sure that your answers are clear and to the point.

2. Computers have already revolutionized our lives. They make it possible for us to do many things we take for granted. Soon a computer will be as much a part of a home as a television is.

3. Credit cards make it easy for a college student to go into debt. They make you feel as if you are getting something for nothing. And they also encourage impulse buying.

4. Taking a vacation does not have to cost a lot of money. There are ways a traveler can cut expenses and still have an enjoyable time. Of

course you won't be staying in a luxurious room with a view or eating a five-course meal every evening, but you will be doing many of the same things that people spending much more are also doing.

B. Go through several of your own essays and find examples of the basic patterns of paragraph development we have discussed.

C. Determine one possible method of development for a paragraph on each of these topics.

1. What love is	6. The connection between sleep and memory
2. How to cope with stress	
3. What kinds of people attend rock concerts	7. Dressing for success
	8. Responsibility
4. My worst job	9. Making the perfect meal
5. American vs. Japanese cars	10. Drinking and driving

D. Write a paragraph on one of the topics in Exercise C.

E. Write a well-developed paragraph on one of the following topics.

1. Learning to drive (process)
2. Studying (cause and effect)
3. Types of friends (classification)
4. A vacation you took (narration)
5. Smokers vs. nonsmokers (comparison and contrast)
6. What is success? (definition)
7. Something right or wrong with television (exemplification)
8. A picture of a person, place, or thing (description)

4f Writing Special Kinds of Paragraphs

So far we have been talking only about the paragraphs that carry the weight of your discussion by presenting your ideas to your readers. Other paragraphs have different functions, however, and do not follow all the principles we have discussed. Even so, they have a significant impact on how readers respond to your ideas. Now let us focus on paragraphs that act as an essay's introduction and conclusion and that provide transition.

(1) Writing introductions

An **introduction** prepares an audience for your essay. The preparation needed will depend on your subject, your audience, and your purpose. A strong introduction brings readers into the world of your essay. A weak one leaves them outside. Not only must you bring readers into your essay through your introduction, you must also create interest and establish your thesis. Your introduction, usually a full paragraph of several sentences and almost never a single sentence, must make clear to your audience what follows.

Some introductions are straightforward, concerned primarily with presenting information. They begin by announcing your subject, limiting it, and then stating your thesis. The following introduction is an example of this pattern.

> Although modern architecture is usually not intricate in design, it often involves remarkable engineering accomplishments. Most people do not realize the difficulties an architect encounters when designing a "great" modern structure. The new wing of the Smithsonian in Washington, in its simplicity, is such a masterpiece of engineering and design. (Student)

The first two sentences introduce and limit the subject of modern architecture. The third sentence focuses on a specific building and presents the thesis of the essay.

Not all subjects appeal to all readers, and at times you must find a way to capture your audience's attention. Effective introductions of this sort can be difficult to conceive and to arrange. One approach is to begin with a *quotation* that leads to the thesis.

> "It's far easier to explain why the moon shouldn't be there," says M.I.T. geophysicist Nafi Toksoz, "than to explain its existence." That may sound strange when the data amassed by the manned Apollo lunar missions should have settled, it seems, the age-old question of the moon's origin once and for all. But that just did not happen. Even after a decade of intensive study, lunar scientists are still trying to recreate the story of how the moon came to be. (Ben Patrusky, "Where Did the Moon Come From?")

Another approach is to introduce an essay with a *question*. This technique creates interest if it focuses on some concern of the reader.

> What kind of person goes to the movies at least three times a week? A film buff, that's who. Film buffs will go anywhere, almost any time, to see a movie they have missed. They spend much of their lives sitting in uncomfortable seats in darkened movie theaters. Even so, their hobby can be interesting, exciting, and rewarding. (Student)

You may also begin an essay with a *definition* of an important term. This technique is especially useful in examinations or research papers.

> Moles are collections of cells that appear on any part of the body. With occasional exceptions, moles are absent at birth. They first appear in the early years of life, between ages two and six years, and occur anywhere. Frequently moles appear at puberty. New moles, however, can continue to appear throughout life. During pregnancy new moles may appear and old ones darken. There are three major designations of moles, each with its own characteristics. (Student)

Unusual *comparisons* often shed light on a subject and attract a reader's attention.

> Once a long time ago, people had special little boxes called refrigerators in which milk, meat, and eggs could be kept cool. The grandchildren of these simple devices are large enough to store whole cows, and they reach temperatures comparable to those at the South Pole. Their operating costs increase each year, and they are so complicated that few home handymen attempt to repair them on their own. Why has this change in size and complexity occurred in America? It has not taken place in many areas of the technologically advanced world (the average West German refrigerator is about a yard high and less than a yard wide, yet refrigeration technology in Germany is quite advanced). Do we really need (or even want) all that space and cold? (Appletree Rodder, "Why Smaller Refrigerators Can Preserve the Human Race")

An *opinion* that seems extreme, outspoken, or outrageous can create immediate interest. It is effective, however, only if you can tie it to your subject and then make a case for your thesis.

> Most men live in harness. Richard was one of them. Typically he had no awareness of how his male harness was choking him until his personal and professional life and his body had nearly fallen apart. (Herb Goldberg, *The Hazards of Being Male*)

Your introduction must talk about the subject of your paper. It cannot be at odds with your subject or seem imposed on it. And it must also fit with the purpose, tone, and style of the rest of your essay. A serious, formal discussion should have the same kind of introduction. If your discussion is relaxed and informal, your introduction should be so, too.

¶
4f

(2) Writing conclusions

Most essays have a **conclusion**, a carefully constructed ending that reinforces major ideas and gives readers a sense of completion. Usually a full paragraph, in long essays the conclusion can run two paragraphs or more. By restating your thesis, the conclusion gives readers the chance to make sure that they have understood your essay. Your conclusion must therefore be clearly connected to your essay—containing the echo of a powerful image, for instance, or a reference to your introduction. By tying your conclusion to your introduction, you frame your essay and bring it full circle.

The following conclusion *reviews the essay's main points.* By pointing back to ideas stated earlier, the writer sums up his reasons for admiring his grandmother. *As you can see* signals the start of the conclusion, and sentences 2 and 3 lead to a final sentence calculated to stay with the audience after they have finished reading.

As you can see, my grandmother is an unusual person. She is a dedicated nurse and a loving parent and grandparent. She has fought for the rights of others all her life, and she has raised children—both male and female—who follow her example. I am glad that I have had the opportunity to know her and to use her as a model for my own life. (Student)

John Pheiffer ends an essay differently. After taking a look at primitive cultures, he concludes by *predicting* the future of the human race.

Looking ahead, prospects may not be quite as dismal as they seem. As a matter of fact, we are not doing so badly. It is something of a miracle that creatures who evolved as nomads in an intimate, small-band, wide-open-spaces context manage to get along at all as villagers or surrounded by strangers in cubicle apartments. Considering that our genius as a species is adaptability, we may yet learn to live closer and closer to one another, if not in utter peace, then far more peacefully than we do today. (John Pheiffer, "Seeking Peace, Making War")

You can also conclude an essay by *stating an opinion.* Donald Murray concludes an essay on revision with this observation about the subject.

A piece of writing is never finished. It is delivered to a deadline, torn out of the typewriter on demand, sent off with a sense of accomplishment and shame and pride and frustration. If only

¶
4f

there were a couple more days, time for just another run at it, perhaps then . . . (Donald Murray, "The Maker's Eye: Revising Your Own Manuscripts")

Or you may use a *quotation*. In this paragraph a student quotes *Alice in Wonderland* to express his feelings about the complexity of the tax system.

> "Curiouser and curiouser," says Alice as she journeys through Wonderland. The same can be said by anyone who wanders through the maze of regulations contained in the tax code. Possibly someday our lawmakers will remedy this situation, but until then we are all victims of a tax system that is too complex for most people to understand and too unwieldy for the government to control. (Student)

Your conclusion should fulfill the promises you make in your introduction. It should not introduce new ideas or go off in new directions. Your conclusion is your last word, and readers base their impressions of your writing on it. A weak or uninteresting ending detracts from an otherwise strong essay. Therefore, do not apologize ("I may not be an expert" or "At least this is my opinion") or in any way undercut your concluding points.

(3) Writing transitional paragraphs

The sole function of a paragraph may be to provide **transition** from one section of an essay to another. This kind of paragraph signals a change in subject and provides a bridge between units.

At their simplest, transitional paragraphs can be single sentences that move readers from one point to the next.

Let us examine this point further.

This idea works better in theory than in practice.

Of course there are other avenues we can explore.

Let us begin with a few estimates.

Sometimes writers use a transitional paragraph to present a concise summary of what they have already said. This technique allows readers to pause momentarily to consider what they have read and also reinforces important concepts. The following transitional paragraph uses a series of questions to restate some frightening points about overpopulation. The author goes on to answer these questions in the next part of his essay.

¶
4

Can we bleed off the mass of humanity to other worlds? Right now the number of human beings on Earth is increasing by 80 million per year, and each year that number goes up by 1 and a fraction percent. Can we really suppose that we can send 80 million people per year to the Moon, Mars, and elsewhere, and engineer those worlds to support those people? And even so, nearly remain in the same place ourselves? (Isaac Asimov, "The Case Against Man")

When you revise, look for abrupt shifts in content that occur at natural breaks in your essay. Then supply the transitional paragraph that moves readers from one section to another.

Student Writer at Work: Writing Paragraphs

A. Following are an introduction, a conclusion, and a list of points for the body paragraphs of a student's essay. Using the introduction and conclusion, write an essay that follows the order and emphasis of the points in the outline. Make certain that the body paragraphs are unified, coherent, and well developed.

Introduction   A party is a gathering at which people are supposed to have fun. Judging from the number of bad parties I have attended lately, knowing how to give an interesting party is a lost art. For this reason I have decided to share my secrets for successful entertaining.

List of   Invite lots of people
points   Invite several people who will liven things up
                   Invite one or two close friends to help
                   Have good food
                   Have a variety of food
                   Have some unusual food
                   Have enough food
                   Mingle with guests
                   Don't stay in the kitchen
                   Introduce guests
                   Stimulate conversation

Conclusion   Even though this advice may seem obvious, you
would be amazed how many people ignore it. The re-
sult is tired, boring parties that everyone cannot wait
to leave. So the next time you have a party, try these
simple rules and you will be surprised at the results.

B. The following draft of a student essay has a weak introduction
and conclusion. Rewrite them to increase their effectiveness.

There are a number of things we can do to reduce traffic deaths.

A passive restraint system automatically protects both
driver and passenger in the event of a collision. Fifteen years
ago the government funded air bag research that it hoped would
fill the need for such a system. The air bag, which is supposed
to inflate upon impact, would automatically shield collision victims from injury. A decline in American auto sales and pressure from auto manufacturers have caused the government to
pull back from its commitment. Ironically, Mercedes Benz, manufacturers of a high-priced German automobile, offers air bags
as an option in some of its models. This is not to say, however,
that air bags do not have critics. Some people feel that they are
both costly and unreliable. You never know for certain that air
bags will work until you are in an accident. Even so, many experts feel that the problems with this system can be solved if
they are deployed.

Combination seat belt and shoulder harnesses are the best
and simplest way to protect passengers in a crash. Volkswagen
has perfected an interlock system that automatically buckles
people into place when the door of the car closes. Most American and Japanese car manufacturers have not adopted this system, preferring instead the tradition of the driver-fastened har-
ness. Whatever system manufacturers use, government studies
show that seat belts could reduce the annual auto death rate by
ten to twelve thousand people. The problem, however, is that
people just will not use seat belts. Insurance statistics show
that only eleven to seventeen percent of all drivers wear their
seat belts regularly.

¶
4

What can be done? First, the federal government should move ahead with the air bag system, offering tax subsidies or credits to consumers who buy it. The money saved in medical costs alone would more than offset the cost to the government. Second, state governments should pass laws requiring riders to use seat belts. People riding without fastened seat belts would receive tickets, just as they would if they were speeding. In several European countries where laws like this are in effect, automobile injuries and deaths have decreased significantly.

Certainly all these things would help.

Constructing a Logical Argument

As you now have learned, the major purpose of some essays is to convey information. In these essays you use factual statements for explanation and expect readers to accept them at face value. In argument, however, factual statements are used to support the assertions you want to prove. You assume that your audience needs to be convinced that certain claims are valid.

The line between explanation and argument is not always clear, of course. Thus, to make all your writing more convincing you should be familiar with the techniques of argument and learn to use them appropriately.

The uses of argument

Argument has a number of important functions. First and foremost, it allows you to test your ideas. By expressing them you see how well your ideas hold up against those of others. Argument forces you to take a stand, to consider an audience, to marshal evidence, to defend your position, and (most important) to draw a conclusion. If you find that your ideas do not hold up during this process, you must change them. Argument thus enables you not only to test, revise, and express your ideas but also to evaluate the ideas of others.

Argument versus persuasion

Argument is one subcategory of a more general class, **persuasion.** Persuasion relies on various appeals—to emotion, reason, and self-interest—to influence people. We encounter persuasion everywhere. Manufacturers of laundry detergents assure us that their products get clothes whiter than white, brighter than bright. Toothpaste commercials promise that our teeth will shine and have fewer cavities, too. For the most part, commercials are nonrational, appealing to the emotions or to self-interest. (Occasionally, of course, they may appeal to reason.)

Although most effective arguments appeal to the emotions to some degree, their primary appeal is to reason. Argument attempts to accommodate an audience—to consider your readers' knowledge of a subject as well as their attitudes and values—while refuting opposing points of view. It also follows rules that assure that ideas are presented fairly and logically. These considerations are central to argument, and they inform every stage of the writing process.

5a Planning Your Argument

When you construct a written argument, you use the same process you use to construct any essay: you plan, you shape your material, and you write and revise. Your purpose, however, requires some special strategies: you must choose an arguable—and defensible—topic, take a stand, define your terms, accommodate your audience, gather evidence, present your points logically and fairly, and deal with opposing arguments.

(1) Choosing a topic

You can base an argumentative essay on any *debatable* topic. (Keep in mind that debatable does not necessarily mean controversial.) Any topic about which people disagree is suitable for argument. "Chromium is a metallic element" is not debatable; it is a fact. Like it or not, people have to accept it. But "We should not support the government of South Africa even though we need South African chromite" is very debatable. Reasonable people could dispute this statement by presenting evidence for or against it.

It helps if you care about your topic, but that is not an absolute requirement. In fact, when you feel very strongly about something, you may not view it objectively. If this is the case, you should consider another topic. Your feelings about an issue should never cloud your reasoning or your perspective as you state your case.

You must also know something about your topic. The more

data you can provide—facts, figures, examples—the more likely you are to sway your audience. General knowledge is seldom convincing by itself, so you will probably have to do some reading and perhaps some research (see Chapter 36). If you find as you read that your topic is too broad, you will have to narrow it. Your topic should also allow you to do more than rehash tired arguments that everyone has already heard. Unless you have something new to say, stay away from topics such as abortion, nuclear war, legalization of marijuana, and the death penalty.

log
5a

Finally, you have to decide what you want to accomplish in your essay. If you cannot state your goal briefly and easily, your topic is probably unfocused. Your purpose is to change or clarify your readers' view of an issue: unclear, unfair, or unrealistic approaches will not accomplish this end. At the very least, you must be able to define both sides of an issue, isolate crucial points, and state your own ideas.

(2) Taking a stand

Your next step is to take a stand—to state your position in a single declarative sentence, usually at the beginning of your essay. Your thesis should be arguable: it should assert or deny something about your topic. Properly cast, this thesis lays the foundation for the rest of your argument.

You can test whether your thesis is arguable by seeing whether it yields a good **antithesis**—a statement that is the negation of your thesis.

> THESIS: Boxing should be regulated by the federal government.

> ANTITHESIS: Boxing should not be regulated by the federal government.

If your thesis does yield a workable antithesis, you can be sure that it is debatable and therefore suitable for argument.

Just when you arrive at your thesis depends on how much you know about your topic. If you already know a lot about something, you may have a thesis in mind before you do any reading or writing. (Of course you must modify your thesis if you uncover information that causes you to change your mind.) But usually you will have to read and possibly do some freewriting or brainstorming to find a thesis. Students often try to arrive at a thesis before they have a good grasp of the topic and their views on it. Review your notes and think about what you want to say before you work up a thesis. If you are having problems settling on one, read some more. If you are still having trouble, begin writing without a thesis. Freewriting often helps you draw out your ideas and discover what you want to say (see 1b.3). After you finish your freewriting, go through what you have written and see if it suggests a thesis. If it does, put your freewriting aside and start a draft with this thesis as your guide.

(3)   Defining your terms

You and your readers must agree about the terms you use in your argument. Words convey different meanings to different people. An argument that one rock group is superior to another means nothing unless your audience knows how *you* define a "superior rock group." Never assume that everybody will know exactly what you mean.

As a rule you should avoid words that convey a moral or ideological stance. When you decide on a thesis, watch for the use of such words as *wrong, bad, good, right,* and *immoral,* which involve judgments that cannot be demonstrated because they are based on beliefs. You may give your reasons for believing what you do, but stating your beliefs alone is not likely to convince a skeptical reader. In argument you must supply facts and reasons to support your beliefs. You can and should restate a thesis that relies on loaded terms.

> ORIGINAL: Censorship of pay TV would be wrong.

> REVISED: Censorship of pay TV would unfairly limit free trade.

The original thesis rests on a moral judgment; the revised thesis focuses on an issue that can be debated. Whatever you believe, you can debate the question of censorship and free trade using court decisions, authoritative opinion, and expert testimony, for instance, and make a good case.

▶
EXERCISE 1

Which of the following would be suitable thesis statements for an argumentative essay? Justify your choices, and explain why you eliminated the statements you did.

1. Getting unemployment benefits is difficult if you are a student.
2. Physical education courses in college are a waste of time and money.
3. The Fish and Wildlife Commission should do more to protect endangered species.
4. Arguing your own case in small-claims court can be an exciting and educational experience.
5. Honesty and integrity are qualities that seem to be missing in modern life.
6. American farm policy is bad for the small farmer.
7. Learning to use a word processor can change a student's attitude toward writing.
8. Despite high initial gains, the home video-game industry has declined in recent years.
9. The history of the Ku Klux Klan—its immoral objectives and propaganda—is something that schools cannot afford to ignore.
10. After soaring in the sixties and seventies, the divorce rate among Americans seems to be edging downward.

log
5a

▶
EXERCISE 2

Look at Exercise 1 and identify the words in each statement that are open to interpretation. Choose one word and rewrite the statement in which it appears so that the word's meaning is clear.

(4) Accommodating your audience

Whatever you write, always consider what your audience knows about your subject. When writing arguments you should also assess what readers like and dislike and their opinions, attitudes, and values. When you attempt to convince people to consider your position, give serious thought to their concerns.

Plan your strategy with a specific audience in mind. The ideal situation is to address an audience with which you are familiar, but ideal situations are rare. Who are your readers? Are they disinterested observers or people deeply involved in the issue you plan to discuss? Can they be cast in a specific role— concerned parents, victims of discrimination, irate consumers— or are they so diverse that they cannot be categorized? If you cannot be certain who your readers are, you will have to direct your arguments to a general audience.

In an argument your aim is to bring your audience to a

position closer to your own. You cannot do this effectively if you expect your readers to accept what you say unquestioningly. You must instead use evidence to move from your thesis to a conclusion that your audience can readily accept.

(5) Gathering evidence

Most arguments consist of **assertions** (claims you make about your topic) backed by **evidence** (facts or expert testimony that reinforces your argument). You could, for instance, assert that law-enforcement techniques have improved in the past few years. You could then support this assertion by referring to a government report stating that violent crime in the ten largest U.S. cities has declined during that time. This report would be one piece of persuasive evidence.

Certain assertions need no proof: statements that are *self-evident* ("All human beings are mortal"), statements that are true by *definition* (2 + 2 = 4), and *statements of fact* that you can expect the average person to know ("The Atlantic Ocean separates England and America"). All other kinds of assertions need supporting evidence.

One source of evidence is facts that you gather from your experience, course work, or research. Facts are verifiable statements that something is true or that something happened. We accept many facts because our senses confirm them: that the sky is blue, that water is wet, and that a baseball team has a certain number of players. Other facts, those we get from reference books or from various media, are more complex, and we accept them because we trust the sources. The *Encyclopaedia Britannica,* for example, is widely respected, so most people accept the facts reported by this source. Keep in mind, however, that facts change as new information is uncovered or as situations change. Several years ago it was a fact that a person could not be given an artificial heart; today this procedure is carried out at a number of hospitals. As you write remember that a good argument includes more than assertions; it includes the facts that back them up.

Facts are not the only kind of evidence that can bolster your argument. The testimony of experts in the field you are writing about can also support your claims. Notice how Rachel Carson uses the words of a noted entomologist to substantiate her argument.

Yet such a world is pressed upon us. The crusade to create a chemically sterile, insect-free world seems to have engendered a fanatic zeal on the part of many specialists and most of the so-called control agencies. On every hand there is evidence that those engaged in spraying operations exercise a ruthless power. "The regulatory entomologists . . . function as prosecutor, judge and jury, tax assessor and collector and sheriff to enforce their own orders," says Connecticut entomologist Neely Turner. The most flagrant abuses go unchecked in both state and federal agencies. (Rachel Carson, *Silent Spring*)

To be useful, an authority's words must pertain specifically to your topic. Furthermore, the opinion of an authority has meaning only in his or her field. In other areas the individual's testimony should have no more weight than that of any reasonably intelligent person. For example, though Paul Newman's opinions on acting are credible, his opinions on arms control do not carry the same weight as Alexander Haig's. After all, Alexander Haig is a former secretary of state and as such can be assumed to have an in-depth knowledge of foreign affairs.

As you gather evidence, keep several things in mind. First, maintain a precise record of your sources and document the information you use (see Chapter 38). An anonymous source may suffice for a newspaper article but not for an argumentative essay. Remember, documentation allows readers to trace the facts to their source, thereby adding credibility to your argument. Next, examine a cross section of opinion on your topic. You should know *all* sides of the issue, not just those that support your stand. Failing to address opposing points of view seriously limits your chance of being convincing.

Write down all your references rather than relying on your memory. Incorrect dates, inaccurate facts, and misspelled book titles and authors' names cast doubt on the accuracy of your entire essay.

Finally, understand that argumentation never proves a thesis conclusively—if it did, there would be no argument. The best you can do is to establish a high probability that your thesis is reasonable. Choose your evidence with this idea in mind.

How do you know when you have enough evidence? When writing you constantly run the risk of basing conclusions on too little evidence. If you say that all Sony television sets are defective because of your experience with two that you bought, you have made a **hasty generalization.** Two examples do not make a rule or warrant a conclusion. Furthermore, your two sets do not represent the entire line.

Occasionally one or two examples do lead to a valid conclusion: just one case of the flu convinces most people that the disease is debilitating (although you would not be likely to argue this point). More often, you must present additional evidence to support a conclusion. A scientist claiming to have discovered a cure for cancer would have to offer many examples to convince colleagues that the conclusion was valid.

▶

EXERCISE 3

Write a paragraph supporting the assertion below with evidence from the list that follows. Include enough evidence to convince a general audience that what you are saying is worth believing. Be able to explain why you chose some pieces of evidence and rejected others.

> *A college degree does not automatically result in higher salaries.*
> According to several studies, status—not education—is a major indicator of income.
> Persons from high-status families make more money than those from low-status families.
> There seems to be a new push to train students for jobs.
> One-third of those who go to college do not make more than they would had they not gone to college.
> Colleges fail to warn students that a good job is hard to get.
> Engineering students and computer science majors make the most money after graduating.
> Liberal arts majors have the most difficult time finding employment.
> Many colleges "overproduce" students for certain careers, such as education, psychology, and law.
> Of thirty psychology majors who graduated from one college, only five had jobs in the field a year later.
> The cost of a college education has doubled in the past five years.
> The tuition of Ivy League colleges is above $10,000 a year.
> The Department of Labor thinks that law schools are graduating more than twice as many lawyers as are necessary. (Adapted from Caroline Bird, *The Case Against College*)

(6) Being fair

The line between being persuasive and being unfair is a fine one and, unfortunately, there are no clear-cut rules to help you make this distinction. Writers of effective and sometimes brilliant argu-

log
5a

mentative essays are often less than fair to their opponents. We could hardly call Jonathan Swift "fair" when he in "A Modest Proposal" implies that the English are cannibals. A supporter of George III would argue that Thomas Jefferson and the other writers of the Declaration of Independence were less than fair when they criticized British policy in America.

Of course, "A Modest Proposal" is bitter satire, and Swift employs overstatement to express his rage at social conditions. In justifying their break with England, the writers of the Declaration of Independence did not intend to be fair to the king. Argument promotes one point of view, so it is seldom objective. Even so, writers of effective arguments know that they must seem fair and reasonable to their readers. If they falsify or distort evidence, many people will not accept their claims.

College writing requires that you stay within the bounds of fairness. To be sure that your evidence is not misleading or distorted, you should learn to avoid the following.

DISTORTING EVIDENCE. Distortion is misrepresentation. Writers sometimes intentionally misrepresent their opponents' views by exaggerating them and then attacking this extreme position. For example, Senator Fratori delivered a speech in which he said that unless something was done soon, the Social Security Trust Fund would run out of money in ten years. He added that a possible solution was to eliminate certain cost-of-living increases that were due to go into effect. His opponent, Ms. Ryan, attacked him by saying that clearly he was in favor of curtailing benefits to older Americans. Where would he stop? Would he eliminate benefits? Would he scrap the whole Social Security System? What about Medicare? Medicaid? Welfare? Anyone who could support such actions, Ms. Ryan said, did not deserve public office.

Senator Fratori said only that something had to be done to keep the Social Security system solvent. Ms. Ryan could have challenged Senator Fratori's assertion and his proposed solution with facts, figures, and other data. Instead, by distorting his position she attacked it unfairly.

QUOTING OUT OF CONTEXT. A writer or speaker quotes out of context by taking someone's words from their original setting and using them in another. When you select certain words from a statement and ignore others, you can change the meaning of what someone has said or implied. Consider this example.

(Mr. N, township resident)

I don't know why you are opposing the new highway. According to your own statements the highway will increase land value and bring more business into the area.

(Mrs. L, township supervisor)

I think you should look at my statements more carefully. I have a copy of the paper that printed my interview and what I said was [*reading*]: "The highway will increase land values a bit and bring some business to the area. But at what cost? One hundred and fifty families will be displaced and the highway will divide our township in half." My comments were not meant to support the new highway but to underscore the problems that its construction will cause.

By repeating only some of Mrs. L's remarks, Mr. N alters her meaning to suit his purpose. In context, Mrs. L's words indicate that although she acknowledges the highway's few benefits, she believes that its drawbacks outweigh them.

SLANTING EVIDENCE. When you select information that supports your case and ignore information that does not, you are slanting evidence. For example, if you support your position that smoking should not be prohibited in public places by choosing only evidence provided by the American Tobacco Institute, you are guilty of slanting evidence. Inflammatory language also biases your writing. A national magazine slanted evidence, to say the least, when it described a reputed criminal as a "hulk of a man who looks as if he could burn out somebody's eyes with a propane torch." Although one-sided presentations do appear in newspapers and magazines, avoid these distortions in your own writing.

(7) Dealing with opposing arguments

To argue effectively, you must also know how to refute opposing arguments. By addressing obvious objections to your thesis, you can defuse them before stating your case. You thereby present yourself as a reasonable person who has considered all sides of an issue before reaching a conclusion. When you acknowledge an opposing view, do not distort it or present it as ridiculously weak. This tactic, called creating a **straw man**, will not fool careful readers.

You can refute opposing views by showing that they are untrue, unfair, unimportant, or irrelevant. In an essay criticizing the unfair practices associated with whaling, a student refutes an argument against her position.

> Of course there are some who say Sea World only wants to capture a few whales. George Will makes this point in a *Newsweek* article. He points out how valuable the research on whales would be. Unfortunately, Will downplays the fact that Sea World wants to capture a hundred whales, not just "a few." And after releasing ninety whales, Sea World intends to keep ten for "further work." At hearings in Seattle last week, several noted marine biologists went on record condemning Sea World's research program. We must wonder, as they do, why Sea World needs such a large number of whales to carry out its project. (Student)

After acknowledging her opponent's position, the student questions its honesty and supports her case with the testimony of several marine biologists.

When an opponent's position is so strong that it cannot be dismissed, concede the point. Admit that it is well taken, and then, if possible, discuss its limitations. Martin Luther King, Jr., uses this tactic in his "Letter from Birmingham Jail."

> You express a great deal of anxiety over our willingness to break laws. This is certainly a legitimate concern. Since we so diligently urge people to obey the Supreme Court's decision of 1954 outlawing segregation in the public schools, at first glance it may seem rather paradoxical for us consciously to break laws. One may well ask: "How can you advocate breaking some laws and obeying others?" The answer lies in the fact that there are two types of laws: just and unjust. I would be the first to advocate obeying just laws. One has not only a legal but a moral responsibility to obey just laws. Conversely, one has a moral responsibility to disobey unjust laws. I would agree with St. Augustine that "an unjust law is no law at all."

King first acknowledges his audience's legitimate concern about his willingness to break laws. He then counters their objections by distinguishing between just and unjust laws. With this concession King hopes to overcome audience resistance and gain a hearing for his views.

When you are planning your argument, list the major arguments against your thesis and pick out those you can refute. Most experienced writers feel that only after recognizing their opposition can they construct a persuasive argument.

5b Shaping Your Argument

Effective and reasonable arguments do not follow automatically from the evidence presented. Arguments move from facts to conclusions in two basic ways: **deductively** (starting with an assumption that some general statement is true and then supporting it with detailed evidence) or **inductively** (starting with examples that lead to a general conclusion). Whether you proceed inductively or deductively depends on your material, your audience, and your purpose. Many—probably most—arguments use a combination of deduction and induction, relying both on general assumptions and on conclusions drawn from examples. For now, however, we will consider deduction and induction separately.

(1) Deduction

The basic form of deduction is the **syllogism,** a three-part set of assumptions that contains a *major premise,* a *minor premise,* and a *conclusion.*

> MAJOR PREMISE: All books from that store are new.
>
> MINOR PREMISE: These books are from that store.
>
> CONCLUSION: Therefore these books are new.

In deduction the premises contain all the information contained in the conclusion: no terms are introduced that have not already appeared in the major and minor premises.

In a deductive argument, then, your conclusion must follow from your premises. No new terms are allowed. Suppose you believe that the government should take steps to protect people who live near nuclear power plants. You begin by stating that the government is obliged to provide for its citizens' safety. You then say that people who live near nuclear power plants are citizens. Your conclusion—that the safety of these residents should therefore be ensured—follows from these assumptions. Stated as a syllogism, your argument looks like this.

> MAJOR PREMISE: The safety of all citizens should be provided for by the government.

MINOR PREMISE: People who live around nuclear power plants are citizens.

CONCLUSION: Therefore, the safety of people who live around nuclear power plants should be provided for by the government.

log
5b

The strength of a deductive argument is that if your readers accept your premises, they usually grant your conclusion. But you must persuade them to accept your premises. Sometimes your readers will accept both your major and minor premises. Other times you must present evidence to persuade readers to accept one or more of your premises. Often it is a good idea to choose as your major premise an idea that your audience already accepts. Once you have established your premises, the force of logic alone should lead readers to accept your conclusion.

When you construct a deductive argument, you may state your conclusion at the beginning or at the end. Your choice depends on whether you want to state a conclusion explicitly and then support it or to lead up to a conclusion that is implied throughout. If your audience is likely to agree with your conclusion, state it at the outset. If not, you should probably proceed gradually. Here is an example of a deductive argument whose conclusion appears at the end.

> The primary function of a university is to discover and disseminate knowledge by means of research and teaching. To fulfill this function a free interchange of ideas is necessary not only within its walls but with the world beyond as well. It follows that the university must do everything possible to ensure within it the fullest degree of intellectual freedom. The history of intellectual growth and discovery clearly demonstrates the need for unfettered freedom, the right to think the unthinkable, discuss the unmentionable, and challenge the unchallenged. To curtail free expression strikes twice at intellectual freedom, for whoever deprives another of the right to state unpopular views necessarily also deprives others of the right to listen to those views. (Yale Committee, "Freedom of Expression at Yale")

The author begins this argument with the major premise. The rest of the paragraph leads logically to the conclusion, stated in the final sentence.

(2) Induction

**log
5b**

Inductive arguments can be very persuasive. By accumulating data that support your conclusion, you have an excellent chance of overcoming your readers' resistance and gaining their support. If you think that your audience will not accept a deductive premise—one that is controversial or hard to establish—use induction.

Unlike deduction, induction is not limited by premises. It begins with an initial **hypothesis,** a question you want your essay to answer; cites proof; and moves to a general conclusion. Its conclusions, however, are never certain, only highly probable. They are arrived at by what is called an **inductive leap.** The more observations you make and the more information you gather, the better your chances of drawing a sound conclusion. When, for example, you look out the window, see dark clouds, and predict that it will rain, you are making an inductive leap. Your conclusion is sound because you have often observed similar situations in the past.

Despite their variety of detail, inductive arguments follow a certain general pattern. First, you state your hypothesis. Next, you investigate the question by gathering a broad sample of evidence, usually examples. Finally, you reach a conclusion based on your evidence. Here is just such an inductive argument.

> Suppose, said Galileo, that you drop two unequal balls from the tower at the same time. And suppose that Aristotle is right—suppose that the heavy ball falls faster, so that it steadily gains on the light ball, and hits the ground first. Very well. Now imagine the same experiment done again, with only one difference: this time the two unequal balls are joined by a string between them. The heavy ball will again move ahead, but now the light ball holds it back and acts as a drag or brake. So the light ball will be speeded up and the heavy ball will be slowed down; they must reach the ground together because they are tied together, but they cannot reach the ground as quickly as the heavy ball alone. Yet the string between them has turned the two balls into a single mass which is heavier than either ball—and surely (according to Aristotle) this mass should therefore move faster than either ball. Galileo's imaginary experiment has uncovered a contradiction; he says trenchantly, "You see how, from your assumption that a heavier body falls more rapidly than a lighter one, I infer that a (still) heavier body falls more slowly." There is only one way out of the con-

tradition: the heavy ball and the light ball must fall at the same rate, so that they go on falling at the same rate when they are tied together. (Jacob Bronowski, *Science and Human Values*)

Bronowski begins his argument with Galileo's hypothesis. He then examines the results of Galileo's experiments and reaches a conclusion based on these observations.

For an inductive argument to be convincing, your audience must accept your evidence. Such evidence must represent general opinion on your topic and must not be debatable; otherwise you will confuse your readers by opening up other arguments. You must also cite enough examples to establish your point, and they must clearly support your conclusion. Too loose a connection between examples and conclusion suggests faulty reasoning.

5c Writing and Revising Your Argument

You write the first draft of your argument just as you write the first draft of any essay (see Chapter 3): you get your ideas down on paper so that you can react to them and begin revising. In addition to using the revision criteria that apply to all essays (see 3d), concentrate on the distinguishing characteristics of arguments as you revise. Make sure that you have enough evidence, that you have presented it fairly and effectively, and that you have dealt with opposing points of view. Pay particular attention to the organization of your essay. Is your essay inductive, deductive, or both? Does its structure suit your material and your audience? Outline its points to make sure that it is well balanced and covers sufficient material but not too much. Do you need to make additional points? Are certain sections weak?

Once you are satisfied with these criteria, focus on two other areas: correct any fallacies in logic, and put in the transitional words and phrases that argument requires.

(1) Fallacies

Fallacies are indefensible flaws in arguments. Because they closely resemble sound arguments, fallacious arguments can seem very convincing. Unscrupulous writers intentionally use such arguments, but well-intentioned writers sometimes slip into them without realizing it. When readers detect these fallacies, they see the writer as illogical—or, worse, dishonest. Here are some common fallacies to watch for when you revise.

EQUIVOCATION. You are guilty of **equivocation** when you shift the meaning of a key word during an argument so that your conclusion seems to follow logically from your premises.

Equivocation can be subtle. Consider this statement.

> It is in the public interest for the government to provide for the welfare of those who cannot help themselves. The public's interest becomes aroused, however, when it hears of welfare recipients getting thousands of dollars by cheating or by fraud.

In the first sentence, *public interest* refers to social good, and *welfare* to well-being. In the second sentence, the *public's interest* refers to self-interest and *welfare* to financial assistance provided by the government.

Do not shift the meaning of key terms from one statement to another. To see if you have equivocated, reread your paper with your intended definition in mind.

THE EITHER/OR FALLACY. You commit the **either/or fallacy** when you analyze a complex situation as if it has only two sides when actually it has more. If you ask whether American involvement in Central America is beneficial or harmful, you admit only two possibilities, ruling out all others. In fact, American involvement in some Central American countries may be beneficial, but in others it may be harmful. Or in any given country it may be *both* beneficial and harmful. Avoid the either/or fallacy by acknowledging the complexity of an issue. Do not misrepresent issues by limiting them.

Of course, *some* either/or situations lead to valid conclusions. In a physics exam, an answer is either correct or incorrect. In biology lab a test either will or will not indicate the presence of a certain enzyme. To be valid, an either/or statement must encompass *every* possible alternative. The premise "Either Kim took the test or she did not" is valid. There are no other possibilities. But the premise "Either Kim took the test or she went to the health service" commits the either/or fallacy. To disprove it, all someone has to do is to point out that Kim went somewhere else.

POST HOC, ERGO PROPTER HOC. *Post hoc, ergo propter hoc*
is Latin for "after this, therefore because of this." Many arguments depend on establishing cause-and-effect relationships,
but the link between the causes and effects presented must actually exist. In some arguments this is not the case. For example,
after the United States sold wheat to the U.S.S.R., the price of
wheat and wheat products rose dramatically. Many people
blamed the wheat sale for this rapid increase. One event followed
another closely in time, so they falsely assumed that the first
event caused the second. In fact, a complicated series of farm-
price controls that had been in effect for years was the actual
cause of increases in wheat prices.

log
5c

   Make certain that you identify the actual causes and effects
of the events you discuss. Cause-and-effect relationships are difficult to prove, so you may have to rely on expert testimony to
support your claim.

   BEGGING THE QUESTION. You are **begging the question**
when you state a debatable premise as if it were true instead of
offering proof for it. Readers may assume in error that something
has been proved when it has not. Simple cases of begging the
question are usually easy to spot.

> Ancient Egyptian monuments should be preserved because they
> are old.
>
> The wealthy should be heavily taxed because they have a lot of
> money.
>
> White-collar criminals should be punished because they break the
> law.

These statements are not arguments but *tautologies:* they end
where they begin, saying the same thing twice without offering
proof.

   Academic writing offers many opportunities for unintentionally begging the question. Here is an example from a research
paper.

> Recently there has been a great deal of debate about restricting the
> importing of Japanese cars. The big three automobile manufactur-
> ers seem to support quotas—despite their lip service to free trade.
> But there is one point that even they concede. Import quotas are a
> dangerous policy because they restrict free trade. (Student)

Because this argument is drawn out, the fallacy may escape a reader's attention. Import quotas restrict free trade by definition. Whether or not they are dangerous has to be established.

Watch for this fallacy whenever you revise an argumentative essay. If you encounter it, either remove the assumption or provide proof to back it up.

ARGUMENT AD HOMINEM. Arguments *ad hominem* ("to the man" in Latin) attack a person rather than an issue. By casting aspersions on an opponent, you turn attention from the facts of the case. Here are some examples.

> That woman has criticized the president's commitment to equal rights for women. But she believes in parapsychology. She thinks that she can communicate with the dead.
>
> Senator Rodriguez supports the deployment of the MX missile. What do you expect from a man who worked for a defense contractor before he ran for public office?

When a topic is controversial, this tactic can work. But although you may persuade some people, others will recognize the fallacy and withdraw their support.

Occasionally you *should* question a person's character. A witness at a criminal trial who has a history of lying should be challenged. A researcher who has falsified data in the past has less credibility than one who has not. Remember, though, that past dishonesty does not mean that a person will always be dishonest. Past circumstances may undermine someone's credibility, but they do not negate it.

RED HERRING. The **red herring** fallacy occurs when you change the subject to distract your audience from the actual issue. Consider, for example, "This company may charge high prices, but they do give a great deal of money to charity each year." The latter observation has nothing to do with the former but somehow manages to obscure it.

Many people use this fallacy when backed into a corner. By switching the subject, they hope to change direction and begin their argument on safer ground. Here is an example from a student essay.

> The appeals court should uphold the lower court's decision to allow females to attend previously all-male Central High School. A number of experts agree that Central High provides the best sec-

ondary education in the city. One can only wonder if the school board members who oppose this decision do not have more pressing things to do. Perhaps they should spend more time wondering how they will finance public education in this city next year. (Student)

This argument avoids discussing what it sets out to prove. Instead of supporting the assertion about women attending Central High, the writer introduces an irrelevant point about financing public education.

TU QUOQUE.   In Latin *tu quoque* means "you also." This fallacy occurs when you accuse a person of not upholding the position he or she advocates.

If you think that I should exercise, why are you so fat?

You're telling me to invest wisely? Look at how much money you lost in the commodities market last year.

In argumentative essays, *tu quoque* is not usually so straightforward. Frequently, it takes the form of "You would do it too if you had the opportunity."

It is difficult to understand why Congress wants to limit the authority of the CIA. After all, the KGB operates all over the world without any restraints.

Why should Eddie Coyle go to jail? Wouldn't you have taken a million dollars if it dropped out of a truck in front of you?

When you revise, keep in mind that the *tu quoque* fallacy does not prove anything. You must focus on the issues being debated, not the person making the opposing argument.

FALSE ANALOGY.   **Analogies**—extended comparisons—are useful in arguments. They enable you to explain something unfamiliar by comparing it to something familiar. By itself, an analogy establishes nothing; it is no substitute for evidence. Skillfully used, however, an analogy can be quite convincing. Henry David Thoreau illustrates the futility of warfare by comparing an ant battle to a human battle. In a freshman essay you might compare students at registration to rats in a maze: both are rewarded if they succeed and punished if they do not. But people are not rats, and you would still have to provide evidence if your purpose is to criticize the registration process.

A **false analogy** (or faulty analogy) assumes that because issues or concepts are similar in some ways, they are similar in other ways. On a television talk show recently a psychiatrist was asked to explain why people commit crimes.

> "Some people," he said, "commit crimes because they are selfish or psychotic. Others are like pregnant women who know they shouldn't smoke but do anyway. They have a craving that they have to give in to. The answer is not to punish this group of criminals, but to understand their behavior and to try to change it."

Admittedly, this analogy is convincing. However, it oversimplifies the issue. A pregnant woman does not intend to harm her unborn child by smoking; many criminals do intend to harm their victims. To undercut the doctor's whole argument you need only point out the shortcomings of his analogy.

(2)   Transitional words and phrases

When you revise an argumentative essay, it is particularly important that you use verbal signals that indicate the relationships among ideas. Certain words and phrases tell your readers that you are presenting one statement in support of another.

> There are thousands of harmful insects that are not native to the United States. <u>For this reason</u> we must strictly enforce the laws restricting foreign fruit, vegetables, and meat.

In this passage the phrase *For this reason* indicates that the writer is drawing a conclusion. Without this phrase, readers would have difficulty seeing the relationship between the two sentences.

Therefore indicates a thought process inherent in both deductive and inductive argument. It tells readers that you are reaching a conclusion.

> The Lawyer's Code of Professional Responsibility says that all defendants are entitled to a defense. Despite the nature of his crimes, Michael Bolino is a defendant in our legal system, and <u>therefore</u> he is entitled to a vigorous and competent defense.

Other words central to argument include *because, although, thus, so,* and *consequently.* Because these words have specific functions, you should not use them haphazardly. Consider this example.

> The work of many American composers is never performed. <u>Consequently</u> there should be more support for the arts in this country.

The word *consequently* indicates a cause-and-effect relationship between the second sentence and the first. But closer examination reveals no such connection. The student who wrote this passage is guilty of faulty reasoning.

log
5c

▶

EXERCISE 4

Identify the fallacies in the following statements. List the fallacy by name and rewrite the statement to correct the problem.

1. Dr. Spock is a brilliant physician. He should use his education to help the sick instead of criticizing the administration's nuclear policy.
2. My opponent says that he wants to be mayor. He has been divorced twice. Obviously, he should get his own life in order before he thinks of running for public office.
3. How can we not support railroads? Railroads are the arteries of our nation, and the trains are the life blood that brings sustenance to all parts of the country.
4. The school's mail-in registration program will either make things easier for students or result in total chaos.
5. During the last flight of the space shuttle, there was heavy rainfall throughout the entire Northeast. Therefore the launch must have disturbed the weather patterns for that region of the country.
6. I just received a pamphlet that urges people to buy savings bonds. How can the government talk about saving? Look how much money it wastes on cost overruns each year.
7. What President Nixon did was wrong, but many people in public office have done a lot worse.
8. For punishment to be effective it must really punish.
9. All of us must accept responsibility for the actions of the utility company. Therefore we should make certain that everyone gets heat this winter.

▶

EXERCISE 5

Write an essay arguing for or against one of the following thesis statements.

1. A terminally ill patient should be allowed to take his or her life.
2. Despite the expense, a college education is a good investment in the future.
3. Video games may seem useless to some people, but they serve some very useful functions.
4. In many colleges grading has outlived its usefulness.
5. Females should be required to register for the draft.

6. Every college freshman should have to take a course in computer programming.
7. Cigarette smokers should not be allowed to smoke in public places.
8. The Supreme Court should reverse itself on the issue of school prayer.
9. Americans should spend less time making money and more time improving the quality of their lives.
10. Despite efforts to conserve, Americans still use too much energy.

Student Writer at Work: Constructing a Logical Argument

Revise the following draft of an argumentative essay. Pay particular attention to audience, logic, and evidence. Be able to explain what changes you made and how they make the essay more convincing:

The Gun Question

Years ago, guns were essential for obtaining food to feed many families. However, since we started domesticating animals, guns have become less important for obtaining food. Instead, they have been widely used for crimes and have caused many accidents. When respected and used properly, however, guns can improve, protect, and even save many people's lives.

Some people feel that if guns were outlawed there would be fewer murders, robberies, and gun-related accidents. These people do not know what they are talking about. If guns are taken away, only the honest citizens will give up their guns. The criminals and the government will be the only people who have guns. We will be at the mercy of outlaws and the good will of the government. Perhaps the people who oppose guns should worry more about tyranny than about criminals who have their rights violated.

Opponents of guns often suggest that all firearms in this country should be registered. The registration of firearms, however, is the first step toward confiscation. If firearms were confiscated, this would be the first step toward an authoritarian government. There would be no armed citizenry to assure that the Bill of Rights is enforced. Would the people who favor the registration of guns like it if the government took away their houses, their cars, or even their money?

The Constitution guarantees all citizens the right to bear arms. The Founding Fathers realized that an armed citizenry is the best defense against tyranny. Look at some of the countries that have forbidden private citizens from owning guns. In Nazi Germany only the army could have guns. If a citizen was caught with a gun, he or she was killed. In Russia only certain people can own weapons. Anyone else who has a gun is thought to be an enemy of the state. The same holds true for Uganda, Chile, Iran, and China.

In addition to protecting our rights, guns enable citizens to protect their lives. In every issue of *The American Rifleman* there are at least a dozen or more examples of honest people using guns to protect their lives and their possessions. These articles show how different types of people have been able to stop criminals. Store owners, housewives, and even children have used guns for protection against criminals. Anyone who cannot accept this evidence obviously has trouble accepting the truth.

Although some people fear guns and their misuse, guns are an important and beneficial factor in our lives. If guns were outlawed, only the criminals and the government would have guns. This fact should be enough to convince anyone how necessary guns are.

Composing Sentences

Building Simple Sentences

6a Identifying the Basic Sentence Elements

A **sentence** is an independent grammatical unit that contains a subject and a predicate and expresses a complete thought.

> <u>My sister</u> <u><u>decided</u></u> to major in business.
>
> <u>It</u> <u><u>came</u></u> from outer space.
>
> <u>Easter Island</u> <u><u>is</u></u> a Chilean island in the South Pacific.

In these three sentences, the **simple subjects** are <u>sister</u>, <u>it</u>, and <u>Easter Island</u>, and the **simple predicates** are <u><u>decided</u></u>, <u><u>came</u></u>, and <u><u>is</u></u>. A simple subject is a noun or noun substitute that tells who or what the sentence is about. A simple predicate, a verb or verb phrase, tells or asks something about the subject. The **complete subject** of a sentence, however, includes all the words associated with the subject, and the **complete predicate** includes not just the verb or verb phrase but all the words associated with it.

▶

EXERCISE 1

Identify and label the complete subjects and predicates in the following sentences.

> EXAMPLE: <u>The quick brown fox</u> <u><u>jumped over the lazy dog.</u></u>
> *s* *p*

1. Chad became an independent republic in 1960.
2. The rain in Spain falls mainly on the plain.
3. A Better Chance was designed to increase minority enrollment in private secondary schools.
4. Necessity is the mother of invention.
5. Each year the underground economy siphons off millions of potential tax dollars.
6. Ohio State's Archie Griffin won the Heisman Trophy in both 1974 and 1975.
7. The New York home of architect Stanford White contained a special mirror room.
8. Vitamin K is essential for blood clotting.

9. *For Colored Girls Who Have Considered Suicide/When the Rainbow Is Enuf* is a play by Ntozake Shange.
10. "Leaping Lizards" is Little Orphan Annie's favorite expression.

▶

sent **EXERCISE 2**
6b
Write two original sentences for each of the following subjects and predicates.

Subjects	Predicates
1. I	need
2. Life	is
3. Winter	brought
4. The library	seemed
5. Catherine	waited

6b Constructing Basic Sentence Patterns

In its basic form, a simple sentence consists of one subject and one predicate. These five sentences illustrate the various combinations of elements from which the most basic English sentences may be built.

Subject	Predicate
1. The economy	improved.
2. The band	played a medley.
3. The class	elected Bridget treasurer.
4. The injection	was painless.
5. Jim	gave her his word.

(1) Subject and intransitive verb (s + v)

The simplest sentence pattern consists of just a subject and a verb or verb phrase.

$$\underset{\text{The economy}}{\overset{s}{\underline{\hspace{2.5cm}}}}\ \underset{\text{improved}}{\overset{v}{\underline{\hspace{1.5cm}}}}.$$

$$\underset{\text{The price of gold}}{\overset{s}{\underline{\hspace{2.5cm}}}}\ \underset{\text{rose}}{\overset{v}{\underline{\hspace{1.5cm}}}}.$$

$$\underset{\text{Stock prices}}{\overset{s}{\underline{\hspace{2.5cm}}}}\ \underset{\text{may fall}}{\overset{v}{\underline{\hspace{1.5cm}}}}.$$

In each of these sentences the verbs (*improved, rose, may fall*) are **intransitive**—that is, they have no direct object. (A dictionary can tell you which verbs are transitive, which are intransitive, and which may be either, depending on context.)

**sent
6b**

(2) Subject + transitive verb + direct object (s + v + do)

In another pattern the sentence consists of the subject, a transitive verb, and a direct object. A **transitive** verb is one that requires an object to complete its meaning in the sentence. A **direct object** indicates where the verb's action is directed and who or what is affected by it.

s   *v*   *do*
The band played a medley.

s   *v*   *do*
Van Gogh painted "The Starry Night."

s   *v* *do*
Caroline hit Jake.

In each sentence the direct object tells *who* or *what* is the recipient of the verb's action.

(3) Subject + transitive verb + direct object + object complement (s + v + do + oc)

This pattern, similar to the one above, includes an **object complement** that renames or describes the direct object.

s   *v*   *do*   *oc*
The class elected Bridget treasurer.

s *v*   *do*   *oc*
I found the exam easy.

In the first sentence the object complement is a noun that renames the object; in the second it is an adjective that describes the object. In this kind of sentence pattern the noun or adjective following the direct object is an object complement if inserting the infinitive *to be* between them makes sense.

(4) Subject + linking verb + subject complement (s + v + sc)

This kind of sentence consists of a subject, a **linking verb** (a verb that connects a subject to its complement) and the **subject complement** (the word or phrase that describes or renames the subject).

s   *v*   *sc*
The injection was painless.

s   *v*   *sc*
The animals seemed restless.

$$\overset{s}{\underline{Darryl}} \; \overset{v}{\underline{\underline{is}}} \; \overset{sc}{a \; real \; friend.}$$

Darryl is a real friend.

Thatcher became prime minister.

**sent
6b**

In the first two sentences the subject complement is an adjective, called a **predicate adjective,** that describes the subject; in the other two, the subject complement is a noun, called a **predicate nominative,** that renames the subject. In each case the linking verb can be seen as an equal sign, equating the subject with its complement (*Thatcher = prime minister*).

(5)   Subject + transitive verb + indirect object + direct object (s + v + io + do)

In this sentence pattern the direct object tells who or what received the verb's action, and the **indirect object** tells to or for whom the verb's action was done:

Jim gave her his word. (Jim gave his word to her.)

The waiter brought us the check. (The waiter brought the check to us.)

The officer handed Frank a ticket. (The officer handed a ticket to Frank.)

▶

EXERCISE 3

In the following sentences, underline the subject once, underline the verb twice, and label direct objects, indirect objects, subject complements, and object complements.

EXAMPLE: Scarlett O'Hara wore a green velvet dress.

1.   Metro-Goldwyn-Mayer released the film version of Margaret Mitchell's novel *Gone with the Wind* in 1939.
2.   Vivien Leigh played the fiery Scarlett O'Hara, a beautiful Southern belle.
3.   Clark Gable co-starred as Rhett Butler.
4.   Scarlett loved her home, the plantation called Tara.
5.   Yankee soldiers looted and vandalized Tara.
6.   Scarlett was angry.
7.   She was also desperate.

8. She paid Rhett Butler a visit.
9. Scarlett requested a $300 loan from Rhett to pay Tara's taxes.
10. She painted Rhett an optimistic picture.
11. Rhett called her a liar.
12. Moreover, he refused her the loan.

6c Forming Questions and Commands

The five basic sentence patterns are alike in one respect: all are statements that present first the subject and then the predicate. This standard word order varies for questions and commands.

(1) Forming questions

Questions in English can be formed in several ways. Most often, we invert subject and verb (This is Maggie's farm. → Is this Maggie's farm?). Sometimes we invert and add a form of *do* before the subject (Maggie lives here. → Does Maggie live here?). Sometimes we also indicate a question by beginning a sentence with *who, what, why, where, when,* or *how.* (Wes was late again. → Why was Wes late again?). In some cases we can simply add a question mark to a statement (This is Maggie's farm? Wes was late again?) or add a phrase with inverted subject and verb at the end of the sentence (This is Maggie's farm, isn't it? Wes was late again, wasn't he?). In these instances, the word order of the original statement remains unchanged.

(2) Forming commands

To form commands, either use the second person singular (You stop that!) or simply leave out the sentence's subject (you), which is understood.

> Go to your room.
> March.
> Stop that!

6d Identifying Phrases and Clauses

Individual words may be joined to build *phrases* and *clauses.*

(1)   Identifying phrases

A **phrase** is a grammatically ordered group of related words that lacks a subject or predicate or both and functions as a single part of speech.

A **verb phrase** consists of the word or words that denote the subject's action or state of being. (Time *is running* out.)

A **noun phrase** includes a noun or pronoun plus all related modifiers. (I'll climb *the highest mountain*.)

A **prepositional phrase** consists of a preposition, its object, and any modifiers of that object (see 6f.1).

> They discussed the ethical implications of the operation.
>
> He was last seen heading into the sunset.

A **verbal phrase** consists of a verbal and its related objects, modifiers, or complements (see 6f.2). A verbal phrase may be a participial phrase, a gerund phrase, or an infinitive phrase.

> Encouraged by the voter turnout, the candidate predicted a victory. (participial phrase)
>
> Taking it easy always makes sense. (gerund phrase)
>
> The jury recessed to evaluate the evidence. (infinitive phrase)

An **absolute phrase** usually consists of a noun or pronoun and a participle, accompanied by modifiers (see 6f.3).

> Their toes tapping, they watched the auditions.

(2)   Identifying clauses

A **clause** is a group of related words that includes a subject and a predicate. An **independent** (main) **clause** may stand alone as a sentence, but a **dependent** (subordinate) **clause** must always be accompanied by an independent clause.

> [Lucretia Mott was an abolitionist.] [She was also a pioneer for women's rights.] (two independent clauses)
>
> [Lucretia Mott was an abolitionist] [who was also a pioneer for women's rights.] (independent clause, dependent clause)
>
> [Although Lucretia Mott was most widely known for her support of women's rights,] [she was also a prominent abolitionist.] (dependent clause, independent clause)

Depending on how they function in a sentence, subordinate clauses may be classified as adjective, adverb, or noun clauses.

Adjective clauses modify nouns or pronouns. Sometimes called **relative clauses,** they are introduced by relative pronouns (see 7b). The adverbs *where* and *when* can be used as relative pronouns when the adjective clause modifies a place or time.

sent
6d

> The television series *M*A*S*H,* which depicted life in an army hospital in Korea during the Korean War, ran for eleven years. (adjective clause modifies the noun *M*A*S*H*)

> Celeste's grandparents, who were born in Rumania, speak little English. (adjective clause modifies the noun *grandparents*)

> The Pulitzer Prizes for journalism are prestigious awards that are presented in areas like editorial writing, photography, editorial cartooning, and national and international reporting. (adjective clause modifies the noun *awards*)

> *Sophie's Choice* is set in Brooklyn, where the narrator lives in a house painted pink. (adjective clause modifies the noun *Brooklyn*)

NOTE: Adjective clauses follow the nouns or pronouns they modify.

Adverb clauses modify single words (verbs, adjectives, or adverbs) or entire phrases or clauses. They are always introduced by subordinating conjunctions (see 7b).

> Exhausted after the match was over, Kim decided to take a long nap. (adverb clause modifies the participle *exhausted*)

> To get to the coach before it turned into a pumpkin, Cinderella had to hurry. (adverb clause modifies the infinitive phrase *to get to the coach*)

> Because 75 percent of its exports are fish products, Iceland's economy is heavily dependent on the fishing industry. (adverb clause modifies independent clause; tells *why* fishing industry is so important)

> Her unemployment insurance benefits were reduced when she found a part-time job. (adverb clause modifies independent clause; tells *when* benefits were reduced)

Adverb clauses provide information to answer the questions *how? where? when? why?* and *to what extent?*

Noun clauses act as nouns (as subjects, direct objects, indirect objects, or complements) in a sentence. A noun clause may be introduced by a relative pronoun or by *whether, when, where, why,* or *how.*

> <u>Whatever happens to us</u> will be for the best. (noun clause serves as subject of sentence)

> <u>What really bothered me</u> was the constant noise. (noun clause serves as subject of sentence)

> They finally decided <u>which candidate was best</u>. (noun clause serves as direct object of verb *decided*)

> What you see is <u>what you get</u>. (noun clause serves as subject complement)

Elliptical clauses are grammatically incomplete—that is, a part of the subject or predicate or the entire subject or predicate is missing. If the missing part can be easily inferred from the context of the sentence, such constructions are acceptable.

> <u>Although</u> [they were] <u>full</u>, they could not resist dessert.

> He has never been able to read maps <u>as well as his brother</u> [can read maps].

▶
EXERCISE 4

Which of the following groups of words are independent clauses (sentences)? Which are dependent clauses? Which are phrases? Mark each word group S, C, or P.

> EXAMPLE: Coming through the rye. (P)

1. Beauty is truth.
2. When knights were bold.
3. In a galaxy far away.
4. He saw stars.
5. I hear a symphony.
6. Whenever you are near.
7. The clock struck ten.
8. The red planet.
9. Slowly I turned.
10. For the longest time.

6e Building Simple Sentences with Individual Words

The simple sentence can consist of as little as a subject and a predicate.

> Jessica <u>fell</u>.

Simple sentences, however, can be considerably more elaborate than this.

Jessica fell in love.

Jessica fell in love with Henry.

Jessica almost immediately fell in love with Henry.

Jessica and her sister almost immediately fell in love with Henry.

Jessica and her younger sister Victoria almost immediately fell in love with the dashing Henry Goodyear.

Jessica and her lively younger sister Victoria almost immediately fell hopelessly in love with the very dashing and mysterious Henry Goodyear.

sent
6e

The addition of modifying words (*older, dashing,* and so on) and phrases (*with the dashing Henry Goodyear*) and the creation of compounds (*Jessica and her sister, dashing and mysterious*) have changed the substance and the meaning of *Jessica fell* quite substantially.

(1) Building simple sentences with adjectives and adverbs

Descriptive adjectives and adverbs enrich the meaning of a sentence. In our sample sentence

Jessica and her lively younger sister Victoria almost immediately fell hopelessly in love with the very dashing and mysterious Henry Goodyear.

four adjectives describe nouns

Adjective	Noun
lively	sister
younger	sister
dashing	Henry Goodyear
mysterious	Henry Goodyear

and four adverbs describe the action of verbs and modify adjectives or other adverbs.

Adverb	
almost	immediately (adverb)
immediately	fell (verb)
hopelessly	fell (verb)
very	dashing and mysterious (adjectives)

(For more about adjectives and adverbs, see Chapter 24.)

▶
EXERCISE 5

Label all descriptive adjectives and adverbs in the following sentences.

           adj   *adv*

EXAMPLE: The red house perched unsteadily on the edge of the

       hill.

1. The matchmaker appeared one night out of the dark fourth-floor hall-way of the graystone rooming house where Finkle lived, grasping a black, strapped portfolio that had been worn thin with use. (**Bernard Malamud**, "The Magic Barrel")

2. During these last decades the interest in professional fasting has markedly diminished. It used to pay very well to stage such great performances under one's own management, but today that is quite impossible. We live in a different world now. (**Franz Kafka**, "A Hunger Artist")

3. A school of minnows swam by, each minnow with its small individual shadow, doubling the attendance, so clear and sharp in the sunlight. (**E. B. White**, "Once More to the Lake")

4. Poetry is as universal as language and almost as ancient. (**Laurence Perrine**, *Sound and Sense*)

5. Every town and village along that vast stretch of double river frontage had a best dwelling, finest dwelling, mansion,—the home of its wealthiest and most conspicuous citizen. (**Mark Twain**)

▶
EXERCISE 6

Expand these five simple sentences by modifying the subject with adjectives and the predicate with adverbs. Label the adjectives and adverbs in your sentences.

     EXAMPLE: The horn blew.

     adj   *adv*

The shiny French horn blew sharply.

1. The kangaroo jumped in its cage.
2. The fire burned the house down.
3. The daffodils began coming up in March.
4. Fans cheered the team to victory.
5. The butler did it.

▶
EXERCISE 7

Using these five sentences as models, write five original simple sentences. Use adverbs and adjectives where the model sentences use them, and then underline and label these modifiers.

EXAMPLE: Cathy <u>carefully</u> put the <u>baby</u> bird in the nest.

He <u>angrily</u> called the <u>old</u> man into the kitchen.

1. Nick turned his head carefully away smiling sweatily. (Ernest Hemingway, *In Our Time*)
2. Outside, the fire-red, gas-blue, ghost-green signs shone smokily through the tranquil rain. (F. Scott Fitzgerald, "Babylon Revisited")
3. The pavement was wet, glassy with water. (Willa Cather, "The Old Beauty")
4. The therapy used for treating burns has been improved considerably in recent years. (Lewis Thomas, "On Medicine and the Bomb")
5. There was a strange, inflamed, flurried, flighty recklessness of activity about him. (Herman Melville, *Bartleby the Scrivener*)

(2)   Building simple sentences with nouns and verbals

Words other than adjectives and adverbs can help you build richer simple sentences. These include **nouns** and **verbals,** verb forms that act as modifiers or as nouns.

Nouns
Certain nouns can act as adjectives modifying other nouns.

He needed the <u>cake</u> pans for the <u>layer</u> cake.

"Silent Night" is a <u>Christmas</u> carol.

Dave is a <u>soccer</u> coach.

Verbals
Certain verb forms, called verbals (see 20c), can be used in sentence building. Verbals include present and past participles, infinitives, and gerunds.

Verbals may be used as modifiers.

All three <u>living</u> former presidents attended the funeral. (present participle serves as adjective)

The Grand Canyon is the attraction <u>to visit</u>. (infinitive serves as adjective)

The puzzle was impossible <u>to solve</u>. (infinitive serves as adverb)

Or verbals may serve as nouns.

When the <u>going</u> gets tough, the tough get going. (gerund serves as noun)

<u>To err</u> is human. (infinitive serves as noun)

It took me an entire three-hour lab period to identify my <u>unknown</u>. (past participle serves as noun)

sent
6e

► EXERCISE 8

Circle the nouns and verbals (participles or infinitives) used as modifiers in this paragraph and indicate whether each functions in the sentence as an adjective or as an adverb. Underline any verbals (gerunds, participles, or infinitives) used as nouns.

> Americans are more aware than ever of the importance of regular exercise. Sales of running shoes, exercise equipment, and memberships in gyms readily attest to this. Everyone from college students to senior executives seems to be spending his or her time jogging, playing squash or racquetball, riding a bicycle, or working out with weights; they all seem to have decided that the court, gym, and track are the places to be. Not only do health-conscious individuals exercise regularly to keep fit, they also exercise to lose weight. In fact, exercising becomes almost an obsession for some of the most devoted.

► EXERCISE 9

1. List ten nouns that can be used as modifiers.

   EXAMPLE: <u>word</u> processor, <u>truck</u> stop, <u>peanut</u> butter

2. List ten participles that can be used as modifiers.

   EXAMPLE: crushed, ringing

3. Choosing words from your lists, write five original sentences, each of which includes both a noun and a participle used as modifiers.

   EXAMPLE: The <u>word</u> processor was a <u>crushed</u> mass of metal and plastic.

4. Then add adjectives and adverbs to enrich the sentence further.

   EXAMPLE: The <u>new</u> word processor was a <u>gruesomely</u> crushed mass of metal and plastic.

► EXERCISE 10

For additional practice in building simple sentences using individual words, combine each of the following groups of sentences into one simple sentence with several modifiers. You will have to add, delete, or reorder words.

> EXAMPLE: The night was cold. The night was wet.
> The night scared them. They were terribly scared.

> REVISED: The cold, wet night scared them terribly.

sent
6f

1. The ship landed. The ship was from space. The ship was tremendous. It landed silently.
2. It landed in a field. The field was grassy. The field was deserted.
3. A dog appeared. The dog was tiny. The dog was abandoned. The dog was a stray.
4. The dog was brave. The dog was curious. He approached the spacecraft. The spacecraft was burning. He approached it carefully.
5. A creature emerged from the spaceship. The creature was smiling. He was purple. He emerged slowly.
6. The dog and the alien stared at each other. The dog was little. The alien was purple. They stared meaningfully.
7. The dog and the alien walked. They walked silently. They walked carefully. They walked toward each other.
8. The dog barked. He barked tentatively. He barked questioningly. The dog was uneasy.
9. The alien extended his hand. The alien was grinning. He extended it slowly. The hand was hairy.
10. In his hand was a bag. The bag was of canvas. The bag was green. The bag was for laundry.

6f Building Simple Sentences with Phrases

You can also enrich your sentences by building with phrases (see 6d.1). Because a phrase lacks a subject or predicate (or both), it cannot stand alone as a sentence. But within a sentence phrases add information and provide connections between ideas. This sentence, for instance, contains only a subject, a linking verb, and two adjectives.

> The peach was firm but ripe.

In the following version, however, a series of phrases is used to build a richer, more detailed sentence.

> The peach was firm but ripe, with rosy, pinkish-yellow skin, a juicy interior, and a sweet taste.

The added phrases describe the peach more fully than the two adjectives alone can.

(1)   Building simple sentences with prepositional phrases

Nearly every sentence written includes **prepositions,** which relate a noun or noun substitute to the rest of the sentence. (For a list of the most commonly used prepositions, see 20f.)

The preposition, its object (the noun or noun substitute), and any modifiers of that object constitute a **prepositional phrase.**

Preposition	Object	Modifiers
after	dark	
before	the war	to end all wars
around	the bend	
over	the river	that flows swiftly
through	the woods	

In each case the preposition *precedes* its object. Occasionally in writing and often in speech, however, the preposition appears after the object.

obj   *prep*
He is the <u>person</u> you are looking <u>for</u>.

Prepositional phrases can function in a sentence as adjectives or as adverbs.

Cumulus clouds are towers <u>on horizontal bases</u>. (prepositional phrase functions as adjective modifying the noun *towers*)

Carry Nation was an agitator <u>for temperance</u>. (prepositional phrase functions as adjective modifying the noun *agitator*)

William the Conqueror invaded England <u>in 1066</u>. (prepositional phrase functions as adverb modifying the verb *invaded*)

The Madeira River flows <u>into the Amazon</u>. (prepositional phrase functions as adverb modifying the verb *flows*)

▶
EXERCISE 11

Read the following sentences. Underline each prepositional phrase and then identify the word it modifies. Finally, tell whether each phrase functions as an adjective or an adverb.

> EXAMPLE: Herz looked harassed enough to be the father <u>of three or four small, mean, colicky children</u>. (Philip Roth, *Letting Go*) (prepositional phrase functions as an adjective)

1. He stumbled down the back steps, hugging the thick book under his arm. (**Richard Wright, "The Man Who Was Almost a Man"**)
2. She looked at me, sitting in the chair before the cold stove, the sailor hat on her head. (**William Faulkner "That Evening Sun"**)
3. It was Paul's afternoon to appear before the faculty of the Pittsburgh High School to account for his various misdemeanors. (**Willa Cather, "Paul's Case"**)
4. It struck the trunk of the apple tree, bounced back at an angle, and rolled steadily and stupidly onto the cement apron in front of the firehouse, where one of the trucks was parked. (**Richard Wilbur, "A Game of Catch"**)
5. Outside the town, along the tracks, there were barren trees and bushes below the embankment, snow-gray in the dark. And down among the trees and bushes there were makeshift houses made out of boxes and tin and old pieces of wood and canvas. You couldn't see them in the dark, but you knew they were there if you'd ever been on the road, if you had ever lived with the homeless and hungry in a depression. (**Langston Hughes, "On the Road"**)

sent
6f

▶
EXERCISE 12

1. List twenty prepositional phrases.

> EXAMPLES: in the best interests of the child
>
> with all due respect
>
> on the Orient Express
>
> with liberty and justice

2. Using as many of the prepositional phrases on your list as you can, create five original simple sentences.

> EXAMPLE: With all due respect, your honor, I doubt your decision is really in the best interests of the child.

▶
EXERCISE 13

For additional practice in using prepositional phrases, combine each pair of sentences to create one simple sentence that includes a prepositional phrase. You may add, delete, or reorder words. Some sentences may have more than one correct version.

> EXAMPLE: America's drinking water is being contaminated. Toxic substances are contaminating it.
>
> America's drinking water is being contaminated by toxic substances.

1. Toxic waste disposal presents a serious problem. Americans have this problem.
2. Hazardous chemicals pose a threat. People are threatened.
3. Some towns, like Times Beach, Missouri, have been completely abandoned. Their residents have abandoned them.
4. Dioxin is one chemical. It has serious toxic effects.
5. Dioxin is highly toxic. The toxicity affects animals and humans.
6. Toxic chemical wastes like dioxin may be found. Over fifty thousand dumps have them.
7. Industrial parks contain toxic wastes. Open pits, ponds, and lagoons are where the toxic substances are.
8. Toxic wastes pose dangers. The land, water, and air are endangered.
9. In addition, toxic substances are a threat. They threaten our public health and our economy.
10. Immediate toxic waste cleanup would be a tremendous benefit. Americans are the ones who would benefit.

(2)   Building simple sentences with verbal phrases

A **verbal phrase** consists of a verbal (participle, gerund, or infinitive) and its related objects, modifiers, or complements. Like verbals, verbal phrases can also help you build sentences.

Some verbal phrases act as nouns. **Gerund phrases,** for example, like gerunds themselves, are always used as nouns, and **infinitive phrases** may also be used as nouns.

> Making a living isn't always easy. (gerund phrase serves as sentence's subject)

> Wendy appreciated Tom's being honest. (gerund phrase serves as object of verb *appreciated*)

> The entire town was shocked by their breaking up. (gerund phrase is object of preposition *by*)

> To know him is to love him. (infinitive phrase *To know him* serves as sentence's subject; infinitive phrase *to love him* is subject complement)

Some verbal phrases are also used as modifiers. **Participial phrases** are always used to modify nouns or pronouns, and infinitive phrases may function as adjectives or as adverbs.

> Fascinated by Scheherazade's story, they waited anxiously for the next installment. (participial phrase modifies pronoun *they*)

Wandering through the jungle, the explorers encountered Tarzan. (participial phrase modifies noun *explorers*)

He found the letter sitting right on the mantlepiece. (participial phrase modifies noun *letter*)

The next morning young Goodman Brown came slowly into the street of Salem Village, staring around him like a bewildered man. (Nathaniel Hawthorne) (participial phrase modifies noun *Goodman Brown*)

Henry M. Stanley went to Africa to find Dr. Livingstone. (infinitive phrase modifies verb *went*)

It wasn't the ideal time to do homework. (infinitive phrase modifies noun *time*)

sent

6f

NOTE: When you use verbal phrases as modifiers, be especially careful not to create misplaced or dangling modifiers (see 13b and 13c).

▶

EXERCISE 14

Identify the verbals (participles, gerunds, infinitives) and verbal phrases in the following paragraph, and indicate whether each is used as a noun, an adjective, or an adverb. Draw an arrow to indicate the word or word group each adjective or adverb modifies.

gerund phrase   *participle used*
used as noun   *as adjective*

EXAMPLE: Running a business requires hard work, working capital, and blind faith.

Creating a long-running television show isn't easy. Such a show should have lasting appeal to its viewers, remaining fresh and absorbing for years. For some reason, the situation comedy *Gilligan's Island* turned out to be an enduring winner. Even though it ran only three seasons, it appeared in reruns for many years. To study the show's central character is to remain baffled by the program's success. Gilligan, bewildered by life's subtleties, always means well. He wanders around the island in a daze, hoping to discover something new and exciting. But he always seems to wind up in trouble—hanging upside down from a tree, for instance. The other stranded survivors of the S.S. *Minnow* are no more compelling. In fact, the whole premise of the show is juvenile. The characters' struggles to survive on an uncharted island in the South Pacific and their endless efforts to be rescued are annoying and tedious.

▶
EXERCISE 15

1. List ten participial phrases, five gerund phrases, and five infinitive phrases.

      EXAMPLES: absorbing him (participial phrase)

                   going in style (gerund phrase)

                   to be king (infinitive phrase)

2. Choosing phrases from your list, use as many as you can in five original sentences.

      EXAMPLE: To be king was Fred's goal, absorbing him completely.

3. Then label each verbal phrase, and indicate whether it functions in your sentence as a noun or a modifier.

      EXAMPLE: **infinitive phrase**   **participial phrase**
                 To be king was Fred's goal, absorbing him completely.
                 (functions as noun)   (functions as modifier)

▶
EXERCISE 16

For additional practice in using verbal phrases, combine each of these sentence pairs to create one simple sentence that contains a participial phrase, a gerund phrase, or an infinitive phrase. Underline and label the verbal phrase in your sentence. You will have to add, delete, or reorder words, and you may find more than one way to combine each pair.

      EXAMPLE: Judy decorated her new pair of jeans.

                 She painted them with pink and yellow flowers.

                         participial phrase
      Judy decorated her new pair of jeans, painting them with pink and yellow flowers.

1. In 1912, the textile workers of Lawrence, Massachusetts, went on strike. They were striking for "Bread and Roses, too."
2. The workers wanted higher wages and better working conditions. They felt trapped in their miserable jobs.
3. Mill workers toiled six days a week. They earned about $1.50 for this.
4. Most of the workers were women and children. They worked up to sixteen hours a day.
5. The mills were dangerous. They were filled with hazards.
6. Many mill workers joined unions. They did this to fight exploitation by their employers.

7. They wanted to improve their lives. This was their goal.
8. Finally, twenty-five thousand workers walked off their jobs. They knew they were risking everything.
9. The police and the state militia were called in. Attacking the strikers was their mission.
10. After 63 days, the American Woolen Company surrendered. This ended the strike with a victory for the workers. (Adapted from William Cahn, *Lawrence 1912: The Bread and Roses Strike*)

sent
6f

(3) Building simple sentences with absolute phrases

Absolute phrases can also help you build more detailed sentences. Although they act as modifiers, absolute phrases are not connected grammatically to any particular word or phrase in a sentence. Instead, an absolute phrase modifies the whole independent clause to which it is linked. An **absolute phrase** is usually composed of a noun or pronoun and a past or present participle, along with its modifiers. Sometimes, however, an infinitive phrase functions absolutely.

> <u>To make a long story short</u>, our team lost.
>
> <u>To tell the truth</u>, quiche isn't my favorite dish.
>
> <u>His head bowed</u>, the prisoner awaited sentencing.
>
> She smiled, <u>her lips curling up</u>, <u>her eyes blinking rapidly</u>.
>
> <u>All things considered</u>, I prefer Maine's cold winters to California's smog.

NOTE: When the participle in an absolute phrase is a form of the verb *be*, it is usually omitted.

> They worked frantically, their time [being] almost up.

▶
EXERCISE 17

For practice in using absolute phrases, combine each group of sentences to create one simple sentence that includes an absolute phrase. You will have to change, add, delete, or reorder some words.

EXAMPLE: Paris was beautiful.
Its streets were exceptionally clean.

Paris was beautiful, its streets exceptionally clean.

1. Notre Dame stood majestically.
   Its Rose Window glowed in the darkness.
2. We took a boat ride down the Seine.
   Our feet were tired.
3. The Louvre is open six days a week.
   Its doors are closed on Tuesdays.
4. The Jeu de Paume displays Impressionist paintings.
   Its exhibits showcase Manet, Degas, Renoir, and van Gogh.
5. We were forced to cut our vacation short.
   Our francs were spent.

(4) Building simple sentences with appositives

An **appositive** is a noun or a noun phrase that identifies, in different words, the noun or pronoun it follows. In these two sentences, for instance,

> Roy Rogers' horse <u>Trigger</u> was a movie star.
>
> Farrington hated his boss, <u>a real tyrant</u>.

Trigger is an appositive that identifies the noun *horse*, and *a real
tyrant* is an appositive that identifies the noun *boss*.

Appositives expand a sentence by defining the nouns or
pronouns they modify, giving them a new name or adding identifying detail. Appositives can substitute for the nouns or pronouns they refer to.

> Francie Nolan, <u>the protagonist of Betty Smith's novel *A Tree Grows
> in Brooklyn*,</u> is determined to finish high school and make a better
> life for herself. (Francie Nolan = the protagonist of the novel)

> Grant, <u>the son of a tanner on the Western frontier,</u> was everything
> Lee was not. (Grant = the son of a tanner) (Bruce Catton)

As in the examples above, appositives are frequently used
without special introductory phrases. They may also be introduced by *such as, or, that is, for example,* or *in other words.*

> Regional airlines, <u>such as Piedmont and Western,</u> frequently ac-
> count for more than half the departures at so-called second-tier
> airports.

> Rabies, <u>or hydrophobia,</u> was nearly always fatal until Pasteur's
> work.

(For information on punctuation with appositives, see 26d.)

In addition to providing clarifying information, appositives
also help make sentences more concise (see 9b).

▶
EXERCISE 18

For practice in using appositives when you write, build ten new simple sentences by combining each of the following pairs. Make one sentence in each pair an appositive. You may need to delete or reorder words in some cases.

sent
6f

EXAMPLE: Rasputin was a religious mystic and faith healer.
Rasputin died in Russia just before the Revolution.

Rasputin, a religious mystic and faith healer, died in Russia just before the revolution.

1. The Rocky Mountains are a mountain range over 300 miles long.
   The Rocky Mountains extend from Mexico to Alaska.
2. *General Hospital* is a popular television soap opera.
   It is set in a hospital in Port Charles, New York.
3. Joyce Carol Oates is a prolific fiction writer.
   She often writes of violence and madness.
4. Grant and Lee were two Civil War generals.
   Grant was a northerner and Lee was a southerner.
5. Could he ever hope to repay her?
   He was a penniless schoolteacher.
6. Disney World is central Florida's most popular attraction.
   Disney World is a huge commercial success.
7. Many formerly deadly diseases have all but disappeared in the United States.
   These include such diseases as measles and polio.
8. A terrarium requires little care.
   A terrarium is a garden enclosed in a glass container.
9. The Hardy Boys led charmed lives.
   The Hardy Boys were amateur detectives.
10. India and Sri Lanka are neighboring countries.
    Before 1972, Sri Lanka was known as Ceylon.

(5) Building simple sentences with compound constructions

Compound constructions consist of two or more grammatically equivalent words or phrases, parallel in importance. These equivalent parts may be joined in one of three ways.

WITH COMMAS (see 26b)

He took one long, loving look at his '57 Chevy.

**sent
6f**

WITH THE COORDINATING CONJUNCTIONS *and, but, nor, or,* or *yet* (see 20g)

He is <u>strong but gentle</u>.

Beethoven composed <u>nine symphonies and an opera</u>.

She was not <u>glib or quick</u> in a world where <u>glibness and quickness</u> were easily confused with ability to learn. (Tillie Olsen, "I Stand Here Ironing")

They <u>reeled</u>, <u>whirled</u>, <u>swiveled</u>, <u>flounced</u>, <u>capered</u>, <u>gamboled</u>, and <u>spun</u>. (Kurt Vonnegut, Jr., "Harrison Bergeson")

WITH A PAIR OF CORRELATIVE CONJUNCTIONS *(both/and, not only/but also, either/or, neither/nor, whether/or)* (see 20g)

<u>Neither Sylvia Plath nor Emily Dickinson</u> achieved recognition during her lifetime.

<u>Both milk and carrots</u> contain Vitamin A.

<u>Either Cathy or Evan</u> will probably be in class today.

(For information on parallelism with correlative conjunctions, see 14a.2).

The parts that are linked in compound constructions may be single words or groups of words. These compounds add information without producing a string of short sentences like these.

Auto emissions pollute the air. Industrial wastes pollute the air. Auto emissions destroy forests. Industrial wastes destroy forests.

Instead, compounding can be used to expand simple sentences.

<u>Auto emissions</u> pollute the air.

<u>Auto emissions and industrial wastes</u> pollute the air. (compound subject)

<u>Auto emissions and industrial wastes</u> <u>pollute the air and destroy forests</u>. (compound predicate)

<u>Auto emissions and industrial wastes</u> are <u>annoying and dangerous</u>. (compound complement)

In these examples sentences are expanded when words or word groups that are closely related in function are combined with the coordinating conjunction *and*. Compounding is useful not just for expanding sentences but also for combining sentences to eliminate wordiness (see 9b).

► EXERCISE 19

A. Expand each of the following sentences by using compound subjects and/or predicates.

> EXAMPLE: The kitten yawned.
>
> The kitten and the mother cat yawned and stretched.

sent
6f

B. Then expand your simple sentence with modifying words and phrases, using compound phrases whenever possible.

> EXAMPLE: Absorbed in their ritual and paying no attention to us, the kitten and the mother cat yawned and stretched.

1. Columbus set sail for the East Indies.
2. The Yankees competed.
3. The Beach Boys performed.
4. The miller's daughter could spin straw into gold.
5. Dracula wore a black cape.

► EXERCISE 20

To practice building sentences with compound subjects, predicates, and modifiers, combine the following groups of sentences into one.

> EXAMPLE: Lester laughed. Ted laughed. They laughed loudly. They laughed heartily.
>
> Lester and Ted laughed loudly and heartily.

1. John McEnroe plays tennis. Jimmy Connors plays tennis. Ivan Lendl plays tennis. Chris Evert Lloyd plays tennis. Martina Navratilova plays tennis.
2. Professional tennis players compete in tournaments. They play exhibition games.
3. Tennis superstars earn money by making personal appearances. They earn money by endorsing tennis-related products. They earn money by endorsing products unrelated to tennis.
4. Top players endorse tennis racquets. They endorse tennis clothing. They endorse sneakers.
5. Nike sneakers are endorsed by tennis players. Lacoste clothing is endorsed by tennis players. Dunlop racquets are endorsed by tennis players.
6. Tennis players do magazine ads. They do television commercials. They sell all kinds of products.
7. Bjorn Borg, now retired from competition, endorsed comic books in Sweden. He endorsed motor scooters in Japan.

8. John McEnroe was a spokesman for the Australian Dairy Group. He was a spokesman for Toyota in Japan. He was a spokesman for Top Spin, an Italian soft drink.

9. In this country, McEnroe endorsed Bic shavers. He endorsed Omega watches.

sent
6f

10. Top-ranking tennis players can become extremely well known. They can become extremely rich.

7

Building Compound and Complex Sentences

7a Building Compound Sentences

The pairing of similar elements—words, phrases, or clauses—to give equal weight to each is called **coordination.** Coordination can be used in simple sentences to link similar elements to form compound subjects, predicates, complements, or modifiers. It can also link two independent clauses to form a **compound sentence.**

A compound sentence is formed when two or more simple sentences (independent clauses) are connected with coordinating conjunctions, conjunctive adverbs, correlative conjunctions, semicolons, or colons. Compound sentences most often communicate addition (through *and, in addition to, not only . . . but also,* or the use of a semicolon); contrast (*but, however*); cause and effect (*so, therefore, consequently*); or a choice of alternatives (*or, either . . . or*).

> The government was overthrown, <u>but</u> poverty remained.
>
> Some votes were challenged; <u>however</u>, the general was declared the winner.
>
> <u>Either</u> reform will begin, <u>or</u> the people will continue to suffer.
>
> Unemployment is high; prospects for the future are not encouraging.
>
> Finally the picture is becoming clear: conditions will not improve soon.

In compound sentences, the ideas in the paired sentences are of equal weight. Neither idea is less important than or dependent on the other.

(1)   Using coordinating conjunctions

**sent
7a**

When two independent clauses are joined by a coordinating conjunction, the first is nearly always followed by a comma. The comma may be omitted in very short sentences (see 26a.2). The seven coordinating conjunctions are *and, or, nor, but, for, so,* and *yet* (see 20g).

> [Congress overrode the president's veto], <u>so</u> [the bill was passed].
>
> [You can declare your major now], <u>or</u> [you can wait until next semester].
>
> [The cowboy is a workingman], <u>yet</u> [he has little in common with the urban blue-collar worker]. (John R. Erickson, *The Modern Cowboy*)
>
> [In the fall the war was always there], <u>but</u> [we did not go to it anymore]. (Ernest Hemingway, "In Another Country")
>
> [She carried a thin, small cane made from an umbrella], <u>and</u> [with this she kept tapping the frozen earth in front of her]. (Eudora Welty, "A Worn Path")

(2)   Using conjunctive adverbs and other transitional expressions

When two independent clauses are joined by a conjunctive adverb or by any other transitional expression to form a compound sentence, the transitional phrase is always preceded by a semicolon and usually followed by a comma.

> [Peter dropped Modern History]; <u>instead</u>, [he decided to take Educational Methods].
>
> [The saxophone does not belong to the brass family]; <u>in fact</u>, [it is a member of the woodwind family].
>
> [Aerobic exercise can help lower blood pressure]; <u>however</u>, [those with high blood pressure should still limit salt intake].

Commonly used conjunctive adverbs include *consequently, finally, still,* and *thus.* For a complete list, see 20e. Other commonly used transitional expressions include *for example, in fact, on the other hand,* and *for instance.* (A complete list of transitional expressions appears in 4c.4; for information on how to punctuate conjunctive adverbs and other transitional expressions in various positions within a sentence, see 26c.3, 26d.3, and 27c.)

(3)   Using correlative conjunctions

Just as correlative conjunctions (see 20g) can link single words or phrases (see 6f.5), they can also connect two independent clauses to form a compound sentence.

> Sharon <u>not only</u> passed the exam, <u>but</u> she <u>also</u> received the highest grade in the class.
>
> <u>Either</u> he left his coat in his locker, <u>or</u> he left it on the bus.

(4)   Using semicolons

A semicolon can link two closely related independent clauses (see 27a).

> [Alaska is the largest state]; [Rhode Island is the smallest].
>
> [Theodore Roosevelt was president after the Spanish American War]; [Andrew Johnson was president after the Civil War].

(5)   Using colons

A colon can sometimes link two independent clauses (see 30a).

> He got his orders: he was to leave for France on Sunday.
>
> They thought they knew the outcome: Truman would lose to Dewey.

▶

EXERCISE 1

Bracket the independent clauses in these compound sentences.

> EXAMPLE: [He was a man of few words], but [those few words were judiciously selected, weighed for quality, and delivered with expertise]. (Anita Brookner, *Hotel du Lac*)

1. We stand on the threshold of a great age of science; we are already over the threshold; it is for us to make that future our own. (Jacob Bronowski, *Science and Human Values*)
2. The players were not two persons, but two illustrious families; the game had been going on for centuries. (Jorge Luis Borges, "The Secret Miracle")
3. He blew the candle out suddenly, and we went inside. (Joseph Conrad, *Heart of Darkness*)
4. They had not shown much interest in the elephant when he was merely ravaging their homes, but it was different now that he was going to be shot. (George Orwell, "Shooting an Elephant")

5. The contempt of joggers and runners for the rest of humanity is often quite sincere, but I am not sure that it is deserved. (Joseph Epstein, *Familiar Territory*)

▶
EXERCISE 2

After reading the following paragraph, use coordination to build as many compound sentences as you think your readers need to understand the links between ideas. When you have finished, bracket the independent clauses and underline the coordinating conjunctions, correlative conjunctions, or punctuation marks that link clauses.

> Alan Bakke applied to medical school at the University of California at Davis. He was rejected in 1973 and 1974. Bakke's grades were good. He said he was the victim of reverse discrimination. The medical school had designated sixteen out of every hundred slots for minority students. Bakke was white. Bakke said some minority students, less qualified than he, had been admitted. Bakke sued the University of California. The case went to the Supreme Court. In 1978, Bakke won his suit. Today, Bakke is a doctor.

▶
EXERCISE 3

Add appropriate coordinating conjunctions, conjunctive adverbs, or correlative conjunctions as indicated to combine each pair of sentences into one well-constructed compound sentence that retains the meaning of the original pair. Be sure to use correct punctuation.

> EXAMPLE: *Mad* was first published in 1952. It did not become a true magazine until July 1955. (coordinating conjunction)
>
> *Mad* was first published in 1952, but it did not become a true magazine until July 1955.

1. The average American consumes 128 pounds of sugar each year. Most of us eat much more sugar than any other food additive, including salt. (conjunctive adverb)
2. Many of us are determined to reduce our sugar intake. We have consciously eliminated sweets from our diets. (conjunctive adverb)
3. Unfortunately, sugar is not found only in sweets. It is also found in many processed foods. (correlative conjunction)
4. Processed foods like puddings and cake contain sugar. Foods like ketchup and spaghetti sauce do, too. (coordinating conjunction)
5. We are trying to cut down on sugar. We find this extremely difficult. (coordinating conjunction)

6. Processors may use sugar in foods for taste. They may also use it to help prevent foods from spoiling and to improve their texture and appearance. (correlative conjunction)
7. Sugar comes in many different forms. It is easy to overlook it on a package label. (coordinating conjunction)
8. Sugar may be called sucrose or fructose. It may also be called corn syrup, corn sugar, brown sugar, honey, or molasses. (coordinating conjunction)
9. No sugar is more nourishing than the others. It really doesn't matter which is consumed. (conjunctive adverb)
10. Sugars contain empty calories. Whenever possible, they should be avoided. (conjunctive adverb) (Adapted from *Jane Brody's Nutrition Book*)

sent
7b

▶
EXERCISE 4

Write two sentences imitating the following. Use the same parts of speech in making substitutions, and retain the function words (articles, prepositions, and conjunctions) of the model.

> His clothes were a trifle outgrown, and the tan velvet on the collar of his open overcoat was frayed and worn; but for all that there was something of the dandy about him, and he wore an opal pin in his neatly knotted black four-in-hand, and a red carnation in his buttonhole. (**Willa Cather**, "**Paul's Case**")

7b Building Complex Sentences

When you want to indicate that one idea is less important than another, you subordinate the secondary idea to the primary one. You might put the secondary idea in a modifying phrase or in another, less emphatic position in the sentence (see 8a). Another way to subordinate one idea to another is to place the main idea in an independent clause and the less important idea in a dependent clause. The result is a complex sentence.

A **complex sentence** consists of one simple sentence, which functions as an independent or main clause in the complex sentence, and at least one dependent or subordinate clause, a clause introduced by a subordinating conjunction or a relative pronoun. **Independent clauses** can stand alone as sentences.

The hurricane began.

The town was evacuated.

Dependent clauses, introduced by a subordinating conjunction or relative pronoun, cannot stand alone.

> When the hurricane began
>
> After the town was evacuated
>
> Which threatened to destroy the town
>
> Because the hurricane presented a great danger

Dependent clauses must be combined with independent clauses to form sentences.

> dependent clause   independent clause
> [When the hurricane began], [the town was evacuated].

> dependent clause   independent clause
> [After the town was evacuated], [the hurricane began].

> independent clause   dependent clause
> [The town was evacuated] [because the hurricane presented a great danger].

> independent clause   dependent clause
> [Officials watched the storm], [which threatened to destroy the town].

Sometimes, a dependent clause may be placed within an independent clause.

> dependent clause
> The storm, [which began slowly], turned into a hurricane.

> dependent clause
> Town officials, [who were very concerned], watched the storm.

The subordinating conjunction or relative pronoun links the independent and dependent clauses and shows the relationship between them.

> dependent clause   independent clause
> [Because he needed money], [he looked for a summer job].

> independent clause   dependent clause
> [I want to spend my junior year] [where I used to live].

Depending on their function in a sentence, subordinate clauses may be adverb, adjective, or noun clauses. Adverb clauses function in a sentence as adverbs, adjective clauses as adjectives, and noun clauses as nouns (see 6d).

> When the school board voted to ban Judy Blume's books, parents protested. (adverb clause)

The Graduate was the film that launched Dustin Hoffman's career.
(adjective clause)

How the fight started remained a mystery. (noun clause)

Subordinating conjunctions introduce adverb clauses. The
most commonly used subordinating conjunctions include

sent
7b

after	rather than
although	since
as	so that
as if	that
as though	though
because	unless
before	until
even though	when
if	whenever
in order that	where
now that	wherever
once	while

Relative pronouns introduce adjective clauses. The relative
pronouns include:

that	who (whose, whom)
what	whoever (whomever)
whatever	
which	

Noun clauses may be introduced by relative pronouns or by
whether, when, where, why, or *how.* For information on punctuating complex sentences see 26c.1.

▶
EXERCISE 5

Bracket and label the independent and dependent clauses in these sentences, and then underline and label the subordinating conjunctions or
relative pronouns. Finally, indicate the function of each subordinate
clause.

sub.

ind. clause   conj.   dep. clause
EXAMPLE: ["Jet-stream art" is created] [when paint thrown into
the exhaust of a jet engine is spattered onto a giant
canvas]. (subordinate clause serves as an adverb)

1. The people were clustered thickly about the old man, all of them
    intermittently flicking glances toward me as they talked animatedly
    in their Mandinka tongue. (Alex Haley, *Roots*)

2. When professional writers complete a first draft, they usually feel that they are at the start of the writing process. (Donald M. Murray, "The Maker's Eye")

3. We cannot help regarding a camel as aloof and unfriendly because it mimics, quite unwittingly and for other reasons, the "gesture of haughty rejection" common to so many human cultures. (Stephen Jay Gould, *The Panda's Thumb*)

4. While the generational struggle continued for decades, it would be some years before it seriously threatened the coherence of the immigrant community. (Irving Howe, *World of Our Fathers*)

5. These are both hopeful and frustrating times for those who want to improve the nation's science and math education. (Arlen J. Large, *Wall Street Journal*)

6. Because they are so near the time to actual events, crime films provide a useful means to review a major strain of American violence along a dynamic continuum. (Carlos Clarens, *Crime Movies: An Illustrated History*)

7. When bacteria or viruses enter the body, white blood cells called macrophages release a hormone, interleukin-1. *(Newsweek)*

8. Although there was always generosity in the Negro neighborhood, it was indulged on pain of sacrifice. (Maya Angelou)

9. That no one dies of migraine seems, to someone deep into an attack, an ambiguous blessing. (Joan Didion, *The White Album*)

10. If you don't already have a word processor, you probably can't imagine why you need one. If you do have one, you probably wonder how you ever got along without it. (David Gabel, *Personal Computing*)

▶
EXERCISE 6

Bracket the independent and dependent clauses in the following complex sentences. Then, using these sentences as models, create two new complex sentences in imitation of each. For each set of new sentences, use the same subordinating conjunction or relative pronoun that appears in the original.

1. Life is what happens while you're making other plans.
2. Mercury is the planet that is closest to the sun.
3. After she returned from the ball, Leila felt exhausted but exhilarated.
4. That vocational programs were becoming more important was obvious to the accreditation team.
5. Gertrude remarried before Hamlet had accepted his father's death.

▶
EXERCISE 7

Use a subordinating conjunction or relative pronoun to combine each of the following pairs of sentences into one well-constructed sentence. The conjunction or pronoun you select must indicate the relationship between the two sentences. You will have to change or reorder words, and in most cases you have a choice among connecting words.

EXAMPLE: College admissions requirements are easing.

The pool of students is growing smaller.

Because the pool of students is growing smaller, college admissions requirements are easing.

sent
7c

1. Some twelve million people are currently out of work. They need new skills for new careers.
2. In the 1960's and 1970's, talented high school students were encouraged to go to college. Some high school graduates are now starting to see that a college education may not guarantee them a job.
3. A college education can cost a student more than $50,000. Vocational education is becoming increasingly important.
4. Students complete their work in less than four years. They can enter the job market more quickly.
5. Nurses' aides, paralegals, travel agents, and computer technicians do not need college degrees. They have little trouble finding work.
6. Some four-year colleges are experiencing growth. Public community colleges and private trade schools are growing much more rapidly.
7. Vocational schools are responsive to the needs of local businesses. They train students for jobs that actually exist.
8. For instance, a school in Detroit might offer advanced automotive design. A school in New York City might focus on fashion design.
9. Other schools offer courses in horticulture, respiratory therapy, and computer programming. They are able to place their graduates easily.
10. Laid-off workers, returning housewives, recent high school graduates, and even college graduates are reexamining vocational education. They all hope to find rewarding careers.

7c Building Compound-Complex Sentences

A **compound-complex sentence** consists of two or more independent clauses and at least one dependent clause.

dependent clause
[When small foreign imports began dominating the U.S.

independent clause
automobile industry], [consumers were very responsive],

independent clause
but [American auto workers were dismayed].

dependent clause   *independent clause*
[As the ferry entered the harbor], [she stood up and made her way down the deck against the light salt wind], and

dependent clause within independent clause
[Baxter], [who had returned to the island indifferently],

independent clause
[felt that summer had begun]. (John Cheever, "The Chaste Clarissa")

▶

EXERCISE 8

In each of these sentences, identify subjects and verbs; bracket and label dependent and independent clauses; and identify each sentence as simple, compound, complex, or compound-complex.

1. Use of the telephone involves personal risk because it involves exposure; for some, to be "hung up on" is among the worst fears; others dream of a ringing telephone and wake up with a pounding heart. (John Brooks, *Telephone: The First Hundred Years*)

2. Although Intourist, the government travel organization, has made great strides in improving tourist facilities and the variety of things to do, the Soviet state still regards the foreign tourist as a blend of spy and ideological alien—a person to be watched, carefully segregated from the citizenry and, to the extent possible, educated in the wonders of Socialist democracy and achievements. (*New York Times*)

3. Though she was stout in build and stood erect, her slow eyes and parted lips gave her the appearance of a woman who did not know where she was or where she was going. (James Joyce, "The Dead")

4. This nation is even more litigious than religious, and the school prayer issue has prompted more, and more sophisticated, arguments about constitutional law than about the nature of prayer. (George F. Will, *Newsweek*)

5. The first time I ever went naked in mixed company was at the house of a girl whose father had a bad back and had built himself a sauna in the corner of the basement. (Garrison Keillor, *New Yorker*)

6. I am the son of Mexican-American parents, who speak a blend of Spanish and English, but who read neither language easily. (Richard Rodriguez, *Aria: Memoirs of a Bilingual Childhood*)

7. Winter was always the effort to live; summer was tropical license. (Henry Adams, *The Education of Henry Adams*)

8. Of course, only in extreme cases do graduates become dull immediately. (Wilfred Sheed, *New York Times*)

9. The most alarming of all man's assaults upon the environment is the contamination of air, earth, rivers, and sea with dangerous and even lethal materials. (Rachel Carson, *Silent Spring*)

10. At the age of 80, my mother had her last bad fall, and after that her mind wandered free through time. (Russell Baker, *Growing Up*)

Student Writer at Work: Building Sentences

A student in a freshman composition class was assigned to interview a grandparent and write a short report about his or her life. When she set out to turn her grandmother's words into a report, the student faced a set of choppy notes—words, phrases, and simple sentences—that she had jotted down as her grandmother spoke. She needed to fill out and combine these fragments and short sentences to produce varied, interesting sentences that would establish the relationships among her ideas. Read the notes and combine sentences wherever it seems appropriate. Your goal is to build simple, compound, and complex sentences enriched by modifiers—without adding any information.

Notes

Grandmother is 67 years old. Born in Lykens, PA (old coal-mining town). Got her first paying job at 13. Her parents lied about her age. Working age was 14. Parents couldn't afford all the mouths they had to feed. Before that, she helped with the housework. At work, she was a maid. Got paid only about a dollar a week. Most of that went to her parents. Ate her meals on job. Worked in house where 3 generations of men lived. They all worked in the mines. She had to get up at 4 A.M. Her first chore was to make lunch for the men. She'd scrub the metal canteens. Then she'd fill them with water. Then she'd make biscuits and broth. Then she'd start breakfast. Mrs. Muller would help. Cooking for 6 hungry men was a real job. Then she did the breakfast dishes. Then she did the chores. The house had 3 stories. She had to scrub floors, dust, and sweep. It wasn't easy. Then Mrs. Muller would need help patching and darning. She had just enough time to get dinner

started. She grabbed her meals after the family finished eating.
She had no spare time. When she wasn't working she had
chores to do at home. In spring and summer she would grow
vegetables. She canned vegetables for her family. What was left
over, she sold. When she was 16, she got married.

sent

7

8

Writing Emphatic Sentences

When speaking, you add attitude and emphasis to your ideas with facial expressions, gestures, and such vocal cues as raising or lowering your voice. When writing, you must find other techniques to highlight important points. Careful sentence construction is the solution to this problem. The skillful arrangement of words, phrases, and clauses; the proper selection of strategies like parallelism and repetition; and the appropriate choice of voice and sentence patterns all help you stress certain points and qualify others.

8a Achieving Emphasis Through Word Order

Manipulating word order can help strengthen and clarify your intention. Where you place your words, phrases, and clauses within a sentence emphasizes or deemphasizes their importance. For instance, placing a word or word group either at the *beginning* or at the *end* of a sentence tends to focus attention on it. Departures from expected word order also attract attention.

(1) Beginning with important ideas

Readers focus on the *beginning* and *end* of a sentence, expecting the most important information to appear there. To convey emphasis clearly and forcefully, take care to fulfill these expectations. Look at the following sentence.

> In a landmark study of alcoholism, Dr. George Vaillant of Harvard followed 200 Harvard graduates and 400 inner-city, working-class men from the Boston area.

This sentence carries its key idea at the beginning. Greatest emphasis is therefore placed on the study itself, not on those who conducted it or who participated in it. Rephrasing changes the emphasis by focusing attention on the researcher and relegating the information about his work to a parenthetical phrase.

> Dr. George Vaillant of Harvard, in a landmark study of alcoholism, followed 200 Harvard graduates and 400 inner-city, working-class men from the Boston area.

Situations that demand a straightforward presentation—laboratory reports, memos, technical papers, business correspondence, and the like—call for sentences that present vital information first and qualify ideas later.

> The possibility of treating cancer with interferon has been the subject of a good deal of research.

> Whether or not dividends will be paid depends on the vote of the stockholders.

The first sentence emphasizes the new treatment, not the research; the second sentence stresses the question of dividends, not the vote. For technical and business audiences artificially created suspense is inappropriate—especially if it means readers must wade through a series of qualifiers to get the point. NOTE: Because sentence beginnings are so strategic, the use of unemphatic, empty phrases like *there is* or *there are* in this position is generally ineffective.

> UNEMPHATIC: There is heavy emphasis placed on the development of computational skills at MIT.

> EMPHATIC: MIT places heavy emphasis on the development of computational skills.

(2)   Ending with important ideas

The close of a sentence can be an even more dramatic position for important ideas. Key elements may be placed at the end of a sentence in a number of conventional ways. A colon or a dash can add emphasis by isolating an important word or phrase at the end of a sentence.

> Beth had always dreamed of owning one special car: a 1953 Corvette.

> The elderly need a good deal of special attention—and they deserve that attention.

In addition, putting modifiers or other subordinate elements at the beginning of a sentence allows you to place more important elements in the naturally emphatic position at its end.

> UNEMPHATIC: The Philadelphia Eagles and the Pittsburgh Steelers became one professional football team, nicknamed the Steagles, during World War II because of the manpower shortage. (modifying phrases at end detract from main idea and weaken sentence)

> EMPHATIC: Because of the manpower shortage during World War II, the Philadelphia Eagles and the Pittsburgh Steelers became one professional football team, nicknamed the Steagles. (correctly emphasizes the newly created team)

**emp
8a**

One special way writers use the emphatic end-of-sentence position is called **climactic word order.** Climactic word order moves in a series from the least to the most important point in the sentence. This sentence pattern stresses the key idea—the last point in the sentence—while building suspense and heightening interest.

When the key idea is buried in the middle of a sentence, the sentence will lack emphasis.

> Duties of a member of Congress include serving as a district's representative in Washington, making speeches, and answering mail. (which duty is most important?)

When you use climactic word order, placing the key idea at the end, the momentum of the sentence gives this idea added force.

> The nation's most prominent orchestras all boast large annual budgets, locations in important cities, and the most talented musicians and conductors. (talent is the key idea)

> Foreign cars are capturing the American market because of their styling, performance, and fuel economy. (fuel economy is the key idea)

NOTE: Unless you have a very good reason to do so, do not waste the end of a sentence on qualifiers such as conjunctive adverbs. In that position a qualifier loses its power as a linking expression that indicates the relationship between ideas. Put transitional phrases earlier, where they can fulfill their functions and add emphasis.

LESS EMPHATIC: Smokers do have rights; they should not try to impose their habits on others, however. (conjunctive adverb at end of clause)

MORE EMPHATIC: Smokers do have rights; however, they should not try to impose their habits on others. (conjunctive adverb at beginning of clause)

LESS EMPHATIC: We wanted the shelves to be water-resistant; we applied three coats of polyurethane for this reason. (transitional expression at end of clause)

MORE EMPHATIC: We wanted the shelves to be water-resistant; for this reason, we applied three coats of polyurethane. (transitional expression at beginning of clause)

▶
EXERCISE 1

Underline the most important word group in each sentence of the following paragraph. Then identify the device the writer used to emphasize those key words. Are the key ideas placed at the beginning or end of a sentence? Does the writer use climactic order?

> Buried in the basement of the computer center, often for hours on end, the campus computer hackers work. Day after day they sit at their terminals, working on games, class assignments, research projects, or schemes to conquer the world. Some computer hackers are totally absorbed in their terminal keyboards, pausing only for occasional meals or classes. A few hackers become almost reclusive, spending little time on recreational activities or social relationships. Sacrificing grades, exercise, dating, and contact with the outdoors, hackers structure their lives around their computers. With their own slang, their own habits, and their own hangouts, computer hackers tend to set themselves apart from their fellow students. But these computer addicts feel that the computer experience is worth the sacrifices they must make: computers have opened up a whole new world for them.

(3) Departing from expected word order

The word order of most sentences is subject-verb-object (or complement). When you change this order, you call attention to the word, phrase, or clause that you have inverted. You may even call attention to the entire sentence.

emp 8a

> More modest and less inventive than Turner's paintings are John
> Constable's landscapes.

Here the writer calls special attention to the modifying phrase
more modest and less inventive than Turner's paintings by turning the sentence around to stress the comparison with Turner's
work.

emp
8b

    This stylistic technique must be used appropriately and in
moderation. Misuse of inverted sentences can distort your meaning; overuse makes your writing stiff and unnatural. (See also
10e.1 on sentence variety.)

▶

EXERCISE 2

Revise the following sentences to make them more emphatic. For each,
decide which ideas should be highlighted, and group key phrases at
sentence beginnings or endings, using climactic order or inverted order
where appropriate.

1. Out-of-wedlock births among all women rose by over 11 percent in
   1980, the last year for which census figures are available.
2. There are increasing numbers of middle-class, well-educated
   women who are electing to become single mothers.
3. This development is not surprising if we see it as the logical consequence of recent trends toward delayed parenting and more women
   entering the work force and becoming independent.
4. These single women have decided that they do not want to be child-
   less all their lives; they do not necessarily want to marry, however.
5. Still, they worry about what will happen to their children if they
   should die, about what to tell family and friends about their decision
   to have a child, and about how to pay for day care.

8b Achieving Emphasis Through Sentence Structure

Supporting details are ideas that are subordinate to the sentence's main idea. Such details are placed in modifying phrases
or dependent clauses. Skillful use of **subordination** can clarify a
sentence's emphasis by deemphasizing less important ideas and
emphasizing more important ones (see 7b). Subordination can be
achieved through either a cumulative or a periodic structure.

emp
8b

(1) Using cumulative sentences

Most English sentences are classified as cumulative. A **cumulative sentence** begins with a main (independent) clause that is followed by additional words, phrases, or clauses that expand or develop it. Here is a basic sentence.

> She holds me in strong arms.

It can be expanded with phrases and clauses.

> She holds me in strong arms, arms that have chopped cotton, dismembered trees, scattered corn for chickens, cradled infants, shaken the daylights out of half-grown upstart teenagers. (Rebecca Hill, *Blue Rise*)

The main clause appears at the beginning of the sentence, and modifiers follow it; therefore the sentence is cumulative. In subordinating the secondary details to the main clause the writer achieves the emphasis she desires.

(2) Using periodic sentences

A **periodic sentence** moves from a number of specific examples to a conclusion. Modifiers and other supporting details appear first, followed by the main clause. The effect is a gradual building of intensity, sometimes of suspense, until a climax is reached in the main clause. Such sentences can be forceful indeed.

> The problems of soiled artificial flowers, soggy undercrust, leaky milk cartons, sour dishrags, girdle stays jabbing, meringue weeping, soda straws sticking out of bag lunches, shower curtains flapping out of the tub, creases in the middle of the tablecloth sticking up, wet boxes in the laundry room, roach eggs in the refrigerator motor, shiny seam marks on the front of recently ironed ties, flyspecks on chandeliers, film on bathroom tiles, steam on bathroom mirrors, rust in Formica drain-boards, road film on windshields—all were acknowledged and certified, probably for the first time ever, in "Hints from Heloise." (Ian Frazier, *New Yorker*)

Here the writer gains force by presenting a long and convincing catalog of details that culminate in the statement of the main clause. Again, putting less important details in modifying phrases places emphasis on the main clause and helps the writer achieve his purpose.

In this less elaborate sentence from an article about Wacky Wall Walkers, the writer adds emphasis to the main clause by keeping readers waiting. As the main clause at the end of the sentence ties the modifying clauses together, the writer's point emerges clearly.

> Unlike the Pet Rock, which insulted the intelligence, and Rubik's Cube, which defied it, a big new hit on the toy scene tickles the imagination and captivates the eye. *(Time)*

In some periodic sentences the modifying phrase or clause comes between subject and predicate so that only the predicate of the main clause is delayed until the end.

> Columbus, after several discouraging and unsuccessful voyages, finally reached America.

Here, too, the result is an emphatic sentence that serves the writer's purpose.

▶
EXERCISE 3

A. Bracket the main clause(s) in each sentence, and underline the modifying phrases.
B. Label each sentence cumulative or periodic. Then relocate the modifiers to make cumulative sentences periodic and periodic sentences cumulative.
C. Be prepared to explain how the word order chosen by each writer conveys the emphasis that best serves his or her purpose.

> EXAMPLE: [Thousands of fans lined the streets], <u>watching the victory parade</u>. (cumulative)
>
> Watching the victory parade, thousands of fans lined the streets. (periodic)

1. Andy is one of approximately 400,000 American youngsters suffering from a newly recognized childhood illness: depression. (**Alice Lake,** **Woman's Day**)
2. . . . Monhegan islanders are trading their kerosene lamps for photovoltaic solar cells, the same technology used to power hundreds of U.S. satellites in orbit. *(Newsweek)*
3. Given the constant changes in air fares, any list of travel bargains would almost certainly be out of date even before it was published. *(Consumer Reports)*
4. On the basis of fake résumés, a man with a high school diploma was

hired as a safety engineer at a nuclear power plant, a woman without a medical degree worked as a doctor at four New York City hospitals, and a man who had never passed the bar was taken on as a
lawyer by the brokerage firm of Paine Webber. *(Time)*

**emp
8b**

5. [Henry] Moore's personal history is as familiar in outline as are his
sculptures: his birth in 1898 as the seventh child of a Yorkshire coal-
mining family; his early skill at carving; a conservative artistic education at the Royal College of Art, in London. (Kay Larson, *New York
Magazine*)

▶

EXERCISE 4

A. Combine each of the following sentence groups into one cumulative
sentence, subordinating supporting details to main ideas.
B. Then combine each group into one periodic sentence. Each group
can be combined in a variety of ways, and you will have to add, delete,
change, or reorder words.
C. Decide which sentence is more effective in each case, the cumulative
or the periodic.

> EXAMPLE: More blacks than ever are registering to vote. They
> are encouraged by the success of minority candi-
> dates.

> CUMULATIVE: More blacks than ever are registering to vote, en-
> couraged by the success of minority candidates.

> PERIODIC: Encouraged by the success of minority candidates,
> more blacks than ever are registering to vote.

1. Many politicians oppose the MX missile. They believe it is too expensive. They feel that a smaller, single-warhead missile is preferable.
2. Smoking poses a real danger. It is associated with various cancers. It
is linked to heart disease and stroke. It may even threaten nonsmokers.
3. Infertile couples who want children sometimes go through a series
of difficult processes. They may try adoption. They may also try artificial insemination or in vitro fertilization. They may even seek out
surrogate mothers.
4. The Thames is a river that meanders through southern England. It
has been the inspiration for literary works like *Alice in Wonderland*
and *The Wind in the Willows.* It was also captured in paintings by
Constable, Turner, and Whistler.
5. Black-footed ferrets are rare North American mammals. They prey

on prairie dogs. They are primarily nocturnal. They have black feet and black-tipped tails. Their faces have racoonlike masks.

▶

EXERCISE 5

Combine each of the following sentence groups into one sentence in which you subordinate supporting details to main ideas. In each case, create either a periodic or a cumulative sentence, depending on which structure you think will best convey the sentence's emphasis. Add, delete, change, or reorder words when necessary.

> EXAMPLE: The fears of today's college students are based on reality. They are afraid there are too many students and too few jobs.
>
> The fears of today's college students—that there are too many students and too few jobs—are based on reality. (periodic)

1. Today's college students are under a good deal of stress. Job prospects are not very good. Financial aid is not as easy to come by as it was in the past.
2. Education has grown very expensive. The job market has become tighter. Pressure to get into graduate and professional schools has increased.
3. Family ties seem to be weakening. Students aren't always able to count on family support.
4. Students have always had problems. Now college counseling centers report more—and more serious—problems among college students.
5. The term *student shock* has recently been coined. This term describes a syndrome that may include depression, anxiety, headaches, and eating and sleeping disorders.
6. Many students are overwhelmed by the vast array of courses and majors offered at their colleges. They tend to be less decisive. They take longer to choose a major and to complete school.
7. Many drop out of school for brief (or extended) periods, or switch majors several times. Many take five years or longer to complete their college education.
8. Some colleges are responding to the pressures students feel. They hold stress-management workshops and suicide-prevention courses. They advertise the services of their counseling centers. They train students as peer counselors. They improve their vocational counseling services.

8c Achieving Emphasis Through Parallelism and Balance

emp
8c

The symmetry of **parallelism** highlights corresponding elements and gives a sentence emphasis and clarity. (For a detailed discussion of parallelism, see Chapter 14.) Parallelism is frequently used in classified advertisements:

> We seek an individual who is a self-starter, who owns a late-model automobile, and who is willing to work evenings.

in instructions

> Do not pass go; do not collect $200.

in examination questions

> Discuss the role of women in the short stories of Ernest Hemingway and F. Scott Fitzgerald, paying special attention to their relationships with men, to their relationships with other women, and to their roles in their jobs and/or marriages.

in examination answers

> The Faust legend is central in Benét's *The Devil and Daniel Webster*, in Goethe's *Faust*, and in Marlowe's *Dr. Faustus*.

and in any other situations where information must be conveyed clearly, quickly, and emphatically.

A sentence neatly divided between two parallel structures is said to be **balanced**. Balanced sentences are typically compound sentences made up of two parallel clauses, but the parallel clauses of a complex sentence can also be balanced. The symmetrical structure of a balanced sentence highlights correspondences or contrasts between clauses.

A balanced sentence can be exactly parallel, matching element for element

> In the fifties, the electronic miracle was the television; in the eighties, the electronic miracle is the computer.

or it can be parallel only when it comes to major elements.

> When guns are outlawed, only outlaws will have guns.

> Alive, the elephant was worth at least a hundred pounds; dead, he would only be worth the value of his tusks, five pounds, possibly. (George Orwell, "Shooting an Elephant")

Beyond helping you achieve emphasis, parallelism and balance can help you combine ideas and thus write more economically (see 9b). The judicious use of balanced sentences also helps you achieve sentence variety (see Chapter 10).

8d Achieving Emphasis Through Repetition

Ineffective repetition makes sentences dull, monotonous, and wordy.

> He had a good arm and <u>also</u> could field well and he was <u>also</u> a fast runner.

> We got three estimates, and <u>the one we got from</u> the Johnson Brothers seemed more reasonable than <u>the one we got from</u> County Carpenters.

Effective repetition of key words can place emphasis on key words or ideas. Repetition may be effective when a word or word group is repeated in a parallel series:

> They decided to begin again: <u>to begin</u> hoping, <u>to begin</u> trying to change, <u>to begin</u> working toward a goal.

or when a key word or phrase is repeated just once:

> During those years when I was just learning to speak, my mother and father addressed me only <u>in Spanish</u>; <u>in Spanish</u> I learned to reply. (Richard Rodriquez, *Aria: Memoirs of a Bilingual Childhood*)

> If ever <u>two groups</u> were opposed, surely those <u>two groups</u> are runners and smokers. (Joseph Epstein, *Familiar Territory*)

Repetition may be confined to a sentence, or it may continue throughout a paragraph—or even a group of paragraphs—contributing to coherence (see 4c). In this group of sentences, the parallel structure and repetition of the *still* add emphasis, stressing how hard the author's mother worked.

> <u>Still</u> she sewed—dresses and jackets for the children, housedresses and aprons for herself, weekly patching of jeans, overalls, and denim shirts. She <u>still</u> made pillows, using the feathers she had plucked, and quilts every year—intricate patterns as well as patchwork, stitched as well as tied—all necessary bedding for her family. Every scrap of cloth too small to be used in quilts was carefully saved and painstakingly sewed together in strips to

make rugs. She <u>still</u> went out in the fields to help with the haying whenever there was a threat of rain. (Donna Smith-Yackel, "My Mother Never Worked")

emp
8d

▶
EXERCISE 6

Revise the sentences in this paragraph, using parallelism and balance whenever possible to highlight corresponding elements and using repetition of key words and phrases to add emphasis. (To achieve repetition, you must change some synonyms.) You may combine sentences and add, delete, or reorder words.

Many readers distrust newspapers. They also distrust what they read in magazines. They don't trust what they hear on the radio and what television shows them either. Newspapers have been most responsive to audience criticism. Some newspapers even have ombudsmen. They are supposed to listen to reader complaints. They are also charged with acting on these grievances. One complaint many people have is that newspapers are inaccurate. Newspapers' disregard for people's privacy is another of many readers' criticisms. Reporters are seen as arrogant, and readers feel that journalists can be unfair. They feel reporters tend to glorify criminals, and they believe there is a tendency to place too much emphasis on bizarre or offbeat stories. Finally, readers complain about poor writing and editing. In any case, polls show there is more hostility to the press now than there has been in years, and also more anger directed toward other media. (Adapted from *Newsweek*)

8e Achieving Emphasis Through Active Voice

The active voice is generally more emphatic—and frequently more concise—than the passive voice (see 22j).

> PASSIVE: The prediction that oil prices will not rise significantly can now be made by economists.

> ACTIVE: Economists can now predict that oil prices will not rise significantly.

The passive voice tends to focus your readers' attention on the action or on its receiver rather than on who is performing it. The subject of the passive sentence receives the action, and the actor tends to fade into the background *(by economists)* or even to be omitted *(The prediction can now be made)*. This deemphasis of the actor can make a sentence seem off-balance and lacking in force.

Sometimes, of course, you want to present the recipient of the action prominently. If so, it makes sense to use the passive voice. To stress the opening of the Western frontier you would write

emp
8e

> PASSIVE: The West was opened by Lewis and Clark. (*or* The West
> was opened.)

To stress the contribution of Lewis and Clark, however, you would write

> ACTIVE: Lewis and Clark opened the West.

The passive is also used when the identity of the actor is irrelevant or unknown.

> The course was canceled.
>
> Littering is prohibited.
>
> The beaker was filled with a saline solution.

The passive voice occurs frequently in scientific and technical writing, where convention has long dictated that writers avoid the first person singular. Because the focus is on what is done, not on who is doing it, passive voice is appropriate in this type of writing.

▶
EXERCISE 7

Revise this paragraph to eliminate awkward or excessive use of passive constructions.

> Jack Dempsey was the heavyweight champion between 1919 and 1926. He was considered one of the greatest boxers of all time. Dempsey began fighting as "Kid Blackie," but his career didn't take off until 1919, when Jack "Doc" Kearns became his manager. Dempsey won the championship when Jess Willard was defeated by him in Toledo, Ohio, in 1919. Dempsey immediately became a popular sports figure; Franklin Delano Roosevelt was one of his biggest fans. Influential friends were made by Jack Dempsey. Boxing lessons were given by him to the actor Rudolph Valentino. He made friends with Douglas Fairbanks, Sr., Damon Runyon, and J. Paul Getty. Hollywood serials were made by Dempsey, but the title was lost by him to Gene Tunney, and Dempsey failed to regain it the following year. Meanwhile, his life was marred by unpleas-

ant developments such as a bitter legal battle with his manager and his 1920 indictment for draft evasion. In subsequent years, after his boxing career declined, a restaurant was opened by Dempsey and many major sporting events were attended by him. This exposure kept him in the public eye until he lost his restaurant. Jack Dempsey died in 1983.

emp
8

Student Writer at Work: Writing Emphatic Sentences

Identify the strategies a freshman composition student has used in this draft to add emphasis. Then revise it to make sentences more emphatic.

Nuclear Power Plants: Threat to the Public

Nuclear power is a relatively new source of energy. Our reliance upon nuclear power increases as conventional sources of energy, such as coal and petroleum, are depleted. There has been much controversy concerning the safety of the reactors currently in use. Nuclear power plants are a constant threat to the public and to the environment.

It has been claimed by the nuclear power industry that its plants are safe. The industry points out that its safety devices and procedures are rigid and that its plants hold a safety record equal to that of conventional plants using coal or petroleum. These nuclear plants do not use coal or petroleum, however. Instead, they use highly radioactive substances. Safety standards at nuclear power plants should be even more rigidly enforced for this reason.

Many nuclear power plants are poorly built and designed. Some unscrupulous construction firms have been caught altering specifications or using shoddy materials to increase their profit margins. One nuclear reactor in California was designed to withstand massive earthquakes. However, some of the specifications have been altered to the extent that the foundation may have to be replaced or modified in order to withstand an earthquake. Many nuclear plants have been plagued with faulty valves installed by firms that allegedly were aware of the defects.

A large number of poorly trained or inexperienced workers are among those employed as plant operators. The extent of the damage at Three Mile Island would not have been so great if the operators had been more experienced or better trained. Many operators failed their licensing test at Three Mile Island recently. This left only the minimum number of personnel required to "safely" operate the reactor.

Until more research is done with regard to safety procedures, design, and personnel of nuclear power plants, these plants should be considered a threat to our environment and to our lives. No more plants should be built, and existing ones should be modified or shut down. Nuclear energy should not be used unless facilities are redesigned and thoroughly tested, although it can be a good source of energy. Tighter government controls should be imposed to protect the people and their environment.

emp
8

Writing Concise Sentences

A concise sentence contains just the number of words necessary to achieve its effect: it says what you want to say in as few words as possible. Wordy sentences try your readers' patience, making them lose interest. But a sentence is not concise simply because it is short. Conciseness is always related to content: how much you have to say. If you can eliminate words without reducing the amount of information you present, you should do so.

Every word serves a purpose in a concise sentence. Because they are free of unnecessary words and convoluted constructions that come between you and your readers, concise sentences are also clear and emphatic. To write such sentences you must control your diction, limiting your words to the essential.

9a Eliminating Nonessential Words

One way to find out which words are essential to the meaning of a sentence is to underline the key words. Then, looking carefully at the remaining ones, you can see which are unnecessary or meaningless and delete them.

> It seems to me that it doesn't make sense to allow any <u>bail</u> to be <u>granted</u> to anyone who has ever been <u>convicted</u> of a <u>violent</u> crime.

The underlining shows you immediately that none of the words in the long introductory phrase are essential. In revising, you might write

> Bail should not be granted to anyone who has ever been convicted of a violent crime.

The new sentence includes all the key words and the minimum number of other words needed to give the key ideas coherence.

Dispensable words fall into three loose classifications: *deadwood, utility words,* and *circumlocution.*

(1) Deadwood

Deadwood refers to unnecessary phrases that take up space and add nothing to meaning. For instance, *to be* can be eliminated in certain contexts.

Kareem Abdul-Jabbar is considered <u>to be</u> a great center.	Kareem Abdul-Jabbar is considered a great center.

Often you can also delete *who are, which are, that is,* and similar phrases that introduce adjective clauses, with no loss of meaning.

Wordy	*Concise*
Shoppers <u>who are</u> looking for bargains often patronize outlets.	Shoppers looking for bargains often patronize outlets.
They played a racquetball game <u>which was</u> exhausting.	They played an exhausting racquetball game.
The box <u>that was</u> in the middle contained a surprise.	The box in the middle contained a surprise.

Removing deadwood from these wordy sentences turns the adjective clauses into simple modifying words or phrases, which in turn helps prevent rambling sentences (see 9c.2).

There is, there are, there were, and *it is* at the beginning of a sentence may also be deadwood. These phrases are frequently unnecessary.

<u>There were</u> many factors that influenced his decision to become a priest.	Many factors influenced his decision to become a priest.
<u>It was</u> lucky that he was able to get his friends to help him move.	He was lucky to get his friends to help him move.

Certain empty self-justifications and pompous sentence extenders too often appear as introductory phrases.

Wordy	*Concise*
<u>With reference to</u> your memo, the points you make are worth considering.	The points in your memo are worth considering.
<u>In my opinion,</u> the characters seem undeveloped.	The characters seem undeveloped.

As far as this course is con-   This course looks interesting.
cerned, it looks interesting.

For all intents and purposes,   The two brands are alike.
the two brands are alike.

It is important to note that   The results were identical in
the results were identical in   both clinical trials.
both clinical trials.

These and other expressions—*obviously, as the case may be, I
feel, it seems to me, all things considered, without a doubt, in
conclusion,* and *by way of explanation*—are simply padding. You
may think they balance or fill out a sentence or make your writing sound more authoritative, but the reverse is the case. Such
phrases add nothing to your meaning, and you should avoid
them.

(2)   Utility words

Utility words are vague, all-purpose words used as fillers. They
may be nouns, usually abstract nouns (*factor, kind, type, quality,
aspect, thing, sort, field, area, situation,* and so on); adjectives,
usually those with broad meanings (*good, nice, bad, fine, important, significant*); or adverbs, usually common ones concerning
degree (*basically, completely, actually, very, definitely, quite*).
Whatever they are, they contribute nothing to a sentence.

Wordy   *Concise*

The field of computer science   Computer science offers many
offers many employment   employment opportunities.
opportunities.

The registration situation was   Registration was disorganized.
disorganized.

His offer to share his lunch   His offer to share his lunch
was a nice gesture.   was a generous gesture.

The scholarship offered Fran a   The scholarship offered Fran
good opportunity to study   an opportunity to study
Spanish.   Spanish.

It was actually a worthwhile   It was a worthwhile book, but I
book, but I didn't com-   didn't finish it.
pletely finish it.

When you find yourself using a utility word, try to delete it or to
replace it with a more specific word. The result will be a more
economical sentence.

(3) Circumlocution

Taking a roundabout way to say something (using ten words when five will do) is called **circumlocution**. When you use big words, complicated phrases, and rambling constructions instead of short, concrete, commonly used words and phrases, you cannot write concise sentences. Notice how the revised versions of these sentences use fewer words and simpler constructions to say the same thing.

Wordy	*Concise*
The curriculum was of a unique nature.	The curriculum was unique.
It is not unlikely that the trend toward smaller cars will continue.	The trend toward smaller cars will probably continue.
Joel was in the army during the same time that I was in college.	Joel was in the army while I was in college.
It is entirely possible that the lake is frozen.	The lake may be frozen.

Wordy phrases can almost always be controlled or avoided. Always choose simple, easily understood terms; when you revise, strike out wordy, convoluted constructions.

Instead of	*Use*
at the present time	now
at this point in time	now
for the purpose of	for
due to the fact that	because
on account of the fact that	because
until such time as	until
in the event that	if
by means of	by
in the vicinity of	near
have the ability to	be able to

Writers use circumlocution for much the same reasons they use deadwood and utility words: either they are not paying close attention to what they are writing, or they think that more and longer words make their writing seem polished and substantial. Nothing could be further from the truth. When you pad a sentence with meaningless words, you interfere with communication.

con
9a

▶
EXERCISE 1

Revise the following paragraph to eliminate deadwood, utility words, and circumlocution. When a word or phrase seems superfluous, delete it or replace it with a more concise expression.

> Sally Ride is an astrophysicist who was selected to be the first American woman astronaut. It seems that there were many good reasons why she was chosen. She is a first-rate athlete, and she did graduate work in x-ray astronomy and free-electron lasers. As a result of these and other factors, NASA accepted Ride as a "mission specialist" astronaut in the year 1978. Prior to that time, Ride had been a graduate student at Stanford who knew she had the capability of becoming a specialist in the area of theoretical physics. At NASA she helped to design the remote manipulator arm of the space shuttle, and at a later point she relayed flight instructions to astronauts until such time as she was assigned to a flight crew. At this point in time she is something quite definitely special: America's first woman in space.

9b   Eliminating Needless Repetition

Repetition of words or concepts can add clarity and emphasis to your writing (see 8c), but unnecessary repetition annoys readers and distorts your meaning. Repeated words and redundant word groups (words or phrases that say the same thing in different words) are the chief problems. For instance:

> Ernest Hemingway, one of the most <u>famous</u> and <u>well-known</u> <u>authors</u> in American literary history, is the <u>author</u> of <u>novels</u> like *The Sun Also Rises* and other <u>novels</u>.

Famous and *well-known* are redundant, while *author* and *novels* are repeated needlessly. The result is an overblown sentence. Compare

> Ernest Hemingway, one of the most famous writers in American literary history, is the author of *The Sun Also Rises* and other novels.

In the next sentence careless repetition of *complex* and *political* gives these words undeserved emphasis and makes the sentence tedious.

Today's <u>complex</u> <u>political</u> climate creates a series of <u>complex</u> challenges for both major <u>political</u> parties.

The revision is just as clear and more economical.

Today's complex political climate creates a series of challenges for both major parties.

con
9b

Redundant phrases weaken the following sentences.

Mark Twain dictated the <u>autobiography of his life</u>.

We wound up the <u>old antique</u> record player.

<u>At first</u> her <u>preliminary</u> plan was to look for work in the Sunbelt.

We got <u>free complimentary</u> tickets to the concert.

Raid <u>kills</u> bugs <u>dead</u>.

The underlined words say the same thing twice. In these revisions the redundant word is deleted.

Mark Twain dictated his autobiography.

We wound up the antique record player.

Her preliminary plan was to look for work in the Sunbelt.

We got complimentary tickets to the concert.

Raid kills bugs.

Other commonly encountered redundant phrases include *repeat again, predicted future,* and *few in number*—but not all redundancies are short stock phrases. For instance

<u>Unpopular</u> courses <u>that are not well liked</u> usually fill up slowly.

You can correct needless repetition in a number of ways.
1. You can simply delete repetition or redundancy.

Wordy	*Concise*
The childhood disease chicken pox occasionally leads to dangerous complications such as the disease known as Reye's Syndrome.	The childhood disease chicken pox occasionally leads to dangerous complications such as Reye's Syndrome.
The speech the president made was the fourth he had made that month.	The speech was the fourth the president had made that month.

2. You can substitute a pronoun for a repeated noun.

Wordy	*Concise*
Agatha Christie's Hercule Poirot has an egg-shaped head. Hercule Poirot also has a large mustache.	Agatha Christie's Hercule Poirot has an egg-shaped head. He also has a large mustache.

3. You can use elliptical clauses, substituting commas for omitted words (see 26f.1).

Wordy	*Concise*
The Quincy Market is a popular tourist attraction in Boston; the White House is a popular tourist attraction in Washington, D.C.; and the Statue of Liberty is a popular tourist attraction in New York City.	The Quincy Market is a popular tourist attraction in Boston; the White House, in Washington, D.C.; and the Statue of Liberty, in New York City.

4. You can use appositives.

Wordy	*Concise*
Red Barber was a sportscaster. He was known for his colorful expressions.	Red Barber, a sportscaster, was known for his colorful expressions.

5. You can combine sentences to create compound subjects, compound objects or complements, or compound predicates. In the following sentence pairs the revised sentences are not only more concise but also less choppy.

Wordy	*Concise*
Wendy found the exam difficult and Karen also found it hard. Ken thought it was tough, too.	Wendy, Karen, and Ken all found the exam difficult. (compound subject)
Huckleberry Finn is an adventure story. It is also a sad account of an abused, neglected child.	*Huckleberry Finn* is both an adventure story and a sad account of an abused, neglected child. (compound complement)

In 1964 Ted Briggs was discharged from the Air Force.
He then got a job with Maxwell Data Processing. He
married Susan Thompson
that same year.

In 1964 Ted Briggs was discharged from the Air Force,
got a job with Maxwell Data
Processing, and married
Susan Thompson. (com-
pound predicate)

6. Finally, you can combine sentences so that one clause is
subordinate to the other.

Wordy

One issue in the campaign was
police brutality. Police brutality was on many voters'
minds.

Concise

One issue in the campaign was
police brutality, which was
on many voters' minds.

The first polio vaccine was
developed by Jonas Salk.
Salk was a physician and a
bacteriologist.

The first polio vaccine was
developed by Jonas Salk,
who was a physician and
bacteriologist.

▶

EXERCISE 2

Delete unnecessary repetition of words or ideas from this paragraph.
Also delete any deadwood, utility words, or circumlocution that you
notice.

More and more people today in the 1980's are choosing a
vegetarian diet. There are three kinds of vegetarian diets: strict
vegetarians eat no animal foods at all; lactovegetarians eat dairy
products but they do not eat meat, fish, poultry, or eggs; and
ovolactovegetarians eat eggs and dairy products but they do not
eat meat, fish, or poultry. Famous vegetarians include such well-
known people as George Bernard Shaw, Leonardo da Vinci, Ralph
Waldo Emerson, Henry David Thoreau, and Mahatma Gandhi.
These and other vegetarians first became vegetarians for a variety
of reasons. For instance, some religions recommend a vegetarian
diet. Some of these religions are Buddhism, Brahmanism, and
Hinduism. Other people turn to vegetarianism for reasons of
health or for reasons of hygiene. These people feel that meat is a
source of potentially harmful chemicals and they believe meat
contains infectious organisms. Other people feel meat may cause
digestive problems and may lead to other difficulties as well. Other
vegetarians adhere to a vegetarian diet because they feel it is eco-
logically wasteful to kill animals after we feed plants to them.

These vegetarians believe *we* should eat the plants. Finally, there are facts and evidence to suggest that a vegetarian diet may possibly help people live longer lives. A vegetarian diet may do this by reducing the incidence of heart disease and lessening the incidence of some cancers. (Adapted from *Jane Brody's Nutrition Book*)

9c   Tightening Rambling Sentences

Rambling, out-of-control sentences are the inevitable result of using nonessential words, unnecessary repetition, and complicated syntax. Making such sentences concise involves more than simply deleting a word or two. For example

> Once the statistics were presented, the report backed them up with (in my opinion) something more appealing, because the reader could relate more easily to things such as real-life examples or relate to the fact that certain well-known organizations such as the World Health Organization were involved in the topic, than they could relate to numbers and percentages.

You would hardly know where to begin revising this sentence. You could eliminate obvious deadwood *(in my opinion)*, utility words *(things)*, and phrases repeated unnecessarily *(such as* and *relate to)*, but the sentence would still be wordy. A total rewrite is needed.

> After the report presented the statistics, it backed them up with material that was more appealing to readers: not just numbers and percentages, but real-life examples and information about the involvement of prominent groups like the World Health Organization.

This revision eliminates nineteen words from the original, with no loss of meaning. It deletes deadwood, utility words, and unnecessary repetition and rearranges the remaining words in an orderly fashion.

Revising rambling sentences requires ruthless deletion. Several techniques should help you avoid the need to delete in the first place. Whenever possible, use one word instead of several and phrases instead of clauses. Avoid excessive coordination and subordination and unnecessary use of the passive voice. Finally, try to identify weak constructions that rely on prepositional phrases instead of single adjectives or adverbs or on convoluted noun constructions instead of strong verbs.

(1)   Excessive coordination

Excessive coordination results from stringing together too many clauses with coordinating conjunctions. Not only does it lead to wordiness, it also causes confusion by presenting all your ideas as if they have equal weight when they do not.

con
9c

Wordy	*Concise*
Puerto Rico is the fourth largest island in the Caribbean, and it is predominantly mountainous and it has steep slopes and they fall to gentle coastal plains.	Fourth largest island in the Caribbean, Puerto Rico is predominantly mountainous, with steep slopes falling to gentle coastal plains. *(National Geographic)*

To revise this sentence, first identify the main idea and then subordinate the supporting details. The revised sentence emphasizes the mountainous nature of Puerto Rico and recasts the other details as modifiers.

Here is another example.

Wordy	*Concise*
"Big Bill" Haywood was once a cowboy and a prospector and later he was an organizer for the Industrial Workers of the World, a militant labor union.	"Big Bill" Haywood, once a cowboy and a prospector, was later an organizer for the Industrial Workers of the World, a militant labor union.

The wordy sentence gives equal weight to Haywood's early years and the more prominent career he had later. In the revision, subordination not only shortens the sentence but also emphasizes Haywood's later career. For information on specific strategies for revising excessive coordination, see 9c.1.

(2)   Excessive subordination

When you use a series of adjective clauses instead of concise modifying words or phrases, you are likely to produce a rambling sentence.

Wordy	*Concise*
The *Star Wars* trilogy, which includes *Star Wars*, *The Empire Strikes Back*, and	The *Star Wars* trilogy, including *Star Wars*, *The Empire Strikes Back*, and *Return of*

con
9c

Return of the Jedi, was conceived by George Lucas, who directed *Star Wars* and who produced all three films, which are popular.	*the Jedi*, was conceived by George Lucas, director of *Star Wars* and producer of all three popular films.

Notice how the four subordinate clauses in the first sentence have been turned into more economical modifiers. *Including* gives further information about the trilogy, *director of* and *producer of* are appositives identifying *George Lucas*, and the adjective *popular* is a single-word modifier describing *films*.

(3)   Passive constructions

The active voice is more economical than the passive. Although some situations call for passive voice (see 8e), the active voice, which communicates the same information in fewer words, is usually more emphatic.

Wordy	*Concise*
"Buy American" rallies are being organized by concerned Americans who hope jobs can be saved by such gatherings.	Concerned Americans are organizing "Buy American" rallies, hoping such gatherings can save jobs.
Water rights are being fought for in court by Indian tribes like the Papago in Arizona and the Pyramid Lake Paiute in Nevada.	Indian tribes like the Papago in Arizona and the Pyramid Lake Paiute in Nevada are fighting in court for their water rights.

(4)   Wordy prepositional phrases

Often you can tighten a rambling sentence by replacing wordy prepositional phrases used as modifiers with single adjectives or adverbs.

Wordy	*Concise*
The trip was one of danger but also one of excitement.	The trip was dangerous but exciting.

The first example uses eleven words to say exactly what the revised example says in six. The substitution of two adjectives for two prepositional phrases makes the sentence more direct.

<table>
<tr><td>

Wordy
He spoke in a confident man-
ner.

</td><td>

Concise
He spoke confidently.

</td></tr>
</table>

Here one adverb replaces a four-word prepositional phrase.
Again, the second sentence is more economical and more direct.

(5) Wordy noun constructions

You can also tighten a rambling sentence by substituting strong
verbs for convoluted noun phrases.

<table>
<tr><td>

Wordy
The normalization of commer-
cial relations between the
United States and China in
1979 led to an increase in
trade between the two
countries.

</td><td>

Concise
When the United States and
China normalized commer-
cial relations in 1979, trade
between the two countries
increased.

</td></tr>
</table>

In the revision one-word verbs replace long phrases. The result is
a much more effective sentence.

<table>
<tr><td>

Wordy
We have made the decision to
postpone the meeting until
after the appearance of all
the board members.

</td><td>

Concise
We have decided to postpone
the meeting until all the
board members <u>appear</u>.

</td></tr>
</table>

Here two noun constructions are replaced by verbs. Again, this
substitution produces a more forceful sentence.

▶
EXERCISE 3

Revise the rambling sentences in this paragraph by eliminating excessive coordination and subordination, unnecessary use of the passive
voice, and overuse of wordy prepositional phrases and noun constructions. As you revise, make your sentences more concise by deleting nonessential words and superfluous repetition.

> Some colleges that have been in support of fraternities for a
> number of years are at this time in the process of conducting a
> reevaluation of the position of those fraternities on campus. In
> opposition to the fraternities are a fair number of students, faculty
> members, and administrators, who claim fraternities are inher-
> ently sexist, which they say makes it impossible for the groups to

exist in a coeducational institution, which is supposed to offer equal opportunities for members of both sexes. And, more and more members of the college community see fraternities as elitist as well as sexist and favor their abolition. The situation has already begun to be dealt with at some colleges. For instance, Williams College made a decision in favor of the abolition of fraternities, and Bowdoin College got its fraternities to agree to the admittance of women. In some cases, however, students, faculty, and administration remain wholeheartedly in support of fraternities, which they believe are responsible for helping students make the acquaintance of people and learn the leadership skills which they believe will be of assistance to them in their future lives as adults. Supporters of fraternities believe students should retain the right to make their own social decisions and that joining a fraternity is one of those decisions, and they also believe fraternities are responsible for providing valuable services and some of these are tutoring, raising money for charity, and running campus escort services. Therefore, they are not of the opinion that the abolition of fraternities makes sense.

Student Writer at Work: Writing Concise Sentences

Revise this excerpt from an essay examination in American literature to make it more concise.

Oftentimes in the course of a literary work, characters may find themselves misfits in the sense that they do not seem to be a real part of the society in which they find themselves. This problem often leads to a series of genuinely serious and severe problems, conflicts either between the misfits and their own identities or possibly between them and that society into which they so poorly fit.

In "The Minister's Black Veil" Reverend Hooper all of a sudden gives to the townspeople and members of his parish a surprise: a piece of black material which he has wrapped over his face, which causes the reader to be as completely and thoroughly confused as the townspeople about the possible reason for the minister's decision to hide his face, until we learn, in his sermon, that he is covering his face (from God, his fellow man, and himself) to atone for the sins of mankind. As far as I can tell, we are never quite sure exactly why he is in possession of the notion that this act must be carried out by him, and we are never completely sure whether Reverend Hooper feels this guilt for some sin that may exist in his own past or for those sins that may have been committed by mankind in general, but in any case it is clear that he feels it is his duty to place himself in isolation from the world at large around him. To the Reverend, there is no solution to his problem, and he lives his whole entire life wearing the veil. Even after his death he insists that the veil remain covering his features, for it is said by the Reverend that his face could not be revealed on earth.

For Reverend Hooper, a terrible conflict exists within himself, and so Reverend Hooper voluntarily makes himself a misfit even at the expense of losing everything, even his true love Elizabeth.

con
9

10

Writing Varied Sentences

Sentences that differ in length, type, and word order are not intrinsically better than sentences that are alike in these respects. But varying your sentences helps you to convey emphasis and, more important, to capture and hold reader interest.

The following paragraph is hard to read. Although it is crammed with information, it does not distinguish main ideas from subordinate ones, does not clarify relationships between adjacent sentences, and lacks emphasis. Moreover, the repetitive sentence structure (nearly every sentence begins with the subject, and all sentences are about the same length) makes it dull.

> Queen Mary landed at Crail in Fife on 10th June, 1538. She was accompanied by a navy of ships under Lord Maxwell. She was also accompanied by 2,000 lords and barons. Her husband had sent them from Scotland to fetch her away. It was just over a year since the landing of Queen Madeleine. Queen Mary was formally received by the king of St. Andrews a few days later. Pageants and plays were performed in her honour. There was a great deal of generally blithe rejoicing. She was remarried the next morning in the cathedral at St. Andrews. Immediately afterwards she was received into the king's palace with trumpets and still more pageants. Sir David Lyndsay of the Mount played a prominent part in all the celebrations. He was later to become famous for his denunciation of the state of the Scottish Church, *The Satire of the Three Estates*. The next day the royal couple were conveyed on a tour of churches, colleges and universities within the town by the provost and burgesses.

The paragraph as it was actually written is quite different.

> Accompanied by a navy of ships under Lord Maxwell, and 2,000 lords and barons whom her new husband had sent from Scotland to fetch her away, Queen Mary landed at Crail in Fife on 10th June, 1538, just over a year since the landing of Queen Madeleine. She was formally received by the king at St. Andrews a few

days later with pageants and plays performed in her honour, and a great deal of generally blithe rejoicing, before being remarried the next morning in the cathedral of St. Andrews. Immediately afterwards she was received into the king's palace with trumpets and still more pageants, in all the celebrations a prominent part being played by Sir David Lyndsay of the Mount, later to become famous for his denunciation of the state of the Scottish Church, *The Satire of the Three Estates.* The next day the royal couple were conveyed on a tour of churches, colleges and universities within the town by the provost and burgesses. (Antonia Fraser, *Mary Queen of Scots*)

var
10a

This paragraph has only four sentences, as compared with thirteen in the first one, and they vary in length, structure, and style. For example, the relatively short sentence at the end is preceded by several long sentences that pile up detail. The impression given is of a simple conclusion to a complex series of events. Fraser varies her sentence openings: sentence 1, a periodic sentence, begins with a participial phrase; sentence 2, a cumulative sentence, like the two that follow, with the subject; sentences 3 and 4, with transitional phrases. Throughout the paragraph the author uses modifying phrases and clauses to indicate subordination, and compounds to coordinate ideas. Obviously, the effort to create sentence variety pays off in clarity and readability.

To avoid monotonous writing, you can adopt a number of revision strategies: vary sentence length; combine choppy simple sentences; break up strings of compounds; and vary sentence types, openings, and word order.

10a Varying Sentence Length

Before you set out to vary your sentences, give careful thought to the effects you want to achieve. If your work sounds a bit monotonous or flat, varying sentence length is one obvious solution. A mixture of long and short sentences gives a pleasing texture to your writing, and their juxtaposition keeps readers interested.

(1) Mixing long and short sentences

A paragraph consisting entirely of short sentences (or entirely of long ones) can be dull.

> Drag racing began in California in the 1940's. It was an alternative to street racing, which was illegal and dangerous. It flourished in the 50's and 60's. Eventually, it became almost a rite of passage. Then, during the 70's, almost one-third of America's racetracks closed. Today, however, drag racing is making a modest comeback.

Although these sentences are varied in structure and have different openings, they are all about the same length. The revision combines sentences to create units of various lengths.

> Drag racing began in California in the 1940's as an alternative to street racing, which was illegal and dangerous. It flourished in the 50's and 60's, eventually becoming almost a rite of passage. Then, during the 70's, almost one-third of America's racetracks closed. Today, however, drag racing is making a modest comeback.

(2)   Following a long sentence with a short one

Using a short sentence after one or more long ones immediately attracts reader attention. This gear-shifting emphasizes the short sentence and its content while adding variety to the passage. For example,

> There are two social purposes for family dinners—the regular exchange of news and ideas and the opportunity to teach small children not to eat like pigs. These are by no means mutually exclusive. (Judith Martin, "Miss Manners," *Redbook*)

> In arguing the need for [vitamin] supplements, doctors like to point out that the normal diet supplies the RDA (Recommended Dietary Allowance) minimums. Nutritionists counter that the RDA, as established by the National Academy of Sciences, is only the minimum daily dose necessary to prevent the diseases associated with particular vitamin deficiencies. Over the years, vitamin boosters say, a misconception has grown that as long as there are no signs or symptoms of say, scurvy, then we have all of the vitamin C we need. Although we know how much of a particular vitamin or mineral will prevent clinical disease, we have practically no information on how much is necessary for peak health. In short, we know how sick is sick, but we don't know how well is well. (*Philadelphia Magazine*)

In both examples a relatively short sentence punctuates a group of longer sentences. Readers are thus forced to focus on the short sentence and to look again at what precedes or follows it.

▶
EXERCISE 1

A. Combine each of the following sentence groups into one long sentence.

B. Then compose a relatively short sentence to follow each long one.

C. Finally, connect all the sentences into a paragraph, adding any transitions necessary for coherence. Proofread your paragraph to make sure the sentences are varied in length.

var
10b

1. Chocolate is composed of over 300 compounds. Phenylethylamine is one such compound. Its presence in the brain may be linked to the emotion of falling in love.
2. Americans now consume a good deal of chocolate. They eat an average of over nine pounds of chocolate per person per year. Belgians, however, consume almost fifteen pounds per year.
3. In recent years, Americans have begun a serious love affair with chocolate. Elegant chocolate boutiques sell exquisite bonbons by the piece. At least one hotel offers a "chocolate binge" vacation. The bimonthly *Chocolate News* for connoisseurs is flourishing. (Adapted from "America's Chocolate Binge," *Newsweek*)

10b Combining Choppy Simple Sentences

Strings of disconnected simple sentences are nearly always tedious—and sometimes hard to follow as well. Revise such sentences by combining them with adjacent sentences, using coordination, subordination, or embedding.

(1) Using coordination

Coordination is one way to revise choppy simple sentences, as illustrated by these notes for part of a short paper on freedom of the press in America.

> John Peter Zenger was a newspaper editor. He waged and won an important battle for freedom of the press in America. He criticized the policies of the British governor. He was charged with criminal libel as a result. Zenger's lawyers were disbarred by the governor. Alexander Hamilton defended him. Hamilton convinced the jury that Zenger's criticisms were true. Therefore, the statements were not libelous.

The information is here, but the presentation is flat and lacks some of the links necessary for coherence. Coordination can add interest and clarity.

> John Peter Zenger was a newspaper editor. He waged and won an important battle for freedom of the press in America. He criticized the policies of the British governor, and as a result, he was charged with criminal libel. Zenger's lawyers were disbarred by the governor. Alexander Hamilton defended him. Hamilton convinced the jury that Zenger's criticisms were true. Therefore, the statements were not libelous.

This revision links two of the choppy simple sentences with *and* to create a compound sentence. The result is a slightly smoother paragraph.

(2) Using subordination

Subordination can clarify the relationships between ideas. This revision changes two simple sentences into dependent clauses to create two complex sentences.

> John Peter Zenger was a newspaper editor who waged and won an important battle for freedom of the press in America. He criticized the policies of the British governor, and as a result, he was charged with criminal libel. When Zenger's lawyers were disbarred by the governor, Alexander Hamilton defended him. Hamilton convinced the jury that Zenger's criticisms were true. Therefore, the statements were not libelous.

Now the paragraph includes two complex sentences: one links ideas with a relative pronoun *(who)* and one with a subordinating conjunction *(when)*.

(3) Using embedding

Embedding—changing some sentences into modifying phrases and working them into other sentences—is another strategy for varying sentence structure.

> John Peter Zenger was a newspaper editor who waged and won an important battle for freedom of the press in America. He criticized the policies of the British governor, and as a result, he was charged with criminal libel. When Zenger's lawyers were disbarred by the governor, Alexander Hamilton defended him, convincing the jury that Zenger's criticisms were true. Therefore, the statements were not libelous.

In this revision the sentence *Hamilton convinced the jury. . . .* has been reworded to create a phrase *(convincing the jury)* that modifies the independent clause *Alexander Hamilton defended him.* The result is a varied, readable paragraph that uses coordination, subordination, and embedding to vary sentence length but retains the final short simple sentence for emphasis. This revision, of course, represents only one of the many possible ways to achieve sentence variety.

var

10c

▶

EXERCISE 2

Using coordination, subordination, and embedding, revise this string of choppy simple sentences into a more varied and interesting paragraph.

> The first modern miniature golf course was built in New York in 1925. It was an indoor course with 18 holes. Entrepreneurs Drake Delanoy and John Ledbetter built 150 more indoor and outdoor courses. Garnet Carter made miniature golf a worldwide fad. Carter built an elaborate miniature golf course. He later joined with Delanoy and Ledbetter. Together they built more miniature golf courses. They abbreviated playing distances. They highlighted the game's hazards at the expense of skill. This made the game much more popular. By 1930, there were 25,000 miniature golf courses in the United States. Courses grew more elaborate. Hazards grew more bizarre. The craze spread to London and Hong Kong. The expansion of miniature golf grew out of control. Then interest in the game declined. By 1931, most miniature golf courses were out of business. The game was revived in the early fifties. Today there are between eight and ten thousand miniature golf courses. The architecture of miniature golf remains an enduring form of American folk art. (Adapted from *Games*)

10c Breaking Up Strings of Compounds

An unbroken series of compound sentences can also be dull—and unemphatic (see 9c.1). By tediously repeating coordinating conjunctions you may fail to indicate emphasis or relationships accurately. For example,

> A volcano that is erupting is considered *active*, but one that may erupt is designated *dormant*, and one that has not erupted for a long time is called *extinct*. Most active volcanoes can be extremely destructive. Italy's Vesuvius erupted in 79 A.D. and it destroyed the town of Pompeii. In 1883 Krakatoa, located between the Indonesian islands of Java and Sumatra, erupted and it caused a tidal wave, and more than 36,000 people were killed. Martinique's Mont Pelée erupted in 1902 and its lava and ash killed 30,000 people and this completely wiped out the town of St. Pierre.

var

10c

One way to clarify the relationships among these sentences while varying their form is to change some main clauses into modifying clauses, thereby creating complex sentences to replace some of the compound sentences. Another way is to break down some of the compound sentences into separate simple sentences. Finally, you can create new simple sentences and expand them with compound predicates or with modifiers or appositives. The following revision employs a number of these strategies.

> A volcano that is erupting is considered *active;* one that may erupt is designated *dormant;* and one that has not erupted for a long time is called *extinct.* [compound sentence] Most active volcanoes are located in "The Ring of Fire," a belt that circles the Pacific Ocean. [simple sentence with appositive] Active volcanoes can be extremely destructive. [simple sentence] Erupting in 79 A.D., Italy's Vesuvius destroyed the town of Pompeii. [simple sentence with modifier] When Krakatoa, located between the Indonesian islands of Java and Sumatra, erupted in 1883, it caused a tidal wave that killed 36,000 people. [complex sentence with modifier] The eruption of Martinique's Mont Pelée in 1902 produced lava and ash that killed 30,000 people, completely wiping out the town of St. Pierre. [complex sentence with modifier]

▶

EXERCISE 3

Revise the compound sentences in this paragraph so that the sentence structure is varied and the writer's emphasis is clear.

> Dr. Alice I. Baumgartner and her colleagues at the Institute for Equality in Education at the University of Colorado surveyed 2,000 Colorado school children, and they found some startling results. They asked, "If you woke up tomorrow and discovered that you were a (boy) (girl), how would your life be different?" and the answers were sad and shocking. The researchers assumed they would find that boys and girls think there are advantages to being either male or female, but instead they found that both boys and girls had a fundamental contempt for females. Many elementary school boys titled their answers "The Disaster" or "Doomsday," and they described the terrible lives they would lead as girls, but the girls seemed to feel they would be better off as boys, and they expressed feelings that they would be able to do more and have easier lives. Boys and girls alike realized that girls are judged by their looks more than boys and both felt girls had to pay more

attention to their looks, so all children perceived boys as having an advantage. In addition, boys and girls both valued boys' activities more highly and boys and girls agreed that "women's work" is less valuable and less valued than "men's work." Both boys and girls also felt that boys are expected to behave differently and they felt that boys could get away with more and be more active but girls did have one advantage and that was that they could express their feelings openly. Finally, both boys and girls agreed that boys are treated better and respected more than girls, so in other words there is a prejudice against females among both boys and girls and this sex stereotyping is a psychological handicap for both men and women. (Adapted from *Redbook*)

10d   Varying Sentence Types

You can ensure a variety of sentence types by mixing simple, compound, and complex sentences; by mixing cumulative and periodic sentences (see 8b); and by using balanced sentences where appropriate (see 8c). You can also vary sentence types by mixing declarative sentences (statements) with occasional imperative sentences (commands or requests), exclamations, and rhetorical questions (questions that the reader is not expected to answer). When a question, exclamation, or command is appropriate for your audience and purpose, use it. The addition of a question, exclamation, or command adds stylistic variety to each of the following paragraphs.

Here the humorous rhetorical question at the beginning gives focus and variety.

> Was it any wonder that seven members of the Continental Congress who had seen the draft of the Declaration of Independence had fled to Philadelphia, threatening to defect to King George III? Still, John Hancock had stood firm. Faithful John Hancock. Even now Hancock was scouring Philadelphia chicken coops, searching for a newborn chick with a quill so small that no one would be able to decipher his signature without a microscope. (Russell Baker, *New York Times Magazine*)

Here a pair of exclamations add emphasis.

> Tracks! Tracks! It seemed to the visionaries who wrote for the popular magazines that the future lay at the end of parallel rails. (E. L. Doctorow, *Ragtime*)

In this short paragraph an imperative sentence breaks up the series of declarative sentences.

> Modern dude ranches mix activities found at conventional resorts—golf, swimming, tennis, dances—with elements of the Old West. But some rather elaborate ranches may be quite expensive. Before planning a dude ranch vacation, then, consider your needs and interests carefully. You may be happier in a more modest (and less costly) setting.

▶

EXERCISE 4

The following paragraph is composed entirely of declarative sentences. To make it more varied, add three sentences—one exclamation, one rhetorical question, and one command—anywhere you like. Make sure the sentences you create are consistent with the paragraph's purpose and tone.

> When the fourth of July comes around, the nation explodes with patriotism. Everywhere we look we see parades and picnics, firecrackers and fireworks. An outsider might wonder what all the fuss is about. We could explain that this is America's birthday party, and all the candles are being lit at once. There is no reason for us to hold back our enthusiasm—or to limit the noise that celebrates it. The fourth of July is watermelon and corn on the cob, American flags and sparklers, brass bands and more. And a good time is had by all.

10e Varying Sentence Openings

In addition to varying sentence length and type, you can also create variety by choosing different openings for your sentences. Rather than resigning yourself to beginning every sentence with the subject, strengthen your emphasis and clarify the relationship of the sentence to those that surround it by opening some sentences with modifying words, phrases, or clauses. For instance, you can begin with one or more *adjectives* or *adverbs* or with an *adverbial clause*

> <u>Proud</u> and <u>relieved</u>, they watched their daughter receive her diploma. (adjectives)
>
> <u>Hungrily</u>, he devoured his lunch. (adverb)
>
> <u>While Woodrow Wilson was incapacitated by a stroke</u>, his wife unofficially performed many presidential duties. (adverbial clause)

or with a *prepositional phrase* or a *participial phrase*.

> For better or worse, alcohol has been a part of human culture through the ages. *(Consumer Reports)* (prepositional phrase)

> Located on the west coast of Great Britain, Wales is part of the United Kingdom. (participial phrase)

var
10e

To clarify the connection between two sentences, you can begin the second sentence with a *coordinating conjunction*, a *conjunctive adverb*, or a *transitional expression*.

> The Big Bang may be the beginning of the universe, or it may be a discontinuity in which information about the earlier history of the universe was destroyed. But it is certainly the earliest event about which we have any record. (Carl Sagan, *The Dragons of Eden*) (coordinating conjunction)

> Pantomime was first performed in ancient Rome. However, it remains a popular dramatic form today. (conjunctive adverb)

> Robert Peary explored Greenland in the late nineteenth century. In later years, he was the first person to reach the North Pole. (transitional expression)

Or you can begin a sentence with an *inverted appositive* or with an *absolute phrase*.

> A British scientist, Alexander Fleming is famous for having discovered penicillin. (inverted appositive)

> His interests widening, Picasso designed ballet sets and illustrated books. (absolute phrase)

The sentences of this paragraph all begin with the subject.

> Chicago set the tone for condominium development across the United States. It is now a city of owners, not renters. Chicago has led the nation in condominium development in recent years. Almost every building on the Gold Coast beside Lake Michigan has been converted. A small unit that sold for $85,000 a few years ago now sells for close to $200,000—if you can find one. Developers have now shifted their sights to secondary markets and are redeveloping offices, hotels, and even lofts. One expert estimates that soon there will be almost no rental property left in the city.

The revision employs a variety of opening strategies.

> Setting the tone for condominium development across the United States, Chicago is crowded with condos. [participial phrase] Once a city of renters, it is now a city of owners. [inverted

appositive] <u>In recent years</u>, Chicago has led the nation in condominium conversion. [prepositional phrase] <u>Today</u> almost every building on the Gold Coast beside Lake Michigan has been converted. [transitional expression] <u>A small unit</u> that sold for $85,000 a few years ago now sells for close to $200,000—if you can find one. [subject] <u>Now</u> developers have shifted their sights to secondary markets and are redeveloping offices, hotels, and even lofts. [transitional expression] <u>One expert</u> estimates that soon there will be almost no rental property left in the city. [subject]

▶

EXERCISE 5

Each of these sentences begins with the subject. Rewrite each so that it has a different opening, and then identify the opening strategy you used.

> EXAMPLE: Doug signed up for the ski trip and immediately began taking lessons.
>
> After he signed up for the ski trip, Doug immediately began taking lessons. (adverbial clause)

1. The first lesson taught him how to put on his boots and skis and how to hold his poles; it was easy.
2. The second lesson concentrated on finer points, teaching Doug how to walk with skis on and how to turn around while wearing them.
3. The third lesson, which was a bit more difficult, focused on such minor details as how to start and how to stop.
4. Doug found himself poised on the beginners' slope ready to head downhill at the start of lesson four.
5. Doug decided, when he looked down the slope, to cancel the ski trip and take up backgammon.

10f   Varying Standard Word Order

You can use two variations on the usual word order of subject-verb-object (or complement): intentionally inverting this order, or placing words between subject and verb.

(1)   Inverting word order

Inverting conventional word order adds both emphasis (see 8a) and variety if used in moderation. Used repeatedly, however, inversion loses its force and sounds odd.

You can place the complement or direct object *before* the

verb instead of in its conventional position or place the verb *before* the subject instead of after it. For example:

> *(subject)*
> Nature ┬ loved and, next to Nature, Art. (Walter Savage Landor)
> *(object)*   *(verb)*

> *(complement)*
> The book was extremely helpful; especially useful was
> its index.   *(verb)*
>   *(subject)*

Even in these individual sentences, the unusual word order draws attention to what has been inverted. In a group of sentences, inverted word order adds variety while calling attention to the content of the inverted sentence.

> As an economic entity, greater Los Angeles is world class: if the area seceded, it would have a G.N.P. larger than that of Mexico and Australia. The movie and TV business is only the hot tip of L.A.'s biggest job sector, its service industries, which together employ 882,000 people. There is a muscular side as well, with 869,000 workers in manufacturing, about a third in aerospace and other clean, high-tech industries. But parts of the city could pass for Buffalo. On the waterfront in Long Beach sit stacks of blue and orange cargo containers. In Lynwood, railroad tracks run past auto salvagers, truck-winch manufacturers, scrap-metal piles. *(Time)*

(2)   Separating subject from verb

Placing words or phrases between subject and verb is another way to vary standard word order.

> Several states require that infants and young children ride in government-approved car seats because they hope this will reduce needless fatalities. (subject and verb together)

> Several states, hoping to reduce needless fatalities, require that infants and young children ride in government-approved car seats. (subject and verb separated)

If you use this strategy, however, be very careful to avoid obscuring the relationship between subject and verb (see 13d).

▶
EXERCISE 6

The following sentences use conventional word order. Revise each in two ways.
A. First, invert the sentence.

B. Then vary the order by placing words between subject and verb.
C. Finally, create a varied five-sentence paragraph, choosing one version of each sentence.

var
10

What do your choices tell you about the use of inverted word order and about the technique of placing words between subject and verb?

EXAMPLE: Exam week is invariably hectic and not much fun.

Invariably hectic and not much fun is exam week.

Exam week, invariably hectic, is not much fun.

1. The Beach Boys formed a band in 1961, and the group consisted of Brian Wilson, his brothers Carl and Dennis, their cousin Mike Love, and Alan Jardine, a friend.
2. Their first single was "Surfin'," which attracted national attention.
3. Capitol Records signed the band to record "Surfin' Safari" because the company felt the group had potential.
4. The Beach Boys had many other top-twenty singles during the next five years, and most of these hits were written, arranged, and produced by Brian Wilson.
5. Their songs focused on California sun and good times and included "I Get Around," "Be True to Your School," "Fun, Fun, Fun," and "Good Vibrations."

Student Writer at Work:
Writing Varied Sentences

Read this draft of a student essay carefully and revise it to achieve greater sentence variety by varying the length, type, openings, and word order of the sentences.

Advertising: Newspapers versus Television

Advertising persuades by provoking the senses. It is big business. It exploits every conceivable method of enticing you to buy. Ads can be straightforward and informational. Or, they can be filled with intrigue, hilarity, or sexuality. They can prod the minds of the hungry, the self-indulgent, the imaginative, and the gullible. Every conceivable medium is used to advertise. Each has the same objective: to sell. Television and the newspaper are perhaps the two most influential means of advertising.

They reach the greatest number and widest range of people.

Advertisements in local newspapers lace the pages like a net. They lure the prospective catch with bait. This bait appears in the form of bold lettering and small dollar signs. But newspapers are for the serious-minded. People tend to believe things they read in black and white. So newspapers tend to report the facts. They announce store hours and liquidation sales. They support everything with numerous figures. Newspaper ads are concise and informative. They are also unpretentious and sensible. They attract your attention to everything from barbells to diamond rings, using (for the most part) only facts.

Television is a completely different medium. It plays with emotion, fantasy, and impulse. It seeks to invoke an immediate response. You must remember a time when you got up from the couch to race to the refrigerator, victim of a commercial that promised Heavenly Hash satisfaction. Television uses only two of the five senses, sound and sight, but with careful calculation touch, smell, and taste can also be triggered. Therein lies its strength. Viewers feel the excitement of driving a Pontiac LeMans up a mountain. They grind their teeth as they prepare to sail in a hang glider over the craggy California coast (chewing Wrigley's spearmint gum, of course). Emotionally charged sensationalism gets the message across.

Television ads roll right into your living room. They sneak up to you. They play on your emotions. The ads appeal to greed, to competitiveness, to a desire for comfort and luxury. Newspaper ads finish the job. They tell you where and when to buy. You already know why.

var
10

Solving Common Sentence Problems

11

Sentence Fragments

A **sentence fragment** is an incomplete sentence, a phrase or clause punctuated as if it were a complete sentence. A sentence may be incomplete because it lacks certain elements.

> The tour was supposed to arrive in Germany on Friday. <u>But got there the next day</u>. (subject missing)
>
> At last he saw the kite. <u>Stuck in a tree beside the house</u>. (finite verb missing)
>
> First in line were the Tyson twins. <u>Two enormous, husky fellows</u>. (both subject and finite verb missing)

NOTE: Participles and infinitives are *not* finite verbs and therefore cannot serve as main verbs in a sentence. (For more information on verbals, see 20c.)

Or a sentence may be incomplete because it is actually a dependent clause, introduced by a subordinating conjunction

> I lost my temper. <u>Because I had asked him over and over again not to bother us</u>.

or by a relative pronoun.

> Rocky Road is the flavor. <u>That is Mike's favorite</u>.

Some sentence fragments are acceptable and effective. We commonly use fragments in speech,

> See you later.
>
> Back soon.
>
> No sweat.
>
> Could be trouble.

in informal writing,

> Just a note to let you know I got the loan. Sure will make things a lot easier next semester.

in advertising,

> Be all curls. <u>Not all nerves</u>.
>
> <u>Finally</u>. <u>Vegetables with no salt added</u>.

> Lighten up! With low-tar Belair.
> Great taste in every bite, and only ½ the sugar.

in journalism,

> They tell me that apathy is in this year. Very chic. (Ellen Goodman,
> *Close to Home*)

and in literature—for instance, to represent casual conversation
or to convey disconnected thinking.

> Then the curtains breathing out of the dark upon my face, leaving
> the breathing upon my face. A quarter hour yet. And then I'll not
> be. The peacefullest words. (William Faulkner, *The Sound and the
> Fury*)

frag
11a

It is not a good idea, however, to use incomplete sentences
until you know how to distinguish between effective and ineffective ones. When readers cannot see where sentences begin and
end, they cannot understand what you have written. For instance, it is impossible to tell to which independent clause the
fragment in the following sequence belongs.

> The course requirements were changed last year. Because a new
> professor was hired at the very end of the spring semester. I was
> unable to find out about this change until after preregistration.

These criteria will help you examine any sentence for completeness.

> A sentence must include a subject.
> A sentence must have a finite verb.
> A sentence cannot consist of a dependent clause alone. (A sen-
>   tence cannot consist of a single clause that begins with a sub-
>   ordinating conjunction; unless it is a question, it cannot con-
>   sist of a single clause beginning with *how, who, which, where,
>   when,* or *why.*)

If your sentence does not pass these three tests, it is a fragment
and should be revised.

Knowing why sentence fragments occur should help you
avoid writing them. At the least it should help you spot and correct them when they do appear.

11a Punctuating Subordinate Clauses

A **subordinate clause** contains a subject and a verb, but it cannot
stand alone as a sentence. Because it needs an independent
clause to complete it, a subordinate clause (also called a depend-

ent clause) must always be attached to at least one independent
clause (see 7b). You can correct fragments that result from punctuating subordinate clauses incorrectly in one of two ways.

You can join the subordinate clause to a neighboring independent
clause.

You can delete the subordinating conjunction or relative pronoun,
leaving behind a complete sentence with a subject and a finite
verb. (In many cases, you will have to replace the relative pronoun with another word that can serve as the clause's subject.)

frag
11a

For example,

FRAGMENT: The United States declared war. <u>Because the Japanese</u>
<u>bombed Pearl Harbor.</u> (subordinate clause punctuated
as a sentence)

REVISED: The United States declared war because the Japanese
bombed Pearl Harbor. (subordinate clause attached to
an independent clause to create a complete sentence)

REVISED: Because the Japanese bombed Pearl Harbor, the United
States declared war. (subordinate clause attached to an
independent clause to create a complete sentence)

REVISED: The United States declared war. The Japanese bombed
Pearl Harbor. (subordinating conjunction deleted; result is a complete sentence)

FRAGMENT: The battery is dead. <u>Which means the car won't start.</u>
(subordinate clause punctuated as a sentence)

REVISED: The battery is dead, which means the car won't start.
(subordinate clause attached to an independent clause
to create a complete sentence)

REVISED: The battery is dead. This means the car won't start.
(relative pronoun deleted; substitution of *this* creates a
complete sentence)

▶
EXERCISE 1

Identify the sentence fragments in the following paragraph and revise
them either by attaching the fragment to an independent clause or by
deleting the subordinating conjunction or relative pronoun to create a
sentence that can stand alone. In some cases you will have to replace a
relative pronoun with another word that can serve as the subject of an
independent clause.

The drive-in movie came into being just after World War II.
When both movies and cars were central to the lives of many

Americans. Drive-ins were especially popular with teenagers and young families during the 1950's. When cars and gas were relatively inexpensive. Theaters charged by the carload. Which meant that a group of teenagers or a family with several children could spend an evening at the movies for a few dollars. In 1958, when the fad peaked, there were over 4,000 drive-ins in the United States. While today there are only about 3,000. Many of these are in the Sunbelt, with most in California. Although many sunbelt drive-ins continue to thrive because of the year-round warm weather. Many northern drive-ins are in financial trouble. Because land is so expensive. Some drive-in owners break even only by operating flea markets or swap meets in daylight hours. While others, unable to attract customers, are selling their theaters to land developers. Soon drive-ins may be a part of our nostalgic past. Which will be a great loss for many who enjoy them.

11b Punctuating Prepositional Phrases

A **prepositional phrase** consists of a preposition, its object, and any modifiers of the object (see 6f.1). It cannot stand alone as a sentence. To correct this kind of fragment, attach it to the independent clause that contains the word or word group modified by the prepositional phrase.

> FRAGMENT: President Lyndon Johnson decided not to seek reelection. <u>For a number of reasons.</u> (prepositional phrase punctuated as a sentence)
>
> REVISED: President Lyndon Johnson decided not to seek reelection for a number of reasons. (prepositional phrase attached to an independent clause)
>
> FRAGMENT: He ran sixty yards for a touchdown. <u>In the final minutes of the game.</u> (prepositional phrase punctuated as a sentence)
>
> REVISED: He ran sixty yards for a touchdown in the final minutes of the game. (prepositional phrase attached to an independent clause)

▶
EXERCISE 2

Read the following passage and identify the sentence fragments. Then correct each one by attaching it to the preceding independent clause to form a sentence.

Most college athletes are caught in a conflict. Between their athletic and academic careers. Sometimes college athletes' responsibilities on the playing field make it hard for them to be good students. Often athletes must make a choice. Between sports and a degree. Some athletes would not be able to afford college. Without athletic scholarships. But, ironically, their commitments to sports (training, exercise, practice, and travel to out-of-town games, for example) deprive athletes of valuable classroom time. The role of college athletes is constantly being questioned. Critics suggest athletes exist only to participate in and promote college athletics. Because of the importance of this role to academic institutions, scandals occasionally develop. With coaches and even faculty members arranging to inflate athletes' grades to help them remain eligible. For participation in sports. Some universities even lower admissions standards. To help remedy this inequity, the controversial Proposal 48, passed at the NCAA convention in 1982 and scheduled to take effect in 1986, establishes minimum scores on aptitude tests. But many people feel that the NCAA remains overly concerned. With profits rather than with education. As a result, college athletic competition is increasingly coming to resemble pro sports. From the coaches' pressure on the players to win to the network television exposure to the wagers on the games' outcomes.

frag
11c

11c Punctuating Verbal Phrases

A **verbal phrase** consists of a present participle *(walking)*, past participle *(walked)*, infinitive *(to walk)*, or gerund plus related objects and modifiers *(walking along the lonely beach)*. Because a verbal phrase does not contain a finite verb, it is not a complete sentence and should not be punctuated as one (see 6f.2).

To correct the fragment that results when a verbal phrase is punctuated as a sentence, either attach the verbal phrase to a related independent clause, or change the verbal to a finite verb and add a subject to create a sentence that can stand alone. For example,

FRAGMENT: In 1948 India became independent. <u>Divided into the nations of India and Pakistan.</u> (participial phrase punctuated as a sentence)

REVISED: Divided into the nations of India and Pakistan, India became independent in 1948. (participial phrase at-

REVISED: In 1948 India became independent. It was divided into
the nations of India and Pakistan. (finite verb *was* and
subject *it* added; result is a separate independent
clause)

FRAGMENT: The pilot changed course. Realizing the weather was
worsening. (participial phrase punctuated as a sentence)

REVISED: The pilot changed course, realizing the weather was
worsening. (participial phrase attached to the related
independent clause to create a complete sentence)

REVISED: The pilot changed course. She realized the weather
was worsening. (finite verb *realized* substituted for the
verbal *realizing* and subject *she* added; result is a separate independent clause)

▶

EXERCISE 3

Identify the sentence fragments in the following paragraph and correct
each. Either attach the fragment to a related independent clause or add
a subject and a finite verb to create a new independent clause.

Many food products have well-known trademarks. Identified by familiar faces on product labels. Some of these symbols
have remained the same, while others have changed considerably.
Products like Sun-Maid raisins, Betty Crocker potato mixes,
Quaker Oats, and Uncle Ben's rice use faces. To create a sense of
quality and tradition and to encourage shopper recognition of the
products. Many of the portraits have been updated several times.
To reflect changes in society. Betty Crocker's portrait, for instance,
has changed five times since its creation in 1936. Symbolizing
women's changing roles. The original Chef Boy-ar-dee has also
changed. Turning from the young Italian chef Hector Boiardi into
a white-haired senior citizen. Miss Sunbeam, trademark of Sunbeam bread, has had her hairdo modified several times since her
first appearance in 1942; the Blue Bonnet girl, also created in 1942,
now has a more modern look, and Aunt Jemima has also been
changed. Slimmed down a bit in 1965. Similarly, the Campbell's
Soup kids are less chubby now than in the 1920's when they first
appeared. But the Quaker on Quaker Oats remains as round as he
was when he first adorned the product label in 1877. The Morton
Salt girl has evolved gradually. Changing several times from blonde
to brunette and from straight- to curly-haired. But manufacturers

are very careful about selecting a trademark or modifying an existing one. Typically spending a good deal of time and money on research before a change is made. After all, a trademark of long standing can help a product's sales. Giving shoppers the sense that they are using products purchased and preferred by their parents and grandparents.

11d Punctuating Absolute Phrases

frag
11d

An **absolute phrase**—a modifying phrase that is not connected grammatically to any one word in a sentence—usually consists of a noun or pronoun plus a participle and any related modifiers. (Infinitive phrases can also be absolutes; see 6f.3.) An absolute phrase may contain a subject, but it lacks a finite verb and therefore cannot stand alone as a sentence.

To correct this kind of fragment, attach the absolute phrase to the clause it modifies, or substitute a finite verb for the participle or infinitive in the absolute phrase.

FRAGMENT: India has over 16 million child laborers. <u>Their education cut short by the need to earn money.</u> (absolute phrase punctuated as a sentence)

REVISED: India has over 16 million child laborers, their education cut short by the need to earn money. (absolute phrase attached to the clause it modifies)

FRAGMENT: The Vietnam War memorial is a striking landmark. <u>Its design featuring two black marble slabs meeting in a V.</u> (absolute phrase punctuated as a sentence)

REVISED: The Vietnam War memorial is a striking landmark. Its design features two black marble slabs meeting in a V. (finite verb substituted for participle)

▶
EXERCISE 4

Identify the sentence fragments in the passage below and correct each by attaching the absolute phrase to the clause it modifies or by substituting a finite verb for the participle or infinitive in the absolute phrase.

The domestic responsibilities of colonial women were many. Their fate sealed by the lack of the mechanical devices that have eased the burdens in recent years. Washing clothes, for instance, was a complicated procedure. The primary problem being the moving of some 50 gallons of water from a pump or well to the stove (for heating) and washtub (for soaking and scrubbing). Home cooking also presented difficulties. The main challenges for the housewife being the danger of inadvertently poisoning her family and the rarity of ovens. Even much later, housework was extremely time-consuming, especially for rural and low-income families. Their access to labor-saving devices remaining relatively limited. (Just before World War II, for instance, only 35 percent of farm residences in the United States had electricity!)

11e   Punctuating Appositives

An **appositive**—a noun or noun phrase that identifies or renames the person or thing it follows—cannot stand alone as a sentence (see 6f.4). An appositive must directly follow the person or thing it renames, and it must do so within the same sentence. To correct a fragment created when an appositive is incorrectly punctuated as a sentence, attach the appositive to the independent clause that contains the word or word group the appositive renames.

> FRAGMENT: Piero della Francesca was a leader of the Umbrian school. A school that remained close to the traditions of Gothic art. (appositive, a fragment that renames *the Umbrian school*, punctuated as a complete sentence)

> REVISED: Piero della Francesca was a leader of the Umbrian school, a school that remained close to the traditions of Gothic art. (appositive attached with a comma to the noun it renames)

Appositives included for clarification are sometimes introduced by a word or phrase like *or, that is, for example, for instance, namely,* or *such as.* These additions do not change anything: appositives still cannot stand alone as sentences. Once again, the easiest way to correct such fragments is to attach the appositive to the preceding independent clause.

> FRAGMENT: Fairy tales are full of damsels in distress. <u>Such as Snow White, Cinderella, and Rapunzel.</u> (appositive, a phrase that identifies *damsels in distress*, punctuated as a sentence)

REVISED: Fairy tales are full of damsels in distress, such as Snow White, Cinderella, and Rapunzel. (appositive attached with a comma to the noun it renames)

Sometimes an appositive can be set within a sentence rather than attached to the end of it.

FRAGMENT: Some popular novelists are highly respected by later generations. For example, Mark Twain and Charles Dickens. (appositive, a phrase that identifies *some popular novelists*, punctuated as a sentence)

REVISED: Some popular novelists—for example, Mark Twain and Charles Dickens—are highly respected by later generations. (appositive is embedded within the preceding independent clause, next to the noun it renames)

frag

11e

NOTE: For information on correct punctuation with appositives, see Chapter 26.

▶
EXERCISE 5

Identify the fragments in this paragraph and correct them by attaching each to the independent clause containing the word or word group the appositive modifies.

The Smithsonian Institution in Washington, D.C., is composed of thirteen different buildings. Museums and art galleries. These include well-known landmarks. Such as the Air and Space Museum and the National Gallery of Art. The Smithsonian also includes the National Zoo. Home of the giant pandas Ling-Ling and Hsing-Hsing. One museum is not located in Washington. Namely, the Cooper-Hewitt Museum in New York. The Smithsonian contains many entertaining and educational exhibits. For example, the Wright Brothers' plane, Lindbergh's Spirit of St. Louis, and a moon rock. The Smithsonian also includes ten other museums. The Museum of American History, the Museum of Natural History, the Hirshorn Museum, the Freer Gallery of Art, the Arts and Industries Building, the Portrait Gallery, the Museum of American Art, the Renwick Gallery, the Museum of African Art, and the Anacosta Neighborhood Museum. The American History Museum contains one especially historic item. Edison's first light bulb. The Natural History Museum also includes a spectacular exhibit. A giant squid that washed ashore in Massachusetts in 1980. These and other entertaining and educational exhibits make up the Smithsonian. An attraction that should not be missed.

11f   Punctuating Compounds

When detached from its subject, the last part of a **compound predicate** (see 6f.5) cannot stand alone as a sentence. To correct this kind of fragment, reconnect the detached part of the compound predicate to the rest of the sentence.

FRAGMENT: People with dyslexia have trouble reading. <u>And may also find it difficult to write.</u> (fragment, part of the compound predicate *have . . . and may find,* punctuated as a sentence)

REVISED: People with dyslexia have trouble reading and may also find it difficult to write. (fragment corrected when the detached part of the compound predicate is reconnected to the rest of of the sentence)

FRAGMENT: The novel was a critical success. <u>But sold only a few thousand copies.</u> (fragment, part of the compound predicate *was . . . but sold,* punctuated as a sentence)

REVISED: The novel was a critical success but sold only a few thousand copies. (fragment corrected when the detached part of the compound predicate is reconnected to the rest of the sentence)

The last part of a **compound object** or **compound complement** (see 6f.5) cannot stand alone as a sentence either. Make sure to attach it to the rest of the sentence.

FRAGMENT: They took only a compass and a canteen of water. <u>And some trail mix.</u> (fragment, part of the compound object *compass . . . canteen . . . trail mix,* punctuated as a sentence)

REVISED: They took only a compass, a canteen of water, and some trail mix. (fragment corrected when the detached part of the compound object is reconnected to the rest of the sentence)

FRAGMENT: When their supplies ran out, they were surprised. <u>And hungry.</u> (fragment, part of the compound complement *surprised and hungry,* punctuated as a sentence)

REVISED: When their supplies ran out, they were surprised and hungry. (fragment corrected when the detached part of the compound complement is reconnected to the rest of the sentence)

▶
EXERCISE 6

Identify the sentence fragments in this passage and correct them by attaching each detached compound predicate, object, or complement to the rest of the sentence.

One of the phenomena of the 70's and 80's is the number of parents determined to raise "superbabies." Many affluent parents, professionals themselves, seem driven to raise children who are mentally superior. And physically fit as well. To this end they enroll babies as young as a few weeks old in baby gyms. And sign up slightly older preschool children for classes that teach computer skills or violin. Or swimming or Japanese. Such classes are important. But are not the only source of formal education for very young children. Parents themselves try to raise their babies' IQ's. Or learn to teach toddlers to read or to do simple math. Some parents begin teaching with flash cards when their babies are only a few months—or days—old. Others wait until their children are a bit older. And enroll them in developmental day-care programs designed to sharpen their skills. Or spend thousands of dollars on "educational toys." Some psychologists and child-care professionals are favorably impressed by this trend toward earlier and earlier education. But most have serious reservations, feeling the emphasis on academics and pressure to achieve may stunt children's social and emotional growth.

11g Punctuating Incomplete Clauses

Not all sentence fragments are short. In the process of adding modifiers it is easy to lose track of the direction of a long sentence and fail to finish it. To correct such a fragment, you must add, delete, or alter words to create a complete independent clause.

FRAGMENT: *Ancient Evenings,* Norman Mailer's 1983 novel, more than ten years in the making and considered by critics to be a major work, which is set in Egypt before the birth of Christ. (subject *Ancient Evenings* has no predicate)

REVISED: *Ancient Evenings,* Norman Mailer's 1983 novel, more than ten years in the making and considered by critics to be a major work, is set in Egypt before the birth of

Christ. (relative pronoun *which* deleted; *is set* is now the predicate of a complete independent clause)

FRAGMENT: Because of Wright Morris's ambition to become a writer, which led him to travel to Paris just as Ernest Hemingway, Gertrude Stein, Samuel Beckett, and Henry Miller had. (contains no independent clause)

REVISED: Wright Morris's ambition to become a writer led him to travel to Paris just as Ernest Hemingway, Gertrude Stein, Samuel Beckett, and Henry Miller had. (subordinating conjunction *because* and relative pronoun *which* deleted, leaving one complete independent clause)

REVISED: Because of Wright Morris's ambition to become a writer, he traveled to Paris just as Ernest Hemingway, Gertrude Stein, Samuel Beckett, and Henry Miller had. (relative pronoun *which* deleted and some words changed, leaving a complete independent clause preceded by a dependent clause)

▶

EXERCISE 7

Identify the fragments in the following paragraph and correct each by adding, deleting, or altering words to create a complete independent clause.

The Brooklyn Bridge, completed in 1883 and the subject of poems, paintings, and films for many years, which helped it to capture the imagination of the public as well as the artist as few other structures have. Because artists like George Bellows, Georgia O'Keeffe, Andy Warhol, and Joseph Stella have used the bridge as a subject, and because it has appeared in the novels of John Dos Passos and Thomas Wolfe and the poems of Hart Crane and Marianne Moore, who have all seen it as a major symbol of America. The Brooklyn Bridge, also making an appearance in essays by writers like Henry James and Lewis Mumford and seen in films from *Tarzan's New York Adventure* and Laurel and Hardy's *Way Out West* to *Annie Hall* and *Sophie's Choice*, which ensured its visibility to the public. Over the years, the bridge has also turned up in songs, in Bugs Bunny cartoons, and on product labels, record jackets, and T-shirts, making it one of the most recognizable structures in America.

frag
11g

Student Writer at Work: Sentence Fragments

Read carefully this excerpt from a draft of a student essay. Identify all the sentence fragments, and determine why each is a fragment. Finally, correct each sentence fragment by adding, deleting, or modifying words to create a sentence or by attaching the fragment· to a neighboring independent clause.

Ab Snopes: A Trapped Man

Abner (Ab) Snopes, the father in William Faulkner's story "Barn Burning," is trapped in a hopeless situation. Disgusted with his lack of status, yet unable to do much to remedy his dissatisfaction. He has little control over his life, but he still struggles. Fighting his useless battle as best he can.

Ab is a family man. Responsible for a wife, children, and his wife's sister. Unfortunately, he is unable to meet his responsibilities. Such as providing a stable home for his family. Evicted because of Ab's "barn burnings," the family constantly moves from town to town. With all their belongings piled on a wagon. But Ab continues to burn barns. Because he hopes that these acts will give him power as well as revenge.

To the rich landowners he works for, Ab is of little significance. Poor, uneducated, uncultured. There are many men just like him. Who can work the land. Ab knows this. But is unwilling to accept his inferior status. Consequently, he approaches new employers with arrogance. His actions and manner soon causing trouble. This, of course, ensures his eventual dismissal. Ab feels that since he can never gain their respect. He should not even bother behaving in a civilized manner. So he insists on playing the role. Of a belligerent, raging man.

This behavior sets in motion a self-fulfilling prophecy. Each time Ab's behavior causes an employer to ask him to leave, his prophecy that he will be mistreated is fulfilled. He pretends that the failure is his employer's, not his own. And vents his frustration. By destroying their property with fire. He also feels that such actions will earn him respect. People will be frightened of him, and he will create a name for himself. Only Ab's son, Sarty, sees the truth. That Ab is to his employers "no more . . . than a buzzing wasp."

frag
11

Comma Splices and Fused Sentences

12

12

Two or more independent clauses may be separated by a period.

> Math and science teachers are becoming increasingly scarce. Many schools are actively trying to recruit them.

Or they may be joined in compound sentences in one of several ways (see 7a). For instance, they may be connected by a semicolon,

> Math and science teachers are becoming increasingly scarce; many schools are actively trying to recruit them.

by a comma and a coordinating conjunction,

> Math and science teachers are becoming increasingly scarce, and many schools are actively trying to recruit them.

or by a semicolon or period accompanied by a conjunctive adverb or other transitional expression.

> Math and science teachers are becoming increasingly scarce; in fact, many schools are actively trying to recruit them.

A **run-on sentence** results when the proper connective or punctuation does not appear between independent clauses. A run-on occurs either as a *comma splice*, two independent clauses joined only by a comma, or as a *fused sentence*, two independent clauses joined with no punctuation.

> COMMA SPLICE: Charles Dickens created the character of Mr. Micawber, he also created Uriah Heep.
>
> FUSED SENTENCE: Charles Dickens created the character of Mr. Micawber he also created Uriah Heep.
>
> REVISED: Charles Dickens created the character of Mr. Micawber. He also created Uriah Heep.

Both kinds of run-on sentences confuse readers. Avoid them, and be sure to revise when they occur in your writing.

227

The Comma Splice

A **comma splice** is created when two independent clauses are incorrectly joined by a comma. It results from a writer's carelessly omitting a needed coordinating conjunction or wrongly assuming that a conjunctive adverb or other transitional expression can take the place of a coordinating conjunction in a sentence.

cs
12a

COMMA SPLICE: Picasso was a Spanish artist who lived in France, Turner and Gainsborough were English. (coordinating conjunction omitted)

COMMA SPLICE: Picasso was a Spanish artist who lived in France, however Turner and Gainsborough were English. (conjunctive adverb incorrectly used in place of a coordinating conjunction)

Comma splices like these can be corrected in one of four ways.

12a   Substituting a Period for the Comma

Using a period to separate independent clauses creates two separate sentences. A comma splice can be revised in this way when the clauses are of equal importance but are not linked closely enough to be joined in one sentence.

COMMA SPLICE: In the late nineteenth century Alfred Dreyfus, a Jewish captain in the French army, was falsely convicted of treason, his struggle for justice pitted the army and the Catholic establishment against the civil libertarians.

REVISED: In the late nineteenth century Alfred Dreyfus, a Jewish captain in the French army, was falsely convicted of treason. His struggle for justice pitted the army and the Catholic establishment against the civil libertarians.

Substituting a period is also the best way to revise a comma splice resulting from the incorrect punctuation of a broken quotation.

COMMA SPLICE: "This is a good course," Eric said, "in fact, I wish I'd taken it sooner."

REVISED: "This is a good course," Eric said. "In fact, I wish I'd taken it sooner."

NOTE: This method of correcting comma splices does have some stylistic limitations. See Chapter 10, Writing Varied Sentences.

12b Substituting a Semicolon for the Comma

If the two clauses of equal importance are closely related, and if you want to underscore that relationship, use a semicolon.

COMMA SPLICE: In pre-World War II Western Europe, only a small elite had access to a university education, this situation changed dramatically after the war.

REVISED: In pre-World War II Western Europe, only a small elite had access to a university education; this situation changed dramatically after the war.

You can also use a semicolon to revise a comma splice when the ideas in the joined clauses are presented in parallel terms.

COMMA SPLICE: Chippendale chairs have straight legs, Queen Anne chairs have curved legs.

REVISED: Chippendale chairs have straight legs; Queen Anne chairs have curved legs.

In such cases, the semicolon emphasizes the symmetry between the two clauses (see 14a).

12c Adding a Coordinating Conjunction

If two closely related clauses are of equal importance but a semicolon alone does not show how they are related, use an appropriate coordinating conjunction to indicate whether the clauses are linked by addition (*and*), contrast (*but, yet*), causality (*for, so*), or a choice of alternatives (*no, nor*).

COMMA SPLICE: Elias Howe invented the sewing machine, Julia Ward Howe was a poet and social reformer.

REVISED: Elias Howe invented the sewing machine, but Julia Ward Howe was a poet and social reformer. (coordinating conjunction *but* shows emphasis is on contrast)

cs
12c

Neither a conjunctive adverb *(however, nevertheless, therefore)* nor any other transitional expression *(for example, in fact, on the other hand)* substitutes for a coordinating conjunction. These phrases can connect two independent clauses *only in combination with a semicolon or a period.* Thus,

> Elias Howe invented the sewing machine, however Julia Ward Howe was a poet and social reformer.

cs

12c

is still a comma splice.

When a comma splice results from the incorrect use of a conjunctive adverb or transitional expression, it is most easily corrected with the addition of a period or a semicolon to separate the clauses.

COMMA SPLICE: The International Date Line is drawn north and south through the Pacific Ocean, largely at the 180th meridian, thus, it separates Wake and Midway Islands.

REVISED: The International Date Line is drawn north and south through the Pacific Ocean, largely at the 180th meridian; thus, it separates Wake and Midway Islands.

REVISED: The International Date Line is drawn north and south through the Pacific Ocean, largely at the 180th meridian. Thus, it separates Wake and Midway Islands.

Although coordinating conjunctions must always appear between the clauses they link, conjunctive adverbs and transitional expressions can appear in several positions. For example,

> Jason forgot to register for chemistry. However, he managed to sign up during the drop/add period. (conjunctive adverb placed at beginning of sentence)

> Jason forgot to register for chemistry; however, he managed to sign up during the drop/add period. (conjunctive adverb placed at beginning of clause)

> Jason forgot to register for chemistry. He managed, however, to sign up during the drop/add period. (conjunctive adverb set within sentence)

> Jason forgot to register for chemistry. He managed to sign up during the drop/add period, however. (conjunctive adverb placed at end of sentence)

For information on punctuating conjunctive adverbs or other transitional expressions, see 27c.

12d Adding a Subordinating Conjunction or Relative Pronoun

When the ideas in two clauses are not of equal importance, correct the comma splice by subordinating the less important idea to the more important one, placing the less important idea in a dependent clause. The subordinating conjunction or relative pronoun clearly establishes the nature of the relationship between the clauses.

> COMMA SPLICE: Stravinsky's ballet *The Rite of Spring* shocked Parisians in 1913, its rhythms and the dancers' movements seemed erotic.

> REVISED: Because its rhythms and the dancers' movements seemed erotic, Stravinsky's ballet *The Rite of Spring* shocked Parisians in 1913. (subordinating conjunction *because* added to subordinate the original sentence's second clause to its first; the result is one complex sentence)

> COMMA SPLICE: Lady Mary Wortley Montagu had suffered from smallpox herself, she helped spread the practice of inoculation against the disease in eighteenth-century England.

> REVISED: Lady Mary Wortley Montagu, who had suffered from smallpox herself, helped spread the practice of inoculation against the disease in eighteenth-century England. (relative pronoun *who* added to subordinate the original sentence's first clause to its second; the result is one complex sentence)

Subordination is a good deal more effective than two separate sentences when ideas do not have equal importance.

> COMMA SPLICE: Glen had never tried skiing before, he found he was good at it.

> REVISED: Glen had never tried skiing before. He found he was good at it. (correct, but relationship between clauses is not clear)

CLEARER: Although Glen had never tried skiing before, he found he was good at it. (relationship between clauses is now clear: writer considers Glen's mastery of skiing to be the most important idea)

12e   Using Comma Splices Effectively

**cs
12e**

In rare cases comma splices may be acceptable. For instance, commas may connect two short *balanced* independent clauses,

My nose is stuffed, my throat is sore.

or two or more short parallel independent clauses, especially when one clause contradicts the other.

Writers aren't born, they're made.

Commencement isn't the end, it's the beginning.

However, until you are certain that you know when comma splices are acceptable and effective, avoid the temptation to use them.

Finally, a comma is always correct between a statement and a tag question, even though each is a separate independent clause.

This is Ron's house, isn't it?

I'm not late, am I?

▶
EXERCISE 1

Find the comma splices in the following paragraphs. Correct each in *two* of the four possible ways.

1. Substitute a period for the comma.
2. Substitute a semicolon for the comma.
3. Add an appropriate coordinating conjunction.
4. Subordinate one clause to the other.

EXAMPLE: The fans rose in their seats, the game was almost over.

The fans rose in their seats; the game was almost over.

The fans rose in their seats, for the game was almost over.

If a sentence is correct, leave it alone.

Entrepreneurship is the study of small businesses, college students are embracing it enthusiastically. Many schools offer one or more courses in entrepreneurship, these courses teach the theory and practice of starting a small business. Students are signing up for courses, moreover they are even starting their own businesses. One student started with a car-waxing business, now he sells condominiums. Others are setting up catering services, they supply everything from waiters to bartenders. One student has a thriving cake-decorating business, in fact she employs fifteen students to deliver the cakes. All over the country, student businesses are selling everything from tennis balls to bagels, the student owners are making impressive profits. Formal courses at the graduate as well as undergraduate level are attracting more business students than ever, several business schools (such as Baylor University, the University of Southern California, and Babson College) even offer degree programs in entrepreneurship. Many business school students are no longer planning to be corporate executives, instead they plan to become entrepreneurs.

fs
12f

The Fused Sentence

A **fused sentence** occurs when two independent clauses are joined without suitable punctuation or a coordinating conjunction.

FUSED SENTENCE: The first manned orbital flight took place in 1961 eight years later men walked on the moon. (neither coordinating conjunction nor appropriate punctuation joins independent clauses)

FUSED SENTENCE: Theodore Roosevelt was the youngest man to become president however John Kennedy was the youngest to be elected president. (neither coordinating conjunction nor appropriate punctuation joins independent clauses)

Fused sentences such as these can, like comma splices, be corrected in one of four ways.

12f Adding a Period

You may revise a fused sentence by adding a period between clauses to create two separate sentences.

FUSED SENTENCE: Buffalo Bill's Wild West Show was introduced to America in 1883 two years later sharpshooter Annie Oakley joined the show.

REVISED: Buffalo Bill's Wild West Show was introduced to America in 1883. Two years later sharpshooter Annie Oakley joined the show.

12g   Adding a Semicolon

Adding a semicolon between clauses can also correct a fused sentence.

FUSED SENTENCE: A group of elephants is known as a herd a group of kangaroos is called a mob.

REVISED: A group of elephants is known as a herd; a group of kangaroos is called a mob.

12h   Adding a Comma and a Coordinating Conjunction

You may also add a comma and an appropriate coordinating conjunction between clauses.

FUSED SENTENCE: The ERA was supported by many Americans the amendment failed to win passage in the allotted time.

REVISED: The ERA was supported by many Americans, but the amendment failed to win passage in the allotted time.

12i   Using Subordination

Finally, you can correct a fused sentence by subordinating one clause to the other, adding an appropriate subordinating conjunction or relative pronoun.

FUSED SENTENCE: Texas is the largest state in the continental United States Alaska is actually the largest state in the union.

REVISED: Although Texas is the largest state in the continental United States, Alaska is actually the largest state in the union.

▶

EXERCISE 2

Find the fused sentences in the following paragraph, and correct each in *two* of the possible four ways.

    1. Add a period between clauses.
    2. Add a semicolon between clauses.
    3. Add a comma and an appropriate coordinating conjunction.
    4. Subordinate one clause to the other.

fs
12i

    EXAMPLE: Amy applied to four colleges she was accepted at three.

                  Amy applied to four colleges; she was accepted at three.

                  Amy applied to four colleges, and she was accepted at three.

        Animals are disappearing from the earth about one species has become extinct every year since 1900. Enormous dinosaurs once roamed the earth they became extinct some 65 million years ago. Huge mammals later flourished they included mastodons and mammoths. Over one hundred different species of these large mammals lived on earth some of them were alive only 11,000 years ago. But these animals all vanished no one is quite sure exactly why this happened. Hundreds of other species had developed and eventually died out before humans existed however after man appeared in North America extinction increased dramatically. Hunters killed animals for food thus some scientists believe it is possible that hunters exterminated the large animals. Other scientists attribute the animals' disappearance to climatic changes during the Ice Age. For instance, marked drops in temperatures ruined grazing lands many animals died from exposure and starvation. Droughts also killed many animals the competition for grasslands was too much for them. Finally, it has been suggested that man did eliminate the animals however many had already been weakened by natural forces like disease and climatic changes.

▶

EXERCISE 3

Combine each of the following sentence pairs into one sentence without creating comma splices or fused sentences. In each case, either connect the clauses into a compound sentence with a semicolon or with a comma and a coordinating conjunction, or subordinate one clause to the other to create a complex sentence. You may have to add, delete, reorder, or change words or punctuation.

1. It is true that caring for pets can be expensive and time-consuming. They can help their owners in many ways.
2. Dogs and cats are extremely popular pets. Moreover, they can help improve the mental and physical health of their owners.
3. Pets can protect their owners. In addition, they can provide companionship.
4. Pets can also give people something to love. The pet is bound to return the owner's love.
5. Pets can help isolated people to make friends. Thus, they can help fight loneliness and depression.
6. Pets can help people to structure their days. A dog, for instance, needs to be walked and fed at set times.
7. Children who own pets can learn to be more responsible. They can learn loyalty and compassion at the same time.
8. Pets can even help sick and disabled people. Seeing-eye dogs and "hearing-ear" dogs for the deaf are two examples.
9. Doctors have found pets can be valuable in treating mentally ill people. Pets can coax withdrawn mental patients out of their shells.
10. More than half of all American families own some kind of pet. Considering pets' many benefits, this seems to make sense.

fs
12i

▶

EXERCISE 4

Find and correct any unjustified comma splices or fused sentences in the paragraph below.

For over two centuries a debate has gone on among educators about the best way to teach deaf children to communicate. The manualists are on one side, the oralists are on the other. Manualists believe communication should center on sign language however oralists believe deaf children should learn to read lips. Oralists believe deaf people cannot truly be part of society unless they speak otherwise they will be isolated. Manualists consider lip reading too difficult it is largely guesswork moreover the speech of profoundly deaf people is very hard to understand. In addition, deaf children acquire oral skills very slowly as a result they can be deprived for years of virtually all communication. Deaf children who learn to sign, however, build a manual vocabulary as quickly as their hearing counterparts build a spoken one. During the 1960's the handicapped rights movement began at this time a new philosophy called Total Communication was developed in the United States. Total Communication uses a combination of speech, lip reading, hearing aids, and sign language, sign language

is stressed. Many people feel this is a good compromise nevertheless oralism is still dominant in most other countries.

Student Writer at Work:
Comma Splices and Fused Sentences

Read the following answer to an economics examination question that asked students to discuss the provisions of the 1935
Social Security Act; correct all comma splices and fused sentences.

fs
12

In June of 1934, Franklin D. Roosevelt selected Frances
Perkins to head the new Committee on Economic Security, the
committee's report was the basis of our current Social Security
program. The committee formulated two policies, one dealt with
the employable the other with the unemployable. Roosevelt in-
sisted that these programs be self-financing, as a result employer and employee social insurance was required. In 1935 the
Social Security Act was passed it attempted to categorize the
poor and provided for federal sharing of the cost, but under local
control. (The Social Security Act did not include a public works
program, this was one aspect of the New Deal that was eliminated.)

Unemployment insurance was one major part of the act.
Funds were to be payable through public employment offices,
also the money was to be paid into a trust fund. It was to be
used solely for benefits an individual could not be denied funds
even if work were available. The program provided for payroll
taxes, in addition separate records were to be kept by each state.
Old Age Survivor Insurance, another major provision of the Act,
was for individuals over sixty-five it was amended in 1939 to
cover dependents. A quarter of the total recipients were disabled.
Public Assistance was the third major part of the act this program was designed to help children left alone by the death or
absence of the parents and children with mental or physical

disabilities. General assistance covered everything not covered under the Public Assistance Program this varied from state to state.

The Social Security Act stressed public administration of federal emergency relief assistance thus it forced reorganization of public assistance. These efforts differed from previous efforts earlier there were no clear guidelines defining which individuals should get aid and why. The Social Security Act attempted to eliminate gaps and overlaps in services.

fs
12

13

Misplaced and Dangling Modifiers

Modifiers add information and show connections between ideas. They also expand and enrich sentences, helping you communicate meaning accurately and precisely to your readers. Normally, a modifier is placed close to its **headword,** the word or phrase it modifies, and readers expect to find it there. **Faulty modification**—the awkward or confusing placement of modifiers or the modification of nonexistent words—blurs your message.

Faulty modification commonly takes two forms: *misplaced modifiers* and *dangling modifiers.* A misplaced modifier is placed to suggest that it modifies one word or phrase when it is intended to modify another. A dangling modifier does not modify any word or word group in the sentence.

Misplaced Modifiers

Misplaced modifiers have no clear relationship with their headword. Modifiers placed far from their headwords, for example, can cause a good deal of confusion.

> Faster than a speeding bullet, the citizens of Metropolis saw Superman flying overhead.

The placement of the introductory phrase makes it appear to modify *citizens,* yet it should modify *Superman.* Here is a corrected version.

> The citizens of Metropolis saw Superman flying overhead, faster than a speeding bullet.

Sometimes, as in the first example above, the misplaced modifier seems to modify the wrong headword. At other times, it is impossible to tell what the misplaced modifier is meant to modify. When writing and revising, take care to put modifying words, phrases, and clauses in a position that clearly identifies the headword.

Another problem occurs when a modifier's placement in the sentence is intrusive—for instance, when it separates a subject and verb. This placement can create an unnatural-sounding, hard-to-follow sentence (see 13d).

13a Recognizing Misplaced Words

Imprecise placement of modifying words can cause confusion. For example,

Dark and threatening, Wendy watched the storm.

Because the adjectives *dark* and *threatening* are adjacent to *Wendy*, they seem to describe her instead of the storm. Compare:

Wendy watched the storm, dark and threatening.

Readers expect to find modifiers directly before or directly after their headwords. Conforming to these expectations helps you compose more readable sentences.

Certain modifiers—such as *almost, only, even, hardly, merely, nearly, exactly, scarcely, just,* and *simply*—should always immediately precede the words they modify. Different placements of these modifiers change the meaning of your sentence.

He *only* had three dollars in his pocket.
  [He had nothing else in his pocket.]

He had *only* three dollars in his pocket.
  [He had no more dollars in his pocket.]

Only he had three dollars in his pocket.
  [No one else had three dollars.]

He had three dollars in his *only* pocket.
  [He had just one pocket.]

Nick *just* set up camp at the edge of the burned-out town.
  [He set up camp just now.]

Just Nick set up camp at the edge of the burned-out town.
  [He set up camp alone.]

Nick set up camp *just* at the edge of the burned-out town.
  [His camp was precisely at the edge.]

To avoid confusion, always place these modifiers directly before the words you intend them to modify.

The imprecise placement of a modifier sometimes produces a **squinting modifier**, one that seems to modify either a word before it or one after it and to convey different meanings in each case.

SQUINTING: The life that everyone thought would fulfill her [totally] bored her.

[*Was she supposed to be totally fulfilled, or is she totally bored?*]

REVISED: The life that everyone thought would totally fulfill her bored her.
[*Everyone expected her to be totally fulfilled.*]

REVISED: The life that everyone thought would fulfill her bored her totally.
[*She was totally bored.*]

mm
13b

EXERCISE 1

In the following sentence pairs, the modifier in each sentence points to a different headword. Underline the modifier and draw an arrow to the word it limits. Then paraphrase the meaning of each sentence.

EXAMPLE: She just came in wearing a hat.
[She just now entered.]

She came in wearing just a hat.
[She wore only a hat.]

1. He wore his almost new jeans.
   He almost wore his new jeans.
2. Draw only one graph.
   Only draw one graph.
3. I don't even like fresh-water fish.
   I don't like even fresh-water fish.
4. I go to the beach only on Saturdays.
   I go only to the beach on Saturdays.
5. He simply hated living.
   He hated simply living.

13b Recognizing Misplaced Phrases

Placing a modifying phrase illogically can create a sentence that is hard to decipher.

Certain *verbal phrases* act as modifiers (see 6f.2). As a rule,

place them directly before or directly after the nouns or pronouns they modify.

> She watched the car [rolling down the hill].

> [Absorbed in the story], he listened intently.

> It was a good year [to plant a victory garden].

mm
13b

The incorrect placement of a verbal phrase that acts as a modifier
can make a sentence convey an entirely different meaning,

> [Rolling down the hill], she watched the car.

or make no sense at all.

> Jane watched the boats [roller skating along the shore].

When a *prepositional phrase* is used as an adjective (see
6f.1), it nearly always directly follows the word it modifies.

> He bought the camera [with the wide-angle lens].

> This is a Dresden figurine [from Germany].

> She chose the specimen [in the middle].

> Created by a famous artist, Venus de Milo is a statue [with no
> arms].

Incorrect placement can give rise to confusion or even unintended humor.

> Venus de Milo is a statue created by a famous artist [with no arms].

When used adverbially, prepositional phrases also usually
follow their headwords.

> It's important to read [between the lines].

> Cassandra looked [into the future].

> Alice traveled [through the looking glass].

As long as the meaning of the sentence is clear, and as long as the
headword is clearly identified, you can place an adverbial modifier in any alternative position.

> He had been waiting anxiously at the bus stop [for a long time].

But be careful to avoid ambiguous placement of prepositional phrases serving as adverbs.

MISPLACED: She saw the house she built in her mind.

REVISED: [In her mind], she saw the house she built.

REVISED: She saw [in her mind] the house she built.

▶

EXERCISE 2

Underline the modifying verbal or prepositional phrases in each sentence, and draw arrows to their headwords.

mm

13c

EXAMPLE: Calvin is the democrat running for town council.

1. The bridge across the river swayed in the wind.
2. The spectators on the shore were involved in the action.
3. Mesmerized by the spectacle, they watched the drama unfold.
4. The spectators were afraid of a disaster.
5. Within the hour, the state police arrived to save the day.
6. They closed off the area with roadblocks.
7. Drivers approaching the bridge were asked to stop.
8. Meanwhile, on the bridge, the scene was chaos.
9. Motorists in their cars were paralyzed with fear.
10. Struggling against the weather, the police managed to rescue everyone.

▶

EXERCISE 3

Use the word or phrase that follows each sentence as a modifier in that sentence. Then draw an arrow to indicate its headword.

EXAMPLE: He approached the lion. (timid)

Timid, he approached the lion.

1. The lion paced up and down in his cage, ignoring the crowd. (watching Jack)
2. Jack stared back at the lion. (fascinated yet curious)
3. The crowd around them grew. (anxious to see what would happen)
4. Suddenly Jack heard a growl from deep in the lion's throat. (terrifying)
5. Jack ran from the zoo, leaving the lion behind. (scared to death)

13c   Recognizing Misplaced Subordinate Clauses

Subordinate clauses that serve as modifiers—adjective clauses and adverb clauses—must also be clearly related to their headwords. Adjective clauses usually appear immediately after the words they modify.

During the Civil War, Lincoln was the president [who governed the United States].

Adverb clauses can appear in any of several positions, as long as the relationship to the clause each modifies is clear and their position conveys the intended emphasis.

During the Civil War Lincoln was president.

Lincoln was president during the Civil War.

mm
13c

Misplaced subordinate clauses change or obscure the meaning of a sentence.

MISPLACED: This diet program will limit the consumption of pos-
(adjective   sible carcinogens, [which will benefit everyone].
clause)   *[Will carcinogens benefit everyone?]*

REVISED: This diet program, [which will benefit everyone], will
            limit the consumption of possible carcinogens.

MISPLACED: "The Mind Machines" was a one-hour episode of the
(adjective   science-oriented series *Nova*, [which dealt with com-
clause)   puters].
             *[What dealt with computers: the one episode or the en-
             tire series?]*

REVISED: "The Mind Machines," [which dealt with computers],
            was a one-hour episode of the science-oriented series
            Nova.

MISPLACED: They decided the house was haunted, but they
(adverb   changed their minds [when purple grass started grow-
clause)   ing out of the fireplace].
             [This bizarre phenomenon reassured them?]

REVISED: They decided the house was haunted when purple
            grass started growing out of the fireplace, but they
            changed their minds.

REVISED: When purple grass started growing out of the fire-
            place, they decided the house was haunted, but they
            changed their minds.

▶

EXERCISE 4

Relocate the misplaced verbal or prepositional phrases or subordinate clauses so that they clearly point to the words or word groups they modify.

EXAMPLE: *Silent Running* is a film about a scientist left alone in
(misplaced   space with Bruce Dern.
modifier)

> *Silent Running* is a film with Bruce Dern about a scientist left alone in space.

1. She realized she had married the wrong man after the wedding.
2. He savored his memory of the bachelor party, expecting it to last forever.
3. The house was designed by a team of architects with unusual moldings.
4. A front-page story announced the merger of the two companies in the *Wall Street Journal.*
5. The comedian was reviewed by the television station's entertainment critic, who had a habit of throwing pies at people.
6. Santa Claus and his eight reindeer were spotted by 200 birdwatchers on the top of the house.
7. *The Prince and the Pauper* is about an exchange of identities by Mark Twain.
8. The energy was used up in the ten-kilometer race that he was saving for the marathon.
9. He loaded the bottles and cans into his new Porsche, which he planned to leave at the recycling center.
10. The manager explained the sales figures to the board members using a graph.

13d Recognizing Intrusive Modifiers

For occasional emphasis a modifier—*word, phrase,* or *clause*—may be placed so that it interrupts a sentence. Do try, however, to avoid awkward interruptions. Readers expect to see each verb phrase (an auxiliary plus a main verb) and infinitive presented as a unit. They expect to be able to see immediately the connections between subjects and their verbs and between verbs and their objects or complements. When these connections are not clear, the result is a clumsy or incoherent sentence. When you revise, make sure each modifier is placed so that its link to its headword is apparent at a glance.

Revise when modifiers interrupt a verb phrase.

AWKWARD: She <u>had</u>, without giving it a second thought or considering the consequences, <u>planned</u> to reenlist.

REVISED: Without giving it a second thought or considering the consequences, she <u>had planned</u> to reenlist.

AWKWARD: He <u>will</u>, if he ever gets his act together, <u>be</u> ready to leave on Friday.

REVISED: If he ever gets his act together, he <u>will be</u> ready to leave on Friday.

A brief modifier can usually interrupt a verb phrase.

She <u>had</u> always <u>planned</u> to reenlist.

He <u>will</u>, however, <u>be</u> ready to leave on Friday.

mm
13d

Longer interruptions, however, may cloud your meaning. *Revise when modifiers interrupt an infinitive.*

As a rule, the parts of an infinitive should be together. When a modifier splits an infinitive—that is, comes between the word *to* and the infinitive form itself—the sentence often becomes awkward.

AWKWARD: He hoped <u>to</u> quickly and easily <u>defeat</u> his opponent.

REVISED: He hoped <u>to defeat</u> his opponent quickly and easily.

AWKWARD: He decided <u>to</u> after he considered the possible risks <u>invest</u> all his money in stocks.

REVISED: After he considered the possible risks, he decided <u>to invest</u> all his money in stocks.

Although the general rule in writing is never to split an infinitive, it is occasionally necessary to do so. When the intervening modifier is short, and when the alternative is awkward or ambiguous, a split infinitive is permissible. For example,

She expected <u>to not quite beat</u> her previous record.

Here a reader would have no trouble connecting the parts of the infinitive. Moreover, any revision using the same words is awkward

She expected <u>not quite</u> to beat her previous record.

or incoherent.

She expected to beat <u>not quite</u> her previous record.

The only way to avoid a split infinitive in this case is to reword the original sentence.

She expected her score to be close to her previous record.

But revisions often do not say exactly what the original said, and it makes sense to allow split infinitives when absolutely necessary. Before you decide to split an infinitive, however, make sure there is no other reasonable place for the modifier.

Revise when modifiers interrupt a subject and its verb or a verb and its object or complement.

It is standard practice to place even a complex or lengthy adjective phrase or clause between a subject and a verb or between a verb and its object or complement. An adverb phrase or clause in this position, however, may not be natural-sounding or clear.

mm
13d

ACCEPTABLE: Major <u>films</u> that were financially successful in the thirties <u>include</u> *Gone with the Wind* and *Citizen Kane*. (adjective clause between subject and verb does not obscure sentence's meaning)

CONFUSING: The <u>election</u>, because officials discovered that some people voted twice, <u>was</u> contested. (adverb clause intrudes between subject and verb)

REVISED: Because officials discovered that some people voted twice, the <u>election was</u> contested. (subject and verb no longer separated)

CONFUSING: A. A. Milne <u>wrote</u>, when his son Christopher Robin was a child, *Winnie-the-Pooh*. (adverb clause intrudes between verb and object)

REVISED: When his son Christopher Robin was a child, A. A. Milne <u>wrote *Winnie-the-Pooh*</u>. (verb and object no longer separated)

When you reread a sentence, if you have any doubts about letting a modifier stand between subject and verb or verb and object or complement, relocate the modifier.

▶
EXERCISE 5

Revise these sentences so that the modifying phrases or clauses do not interrupt the parts of a verb phrase or infinitive or separate a subject from a verb or a verb from its object or complement.

EXAMPLE: A play can sometimes be, despite the playwright's best efforts, mystifying to the audience.

Despite the playwright's best efforts, a play can sometimes be mystifying to the audience.

1. The audience, when they saw that the play was about to begin and realized that the orchestra had finished tuning up and had begun the overture, finally quieted down.

2. They settled into their seats, expecting to very much enjoy the first act.

3. However, most people were, even after watching and listening for twenty minutes and paying close attention to the drama, completely baffled.

4. In fact, the play, because it had nameless characters, no scenery, and a rambling plot that didn't seem to be heading anywhere, puzzled even the drama critics.

5. Finally one of the three major characters explained, speaking directly to the audience, what the play was really about.

**dm
13**

Dangling Modifiers

When the true headword of a modifier does not appear in a sentence, the modifier is left dangling. A **dangling modifier** drifts in a sentence because it has nothing to attach itself to. Look at this sentence, for instance.

> Many undesirable side effects have been seen <u>using this drug</u>.

Because the modifier has no headword, *using this drug* appears to modify *side effects*, but of course this makes no sense. To correct such an inaccuracy, you must add to the sentence something for the dangling modifier to modify.

> Many undesirable side effects are seen <u>in patients using this drug</u>.

Or the dangling modifier must be changed to a subordinate clause.

> Many undesirable side effects are seen <u>when patients use this drug</u>.

To correct dangling modifiers, you may do one of two things.

1. Change the subject of the sentence's main clause, creating a subject that can logically serve as the headword of the dangling modifier.
2. Add words that transform the dangling modifier into a subordinate clause.

The three most frequently encountered kinds of dangling modifiers are dangling verbal phrases, dangling prepositional phrases, and dangling elliptical clauses.

13e Recognizing Dangling Verbal Phrases

Verbal phrases used as modifiers sometimes dangle in a sentence.

dm
13f

DANGLING: Using a pair of forceps, the skin of the rat's abdomen
(participial   was lifted and a small cut was made into the body
phrase)   with scissors. (sentence contains no word the participial phrase can logically modify)

REVISED: Using a pair of forceps, the technician lifted the skin
of the rat's abdomen and made a small cut into the
body with scissors. (subject of main clause changed
from *the skin* to *the technician,* a headword the participial phrase can logically modify)

DANGLING: Paid in three installments, Brad felt the grant would
(participial   last all year. (sentence contains no word the particip-
phrase)   ial phrase can logically modify)

REVISED: Because the grant was paid in three installments,
Brad felt it would last all year. (modifying phrase now
a subordinate clause)

DANGLING: To make his paper more accurate, all references were
(infinitive   checked twice. (sentence contains no word the infini-
phrase)   tive phrase can logically modify)

REVISED: To make his paper more accurate, Don checked all
references twice. (subject of main clause changed
from *references* to *Don,* a headword the infinitive
phrase can logically modify)

DANGLING: Music seemed to carry the children's minds away
(infinitive   from reality to dream about the future. (sentence
phrase)   contains no word the infinitive phrase can logically
modify)

REVISED: Music seemed to carry the children's minds away from
reality so that they were able to dream about the future.
(infinitive phrase now a subordinate clause)

13f Recognizing Dangling Prepositional Phrases

Prepositional phrases can also dangle in a sentence.

DANGLING: With fifty pages to read, *War and Peace* was absorbing.
(sentence contains no word the prepositional phrase
can logically modify)

dm
13g

REVISED: <u>With fifty pages to read</u>, Meg found *War and Peace* absorbing. (subject of main clause changed from *War and Peace* to *Meg,* a word the prepositional phrase can logically modify)

DANGLING: <u>On the newsstands only an hour</u>, its sales surprised everyone. (sentence contains no word the prepositional phrase can logically modify)

REVISED: <u>Because the magazine had been on the newsstands only an hour</u>, its sales surprised everyone. (prepositional phrase now a subordinate clause)

Frequently, dangling modifiers involving prepositional phrases occur when the object of the preposition *by* is a gerund (e.g., *by taking a shortcut*). This sort of error often involves a passive construction.

DANGLING: The exhibit was very efficiently presented <u>by using diagrams and photographs</u>. (sentence contains no word the prepositional phrase can logically modify)

REVISED: <u>By using diagrams and photographs</u>, they presented the exhibit very efficiently. (subject of main clause has been changed from *the exhibit* to *they,* a word the prepositional phrase can logically modify)

DANGLING: <u>By moving the microscope's mirror</u>, light can be reflected off its surface up into the viewing apparatus. (sentence contains no word the prepositional phrase can logically modify)

REVISED: <u>When the microscope's mirror is moved</u>, light can be reflected off its surface up into the viewing apparatus. (prepositional phrase now a subordinate clause)

13g   Recognizing Dangling Elliptical Clauses

Elliptical clauses are subordinate clauses from which part of the subject or predicate or the entire subject or predicate is missing. The absent words, therefore, must be inferred from the context (see 6d.2). When such a clause cannot logically modify the subject of the sentence's main clause, it too dangles.

DANGLING: <u>While still in the Buchner funnel</u>, you should press the crystals with a clear stopper to eliminate any residual solvent. (elliptical clause cannot logically modify subject of main clause)

REVISED: While still in the Buchner funnel, the crystals should be pressed with a clear stopper to eliminate any residual solvent. (subject of main clause changed from *you* to *crystals*, a word the elliptical clause can logically modify)

DANGLING: Though a high-pressure field, I find great personal satisfaction in nursing. (elliptical clause cannot logically modify subject of main clause)

REVISED: Though it is a high-pressure field, I find great personal satisfaction in nursing. (elliptical clause expanded into a complete subordinate clause)

dm
13g

▶

EXERCISE 6

Eliminate the dangling modifier from each of the sentences below. You may either change the subject of the main clause to one the dangling modifier can logically modify or revise the dangling modifier to make it a subordinate clause.

EXAMPLE: Medical care will be greatly improved using atomic power to treat disease. (dangling modifier)

Medical care will be greatly improved when atomic power is used to treat disease. (subordinate clause)

Using atomic power to treat disease, physicians will provide greatly improved medical care. (subject of main clause changed)

1. Fortunately, vitamin B^6 has so far been proven safe when taking supplements.
2. By lowering the drinking age to eighteen, the high schools will be filled with students under the influence of alcohol.
3. Unemployment creates tension in the family when wondering where the next dollar is going to come from.
4. By using a piece of filter paper, the ball of sodium is dried as much as possible and placed in a dry test tube.
5. After sitting through the dull program, the show failed to reach any conclusions.
6. By purchasing only the necessary amounts of food for each member of the family, extra expenses will be eliminated.
7. The enzyme activity of these solutions was immediately stopped by adding the samples to a strong acid solution.
8. To build a house, good blueprints are needed.
9. When voting for president, newspaper polls can be very powerful.
10. Being a freshman, my study habits were not very good.

▶
EXERCISE 7

Combine each sentence pair into a single sentence by rewording one sentence so that it modifies the other. Be careful not to create dangling modifiers, and make sure that each modifier clearly and unambiguously points to a headword it can logically modify.

EXAMPLE: He climbed to the top of the mountain. He discovered a wonderful view.

Climbing to the top of the mountain, he discovered a wonderful view. (Revised)

When he climbed to the top of the mountain, he discovered a wonderful view. (Revised)

1. Carol was notified that she had just won a music scholarship. She was notified at three-thirty in the afternoon.
2. She stared at the letter. She was too excited to move.
3. She called her mother. Her mother was at work.
4. Her mother said she was thrilled. She said it over the telephone.
5. Carol sat down at her desk. She was trying to consider the pros and cons of accepting the scholarship.
6. She was still sitting there at five-thirty. Her mother arrived home then.
7. Her mother tried to make Carol's decision easy. Instead, she gave her more to think about.
8. Possibilities filled Carol's mind. The possibilities included accepting the scholarship, waiting, or turning it down.
9. She wanted to accept it. She hoped very much to study music.
10. She made up her mind. Then she began to answer the letter.

Student Writer at Work: Misplaced and Dangling Modifiers

Read this draft of a student's technical description of a 10cc syringe, and revise it to correct misplaced and dangling modifiers.

Designed to inject liquids into, or withdraw them from, any vessel or cavity, the function of a syringe is often to inject drugs into the body or withdraw blood from it. Syringes are also used to precisely measure amounts of drugs or electrolytes that must be added to large intravenous solutions.

There are available on the market today many different

types of syringes, but the one most commonly utilized in hospital pharmacy practice is the 10-cubic-centimeter disposable syringe. Approximately 5 inches in length, the primary composition of this particular syringe is transparent polyethylene plastic. The 10cc syringe and the majority of other syringes all share the design of a round plunger or piston within a barrel.

The barrel of a syringe is a round, hollow cylinder about 4½″ long with a diameter of 3/8″. The bottom end of the barrel has two outward extensions on its opposite sides, which are perpendicular to the cylinder. With a width equal to the diameter of the barrel, the length of these extensions is about ½″. The purpose of these extensions is to enable one to hold with the forefinger and middle finger the barrel of the syringe while withdrawing the plunger with the thumb and third finger.

The barrel of the syringe is calibrated on the side in black ink subdivided into gradations of .2cc. At the top of the syringe the barrel abruptly narrows to a very small cylinder, 1/8″ in diameter and 1/4″ in length. This small cylinder is surrounded by another hollow cylinder with a slightly larger diameter. The inside wall of the outer cylinder is threaded like a corkscrew. The purpose of this thread is to secure the needle in place.

The other major part of the syringe is the plunger. The plunger is a solid, round cylinder that fits snugly into the barrel made of plastic. At the bottom of the plunger is a plastic ring the size of a dime, which provides something to grasp while withdrawing the plunger. The body of the plunger connects the bottom rim with the tip of the plunger, which is made of black rubber.

**dm
13**

14

Faulty Parallelism

Parallelism is the use of similar grammatical elements in sentences or parts of sentences. It ensures that elements sharing the same function also share the same grammatical form—for instance, that verbs match corresponding verbs in tense, mood, and number. Words, phrases, clauses, or complete sentences may be parallel, and parallel items may be paired or presented in a series.

PARALLEL WORDS: We studied <u>Romanticism</u>, <u>Naturalism</u>, and <u>Transcendentalism</u>. (nouns)

The bill was <u>signed</u>, <u>sealed</u>, and <u>delivered</u>. (verbs)

College is <u>broadening</u> but <u>exhausting</u>. (adjectives)

PARALLEL PHRASES: . . . government of the people, by the people, and for the people shall not perish from the earth. (prepositional phrases) (Abraham Lincoln, Gettysburg Address)

He has plundered our seas, ravaged our coasts, burnt our towns, and destroyed the lives of our people. (verbs plus objects) (Thomas Jefferson, The Declaration of Independence)

PARALLEL CLAUSES: Go back to Mississippi, go back to Alabama, go back to South Carolina, go back to Georgia, go back to Louisiana, go back to the slums and ghettos of our northern cities, knowing that somehow this situation can and will be changed. (Martin Luther King, Jr., "I Have a Dream")

PARALLEL SENTENCES: The first mistake is to think of mankind as a thing in itself. It isn't. It is part of an intricate web of life. And we can't think even of life as a thing in itself. It isn't. It is part of the intricate structure of a planet bathed by energy from the sun. (Isaac Asimov, "The Case Against Man")

Effective parallelism adds force, unity, balance, and symmetry to your writing. It makes sentences clear and easy to follow and emphasizes relationships among equivalent ideas. It helps you and your reader keep track of ideas, and it makes sentences more emphatic (see 8c), more concise (see 9b), and more varied.

14a Using Parallelism

14a

When like items are presented in a series or are paired, the use of parallelism provides coherence. If it is not used, the sentence will be likely to sound awkward or incoherent.

(1) With items in a series

Coordinate elements—words, phrases, or clauses—in a series should be in parallel form.

> As a vegetarian, he avoided <u>meat</u>, <u>fish</u>, and <u>eggs</u>.
>
> <u>Marijuana use</u>, <u>baby food consumption</u>, and <u>toy production</u> are all starting to decline as the United States population grows older.
>
> <u>Eat</u>, <u>drink</u>, and <u>be</u> merry.
>
> I came; I saw; I conquered.
>
> Three factors influenced him: <u>his desire to relocate</u>; <u>his need for greater responsibility</u>; and <u>his dissatisfaction with his current job</u>, which involved long hours.

Elements in a series may also appear in list form, and these too should be presented in parallel terms.

> Major causes of the Irish potato famine included:
> 1. The establishment of the landlord-tenant system
> 2. The failure of the potato crop
> 3. The reluctance of England to offer adequate financial assistance
> 4. The passage of the Corn Laws

(2) With paired items

Paired points or ideas (words, phrases, or clauses) should be presented in parallel terms. Parallelism conveys their correspondence and connects points to each other.

> Her note was <u>short</u> but <u>sweet</u>.
>
> <u>Speech is silver</u>, but <u>silence is golden</u>.

We can go to the movies, or we can stay home.

Roosevelt represented the United States, and Churchill represented Great Britain.

The research focused on muscle tissue and nerve cells.

The more you study, the more you learn.

High school was over; real life was beginning.

Ask not what your country can do for you; ask what you can do for your country.   (John F. Kennedy, Inaugural Address)

14a

Correlative conjunctions (like *not only/but also, both/and, either/or, neither/nor,* and *whether/or*) are frequently used to link paired elements. These phrases convey balance, so the terms they introduce should be parallel.

The design team paid close attention not only to color but also to texture.

Either repeat physics or take calculus.

Both cable television and videocassette recorders threaten the dominance of the three major television networks.

Parallelism can also be used to highlight opposition between paired elements linked by the word *than.*

It is better to light a candle than to curse the darkness.

Richard Wright and James Baldwin chose to live in Paris rather than to remain in the United States.

Spending money is easier than earning it.

▶
EXERCISE 1

Identify the parallel elements in these sentences by underlining parallel words and bracketing parallel phrases and clauses.

> EXAMPLE: He is 81 now, [a tall man in a dark blue suit], [a smiling man with a nimbus of snowy white hair], and much of the world knows him [as the proponent of vitamin C to cure colds], [as a quixotic, vaguely ridiculed figure on the fringes of medicine]. (Maralyn Lois Polak, *Philadelphia Inquirer*)

1. You have lived an American dream when you begin the year setting pressure gauges for the Caterpillar Tractor Company in Peoria and end it building rocking chairs for your grandchildren. (*Newsweek*)

2. The public image [of the American woman] in the magazine and television commercials is designed to sell washing machines, cake mixes, deodorants, detergents, rejuvenating face creams, hair tints. (Betty Friedan, *The Feminine Mystique*)

3. Right answers are what the school wants, and [the child] learns countless strategies for prying answers out of the teacher, for conning her into thinking he knows what he doesn't know. (John Holt, *Saturday Evening Post*)

4. Surgery restores to function broken limbs and damaged hearts with amazing safety and little suffering; sanitation removes from our environment many of the germs of disease; new drugs are constantly being developed to relieve physical pain, to help us sleep if we are restless, to keep us awake if we feel sleepy, and to make us oblivious to worries. (René Dubos, *Medical Utopias*)

5. For several years now, college graduates have been abandoning the classroom for more lucrative careers in the boardroom, the courtroom, and the operating room. (*Newsweek*)

6. The society that was once uniform is now a patchwork of rich and poor, old and young, men and women, blacks, whites, Hispanics, and Indians. (Frances FitzGerald, *America Revised*)

7. She had no chance of learning grammar and logic, let alone of reading Horace and Virgil. (Virginia Woolf, "If Shakespeare Had a Sister")

8. Theoretically—and secretly, of course—I was all for the Burmese and all against their oppressors, the British. (George Orwell, "Shooting an Elephant")

9. As nations, we can apply to affairs of state the realism of science: holding to what works and discarding what does not. (Jacob Bronowski, *A Sense of the Future*)

10. In the final assembly area of their new plant long lines of young Japanese women wired together electronic products on a piecerate system: the more you wired, the more you got paid. (William Ouchi, *Theory Z*)

14a

▶
EXERCISE 2

Combine each of the following sentence pairs or sentence groups into one sentence that uses parallelism effectively. Be sure all parallel words, phrases, and clauses are expressed in parallel terms.

1. Originally, there were five performing Marx Brothers. One was nicknamed Groucho. The others were called Chico, Harpo, Gummo, and Zeppo.

2. Groucho was very well known. So were Chico and Harpo. Gummo soon dropped out of the act. And later Zeppo did, too.

3. They began in vaudeville. That was before World War I. Their first show was called *I'll Say She Is*. It opened in New York in 1924.

4. The Marx Brothers' first movie was *The Coconuts*. The next was *Animal Crackers*. And this was followed by *Monkey Business, Horsefeathers,* and *Duck Soup*. Then came *A Night at the Opera*.

5. In each of these movies, the Marx Brothers made people laugh. More importantly, they established a unique, zany comic style.

6. Each man had a set of familiar trademarks. Groucho had a mustache and a long coat. He wiggled his eyebrows and smoked a cigar. There was a funny hat that Chico always wore. And he affected a phony Italian accent. Harpo never spoke.

7. Groucho was always cast as a sly operator. He always tried to cheat people out of their money. He always tried to charm women.

8. In *The Coconuts* he played Mr. Hammer, proprietor of the run-down Coconut Manor, a Florida hotel. In *Horsefeathers* his character was named Professor Quincy Adams Wagstaff. Wagstaff was president of Huxley College. Huxley also had financial problems.

9. In *Duck Soup* Groucho played Rufus T. Firefly, president of the country of Fredonia. Fredonia had formerly been ruled by the late husband of a Mrs. Teasdale. Fredonia was now at war with the country of Sylvania.

10. Groucho's leading lady was often Margaret Dumont. She played Mrs. Teasdale in *Duck Soup*. In *A Night at the Opera* she played Mrs. Claypool. Her character in *The Coconuts* was named Mrs. Potter.

11. One scene in *Horsefeathers* is quite well known. It occurs on a football field, where Huxley College plays against rival Darwin College. An even more famous scene, in *A Night at the Opera*, takes place in a crowded stateroom aboard an ocean liner.

12. Marx Brothers films were written by some talented artists. S. J. Perelman was one. And George S. Kaufman was another.

14b   Revising Faulty Parallelism

When elements that have the same function in a sentence are not presented in the same terms, the sentence is flawed by **faulty parallelism.** For example,

> FAULTY
> PARALLELISM: Many people in third-world countries suffer because the countries lack sufficient housing to accommodate them, sufficient food to feed them, and their health-care facilities are inadequate.

Because all these points have the same weight and are presented in a series connected by the coordinating conjunction *and,* readers expect them to be expressed in parallel terms. The first two elements satisfy this expectation.

sufficient housing to accommodate them . . .

sufficient food to feed them . . .

The third item in the series, however, breaks this pattern.

their health-care facilities are inadequate.

For a clear, emphatic sentence, all three elements should be presented in the same terms.

> Many people in third-world countries suffer because the coun-tries lack <u>sufficient housing to accommodate them</u>, <u>sufficient food to feed them</u>, and <u>sufficient health-care facilities to serve them</u>.

14b

(1) Repeating parallel elements

Faulty parallelism occurs when a writer does not use parallel elements in a series or in paired points. Nouns must be matched with nouns, verbs with verbs, phrases and clauses with similarly constructed phrases and clauses, and so on, in places where they are expected.

FAULTY PARALLELISM	REVISED
New trends in exercise for women include aerobic dancing, weight lifters, and jogging. (*dancing* and *jog-ging* are gerunds; *weight lifters* is a noun phrase)	New trends in exercise for women include aerobic <u>dancing</u>, weight <u>lifting</u>, and <u>jogging</u>. (three gerunds)
Some of the side effects are skin irritation and eye irri-tation, and mucous mem-brane irritation may also develop. (*skin irritation* and *eye irritation* are noun phrases; *mucous mem-brane irritation may also develop* is an independent clause)	Some of the side effects that may develop are <u>skin</u>, <u>eye</u>, and <u>mucous</u> membrane ir-ritation. (three nouns used as modifiers of *irritation*)
I look forward to hearing from you and to have an oppor-tunity to tell you more about myself. (*hearing from you* is a gerund phrase; *to have an opportunity* is an infinitive phrase)	I look forward to <u>hearing from you</u> and to <u>having an op-portunity</u> to tell you more about myself. (two gerund phrases)

(2)   Repeating signals of parallelism

Faulty parallelism also occurs when a writer does not repeat
words that signal parallelism: prepositions, articles, the *to* that
goes with the infinitive, or the word that introduces a phrase or
clause. Although similar grammatical structures (verbs that
match verbs, nouns that match nouns, and so on) may sometimes be enough to convey parallelism, sentences are clearer and
more emphatic if other key words in parallel constructions are
also parallel. Repeating these signals makes the boundaries of
each parallel element clear. But be sure to include the same signals with *all* the elements in a series. Broken parallelism creates
ambiguity.

14b

FAULTY PARALLELISM	REVISED
Computerization helps industry by not allowing labor costs to skyrocket, increasing the speed of production, and improving efficiency (Does *not* apply to all three phrases, or only the first?)	Computerization helps industry <u>by not allowing labor costs to skyrocket</u>, <u>by increasing the speed of production</u>, and <u>by improving efficiency</u>. (Preposition *by* is repeated to clarify the boundaries of the three parallel phrases.)
I have always had a high level of tolerance for the pressures of the business world, long hours, and hard work. (Are *long hours* and *hard work* objects of the preposition *of* or *for*?)	I have always had a high level of tolerance <u>for the pressures of the business world</u>, <u>for long hours</u>, and <u>for hard work</u>. (Preposition *for* is repeated to clarify the boundaries of the three parallel phrases.)
The United States suffered casualties in the Civil War, French and Indian War, Spanish-American War and Korean War. (Without the repeated definite article, it is hard for readers to distinguish the four different wars.)	The United States suffered casualties in <u>the Civil War</u>, <u>the French and Indian War</u>, <u>the Spanish-American War</u>, and <u>the Korean War</u>. (The article *the* is repeated for clarity and emphasis.)
It may be easier to try remodeling than abandon a house. (Although *try* and	It may be easier <u>to try</u> remodeling than <u>to abandon</u> a house. (The *to* of the infini-

abandon correspond, the sentence does not highlight their parallel structure; in fact, *remodeling* and *abandon* seem to be the paired elements.)

tive is repeated for clarity and emphasis.)

Koala bears are not as appealing as they look because they have fleas, they have bad breath, and a tendency to scratch. (Are *bad breath* and *a tendency to scratch* reasons that Koalas are unappealing, or are they incidental points?)

Koala bears are not as appealing as they look <u>because they have fleas</u>, <u>because they have bad breath</u>, and <u>because they have a tendency to scratch</u>. (The introductory words *because they* are repeated for clarity and emphasis.)

14b

(3)   Repeating relative pronouns

Faulty parallelism occurs when a writer fails to use a clause beginning with the relative pronoun *who, whom,* or *which* before one beginning with *and who, and whom,* or *and which.*

Like correlative conjunctions, *who/and who* and similar expressions are always paired and always introduce parallel clauses. Omitting the first part of the expression throws readers off balance.

This sentence correctly uses *which/and which.*

> CORRECT: *The Thing,* <u>which</u> was directed by Howard Hawks, <u>and which</u> was released in 1951, featured James Arness as the monster.

Without the *which* clause preceding the *and which* clause, the sentence would lack clarity and emphasis.

> INCORRECT: *The Thing,* directed by Howard Hawks, and which was released in 1951, featured James Arness as the monster.

Of course, if the *and which* were omitted, there would be no need to add the *which.*

> CORRECT: *The Thing,* directed by Howard Hawks and released in 1951, featured James Arness as the monster.

▶

EXERCISE 3

Identify and correct faulty parallelism in these sentences. Then underline the parallel elements—words, phrases, and clauses—in your corrected sentences. If a sentence is already correct, mark it with a C and
underline the parallel elements.

14b

> EXAMPLE: Alfred Hitchcock's films include *North by Northwest,*
> *Vertigo, Psycho,* and he also directed *Notorious* and
> *Saboteur.*
>
> REVISED: Films directed by Alfred Hitchcock include *North by*
> *Northwest, Vertigo, Psycho, Notorious,* and *Saboteur.*

1. The world is divided between those with galoshes on and those
    who discover continents.
2. Clothing can very well give an idea of one's personality, such as if
    one is the quiet type or more outgoing.
3. The more expensive brands [of stockings] will feel silky soft, look
    delicately sheer and the color flatters. Too often off-price hosiery
    feels scratchy, looks more opaque than sheer and color is harsh
    and unattractive. (*Philadelphia Inquirer*)
4. Insurance buyers can choose between five-year renewable term or
    decreasing term policies or they can also choose a whole-life pol-
    icy.
5. Soviet leaders, members of Congress, and the American Catholic
    bishops all pressed the president to limit the arms race.
6. A national task force on education recommended improving public
    education by making the school day longer, higher teachers' sala-
    ries, and integrating more technology into the curriculum.
7. It was difficult to find a stone mason and agreeing on a timetable
    for the necessary work.
8. The fast-food industry is expanding to include many kinds of res-
    taurants: those that serve pizza, fried chicken chains, some offering
    Mexican-style menus, and hamburger franchises.
9. The consumption of Scotch in the United States is declining be-
    cause of high prices, tastes are changing, and increased health
    awareness has led many whiskey drinkers to switch to wine or
    beer.
10. Pocket paging devices are carried not only by physicians but also
    some maintenance personnel and police officers carry them.

Student Writer at Work: Faulty Parallelism

Correct the faulty parallelism in the following partial draft of a student paper written for a class in public health. Here the student discusses factors that must be taken into account by medical practitioners at the Indian Health Service.

14

The average life span of American Indians is considerably lower than that of the general population. Not only is their infant mortality rate four times higher than that of the general population, but they also have a suicide rate that is twice as high as other races. Moreover, Indians both die in homicides more often than other races do and there are more alcohol-related deaths in Indians than in other races. Medical care available for them does not meet their needs and is presenting a challenge for the health professionals who serve them.

The Indian Health Service (IHS), a branch of the U.S. Public Health Service, is responsible for providing medical care to reservation Indians. The IHS has been faulted for its inability to deal with cultural differences between health professionals and Indians—cultural differences that interfere with adequate medical care. In order to diagnose disease states, for prescribing drug therapy, and to counsel patients, health professionals need to incorporate an understanding of Indian culture. They must acquire a working knowledge of Indians' ideas and feelings toward health and also God, relationships, and death. Only then can health professionals communicate their goals, provide quality medical care, and in addition they will be able to achieve patient compliance.

There are many obstacles to effective communication: hostility to white authority and whites' structured, organized society; language is another obvious barrier to communication; Indians' view of sickness, which may be different from Anglos'; and some Indian cultures' concept of time is also different from that of the Anglo health workers. Other problems are more basic: a physician cannot expect a patient to refrigerate medication if no refrigerators are available or dilute dosage forms at home or be changing wet dressings several times a day if clean water is not readily available nor quart/pint measuring devices to dilute stock solutions.

The defects in Indian health care cannot be completely solved by the improvement of communication channels or making these channels stronger. But the health professional's communication with the Indian patient can be effective enough so medical staff can acquire an adequate medical history, monitor drug use, be alert for possible drug interactions, and to provide useful discharge counseling. If health professionals can communicate understanding and respect for Indian culture and concern for their welfare, they may be able to meet the needs of their Indian patients more effectively.

Shifts and Mixed Constructions

15a Recognizing Shifts

A **shift** is a change of tense, voice, mood, person, number, or type of discourse within or between sentences. In some cases these shifts are necessary—to indicate changes of time, for example.

> *The Wizard of Oz* <u>is</u> a film that has enchanted audiences since it <u>was made</u> in 1939.

Problems occur, however, when you make unnecessary or illogical shifts.

(1) Shifts in tense

An unwarranted shift in tense occurs when the tenses of verbs in a sentence or group of sentences do not logically correspond.

Tense Shifts Within a Sentence

The verb tenses in a sentence should not shift without good reason (see 22f). Therefore, the tense of a verb in one clause of a sentence should generally be consistent with the tense of the verbs in the other clauses. For example, the action of the following sentence occurs in the past. The shift to the present (*promises*) in the last clause of the sentence is therefore unwarranted.

> FAULTY: The judge <u>told</u> the defendant that he would not release him unless he <u>promises</u> to undergo therapy.

> REVISED: The judge <u>told</u> the defendant that he would not release him unless he <u>promised</u> to undergo therapy.

The following sentence is about a work of literature, so its action should be described in the present (see 22c). The shift to the past (*drove*) in the subordinate clause is therefore unwarranted.

> FAULTY: The novel is about two friends who drove across the United States.

> REVISED: The novel is about two friends who drive across the United States.

shft
15a

The verbs of this compound sentence shift from past to present tense (*rose, invest*). When you revise, make sure there are no unwarranted tense shifts between independent clauses.

> FAULTY: Throughout 1928 the stock market rose steadily, and as a result, small investors invest heavily in 1929.

> REVISED: Throughout 1928 the stock market rose steadily, and as a result, small investors invested heavily in 1929.

Tense Shifts in Groups of Sentences

Unwarranted tense shifts occur when verb tenses in a series of sentences differ for no logical reason. For example,

> ORIGINAL: One night I was driving late at night. Suddenly I see a dog right in the path of my car. I slam on my brakes and barely avoid hitting it.

Caught up in the action of the narrative, the writer makes an unwarranted shift to the present tense. Putting all the verbs into the past tense improves the presentation.

> REVISED: One night I was driving late at night. Suddenly I saw a dog right in the path of my car. I slammed on my brakes and barely avoided hitting it.

The following passage describes an event that occurs regularly (each summer), so the dominant tense is the present. The shift to the past tense in sentence 4 throws readers off balance.

> ORIGINAL: (1) Each summer I spend a month at the shore. (2) I lie on the beach and let the sun drive away my troubles. (3) The breeze blows over the beach and cools the sand. (4) I listened to a radio on a nearby blanket and watched children playing by the water.

> REVISED: (1) Each summer I spend a month at the shore. (2) I lie on the beach and let the sun drive away my troubles. (3) The breeze blows over the beach and cools the sand. (4) I listen to a radio on a nearby blanket and watch children playing in the water.

▶
EXERCISE 1

Revise any of the following sentences and sentence groups that contain unwarranted shifts in tense. Be prepared to explain the changes you make. If a sentence or sentence group is correct, mark it with a C.

EXAMPLE: The old man fished and catches a shark.

The old man fished and caught a shark.

shft
15a

1. The Holy Roman Empire was established in 962 and is an attempt to revive the traditions of Rome.
2. Dr. Salk looked carefully until he found a vaccine for polio.
3. My dog always runs to greet me when I came home.
4. The reporter was happy; he has just been awarded a Pulitzer Prize.
5. In his novel *The Grapes of Wrath* Steinbeck creates a portrait of a poor family who left Oklahoma and went to California.
6. The cat looks carefully at the mouse. After playing with it for a while, she pounced on it.
7. The surgeon was excited when he is reading of a new technique for removing kidney stones.
8. The station presented programs that discussed ecology.
9. During the nineteenth century there was great unrest in Russia. The peasants are demanding land and workers are calling for unions.
10. Hoover resisted giving federal relief funds to the states. He gave aid, however, to financially weak banks. He hopes that they will put the money to productive use. Early in 1932 he created the Reconstruction Finance Corporation to make loans to banks, railroads, and insurance companies. None of these tactics, though, is able to help the slumping American economy.

(2) Shifts in voice

Shifts in voice from active to passive (see "Voice" in Chapter 22) may be necessary to give a sentence proper emphasis.

Even though consumers protested, controls on the price of natural gas were lifted.

Here the shift from active (*protested*) to passive (*were lifted*) enables the writer to keep the focus on consumer groups and the issue that they protested. To say *Congress lifted the price controls* would change the emphasis of the sentence.

Unwarranted shifts from active to passive, however, can be confusing and misleading.

F. Scott Fitzgerald <u>wrote</u> *This Side of Paradise* and later *The Great Gatsby* <u>was written</u>.

The shift from active (*wrote*) to passive (*was written*) makes this sentence difficult to understand. Although readers are able to tell that Fitzgerald wrote *This Side of Paradise*, they cannot be certain who wrote *The Great Gatsby*. Consistent use of the active voice makes this sentence clear.

shft

15a

F. Scott Fitzgerald <u>wrote</u> *This Side of Paradise* and later <u>wrote</u> *The Great Gatsby*.

Notice the unjustified shifts in these sentences.

INCONSISTENT: As we <u>walked</u>, the sun <u>was seen</u> setting in the distance.

INCONSISTENT: The chemist <u>stirred</u> the mixture for ten minutes and then it <u>was allowed</u> to settle.

INCONSISTENT: Coco Chanel <u>designed</u> dresses and suits and the perfume Chanel No. 5 <u>was</u> also <u>developed</u>.

Consistent voice eliminates confusion.

REVISED: As we <u>walked</u>, we <u>saw</u> the sun setting in the distance.

REVISED: The mixture <u>was stirred</u> for ten minutes and then it <u>was allowed</u> to settle.

REVISED: Coco Chanel <u>designed</u> dresses and suits and also <u>developed</u> the perfume Chanel No. 5.

▶

EXERCISE 2

Eliminate any unwarranted shifts in voice in each of the following sentences.

EXAMPLE: The Etruscans used horses in warfare, and horse races were conducted by them as early as 1500 B.C.

1. The ancient Romans loved horseracing, so highly bred strains of horses were developed by them for chariot racing.
2. The first organized horse race was staged in 1780 by the Earl of Derby, and prizes were awarded by him to the winners.
3. Because the American colonists loved horse racing, races were organized at fairs.
4. Gambling was done by many Americans in the nineteenth century. They ignored the opposition of religious reformers.
5. New York instituted the first legalized off-track betting system, and it was hoped that this would increase state revenue.

(3) Shifts in mood

As with tense and voice, unnecessary shifts in mood (see "Mood" in Chapter 22) can be confusing and annoying.

> INCONSISTENT: It is important that a student <u>buy</u> a dictionary and <u>uses</u> it. (shift from subjunctive to indicative)
>
> REVISED: It is important that a student <u>buy</u> a dictionary and <u>use</u> it. (both verbs in the subjunctive)
>
> INCONSISTENT: Next, <u>heat</u> the mixture in a test tube and <u>you should make sure</u> it does not boil. (shift from imperative to indicative)
>
> REVISED: Next, <u>heat</u> the mixture in a test tube and <u>be sure</u> it does not boil (both verbs in the imperative)
>
> INCONSISTENT: The football player demanded that he <u>get</u> a raise and that he <u>wants to play</u> more often. (shift from the subjunctive to the indicative)
>
> REVISED: The football player demanded that he <u>get</u> a raise and that he <u>play</u> more often. (both verbs in the subjunctive)

shft
15a

▶
EXERCISE 3

Make the following sentences consistent in mood. If a sentence is correct, mark it with a *C*.

> EXAMPLE: To fix a faucet unscrew the handle and you should examine the washer.
>
> To fix a faucet unscrew the handle and <u>examine</u> the washer.

1. Make an incision along the dorsal axis of the frog, and then you peel back the skin.
2. First open the hood of the car and then you should examine the distributor cap.
3. It is necessary that the student fill out the questionnaire and hands it in.
4. The government wants to eliminate the graduated income tax and give a fixed rate to all taxpayers.
5. First mail your résumé and then you call for an interview.

(4) Shifts in person and number

Person is the form a pronoun or verb takes to indicate the person or persons speaking (first person—*I am, we are*), those spoken to (second person—*you are*), and those spoken about (third person—*he, she, it is;* and *they are*). Number indicates one (singular—*novel, it*) or many (plural—*novels, they, them*).

Faulty shifts between the second- and the third-person pronouns cause most errors.

shft
15a

INCONSISTENT: When <u>one</u> looks for a loan, <u>you</u> compare the interest rates from several banks. (shift from second to third person)

REVISED: When <u>one</u> looks for a loan, <u>one</u> compares the interest rates from several banks.

REVISED: When <u>you</u> look for a loan, <u>you compare</u> the interest rates from several banks.

REVISED: When a <u>person</u> looks for a loan, <u>he or she</u> compares the interest rates from several banks.

Shifts in number also create inconsistencies within sentences. Make sure that singular pronouns refer to singular antecedents and plural pronouns to plural antecedents (see 23b).

INCONSISTENT: If <u>a person</u> does not study regularly, <u>they</u> will have a difficult time passing organic chemistry. (shift from singular to plural)

REVISED: If <u>a person</u> does not study regularly, <u>he or she</u> will have a difficult time passing organic chemistry.

REVISED: If <u>students</u> do not study regularly, <u>they</u> will have a difficult time passing organic chemistry.

▶
EXERCISE 4

Read the following sentences and eliminate any shifts in tense, voice, mood, person, or number. Some sentences are correct, and some will have more than one possible answer.

1. Gettysburg is a borough of southwestern Pennsylvania where some of the bloodiest fighting of the Civil War occurs in July 1863.
2. Giotto was born near Florence in 1267 and is given credit for the revival of painting in the Renaissance.
3. The early Babylonians divided the circle into 360 parts and the volume of a pyramid could also be calculated by them.
4. During World War II General Motors expanded its production facilities and guns, tanks, and ammunition were made.
5. Diamonds, the only gems that are valuable when colorless, were worn to cure disease and to ward off evil spirits.
6. First, clear the area of weeds, and then you should spread the mulch in a six-inch layer.

7. When one visits the Grand Canyon, you should be sure to notice the fractures and faults on the north side of the Kaibab plateau.

8. For a wine grape, cool weather means a higher acid content and a sour taste; hot weather means they will have lower acid content and a sweet taste.

9. Mary Wollstoncraft wrote *Vindication of the Rights of Women,* and then she wrote *Vindication of the Rights of Men.*

10. When one looks at the angora goat, you should notice it has an abundant undergrowth.

shft

15a

(5) Shifts from direct to indirect discourse

Shifts from direct to indirect discourse can lead to error because they invite illogical tense shifts.

The first sentence below contains an unwarranted shift from indirect discourse to direct discourse. Recording Howells's statement in either the present tense (direct discourse) or the past tense (indirect discourse) eliminates the problem.

> FAULTY: William Dean Howells said that he <u>felt</u> the equality of things and "I <u>believe</u> in the unity of men."

> REVISED: William Dean Howells said that he <u>felt</u> the equality of things and that he <u>believed</u> in the unity of men.

> REVISED: William Dean Howells said, "I <u>feel</u> the equality of things and I <u>believe</u> in the unity of men."

Direct discourse reports the exact words of a speaker or writer. It is always enclosed in quotation marks and is usually accompanied by an identifying tag *(he says, she said).*

> Commenting on his play, Eugene O'Neill said, "The script is written in blood and tears."

When a question is reported directly, the identifying tag includes a verb that indicates asking and a question mark at the end of the sentence.

> Rousseau asked, "Is it not obvious that where we demand everything, we owe nothing?"

Indirect discourse summarizes the words of a speaker or writer. It does not use quotation marks and often introduces the reported statement with the word *that.* As a rule, both pronouns and verb tenses in a reported statement are different from those in a direct statement.

> DIRECT DISCOURSE: My instructor said, "I want your report by this Friday."
>
> INDIRECT DISCOURSE: My instructor said that he wanted my report by this Friday.

Indirect reporting of a question often includes a word like *who, what, why, whether, how,* or *if.* In addition, the pronouns and verb tenses of the original question change, and the question mark at the end of the sentence becomes a period.

shft

15a

> DIRECT QUESTION: The mayor asked, "Do you want to work in my reelection campaign?"
>
> INDIRECT QUESTION: The mayor asked if I wanted to work in his reelection campaign.

When you write research papers, you must often shift from direct to indirect discourse to avoid too many direct quotations (see 37c). But remember, unwarranted shifts in tense can result. Therefore, when preparing research papers, pay attention to the rules that apply to sequence of tenses (see 22f).

▶

EXERCISE 5

Transform the direct discourse in the following sentences into indirect discourse. In addition, put a check mark next to the sentences that seem better when discourse is direct. Be prepared to explain the reasons for your choices, and remember that general truths stay in the present.

> EXAMPLE: John F. Kennedy said, "Ask not what your country can do for you—ask what you can do for your country."
>
> John F. Kennedy said that you should not ask what your country can do for you, but what you can do for your country.

1. Thoreau said, "I went to the woods because I wished to live deliberately."
2. Martin Luther King, Jr., said, "I would be the first to advocate obeying just laws."
3. Steven Muller said, "I see an American society sadly in need of social services."
4. To the psychologist B. F. Skinner, "Cultures are often judged by the extent to which they encourage self-observation."
5. "Why," asked Freud, "does our memory lag behind all our other psychic activities?"

15b Recognizing Mixed Constructions

Mixed constructions occur when you begin a sentence with one grammatical strategy and then switch to another without completing the first. Because the two parts of the sentence are at odds with each other, readers have trouble determining your meaning.

mix
15b

(1) Adverb clauses as subjects

Using an adverb clause as the subject of a sentence results in a mixed construction. You can avoid this problem by recasting the sentence.

> MIXED: Even though he published a paper on the subject does not mean he should get credit for the discovery. (adverb clause used as the subject)

> REVISED: Even though he published a paper on the subject, he should not necessarily get credit for the discovery.

> REVISED: Publishing a paper on the subject does not necessarily give him credit for the discovery.

(2) Objects as apparent subjects

Using an object as if it were the subject of a sentence results in another kind of mixed construction. Often you make this error because the object is actually more important to you than the subject. By using the object as the apparent subject, you cause readers to redirect their attention in the middle of the sentence. You can correct this problem by determining your focus and making it the true subject of the sentence.

> MIXED: The book we found in the antique store, we took it to the museum to be appraised. (object used as the apparent subject)

> REVISED: We took the book we found in the antique store to the museum to be appraised.

> MIXED: People who had tickets, the ushers told them to line up on the right. (object used as apparent subject)

> REVISED: The ushers told people who had tickets to line up on the right.

(3)   Independent clauses as subjects

Still another kind of mixed construction results when you use an independent clause as the subject of a sentence. You can correct this error by recasting the independent clause.

MIXED: <u>The fall of the Roman Empire occurred in the fifth century</u> was what brought the Dark Ages to Europe. (independent clause used as the subject)

REVISED: The fall of the Roman Empire in the fifth century brought the Dark Ages to Europe.

REVISED: Because of the fall of the Roman Empire in the fifth century, the Dark Ages came to Europe.

REVISED: It was the fall of the Roman Empire in the fifth century that brought the Dark Ages to Europe.

15c   Recognizing Faulty Predication

Faulty predication occurs when the meaning of the subject and the predicate of a sentence are not directly related. Faulty predication is especially common in sentences containing a linking verb—a form of the verb *be*, for example—and a subject complement. It usually occurs when you incorrectly equate the subject and the subject complement. For example,

FAULTY: <u>Mounting costs and declining advertising revenue</u> were <u>the demise</u> of *Look* magazine in 1971.

This sentence states incorrectly that mounting costs and declining advertising *were* the demise of the magazine when, in fact, they were the *reasons* for its demise. You can correct this problem by making sure the subject and its complement are sensibly related to each other.

REVISED: <u>Mounting costs and declining advertising revenue</u> were <u>the reasons</u> for the demise of *Look* magazine in 1971.

FAULTY: In the fifteenth century <u>the production</u> of tapestries was <u>Paris</u> and the <u>Low Countries</u> of France.
[The production was not Paris and the Low Countries.]

REVISED: In the fifteenth century the production of tapestries was carried on in Paris and the Low Countries of France.

Faulty predication commonly arises in the following situations.

(1) Intervening words

When words come between the subject and the verb, confusion can result.

> FAULTY: The <u>development</u> of telescopes <u>was made</u> in considerable numbers and <u>was found</u> throughout Europe soon after their invention.
> *(Telescopes, not <u>development</u>, were made and found.)*

> REVISED: Telescopes were made in considerable numbers and were found throughout Europe soon after their invention.

> FAULTY: The <u>purpose</u> of Napoleon's campaign <u>failed</u> because of the Russian winter.
> *(The <u>campaign</u>, not the <u>purpose</u>, failed.)*

> REVISED: Napoleon's campaign failed because of the Russian winter.

> REVISED: The purpose of Napoleon's campaign was thwarted by the Russian winter.

pred
15c

(2) *When* or *where* clauses

Faulty predication can occur in definitions that begin with *when* or *where* clauses and that contain the verb *be*. These sentences need a noun or a noun phrase as both the subject and the subject complement.

> FAULTY: <u>Taxidermy</u> is <u>where you construct</u> a lifelike representation of an animal using its preserved skin.
> *(In definitions* be *must be preceded and followed by nouns or noun phrases.)*

> REVISED: Taxidermy is the construction of a lifelike representation of an animal by using its preserved skin.

> REVISED: With taxidermy you construct a lifelike representation of an animal by using its preserved skin.

(3) Faulty appositives

A faulty appositive is a type of faulty predication in which two words or word groups are incorrectly equated. A form of the verb *be* has been eliminated.

> FAULTY: The salaries are high in professional athletics, such as football players.
> *(<u>Professional athletics</u> is not the same as <u>football players</u>.)*

REVISED: The salaries are high for professional athletes, such as football players.

REVISED: Professional athletes, such as football players, receive high salaries.

▶
EXERCISE 6

Revise the following sentences so that their parts fit together grammatically and logically. Keep in mind that each sentence has more than one correct format.

1. The war that George III fought, he said it was a bloody and expensive war.
2. By trying to find a short route to India was how Columbus discovered the New World.
3. Copernicus thought that just because Ptolemy said that the world was flat did not make it so.
4. The troops that advanced on Carthage, Scipio Africanus urged them to fight for the glory of Rome.
5. The first printing press had movable type was what made it revolutionary.
6. Depression is where a person has a mood of hopelessness and a feeling of inadequacy.
7. A block and tackle attached to the second floor window would be the obvious place to move the piano.
8. Competition is fierce among athletes, such as fencing and water polo.
9. Because of a defect in design is why the roof of the stadium collapsed.
10. Joseph Lister proved that one of the best germ killers is by coating a wound with carbolic acid.

Student Writer at Work: Shifts and Mixed Constructions

Following is an excerpt from a rough draft of a student's research paper. The information in this paper comes from Irving Howe's book *World of Our Fathers* and concerns a fire that contributed to the creation of better fire safety codes. Read the paragraphs, and correct any mixed constructions, faulty predications, or grammatical shifts that you find.

On March 2, 1911, a terrible fire broke out in the ten-story
Asch Building near Washington Square in New York City. The
fire begins with a cigarette or a spark in a rag bin. Although
the people inside the building tried dousing the flames, efforts
are useless due to the rotted hoses and rusted water valves.

The workers on the ninth floor found to their dismay that
the fire exit doors were locked. People jumped from the windows to avoid the intense fire that swept through the building.
Many people were killed, but miraculously, some survived. Although the effort to escape the fire lasted only eighteen minutes
was what left 146 workers dead. After the tragedy an investigation was carried out to determine the causes of the fire (Howe
304).

**pred
15**

The list of causes of the fire is numerous and terrible.
According to the investigating committee, only one fire escape is
visible from Green Street. It collapsed after fewer than twenty
people escaped. In addition, although sprinkler systems were
invented in 1895, none were present in the Asch building because they were considered too expensive.

Records show that six months before the fire, the building
was cited as a firetrap by the city. The owners were supposed
to make alterations was what the report said. Failure to have
regular fire drills and a lack of clearly marked fire exits are
what caused people not to escape.

Although it was 4:30 p.m. on a Saturday when the fire
broke out meant there were 650 workers in the building, the
majority of whom were women who were forced to work because there was a back-up in production. Ironically, the back-up
was caused by a strike by some workers who want better working conditions.

Another factor that added to the problems during the fire
was that there was no single language spoken by the women
such as Italian or Yiddish. Under ordinary working conditions,
many of the workers had trouble communicating with each
other. In the middle of a fire that spreads panic and confusion,

the situation was even worse. Eyewitnesses describe the fire as spreading chaos and panic. Adding to the confusion was the fact that many of the workers screamed frantically in their native languages (Howe 304).

The investigation never pointed a finger at one particular person or group who took the blame for this disaster. The results of the fire, however, were very encouraging to factory workers. The Ladies Garment Workers Union is established to protect workers from poor working conditions. Fire codes are regulated and carefully watched, and smoking is prohibited in factories. And finally, fire drills, emergency exits, fire escapes, and sprinkler systems are mandatory in all buildings housing workers (Howe 305).

pred
15

SECTION

Using Words Effectively

Choosing Words

Diction refers to word choice, especially with regard to appropriateness, accuracy, and freshness. But this definition does not capture the complexity of choosing the right word. Unfortunately, no clear rule exists for distinguishing the right word from the wrong one. The same word may be fine in one situation and inappropriate in another.

An added difficulty is that many words in English express the same or almost the same idea. The following words, for instance, all denote clothing.

clothing	array
clothes	raiment
apparel	garb
wear	vestments
dress	togs
attire	duds

But these words do not all mean the same thing. Fine stores sell *apparel,* while most other stores sell *clothing* or *clothes.* Prophets in the Bible wear *raiment,* peasants wear *garb,* bridegrooms wear *attire,* children wear *togs,* priests wear *vestments,* and cowboys wear *duds.*

Choosing the right word is difficult. This chapter aims to acquaint you with the subtleties of language and to help you express yourself precisely and originally.

16a   Choosing Appropriate Words

A word is *appropriate* if it suits the audience, occasion, and purpose for which it is intended.

(1)   Adjusting diction for audience and occasion

Different audiences and occasions call for different *levels* of diction. You would think it odd, for example, if your history textbook said that Julius Caesar was the *guy* who ruled Rome, even though *man* and *guy* essentially mean the same thing. When you know who your readers are and what they expect, you can determine whether your level of diction should be *formal, informal,* or *popular.*

Formal Diction

When decorum is in order—in eulogies and other addresses, scholarly articles, formal reports, and some essays—readers expect **formal** or **learned diction.** Formal discourse uses words familiar to an educated audience: *impoverished* rather than *poor, wealthy* or *affluent* rather than *rich, intelligent* rather than *smart, automobile* rather than *car.* Contractions, shortened word forms, and utility words like *nice* (see 9a.2) generally do not appear in formal diction.

Formal English is nevertheless often quite simple. Its major characteristic is grammatical precision. In addition, the writer often remains a neutral observer, using the impersonal *one* or the collective *we* rather than the more personal *I* and *you.*

The following passage from John F. Kennedy's inaugural address illustrates these characteristics.

> The world is very different now. For man holds in his mortal hands the power to abolish all forms of human poverty and all forms of human life. And yet the same revolutionary beliefs for which our forebears fought are still at issue around the globe—the belief that the rights of man come not from the generosity of the state but from the hand of God.
>
> We dare not forget today that we are the heirs of that first revolution. Let the word go forth from this time and place, to friend and foe alike, that the torch has been passed to a new generation of Americans—born in this century, tempered by war, disciplined by a hard and bitter peace, proud of our ancient heritage, and unwilling to witness or permit the slow undoing of those human rights to which this nation has always been committed, and to which we are committed today at home and around the world.

Although formal, the diction is eloquent, graceful, and clear. Word choice remains on a level that fits the occasion, with no shortened forms or colloquialisms.

Academics frequently use formal diction, as the psychologist B. F. Skinner does in the following paragraph.

> We learn to perceive in the sense that we learn to respond to things in particular ways because of the contingencies of which they are a part. We may perceive the sun, for example, simply because it is an extremely powerful stimulus, but it has been a permanent part of the environment of the species throughout its evolution and more specific behavior with respect to it could have been selected by contingencies of survival (as it has been in many other species). The sun also figures in many current contingencies of reinforcement: we move into or out of sunlight depending on the temperature; we wait for the sun to rise or set to take practical action; we talk about the sun and its effects; and we eventually study the sun with the instruments and methods of science. Our perception of the sun depends on what we do with respect to it. Whatever we do, and hence however we perceive it, the fact remains that it is the environment which acts upon the perceiving person, not the perceiving person who acts upon the environment. (B. F. Skinner, *Beyond Freedom and Dignity*)

wds
16a

Expecting his audience to be familiar with his terminology, Skinner uses such phrases as *powerful stimulus, contingencies of survival,* and *contingencies of reinforcement* for precision. He does not use the personal *I* and *you,* preferring the collective *we* and *our* ("Our perception of the sun depends on what we do with respect to it").

Informal Diction

Informal diction is the language that people use daily in conversation. It includes *colloquialisms, slang, regionalisms,* and occasionally *nonstandard language.* Much good writing makes use of informal diction. In your college writing, however, treat it with great care, limiting its use to imitating speech or dialect or to giving an essay a conversational tone.

COLLOQUIALISMS Whereas formal diction is primarily a language of writing, **colloquial diction** occurs most often in everyday speech. We use it when we are not necessarily concentrating on being grammatically correct, and it is perfectly acceptable in informal situations, where formal diction would be out of place.

Contractions—*isn't, won't, I'm,* and *he'd*—are typical colloquialisms, as are shortened word forms—*phone* for *telephone, TV* for *television, dorm* for *dormitory,* and *exam* for *examination,* for instance. Other colloquialisms include the placeholders *you know, sort of, kind of,* and *I mean* and the utility words *nice* for good or *acceptable*, *funny* for *odd*, and *great* meaning almost anything. Colloquial English also includes combined verbs—*get across* for *communicate*, *come up with* for *find*, and *check out* for *investigate*.

In the following passage from J. D. Salinger's novel *The Catcher in the Rye*, the narrator, Holden Caulfield, uses colloquial diction.

> The book I was reading was this book I took out of the library by mistake. They gave me the wrong book, and I didn't notice it till I got back to my room. They gave me *Out of Africa*, by Isak Dinesen. I thought it was going to stink, but it didn't. It was a very good book. I'm quite illiterate, but I read a lot. My favorite author is my brother D.B., and my next favorite is Ring Lardner.

SLANG **Slang** words are extremely informal. Whether inventions or existing words redefined, they emerge to meet a need. Words like *high, spaced out, dove, hawk, hippie, uptight, groovy, rap, heavy, be-in, happening*, and *rip off* emerged in the 1960's as part of the counterculture surrounding rock music, drugs, and the protest against our involvement in Vietnam. During the 1970's, technology, music, politics, and feminism influenced slang, giving us words and phrases like *input, feedback, disco, stonewalling, Watergate, nuke, burn-out, macho, sexist*, and *male chauvinism*. The 1980's have contributed *Valley talk*, a phenomenon that began in California and quickly spread to other parts of the country, yielding words and expressions like *for sure, tubular, awesome, grody*, and *gag me with a spoon*.

Slang varies with time and place, becomes dated quickly, and fades into disuse. (Consider *beatnik, daddy-o*, and *hepcat*.) You should therefore use it in college writing only when imitating speech or dialect.

REGIONALISMS Some words and expressions that are commonly used in certain geographical areas are not necessarily understood by a general audience. **Regionalisms** include words like *overshoe, fried cake*, and *angledog* and expressions like *take sick* and *come down with a cold*. They also include old forms that have lost their meanings outside a particular area. For example, in Lancaster, Pennsylvania, which has a large Amish population, it is not unusual to hear an elderly person saying *darest* for *dare not* or *daresome* for *adventurous*, expressions that would not be readily understood elsewhere.

In the following passage William Faulkner uses regionalisms of the American South to add color to his writing.

> "It's fixing up to rain," Pa says. "I am a luckless man. I have ever been." He rubs his hands on his knees. "It's that durn doctor, liable to come at any time. I couldn't get word to him till so late. If he was to come tomorrow and tell her the time was nigh, she wouldn't wait." (William Faulkner, *As I Lay Dying*)

Regionalisms can make your writing more vivid. But because they are an informal use of language and often have little meaning to an audience not familiar with a particular region's dialect, use them with care when you address a general audience.

wds 16a

NONSTANDARD LANGUAGE **Nonstandard** (or **substandard**) refers to words that are not generally considered a part of standard English, even though many individuals use them when speaking. Included are words like *ain't, nohow, anywheres, nowheres, hisself,* and *wait on* (instead of *wait for*).

Keep in mind that no absolute rules distinguish standard and nonstandard usage. At present this issue is hotly debated by people concerned with language. Dictionaries and handbooks can at best only attempt to define the norms of language (see 17d.9). In the end, you will have to supplement the guidelines that these books provide with your own assessment of your audience and purpose to determine what is acceptable usage in a particular writing situation.

Popular Diction

Popular diction is the language of mass-audience magazines, newspapers, best sellers, and editorials. Conversational in tone, popular diction falls somewhere between formal and informal English. It does not employ words as precisely as formal English, often relying on colloquialisms, contractions, and the first person. Even so, it generally uses correct grammar and generally avoids slang and nonstandard language.

This passage from *Esquire* illustrates many of these characteristics.

> Decade after decade of mediocre Disney films triumphed and stoked our sensibilities because the art itself, animation, is such a delight. It has been right from the start. In 1928, when Mickey Mouse as Steamboat Willie joins prototype Minne to crank up a

goat's tail in order to see musical notes leave the beast's mouth and dance to the tune of "Turkey in the Straw," the magic is already in full bloom. When Dumbo's ears flap and the ungainly mass finally soars, nobody cares where he's going. We love this creature; indeed we fall for Disney the way we fall in love: what the eye sees is more important than what the eye judges. (Max Apple, "Uncle Walt")

wds
16a

The personal pronouns *we* and *our,* the contraction *he's,* and the colloquial expressions *in full bloom, crank up,* and *fall for* give this piece a relaxed, conversational tone. However, the author also uses relatively formal words like *decade, prototype,* and *indeed* to give a general impression of Disney's work, not to carry out a precise analysis of the films or their meaning.

College Writing

The level of diction appropriate for college writing varies between formal and popular diction, depending on your assignment and your audience. A personal experience essay calls for a natural sound, but a research paper, an examination, or a report calls for a more formal vocabulary and an impersonal tone.

The following passage illustrates the level of diction typical of much college writing.

Deaf students face many problems. Their needs are greater than those of other students. Often rejected, deaf students develop a severe inferiority complex. Their inability to mix in a large group is a partial cause of this problem. Because deaf students communicate by sign language or by lip reading, they usually interact on a one-to-one basis. It is not at all unusual for deaf students to be in a classroom and not even realize that someone in the class is speaking. Other problems occur when people in the class find out that a person has a hearing problem. Often, in an effort to try to help, people begin exaggerating their lip movements. This exaggerated lip movement, called "mouthing," makes it impossible for many deaf students to read lips. For this reason, many deaf students find it better to conceal a hearing impairment than to disclose it.

This passage uses no nonstandard language or technical terminology. Its aim is to instruct a well-educated audience. Despite the occasional use of formal diction, the paragraph moves easily and conversationally.

▶
EXERCISE 1

This paragraph, from Sherwood Anderson's short story "I'm a Fool," is characterized by informal diction. As the speech of a young boy, it is laced with slang and grammatical inaccuracies. Underline the words that identify the diction of this paragraph as informal. Then rewrite the paragraph, using popular diction.

> You know how it is. Gee, she was a peach! She had on a soft dress, kind of a blue stuff and it looked carelessly made, but was well sewed and made and everything. I knew that much. I blushed when she looked right at me and so did she. She was the nicest girl I have ever seen in my life. She wasn't stuck on herself and she could talk proper grammar without being a school teacher or something like that. What I mean is, she was O.K. I think maybe her father was well-to-do, but not rich to make her chesty because she was his daughter, as some are. Maybe he owned a drug store or a drygoods store in their hometown or something like that. She never told me and I never asked.

wds
16a

▶
EXERCISE 2

After reading the following paragraphs, underline the words and phrases that identify each as formal diction. Then choose one of these paragraphs and rewrite it using a level of diction that you would use in your college writing. Use a dictionary if necessary.

> In looking at many small points of difference between species, which, as far as our ignorance permits us to judge, seem quite unimportant, we must not forget that climate, food, etc., have no doubt produced some direct effect. It is also necessary to bear in mind, that owing to the law of correlation, when one part varies and the variations are accumulated through natural selection, other modifications, often of the most unexpected nature, will ensue. (Charles Darwin, *The Origin of Species*)

> I hope you are able to see the distinction I am trying to point out. In no sense do I advocate evading or defying the law, as would the rabid segregationist. That would lead to anarchy. One who breaks an unjust law must do so openly, lovingly, and with a willingness to accept the penalty. I submit that an individual who breaks a law that conscience tells him is unjust, and who willingly accepts the penalty of imprisonment in order to arouse the conscience of the community over its injustice, is in reality expressing the highest respect for law. (Martin Luther King, Jr., "Letter from Birmingham Jail")

An artist, then, expresses feeling, but not in the way a . . .
baby laughs and cries. He formulates that elusive aspect of reality
that is commonly taken to be amorphous and chaotic; that is, he
objectifies the subjective realm. What he expresses is, therefore,
not his own actual feelings, but what he knows about human feeling. Once he is in possession of a rich symbolism, that knowledge
may actually exceed his entire personal experience. A work of art
expresses a conception of life, emotion, inward reality. But it is
neither a confessional nor a frozen tantrum; it is a developed metaphor, a nondiscursive symbol that articulates what is verbally
ineffable—the logic of consciousness itself. (Susanne K. Langer,
Problems of Art)

**wds
16a**

(2)   Selecting diction appropriate to purpose

Your purpose in writing determines the kinds of words you use.
If your purpose is primarily to convey *information*, your words
will be predominantly referential—that is, they will refer to what
you are discussing. If your purpose is to convey your *personal
feelings*, your words will be predominantly expressive. If your
purpose is to *persuade*, you will choose words that will help you
elicit a specific action or response from a reader.

Naturally, your aims overlap. An informative article in a scientific journal, for example, may contain some persuasive or personal phrases. For the sake of clarity, however, we discuss each
type of diction individually.

Informative Writing

Informative writing—the kind that appears in journals,
magazines, newspapers, textbooks, and examinations—conveys
information to its readers. For the most part, it is factual and
avoids words with emotional associations. It often relies on the
third-person pronoun instead of using *I* or *we*. Here is a good
example from a student paper.

One method of disposing of nuclear wastes is to store them in
air-cooled vaults. Most vaults of this type are large reinforced concrete buildings that are cooled by natural convection. An air-
cooled vault requires at least 10,000 square feet of space to hold
nuclear waste discharged from an atomic power plant. Spent fuel
is packaged in lead containers and stored in compartments within
the vault. Air flows through vents that line the inside of the cham-
ber, keeping the vault at a constant temperature. A single air-

cooled vault can store approximately 28.2 million pounds of spent fuel. This method of storage has two major drawbacks. First, it requires a large amount of space, and second, it costs $103 for each kilogram of fuel stored.

In this straightforward description of the storage vault, the writer conveys facts about nuclear storage and evaluates the usefulness of the air-cooled vault without relying on technical terminology.

Personal Writing

Personal writing—the kind found in diaries, journals, letters, and personal experience essays—expresses the feelings of the writer. It uses language that is emotive, explicitly or by association; relies on the personal *I* and *we;* and contains informal language, although it can also be formal, as in some autobiographies and confessionals. The following paragraph is a good example.

wds
16a

> *March 4.*   When will it all end? The idiocy and the tension, the dying of young men, the destruction of homes, of cities, starvation, exhaustion, disease, children parentless and lost, cages full of shivering, staring prisoners, long lines of hopeless civilians plodding through mud, the endless pounding of the battle line. I can scarcely remember what it is like to be where explosions are not going off around me, some hostile, some friendly, all horrible; an exploding shell is a terrible sound. What keeps this war going, now that its end is so clear? What do the Germans think of us, and we of them? I do not think we think of them at all, or much. Do they think of us? I can think of their weapons, their shells, their machine guns, but not of the men behind them. I do not feel as if I were fighting against men, but against machines. (Donald Pearce, *Journal of a War*)

This writer's major concern is to express his frustration about World War II, as indicated by his choice of words: *idiocy, hopeless, endless*, and so on. Many of the words and phrases evoke emotional images, and the use of *I* emphasizes the paragraph's subjectivity.

Persuasive Writing

The purpose of persuasive writing—the kind that appears in political tracts, advertising, editorials, and legal briefs—is to convince someone to do something or to accept something. Words and phrases that reinforce the progression of an argu-

ment—*furthermore, consequently, accordingly,* and *therefore*—
often appear. Persuasive essays use either the first person *I* or *we,*
or the more formal third person *he, she, they,* or *one.* Persuasive
writing may employ technical or other specialized terms to convince an audience of the validity of an assertion. Here is an example of persuasive writing.

> Students at this college wonder just how long they will have
> to put up with the dreadful conditions that exist in the cafeteria.
> The food is often overcooked and tasteless, and the facilities are
> always cramped and dirty. Even more important is that the cafete-
> ria's hours do not correspond to the needs of the students. For the
> past year the cafeteria has served lunch from eleven to one-thirty.
> A recent study conducted by this paper revealed that almost
> thirty-seven percent of all students have classes straight through
> this time period. As a result, these students must miss lunch en-
> tirely or eat "on the run." Accordingly, most students interviewed
> voiced the hope that the cafeteria would serve light snacks and
> sandwiches all afternoon. So far, neither the management of the
> cafeteria nor the administration has responded to these concerns.

**wds
16a**

This editorial uses words and phrases that both emphasize the
structure of the argument and clearly indicate value judgments.

▶
EXERCISE 3

Identify the major purpose of each of the following paragraphs. Underline the words and phrases that help you make your determination.

> At home in Moscow the winter routine was already established;
> the stoves were heated, and in the morning it was still dark when the
> children were having breakfast and getting ready for school, and the
> nurse would light the lamp for a short time. There were frosts already.
> When the first snow falls, on the first day the sleighs are out, it is pleas-
> ant to see the white earth, the white roofs; one draws easy, delicious
> breaths, and the season brings back the days of one's youth. The old
> limes and birches, white with hoar-frost, have a good-natured look; they
> are closer to one's heart than cypresses and palms, and near them one
> no longer wants to think of mountains and the sea. (Anton Chekhov, "The
> Lady with a Pet Dog")

> There also was more than a hint of unseen mass in the finding last
> year by the High Energy Astronomical Observatory that an invisible ring
> of superheated gas circled the constellation Northern Cross like a halo.
> The halo extends 72 quadrillion miles. Its temperature is 3.5 million
> degrees, hot enough to create out of the gas in the halo as many as

10,000 new stars. Carrying powerful X-ray telescopes, HEAO was able to map 90 percent of the halo, which is invisible in space to any but an X-ray telescope. The halo is so hot that its light is paler than the sun's corona; surrounding bright stars and the background light of the galaxy are sufficient to wash out its light by the time it reaches Earth. (Thomas O'Toole, "Will the Universe Die by Fire or Ice?")

Why did I write it down? In order to remember, of course, but exactly what was it I wanted to remember? How much of it actually happened? Did any of it? Why do I keep a notebook at all? It is easy to deceive oneself on all those scores. The impulse to write things down is a peculiarly compulsive one, inexplicable to those who do not share it, useful only accidentally, only secondarily, in the way that any compulsion tries to justify itself. I suppose that it begins or does not begin in the cradle. Although I have felt compelled to write things down since I was five years old, I doubt that my daughter ever will, for she is a singularly blessed and accepting child, delighted with life exactly as life presents itself to her, unafraid to go to sleep and unafraid to wake up. (Joan Didion, *Slouching Toward Bethlehem*)

College, then, may be a good place for those few young people who are really drawn to academic work, who would rather read than eat, but it has become too expensive, in money, time, and intellectual effort to serve as a holding pen for large numbers of our young. We ought to make it possible for those reluctant, unhappy students to find alternative ways of growing up, and more realistic preparation for the years ahead. (Caroline Bird, *The Case Against College*)

wds
16b

16b Using Accurate Words

According to Mark Twain, the difference between the right word and almost the right word is the difference between the lightning and the lightning bug. If you use the wrong words—or even *almost* the right ones—you will confuse your readers. So when you write, be careful to choose just the *right* ones.

(1) Clarifying denotation and connotation

Understanding a word's denotations and connotations is the first step toward effective diction. A word's **denotation** is its explicit meaning, what it stands for without any emotional associations. For example, you make an error in denotation when you say that the jury members should be *uninterested,* when you actually mean *disinterested. Uninterested* means "bored" or "lacking interest" while *disinterested* means "impartial." (For other commonly confused words, see the Glossary of Usage.) If you say *molecule* when you mean *atom*, or *compound* when you mean *mixture*, you confuse the things that the two words refer to—another kind of error in denotation.

More common than errors in denotation, however, are errors in **connotation**—the emotional associations that surround a word. A dictionary can suggest some of these connotations, but only experience and familiarity with language can give you the ability to use them effectively (see 17d.6).

wds
16b

Connotations suggest *feelings*, *attitudes*, *opinions*, and *desires*. The word *group*, for instance, is neutral; *gathering* suggests orderliness; and *mob* brings to mind unruliness, even danger. To say "The *mob* listened to the mayor" suggests that the mayor faced an angry group of people.

Slang or colloquialisms can give an unintended connotation to a sentence. The sentence "In school we *mess around* with computers" gives the impression that your involvement with computers is not serious or important. If indeed your involvement *is* serious, it would be far better to say that in school you *work* with computers.

Errors in connotation generally result from carelessness, from not taking the time to think about a word's associations. If you have any doubt about the connotation of a word, look it up in your dictionary to see if that connotation is labeled as favorable or unfavorable. If you are still not certain, ask your instructor or use a word whose connotation you are certain of.

▶

EXERCISE 4

The following words have negative connotations. For each, list one word with a similar meaning whose connotation is neutral and another whose connotation is favorable.

EXAMPLE: *Negative*   skinny
Neutral   thin
Favorable   slender

1. deceive
2. antiquated
3. egghead
4. pathetic
5. cheap
6. blunder
7. argumentative
8. politician
9. shack
10. stench

▶
EXERCISE 5

Think of a vacation you took. First, write a one-paragraph description that would discourage anyone from taking the same vacation. Next, re-write this paragraph, describing your vacation favorably. Finally, rewrite your paragraph using neutral words that convey no judgments. In all three versions of your paragraph, underline the words that helped you to convey your impressions to your readers.

(2) Avoiding euphemisms

A **euphemism** is a positive or neutral word or phrase used in place of a word or phrase that describes a subject that society considers unmentionable. In the Victorian era, for instance, direct reference to the body and its functions was disdained. Consequently, table supports were delicately referred to as *limbs*, and to avoid saying *leg* and *breast*, people referred to the meat of a turkey as *dark* or *light*.

wds **16b**

People still avoid discussing a number of subjects, such as bodily functions, death, and certain social problems. Thus, *toilets* are *restrooms, lounges, bathrooms,* or *powder rooms.* The word *toilet* itself is a euphemism for *dressing* or *shaving.* We say that the dead have *passed on, gone to their reward,* or *departed,* and we call graveyards *resting places* or *memorial parks.* We refer to *divorce* as *marital dissolution, adultery* as an *affair,* the *elderly* as *senior citizens,* the *poor* as *deprived,* and *retarded children* as *exceptional children.*

Euphemisms are even more prevalent in business and government. *Used cars* are *preowned automobiles,* and *corporate takeovers* are *mergers* or *marriages. Garbage collectors* are called *sanitation engineers* and *barbers, hair stylists.* Government facilities are *relocated,* not *closed,* and budget deficits are called *negative growth.*

College writing is no place for such coyness. Say what you mean—*pregnant* not *expecting, died* not *passed away,* and *strike* not *work stoppage.*

(3) Avoiding offensive language

Racial and ethnic slurs, sexist rhetoric, and obscenities are all truly offensive. Avoid the use of such language in your writing.

Avoiding Racial, Ethnic, and Religious Slurs

When referring to any racial, ethnic, or religious group, use words with neutral connotations or words that the groups use *formally* to refer to themselves. The derogatory terms with which we are all too familiar are unacceptable in your writing.

Racial, ethnic, and religious stereotypes are also offensive. Avoid biased generalizations that brand certain groups as stupid, pushy, or tight with money, for instance. Such generalizations are rooted in prejudice and are always inaccurate.

**wds
16b**

Avoiding Sexism

Sexist language is insulting to both men and women. It entails much more than the use of derogatory words like *broads* and *chicks*. Assuming that some professions are exclusive to one sex—that, for instance, *nurse* denotes only women and *doctor* denotes only men—is also sexist. So is the use of job titles like *postman* for *letter carrier*, *fireman* for *fire fighter*, and *policeman* for *police officer*. Habits of thought and language change slowly, but they do change.

Sexist language also results when a writer fails to use the same terminology when referring to men and women. For example, you should not refer to two scientists with Ph.D.s as Dr. Sagan and Mrs. Yallow, but as Dr. Sagan and Dr. Yallow. You should refer to two writers as James and Wharton, not Henry James and Mrs. Wharton.

In your writing, always use *women*—not *girls*—when referring to adult females. Similarly, use *Ms.* as the form of address when a woman's marital status is unknown or irrelevant. If the woman you are addressing refers to herself as Mrs. or Miss, however, then you should use the form of address she prefers. Finally, avoid using the generic *he* or *him* when your subject could be either male or female. Use the third-person plural or the phrase *he or she* when possible (not *he/she*).

TRADITIONAL: Before boarding, each passenger should make certain that <u>he</u> has <u>his</u> ticket.

REVISED: Before boarding, <u>passengers</u> should make certain that <u>they</u> have <u>their</u> tickets.

REVISED: Before boarding, each <u>passenger</u> should make certain that <u>he or she</u> has a ticket.

Be careful, however, not to create ungrammatical constructions like the following.

> UNGRAMMATICAL: Before boarding, each <u>passenger</u> should be certain that <u>they</u> have <u>their</u> tickets.

Avoiding Obscenities

The freedom to use obscene language when writing is *not* one of the characteristics that distinguishes college students from high school students. An X-rated paper does not establish your sophistication. It does reveal an eagerness to shock and a lack of respect for your audience.

wds
16b

(4)   Selecting specific or general words

Specific words signify particular examples of persons, things, or events, while **general** words signify an entire class or group. *Queen Elizabeth II*, for example, is more specific than *monarch*; *topcoat* is more specific than *clothes*; and *Corvette* is more specific than *automobile*. General words are, of course, useful. Statements that use general words to describe entire classes of things or events are often necessary to convey a point. But such statements must also include specific words for support and clarity.

Using general words when specific words are needed results in vagueness. If you want your readers to visualize a certain building—say, the new wing of the National Gallery in Washington, D.C.—it is not enough to say that it has "an unusual shape." If you want your audience to "see" Picasso's *Guernica*, you must do more than note its "interesting imagery" and "vivid colors." What imagery? What colors? What else can you say about it? You must use specific words to convey information to your readers whenever you can.

Whether a word is general or specific is relative, determined by its relationship to other words. The following word chains illustrate increasing specificity, with the word farthest to the left denoting a general category or class and the one farthest to the right, a specific, tangible member of that class.

> History—American history—Civil War history—History 263
> Apparel—accessory—tie—bow tie
> Human being—official—president—Thomas Jefferson
> Reading matter—book—nonfiction book—*The Fate of the Earth*
> Machine—vehicle—train—bullet train

The more specific your choice of words, the more vivid your writing will be.

The essayist E. B. White uses specific diction in this paragraph.

> Most of the time she simply rode in a standing position, well aft of the beast, her hands hanging easily at her sides, her head erect, her straw-colored ponytail lightly brushing her shoulders, the blood of exertion showing faintly through the tan of her skin. Twice she managed a one-foot stance—a sort of ballet pose, with arms outstretched. At one point the neck strap of her bathing suit broke and she went twice around the ring in the classic attitude of a woman making minor repairs to a garment. The fact that she was standing on the back of a moving horse while doing this invested the matter with a clownish significance that perfectly fitted the spirit of the circus—jocund, yet charming. She just rolled the strap into a neat ball and stowed it inside her bodice while the horse rocked and rolled beneath her in dutiful innocence. The bathing suit proved as self-reliant as its owner and stood up well enough without benefit of strap. (E. B. White, *Points of My Compass*)

White selects specific words and phrases calculated to bring into focus his experience of the young woman and her actions. Here is how the paragraph would read if White had used general words to tell his story.

> Most of the time she rode in a standing position with her hands down at her sides. Twice she managed an off stance. At one point an article of her clothing broke, but she managed to solve the problem and continued to ride.

(5)   Selecting concrete or abstract words

Abstract words—*beauty, truth, justice,* and so on—refer to ideas, qualities, or conditions that cannot be perceived by the senses. **Concrete** words, on the other hand, convey a vivid picture by naming things that readers can *see, hear, taste, smell,* or *touch.* Concrete words are specific: they get your point across. Abstract words are often too general to communicate much about real things.

Abstract	*Concrete*
The ocean was beautiful.	The wind blew across the ocean and whipped it into white, frothy peaks.

The mountain was awesome.	The mountain seemed to dominate the landscape, with the ragged outcroppings in stark contrast to the green valley below.
The man looked happy.	The corners of his mouth turned up into a wide grin.

Of course, as with general and specific words, whether a word is abstract or concrete is relative. The more concrete your words and phrases, the more vivid the image you evoke in the reader.

In the following paragraph, Annie Dillard uses concrete diction to create a vivid picture.

wds 16b

> Where Tinker Creek flows under the sycamore log bridge to the tear-shaped island, it is slow and shallow, fringed thinly in cattail marsh. At this spot an astonishing bloom of life supports vast breeding populations of insects, fish, reptiles, birds, and mammals. On windless summer evenings I stalk along the creek bank or straddle the sycamore log in absolute stillness, watching for muskrats. The night I stayed too late I was hunched on the log staring spellbound at spreading, reflected stains of lilac on the water. A cloud in the sky suddenly lighted as if turned on by a switch; its reflection just as suddenly materialized on the water upstream, flat and floating, so that I couldn't see the creek bottom, or life in the water under the cloud. Downstream, away from the cloud on the water, water turtles smooth as beans were gliding down with the current in a series of easy, weightless push-offs, as men bound on the moon. I didn't know whether to trace the progress of one turtle I was sure of, risking sticking my face in one of the bridge's spider webs made invisible by the gathering dark, or take a chance on seeing the carp, or scan the mudbank in hope of seeing a muskrat, or follow the last of the swallows who caught at my heart and trailed it after them like streamers as they appeared from directly below, under the log flung upstream with their tails forked, so fast. (Annie Dillard, *Pilgrim at Tinker Creek*)

Because Dillard uses strong, sharp sensory details, reading this passage is like seeing a color photograph of the scene.

We need abstract words to discuss concepts. The works of many great writers concentrate on abstractions such as *truth*, *faith*, and *beauty*. But because such terms provide no tangible details, they can create problems for student writers, who often use them—without concrete supporting detail—as a cover for fuzzy, inexact thinking.

Good writing usually describes the abstract with concrete details. In the following paragraph the overuse of abstract words does not conceal the lack of concrete detail.

> Too
> ABSTRACT: *The Balzac Monument* is Rodin's most daring creation. The figure is unusual. Balzac is wrapped in a cloak in an interesting way. He has an unusual expression on his face.

wds
16b

Why is the figure of Balzac unusual? What is interesting about the way the cloak wraps the figure? What is the unusual expression on Balzac's face? When concrete words replace abstract words, the passage is much more informative.

> MORE
> CONCRETE: *The Balzac Monument* is Rodin's most daring creation. The figure is large and resembles a ghost or specter. Balzac seems to tower above us so that from a distance we see only his great size. Upon closer inspection we see that Balzac is wrapped in a cloak. From the indistinct lines of the cloak, Balzac's head emerges godlike, with eyes that stare off into the distance.

Vague diction often results when you use *utility words*— abstract terms like *nice, great,* and *terrific*—that say nothing and could be used in almost any sentence (see 9a.2). These words indicate only enthusiasm. Replace them with more concrete words.

> VAGUE: The movie was <u>nice</u>.

> BETTER: The movie was <u>entertaining</u>.

▶

EXERCISE 6

Good writing usually mixes specific and general words and abstract and concrete words. Read the following passage and underline words that are specific and concrete. How do they make the paragraph more effective? Are any general and abstract words used? How do they function? What impression does the writer want to convey?

> Near the end of March, 1845, I borrowed an axe and went down to the woods by Walden Pond, nearest to where I intended to build my house, and began to cut down some tall arrowy white pines, still in their youth, for timber. It is difficult to begin without borrowing, but perhaps it is the most generous course thus to

permit your fellowmen to have an interest in your enterprise. The owner of the axe, as he released his hold on it, said that it was the apple of his eye; but I returned it sharper than I received it. It was a pleasant hillside where I worked, covered with pine woods, through which I looked out on the pond, and a small open field in the woods where pines and hickories were springing up. The ice in the pond was not yet dissolved, though there were some open spaces, and it was all dark colored and saturated with water. There were some slight flurries of snow during the days that I worked there; but for the most part when I came out on to the railroad, on my way home, its yellow sand heap stretched away gleaming in the hazy atmosphere, and the rails shone in the spring sun, and I heard the lark and pewee and other birds already come to commence another year with us. They were pleasant spring days, in which the winter of man's discontent was thawing as well as the earth, and the life that had lain torpid began to stretch itself. (Henry David Thoreau, *Walden*)

**wds
16c**

▶
EXERCISE 7

Revise this paragraph from a job application by substituting specific, concrete language for general or abstract words and phrases.

I have had several part-time jobs lately. Some of them would qualify me for the position you advertised. In my most recent job, I sold products in a store. My supervisor said I was a good worker who possessed a number of valuable qualities. I am used to dealing with different types of people in different types of settings. I feel that my qualifications would make me a good candidate for your job.

16c Using Fresh Language

Use fresh language when you write by choosing words that are original, vivid, and interesting and avoiding *jargon, neologisms, clichés,* and *pretentious diction,* which deaden writing and leave your meaning unclear.

(1) Avoiding jargon

Jargon refers to the specialized or technical vocabulary of a trade, profession, or academic discipline. Jargon is useful in the field for which it was developed. Outside that field, however, it is often imprecise and pretentious. Medical doctors tell patients that a procedure is *contraindicated* or that they are going to carry out a *differential diagnosis* of the symptoms that patients *present with.* Business executives ask for *feedback* or *input* and want departments to *interface* effectively. On a recent television talk show, a sociologist spoke about the need for *perspectivistic thinking* to achieve organizational goals. Is it any wonder that the befuddled host asked his guest to explain this term to the audience?

Jargon is often accompanied by overly formal diction, the passive voice, and wordy constructions. The following sentence is typical.

wds 16c

ORIGINAL: Procedures were instituted to implement changes in the parameters used to evaluate all aspects of the process.

Here is what this sentence means.

TRANSLATION: We used different criteria to judge the process.

Many students deliberately use jargon to impress their audience. Its effect is usually just the opposite. When writing, avoid jargon and concentrate on a vocabulary that is appropriate for your audience, occasion, and purpose.

(2) Avoiding neologisms

Neologisms are newly coined words that are not part of standard English. New situations call for new words, and occasionally such words become a part of the language. The recent explosion of scientific knowledge, for example, has brought about literally thousands of new words whose use is perfectly acceptable.

quark	A hypothetical subatomic particle
Eurodollar	A U.S. dollar held in Europe
synthesizer	An electronic apparatus for the production of sound
microelectronics	A branch of electronics that deals with the miniaturization of electronic circuits and components

Other coined words, however, are passing fads that do not enter our language. They fill no need because other words already exist for the ideas they express. *Tightish* and *survivability* are just two examples.

Many neologisms are created when the suffixes *-wise* and *-ize* are added to existing words. Police officers say that a criminal must be *Mirandized*. Business people *prioritize* before they *finalize* things *investmentwise*. News commentators seem to attach these suffixes to everything in sight—creating words like *weatherwise, sportswise, timewise, productwise,* and so on, into the night.

If you suspect that a word you are using is a neologism, look it up in your college dictionary. If it is not there, it is probably not standard usage.

(3) Avoiding pretentious diction

In an effort to impress readers, students sometimes elevate their diction, using adjectives and adverbs, learned words, and poetic devices when they are not necessary. Good writing is clear writing, and flowery language is no substitute for thought.

> PRETENTIOUS DICTION: The expectations of offspring may be appreciably different from their parents'.
>
> REVISED: Children's goals may be different from their parents'.
>
> PRETENTIOUS DICTION: Another point to consider is that the economic situation of most women has been ameliorated.
>
> REVISED: Women now have increased economic opportunities.
>
> PRETENTIOUS DICTION: As I fell into slumber, I cogitated about my day ambling through the splendor of the Appalachian Mountains.
>
> REVISED: As I fell asleep, I thought about my day hiking through the Appalachian Mountains.

Pretentious diction is not formal diction used in the wrong situation. Good writing—whether formal or popular—relies on the choice of appropriate words. Whenever you discover pretentious diction in your essays, delete it.

(4) Avoiding clichés

Clichés are expressions that have lost all interest and meaning through overuse. Writers use them to paper over holes in their sentences, cluttering their work with useless phrases that hamper communication (see 16e.1). Sayings like "This isn't my cup of tea," "We're in the same boat," "That's the last straw," and "Let's get down to brass tacks" once had the power to call forth vivid mental images. But they have long since lost their concrete associations and are now ineffective.

Familiar sayings are not the only clichés. In many pat phrases, words have become bound—*inextricably bound*, no doubt—to other words. For example, political, social, or economic situations are often described as *rapidly deteriorating*. *Root causes* need to be uncovered, so *options are explored*, *Herculean efforts* are made, and sometimes *mutually agreeable solutions* are found. If not, *viable alternatives* may allow the two sides to *peacefully coexist*, and so on.

The purpose of academic writing is always to convey information clearly, and the deadening effect of clichés only damages that effort.

**wds
16c**

▶

EXERCISE 8

Rewrite the following passage, eliminating jargon, neologisms, pretentious diction, and clichés. Feel free to add words and phrases and to reorganize sentences to make their meaning clear. If you are not certain about the meaning or status of a word, consult a dictionary.

At a given point in time there coexisted a hare and a tortoise. The aforementioned rabbit was overheard by the tortoise to be blowing his horn about the degree of speed he could attain. The latter quadruped thereupon put forth a challenge to the former by advancing the suggestion that they interact in a running competition. The hare acquiesced, laughing to himself. The animals concurred in the decision to acquire the services of a certain fox to act in the capacity of judicial referee. This particular fox was in agreement, and consequently implementation of the plan was facilitated. In a relatively small amount of time the hare had considerably outdistanced the tortoise and, after ascertaining that he himself was in a more optimized position distancewise than the tortoise, he arrived at the unilateral decision to avail himself of a respite. He made the implicit assumption in so doing that he would anticipate no difficulty in overtaking the tortoise when his suspension of activity ceased. An unfortunate development racewise occurred when the hare's somnolent state endured for a longer-than-anticipated time-frame, facilitating the tortoise's victory in the contest and affirming the concept of unhurriedness and firmness triumphing in competitive situations. Thus the hare was unable to snatch victory out of the jaws of defeat. Years later he was still ruminating about the exigencies of the situation.

▶
EXERCISE 9

List the words and phrases you eliminated from the preceding passage. Then label them jargon, neologisms, pretentious diction, or clichés. Be prepared to discuss your interpretation of each word and the word you chose to put in its place.

16d Using Figurative Language

Language that adheres to fact is called **literal language.** But when writers want to express their personal reactions, they often must go beyond literal meanings. They do so by using **figurative language**—language that uses imaginative comparisons called **figures.** A writer who wanted to express his or her feelings upon seeing the moon could say, "The moon came up fast and was beautiful, large, and white." Figurative language is more expressive: "The moon rose quickly and hung in the sky like a papier-maché ball." Here the comparison conveys the writer's feelings vividly.

Figurative language is not just for literary writing; it has its place in journalism, in academic writing, and even in scientific and technical writing. Although you should not overuse figurative language, do not be afraid to use it when you think it will help you communicate with a reader.

The five most commonly used figures of speech are *simile, metaphor, analogy, personification,* and *allusion.*

(1) Constructing similes

A **simile** is a comparison between two essentially unlike items on the basis of a shared quality. Similes are introduced by a term such as *like* or *as.*

> SIMILE: Like travelers with exotic destinations on their minds, the graduates were remarkably forceful. (Maya Angelou, *I Know Why The Caged Bird Sings*)

> SIMILE: He stared at his hands while I thought about my father who has been opened and closed on the operating table like a book whose first page proves too difficult. (Lee Zacharias, *Lessons*)

> SIMILE: We live in a single-wide trailer shaped like a Velveeta cheese box and made of white metal. (Holley Ballard, *Redbook*)
>
> SIMILE: A cloud in the sky suddenly lighted as if turned on by a switch. (Annie Dillard, *Pilgrim at Tinker Creek*)

These figures present readers with images that enhance their understanding. Without them, the preceding sentences would fall flat.

> The graduates were remarkably forceful.
>
> He stared at his hands while I thought about my father who had just been operated on.
>
> We live in a single-wide trailer made of white metal.
>
> A cloud in the sky suddenly grew bright.

A simile must compare two *dissimilar* things. The following sentence is not a simile.

> My dog is like your dog.

But this sentence is.

> My dog is as sleek as a seashell.

(2) Constructing metaphors

A **metaphor** also compares two essentially dissimilar things, but instead of saying that one thing is *like* another, it *equates* them. Here is a metaphor from a student essay.

> My mother was a beacon illuminating my childhood.

In this metaphor the subject *mother* is equated with, and enhanced by, the image *a beacon illuminating my childhood.* With one effective image, the student sums up his feelings about his mother.

Metaphors are more compressed than similes, and when used successfully, they have great impact. They clarify thought and convey ideas with startling efficiency. Notice the use of metaphors in the following sentences.

> The high grey-flannel fog of winter closed off the Salinas Valley from the sky and all the rest of the world. (John Steinbeck, "The Chrysanthemums")
>
> In its first days of operation, a new telescope orbiting the earth has returned infrared images showing previously unobserved features

of distant galaxies and revealing cosmic "maternity wards" where clouds of interstellar gas appear at various stages of giving birth to stars. (John Noble Wilford, *New York Times*)

Perhaps it is easy for those who have never felt the stinging darts of segregation to say, "Wait." (Martin Luther King, Jr., "Letter from Birmingham Jail")

Science and technology like all creations of the human spirit are unpredictable. If we had a reliable way to label our toys good and bad, it would be easy to regulate technology wisely. (Freeman Dyson, *Disturbing the Universe*)

NOTE: For a metaphor to work, it has to employ images with which readers are familiar. If the comparison is too remote, readers will miss the point entirely. If it is too common, it will become a cliché (see 16e.1).

wds
16d

(3) Constructing analogies

In an **analogy** you explain an unfamiliar object or idea by comparing it to a more familiar one.

An atom is like a miniature solar system.

Robert Frost said that writing free verse is like playing tennis without a net.

The circulatory system runs through the body like a network of rivers and streams.

Analogies can extend over several sentences or even several paragraphs. Extended analogies resemble comparison-and-contrast paragraphs (see 4e.6) with one important difference: whereas comparisons give equal weight to both things being compared, extended analogies use one part of the comparison for the *sole* purpose of shedding light on the other. Here is how one author uses the behavior of people to explain the behavior of ants.

Ants are so much like human beings as to be an embarrassment. They farm fungi, raise aphids as livestock, launch armies into wars, use chemical sprays to alarm and confuse enemies, capture slaves. The families of weaver ants engage in child labor, holding their larvae like shuttles to spin out the thread that sews the leaves together for their fungus gardens. They exchange information ceaselessly. They do everything but watch television. (Lewis Thomas, "On Societies as Organisms")

NOTE: Analogies work only when the subjects you are comparing have something in common. If you compare things that
are too dissimilar, your analogy will not hold up. Drawing an
analogy between tables and ants would be a problem. But explaining ants by comparing them to people—both social animals—works.

(4)   Using personification

wds 16d

Personification gives an idea or inanimate object human attributes, feelings, or powers. We use personification every day in
expressions like

> The wind <u>whispered</u> through the trees.
>
> The engine <u>coughed</u> loudly.
>
> The river moved <u>lazily</u>.
>
> The ocean <u>pounded</u> the shore.
>
> The leaves <u>danced</u> in the wind.
>
> Love is <u>blind</u>.

Personification can make an entity that is abstract or hard to
describe more concrete and familiar. By doing so, it also makes
your writing more precise and more interesting.

> Wit is a lean creature with a sharp inquiring nose. (Charles Brooks,
> *Wit and Humor*)
>
> Truth strikes us from behind, and in the dark, as well as from
> before in broad daylight. (Henry David Thoreau, *The Journals*)
>
> One night I was allowed to stay up until the stars were in full
> command of the sky. (Russell Baker, "Summer beyond Wish")
>
> Institutions, no longer able to grasp firmly what is expected of
> them and what they are, grow slovenly and misshapen and wan-
> der away from their appointed tasks in the Constitutional scheme.
> (Jonathan Schell, *The Time of Illusion*)

(5)   Using allusion

An **allusion** is a reference to a well-known historical or literary
person or event. Allusion enriches a reader's understanding of
your writing by comparing one subject to another that in some
way resembles it. Suppose that you title an essay you have written about your personal goals "Miles to Go Before I Sleep." By
reminding your readers of the concluding lines of Robert Frost's

poem "Stopping by Woods on a Snowy Evening," you suggest your determination and self-discipline.

Literary allusions enrich your expression of feelings. *Biblical* allusions allow you to express a moral attitude ("Eyes have they, but they see not"). *Historical* allusions, such as "When Robert Vesco decided to battle the government, he set the scene for his Dunkirk," elucidate current events by drawing parallels between a current event (Vesco's battle) and an event of historical importance (the retreat of the Allies during WW II).

Once again, for an allusion to work, readers must know what you are alluding to. Family jokes, expressions that your friends use, and esoteric references mean nothing to a general audience.

**wds
16e**

16e Avoiding Ineffective Figures of Speech

Effective figures of speech enrich your diction. Ineffective figures of speech—*dead metaphors* or *similes, mixed metaphors, strained metaphors, overblown imagery*—seriously damage it.

(1) Avoiding dead metaphors and similes

Metaphors and similes stimulate thought by calling up vivid images in a reader's mind. A **dead metaphor** or **simile** has been so overused that it calls up no image. It has become a pat, meaningless cliché. Here are some examples.

> beyond a shadow of a doubt
> crying shame
> sit on the fence
> the bottom line
> green with envy
> pull up stakes
> off the track
> the last straw
> off the beaten path
> a shot in the arm
> smooth sailing
> blind as a bat
> dead as a doornail
> up in arms
> sink or swim

Avoid dead metaphors and similes by taking the time to think of images that make your writing fresher and more vivid.

(2)   Revising mixed metaphors

A **mixed metaphor** results when you combine two or more incompatible images in a single figure of speech. Mixed images leave readers wondering what you are trying to say, or leave them laughing.

> MIXED: The German army advanced <u>ravenously</u> and <u>swept</u> away all opposition. (ravenously sweeping?)

> MIXED: The president extended an <u>olive branch</u> in an attempt to <u>break some of the ice</u> between the United States and the Soviet Union. (break the ice with an olive branch?)

When you revise mixed metaphors, make your imagery consistent. Notice that in the revised versions of the preceding sentences the message is clear.

> REVISED: The German army advanced <u>ravenously</u> and <u>devoured all opposition.</u>

> REVISED: The president extended an <u>olive branch</u> with the hope that the leaders of the Soviet Union <u>would take it up.</u>

(3)   Revising strained metaphors

A **strained metaphor** compares two things that do not have enough in common to justify the comparison or whose connotations do not match.

> STRAINED: The wind rose in the morning like a giant getting out of bed.

> STRAINED: The plane was a fragment of candy falling through the sky.

How is the wind like a giant? And in what sense is a plane comparable to a piece of candy? By comparing things that have a strong basis of comparison, the following revisions create effective metaphors.

> REVISED: The wind rose in the morning like a great wave.

> REVISED: The plane was a wounded bird falling through the sky.

(4) Revising overblown imagery

Overblown, pretentious diction is always out of place. By calling attention to itself, it draws readers away from the point you are making.

> The Tammany Society [a political association] was an all-engulfing weed that rapidly overran and choked New York City's political gardens. Times were filled with danger for those who dared protest this corruption. Even the champion of the people—*The Sun*—refused to encourage the few flowers that dared to rear their heads in that field of briars. Although the situation improved somewhat in the hands of skillful gardeners, much corruption existed for years to come.

This overblown imagery obscures the writer's meaning. Comparing Tammany to a weed is certainly valid, but here it is the imagery that has grown like one. Compare this paragraph, revised for clarity and consistency.

> The Tammany Society was a weed that quickly overran New York City. Times were hard for those who dared to speak against its spread; even *The Sun* did not encourage reformers. Although the situation improved somewhat in the hands of reform-minded politicians, much corruption existed for years to come.

▶

EXERCISE 10

Read the following paragraph from Mark Twain's *Life on the Mississippi* and identify as many figures of speech as you can.

> Now when I had mastered the language of this water, and had come to know every trifling feature that bordered the great river as familiarly as I knew the letters of the alphabet, I had made a valuable acquisition. But I had lost something, too. I had lost something which could never be restored to me while I lived. All the grace, the beauty, the poetry, had gone out of the majestic river! I still keep in mind a certain wonderful sunset which I witnessed when steamboating was new to me. A broad expanse of the river was turned to blood; in the middle distance the red hue brightened into gold, through which a solitary log came floating black and conspicuous; in one place a long, slanting mark lay sparkling upon the water; in another the surface was broken by boiling, tumbling rings, that were as many-tinted as an opal; where the ruddy flush was faintest, was a smooth spot that was

covered with graceful circles and radiating lines, ever so delicately traced; the shore on our left was densely wooded, and the somber shadow that fell from this forest was broken in one place by a long, ruffled trail that shone like silver; and high above the forest wall a clean-stemmed dead tree waved a single leafy bough that glowed like a flame in the unobstructed splendor that was flowing from the sun. There were graceful curves, reflected images, woody heights, soft distances; and over the whole scene, far and near, the dissolving lights drifted steadily, enriching it every passing moment with new marvels of coloring.

wds
16

▶
EXERCISE 11

Rewrite the following sentences, adding one of the figures of speech just discussed above to each sentence to make the ideas more vivid and exciting. Make sure that you identify the technique you use and that you use each of the five figures of speech at least once.

> EXAMPLE: The night was cool and still.
>
> The night was cool and still like the inside of a cathedral.

1. The child was small and carelessly groomed.
2. I wanted to live life to its fullest.
3. The December morning was bright and cloudy.
4. As I walked I saw a cloud floating in the sky.
5. House cats can be a lot like tigers.
6. The sunset turned the lake red.
7. The street was quiet except at the hour when the school at the corner let out.
8. A shopping mall is a place where teenagers like to gather.
9. The president faced an angry Senate.
10. Education is a long process that takes much hard work.

Student Writer at Work: Choosing Words

The following draft was written for a freshman composition class. Revise it for appropriateness, accuracy, and freshness. Change words and rewrite sentences as you see fit.

Computers and Society

Computers are presently addressing many thorny problems that are just begging to be solved. Their widespread use is making advances possible in many fields. At the present time computers are a major part of our environment, cutting down time-consuming chores and making our lives easier.

A computer is a device engineered to make computation easier and faster. Today the computer has taken the image of a highly sophisticated electronic complex. By transforming Base 10 into Base 2, the computer's binary coded hexadecimal system allows it to distinguish numbers through the use of electronic switches. An open switch represents an "0" state and a closed switch represents a "1" state. By the use of programming, you can accomplish a desired result in a matter of milliseconds.

The computer's applications have spread like wildfire to almost every field of endeavor. In the fields of mathematics and science, the computer has been used in activities as diverse as studying the structure of the atom and sending satellites into space. Another recent application is the use of computers in hospitals to detect drugs and toxins in human blood. Doctors will be cognizant of poisoning immediately and can embark upon an appropriate course of action and resuscitate the victim. This technique is a vast improvement over conventional laboratory analysis methods.

Computers can also be used at a person's residence to make daily chores easy to do. A computer can turn on and off lights even though a person is not home. Thus a thief can be thwarted in his attempt to violate a home. Likewise, a computer can direct a remote-controlled vacuum cleaner to make a house super-clean. It can do laundry and dishes through the use of more automatic devices. Taking care of everyday financial matters would be easy as pie. Alarm clocks could be programmed so members of the household could be awakened at different times.

In conclusion, the computer is a useful tool for society. It can be used beneficially in business and industry as well as in the home. And just as the automatic dishwasher has replaced doing dishes by hand, the computer will alter the way we do many things. The computer is an idea whose time has come and an idea that will open the door to the future.

wds
16

17

Using the Dictionary

dict
17a

When asked what single book he would want with him if he were marooned on a desert island, the poet W. H. Auden chose the dictionary. Not everyone shares this extreme enthusiasm, but most experienced writers agree that the dictionary is the most useful reference book they own. It contains considerable information about many subjects, and it is invaluable when you revise your writing.

17a Discovering the Contents of a Dictionary

A dictionary is usually divided into three parts: the *front matter*, the *alphabetical listing*, and the *back matter*.

The **front matter** differs in each dictionary but generally contains a preface explaining how the dictionary is set up and guides for pronunciation and abbreviations. Some dictionaries contain special material in the front matter. *The American Heritage Dictionary*, a standard reference dictionary, has articles focusing on the history of the language, dialects, usage and acceptability, and computers and language analysis.

The **alphabetical listing** is the largest section of every dictionary. Entries tell how a word is spelled, pronounced, and used, and some dictionaries also include information on stress, grammatical function, and history and origin of the word *(etymology)*. On the basis of hundreds of examples of usage, lexicographers also identify word meanings as *regional, slang, preferred,* and so on. Dictionaries may disagree regarding these designations, however.

Meanings under each entry may also be arranged differently from one dictionary to another. Some dictionaries list meanings in historical order, with the oldest usage coming first; others list meanings in order of most frequent usage. Therefore, you cannot assume that the first definition under an entry is its preferred usage. You must look in the front matter to find out what principle of arrangement the lexicographers used.

The **back matter** also differs in each dictionary. Some dictionaries contain a list of weights and measures; others, an essay on punctuation; and still others, a glossary of foreign words. To get the most out of your dictionary, acquaint yourself with its back matter and refer to it when the need arises.

17b Choosing a Dictionary

Many people think that the meanings listed in dictionaries are the only correct meanings of a word. Nothing could be further from the truth. Dictionaries suggest only the *possible* meanings of a word. They provide guidance, especially concerning disputed usage, but in no way do they legislate meaning or cover every use of a word. In addition, because of rapid growth in the communications industry and in scientific research, new words are coming into our language at an unprecedented rate. Ten years ago, who had heard of *quarks, software, microchips, interferon,* or *CAT scans?* Because new words enter the language so rapidly, you should choose a dictionary that is no more than ten years old. Choose an even newer one if you frequently look up specialized terms. When you buy a dictionary, check the date of its edition, *not* its printing, to make certain that you have the most recent one.

Many people also think that all dictionaries are essentially alike. This too is a misconception. Like tools, different dictionaries are designed for different tasks. The most widely used type of dictionary, the one-volume abridged dictionary (called a **desk dictionary** or a **college dictionary**), is ideal for daily use. Other types of dictionaries include multivolume, unabridged dictionaries, which give a great deal of specialized data, and the many special-purpose dictionaries. Each type of dictionary has its special uses.

17c Surveying Abridged Dictionaries

A good hardback **abridged dictionary** will contain about 1,500 pages and about 150,000 entries. Paperback dictionaries usually contain fewer entries, treated in less detail. A paperback dictionary is adequate as a spelling reference that you can easily carry to class, but for home reference, any of the following hardback abridged dictionaries does a better job.

The American Heritage Dictionary of the English Language. 2d Coll. ed. Boston: Houghton Mifflin, 1982.

This extensively illustrated dictionary was first published in 1969. In an effort to create a readable dictionary, the editors keep technical terms and abbreviations to a minimum. The front matter of the dictionary discusses etymology, the history of language, usage and acceptability, dialects, and computers and language analysis. Within the alphabetical listing the principal and most current meaning appears first, with other meanings branching out from it. Throughout the dictionary, the editors have provided *usage notes* based on the responses of a panel of one hundred experts. Synonyms and sometimes antonyms are also listed.

In general, this dictionary gives more guidance than any of the other abridged dictionaries listed here. Its back matter contains biographical and geographical entries, abbreviations, and a list of two-year and four-year colleges.

The Concise Oxford Dictionary. 6th ed. New York: Oxford University Press, 1976.

This no-nonsense dictionary contains no illustrations and gives little guidance on usage. It lists meanings according to the most common usage, includes illustrative quotations, and gives British as well as American spellings. Front and back matter is sparse: there is a short preface, and the back matter includes a table of weights and measures, the Greek and Russian alphabets, and a compendium of the principal monetary units of the world.

The Random House College Dictionary, rev. ed. New York: Random House, 1982.

This is an abridged version of the larger unabridged *Random House Dictionary of the English Language.* It lists meanings according to frequency of use and indicates informal and slang usage. It also gives synonyms and antonyms as well as geographical and biographical names. Illustrations are helpful but less extensive than those in *The American Heritage Dictionary.* Back matter includes a manual of style.

Webster's Ninth New Collegiate Dictionary. Springfield, Mass.: Merriam, 1983.

Like *The Random House College Dictionary,* this dictionary is an abridged version of a larger unabridged dictionary. The first Mer-

dict
17c

riam Webster collegiate dictionary appeared in 1898, and the ninth edition incorporates many of the features of its predecessors. Information is derived from the more than 13 million citations gathered by the G. & C. Merriam Company. Meanings are listed chronologically rather than according to frequency of usage, and historical information precedes each definition. *Webster's Collegiate* contains fewer illustrations than *The American Heritage Dictionary*.

Two new features characterize the ninth edition. First, entries are accompanied by dates, showing how old a word is and when a definition came into use. Second, many entries are now followed by usage notes that discuss problems of usage and diction.

**dict
17d**

The front matter of this dictionary contains a detailed essay on the English language commissioned for this edition. Foreign words and phrases as well as biographical and geographical names appear in separate sections in the back matter. This dictionary also contains a list of American and Canadian colleges and universities, a handbook of style, and an index.

Webster's New World Dictionary. 2d Coll. ed. New York: William Connins and World, 1978.

This good basic dictionary presents meanings in historical order and indicates frequent usage. Foreign terms and geographical and biographical names are included in the alphabetical listing. Back matter includes information on mechanics, manuscript form, and punctuation.

NOTE: The name *Webster*, referring to the great lexicographer Noah Webster, is in the public domain. Because it cannot be copyrighted, it appears in the titles of many dictionaries of varying quality.

17d Using the Dictionary

To put a lot of information into a small space, abridged dictionaries use a system of symbols, abbreviations, and different typefaces. Each dictionary uses a slightly different system, so you should consult the front matter of your dictionary to determine how these devices work.

Two entries with labels from *The American Heritage Dictionary* and *Webster's Ninth New Collegiate Dictionary* are shown in Figures 3 and 4 (on page 316).

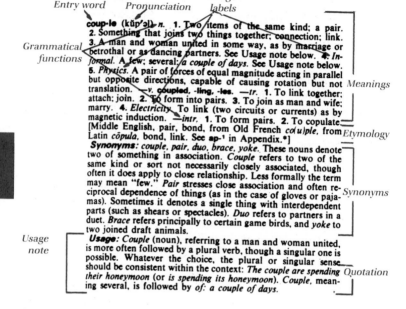

FIGURE 3   THE AMERICAN HERITAGE DICTIONARY

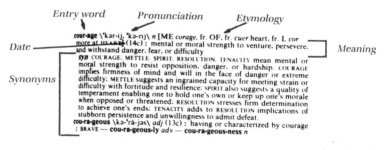

FIGURE 4   WEBSTER'S NINTH NEW COLLEGIATE DICTIONARY

(1)   Using guide words

To help you locate words all dictionaries include a pair of
guide words at the top corner of each page.

Couperin / court-martial

shriek   •   shut

The guide words indicate the first and last entries appearing on
that page. The word on the left shows the first entry on the page,

and the word on the right shows the last. All entries on the page fall alphabetically between these words.

(2) Understanding the entry word

The **entry word**, which appears in boldface at the beginning of the entry, gives the spelling of a word and also its variant forms.

> col • or n. Also chiefly British col • our

An entry word is divided into syllables by small, centered dots.

> cour • age

**dict
17d**

An entry of more than one word will appear as such on the page.

> county seat

If a word is hyphenated, the hyphen will appear as part of the entry.

> vacuum-packed

Dictionaries differ in their treatment of word division and compound words. *The American Heritage Dictionary*, for example, divides the word *creepy* as *creep • y*. *Webster's Ninth New Collegiate Dictionary* shows this word as *creepy*. Similarly, *The American Heritage Dictionary* has *cross fire*, *The Concise Oxford Dictionary* has *cross-fire*, and *Webster's Ninth New Collegiate Dictionary* has *cross fire*.

➡
EXERCISE 1

Use your college dictionary to help you divide the following words into syllables and list all variant spellings. Consult a second college dictionary to see if both dictionaries agree.

1.	cross reference	6.	lovable
2.	dexterous	7.	theater
3.	aesthetic	8.	judgment
4.	although	9.	counselor
5.	austerity	10.	flavor

(3) Understanding the pronunciation guide

The pronunciation of a word appears in parentheses after the main entry (or between slashes [/ /] in *Webster's Ninth New Collegiate Dictionary*). Dictionaries use symbols to represent sounds, and an explanation of these symbols usually appears at the bottom of each page or across the bottom of facing pages throughout the alphabetical listing. (A full guide to pronunciation appears as part of the front matter of the dictionary.) The stressed syllable of a word is indicated by an accent mark ('). A secondary stress is indicated with a similar but lighter mark ('). In *The American Heritage Dictionary*, the accent mark follows the stressed syllable.

> (kûr′ĭj)
> (dĭ-prē′shē-āt′)

dict
17d

In *Webster's Ninth New Collegiate Dictionary*, the accent precedes the stressed syllable.

> /`kar-ij,`ka-rij/

Dictionaries will often include more than one pronunciation of a word, but they rarely include all its regional variations. Therefore, they are not perfect guides to pronunciation. They are most reliable for the pronunciation of unusual words that are used more in writing than in speech and therefore have no colloquial variants.

▶
EXERCISE 2

Determine the pronunciation of the following words by looking up each in your college dictionary. Write out the symbols that the dictionary uses, and include variant pronunciations.

1.	Cartesian	6.	sangfroid
2.	entablement	7.	tiara
3.	narwhal	8.	malamute
4.	insouciance	9.	cavil
5.	chimera	10.	envoi

(4) Using grammatical function labels

Dictionaries use part-of-speech labels to indicate grammatical categories. These are the labels for the eight traditional parts of speech.

> de • cep • tive   adj [adjective]
> hap • pi • ly   adv [adverb]

be • cause	conj [conjunction]
hey	interj [interjection]
cour • age	n [noun]
of	prep [preposition]
they	pron [pronoun]
re • lax	vb [verb]

If a verb is regular, the entry provides only the base form of the verb.

help . . . vb

If a verb is irregular, the entry lists the principal parts of the verb.

with • draw . . . vb -drew . . . ; -drawn . . . ; -drawing . . .

The entry also indicates whether a verb is transitive, intransitive, or both.

in • fect . . . vt

va • ca • tion . . . vi

pen • e • trate . . . vb . . . vt . . . vi

Part-of-speech labels indicate the plural form of irregular nouns.

fly . . . n pl flies

to • ma • to . . . n pl -toes

a • lum • nus . . . n pl -ni

moth • er-in-law . . . n pl moth • ers-in-law

When the plural form is regular, it is not shown.

Dictionaries usually show the comparative and superlative forms of both regular and irregular adjectives and adverbs.

red . . . adj redder; reddest (regular)

bad . . . adv worse; worst (irregular)

Most entries for regular adjectives and adverbs show the comparative and superlative forms with -er and -est. Showing -er and -est does not preclude your using *more* and *most* as an alternate way to form the comparative and the superlative, however. An entry without -er and -est always uses *more* and *most* to form the comparative and the superlative.

▶
EXERCISE 3

Use your college dictionary to answer the following questions about grammatical function.

1. What are the principal parts of the following verbs: *drink, deify, carol, draw,* and *ring?*
2. Which of the following nouns can be used as verbs: *canter, aesthetic, minister, council, command, magistrate, mother,* and *lord?*
3. What are the plural forms of these nouns: *silo, sheep, seed, dry, scissors, genetics,* and *alchemy?*
4. What are the comparative and superlative forms of the following adverbs and adjectives: *fast, airy, good, mere, homey,* and *unlucky?*
5. Are the following verbs transitive, intransitive, or both? Copy the phrase or sentence from the dictionary that illustrates the use of each verb: *bias, halt, dissatisfy, die,* and *turn.*

dict
17d

(5)   Understanding etymology

The **etymology** of a word is its history, its evolution over the years. This information appears in brackets—[ ]—either before or after the list of meanings. The etymology traces a word back to its roots and shows its form when it entered English. For instance, *The American Heritage Dictionary* shows that *couple* came into Middle English (1150–1475) from Old French and into Old French from Latin. *Webster's Ninth New Collegiate Dictionary* shows *cup* to have the same form, *cuppe,* in both Old and Middle English and to have come into English from the Latin *cuppa.*

Here are the most common abbreviations used in etymologies.

OE	Old English	OF	Old French
ME	Middle English	G	German
AS	Anglo Saxon	ON	Old Norse or
	(or Old English)		Early Scandinavian
F	French	L	Latin
MF	Middle French		

▶
EXERCISE 4

Using your college dictionary, trace the etymologies of the following words. Write a paragraph on each explaining how their definitions have changed or remained the same over the years.

1.	atom	6.	car
2.	rampart	7.	capitol
3.	liquor	8.	silly
4.	poll	9.	populace
5.	assassin	10.	custard

(6)   Understanding meanings

Some dictionaries, like *The American Heritage Dictionary*, give the most common usage first and then list less common ones. Others, like *Webster's Ninth New Collegiate Dictionary*, begin with the oldest meaning and move to the most current ones. Regardless of the method your dictionary uses, you should remember certain points when looking up a word's meaning.

dict
17d

First, remember that a dictionary records the meanings that appear most regularly in speech and in writing. If a word is in the process of acquiring new meanings, the dictionary may not yet record them.

Also remember that a dictionary meaning is primarily a record of the **denotations,** or exact meanings, of a word. Its emotional associations, or **connotations,** are not usually among the meanings listed, although some dictionaries do attempt to suggest them. *Webster's New World Dictionary*, for example, says that *scheme* "often connotes either an impractical, visionary plan or an underhanded intrigue." As a rule, however, a word is richer in everyday speech and writing than its dictionary definition suggests.

(7)   Understanding synonyms and antonyms

The main entry often lists synonyms and occasionally antonyms in addition to definitions. **Synonyms** are words that have similar meanings, like *well* and *healthy.* **Antonyms** are words that have opposite meanings, like *courage* and *cowardice.* Dictionaries present synonyms—and sometimes antonyms—because they clarify the meanings of a word and are also useful to a writer. However, no two words are exactly alike, so you must use synonyms carefully, making certain that the connotation of the synonym is as close as possible to that of the original word.

▶

EXERCISE 5

Using your dictionary, as well as your own knowledge, write a paragraph explaining the differences in the connotations of the words in each group.

1. car, automobile, limousine   4. portly, heavy, fat
2. cabin, shack, hovel   5. slumber, sleep, snooze
3. cry, weep, sob

dict
17d

(8) Understanding idioms

Dictionary entries often show how certain words are used with other words in set expressions called **idioms.** Such phrases present problems for some native speakers and especially for nonnative speakers, as you may know from your own study of other languages. For example, what are we to make of the expression *from the shoulder?* That it means "in a direct or outspoken manner of telling" is not at all apparent. Such idiomatic phrases do not follow any rules; they have become fixed through custom and must be memorized.

Dictionaries also indicate the idiomatic use of prepositions. Under a usage note for the word *acquiesce,* for instance, *The American Heritage Dictionary* says that *acquiesce* is used with *in* when it takes a preposition. Similarly, we do not say that we *abide with* a decision or that we *interfere on* a performance. We say *abide by* and *interfere with.* The idiomatic use of prepositions is again a matter of custom.

Most dictionaries list common idiomatic phrases under an individual entry. For example, *The Random House College Dictionary* lists the following idiomatic phrases under the entry *hat.*

> *Pass the hat*
> *Take one's hat off to*
> *Talk through one's hat*
> *Throw one's hat into the ring*
> *Under one's hat*

(9) Understanding usage labels

Dictionaries use special labels to indicate restrictions on word meanings. The most common labels are *nonstandard* or *substandard, informal* or *colloquial, slang, dialect* or *regional, vulgar, obsolete, archaic, rare, poetic,* and *foreign language* and *field* labels. Where such labels involve value judgments, dictionaries differ.

Nonstandard or Substandard
Nonstandard or substandard means that a word is in wide use but is not considered part of standard usage (see 16a.1). **Nonstandard** refers to words that have existed side by side with standard forms but have never been accepted as standard usage. **Substandard** refers to words even more removed from the mainstream than those designated nonstandard. Dictionaries disagree about which words are nonstandard or substandard. For instance, *The American Heritage Dictionary* says that nonstandard usage includes forms such as *ain't. Webster's Ninth New Collegiate Dictionary,* however, labels *ain't* substandard.

dict
17d

Informal or Colloquial
Within standard English there are two levels of usage: formal and informal (see 16a.1). **Informal** or **colloquial** discourse is the language of conversation, and it is acceptable in informal situations. Its use does not imply ignorance of standard forms. Rather, it occurs when people concentrate more on what they are saying than on how they are saying it. Most words are correctly used in both formal and informal situations, but some words usually appear only in speech or informal writing—contractions such as *I've* for *I have* and the word *sure* for the more formal *surely,* for example.

Slang
Words labeled **slang** by the dictionary are appropriate only in extremely informal situations but, unlike regionalisms, are widely used. *Clip joint* and *prof* (for professor) are good examples. Certain words are acceptable in some usages but are considered slang in others. *"The pig squeals,"* for example, is standard usage of the word *squeals.* But when used to mean informing on someone, this word is slang. Use of slang does not imply that one is illiterate. In writing it can be used intentionally to produce an irreverent or exaggerated effect or to record dialect.

Dialect or Regional

These labels indicate that a word or meaning of a word is limited to a certain geographical region. The term *hero sandwich* is a good example: its many names include *hoagie, grinder, submarine, zeppelin,* and *poor boy.* Although some dictionaries label those words *slang,* others consider them **regionalisms;** *grinder,* for instance, is used almost exclusively in New England. Other regionalisms include *arroyo,* a word used in the Southwest to mean "deep gully," and *potlatch,* a word used in the Northwest to mean celebration.

Vulgar

Words so labeled are offensive. **Vulgar** words differ from slang in that some social taboo is usually attached to them. This category includes words labeled **obscene,** which are extremely offensive, and words labeled **profane,** which show disrespect for the Diety.

Obsolete

This label indicates that a word is no longer in use. The word *egal,* meaning equal, is **obsolete.** Note, however, that just because the thing a word refers to is obsolete does not mean that the word itself is obsolete. A *ruff,* for example, is a stiff collar worn by men and women in the late sixteenth century. Ruffs are no longer in fashion, but their name still exists. The label *obsolete* applies only to words that have disappeared from the language.

Archaic and Rare

The label **archaic** indicates that a word or meaning of a word was once common but now occurs rarely. Archaic differs from **rare,** which means that a word was never in common usage. For example, *affright,* meaning "to arouse fear or terror," was once widely used but now is no longer in general use. On the other hand, *nocent,* meaning "guilty or causing injury," has not been used since Middle English and was not in common usage then.

Poetic

This label refers to words that are or were used commonly only in poetry. These words include shortened forms such as *eve* for *evening* and *o'er* for *over.*

Foreign Language Labels

These labels identify expressions or words from other languages that are commonly used by English-speaking people but are not felt to belong to English. Examples are *adios*, Spanish for "goodbye," and *sine qua non*, Latin for "something that is essential."

Field Labels

These labels (*Mathematics*, *Chemistry*, *Biology*, *Military*, etc.) indicate that a word or meaning of a word is limited to a certain field or discipline. For example, *The American Heritage Dictionary* uses the labels *Physics* and *Electricity* to indicate special meanings of the word *couple.*

**dict
17d**

▶
EXERCISE 6

Use your college dictionary to find the restrictions on the use of the following words.

1. hornswoggle
2. apse
3. flunk
4. lorry
5. kirk
6. ope
7. nice (silly)
8. integer
9. bannock
10. blowhard

(10) Finding general information

In addition to containing information about words, your abridged dictionary is an excellent source of general information. Most abridged dictionaries contain lists of geographical and biographical names as well as references to topics of general interest. If you wanted to find out the year in which John Glenn orbited the earth, you would look up the entry *Glenn, John* in the biographical listing. If you needed to find out after whom the Davis Cup is named, you would look up *Davis Cup* in the alphabetical listing. Thus, when no other references are handy, your abridged dictionary can serve as a valuable source of information.

▶
EXERCISE 7

To test the research capability of your dictionary, use it to answer the following questions.

1. Where is Kitty Hawk, the site of Wilbur and Orville Wright's first heavier-than-air powered flight?
2. How many satellites does the planet Uranus have?
3. What is the population of Los Angeles?
4. In what year did Martin Luther King, Jr., win the Nobel Peace Prize?
5. In what year did Edward VII of England abdicate?
6. Who was Grandma Moses?
7. After whom was the ferris wheel named?
8. What is the atomic weight of sulfur?
9. What was Joseph Conrad's original name?
10. What is surrealism?

17e   Using Unabridged Dictionaries

In some situations you may need more information than your college dictionary offers. When you are looking for a detailed history of a word or when you want to look up an especially rare usage, you need to consult an **unabridged dictionary.** An unabridged dictionary gives a wider and more detailed treatment of entries than an abridged dictionary, and its comprehensive listings may extend over several volumes. The following unabridged dictionaries are excellent sources of information and are available at your college library.

The Random House Dictionary of the English Language. New York: Random House, 1980.
This short unabridged dictionary—the shortest listed here—contains about 260,000 entries. It includes appendices with short dictionaries of Italian, French, German, and Spanish.

Webster's Third International Dictionary of the English Language. Springfield, Mass.: Merriam, 1981.
This unabridged dictionary contains over 450,000 entries along with illustrations, some in color. Meanings appear in chronological order and are extensively illustrated with quotations. This dictionary does not, however, give much guidance on usage.

The Oxford English Dictionary. New York: Oxford University Press, 1976.
Consisting of thirteen volumes plus four supplements, two of which are completed, *The Oxford English Dictionary* offers over 500,000 definitions, historically arranged, and 2 million supporting quotations. The quotations begin with the earliest recorded use of a word and progress through each century either until the

word becomes obsolete or until its latest meaning is listed. For this reason, many scholars consider *The Oxford English Dictionary* the best place to find the history of a word or to locate illustrations of its usage. However, *The Oxford English Dictionary* emphasizes British usage and does not treat American usage fully.

Also available is the compact edition, a photographic reduction of the entire thirteen-volume edition into two volumes. The one drawback of the compact edition is that it must be read with a magnifying glass.

The entry from *The Oxford English Dictionary*, shown in Figure 5, illustrates the in-depth coverage offered by an unabridged dictionary. Compare this entry on *courage* to the one on page 316.

dict
17f

Courage (kʊˈrɪdʒ), *sb.* Forms: 4-7 **corage,** curage, (4 6 **corrage,** 5 **curag, coreage,** 6 **currage, courra(d)ge,** 7 **corege**). 5- **courage.** [ME. *corage,* a. OF. *corage, curage,* later *courage* Pr. and Cat. *coratge,* Sp. *corage,* It. *coraggio,* a Common Romanic word, answering to a L. type **coraticum,* f. *cor* heart. Cf. the parallel *ætāticum* from *ætāt-em* (AGE); and see -AGE.]

†**1.** The heart as the seat of feeling, thought, etc.; spirit, mind, disposition, nature. *Obs.*

c 1300 *K. Alis.* 3559 Archelaus, of proud corage. *c* 1386 CHAUCER *Prol.* 11 Smale fowles maken melodie..So priketh hem nature in here corages. *c* 1430 *Pilgr. Lyf Manhode* 1. xxxiii. 1369) 20 What thinke.t in thi corage? *c* 1430 *Stans Puer* 5 To all norture thi corage to enclyne. *c* 1500 *Knt. Cur'esy* 407 in Ritson *Met. Rom.* III. 213 In his courage he was full sad. **1593** SHAKS. 3 *Hen. VI,* ii. ii. 57 This soft courage makes your Followers faint. **1638** DRUMM. OF HAWTH. *Irene* Wks. (1711) 163 Men's courages were growing hot, their hatred kindled. **1659** B. HARRIS *Parival's Iron Age* 41 The Spaniards..attacked it with all the force and maistry the greatest courages were able to invent.

†**b.** *transf.* Of a plant. *Obs.* (Cf. ' To bring a thing into *good heart.*')

c 1420 *Palladius on Husb.* XI. 90 In this courage Hem forto graffe is goode.

†**c.** Applied to a person: cf. *spirit. Obs.*

1561 T. HONY tr. *Castiglione's Courtyer* (1577) V j b, The prowes of those diuine courages [viz. Marquesse of Mantua, etc.]. **1647** W. BROWNE *Polex.* II. 197 These two great **courages** being met, and followed by a small companie of the most resolute pirates.

†**2.** What is in one's mind or thoughts, what one is thinking of or intending; intention, purpose; desire or inclination. *Obs.* (Cf. ' To speak one's *mind* ', ' to tell all one's *heart* '.)

c 1300 *Seuyn Sag.* (W.) 2446 Lo her, sire, a litel page! That schal sai the thi corage. *c* 1386 CHAUCER *Merch. T.* 10 Swich a greet corage Hadde this knyght to been a wedded man. **1484** CAXTON *Chivalry* 7 Fayr frend what is

your corage or entent. *c* 1530 LD. BERNERS *Arth. Lyt. Bryt.* (1814) 277 Ye mayster dyscouered to her all his courage, how that he loued her. **1557** NORTH tr. *Gueuara's Diall Pr.* 93 b/1 The romaines had a great corage to conquere straunge realmes. **1568** GRAFTON *Chron.* II. 289 Many were taken of their owne courage, which might have scaped if they had list. **1607** SHAKS. *Timon* III. iii. 24 I'de such a courage to do him good. *a* 1626 BACON *Max. & Uses Com. Law* xxii. 81 The law..shall..make construction that my minde and courage is not to enter into the greater bond for any menace.

†**3.** Spirit, liveliness, lustiness, vigour, vital force or energy; also *fig. Obs.*

a 1400 WARKW. *Chron.* (Camden) 2 Thei..were greved with colde and rayne, that thei hade no coreage to feg t. **1565** JEWEL *Def. Apol.* (1611) 305 In the Cardinals of Rome, Pride, Auarice, and Lechery are in their greatest Courage. **1630** R. *Johnson's Kingd. & Commw.* 247 They have horses of excellent courage. **1705** *Lond. Gaz.* No. 4182/4 A Chesnut Mare..of great Courage.

†**b.** Anger, wrath; **c.** Haughtiness, pride; **d.** Confidence, boldness.

c 1386 CHAUCER *Knt.'s T.* (Harl.) 1154 The hunt[e] strangled with wilde bores courage. **1483** CAXTON *G. de la Tour* F iij b, [She] became..so grete of courage that also to the kynge her lord she bare not so grete reuerence as she ought. **1568** GRAFTON *Chron.* II. 285 Every man cryed and besought the king to have mercy..for Gods sake refraine your courage, ye have the name of sovereigne noble. esse. **1590** SPENSER *F. Q.* III. x. 30 Trompart..Besought him his great corage to appease, And pardon simple man. **1608** MIDDLETON *Trick to catch* I. i, I will..set so good a courage on my state, That I will be believed.

†**e.** Sexual vigour and inclination; lust. *Obs.*

1541 BARNES *Wks.* (1573) 329/1 By the reason that priestes are so hoate of courage, and can not keepe theyr chastitie. **1577** B. GOOGE *Heresbach's Husb.* III. 158b) 129 If the Bull be not lusty enough about his businesse..his courage is also stirred up by the like odours. **1606** G. W[OODCOCKE] tr. *Justin* 56 Darius horse..by reason of the courage had to the Mare, forthwith neighed alowde. **1615** CROOKE *Body of Man* 45 If they be taken away, the iollity and courage of the Creature is extinguished.

FIGURE 5   THE OXFORD ENGLISH DICTIONARY

17f   Using Special-Purpose Dictionaries

Special-purpose dictionaries focus on one particular field of interest or endeavor, providing more information on these topics than standard dictionaries do. The following dictionaries may be of help.

Dictionaries of Usage

These works list words and phrases that commonly cause trouble.

> Bryant, Margaret M. *Current American Usage.* (1969).
> Follett, Wilson. *Modern American Usage: A Guide* (1966).
> Fowler, H. W. *A Dictionary of Modern English Usage* (2d ed. rev., 1965).
> Hornby, Albert S. *Guide to Patterns of Usage in English* (2d ed., 1975).
> Morris, William and Mary Morris. *Harper Dictionary of Contemporary Usage* (1975).

Dictionaries of Synonyms

These works list words whose meanings are closely related.

> Hayakawa, S. I. *Modern Guide to Synonyms and Related Words* (1968).
> Kay, Mairé Weir. *Webster's Collegiate Thesaurus* (1976).
> Lewis, Norman. *The New Roget's Thesaurus of the English Language in Dictionary Form* (1964).

NOTE: *Thesaurus,* from the Greek word *treasure,* and *Roget,* the name of a man who published a well-known thesaurus, are not copyrighted names and can be attached to any dictionary of synonyms.

Dictionaries of Slang and Idioms

These works list slang origins and idiomatic constructions.

> Makkai, Adam. *A Dictionary of American Idioms* (rev. ed., 1975).
> Partridge, Eric. *Dictionary of Slang and Unconventional English* (1970).
> Wentworth, Harold, and Stuart B. Flexner. *Dictionary of American Slang* (2d ed., 1975).
> Wood, Frederick T. *English Prepositional Idioms* (1967).

Dictionaries of Etymologies

These works give detailed information about the origin of words.

> Morris, William, and Mary Morris. *Dictionary of Word and Phrase Origins* (1977).
> Onions, C. T. *The Oxford Dictionary of English Etymology* (1966).
> Partridge, Eric. *Origins: A Short Etymological Dictionary of Modern English* (1966).

Dictionaries of Foreign Terms

These works list non-English phrases likely to be encountered in books and periodicals.

> Guinagh, Kevin. *Dictionary of Foreign Phrases and Abbreviations*
> (2d ed., 1972).
> Mawson, C. O. Sylvester, and Charles Berlitz. *Dictionary of Foreign
> Terms* (2d ed., 1975).
> Pei, Mario, and Salvatore Ramondino. *Dictionary of Foreign Terms*
> (1974).

For more special-purpose dictionaries, see 36b.1.

▶

dict
17f

EXERCISE 8

Use special-purpose dictionaries to answer the following.

1. Find as many synonyms as you can for these words: *navigator, fra-
    grance, boast, memory,* and *zigzag.*
2. Find the origins of the following slang terms: *vamoose, highbrow,
    clip joint,* and *humongous.*
3. Give the etymologies of these words: *gargantuan, amazon, doily, gal-
    vanize, hygiene, fathom,* and *maverick.*
4. Find the meaning of the following foreign phrases: *quid pro quo, tout
    passe, todo el mundo, idée fixe, con brio,* and *dos-à-dos.*

18

Building a Vocabulary

18a Analyzing Your Vocabulary

Your vocabulary comprises all the words you know. But this definition oversimplifies the situation. Actually you have four overlapping vocabularies that you use in various situations. First, you have a **speaking vocabulary**, the words you use in general conversation. For most people this vocabulary consists of the few hundred words they use when talking with friends. Next, you have a **writing vocabulary**, the words you use when writing. This vocabulary is considerably larger than your speaking vocabulary, consisting of about 10,000 to 45,000 words. Many of the words in your spoken vocabulary are also part of your written vocabulary. But certain words like *satire, analogy, positron,* and *logarithm* belong almost exclusively to your writing vocabulary. The colloquialisms and slang that are part of your spoken vocabulary are usually excluded from your writing vocabulary.

You also have a **reading vocabulary**, the words whose meanings you know but do not necessarily use in writing or in conversation. Words like *plutocrat, elucidate,* and *equivocate* might fall into this category. Most college students have a reading vocabulary of between 50,000 and 100,000 words. Finally, there is your **guess vocabulary**, words whose meanings you do not know exactly but can infer because the words are similar to ones you already know or because their context gives clues to their meanings.

Beyond these are words that you do not know and that you cannot figure out. These words you must look up in a dictionary.

18b Why Build a Vocabulary?

Why should you spend time increasing your vocabulary? One reason is that people who can express their thoughts accurately have an advantage over people who cannot. In college a good vocabulary not only strengthens your performance on written examinations, papers, and oral reports, but it also increases your ability to comprehend reading material and your instructors' comments in class. Without a good vocabulary, your ability to learn is limited.

Think for a moment about how much time your instructors spend explaining the basic vocabulary of any discipline. You cannot study psychology without knowing the meaning of *neurosis*, *psychosis*, and *conditioning* or understand sociology without knowing the meaning of *class*, *ethnocentrism*, and *culture*. Broadly speaking, then, education is the learning of a new vocabulary, the words with which you express new ideas.

Many of the new terms you learn will go into your writing and reading vocabularies, and some will even become a part of your speaking vocabulary. Many words whose popular meanings you know will acquire new, specialized meanings in an academic setting. The word *irony*, for example, means one thing in everyday conversation and another thing in a literature class. Certain words that are specific to a subject simply have to be memorized. In biology, for example, your previous experience has probably not prepared you to guess the meaning of *mitosis*, *mitochondria*, or *pineal body*. You must also cope with a general group of "learned" words—*aesthetic*, *concomitant*, and *penultimate*, for example—that occur often enough in an academic setting to cause trouble if you cannot understand them readily.

18c Avoiding Ineffective Vocabulary Building

When trying to increase their vocabularies, many people overlook the distinctions between their speaking, writing, reading, and guess vocabularies. Books that claim to build "word power" often make the same mistake. They list complicated words that you are to memorize and practice using every day. If you do so, you put words into your speaking vocabulary that belong in your reading or writing vocabularies. Imagine how your friends would react, for example, if you said

> After I admonished him about his table manners, my brother masticated his food more thoroughly.

Memorizing lists of words has other limitations as well.

Words that are not regularly used are quickly forgotten. Furthermore, one is not usually motivated to memorize someone else's vocabulary list. If you do not need to learn a new word, the chances are that you will rapidly forget it.

Reading will not automatically increase your vocabulary either. It does so only if you constantly look up and study new words. But students who must read extensively, especially while studying for examinations, often do not take the time to do this. Nor will your vocabulary somehow increase as you get older. Unless you work at it, your vocabulary *decreases*. As you can see, building a vocabulary takes a conscious effort and considerable work.

18d Building a Better Vocabulary: Preliminaries

Learning new words takes work and, at first, a good deal of time. But as you proceed, your vocabulary increases and your task gets easier. Here are some ideas for beginning a program of vocabulary development.

(1) Becoming a reader

One way to build your vocabulary is to make a habit of reading. Set aside a certain amount of time each day—say, an hour—and do your private reading. Having to read for your courses will occasionally throw off your schedule, but whenever you can, read.

Reading in itself will not increase your vocabulary. But focusing on words as you read is one of the best ways of learning new words. Seeing words in context, remembering the sentences in which they appear and the ideas with which they are associated, helps you recall them later. Get into the routine of looking up new words as you encounter them and then writing them down along with their meanings. As your vocabulary grows, you will have to do this less often.

(2) Keeping a vocabulary journal

A vocabulary journal is a systematic record of the words you look up as you read. In the following sample the student not only includes the definition of a word but also an example of its usage.

Word	*Meaning*	*Example*
intervene	to come be-tween	The governor <u>intervened</u> in the truckers' strike.
satire	a work in which wit is used to expose folly or wicked-ness	"A Modest Proposal" by Jonathan Swift is a <u>satire</u> that attacks Britain's oppression of Ireland.
aberrant	deviating from the proper course	The patient was institutionalized because of his <u>aberrant</u> behavior.
nadir	the lowest point	By 1868 Andrew Johnson had reached the <u>nadir</u> of his political career.
acrid	harsh in taste or smell	The fertilizer plant covered the town with <u>acrid</u> smoke.

voc 18e

By regularly reviewing the words in your journal, you will gradually build your reading vocabulary. Once you acquire a good working vocabulary, you can move on to more advanced methods of vocabulary building.

▶
EXERCISE 1

Keep a vocabulary journal for a week. Enter in it words you encounter in your academic and personal reading. Bring your journal to class and compare its entries with those of your classmates. Do certain words appear regularly? Why? What words do you expect to be of little use to you? Explain.

18e Building a Better Vocabulary: Continuing the Program

Surrounding a word with associations helps you remember it. You can use a number of techniques to create such associations.

(1)   Learning the histories of words

Many of the words you encounter have interesting histories, or etymologies. Knowing the **etymology** of a word will help you remember its definition. For example, *cliché*, meaning a worn-out expression, is a French word that refers to a plate used for printing. It thus suggests the idea of being cast in metal from a mold; in other words, unalterably fixed. Hence a *cliché* is a fixed form of expression.

voc
18e

The word *vandal* is another interesting example. An ancient Germanic tribe, the Vandals, destroyed temples, buildings, books, and works of art as they overran Rome in the fifth century A.D. From then on, *vandal* became synonomous with anyone who willfully destroys or defaces property.

You can find the history of a word in any good college dictionary, or you can consult a specialized dictionary of etymology (see 17f). As you build your vocabulary, see if the history of a word provides associations that help you remember it.

▶
EXERCISE 2

Using your college dictionary, look up the histories of the following words. How does the history of each word help you remember its definition?

1.	mountebank	6.	cicerone
2.	pyrrhic	7.	fathom
3.	pittance	8.	gossamer
4.	protean	9.	rigamarole
5.	gargantuan	10.	maudlin

(2)   Learning roots, prefixes, and suffixes

The words you encounter in your college studies are sometimes long and complex. Often, however, a word can be broken down into smaller units that give you clues to its meaning. For instance, *bigamy* can be divided into the Greek prefix *bi*, meaning "two," and the root *gamos*, meaning "marriage," thus revealing *bigamy* to mean being married to two people at once. Over half the words in English come from Latin and Greek sources, so knowing something about Latin and Greek roots, prefixes, and suffixes can help you determine what these words mean and remember their definitions once you learn them. Once you see how roots, prefixes, and suffixes work in the words you already know, you can discover the meaning of new words based on these forms. Thus, once you know the derivation of *bigamy*, you can probably guess the meaning of *bicolor*, *biconvex*, and *polygamy*.

Roots

A **root** is a word from which other words are formed. Both *hypodermic* and *dermatologist*, for example, come from the Greek root *derma*, meaning "skin." *Manual* means working by hand, *manuscript* refers to a handwritten draft of a book, and *manufacture* literally means making a product by hand. All these words derive from the Latin root *manus*, meaning "hand."

Many scientific words are based on Latin and Greek roots. *Biography* contains the Greek root *graph*, meaning "to write," and *vacuum* contains the Latin root *vac*, meaning "empty." *Biology* contains the Greek root *bios*, meaning "life," as do *biosphere*, *biophysics*, *bionics*, and *biopsy*. When you come across words that contain *bio*, you already know half their meaning.

NOTE: Be careful when making generalizations based on roots, prefixes, and suffixes. Some words appear to have the same root but do not—for instance, *homosexual* (from the Greek *homos*, meaning "same"), *homo sapiens* (from the Latin *homo*, meaning "man").

Here are some common Latin and Greek roots whose meanings can help you identify and remember new words.

voc
18e

Latin Roots

1. æqus	equal	equivocal, equinox
2. amare, amatum	to love	amiable
3. annus	year	annual
4. audire	to hear	audible
5. capere, captum	to take	capture
6. caput	head	caption, capital
7. dicere, dictum	to say, to speak	edict, diction
8. duco, ductum	to lead	aqueduct
9. facere, factum	to make, to do	manufacture
10. loqui, locutum	to speak	eloquence
11. lucere	to be light	elucidate, translucent
12. manus	hand	manual, manuscript
13. medius	middle	mediate
14. mittere, missum	to send	admit, permission

15. omnis	all	omnipotent
16. plicare, plicatum	to fold	implicate
17. ponere, positum	to place	post, depose
18. portare, portatum	to carry	porter
19. quarere, quaesitum	to ask, to question	inquire
20. rogare, ragatum	to ask	interrogate
21. scribere, scriptum	to write	scribble
22. sentire, sensum	to feel	consent, sense
23. specere, spectrum	to look at	inspect
24. spirare, spiratum	to breathe	inspire, conspire
25. tendere, tentum	to stretch	extend, attend
26. verbum	word	verb, verbiage

voc

18e

Greek Roots

1. bios (bio-)	life	biology, biography
2. chronos (chrono-)	time	chronology
3. derma (derma-)	skin	dermatologist, hypodermic
4. ethos (ethno-)	race, tribe	ethnic
5. gamos (-gamy, -gamous)	marriage, union	bigamy, bigamous
6. genos (gene-)	race, kind, sex	genetics, genealogy
7. geo-	earth	geology, geography
8. graphein (-graph)	to write	paragraph
9. helios (helio-)	sun, light	heliotrope
10. krates (-crat)	member of a group	plutocrat, democrat
11. kryptos (crypto-)	hidden, secret	cryptic, cryptogram
12. metron (-meter, metro-)	to measure	barometer, metronome
13. morphe (morph)	form	morphology
14. osteon (osteo-)	bone	osteopath, osteomyelitis
15. pathos (patho-, -pathy)	suffering, feeling	sympathy
16. phagein (phag)	to feed, to consume	bacteriophage
17. philos (philo-, -phile)	loving	bibliophile, philosophy
18. phobos (-phobe, phobia)	fear	Anglophobe, claustrophobia
19. photos (photo-)	light	photograph
20. pneuma	wind, air	pneumatic
21. podos (-pod, -poda)	foot	tripod, hexapoda
22. pseudein (pseudo-)	to deceive	pseudonym
23. pyr (pyro-)	fire	pyrotechnical
24. soma (soma-)	body	psychosomatic
25. tele-	distant	telephone
26. therme (thermo-, -therm)	heat	thermometer

▶

EXERCISE 3

Using the above list of roots, speculate on the meaning of the following words. If you cannot determine the exact meaning of a word, make the best guess you can. Check your definition against one that you find in your college dictionary.

1.	amateur amative	**4.**	audio audiometer
2.	pathology pathetic	**5.**	verbalize verbose verbalist
3.	photosensitive photoengraver photoelectric		

Prefixes

A **prefix** is a letter or group of letters put before a root or word that adds to, changes, or modifies it. The prefix *anti-*, for example, means "against." When combined with other words it forms new words.

antiaircraft	A weapon used against aircraft
antibiotic	A substance used to combat microorganisms
anticoagulant	A substance that suppresses the clotting of the blood
antidote	A remedy that counteracts poison
antifreeze	A substance used to stop a liquid from freezing

Knowing even a few prefixes can help you deduce the meanings of a great many words. Here is a list of prefixes that, combined with different roots, form thousands of words.

Prefixes Indicating Number

Prefix	Meaning	Example	Definition
uni-	one	unify	To make into a unit
bi-	two	bimonthly	Every two months
duo-	two	duotone	Printed in two tones of the same color
tri-	three	triad	A group of three
quadri-	four	quadruped	A four-footed animal
tetra-	four	tetrachloride	A chemical with four chlorine atoms
quint-	five	quintuplets	Five offspring born in a single birth
pent-	five	pentagon	A five-sided figure
multi-	many	multilateral	Having many sides
mono-	one	monogamy	Having one spouse
poly-	many	polygamy	Having many spouses
omni-	all	omnivore	Eating all kinds of food

VOC
18e

Prefixes Indicating Smallness

Prefix	Meaning	Example	Definition
micro-	small	microscope	An instrument for observing small things
mini-	small	minibus	A small bus

Prefixes Indicating Sequence and Space

Prefix	Meaning	Example	Definition
ante-	before	antebellum	Before the war
pre-	before	prehistory	Before history
intro-	within	introspective	Looking into oneself
post-	after	postscript	A message written after the body of the letter
re- #	back, again	review	To look at again
sub-	under	submarine	An underwater ship
super-	above	supervise	To look over the performance of others
inter-	between	international	Between nations
intra-	within	intramural	Within the bounds of an institution
in-	in, into	incorporate	To write as a body
ex-	out, from	exhale	To breathe out
circum-	around	circumnavigate	To sail or fly around (the earth, an island, etc.)
con-	with, together	congregate	To meet together

voc
18e

Prefixes Indicating Negation

Prefix	Meaning	Example	Definition
non-	not	nonpartisan	Not affiliated
in-	not	inactive	Not active
un-	not, the opposite of, against	unequal	Not equal
anti-	against	antiseptic	Against infection
counter-	opposing	countermand	To revoke an order with another order
contra-	against	contradict	To speak against
dis-	not, the opposite of	dislike	To not like
mis-	wrong, ill	mislead	To give bad advice
mal-	bad, wrong, ill	malformed	Incorrectly shaped
pseudo-	false	pseudonym	A false name

▶
EXERCISE 4

Review the above list of prefixes and list one additional word and definition for each prefix.

▶
EXERCISE 5

Using the lists of prefixes and roots above, determine the meanings of the following words.

voc

18e

1. bilateral
    a) divided
    b) composed of delegates
    c) having two sides
    d) deceitful
2. malediction
    a) a chemical compound
    b) a curse
    c) a prophesy
    d) a tropical plant
3. postnatal
    a) after birth
    b) a back door or gate
    c) quick
    d) a result of trauma
4. extrinsic
    a) unravel
    b) remote
    c) a mathematical function
    d) originating outside
5. omniscient
    a) eating plants
    b) an ancient unit of measurement
    c) understanding everything
    d) made of one piece

Suffixes

Suffixes are syllables added to the end of a word or root that change its part of speech. For example, suffixes added to the verb *believe* form two nouns, an adjective, and an adverb.

<u>verb</u>	believe
<u>noun</u>	believer

noun	believability
adjective	believable
adverb	believably

English has relatively few suffixes that form verbs and adverbs. A large number of suffixes, however, form nouns and adjectives. Knowing the most common ones helps you to identify several words from a single base word.

voc

18e

Verb Suffixes

Suffix	Meaning	Example
-en	to cause to or become	cheapen, redden
-ate	cause to be	activate, animate
-ify, -fy	to make or cause to be	fortify, magnify
-ize	to make, to give, to practice	memorize, modernize

Adverb Suffixes

The only regular suffix for adverbs is -ly, as in *slowly, wisely,* and *energetically.*

Adjective Suffixes

Suffix	Meaning	Example
-al	capable of, suitable for	comical
-ial	pertaining to	managerial
-ic	pertaining to	democratic
-ly	a resemblance	sisterly
-ly	at specific intervals	hourly
-ful	abounding in	colorful
-ous, -ose	full of	porous, verbose
-ive	quality of, that which	creative, adaptive
-less	lack of, free of	toothless
-ish	having the qualities of, preoccupied with	childish, bookish

Noun Suffixes

Suffix	Meaning	Example
-ance, -ence	quality or state of	insurance, competence
-acy	quality or state of	piracy, privacy
-or	one who performs an action	doctor
-arium, orium	place for	aquarium, auditorium
-ary	place for, pertaining to	dictionary
-cide	kill	suicide, homicide
-icle, -cle	a diminutive ending	icicle, corpuscle
-hood	state or condition of	childhood
-ism	quality or doctrine of	Marxism, conservatism
-ity	quality or state of	acidity

Suffix	Meaning	Example
-itis	inflammation of	appendicitis
-ics	the science or art of	economics
-ment	act or condition of	resentment
-mony	resulting condition	testimony
-ology	the study of	biology, psychology

(3) Learning words according to a system

Learning related words according to some system is far more effective than memorizing words at random. Consider the following pair of words.

**voc
18e**

duct	a tubular passage
aqueduct	a conduit designed to transport water

Both words share the Latin root *ducere* (to lead). Because you are already familiar with the word *duct*, you have a clue to the meaning of *aqueduct*. If you know that *aqua* is a Latin word meaning "water," you can easily remember the definition of the word.

Other words also share the root *ducere*.

conduct	to direct the course of
induct	to install, to admit as a member
viaduct	a series of spans used to carry a railroad over a valley or other roads
abduct	to carry off
deduct	to take away
ductile	capable of being fashioned into a new form

Learning these related words together would clearly be easier than learning them at random.

Other word groupings also facilitate learning. You can, for example, study together words that are confusing because they *sound* so much alike.

imminent	about to occur
eminent	prominent
elicit	to draw out
illicit	improper, unlawful
assure	to promise
ensure	to make certain
insure	to provide or obtain insurance (sometimes used interchangeably with *ensure*)
ascent	a rise

assent	agreement
capital	a seat of government
capitol	the building where the legislative body meets
principal	the most important; the head of a school
principle	a basic law or truth

You can also study together words that are confusing because they *look* somewhat alike.

marital	referring to marriage
martial	referring to war
casual	informal
causal	acting as a cause
descent	a downward movement
decent	characterized by good taste or morality

Finally, you can study together words that are confusing because their meanings are so *closely associated* with each other.

imply	to suggest
infer	to conclude
convince	to change a person's opinion
persuade	to move a person to action
explicit	stated outright
implicit	implied, unsaid

See the Glossary of Usage for additional examples of confusing word pairs.

(4)   Keeping a vocabulary file

Get in the habit of writing new words down on 3″ × 5″ cards and grouping together cards that you associate with one another. One section of your vocabulary file might consist of words whose roots are the same; another might contain look-alike or sound-alike words. On each card list synonyms, antonyms, roots, and any other associations that help you remember the definition.

SIDE 1

1. The word
2. A sentence in which the word appears
3. The word with its syllables along with its pronounciation

SIDE 2

1. Prefix, root, and suffix (if applicable)
2. Definitions
3. Synonyms, antonyms, root words, or other words that are related.

Carry a packet of these cards around with you and look at them whenever you have a spare moment. When you feel that you have learned the words in the stack, return them to your card file and take out another stack. Review the cards periodically so you do not forget what you have learned.

Be on the lookout for ways to categorize a series of words for easy recall. After learning a word, look up its synonyms and antonyms and learn them, too. Find other words that contain the same prefix, suffix, or root. After a while, you will find that you have a surprisingly large number of words and cross-references in your card file and an expanded vocabulary at your command.

voc

18e

▶

EXERCISE 6

Select word pairs from your vocabulary journal that fall into the categories mentioned above: (1) words that have the same root, (2) words that sound alike, (3) words that look alike, and (4) words that are closely associated with each other. Make out 3″ × 5″ cards for each pair and begin your own vocabulary file.

19

Improving Spelling

Contrary to popular opinion, spelling usually *does* count on examinations, essays, and reports, and many instructors do not hesitate to lower a grade on a paper that contains poor spelling. Spelling errors distract readers and make it difficult for them to understand what you are trying to say. In some cases, incorrectly spelled words actually misrepresent your meanings, as when you use *equivalents* for *equivalence*, for example, or *benzene* for *benzoin.*

If spelling has always given you trouble, you will probably not become a champion speller overnight. But the situation is not hopeless. Most people can spell even difficult words "almost" correctly; usually just a letter or two is wrong. For this reason, memorizing just a few simple rules and their exceptions and learning the correct spelling of the most commonly misspelled words can make a big difference.

19a   Spelling and Pronouncing Words

Because many words in English are not spelled as they are pronounced, sound alone does not necessarily indicate a word's spelling. For instance, *gh* is silent in *light* but pronounced *f* in *cough*; the ō sound is spelled differently in *mow, toe, though, sew,* and *beau.* These and other inconsistencies between English spelling and pronunciation create a number of problem areas to watch for.

(1)   Vowels in unstressed positions

Many unstressed vowels sound exactly alike when we say them. For instance, it is hard to tell from pronunciation alone that the last *i* in *invincible* is not an *a.* In general, the vowels *a, e,* and *i* are impossible to distinguish in the suffixes *-able* and *-ible, -ance* and *-ence,* and *-ant* and *-ent.*

comfortable	compatible
brilliance	excellence
servant	independent

This blurring of sounds is problematic for both native and nonnative speakers of English.

(2) Silent letters in words

A number of words in English contain silent letters. The *b* in *climb* and *dumb* is silent, as is the *t* in *mortgage*. Silent letters at the beginning of a word are especially bothersome because they make its proper spelling difficult to look up in a dictionary. You cannot look up *gnu* (pronounced *new*) if you don't already know that it begins with a *g*. The spelling of words with silent letters follows no rules, so you have to memorize words as you encounter them. Here are some examples.

**sp
19a**

aisle	gnome
bough	knell
condemn	knight
climb	pneumonia
depot	silhouette
gnarl	sovereign

(3) Words that contain letters or syllables not pronounced in informal speech

Most people pronounce words rather carelessly in everyday speech. If they then use pronunciation as a guide to spelling, they leave out, add, or misplace letters. The following words are often misspelled because they are pronounced incorrectly.

literature	nuclear
February	environment
foliage	stubborn
candidate	disastrous
library	modern
government	hundred
perform	lightning
candidate	drowning
quantity	probably
recognize	specific
strictly	surprise

(4)   Variant forms of the same word

Some spelling problems occur because the forms of certain words have different spellings.

In some cases the root of a word changes spelling as it changes form.

nine	ninth
five	fifth
four	forty

Spelling problems can occur when the spellings of the noun and verb forms of a word are different.

advise (v)	advice (n)
renounce (v)	renunciation (n)
announce (v)	annunciation (n)
describe (v)	description (n)
omit (v)	omission (n)

Spelling differences also occur among the principal parts of irregular verbs.

arise arose, arisen
drive, drove, driven
grow, grew, grown
ride, rode, ridden
spring, sprang, sprung
throw, threw, thrown

Irregular nouns change spelling when the plural is formed.

man, men
calf, calves
child, children
goose, geese
wife, wives
woman, women

Some words have more than one accepted spelling, such as *theater/theatre, rime/rhyme, counselor/counsellor.* In addition, some words are spelled one way in America and another way in Great Britain. You should always consult a dictionary to determine the preferred American spelling.

American	*British*
check	cheque
color	colour
judgment	judgement

flavor	flavour
humor	humour
analyze	analyse
offense	offence

(5) Words that sound alike but that are spelled differently

Many words in English are pronounced alike but spelled differently. Such words, called **homonyms**, can cause spelling problems. The following is a partial list of the homonyms that are misspelled most often. For other examples see the Glossary of Usage.

**sp
19a**

accept/except	effect/affect
affect/effect	eminent/imminent
ascent/assent	hear/here
bored/board	hoarse/horse
break/brake	its/it's
capital/capitol	principal/principle
cite/site/sight	stationary/stationery
complement/compliment	there/their/they're
council/counsel	theirs/there's
descent/dissent	weather/whether

▶

EXERCISE 1

Use your dictionary to determine the proper word for each sentence.

1. Two members of the committee registered their descent/dissent.
2. In the short story "Araby," James Joyce makes an allusion/illusion to Sir Walter Scott's *The Abbott.*
3. Mrs. Holdsworth was the principle/principal shareholder of the utility stock.
4. The gangster John Dillinger alluded/eluded capture for years.
5. The scientists warned of eminent/imminent disaster from the volcano.
6. Ted Kennedy decided not to accept/except the 1984 presidential nomination.
7. The Internal Revenue Service allows you a standard deduction for dependence/dependents.
8. The Naval Academy has traditionally maintained strict entrants/entrance requirements.
9. A fine wine is a perfect complement/compliment to dinner.
10. Because its rotation matched the earth's, the satellite appeared stationary/stationery.

19b Learning Spelling Rules

The few reliable rules that govern English spelling can help you overcome the general inconsistency between pronunciation and spelling. These rules have exceptions, but they are still useful guides.

(1) The *ie/ei* combinations

sp
19b

The old rule still stands: use *i* before *e* except after *c* or when pronounced *ay* as in *neighbor.*

i **before** *e*

belief	niece	grief
chief	piece	yield
field	friend	hygiene

ei **after** *c*
ceiling
conceit
deceit
receive
perceive

ei **pronounced** *ay*
neighbor
weigh
freight
eight

There are a few exceptions to this rule: *either, neither, foreign, leisure, weird,* and *seize.* In addition, if the *ie* combination is not pronounced as a unit, the rule does not apply: *atheist, science.*

▶

EXERCISE 2

Fill in the blanks with the proper *ie* or *ei* combination. After completing the exercise, use your dictionary to check your answers.

>   EXAMPLE: conc __ei__ ve

1.	rec _____ pt	6.	misch _____ f
2.	var _____ ty	7.	effic _____ nt
3.	caff _____ ne	8.	v _____ n
4.	ach _____ ve	9.	spec _____ s
5.	kal _____ doscope	10.	suffic _____ nt

(2)   Doubling consonants

Some words double their final consonants before a suffix that begins with a vowel *(-ed, -ing)*; others do not. Fortunately, there is a rule to distinguish them. The only words that double their consonants in this situation are those that

> have one syllable or are stressed on the last syllable;
> contain only one vowel in the last syllable; and
> end in a single consonant.

The word *tap* satisfies all three conditions: it has only one syllable, it contains only one vowel *(a)*, and it ends in a single consonant *(p)*. Thus, the final consonant doubles before a suffix beginning with a vowel *(tapped, tapping)*. The word *relent* meets two of the above criteria (it has one vowel in the last syllable and it is stressed on the last syllable), but it does not end in a single consonant. Thus, its final consonant is not doubled *(relented, relenting)*.

sp
19b

(3)   Prefixes

The addition of a prefix never affects the spelling of the root.

> un + acceptable = unacceptable
> dis + agree = disagree
> mis + spell = misspell
> dis + joint = disjoint
> over + cautious = overcautious
> fore + hand = forehand
> over + haul = overhaul
> poly + morphous = polymorphous
> semi + conductor = semiconductor
> uni + cellular = unicellular

(For a more complete list of prefixes, see 18e.2.)
Some prefixes can cause spelling problems because they are easily confused or because they are pronounced alike although they are not spelled alike. Be especially careful of the prefixes *ante-/anti-, en-/in-, per-/pre-,* and *de-/di-*.

antebellum	antiaircraft
encircle	integrate
perceive	prescribe
deduct	direct

(4)   Suffixes: silent *e*

When a suffix that starts with a consonant is added to a word ending in silent *e*, the *e* is generally kept: *hope/hopeful; lame/lamely; bore/boredom.*

Familiar exceptions include *argument, truly, ninth, wholly, judgment,* and *abridgment.*

When a suffix that starts with a vowel is added to a word ending in silent *e*, the *e* is generally dropped: *hope/hoping; trace/traced; grieve/grievance; love/lovable.*

**sp
19b**

Familiar exceptions include *changeable, noticeable,* and *courageous.* In these cases the *e* is kept so that the *c* or *g* will be pronounced like the initial consonants in *cease* or *gem* and not like the initial consonants in *come* or *game.*

▶
EXERCISE 3

Combine the following words with the suffixes in parentheses. Determine whether you keep or drop the silent *e*, and be prepared to explain your choice.

> Example: fate (al)
>
> fatal

1. surprise (ing)
2. sure (ly)
3. force (ible)
4. manage (able)
5. due (ly)
6. outrage (ous)
7. service (able)
8. awe (ful)
9. shame (ing)
10. shame (less)

(5)   Suffixes: words ending in *y*

When a word ends in *y (beauty, bounty)*, the *y* often changes when a suffix is added. The *y* changes to an *i* when a suffix begins with a consonant *(beautiful, bountiful)*. The *y* is retained, however, when the ending begins with a *vowel (-ed, -ing)*, or when the *y* ends a proper name *(play/played; tally/tallying; Levy/Levys).*

Familiar exceptions include some one-syllable words.

day/daily but days
pay/paid but payment
say/said but says

▶

EXERCISE 4

Add the endings in parentheses to the following words. Change or keep the final *y* as you see fit, and be prepared to explain your choice.

> EXAMPLE: valley (s)
>
> valleys

1. journey (ing)
2. toy (ed)
3. carry (ing)
4. deputy (ize)
5. study (ing)

6. study (es)
7. bury (ed)
8. likely (hood)
9. plenty (ful)
10. supply (er)

(6) Suffixes: *seed* endings

Endings with the sound *seed* are nearly always spelled *cede: precede, intercede, concede,* and so on. The only exceptions are *supersede, exceed, proceed,* and *succeed.*

(7) Suffixes: *-able, -ible*

These endings sound alike, and they often cause spelling problems. Fortunately, there is a rule that can help you distinguish them. If the stem of a word is itself an independent word, the suffix *-able* is most commonly used. If the stem of a word is not an independent word, the suffix *-ible* is most often used.

> *comfort*able   compatible
> *agree*able   incredible
> *dry*able   plausible

(8) Forming plurals

Most nouns form plurals by adding *-s.* This applies to words ending with consonants or with the vowels *a, e, i,* and *u.*

> savage/savages
> girl/girls
> boat/boats
> tortilla/tortillas
> gnu/gnus
> taxi/taxis

There are, however, a number of exceptions.

Exceptions

WORDS ENDING IN *F* OR *FE*   Words ending in *f* or *fe* can form plurals in several ways. Some words ending in *f* or *fe* form plurals by changing the *f* to *v* and adding *-es* or *-s*.

> knife/knives
> life/lives
> wife/wives
> self/selves

Some words ending in *f* or *fe* just add *-s*.

> belief/beliefs
> proof/proofs

A few such words can form plurals either by adding either *-s* or substituting *-ves* for *f*.

> scarf/scarfs/scarves
> hoof/hoofs/hooves

Words ending in double *f* take *-s* to form plurals *(tariff/tariffs)*.
Because of the irregularity of the plural forms of these words, look them up in your college dictionary if you have any questions.

WORDS ENDING IN *Y*   Most words that end in a consonant followed by *y* form plurals by changing the *y* to *i* and adding *-es*.

> baby/babies
> seventy/seventies
> blueberry/blueberries
> worry/worries

Proper nouns, however, are exceptions: the *Kennedys* (never the *Kennedies*).
Words that end in a vowel followed by a *y* form plurals by adding *-s*.

> monkey/monkeys
> turkey/turkeys
> key/keys
> day/days

WORDS ENDING IN *O*   Most words that end in a consonant followed by *o* add *-es* to form the plural.

> tomato/tomatoes
> hero/heroes
> potato/potatoes

Some, however, add -*s*.

> silo/silos
> memo/memos
> piano/pianos
> soprano/sopranos

Still other words that end in *o* add either -*s* or -*es* to form plurals.

> memento/mementos/mementoes
> mosquito/mosquitos/mosquitoes

Words that end in a vowel followed by *o* form the plural by adding -*s*.

> radio/radios
> stereo/stereos
> zoo/zoos

WORDS ENDING IN *S, SS, SH, CH, X,* AND *Z*   These words form plurals by adding -*es*.

> Jones/Joneses
> mass/masses
> rash/rashes
> lunch/lunches
> box/boxes
> buzz/buzzes
> tax/taxes
> latch/latches
> fix/fixes

NOTE: Some one-syllable words that end in *s* or *z* double their final consonants when forming plurals *(quiz/quizzes)*.

COMPOUND NOUNS   Compound nouns—nouns formed from two or more words—usually conform to the rules governing the last word in the compound construction.

> sidestep/sidesteps
> congressman/congressmen
> welfare state/welfare states

However, in compound nouns where the first element of the construction is more important than the second, the plural is formed with the first element *(sister-in-law/sisters-in-law)*.

Irregular Plurals
Some words in English have irregular plural endings. No rules govern these plurals, so you have to memorize them.

child/children   ox/oxen
woman/women   louse/lice
man/men   mouse/mice
goose/geese

Foreign Plurals

Some words, especially those borrowed from Latin or Greek, keep their foreign plurals. When you use these words, you must look up their plural forms in your college dictionary if you do not know them. Here are some of the more common Latin and Greek words and their plurals.

Singular	*Plural*
alga	algae
alumnus	alumni
appendix	appendices
axis	axes
criterion	criteria
datum	data
larva	larvae
memorandum	memoranda
oasis	oases
stimulus	stimuli

Some foreign words have a regular English plural as well as the one from its language of origin.

Singular	*Plural*
hippopotamus	hippopotami, hippopotamuses
antenna	antennae, antennas

No Plural Forms

A few words use the same form for both the singular and the plural.

Singular	*Plural*
apparatus	apparatus
deer	deer
fish	fish (*also* fishes)
sheep	sheep
species	species

19c   Developing Spelling Skills

To form good spelling habits, you must invest time and effort. In addition to studying the rules outlined in 19b, you can do a number of things to help yourself become a better speller.

(1)   Learning commonly misspelled words

Following is a list of some of the most commonly misspelled words. It is a good idea to take a group of these words—say, twenty each day—and learn them. Put them down on 3″ × 5″ cards and review them whenever you have a few extra minutes. Or ask a friend to quiz you on them. After isolating the words you chronically misspell, you can concentrate on learning them.

When you master the following list, you might turn to the look-alike words in the Glossary of Usage.

**sp
19c**

A

absence	acquaintance	analysis/analyze
absorption	across	angel/angle
abundance	address	annual
accessible	advice/advise	apparent
accidentally	aggravate	appearance
acclaim	allotted	argument
accommodate	a lot	atheist
accomplish	all right	attendance
accumulate	already	auxiliary
achievement	amateur	

B

balloon	believe	breathe
barbiturate	benefited	Britain
bargain	biscuit	bouyant
basically	bouillon	bureaucracy
beggar	boundary	business
beginning	breadth/breath	

C

calendar	colossal	consensus
camouflage	column	consistent
cantaloupe	coming	continuous
capital/capitol	committee	controlled
cemetary	commitment	coolly
chagrined	comparative	corollary
challenge/challengeable	competent	correlate
characteristic	completely	correspondence
changing	concede	counselor
chief	conceive	council/counsel
choose/chose	condemn	courteous
cigarette	condescend	courtesy
climbed	conscience	criticize
colonel	consciousness	

D

deceive	desperate	disappoint
defendant	develop	disastrous
deferred	developed	discipline
definitely	development	disease
dependent/dependant	dilemma	dissatisfied
descend	dining	dominant
desirable	disappearance	drunkenness
despair		

E

easily	environment	exhaust
ecstasy	equipped	exhilarate
efficiency	equivalent	existence
eighth	especially	expense
eligible	exaggerate	experiment
embarrass	exceed	explanation
eminent	excellence	extremely
enemy	except	exuberance
entirely		

F

fallacious	fiery	forfeit
fallacy	finally	formerly
familiar	financially	forty
fascinate	forcibly	fourth
February	foreign	fulfill
fictitious	foresee	fundamentally

G

gauge	governor	guard
generally	grammar	guerilla
genius	grievous	guidance
government	guarantee	

H

handkerchief	hemorrhage	hoping
happily	heroes	humorous
harass	hesitancy	hypocrisy
height	hindrance	hypocrite
heinous	hoarse	

I

ideally	implement	indispensible
idiosyncrasy	incidentally	inevitable
ignorance	incredible	innocuous
imaginary	independent	insurance
immediately	indicted	intelligence

inoculate	interpret	irrelevant
intercede	interrupt	irresistible
interference	introduce	island

J

| jealousy | judicial | judgment |
| jewelry | | |

K

knowledge

L

laboratory	license	literally
leisure	lieutenant	loneliness
legitimate	lightning	loose
length	likely	lose
lenient	likelihood	luxury

**sp
19c**

M

magazine	medieval	misspelled
maintain	millionaire	mortgage
maintenance	minor	mosquito
manageable	minutes	mosquitoes
maneuver	miniature	murmur
marriage	mischievous	muscle
mathematics	missile	mysterious
medicine		

N

narrative	neutron	noticeable
naturally	niece	nowadays
necessity	ninety	nuclear
neighbor	ninth	nuisance
neither		

O

obedience	omission	oppression
obstacle	omit	optimism
occasionally	omitted	ordinarily
occurred	opinion	origin
occurrence	opponent	outrageous
official	opportunity	overrun

P

panicky	peculiar	permissible
parallel	penetrate	permitted
parliament	perceive	perseverance
particularly	performance	persistent
peaceable	permanent	physical

physician
picnicked
piece
pitiful
planning
playwright
possessive
potato
potatoes
practically
prairie
precede

preceding
predominant
preference
preferred
prejudice
preparation
prescription
prevalent
primitive
principle
privilege
probably

procedure
proceed
process
professor
prominent
pronounce
pronunciation
propaganda
prophecy/prophesy
psychology
publicly
pursue

_sp_
19c

_Q_
quandary
quarantine

questionnaire

quizzes

_R_
realistically
realize
really
recede
receipt
receive
recognize
recommend

reference
referred
relevant
relieving
religious
remembrance
reminiscence
repetition

representative
resemblance
reservoir
resistance
restaurant
rheumatism
rhythmical
roommate

_S_
sacrifice
safety
salary
satellite
scenery
schedule
secede
secretary
seize
separate
sergeant
several
shining
simile
simply
sincerely

skeptical
skiing
soliloquy
sophomore
souvenir
specifically
specimen
sponsor
spontaneous
statistics
stopped
strategy
strength
strenuous
stubbornness
subordinate

subtle
succeed
succession
sufficient
summary
supersede
suppress
surprise
surround
suspicious
susceptible
synonymous
syllable
symbol
symmetrical

_T_
tangible
technical

technique
temperature

tenant
tendency

than/then	through	tragedy
their/there/they're	though	transferred
themselves	till	truly
theories	tomorrow	twelfth
therefore	tournament	tyranny
thorough	tourniquet	

U

unanimous	unnecessary	usage
unconscious	until	usually
undoubtedly		

V

vacuum	vengeance	villain
valuable	vigilant	violence
varies	village	visible

W

warrant	wherever	women
weather/whether	wholly	writing
Wednesday	whose/who's	written
weird	woman	

XYZ

yacht	your/you're	zoology
yield		

sp
19c

(2) Making your own spelling list

Each of us has individual spelling problems, so you should compile a list of your own problem words. When you write a first
draft, circle any words whose spelling you are unsure of. Then
look them up in your dictionary as you revise, and add them all
(even those you have guessed correctly) to your list. When your
instructor returns a paper, you should also record any words
you have misspelled. In addition, record words that you encounter when reading, including those from class notes and textbooks. It is especially important that you master words that are
basic to a course or given field of study.

Review your list periodically so that the correct spelling of
your problem words becomes a part of your long-term memory.

(3) Uncovering patterns of misspelling

In addition to studying individual words, review your list as a
whole to see whether any patterns of misspelling emerge. Do you

consistently have a problem with plurals, or with -*ible*/-*able* endings? If so, review the spelling rules that apply to these particular problems. By using this strategy to get at the source of your spelling difficulties, you can eliminate the need to memorize single words.

(4)   Fixing each word in your mind

**sp
19c**

Once you isolate the words that you consistently misspell, take the time to think of associations that will help fix the correct spellings in your mind. For example, you can arrive at the correct spelling of *definite* (often misspelled *definate*) by remembering that it contains the word *finite*, which suggests the concept of *limit*, as does *definite*. You can recall the *a* in *brilliance* (often misspelled *brillience*) by remembering that brilliant people often get A's in their classes. You can master the spelling of *criticism* by remembering that it contains the word *critic*.

Another way of fixing words in your mind is to write them down. When you review your spelling list, do not just reread the words on it; write them down. This repeated copying will help you remember the correct spellings.

▶

EXERCISE 5

Begin your own spelling list by selecting thirty words from the list of commonly misspelled words on pages 355–359. Choose ten especially troublesome words from your list, and think of associations to help you remember them.

Understanding Grammar

20

Identifying the Parts of Speech

The eight basic parts of speech—the building blocks for all English sentences—are *nouns, pronouns, verbs, adjectives, adverbs, prepositions, conjunctions,* and *interjections.* The part of speech to which a word belongs depends on its function in a sentence.

20a Nouns

Nouns name people, places, things, ideas, actions, or qualities.

A **common noun** names any of a class of people, places, or things: *artist, judge, building, event, city.*

A **proper noun,** always capitalized, refers to a particular person, place, or thing: *Mary Cassatt, Learned Hand, World Trade Center, Crimean War, St. Louis.*

A **mass noun** names a quantity that is not countable: *time, dust, work, gold.* Mass nouns are generally treated as singular.

A **collective noun** designates a group of people, places, or things thought of as a unit: *committee, class, navy, band, family.* Collective nouns are generally treated as singular unless the sentence clearly refers to the members of the group as individuals.

An **abstract noun** refers to an intangible idea or quality: *love, hate, justice, anger, fear, prejudice.*

20b Pronouns

Pronouns are words that may be used in place of nouns in a sentence. The noun for which a pronoun stands is called its *antecedent.* There are eight different types of pronouns. Note that different types of pronouns may have the same forms but are distinguished by *their functions in the sentence.*

A **personal pronoun** stands for a person or thing: *I, me, we, us, my, mine, our, ours, you, your, yours, he, she, it, its, him, his, her, hers, they, them, their, theirs.*

She decided to apply for the position.

The company responded to her letter.

They made her an offer she couldn't refuse.

She turned them down.

An **indefinite pronoun** functions in a sentence as a noun but does not refer to any particular person or thing. For this reason, indefinite pronouns do not require antecedents. Indefinite pronouns include *another, any, each, few, many, some, nothing, anyone, everyone, everybody, everything, someone, something, either,* and *neither*.

Many are called, but few are chosen.

A **reflexive pronoun** is one that ends with *-self* and refers back to the sentence's or clause's subject: *myself, yourself, himself, herself, itself, oneself, themselves, ourselves, yourselves*.

They found themselves in downtown Pittsburgh.

An **intensive pronoun** ends with *-self* and emphasizes a noun or pronoun in the sentence.

Darrow himself was sure his client was innocent.

A **relative pronoun** introduces an adjective or noun clause in a sentence: *which, who, whom, that, what, whose, whatever, whoever, whomever, whichever*.

Gandhi was the charismatic man who helped lead India to independence. (introduces adjective clause)

Whatever happens will be a surprise. (introduces noun clause)

An **interrogative pronoun** introduces a question: *who, which, that, whom, whose, whoever, whatever, whichever*.

Who was that masked man?

A **demonstrative pronoun** points to a particular thing or group of things: *this, that, these, those*.

This is one of Shakespeare's early plays.

A **reciprocal pronoun** denotes a mutual relationship: *each other, one another*.

Ah, love, let us be true/to one another! (Matthew Arnold)

20c Verbs

A verb may either express action

> He ran for the train.
>
> The owl and the pussycat went to sea.

or a state of being.

> Elizabeth II became queen after the death of her father George VI.
>
> It seems impossible that they were in elementary school when I last saw them.

Verbs can be classified into two groups: main verbs and auxiliary verbs (sometimes called helping verbs).

Main verbs carry most of the meaning in the sentence or clause in which they appear.

gr
20c

> Bulfinch's *Mythology* contains a discussion of Greek mythology.
>
> Emily Dickinson anticipated much of twentieth-century poetry.

A main verb is a **linking verb** when it is followed by a subject complement, a word or phrase that defines or describes the subject. Linking verbs include *become, seem, appear,* and *be* (see 6b).

> Kevin is bright.
>
> Carbon disulfide smells bad.

Auxiliary verbs such as *be* and *have* combine with main verbs to form *verb phrases.*

> [auxiliary] [main verb]   [auxiliary] [main verb]
> The train has started. We are leaving soon.
>   [verb phrase]   [verb phrase]

Other auxiliary verbs, known as **modal auxiliaries** (*must, will, would, shall, should, may, might, can, could, need [to],* and *ought [to]*) indicate necessity, possibility, willingness, obligation, or ability.

> In the near future farmers might cultivate seaweed as a food crop.
>
> Coal mining would be safer if dust were controlled in the mines.

See Chapter 22 for a detailed treatment of verbs.

Certain verb forms—participles, infinitives, and gerunds—are collectively called **verbals.** In a sentence, these special verb forms do not behave like verbs. Because none of these forms, like *known* or *running* or *to go* are **finite verbs**—verbs that change form to indicate person, tense, and number—none can serve as a sentence's main verb. Only when used with an auxiliary can such a verb form serve as the main verb of a sentence. ("The answer known" and "The water running" are not sentences; "The answer was known" and "The water is running" are.)

Virtually every verb has a **present participle**, which ends in *-ing (loving, learning, going, writing)*, and a **past participle**, which usually ends in *-d* or *-ed (agreed, learned)*. Some verbs have irregular past participles *(gone, begun, written)*. Participles may function in a sentence as adjectives

**gr
20c**

> Twenty brands of <u>running</u> shoes were displayed at the exhibition. (present participle *running* modifies noun *shoes*)
>
> The <u>crowded</u> bus went right by those waiting at the corner. (past participle *crowded* modifies noun *bus*)

or as nouns.

> The <u>wounded</u> were given emergency first aid. (past participle *wounded* serves as sentence's subject)

An **infinitive**—the base form of the verb preceded by *to*—may serve as an adjective, an adverb, or a noun.

> Ann Arbor was clearly the place <u>to be</u>. (infinitive *to be* serves as adjective modifying noun *place*)
>
> They say that breaking up is hard <u>to do</u>. (infinitive *to do* serves as adverb modifying adjective *hard*)
>
> Carla went outside <u>to think</u>. (infinitive *to think* serves as adverb modifying verb *went*)
>
> <u>To win</u> was everything. (infinitive *to win* serves as sentence's subject)

Gerunds, special forms of verbs ending in *-ing,* are always used as nouns.

> <u>Seeing</u> is <u>believing</u>. (gerund *seeing* serves as sentence's subject; gerund *believing* serves as subject complement)
>
> He worried about <u>interrupting</u>. (gerund *interrupting* is object of preposition *about*)
>
> Andrew loves <u>skiing</u>. (Gerund *skiing* is direct object of verb *loves*)

NOTE: When the *-ing* form of a verb is used as a noun, as it is here, it is considered a *gerund;* when it is used as a modifier, it is a *present participle.*

20d Adjectives

Adjectives are words that describe, limit, qualify, or in any other way modify nouns or pronouns.

The largest class of adjectives is **descriptive;** that is, they name a quality of the noun or pronoun they modify.

> Strike while the iron is <u>hot</u>.
>
> They ordered a <u>chocolate</u> soda and a <u>butterscotch</u> sundae.
>
> The <u>little</u> one is the runt of the litter.

Some descriptive adjectives are formed from common nouns or from verbs (friend/friendly, agree/agreeable). Others, called *proper adjectives*, are formed from proper nouns.

> Eubie Blake was a talented <u>American</u> musician who died in 1983.
>
> The <u>Shakespearean</u> or <u>English</u> sonnet has an octave and a sestet.

**gr
20d**

Two or more words may be joined, with or without a hyphen, to form a single modifier (foreign born, well-read). See 33b.1.

Other kinds of words—articles, pronouns, and numbers, for example—may be used to limit or qualify nouns, and are then considered adjectives.

Articles *(a, an, the).*

> The boy found <u>a</u> four-leaf clover.

Possessive adjectives (the personal pronouns *my, your, his, her, its, our, their, one's*, etc.).

> <u>Their</u> lives depended on <u>my</u> skill.

Demonstrative adjectives *(this, these, that, those).*

> <u>This</u> song reminds me of <u>that</u> song we heard yesterday.

Interrogative adjectives *(what, which, whose).*

> <u>Whose</u> book is this?

Indefinite adjectives *(another, each, both, many, any, some,* and so on).

> <u>Both</u> contestants agreed to return <u>another</u> day.

Relative adjectives *(what, whatever, which, whichever, whose, whosever).*

> I forgot <u>whatever</u> reasons I had for leaving.

Numerical adjectives (*one, two, first, second,* and so on).

The <u>first</u> time I played I only got <u>one</u> hit.

20e   Adverbs

Adverbs are words that describe the action of verbs or modify adjectives, other adverbs, or complete phrases, clauses, or sentences. They answer the questions "How?" "Why?" "Where?" "When?" "To what extent?" and "To what degree?"

He walked <u>rather hesitantly</u> toward the front of the room.

It seems <u>so</u> long since we met <u>here yesterday</u>.

<u>Unfortunately</u>, the program didn't run.

Cody's brother and sister were <u>staggeringly</u> unobservant. (Anne Tyler, *Dinner at the Homesick Restaurant*)

<u>Luckily</u>, my <u>very</u> good grades in calculus and history <u>rather easily</u> raised my average. (In this sentence, *very* modifies the adjective *good*; *rather*, the adverb *easily*; and *easily*, the verb *raised*. *Luckily* modifies the entire independent clause.)

The largest group of adverbs are those formed from adjectives, and some of these are identical in spelling to adjectives. ("The *early* bird woke up *early*.") Others are formed when *-ly* is added to the adjective form (serious/seriously, creative/creatively).

Another group of adverbs is derived from prepositions ("He woke *up*"; "I get *around*.")

Many familiar adverbs that indicate time, place, condition, cause, or degree do not derive their forms from other parts of speech: *then, never, maybe, very, also, now, often,* and *there,* for example.

When they ask questions, the words *how, why, where,* and *when* are classified as **interrogative adverbs**. (*Why* did the compound darken?).

Conjunctive adverbs join and relate independent clauses. Following are the most commonly used conjunctive adverbs.

accordingly	furthermore	meanwhile	similarly
also	hence	moreover	still
anyway	however	nevertheless	then
besides	incidentally	next	thereafter
certainly	indeed	nonetheless	therefore
consequently	instead	now	thus
finally	likewise	otherwise	undoubtedly

20f Prepositions

A preposition introduces a word or word group consisting of one or more nouns or pronouns or of a phrase or clause functioning in the sentence as a noun. The word or word group the preposition introduces is called its *object*.

$$\overset{\textit{prep} \quad \textit{obj}}{\frown} \qquad\qquad \overset{\textit{prep} \quad\textit{obj}}{\frown}$$

They received a postcard <u>from</u> Bobby that told them <u>about</u> his trip

$$\overset{\textit{prep} \qquad\quad \textit{obj}}{\frown}$$

<u>to</u> the Soviet Union.

Here is a list of the most frequently used prepositions. Many of them can also be used as other parts of speech, depending on their function in a sentence.

**gr
20g**

about	beneath	inside	since
above	beside	into	through
across	between	like	throughout
after	beyond	near	to
against	by	of	toward
along	concerning	off	under
among	despite	on	underneath
around	down	onto	until
as	during	out	up
at	except	outside	upon
before	for	over	with
behind	from	past	within
below	in	regarding	without

20g Conjunctions

Conjunctions are words used to connect single words, phrases, clauses, or sentences.

Coordinating conjunctions *(and, or, but, nor, for, so, yet)* connect words, phrases, or clauses of equal weight.

He had to choose pheasant <u>or</u> venison. (coordinating conjunction links two nouns)

. . . of the people, by the people, <u>and</u> for the people (coordinating conjunction links three prepositional phrases)

Candy is dandy, <u>but</u> liquor is quicker. (Ogden Nash) (coordinating conjunction connects two independent clauses)

Correlative conjunctions, always used in pairs, also link items of equal weight (see 7a.3). Following are the most frequently used correlative conjunctions.

both . . . and	not only . . . but also
either . . . or	whether . . . or
neither . . . nor	just as . . . so

<u>Both</u> Hancock <u>and</u> Jefferson signed the Declaration of Independence. (pair of correlative conjunctions connects two nouns)

<u>Either</u> I will renew my lease, <u>or</u> I will move. (pair of correlative conjunctions links two independent clauses)

Subordinating conjunctions (*since, because, although, if, after, when, while, before, unless,* and so on) introduce adverbial clauses. Thus, a subordinating conjunction connects the sentence's main (independent) clause with an adverbial (dependent or subordinate) clause (see 7b).

<u>Although</u> drug use is a serious concern for parents, many parents are afraid to discuss it with their children.

It is best to draw a diagram of your garden <u>before</u> you start to plant it.

For a list of the most commonly used subordinating conjunctions, see 7b.

Adverbial conjunctions, also known as conjunctive adverbs, are discussed in 20e.

20h Interjections

Interjections are words used as exclamations: *Oh! Ouch! Wow! Alas! Hey!* These words, which express emotion, are grammatically independent; that is, they do not have a grammatical function in a sentence. Interjections may be set off in a sentence by commas.

The message, <u>alas</u>, arrived too late.

Or, for greater emphasis, they can be punctuated as independent units, set off with an exclamation point.

<u>Alas</u>! The message arrived too late.

Other words besides interjections are also sometimes used in isolation. These include words like *yes, no, hello, good-bye, please,* and *thank you.* All such words, including interjections, may be collectively referred to as **isolates.**

21

Nouns and Pronouns

Case

Case is the form a noun or pronoun takes to indicate how it functions in a sentence. English has three cases: objective, subjective, and possessive.

As the English language developed, nouns generally lost their case distinctions and now change form only in the possessive case: the *cat's* eyes, *Bradley's* book (see 28a). Therefore, discussions of case usually focus on pronouns.

Pronouns take the **subjective** case when they act as the subject of a sentence or clause and the **objective** case when they act as the object of a verb or preposition. Nouns and pronouns take the **possessive** case when they indicate possession of a quality.

In English, only the pronouns *I, we, he, she, they,* and *who* change forms in all cases.

Subjective
| I | he, she | it | we | you | they | who | whoever |

Objective
| me | him, her | it | us | you | them | whom | whomever |

Possessive
| my | his, her | its | our | your | their | whose | |
| (mine) | (hers) | | (ours) | (yours) | (theirs) | | |

21a Using the Subjective Case

A pronoun takes the **subjective case** when it acts as the *subject of a verb;* when it serves as a *subject complement;* when it is the *subject of a clause;* and when it is an *appositive identifying the subject.*

> David and <u>I</u> bought the same kind of ten-speed bicycle. (subject of a verb)

> It was <u>he</u> the men were looking for. (subject complement)

The sergeant asked whoever wanted to volunteer to step forward. (subject of noun clause, *whoever wanted to step forward*)

Both scientists, Oppenheimer and he, worked on the atomic bomb. (appositive identifying the subject *Both scientists*)

NOTE: Using the proper case for subject complements sometimes creates forced-sounding constructions. Most people feel silly saying "It is I" or "It is he," and they use the more natural colloquial constructions "It's me" or "It's him," especially in speech or informal writing. Often you can avoid stilted "proper English" by revising the sentence to make your point.

> STILTED: The students who served on the committee were you and I.

> REVISED: You and I were the students who served on the committee.

21b   Using the Objective Case

A pronoun takes the **objective case** when it acts as a *direct object*, an *indirect object*, an *object of a preposition*, an *object of an infinitive*, an *object of a gerund*, a *subject of an infinitive*, or an *appositive identifying an object*.

Our sociology teacher likes Adam and me. (*me* is a direct object of the verb *likes*)

During the 1950's the *Kinsey Report* gave them quite a shock. (*them* is the indirect object of the verb *gave*)

In 1502 Leonardo da Vinci designed the fortifications of the city for him. (*him* is the object of the preposition *for*)

Hoover did not want to anger Alfred E. Smith or him. (*him* is the object of the infinitive *to anger*)

Finding her was not easy for Marlow. (*her* is the object of the gerund *finding*)

They told him to defend his flank against the French cavalry. (*him* is the subject of the infinitive *to defend*)

Rachel discussed both authors, Hannah Arendt and her. (*Hannah Arendt and her* is an appositive identifying the object, *authors*)

NOTE: Discard the mistaken idea that *I* is somehow always more appropriate than *me*. This impulse to overcorrect is often expressed in compound constructions.

He told Jason and me [not I] to run our computer program. (*me* is the object of the verb *told*)

Between you and me [not I] we own ten shares of stock. (*me* is the object of the preposition *between*)

Let's you and me [not I] go to the art museum. (*me* is in apposition to *us*, direct object of the verb *let*)

21c Using the Possessive Case

A pronoun takes the **possessive case** when it indicates ownership. (*our* car, *your* book). Some possessive forms—*his, hers, mine, ours, yours,* and *theirs*—may be used alone in a noun position in place of a noun.

> Hers is the house at the corner.
>
> The blue Volvo is mine.
>
> Last year we all decided to plant a garden; theirs grew vegetables and ours grew weeds.

In your sentences be sure to distinguish gerunds, which always function as nouns, from present participles functioning as adjectives (see 20c). Keep in mind that in college writing you should use the possessive, not the objective, before the gerund.

> John Glenn's failing to get the nomination disappointed his supporters. (*failing* is a gerund)
>
> Napoleon approved of their ruling Naples. (*ruling* is a gerund)
>
> You do not use the possessive case with a participle.
>
> The astronaut orbiting the earth saw flecks of white crystals. (*orbiting* is a participle that serves as an adjective)

NOTE: Be careful when using the possessive pronoun *its* and the contraction *it's*. *Its* designates possession (*its* leg) while *it's* is the contraction of *it is* ("*It's* a nice day") or *it has* ("*It's* faded in the sunlight").

▶

EXERCISE 1

Choose the correct form of the pronoun within the parentheses.

EXAMPLE: Traveling down the Columbia River, Balboa and (he, him) sighted the Pacific Ocean.

ca
21c

1. Rodin and (he, him) participated in the Paris exhibit.
2. It was (they, them) who fought in the revolution of 1848.
3. Milton Friedman says it is (us, we) who are responsible for the declining dollar.
4. Both writers, Conrad and (he, him), wrote books about the sea.
5. My father gave Brian and (I, me) advice.
6. The heat along with the humidity made (he, him) sick.
7. The foreman agreed to (me, my) working there.
8. Hester was disturbed by (his, him) ignoring her.
9. (Us, We) students deserve better food.
10. Marat, Robespierre, and (he, him) were the most radical members of the cabinet.

ca
21d

21d Correcting Common Errors: Case

(1) Words left out

In constructions where words are left out but definitely understood, the case of a pronoun depends upon the missing verb. Implied comparisons using *than* or *as* are especially troublesome. When a sentence that has implied elements ends with a pronoun, your meaning dictates your choice of pronoun.

> Darcy likes John more than I.
> *[more than I like John]*

> Darcy likes John more than me.
> *[more than she likes me]*

> Alex helps Dr. Elliott as much as I.
> *[as much as I help]*

> Alex helps Dr. Elliott as much as me.
> *[as much as he helps me]*

(2) *Who* and *whom*

The case of the pronouns *who* and *whom* depends on their function within their own clause. Remember, pronoun case does *not* depend on the function of the entire clause, which can serve as a *subject*, *object*, or *modifier*.

Use *who* and *whoever* *for all subjects of a subordinate clause.*

> The Salvation Army gives food and shelter to whoever is in need.
> (*Whoever* is the subject of the verb *is* in the subordinate clause; the entire clause, *whoever is in need*, serves as the object of the preposition *to*.)

Shortly after leaving Oklahoma the Joads were reminded who they were and where they came from. (*Who* is the subject complement of the verb *were* even though the entire clause serves as the object of the verb *reminded*.)

Use whom *and* whomever *for all objects of a subordinate clause.*

I wonder whom Rousseau influenced. (*Whom* is the object of *influenced*; the entire clause *whom Rousseau influenced* is the object of the verb *wonder*.)

Whomever Stieglitz photographed, he revealed. (*Whomever* is the object of *photographed*; the entire clause is the direct object of the verb *revealed*.)

NOTE: Watch out for intervening phrases such as *I think, we know,* or *she* or *he says*. The choice of *who* or *whom* still depends upon how the pronoun functions in its own clause. If intervening phrases cause problems, read the sentence without the intervening phrase.

ca
21d

Isaac Newton is the man who [we know] revolutionized the science of physics. (*Who* is the subject of the clause *who we know revolutionized the science of physics.*)

Determine the case of who *at the beginning of a question by answering the question using the personal pronoun.*

Who wrote *Gone with the Wind?*
   [*She wrote it. Subject*]

Whom do you want for mayor?
   [*I want her. Object*]

For whom is the letter?
   [*It is for him. Object of a preposition*]

NOTE: Although formal writing requires that *whom* be used for all objects, strict adherence to this rule can result in stilted constructions. In all but the most formal situations, current usage accepts *who* at the beginning of questions.

Who do you want for Mayor?

Who is the letter for?

▶

EXERCISE 2

Using the word in parentheses, combine each pair of sentences into a single sentence. You may change word order and add or delete words.

EXAMPLE: Lee is a carpenter. Many people employ him. (whom)

Lee is a carpenter whom many people employ.

1.   Henry Ford was a famous automobile manufacturer.
     He introduced his Model T in 1908. (who)
2.   Christopher Columbus interested the king and queen.
     He met them in Madrid in 1486. (whom)
3.   Does anyone know the author?
     He wrote *Catch 22.* (who)
4.   He mourned for his friend.
     He last saw him in October. (whom)
5.   Wyndham Lewis was a writer.
     He was cofounder and editor of *Blast* magazine in 1914. (who)

**ref
21**

Pronoun Reference

The word or group of words to which a pronoun refers is called its **antecedent.** Pronouns get their meaning from the noun or noun phrase to which they refer.

In the sentence "Melville knew he had written more than a whaling book," *he* refers to the antecedent *Melville.* Now look at this sentence.

> Physicians have more people in their waiting rooms with emotional problems than they have ever had before, but they also have more elderly patients who not only try to live with their decreased physical abilities . . . but who also face loneliness and isolation with all its pains and anguish. (Elizabeth Kübler-Ross)

This sentence has seven pronouns. The first three—*their, they,* and *they*—refer to the antecedent *physicians.* The next three—*who, their,* and *who*—refer to *elderly patients.* The final pronoun *its* refers to *loneliness and isolation.*

Pronouns can also refer to antecedents in other sentences. Consider this passage.

> (1) The telephone and the automobile produced quantum jumps in communication and transportation. (2) They gave ordinary men a mastery over space that not even kings and emperors possessed in the past. (3) They changed not only the patterns of everyday life, but the physical structure of the world—the shapes of our cities, the uses of the land. (Arthur C. Clarke, "Electronic Tutors")

Here the pronoun *they* in sentences 2 and 3 refers to the phrase the *telephone and the automobile* in sentence 1.

Indefinite pronouns such as *everyone, someone, no one, each, every,* and *some* refer to unspecified persons or things, and therefore they require no antecedents (see 20b). Occasionally, a pronoun whose meaning is clearly understood needs no antecedent. When they refer to the narrator or audience of a piece of writing, the pronouns *I, you,* and *we* fall into this category.

But most pronouns do have antecedents. Just as pronouns must be in the proper case, they must also refer clearly to their antecedents.

21e Making Pronoun References Clear

A pronoun reference is clear only when readers can correctly identify the noun or pronoun whose place it takes. You must therefore make sure that your pronouns unmistakably point to their antecedents. In the following passage, notice how the underscored pronouns point clearly to a definite word.

> Warts are wonderful structures. They can appear overnight on any part of the skin, like mushrooms on a damp lawn, full grown and splendid in the complexity of their architecture. Viewed in stained sections under a microscope, they are the most specialized of cellular arrangements, constructed as though for a purpose. They sit there like turreted mounds of dense impenetrable horn, impregnable, designed for defense against the world outside. (Lewis Thomas, *The Medusa and the Snail*)

The pronouns *they* and *their* carry through several sentences, but Thomas has made their references to *warts* in sentence 1 quite clear.

Here is another example.

> For example, many fairy stories begin with the death of a mother or father; in these tales the death of a parent creates the most agonizing problems, as it . . . does in real life. (Bruno Bettelheim, *The Uses of Enchantment*)

Again the meaning of each pronoun is clear. *These* refers to the antecedent *fairy stories,* and *it* refers to *the death of a parent.*

▶
EXERCISE 3

Supply the proper pronoun for the underlined antecedent.

EXAMPLE: Indians occupied North America before the arrival of
            Europeans.

            They are called Indians because Columbus thought he
            had reached the Indies.

1. Indians probably migrated into North America from Asia via the Bering Strait. When _____ arrived in Alaska _____
   spread south.
2. Evidence of Indians in America goes back 25,000 years. Consisting of
   pottery, cave drawings, and artifacts, _____ placed Indians
   in every part of the continent.
3. Many Indians occupied the Northwest Coast area. According to geo-
   logical records, _____ was thickly wooded and temperate.
4. The Plains Indians gave other Indians the horse, the tepee, and
   deerskin clothes. _____ caused great cultural changes.
5. The Plateau Indians occupied the area above the Canadian border.
   _____ winter villages had subterranean lodges with cone-
   shaped roofs.

**ref
21f**

21f Revising Ambiguous or Vague Pronoun References

When a pronoun refers to more than one antecedent its reference is said to be ambiguous. Vague pronoun references occur
when a pronoun refers to a nonexistent antecedent or is too far
from its antecedent for the reference to be obvious.

(1) Pronouns should not refer to more than one antecedent

The meaning of a pronoun is ambiguous if the pronoun appears
to refer to more than one antecedent. The pronouns *this, that,
which,* and *it* are most likely to invite this kind of confusion. To
ensure clarity make sure that each pronoun points to a specific
antecedent.

Here is an example of an ambiguous reference.

The accountant took out his calculator and completed the tax
return. After finishing, he put it in his briefcase.

The pronoun *it* can refer either to *calculator* or to *tax return.* The
ambiguity can be eliminated if a noun is substituted for the pronoun.

The accountant took out his calculator and completed the tax return. After finishing, he put the calculator in his briefcase.

In the following example, the pronoun *this* is the problem.

Some one-celled organisms contain chlorophyl and are considered animals. This is one reason one-celled organisms are difficult to classify.

This can refer either to the fact that some one-celled organisms are animals or to the fact that they contain chlorophyl. It could also refer to the implied idea that some one-celled organisms are not easily classified as plants or animals. Recasting the sentence and repeating the antecedent eliminates this ambiguous reference.

Some one-celled organisms that contain chlorophyl are considered animals. This fact points out the difficulty of classifying single-celled organisms as either animals or plants.

ref
21f

If you are certain that no misunderstanding will occur, you can use *this, that, which,* or *it* to refer to a previous clause.

Visitors would constantly interrupt Edison. This made him angry.

Be careful, however. General references often invite confusion.

(2)   Pronouns should not refer to remote antecedents

The farther a pronoun is from its antecedent, the more difficult it is for readers to make a connection between them. As a result, readers lose track of meaning and must reread a passage to determine the connection. Here is an example.

Rumors of gold, letters from friends and relatives, and newspaper articles praising democracy persuaded many Czechs to come to America. By 1860 about 23,000 Czechs had left their country. Many immigrants were children under the age of twelve. By 1900, 13,000 Czech immigrants were coming to its shores each year.

The pronoun *its* in the last sentence is too far removed from its antecedent, *America,* to be easily understood. For clarity, the antecedent should be restated in the final sentence.

By 1900, 13,000 Czech immigrants were coming to America's shores each year.

(3)   Pronouns should not refer to nonexistent antecedents

A vague pronoun reference occurs when a pronoun refers to an unidentified antecedent.

> Our township has decided to build a computer lab in the elementary school. <u>They</u> feel that children should learn to use computers in fourth grade.

In the second sentence *they* seems to refer to *township* as a collective noun. Actually *they* refers to an antecedent that the writer has neglected to mention. Supplying the noun *teachers* eliminates the confusion.

ref
21f

> Our township has decided to build a computer lab in the elementary school. <u>Teachers</u> feel that children should learn to use computers in fourth grade.

Here is another example.

> (1) In his article M. H. Abrams discusses Milton's use of figurative language. (2) He points out that in *Paradise Lost* Milton uses <u>them</u> to achieve special meaning or effect.

Several of the pronouns in this passage clearly refer to their antecedents. *His* in sentence 1 points to *M. H. Abrams,* as does *he* at the beginning of sentence 2. The writer repeats *Milton* in sentence 2 to avoid having *he* refer to either Abrams or Milton. But a problem occurs with *them* in sentence 2. It might refer to *figurative language,* but *them* is plural and *figurative language* is singular. Here are two possible revisions.

> In his article M. H. Abrams discusses Milton's use of figurative language. He points out that in *Paradise Lost* Milton uses metaphor and simile to achieve special meaning or effect.
>
> or
>
> In his article M. H. Abrams discusses Milton's use of metaphor and simile. He points out that in *Paradise Lost* Milton uses them to achieve special meaning or effect.

▶

EXERCISE 4

Analyze the pronoun errors in each of the following sentences about the Lewis and Clark expedition. After doing so revise each sentence by substituting an appropriate noun or noun phrase for the underlined pronoun.

EXAMPLE: Jefferson asked Lewis to head the expedition, and
            Lewis selected him as his associate.

ANALYSIS: *Him* refers to a nonexistent antecedent.

REVISION: Jefferson asked Lewis to head the expedition, and
            Lewis selected Clark as his associate.

1. The purpose of the expedition was to search out a land route to the
   Pacific and to gather information about the West. The Louisiana Purchase increased the need for it.
2. The expedition was going to be difficult. They trained the men in
   Illinois, the starting point.
3. Clark and most of the men descended the Yellowstone River and
   camped on the bank. It was beautiful and wild.
4. Both Jefferson and Lewis had faith he would be successful in his
   transcontinental journey.
5. The expedition was efficient, and only one man was lost. It was an
   extraordinary feat.

ref
21

Student Writer at Work: Nouns and Pronouns

Following is a draft of a short essay on "A & P," a short story by
John Updike. Read the draft and revise it to correct errors in case
and to eliminate inexact pronoun reference.

John Updike's "A & P" is the fourteenth short story in the
book Pigeon Feathers. It takes place in a small town similar to
Updike's home town. The character who has the significant role
in "A & P" is Sammy, a cashier at the supermarket. Sammy is a
nineteen-year-old boy whom is just out of high school. He analyzes everyone who comes to the A & P to shop. It is him who
is the narrator of the story.

The story takes place on a Thursday afternoon when three
girls in bathing suits walk into the store. They are different
from the other shoppers. Their manner and the way they walk
make them different from them. Sammy notices that one of the
girls, who he calls Queenie, leads the other girls. This appeals
to him. He identifies with her because he feels that he too is a
leader.

When the girls come to his check-out counter, he rings up
their purchase. Suddenly the store manager, Lengel, begins
scolding the girls for coming into the store in bathing suits.
Sammy feels sorry for them, and in a gesture of defiance he
quits. Sammy feels that him quitting is a rejection of him and
all that he stands for. To Sammy, Lengel is a drab person who
represents the narrow morality of the town.

Sammy quitting is the climax of the story. Sammy chooses
to follow his conscience and in doing so pays the price. He feels
that not following his ideals would be bad. Because he is young,
however, he does not realize the significance of his acts. For a
moment Lengel and Sammy face each other, but he does not
change his mind. Sammy feels that he has won his freedom.
His confidence is short-lived though. When he walks out into
the parking lot, the girls are gone and he is alone. It is then he
realizes that the world is going to be hard for him from this
point on.

ref
21

Verbs

Verb Forms

All verbs have four **principal parts** from which their tenses are derived: a **base form** (the form of the verb used with *I, we, you,* and *they* in the present tense), a **present participle,** a **past tense form,** and a **past participle.** Most verbs in English are **regular** and form their principal parts with *-ing, -ed,* or *-d* added to the base form.

Base Form	Present Participle	Past	Past Participle
smile	smiling	smiled	smiled
talk	talking	talked	talked
jump	jumping	jumped	jumped
laugh	laughing	laughed	laughed

Irregular verbs, however, do not follow this pattern.

22a Identifying the Principal Parts of Irregular Verbs

Many irregular verbs change an internal vowel in the past tense and past participle.

Base Form	Present Participle	Past	Past Participle
begin	beginning	began	begun
come	coming	came	come
fly	flying	flew	flown
swim	swimming	swam	swum

Other irregular verbs not only change an internal vowel in the past tense but also add *-n* or *-en* to the past participle.

Base Form	Present Participle	Past	Past Participle
fall	falling	fell	fallen
ride	riding	rode	ridden
rise	rising	rose	risen
write	writing	wrote	written

Still other irregular verbs take the same form in both the past and the past participle forms.

Base Form	Present Participle	Past	Past Participle
bet	betting	bet (betted)	bet
have	having	had	had
shed	shedding	shed	shed
spin	spinning	spun	spun
win	winning	won	won

22b   Using Correct Verb Forms

Consult a dictionary whenever you are uncertain about the form of a verb. If only the base form is listed, the verb is regular and forms both its past tense and past participle by adding *-d* or *-ed*. If the verb is irregular, the dictionary lists its forms, three if the past tense and past participle are different

hide, v (past hid, pp hidden)
fall, v (past fell, pp fallen)

and two if the past tense and the past participle are the same.

make, v (made)
spin, v (spun)

The following list presents the irregular verbs that can cause trouble. If you have problems with some of these verbs, familiarize yourself with their principal parts and refer to this list when you edit your writing.

Base Form	Present Participle	Past	Past Participle
arise	arising	arose	arisen
awake	awaking	awoke, awaked	awoke, awaked
be	being	was/were	been
bear (carry)	bearing	bore	borne
beat	beating	beat	beaten
begin	beginning	began	begun
bend	bending	bent	bent
bet	betting	bet, betted	bet
bid	bidding	bid	bid
bind	binding	bound	bound
bite	biting	bit	bitten

Base Form	Present Participle	Past	Past Participle
bleed	bleeding	bled	bled
blow	blowing	blew	blown
break	breaking	broke	broken
bring	bringing	brought	brought
build	building	built	built
burn	burning	burned, burnt	burned, burnt
burst	bursting	burst	burst
buy	buying	bought	bought
catch	catching	caught	caught
choose	choosing	chose	chosen
cling	clinging	clung	clung
come	coming	came	come
creep	creeping	crept	crept
cut	cutting	cut	cut
deal	dealing	dealt	dealt
dig	digging	dug	dug
dive	diving	dived, dove	dived
do	doing	did	done
draw	drawing	drew	drawn
drink	drinking	drank	drunk
drive	driving	drove	driven
eat	eating	ate	eaten
fall	falling	fell	fallen
feed	feeding	fed	fed
feel	feeling	felt	felt
fight	fighting	fought	fought
find	finding	found	found
fling	flinging	flung	flung
fly	flying	flew	flown
forbid	forbidding	forbade, forbad	forbidden, forbid
forget	forgetting	forgot	forgotten, forgot
forsake	forsaking	forsook	forsaken
freeze	freezing	froze	frozen
get	getting	got	got, gotten
give	giving	gave	given
go	going	went	gone
grind	grinding	ground	ground
grow	growing	grew	grown
hang (suspend)	hanging	hung	hung

vb 22b

vb
22b

Base Form	Present Participle	Past	Past Participle
hang (execute)	hanging	hanged	hanged
have	having	had	had
hear	hearing	heard	heard
hit	hitting	hit	hit
keep	keeping	kept	kept
know	knowing	knew	known
lay	laying	laid	laid
lead	leading	led	led
leap	leaping	leaped, leapt	leaped, leapt
learn	learning	learned, learnt	learned, learnt
lend	lending	lent	lent
let	letting	let	let
lie (recline)	lying	lay	lain
lie (tell an untruth)	lying	lied	lied
light	lighting	lighted, lit	lighted, lit
mow	mowing	mowed	mowed, mown
plead	pleading	pleaded, pled	pleaded, pled
prove	proving	proved	proved, proven
put	putting	put	put
read	reading	read	read
rid	ridding	rid, ridded	rid, ridded
ride	riding	rode	ridden
ring	ringing	rang	rung
rise	rising	rose	risen
run	running	ran	run
see	seeing	saw	seen
seek	seeking	sought	sought
set	setting	set	set
shake	shaking	shook	shaken
shed	shedding	shed	shed
shine	shining	shone	shone
shoe	shoeing	shod, shoed	shod, shoed
shrink	shrinking	shrank, shrunk	shrunk, shrunken
sing	singing	sang	sung
sink	sinking	sank	sunk
sit	sitting	sat	sat
slay	slaying	slew	slain
sow	sowing	sowed	sowed, sown

Base Form	Present Participle	Past	Past Participle
speak	speaking	spoke	spoken
speed	speeding	sped, speeded	sped, speeded
spin	spinning	spun	spun
spring	springing	sprang	sprung
stand	standing	stood	stood
steal	stealing	stole	stolen
stick	sticking	stuck	stuck
strike	striking	struck	struck, stricken
strive	striving	strove	striven
swear	swearing	swore	sworn
swim	swimming	swam	swum
swing	swinging	swung	swung
take	taking	took	taken
teach	teaching	taught	taught
tear	tearing	tore	torn
think	thinking	thought	thought
throw	throwing	threw	thrown
tread	treading	trod	trodden, trod
wake	waking	woke	waked, woke, wakened
wear	wearing	wore	worn
weave	weaving	wove	woven
wed	wedding	wed, wedded	wed, wedded
weep	weeping	wept	wept
win	winning	won	won
wind	winding	wound	wound
wring	wringing	wrung	wrung
write	writing	wrote	written

**vb
22b**

▶

EXERCISE 1

Complete the following sentences with an appropriate form of the verbs in parentheses.

> EXAMPLE: The inhabitants of Easter Island _____ Polynesian. (be)
>
> The inhabitants of Easter Island ___*are*___ Polynesian.

1. John Hancock _____ to write his name first on the Declaration of Independence. (choose)
2. In *The Scarlet Letter* Hester Prynne _____ the consequences of her guilt. (bear)

3. Before mechanization workers _____ the water out of the fabric by hand. (wring)

4. Daedalus warned his son what would happen if he _____ too close to the sun. (fly)

5. John Brown was _____ for his attack on Harpers Ferry, Virginia. (hang)

Tense

Tense is the form of a verb that indicates when an action occurred or when a condition existed. Tense, however, is not the same as time. The present tense, for example, indicates present time, but it can also indicate future time or a generally held belief (see 22c).

English has three tenses. The **simple tenses** consist of the present, past, and future. The **perfect tenses,** formed with the auxiliaries *have* and *had* plus the past participle, include the present perfect, the past perfect, and the future perfect. The **progressive tenses** are formed with the appropriate tense of the verb *be* plus the present participle.

22c   Using the Simple Tenses

(1)   The present tense (*I finish, she* or *he finishes*)

The **present tense** usually indicates that an action is taking place when you are speaking or writing. With subjects other than singular nouns or third-person singular pronouns, the present tense uses just the base form of the verb.

> I <u>smile</u> when I am nervous.
>
> They <u>wear</u> wool in the winter.

With singular nouns or third-person singular pronouns, *-s* or *-es* is added to the base form.

> She <u>smiles</u> when she is nervous.
>
> Scott <u>catches</u> cold easily.
>
> He <u>wears</u> wool in the winter.

In addition to expressing action in the present, the present tense has some special uses.

> The rector <u>opens</u> the chapel every morning at six o'clock. (indicates that something occurs regularly)
>
> The grades <u>arrive</u> next Thursday. (indicates future time)
>
> Studying <u>pays</u> off. (states a generally held belief)
>
> An object at rest <u>tends</u> to stay at rest. (states a scientific truth)
>
> In *The Catcher in the Rye* Holden Caulfield <u>spends</u> a weekend wandering through New York City. (discusses the plot, characters, or meaning of literary works)

NOTE: Some words and phrases, such as *just, always,* and *next* help to indicate time.

(2)   The past tense (*I finished*)

vb
22c

The **past tense** is the form of the verb that indicates that an action has taken place. It is formed by adding *-d* or *-ed* to the base form or, for irregular verbs, by changing the form of the verb. The past tense has two uses.

> Charles Lindbergh <u>flew</u> across the Atlantic Ocean on May 20, 1927. (indicates an action completed in the past)
>
> When he was young, Mark Twain <u>traveled</u> across the mining towns of the Southwest. (indicates actions that recurred in the past but did not extend into the present)

(3)   The future tense (*I will finish*)

The **future tense** indicates that an action will take place. A number of constructions can be used to indicate future action, including the present tense (see 22c.1), but here we discuss future tense verb forms. These verb forms consist of the auxiliaries *will* or *shall* plus the present tense. The future tense has the following uses.

> Halley's Comet <u>will reappear</u> in 2061. (indicates a future action that will definitely occur)
>
> The college has announced it <u>will require</u> all freshmen to buy a microprocessor. (indicates intention)
>
> If you expose white phosphorous to oxygen, a violent reaction <u>will</u> <u>occur</u>. (indicates what will happen if certain conditions occur)
>
> The land boom in Florida <u>will</u> most likely <u>continue</u>. (indicates probability)

Note: At one time, *will* was used exclusively for the second- and third-person future of a verb, and *shall* was used for the first person. Except in legal documents, however, *shall* is now rare in current usage.

22d Using the Perfect Tenses

The perfect tenses designate an action that was or will be completed before another action or condition. The perfect tenses are formed with the appropriate tense form of the auxiliary verb *have* plus the past participle.

(1) Forming the present perfect tense (*I have finished, she* or *he has finished*)

The **present perfect** can indicate three types of continuing action that begin in the past.

> Dr. Kim has finished studying the effects of BHA on rats. (indicates an action that begins in the past and is finished when you are speaking or writing)
>
> My father has invested his money wisely. (indicates an action that begins in the past and extends into the present)
>
> I have read all the books in the *Dune* series by Frank Herbert. (indicates an action that occurred at an unspecified past time)

(2) Forming the past perfect tense (*I had finished*)

The **past perfect** has three uses.

> By 1946 engineers had built the first electronic digital computer. (indicates an action occurring before a certain time in the past)
>
> By the time Alfred Wallace wrote his paper, Darwin had already published *The Origin of Species*. (indicates that one action was finished before another one started)
>
> We had hoped to visit the Kennedy Space Center on our trip to Florida. (indicates an unfulfilled desire in the past)

(3) Forming the future perfect tense (*I will have finished*)

The **future perfect** has two uses.

> By Tuesday the transit authority will have run out of money. (indicates that an action will be finished by a certain future time)

By the time a commercial fusion reactor is developed, the government <u>will have spent</u> billions of dollars in research. (indicates that
one action will be finished before another occurs in the future)

22e   Using the Progressive Tense Forms

The tenses discussed so far, the simple tenses and the perfect
tenses, are called **common forms.** They indicate a completed,
momentary, or habitual action.

English also has **progressive forms** that express continuing
action. The progressive forms consist of the appropriate tense of
the verb *be* plus the present participle.

vb
22e

(1)   Present progressive tense (*I am finishing, she* or *he is finishing*)

The **present progressive** has two specific uses.

The volcano <u>is erupting</u> and lava <u>is flowing</u> toward the town. (indicates that something is happening when you are speaking or
writing)

Law <u>is becoming</u> an overcrowded profession. (indicates that an
action is happening even though it may not be taking place when
you are speaking or writing)

(2)   Past progressive tense (*I was finishing*)

The **past progressive** has two uses.

Roderick Usher's actions <u>were becoming</u> increasingly bizarre. (indicates an action continuing in the past)

The French revolutionary Marat was stabbed to death while he
<u>was bathing</u>. (indicates two actions occurring at the same time in
the past)

(3)   Future progressive tense (*I will be finishing*)

The **future progressive** has two uses.

The Secretary of the Treasury <u>will be</u> carefully <u>monitoring</u> the
money supply. (indicates a continuing action in the future)

Next month NATO forces <u>will be holding</u> military exercises. (indicates a continuing action at a specific future time)

(4) Present perfect progressive tense (*I have been finishing*)

The **present perfect progressive** has only one use.

> The number of women getting lung cancer <u>has been increasing</u> dramatically. (indicates action continuing from the past into the present and possibly into the future)

(5) Past perfect progressive tense (*I had been finishing*)

The **past perfect progressive** has only one use.

**vb
22e**

> Before Julius Caesar was assassinated he <u>had been increasing</u> his power. (indicates that one past action went on until a second occurred)

(6) Future perfect progressive tense (*I will have been finishing*)

The **future perfect progressive** has only one use.

> By eleven o'clock we <u>will have been driving</u> for seven hours. (indicates that an action will continue until a certain future time)

▶
EXERCISE 2

A verb is missing from each of the following sentences. Its base form is supplied in parentheses. Fill in the form of the verb indicated after each sentence. Be prepared to explain why you have used a particular tense in each sentence.

> EXAMPLE: The full moon _____ now. (rise: present progressive)
>
> The full moon __is rising__ now. (the action is happening when you are writing or speaking)

1. April showers _____ May flowers. (bring: present)
2. Before he sailed through the Straits of Magellan, Sir Francis Drake _____ Robert Dudley. (execute: past)
3. The movie *E.T.* _____ the contact between a traveler from outer space and an earth boy. (examine: present)
4. The Securities and Exchange Commission always _____ the interests of the public regarding the sale of securities. (protect: present perfect)
5. The Hindenburg _____ and people _____ to the ground. (burn, jump: present progressive)

6. Four engineers _____ on this system since March. (work: present perfect progressive)
7. The Environmental Protection Agency _____ cleaning up a chemical dump in North Jersey. (finish: present perfect)
8. Columbus _____ when the man on watch sighted land. (rest: past progressive)
9. By 1895 Sigmund Freud _____ the science of psychoanalysis. (develop: past perfect)
10. To Rutherford current models of the atom _____ questionable. (become: past progressive)

22f Using the Correct Sequence of Tenses

The relationship among the verb tenses in a sentence is called the **sequence of tenses.** If the actions of all the verbs in a sentence occur at approximately the same time, the tenses should be the same.

> When Katherine Hepburn <u>walked</u> on stage, the audience <u>rose</u> and <u>applauded</u>.

Often, however, a sentence contains several verbs describing actions that occur at different times. The tenses of the verbs must therefore shift. Which tense to use depends both on meaning and on the nature of the clauses in which the verbs occur.

The tense of verbs that appear in adjacent *independent clauses* can shift as long as their relationships to their subjects and to each other are clear.

> The debate <u>was</u> not impressive, but the election <u>will determine</u> the winner.

However, when a verb or verbal appears in a *subordinate clause* or *verbal phrase*, respectively, its tense depends on the tense of the main verb in the independent clause.

The following examples illustrate a number of possible sequences.

1. When the main verb in the independent clause is in any tense except the past or past perfect, the verb in the subordinate clause may be in any tense needed for meaning.

Main Verb	*Subordinate Verb*
Ryan <u>knows</u>	that Herman Melville <u>wrote</u> *The Confidence Man.*
The mayor <u>will explain</u>	why she <u>changed</u> her position

2. When the main verb is in the past tense, the verb in the subordinate clause is usually in the past or past perfect tense. When the main verb is in the past perfect, the subordinate verb is usually in the past tense.

Main Verb	Subordinate Verb
George Hepplewhite <u>was</u> an English cabinetmaker	who <u>designed</u> distinctive chair backs.
The battle <u>had ended</u>	by the time reinforcements <u>arrived</u>.

3. The *present infinitive* (*to* plus the base form of the verb) indicates an action happening at the same time as or later than the main verb. The *perfect infinitive* (*to have* plus the past participle) indicates action happening earlier than the main verb.

vb
22f

Main Verb	Infinitive
I <u>went</u>	<u>to hear</u> Carlos Fuentes last week. (the going and hearing occurred at the same time)
I <u>want</u>	<u>to hear</u> Carlos Fuentes tomorrow. (wanting is in the present, and hearing is in the future)
I would have <u>liked</u>	<u>to hear</u> Carlos Fuentes last week. (both liking and hearing occur at the same time)
I would <u>like</u>	<u>to have heard</u> Carlos Fuentes lecture. (liking occurs in the present, and hearing would have occurred in the past)

4. The *present participle* indicates action happening at the same time as the action of the main verb. The *past participle* or the *present perfect participle* indicates action occurring before the action of the main verb.

Participle	Main Verb
<u>Addressing</u> the 1896 Democratic Convention,	William Jennings Bryan <u>delivered</u> his Cross of Gold speech. (addressing and the delivery occurred at the same time)
<u>Having published</u> his General Theory of Relativity,	Einstein <u>worked</u> on a Unified Field Theory. (publishing occurred before the work on the Unified Field Theory)

▶

EXERCISE 3

From inside each pair of parentheses, choose the correct verb form. Make certain you check the sequence of the verb forms and are able to explain your choices.

EXAMPLE: When the instructor _____ (speaks, spoke), the class listened.

When the instructor spoke, the class listened. (action occurs at same time as the action of the main verb)

1. Alexandre Dumas was a French novelist who (wrote, writes) *The Three Musketeers.*
2. When the war ends the peasants _____ (will go, will have gone) home.
3. I have stopped writing letters of application because I _____ (have heard, heard) all the jobs are filled.
4. The disgruntled fans left the stadium before the game _____ (had ended, ended).
5. Having studied all night, she _____ (had felt, felt) a sense of accomplishment.
6. Playing poker in a saloon, Wild Bill Hickok _____ (had been shot, was shot) in the back.
7. When the temperature _____ (drops, dropped) below freezing, rain turns to snow.
8. Scientists have studied quasars ever since they _____ (discovered, had discovered) them.

vb
22g

Mood

Mood is the verb form that indicates a writer's basic attitude. For a statement or a question, you use the indicative mood. For a command, you use the imperative mood. And for a wish or a hypothetical condition, you use the subjunctive mood.

22g Using the Indicative Mood

The **indicative** is the mood used to express an opinion, state a fact, or ask a question. It may be used along with a form of *do* for emphasis.

Jackie Robinson had an impact on American professional baseball.

Martin Luther King, Jr., wrote "Letter from Birmingham Jail."

American automobile manufacturers do have a large share of the market.

Did Margaret Mead say that behavioral differences are rooted in culture?

22h   Using the Imperative Mood

The **imperative** is the mood used in commands and direct requests. Often the imperative includes only the base form of the verb without a subject.

> (You) <u>Use</u> a dictionary.
>
> (You) <u>Send</u> the results at once.
>
> (You) Please <u>vote</u> today.

When you include yourself in a command, use *let's* or *let us* before the base form of the verb.

> <u>Let us examine</u> Machiavelli's view of human nature.
>
> <u>Let's go</u> to the movies.

22i   Using the Subjunctive Mood

The **subjunctive mood** is used to state wishes, conditions, and contrary-to-fact statements. It is also used in *that* clauses and in certain idiomatic phrases. It calls for special subjunctive verb forms.

The *present subjunctive* uses the base form of the verb, regardless of the subject. The *past subjunctive* has the same form as the past tense of the verb. The auxiliary verb *be*, however, takes the form *were* regardless of the number or person of the subject. The *past perfect subjunctive* has the same form as the past perfect.

> Dr. Gorman suggested that I <u>study</u> the Cambrian period. (present subjunctive)
>
> I wish I <u>were</u> going to Europe. (past subjunctive)
>
> I wish I <u>had gone</u> to the review session. (past perfect subjunctive)

Although technically correct, the subjunctive mood can seem stiff and unnatural. For this reason the indicative mood has almost displaced subjunctive verb forms. In formal writing, however, the subjunctive is still used in the following cases.

1. The subjunctive is used in *that* clauses after words such as *ask, suggest, require, recommend,* and *demand.*

> The report <u>recommended</u> that juveniles <u>be</u> given mandatory counseling.

> During the 1930's Huey Long <u>suggested</u> that personal fortunes above a certain amount <u>be</u> liquidated.

> Captain Ahab <u>insisted</u> that his crew <u>hunt</u> the white whale.

2. The subjunctive is used in contrary-to-fact clauses beginning with *if* or expressing a wish.

A conditional statement begins with a dependent *if* clause that presents a condition and concludes with an independent clause that presents the effect of that condition. If the effect is even slightly possible, use the indicative mood for the verb in the *if* clause.

> If a nuclear treaty <u>is</u> signed, the world will be safer. (a nuclear treaty is possible)

If the condition is impossible or contrary-to-fact, use the subjunctive mood for the verb in the *if* clause.

> If Teller <u>were</u> there, he would have seen Oppenheimer. (Teller was not there)

NOTE: A conditional clause beginning with *as if* is contrary to fact and should be in the subjunctive mood.

> The father acted as if he <u>were</u> having the baby. (the father couldn't be having the baby)

A wish is a condition that does not exist and so should be expressed in the subjunctive mood.

> I wish I <u>were</u> more organized.

3. The subjunctive is used in certain expressions.

> If need <u>be</u>, we will stay up all night to finish the report.

> <u>Come</u> what may, they will increase their steel production.

> Far <u>be</u> it for me to correct an expert.

> Special interest groups have, as it <u>were</u>, shifted the balance of power.

**vb
22i**

▶
EXERCISE 4

Complete the sentences in the following paragraph by inserting the appropriate form (indicative, imperative, or subjunctive) of the verb in parentheses. Be prepared to explain your choices.

Harry Houdini's real name was Erich Weiss. He _____ (perform) escapes from every type of bond imaginable—

handcuffs, locks, straitjackets, ropes, sacks, and sealed chests underwater. In Germany workers _____ (challenge) Houdini to escape from a packing box. If he _____ (be) to escape, they would admit that he _____ (be) the best escape artist in the world. Houdini accepted. Before getting into the box he asked that the observers _____ (give) it a thorough examination. He then asked that a worker _____ (nail) him in the box. " _____ (place) a screen around the box," he ordered after he had been sealed inside. In a few minutes Houdini _____ (step) from behind the screen. When the workers demanded that they _____ (see) the box, Houdini pulled down the screen. To their surprise they saw the box with the lid still nailed tightly in place.

vb
22j

Voice

Voice indicates whether the subject of a verb acts or is acted upon. When the subject of a verb does something—that is, is acting—the verb is in the **active voice.**

ACTIVE VOICE: Hart Crane <u>wrote</u> *The Bridge.*

The city council <u>introduces</u> legislation.

When the subject of a verb receives the action—that is, is acted upon—the verb is in the **passive voice.**

PASSIVE VOICE: *The Bridge* <u>was written</u> by Hart Crane.

Legislation <u>was introduced</u> by the city council.

The active voice is usually briefer, clearer, and more emphatic than the passive voice (see 8e). Some situations, however, require the passive voice for clarity or emphasis.

22j Using the Passive Voice

The passive voice enables you to emphasize actions when the person or thing acting is unknown or unimportant.

DDT <u>was found</u> in local soil samples.

We <u>were required</u> to embroider and I had trunkfuls of colorful dish towels, pillowcases, runners, and handkerchiefs to my credit. (Maya Angelou, *I Know Why the Caged Bird Sings*)

The passive voice also enables you to emphasize whatever logically receives, or is the logical object of, the action.

Darwin's faith in fixed species <u>was destroyed</u> on his five-year trip on the *Beagle*. (emphasis is on fact that Darwin's faith was destroyed, not on who or what destroyed it)

The art of the Greek sculptors of the great age <u>is known</u> to us by long familiarity. (Edith Hamilton, *The Greek Way*) (the passive emphasizes the art, not what we know about it)

Numerical superiority <u>was achieved</u> by the Allies at the Battle of the Marne. (the passive enables the sentence to focus on superiority)

NOTE: Because constructions involving passive voice can be awkward or wordy, you should use the passive voice carefully and only when you have a good reason. For a discussion of problems concerning the passive voice, see 9c.3.

vb
22k

▶

EXERCISE 5

Read the following paragraph and determine which verbs are active and which are passive. Comment if you can on why the author used the passive voice in each case.

> The human species is now undertaking a great venture that if successful will be as important as the colonization of the land or the descent from the trees. We are haltingly, tentatively breaking the shackles of Earth—metaphorically, in confronting and taming the admonitions of those more primitive brains within us; physically, in voyaging to the planets and listening for the messages from the stars. These two enterprises are linked indissolubly. Each, I believe, is a necessary condition for the other. But our energies are directed far more toward war. Hypnotized by mutual mistrust, almost never concerned for the species or the planet, the nations prepare for death. And because what we are doing is so horrifying, we tend not to think of it much. But what we do not consider we are unlikely to put right. (Carl Sagan, *Cosmos*)

22k Changing from Passive to Active Voice

You can change a verb from passive to active voice by making the subject of the passive verb the object of the active verb. The person or thing performing the action then becomes the subject of the new sentence.

PASSIVE: The novel *Frankenstein* <u>was written</u> by Mary Shelley.

In this sentence the subject, *Frankenstein,* receives the action and the object of the preposition, Mary Shelley, initiates it. To put this verb into the active voice, you must reorganize the sentence.

ACTIVE: Mary Shelley <u>wrote</u> the novel *Frankenstein.*

Now Mary Shelley is the subject and the novel *Frankenstein* is the object. The emphasis therefore shifts from the recipient of the action to the person initiating it.

You can easily change a verb from passive to active if the sentence contains an *agent* that performs the action. Often the word *by* follows the passive verb, indicating the agent that can become the subject of an active verb.

PASSIVE: Robert E. Lee <u>was defeated</u> by Ulysses S. Grant. (agent)
ACTIVE: Ulysses S. Grant <u>defeated</u> Robert E. Lee.

If a passive verb has no agent, supply a subject for the active verb; if you cannot, keep the passive construction.

PASSIVE: Baby elephants are taught to avoid humans. (who are baby elephants taught by?)
ACTIVE: <u>Adult elephants</u> teach baby elephants to avoid humans.

vb
22k

▶
EXERCISE 6

Determine which verbs in the following paragraph should be changed from the passive to the active voice. Rewrite the sentences containing these verbs, and be prepared to explain your changes.

Rockets were invented by the Chinese about A.D. 1000. Gunpowder was packed into bamboo tubes and ignited by means of a fuse. These rockets were fired by soldiers at enemy armies and usually caused panic. In thirteenth-century England an improved form of gunpowder was introduced by Roger Bacon. As a result rockets were used in battles and were a common—although unreliable—weapon. In the early eighteenth century a twenty-pound rocket that traveled almost two miles was constructed by William Congreve, an English artillery expert. By the late nineteenth century thought was given to supersonic speeds by the physicist Ernst Mach. The sonic boom was predicted by him. The first liquid fuel rocket was launched by the American Robert Goddard in 1926. A pamphlet written by him anticipated almost all future rocket developments. As a result of his pioneering work he is called the father of modern rocketry.

22l   Changing from Active to Passive Voice

You can change verbs from active to passive voice by making the object of the active verb the subject of the passive verb. The subject of the active verb then becomes the object of the passive verb.

> ACTIVE: Sir James Murray <u>compiled</u> the *Oxford English Dictionary.*
>
> PASSIVE: *The Oxford English Dictionary* <u>was compiled</u> by Sir James Murray.

When changing verbs from active to passive voice, remember that words modifying the entire clause can remain where they are. Words modifying particular words and phrases, however, should go with the words they modify.

> ACTIVE: (On Halloween night in 1938) Orson Welles's Mercury Theatre presented the radio drama *Invasion from Mars.*
>
> PASSIVE: (On Halloween night in 1938) the radio drama *Invasion from Mars* was presented by Orson Welles's Mercury Theatre.

vb
22l

Remember that an active verb must have an object or it cannot be put into the passive voice. If an active verb has no object, supply the subject or keep the active construction.

> ACTIVE: Shakespeare wrote.
>   _____?_____ was written by Shakespeare.
>
> PASSIVE: *Twelfth Night* was written by Shakespeare.

▶

EXERCISE 7

Determine which sentences in the following paragraphs would be more effective in the passive voice. Rewrite these sentences, making sure that you can explain the reasons for your choices.

> Thomas Eakins was a painter and sculptor who was born in Philadelphia in 1844. Many people consider Eakins one of America's best nineteenth-century artists. Eakins, an innovative artist who knew anatomy and who insisted on working with nude models, led the move toward American realism. As a result, some people forced his resignation from the Pennsylvania Academy in 1886.
>
> Eakins never flattered his subjects. He painted what he saw and relied on photographs to help him paint accurately and to study motion. Many people recognized Eakins as a major painter by his death in 1916. Some people considered *The Surgical Clinic*

of Professor Gross (1875) and *The Swimming Hole* (1883) to be his best paintings. Eakins was unusual in a period when most artists concerned themselves with painting the ideal or the exotic.

Student Writer at Work: Verbs

Revise this draft of a short report on the life of Samuel Pepys, the famous seventeenth-century English diarist. Look for inconsistencies in tense and mood and ineffective use of both passive and active voice. You may add words and phrases and rearrange sentences to make them consistent.

vb 22

Samuel Pepys was born on February 23, 1633, in a house in Shaftsbury Court, where the business of tailoring was carried out by his father. Samuel Pepys was the fifth child and second son of his family. A primary education was secured for Pepys with the aid of his father's cousin, Sir Edward Montagu. In 1650 Pepys enters Trinity College, Cambridge, and after transferring to Magdalene College a Bachelor of Arts Degree and a Master's Degree were secured.

In 1655 Elizabeth Marchant (some sources say Elizabeth Saint Michael) was married by Pepys. The newlyweds took up residence with Sir Edward Montagu where Pepys served as an upper steward. Many government positions were secured by Montagu for Pepys.

In 1665 Pepys entered the navy as a surveyor. During 1666, the year of the great fire, Pepys was on naval duty. Many officers of the navy were saved from the fire by Pepys's intelligent actions. In 1669 Pepys's wife had died and although he was crushed by the loss, Pepys returned to duty.

Between 1672 and 1679 various important offices were held by Pepys. He eventually rises to be secretary of the Admiralty and many important duties were given to him. The revolution of 1688 terminated King James's reign, and also the career of Pepys was ended. Pepys, a person who needed time to carry on a wide correspondence, which included the writers John Eve-

lyn and John Dryden, was awarded an affluent retirement. On
May 25, 1703, Pepys died and was buried beside his wife.

Throughout his life Pepys's true character was probably
not known to those around him. Between 1660 and 1669, however, Pepys recorded his personal observations in his diary.
This document was written in shorthand, French, Spanish,
Latin, Greek, and invented ciphers. More than one hundred
years after Pepys's death six volumes had been discovered by the
Reverend John Smith, and in 1825 the first edition of *The Diary*
was published. In the nine years he kept his diary, a brilliant
and candid picture of Restoration life was given by Pepys. If
Pepys was never born, we would know a lot less about Restoration life than we do. Today Pepys is regarded by most scholars
as the most insightful of the English diarists.

**vb
22**

Agreement

Agreement is the correspondence between words in number, gender, or person. Subjects and verbs agree in **number** (singular or plural) and **person** (first, second, or third); pronouns and their antecedents agree in number, person, and **gender** (masculine, feminine, or neuter).

23a Making Subjects and Verbs Agree

Verbs should agree in number and person with their subjects: singular subjects have singular verbs, and plural subjects have plural verbs.

> SINGULAR: Hydrogen peroxide is an unstable compound.
>
> PLURAL: The characters are not well developed in most of O. Henry's short stories.

Present tense verbs, except *be* and *have*, add *-s* or *-es* when the subject is third-person singular. Third-person singular subjects include nouns; the personal pronouns *he, she, it,* and *one;* and many indefinite pronouns.

> The president has the power to veto congressional legislation.
>
> She frequently cites statistics to support her assertions.
>
> In every group somebody emerges as a natural leader.

Present tense verbs do not add *-s* or *-es* when the subject is first-person singular (*I*), first-person plural (*we*), second-person singular or plural (*you*), or third-person plural (*they*).

> I recommend that dieters avoid processed meat because of its high salt content.
>
> In our Bill of Rights, we guarantee all defendants the right to a speedy trial.
>
> At this stratum, you see rocks dating back fifteen million years.
>
> They say that many wealthy people default on their student loans.

Subject-verb agreement is generally straightforward, but some situations can be troublesome. You can achieve proper agreement if you are familiar with the following conventions.

(1) Intervening prepositional phrases

Even if a prepositional phrase comes between them, your subject and verb should still agree. For example, in the sentence

> The <u>sound</u> of the drumbeats <u>builds</u> in intensity in *The Emperor Jones.*

the subject, <u>sound</u>, is singular and takes a singular verb, <u>builds</u>. The plural *drumbeats*, part of the prepositional phrase that immediately precedes the verb, is not the subject.

> The <u>games</u> won by the intramural team <u>are</u> usually few and far between.

**agr
23a**

Here the plural subject, <u>games</u>, takes the plural verb form, <u>are</u>. *Team*, the object of the preposition *by*, is not the subject.

Even when expressions beginning with phrases such as *along with, as well as, in addition to, including,* and *together with* come between subject and verb, the subject does not change in number.

> Heavy <u>rain</u>, together with high winds, <u>causes</u> hazardous driving conditions along the Santa Monica Freeway.

> Recent <u>advances</u> in filmmaking techniques, along with increased interest in the film as a genre, <u>are</u> encouraging directors to undertake more and more ambitious and costly productions.

(2) Compound subjects

Compound subjects joined by *and* take plural verbs.

> <u>Air conditioning and power steering</u> <u>are</u> two of the available options on most domestic automobiles.

The compound subject <u>air conditioning and power steering</u> takes the plural verb <u>are</u>. Each of the following sentences also has a compound subject joined by *and* and a plural verb.

> <u>Labanotation and the Benesch system</u> <u>are</u> two kinds of dance notation.

> <u>Rice and beans</u> <u>form</u> a complete protein.

The kangaroo, the koala bear, and the opossum are all marsupials.

There are, however, two exceptions to this rule. Some compound subjects joined by *and* stand for a single idea or person. These should be treated as a unit and given singular verbs.

Rhythm and blues is a forerunner of rock and roll.

The chairman of the board and chief executive officer of Todd and Honeywell is Andrew Eastwood, widely known for his innovations in publishing.

When *each* or *every* precedes a compound subject joined by *and*, the subject also takes a singular verb.

agr
23a

Each complaint and contract violation passes through the grievance committee.

Every nook and cranny was searched before the purloined letter was found in plain sight on the mantle.

Compound subjects linked by *or* or by the correlative conjunctions *either . . . or* or *neither . . . nor* may take singular or plural verbs. If both subjects are singular, use a singular verb; if both subjects are plural, use a plural verb.

Either radiation or chemotherapy is combined with surgery for the most effective results. (both parts of the compound subject, *radiation* and *chemotherapy*, are singular, so the verb is singular)

Either radiation treatments or chemotherapy sessions are combined with surgery for the most effective results. (both parts of the compound subject, *treatments* and *sessions*, are plural, so the verb is plural)

When a singular and a plural subject are linked by *or*, or by the correlative conjunctions *either . . . or, neither . . . nor*, or *not only . . . but also*, the verb should agree with the subject that is nearer to it.

Either radiation treatments or chemotherapy is combined with surgery for the most effective results. (singular verb agrees with *chemotherapy*, the part of the compound subject closer to it)

Either chemotherapy or radiation treatments are combined with surgery for the most effective results. (plural verb agrees with *treatments*, the part of the compound subject closer to it)

Sometimes a compound subject is made up of nouns and pronouns that differ in person and therefore require different verb forms. In such cases, the convention is the same: the verb should agree in person as well as number with the element of the compound subject to which it is closer.

> Neither my running mate nor I wish to contest the election.

> Neither I nor my running mate wishes to contest the election.

(3) Indefinite pronouns

In most cases, you should use a singular verb when using an indefinite pronoun as a subject. Although some indefinite pronouns—*both, many, few, several, others*—are always plural, most—*another, anyone, everyone, one, each, either, neither, anything, everything, something,* and *somebody*—are singular. That is, each word generally stands for a single person or thing.

**agr
23a**

> Anyone is welcome to apply for a grant, providing certain financial qualifications are met.

> Something was wrong with the way the results were tabulated.

> Someone is in the kitchen with Dinah.

Some indefinite pronouns—*some, all, any, more, most,* and *none*—can be singular or plural. In these cases the noun to which the pronoun refers determines whether the verb form should be singular or plural.

> Of course, some of this trouble is to be expected. (*some* refers to *trouble*; therefore, the verb is singular)

> Some of the spectators are getting restless. (*some* refers to *spectators*; therefore, the verb is plural)

(4) Collective nouns

Collective nouns, like indefinite pronouns, may take either singular or plural verbs, depending on how they are used. A **collective noun** is a word that is singular in form but denotes a group of persons or things—for instance, *navy, union, association, group.* When a collective noun refers to a group as a unit, it takes a singular verb; when it refers to the individuals or items that make up the group, it takes a plural verb.

> The Security Council votes on matters concerning international politics. (the whole group votes)

To many people the royal family symbolizes Great Britain. (the family, as a unit, is the symbol)

The class file out of the room one by one after the examination. (each student leaves separately)

Sometimes, however, even when usage is correct, a plural verb sounds awkward with a collective noun.

After years of living together, the nuclear family begin to go their separate ways.

If this is the case, rewrite the sentence to eliminate the awkwardness.

After years of living together, the members of the nuclear family begin to go their separate ways.

Phrases that name a fixed amount—*three-quarters, twenty dollars, the majority*—are treated like collective nouns. When the amount is considered as a unit, it takes a singular verb; when it denotes parts of the whole, it takes a plural verb.

Three-quarters of those taking the math anxiety workshop improve dramatically. (all individuals in this group improve)

Three-quarters of his usual Social Security check is not enough. (three-quarters denotes a unit)

Note that *the number* is always singular and *a number* is always plural.

The number of voters has declined.

A number of students have missed the opportunity to preregister.

(5)   Singular subjects that have plural forms

Be sure to use a singular verb with a singular subject, even if the form of the subject is plural.

Hives is a common skin disease.

No news is good news.

Economics is the study of scarcity.

Statistics deals with the collection, classification, analysis, and interpretation of data.

Politics makes strange bedfellows.

The subjects of these sentences might seem at first glance to be plural because of their -*s* endings. But in fact, each is singular and must take a singular verb. In certain contexts, however, some of these words may actually have plural meanings. In these cases, a plural verb should be used.

> Her politics are too radical for her parents.
>
> The statistics prove him wrong.

In the first sentence, *politics* refers not to the science of political government but to political principles or opinions; in the second, *statistics* denotes not a body of knowledge but the numerical facts or data themselves.

Be sure that titles of individual works take singular verbs, even if their form is plural.

> *The New Aerobics* outlines a popular physical fitness program.
>
> *The Grapes of Wrath* describes the journey of migrant workers and their families from the Dust Bowl to California.

This convention also applies to words referred to as words, even if they are plural. For instance,

> *Good vibes* is a 60's slang term meaning positive feelings.

(6)   Inverted verb order

Be sure a verb agrees with its subject, even when a sentence inverts normal word order.

> As Maine goes, so goes the nation.
>
> There but for fortune go you and I.
>
> For every thing there is a season.
>
> There are currently twelve circuit courts of appeals in the federal court system.

Note that the usual word order of a sentence is inverted with constructions involving *there is* or *there are.* Whenever possible, such constructions should be avoided (see 8a.1).

(7)   Linking verbs

Be sure linking verbs agree with their subjects, not with the subject complement.

> The problem was termites.

Here the verb <u>was</u> agrees with the subject <u>problem</u>, not with the subject complement *termites*. If *termites* were the subject, the verb would be plural.

<u>Termites</u> <u>were</u> the problem.

(8) Relative pronouns

When you use a relative pronoun (*who, which, that*) to begin a subordinate clause, the verb in that clause should agree in number with the pronoun's antecedent. Because these pronouns have the same form for singular and plural, they provide no clues to subject-verb agreement.

The farmer is one of the <u>ones</u> who <u>suffer</u> during a grain embargo.

Here the verb <u>suffer</u> agrees with the antecedent <u>ones</u> of the relative pronoun, *who*, but compare

The farmer is the only <u>one</u> who <u>suffers</u> during the grain embargo.

Now the verb agrees with the antecedent <u>one</u>, which is singular.

agr
23a

▶

EXERCISE 1

Each of these ten correct sentences illustrates one of the eight conventions just explained. Read the sentences carefully, and explain why each verb form is used in each case.

> EXAMPLE: "<u>Frankie and Johnny</u>" <u>is</u> a ballad about a woman's revenge against her unfaithful lover. (the verb *is* is singular because the subject *"Frankie and Johnny"* is the title of an individual work even though it is plural in form)

1. Sugar and spice is what little girls are supposedly made of.
2. All is quiet.
3. Weight Watchers was founded by Jean Nidetch.
4. An army marches on its stomach.
5. *Typee*, like *Omoo* and *White-Jacket*, is an early Melville novel.
6. Neither famine nor wars destroy a strong nation.
7. Sir Laurence Olivier is one of the actors who are considered great.
8. *Star Wars* was directed by George Lucas.
9. The time-consuming part of the job is all these credit checks.
10. There is no reason for this kind of delay, and I would appreciate your giving this matter your prompt attention.

▶
EXERCISE 2

Some of these sentences are correct, but others illustrate common errors in subject-verb agreement. If a sentence is correct, mark it with a *C*; if it has an error, correct it.

1. Margaret Farrar is one of the people who is considered important in the history of the crossword puzzle.
2. Mme Dionne's surprise was quintuplets.
3. The bargaining team always prepared their initial demands before meeting with management.
4. Neither Pac Man nor Space Invaders are a substitute for chess.
5. Some say gentrification is destroying our neighborhoods by driving out long-term residents.
6. There is currently specific laws, grants, and tax credits designed to help low-income elderly people.
7. Canada is the country that is directly north of the United States.
8. Dungeons and Dragons are popular with those who like fantasy role-playing games.
9. The *Dune* novels, which revolve around efforts to survive on a desert planet, emphasizes the relationship between people and their environment.
10. Martha's Vineyard, Hilton Head Island, and Mackinac Island continues to attract numerous tourists.

agr
23b

23b   Making Pronouns and Antecedents Agree

Pronouns must agree with their **antecedents** in number, person, and gender. Singular pronouns—such as *he, him, she, her, it, me, myself,* and *oneself*—should refer to singular antecedents. Plural pronouns—such as *we, us, they, them,* and *their*—should refer to plural antecedents. (See Chapter 21 for a complete list of pronouns.) Pronouns must also agree with their antecedents in person (first, second, third) and gender (masculine, feminine, neuter). Several conventions govern pronoun-antecedent agreement.

(1)   More than one antecedent

In most cases use a plural pronoun to refer to two or more antecedents connected by *and,* even if one or more of the antecedents is singular.

> Mormonism and Christian Science were influenced in their beginnings by Shaker doctrines.

In some cases, however, the compound antecedent may denote a single unit—one person or thing or idea. In these instances a singular pronoun should be used to refer to the compound antecedent.

> In 1904 the husband and father brought his family from Poland to America.

The same convention applies when the compound antecedent is preceded by *each* or *every*: here, too, a singular pronoun should be used.

> Every programming language and software package has its limitations.

agr

23b

Use a singular pronoun to refer to two or more singular antecedents linked by *or* or *nor*.

> Neither Thoreau nor Whitman lived to see his work read widely.

However, when one antecedent is singular and one is plural, you should be sure the pronoun agrees in person and number with the closer antecedent.

> Neither Great Britain nor the Benelux nations have experienced changes in their borders in recent years.

Here one antecedent (*Great Britain*) is singular and one (*Benelux nations*) is plural. The pronoun is closer to the plural antecedent, so it is plural.

(2)   Collective noun antecedents

Consider the context and meaning of collective nouns carefully. Collective noun antecedents usually call for singular pronouns, but plural pronouns may occasionally be required. If the meaning of the collective noun antecedent is singular, use a singular pronoun. If its meaning is plural, use a plural pronoun.

> The teachers' union was ready to strike for the new contract its members had been promised. (all the members act as one)
>
> When the whistle blew, the team left their seats and moved toward the court. (each member acts individually)

Within any one sentence a collective noun should be treated consistently as either singular or plural. When one collective noun serves as both the subject of a verb and the antecedent of a pronoun, both verb and pronoun must agree with the noun. In this sentence, verb and pronoun are not consistent.

The teachers' union, ready to strike for the new contract its members had been promised, were still willing to negotiate.

Here the collective noun *union* is singular; the verb *were* is plural and, therefore, incorrect.

(3) Antecedent indefinite pronouns

In most cases use singular pronouns when your antecedent is an indefinite pronoun. Most indefinite pronouns—*each, either, neither, one, anyone,* and the like—are singular in meaning and should take singular pronouns. (Others may be plural—see 23a.3—and require plural pronouns.)

Neither of these men is likely to have his proposal ready by the application deadline.

Each of these neighborhoods is like a separate nation, with its own traditions and values.

Everyone will get basic instruction in the modern foreign language of his choice.

NOTE: *Everyone* presents problems for some writers. Because *everyone* is singular in meaning and does not specify gender, convention says that it should be referred to by the singular pronoun *his.* Indefinite pronouns, however, really denote members of both sexes, so many writers feel that using *his* is inaccurate. Though it can be somewhat cumbersome if overused, one solution to this problem is to use *both* the masculine and feminine pronouns.

Everyone will get basic instruction in the modern foreign language of his or her choice.

Another solution is to change the subject and use a plural pronoun.

All students will get basic instruction in the modern foreign language of their choice.

For more information on avoiding sexist pronoun usage, see 16b.3.

EXERCISE 3

Identify all the pronouns and their antecedents in each of the following sentences and sentence groups.

Example: The bay was mysterious. It lay five miles to the west of the town, but no one ever went to see it.

1. But Pentaquod was not afraid of the storm, and next morning, when it had passed and he surveyed his island, he did not find the damage excessive. He had seen storms before, rather violent ones which swept down the river valley of his home, and although this one had been swifter and more thunderous, it was merely an exaggeration of what he had long known. (James A. Michener, *Chesapeake*)

2. Harrison had been a shining student wherever he went. The best teachers passed him on to each other like a gift. (Michael M. Thomas, *Green Monday*)

3. On a mid-January morning in the early nineteen-seventies, at 2 A.M., Central Standard Time, Jane Clifford lay awake in a Midwestern university town, thinking about insomnia; traditions of insomnia, all the people she knew had it, the poets and artists and saints who had left written testimonies of their sleeplessness. (Gail Godwin, *The Odd Woman*)

4. She wrapped the sandwiches tightly, snugly, like little babies swaddled in giant sheets of heavy white paper that had transparent spatters of grease on them. She put the sandwich on one corner of the paper and then quickly rolled it up, tucking the ends and sealing them with white tape. (Nancy Hayfield, *Cleaning House*)

5. De Gaulle was strong willed and had strong opinions. He spoke the language that dreams are made of. When he spoke, you had the feeling that he had great plans in every area he touched upon, and that he was convinced they would come true. (François Mitterand, *New York Times Magazine*)

▶
EXERCISE 4

Find and correct any errors in subject-verb and/or pronoun-antecedent agreement.

1. Either the Boy Scouts or the 4-H Program are offering special courses and publications to help latchkey children take care of themselves.

2. Gilbert and Sullivan's classic *The Pirates of Penzance* were revived in the early 80's in stage and screen versions.

3. None of the lower forty-eight states is able to match Alaska's coal reserves.

4. A creole is a kind of language that comes into being when several different languages are spoken in an area. To make communication easier, speakers of each of these different languages tend to borrow from all the area's languages.

5. Although some 15 percent of students now enrolled in U.S. dental schools are female, in 1979 there was only one oral pathologist, four endodontists, and six oral surgeons who were women.

agr
23b

6. A number of drugs currently banned in America is still routinely sold to "underdeveloped" countries by American manufacturers.

7. Alcohol use among college students, frequently associated with campus vandalism and traffic fatalities, are on the rise.

8. Since the 1960's, vegetarianism has moved apart from any particular religious, political, or ethical philosophy; now they have become a legitimate nutritional movement instead of a fad.

9. Neither paralegals, systems analysts, radiation therapy technologists, nor physician's assistants was in existence a generation ago.

10. Groups as diverse as the Moral Majority, Phyllis Schlafly's Eagle Forum, NOW, People for the American Way, and the DAR seeks to influence textbook selection committees.

▶
EXERCISE 5

The following ten sentences illustrate correct subject-verb and pronoun-antecedent agreement. To practice writing sentences that have correct agreement, follow the instructions in parentheses after each sentence.

> EXAMPLE: One child in ten suffers from a learning disability. (change *one child in ten* to *ten percent of all children*)
>
> Ten percent of all children suffer from a learning disability.

1. The governess is seemingly pursued by evil as she tries to protect Miles and Flora from those she feels seek to possess the children's souls. (change *the governess* to *the governess and the cook*)

2. Insulin-dependent diabetics are now able to take advantage of new technology that can help alleviate their symptoms. (change *diabetics* to *the diabetic*)

3. All homeowners in shore regions worry about the possible effects of a hurricane on their property. (change *all homeowners* to *every homeowner*)

4. Federally funded job-training programs offer unskilled workers an opportunity to acquire skills they can use to secure employment. (change *workers* to *the worker*)

5. Foreign imports pose a major challenge to the American automobile market. (change *foreign imports* to *the foreign import*)

6. *Brideshead Revisited* tells how one family and its devotion to its Catholic faith affect Charles Ryder. (delete *and their devotion to their Catholic faith*)

7. *Writer's Digest* and *The Writer* are designed to aid novice and experienced writers as they seek markets for their work. (change *writers* to *the writer*)

8. Most American families own a television; in fact, more have televisions than have indoor plumbing. (change *most* to *almost every*)

9. In Montana it seems as though every town's elevation is higher than its population. (change *every town's* to *all the towns'*)

10. A woman without a man is like a fish without a bicycle. (change *a woman/a man* to *women/men*)

Student Writer at Work: Agreement

Read the following draft of an informal article for a college newspaper carefully, correcting all errors in subject-verb and pronoun-antecedent agreement.

A View from the Stands

The setting: Veterans Stadium, Philadelphia. The date: Sunday afternoon, November 5. The event: A football game, the Eagles against Green Bay.

The numbers on my ticket says Section 638, Row 11, Seat 2. For the uninitiated that means I'm at the oxygen mask level (bring binoculars), at the thirty-one yard line, on the Green Bay side of the field. Right now it's 12:23, thirty-seven minutes before game time. The Eagles are all lying together on the field, pretending to stretch out. I think the team just does it because their fans expect it. The Packers, on the other hand, don't have to impress the hometown folks, so they seem to be taking it easy.

Sitting next to me is a nine-year-old, stuffing his face with popcorn and Coke. He hasn't stopped kicking his feet back and forth since I got here, and he doesn't appear to be too interested in the game. He just keeps asking his father for another Coke. On my other side is trouble, in the form of a yeller. The guy has a voice that could pierce steel, and he looks as though he's pretty well fortified for the game.

Now the Eagles, after a brief trip to their lockers, returns to the field. Somehow, as they all run out onto the field and start jumping up and down, the team reminds me of the little kid sitting next to me.

Before the game can start, someone has to sing the National Anthem. The band that plays the music is good. The public address announcer tells us that they have won 130 trophies. Unfortunately, the man singing the National Anthem isn't as good as the band are. He keeps on singing too fast, giving us the words five seconds before we hear the music. None of us really care anyway, and long before the song ends cries of "Let's go Birds" and "C'mon Iggles" erupts in the stands.

The game itself isn't very exciting, but there is a few interesting aspects. Did you ever notice how loud a quarterback's voice is? I am firmly convinced that you don't need a strong arm or a good mind to become a professional quarterback, just that voice. Maybe the yeller next to me should become a pro. Then there's the guys who do nothing—and get paid for it. One official stands with a stick in his hand, marking the spot where each drive starts. That guy is getting paid for standing there holding what looks like an oversized lollipop. Remarkable. Another of the men earning a full salary is the one who is responsible for filling cups with Gatorade. He stands there by the juice table filling those cups for three hours. None of the stars even drinks the stuff; it's the bench warmers who get up once a quarter to make a pilgrimage to the table.

agr
23

Meanwhile, out on the playing field, the Eagles are whipping the Packers. The defense are very tough, and the offense puts together two or three drives of more than eighty yards. Nevertheless, throughout the game, the fans are waiting for the Birds to blow it. When the game ends in an Eagles victory, most of the crowd in the stands are truly surprised.

Adjectives and Adverbs

Adjectives and adverbs are modifiers used alone or in combination to enrich sentences. Both adjectives and adverbs describe, limit, or qualify other words, phrases, or clauses. But they have different functions, forms, and positions in a sentence.

The *function* of a word, not its *form*, determines whether it is classified as an adjective or an adverb. While many adverbs (like *immediately* and *hopelessly*) end in -*ly*, others (like *almost* and *very*) do not. Moreover, some adjectives (like *lively*) end in -*ly*. Only by locating the modified word and determining its part of speech can you identify a modifier as an adjective or adverb.

Adjectives are commonly placed close to the nouns or pronouns they modify. They most often appear immediately *before* nouns,

They bought two shrubs for the yard.

directly *after* linking verbs,

The name seemed familiar. (subject complement)

directly *after* direct objects,

The coach ran them ragged. (object complement)

and directly *after* indefinite pronouns.

Anything sad makes me cry.

Two or more adjectives can be placed *after* the noun or pronoun they modify.

The expedition, long and arduous, ended in triumph.

Adverbs are also usually located close to the words they modify. However, because they modify more kinds of words and word groups than adjectives do, they occur in a greater variety of positions. In addition, in a given sentence an adverb can frequently be located in more than one position.

He walked slowly across the room.

Slowly he walked across the room.

He slowly walked across the room.

He walked across the room slowly.

24a Using Adjectives

Adjectives modify nouns and pronouns (see 20d). Be sure to use an adjective—not an adverb—as a subject complement or an object complement.

A **subject complement** is a word that follows a *linking verb*— a verb that connects the subject to its complement—and that modifies the sentence's subject, not its verb. Words that are or can be used as linking verbs include *seem, appear, believe, become, grow, turn, remain, prove, look, sound, smell, taste, feel,* and forms of the verb *be*. Because a subject complement modifies the subject—a noun or pronoun—it must be an adjective.

> Melissa seemed <u>brave</u>.

Here *seemed* shows no action and is therefore a linking verb. Because *brave* is a subject complement that modifies the noun *Melissa,* the adjective form is used. Compare

> Melissa smiled <u>bravely</u>.

Here *smiled* shows action, so it is not a linking verb. *Bravely* modifies *smiled,* so it takes the adverb form.

Some verbs can either serve as linking verbs or convey action. Compare these two sentences.

> He remained <u>stubborn</u>. (he was still stubborn)

> He remained <u>stubbornly</u>. (he remained, in a stubborn manner)

In the first sentence, *remained* is a linking verb, and *stubborn,* a subject complement, modifies the pronoun *he.* In the second sentence, however, *remained* is used in another sense—to convey action. *Stubbornly* modifies *remained,* so the adverb form is used.

When a word following a sentence's direct object modifies that object and not the verb, it is an **object complement.** Objects are nouns or pronouns, so their modifiers must be adjectives. Here is an example.

> Most people called him <u>shy</u>. (Most people thought he was shy.)

Shy modifies the sentence's direct object (*him*), so the adjective form is correct. But in the following sentence *shyly* modifies the verb (*called*)—not the object—so the adverb form is used.

> Most people called him <u>shyly</u>. (Most people were shy when they called him.)

ad
24a

24b   Using Adverbs

Adverbs modify verbs, adjectives, other adverbs, or entire phrases, clauses, or sentences (see 20e).

> FAULTY: The majority of the class did <u>great</u> on the midterm. (adjective form used to modify verb)
>
> My parents dress a lot more <u>conservative</u> than my friends do. (adjective form used to modify verb)
>
> REVISED: The majority of the class did <u>well</u> (or <u>very</u> <u>well</u>) on the midterm.
>
> My parents dress a lot more <u>conservatively</u> than my friends do.

In informal speech adjective forms like *good, bad, sure,* and *real* are often incorrectly used to modify verbs, adjectives, and adverbs.

> FAULTY: The program ran <u>good</u> the first time we tried it.
>
> The new system performed <u>bad</u>.
>
> The tutoring project <u>sure</u> needs volunteers.
>
> Be <u>real</u> careful when you proofread the bibliography.

In your college writing be sure to avoid these informal modifiers and to use adverbs to modify verbs, adjectives, and other adverbs.

> REVISED: The program ran <u>well</u> the first time we tried it.
>
> The new system performed <u>badly</u>.
>
> The tutoring project <u>surely</u> (or <u>certainly</u>) needs volunteers.
>
> Be <u>really</u> (or <u>extremely</u>) careful when you proofread the bibliography.

Some adverbs ending in *-ly* have short versions that are identical in form and meaning to adjectives—*slow, quick, loud, sharp,* and *wrong,* for instance. These short forms are, for the most part, acceptable as adverbs *only* in informal writing or speech.

> Go <u>slow</u> or you'll miss the turnoff.
>
> Talk <u>loud</u> so they can hear your answer.

Use the *-ly* forms of such words in college writing: *slowly, quickly, loudly, sharply, wrongly.*

▶
EXERCISE 1

Read this paragraph carefully, and label every adjective and adverb. Draw an arrow to indicate the word each adjective or adverb modifies, and then label each of these words to indicate what part of speech it is.

> EXAMPLE:
>
>   *(adj)*   *(noun)*   *(adv)*   *(verb)*   *(adj)*   *(noun)*
> The provisional government greatly feared a military coup.

In recent years, several medical schools have opened up on Caribbean islands like Dominica, Grenada, and Montserrat. Because these are English-speaking islands, the schools draw most of their student body from American college graduates who are unable to get into medical schools in the United States. Some physicians and medical associations have sharply criticized the schools' facilities, curricula, supplies, and faculties. They claim the schools are simply not on a par with most American medical schools. But some other medical professionals see things differently. They claim the schools do prepare their students adequately, and some standardized tests seem to support this view. Other groups also support these new Caribbean schools wholeheartedly. The students who find these schools so attractive are grateful for the opportunity to become doctors. The governments are equally grateful for the increased revenue generated by the schools. And many small, inner-city hospitals, critically short of physicians, are glad to provide the "offshore" medical students with a setting for their clinical training.

ad
24b

▶
EXERCISE 2

Revise each of the incorrect sentences in this paragraph so that only adjectives modify nouns and pronouns and only adverbs modify verbs, adjectives, or other adverbs. Be sure to eliminate informal forms. Put a check mark before any sentence that is correct.

Cruises have become more popular in recent years, in part, because of the popularity of the television show *The Love Boat*. But steamship lines are still trying real hard to promote their cruises, and their upbeat message comes through loud and clear. Most advertisements emphasize the unlimited quantities of gourmet food, the good value, the varied activities, the sense of luxury, and the possibility of romance. As a result, people who sign up for cruises believe they will be able to travel quite cheap—after all, almost everything is included in the prepaid price. They also believe that it is possible to fall in love fairly quick, all the while cruising along slow and easy under the stars. Enjoying a cruise is not hard, and it sure helps if people allow themselves to believe their fantasies can come true.

▶

EXERCISE 3

Being careful to use adjectives—not adverbs—as subject complements and object complements, write five sentences in imitation of each of the following. Be sure to use five different linking verbs in your imitations of each sentence.

1. Julie looked worried.
2. Dan considers his collection valuable.

24c Distinguishing Between Comparative and Superlative Forms

Adjectives and adverbs change their forms to indicate an increase or decrease in the quality described. The **positive** degree (big) simply describes a quality. It indicates no comparisons. The **comparative** (bigger) and **superlative** (biggest) degrees do indicate comparisons—between two qualities (greater or lesser) or among many qualities (greatest or least), respectively. In general, the comparative degree compares two persons or things, and the superlative compares one person or thing with all the others in the class. (John's house is bigger than Hal's; Randy's house is the biggest one on the block.)

NOTE: Some adverbs, particularly those indicating time, place, and degree (*almost, very, here, yesterday,* and *immediately*) do not exist in the comparative or superlative degree.

(1) The comparative degree

Adjectives

To indicate a *greater* degree, all one-syllable adjectives and many two-syllable adjectives (particularly those that end in *-y, -ly, -le, -er,* and *-ow*) add *-er* to form the comparative.

slow	slower
funny	funnier
lovely	lovelier

(Note that a final *y* becomes *i* before *-er* is added.)

Other two-syllable adjectives and all long adjectives form the comparative with *more*.

| famous | more famous |
| incredible | more incredible |

NOTE: Many two-syllable adjectives can form the comparative with either *more* or *-er*—for example, *more lovely* or *lovelier*. All adjectives indicate a lesser degree with the word *less*.

| lovely | less lovely |
| famous | less famous |

Adverbs

Adverbs ending in *-ly* indicate a greater degree with *more*.

| slowly | more slowly |

Other adverbs use the *-er* ending to indicate a greater degree.

| soon | sooner |

Adverbs always indicate a lesser degree with the word *less*.

less slowly
less soon

NOTE: Never use both *more* and *-er* to form the comparative degree.

FAULTY: Nothing could have been more easier.

REVISED: Nothing could have been easier.

(2) The superlative degree

Adjectives

Adjectives that indicate the comparative with *-er* add *-est* to indicate the superlative (the *greatest* degree).

| nicer | nicest |
| funnier | funniest |

Adjectives that indicate the comparative with *more* use *most* to indicate the superlative.

| more famous | most famous |
| more challenging | most challenging |

All adjectives indicate the least degree with the word *least*.

least interesting
least enjoyable

Adverbs

The majority of adverbs are preceded by *most* to indicate the greatest degree.

most quickly
most helpfully
most efficiently

Others use the *-est* ending to indicate the greatest degree.

soonest

All adverbs use *least* to indicate the least degree.

least willingly
least fashionably

ad
24c

NOTE: Never use both *most* and *-est* to form the superlative degree.

FAULTY: Jack is the most meanest person in town.

REVISED: Jack is the meanest person in town.

(3) Irregular comparatives and superlatives

Some adjectives and adverbs do not conform to the rules stated above. Instead of adding a word or an ending to the positive form, they use different words to indicate each degree. You therefore need to familiarize yourself with these irregular forms.

	Positive	*Comparative*	*Superlative*
ADJECTIVES:	good	better	best
	bad	worse	worst
	a little	less	least
	many, some, much	more	most
ADVERBS:	well	better	best
	badly	worse	worst

(4) Illogical comparisons

Many adjectives and adverbs have absolute meanings—that is, they can logically exist only in the positive degree. Good sense suggests that words like *perfect, unique, excellent, impossible,* and *dead* can never be used in the comparative or superlative degree. How can one thing be more excellent or less impossible than another?

Consider the word *unique*. Unique means one of a kind; it can *never* be used in the comparative or superlative degree.

> FAULTY: The vase is the <u>most unique</u> piece in her collection.
>
> REVISED: The vase in her collection is <u>unique</u>.

However, although these constructions should be avoided in college writing, they may be used in informal contexts.

> He revised eight times, always looking for the <u>most perfect</u> draft.
>
> It was the <u>most impossible</u> course I ever took.

NOTE: Absolutes can be modified by words that suggest approaching the absolute state—*nearly* or *almost*, for example.

> He revised until his draft was <u>almost perfect</u>.

ad
24d

▶
EXERCISE 4

Supply the correct comparative and superlative forms for each of the adjectives or adverbs listed below. Then use each form in a sentence.

> EXAMPLE: strange   stranger   strangest
> The story had a *strange* ending. The explanation sounded *stranger* each time I heard it. This is the *strangest* gadget I have ever seen.

1.	many	6.	softly
2.	eccentric	7.	tremendous
3.	confusing	8.	well
4.	bad	9.	often
5.	mysterious	10.	tiny

24d Using Nouns as Adjectives

Many nouns can function as modifiers in a sentence (see 6e.2).

> He made a sandwich of <u>turkey</u> bologna, <u>egg</u> salad, and <u>tomato</u> slices on <u>wheat</u> bread.

The reason for using nouns as adjectives is to create cleaner, more efficient, and more idiomatic sentences—to avoid, for example, having to say

> He made a sandwich of bologna made from turkey, salad made from eggs, and slices of tomato on bread made from wheat.

Many familiar phrases consist of a noun modifying another noun.

space station	dance class
art history	beach towel
flower bed	water color
piano bench	Star Wars
amusement park	police force
baby sitter	house trailer

In each case using a noun as a modifier saves words. But overusing nouns as modifiers can create cluttered, clumsy, and even incoherent sentences.

> CONFUSING: The Chestnut Hill Fathers' Club Pony League beginners spring baseball clinic will be held Saturday.

ad
24d

To avoid such sentences, use as modifiers only two or three short nouns in succession. To revise cluttered sentences like the one above, restructure to break up long series of nouns. You can also substitute equivalent adjective forms, where such forms exist, or possessives for some of the nouns used as modifiers.

> IMPROVED: The Chestnut Hill Fathers' Club's spring baseball clinic for beginning Pony League players will be held Saturday.

Of course, eliminating the passive voice could make this sentence even clearer.

> On Saturday, the Chestnut Hill Fathers' Club will hold its spring baseball clinic for beginning Pony League players.

►
EXERCISE 5

Identify every noun used as a modifier in the following passage. Then revise where necessary to eliminate clumsy or unclear phrasing resulting from overuse of nouns as modifiers. Try substituting adjective or possessive forms, and rearrange word order where you feel it is indicated.

      The student government business management trainee program is extremely popular on campus. The student government donated some of the seed money to begin this management trainee program, which is one of the most successful the university business school has ever offered to undergraduate students. Three core courses must be taken before the student intern can actually begin work. First, there is a management theory course given every spring semester in conjunction with the business school. Then, the following fall semester, students in the trainee program are required to take a course in personnel practices, including employee benefits. Finally, they take a business elective.

During the summer, the student interns are placed in junior management positions in large electronics, manufacturing, or public utility companies. This job experience is considered the most valuable part of the program because it gives students a taste of the work world.

Student Writer at Work: Adjectives and Adverbs

ad
24

Read carefully this draft of an essay, and revise it wherever necessary to correct errors in the use of adjectives and adverbs. Check to make sure adjectives modify nouns or pronouns and adverbs modify verbs, adjectives, or other adverbs; make sure the correct comparative and superlative forms are used; and eliminate any overuse of nouns as modifiers.

Save the Harp Seals

What do rabbits, minks, foxes, and seals all have in common? Each is a victim of fashion. Many people want to own a fur coat real bad, and for those who can afford it, buying one seems to be a simple decision. This is all fine for the fur coat showroom salesperson who earns a commission on the sale, but what about the original owner of the fur? What about the animal who lost its life so its fur could sit on someone's shoulders? Too many animals have been slaughtered for just this reason, and in some cases the animals are skinned quick before they are even completely dead. Something sure must be done to stop the slaughter of these animals before they become extinct. Take the case of the harp seal, for example.

The harp seal has suffered a very large reduction in numbers during recent times because hunters have subjected these seals to a tremendous mass slaughter. The issue is not only that the harp seals are butchered, but also that they are killed in the inhumanest manner possible.

The traditional method uses a gaff, which is a length of wood with a hook at one end and a spike at the other. The hook is struck across the seal's brain. Some people consider this method painlessly; however, sometimes the spike misses the vital spot and the seal, still alive, is skinned by the hunter. Thus the gaff can prove painful indeed. The second method used is clubbing. The hunters use wooden clubs or great iron hooks. Seals often pull in their heads in alarm, covering their skulls with a thick layer of fat. It takes many powerful blows to penetrate the fat and kill the seal.

The seals are being killed in more greater numbers each year, and being killed savagely. Even the existing laws, which are supposed to help save the seals, have no effect. One such law limits the size and weight of the club, but if the clubs are made more lightly it will only require more blows to kill the seal. This law does not prevent the killings. Many other regulations are constantly being broken, and the problem of enforcement remains seriously. Meanwhile, the harp seals are the unwilling victims of brutal killings.

When will this mass slaughter end? If strong, immediate action is not taken, it will be too late for the animals. Something must be done quick before the harp seal becomes extinct.

VI

Understanding Punctuation and Mechanics

25

The Period, the Question Mark, and the Exclamation Point

25a Using Periods

Periods are used to end declarative sentences (statements), mild commands, polite requests, and indirect questions. They are also used in most familiar abbreviations and in dramatic and poetic references.

(1) Marking an end point

Periods signal the end of a statement, a mild command or polite request, or an indirect question.

> Something is rotten in the state of Denmark. (statement)
>
> Dioxin traces were found in nearby bodies of water. (statement)
>
> Be sure to have the oil checked before you start out. (mild command)
>
> When the bell rings, please exit in an orderly fashion. (polite request)
>
> They wondered whether it was safe to go back in the water. (indirect question)
>
> She asked everyone she knew whether they could solve the equation. (indirect question)

NOTE: An indirect question tells what has been asked, but because it does not use the speaker's exact words, it does not take a question mark.

> DIRECT QUESTION: How much is that doggie in the window?
>
> INDIRECT QUESTION: He asked the price of the dog in the window.

(2) Marking an abbreviation

Periods appear in most abbreviations.

Mrs. Robinson	Captain Newman, M.D.	25 B.C.
Mr. Spock	George McGovern, Ph.D.	N.Y., N.Y., U.S.A.
Ms. J. R. Jones	Sue Barton, R.N.	221b Baker St.
Dr. Kildare	9 P.M.	etc.

Be sure to use other punctuation correctly with abbreviations that take periods.

At the end of a sentence

If the abbreviation ends the sentence, do not add another period.

> FAULTY: He promised to be there at 6 A.M..

> REVISED: He promised to be there at 6 A.M.

However, do add a question mark after the abbreviation's final period if the sentence is a question.

> Did he arrive at 6 P.M.?

Within a sentence

25a

If the abbreviation falls within a sentence, use normal punctuation after the abbreviation's final period.

> FAULTY: He promised to be there at 6 P.M. but he forgot his promise.

> REVISED: He promised to be there at 6 P.M., but he forgot his promise.

Some abbreviations do not require periods (see 34b). These include **acronyms,** new words formed from the first letters of a group of words

| NATO | radar | OSHA | scuba |
| NOW | VISTA | SALT | CAT scan |

or abbreviations made from the first few letters of a series of words.

> Fannie Mae (Federal National Mortgage Association)
> Gestapo (Geheime Staats Polizei)
> Modem (modulator demodulator)

In addition, the periods are often dropped from frequently used capital-letter abbreviations of names of corporations, government agencies, and scientific and technical terms.

CIA	WPA	IBM	FBI	WCAU-FM
EPA	CCC	DNA	IRA	AFT
MGM	RCA	HBO	UCLA	UFO

Do not use a period after commonly accepted shortened forms of words (gym, dorm, math, and so on) or after abbreviations that do not require them. If you are unsure whether or not to use a period with a particular abbreviation, consult a good college dictionary. You may find that the dictionary offers more than one alternative—IOU or I.O.U., for instance.

(3) Marking citations

Periods separate act, scene, and line references in plays, and book and line references in long poems.

> DRAMATIC REFERENCE: *Long Day's Journey into Night* II.ii.1–5.

> POETIC REFERENCE: *Paradise Lost* VII.163–67.

▶

EXERCISE 1

Correct these sentences by adding missing periods and deleting superfluous ones. If a sentence is correct, mark it with a C.

> EXAMPLE:

> ORIGINAL: I wonder who's kissing her now?

> REVISED: I wonder who's kissing her now.

1. Julius Caesar was killed in 44 B.C.
2. Please begin speaking when you hear the beep!
3. Carmen was supposed to be at A.F.L.-C.I.O. headquarters by 2 P.M.; however, she didn't get there until 10 P.M..
4. He asked whether anyone had change of a dollar?
5. Representatives from the U.M.W. began collective bargaining after an unsuccessful meeting with Mr. L Pritchard, the coal company's representative.

25b Using Question Marks

Question marks appear at the end of direct questions. They are also used to indicate questionable dates or numbers.

(1) Marking the end of a direct question

Use a question mark to signal the end of a direct question.

> Who was that masked man? (direct question)

> Who was it who asked, "Who was that masked man?" (question within a question)

Did he say where he came from, who his companion was, or where they were headed? (series of direct questions)

Did he say where he came from? Who his companion was? Where they were headed? (series of direct questions with each question asked separately)

Did he say where he came from? who his companion was? where they were headed? (series of direct questions; informal usage does not require capitalization of first word of each question)

"Is this a silver bullet?" they asked. (declarative sentence opening with a direct question)

They asked, "Could he have been the Lone Ranger?" (declarative sentence closing with a direct question)

NOTE: No additional punctuation follows the question mark in any of these sentences. However, a pair of dashes or a pair of parentheses is used around a direct question within a declarative sentence.

?
25b

Someone—a disgruntled office seeker?—is sabotaging the campaign.

Part of the shipment (three dozen cases?) was delayed.

(2)   Marking questionable dates or numbers

Use a question mark in parentheses to indicate that a date or number is uncertain.

The clock struck five (?) and stopped.

Aristophanes, the Greek author of satirical comic dramas, was born in 448 (?) B.C. and died in 380 (?) B.C.

(3)   Editing to eliminate misuse or overuse of question marks

The use of question marks can be redundant or incorrect. Question marks are not used in the following situations.

After an indirect question

An indirect question calls for a period only.

FAULTY: The personnel officer asked if he knew how to type?

REVISED: The personnel officer asked if he knew how to type.

With other punctuation

A question mark is not used along with an exclamation point, comma, semicolon, or period.

FAULTY: "Can it be true?," he asked.

REVISED: "Can it be true?" he asked.

FAULTY: Can you believe this run of good luck?!

REVISED: Can you believe this run of good luck?

In a series

Question marks are not used in a series.

FAULTY: You did what?? Are you crazy??

REVISED: You did what? Are you crazy?

As an indication of attitude

Question marks are not to be used to convey sarcasm.

FAULTY: I refused his generous (?) offer.

Instead, suggest your attitude through word choice.

REVISED: I refused his not-very-generous offer.

?

25b

In an exclamation

A question mark is not used after an exclamation phrased
as a question.

FAULTY: Will you please stop that at once?

REVISED: Will you please stop that at once!

▶
EXERCISE 2

Correct the use of question marks and other punctuation in the following sentences.

EXAMPLE:

ORIGINAL: She asked whether Freud's theories were accepted
during his lifetime?

REVISED: She asked whether Freud's theories were accepted
during his lifetime.

1. He wondered whether he should take a nine o'clock class? Or would
   that be too early?
2. The instructor asked, "Was the Spanish-American War a victory for
   America?"?
3. Are they really going to Peking??!!
4. He took a modest (?) portion of dessert—half a pie.
5. "Is *data* the plural of *datum*?," he inquired.

25c   Using Exclamation Points

An **exclamation point** is used to convey strong feeling—astonishment, drama, shock, and the like—at the end of an emphatic statement, interjection, or command.

(1)   Marking emphasis

Use an exclamation point to signal the end of an emotional or emphatic statement,

> Remember the Maine!
>
> I really mean it this time: no dinner, no dessert!
>
> My long lost brother!
>
> How dare you question my motives!
>
> What a terrific concert!

an emphatic interjection,

> No! Don't leave!
>
> Oh! I didn't see you at first.

or a forceful command.

> Finish this job at once!
>
> Get out of here!

NOTE: An exclamation point can follow a complete sentence ("What big teeth you have!") or a phrase ("What big teeth!")

(2)   Editing to eliminate misuse or overuse of the exclamation point

Like the question mark, the exclamation point has a way of turning up where it does not belong. Except for recording dialogue, exclamation points are almost never appropriate in academic writing. They do not make writing authoritative and emphatic. In fact, they suggest that you feel your words are not sufficiently forceful.

Use exclamation points with care, even in informal writing. Too many exclamation points give readers the impression that you are overwrought, even hysterical. Exclamation points should not be used in the following situations.

With mild statements

Exclamation points are not used with mildly emphatic statements or with mild interjections or commands.

Please close the door behind you.

Oh, don't be such a jerk.

Stand by your man.

In a series

A series of exclamation points is not used for added emphasis.

FAULTY: I could hardly believe my eyes!!!

REVISED: I could hardly believe my eyes!

With other punctuation

An exclamation point is not used with a comma, period, semicolon, or question mark.

FAULTY: "Fire!," he shouted.

REVISED: "Fire!" he shouted.

FAULTY: You can't be serious?!

REVISED: You can't be serious!

As an indication of attitude

Do not use an exclamation point to suggest sarcasm or humor. Use word choice and sentence structure instead.

FAULTY: The team's record was a near-perfect (!) 0 and 12.

REVISED: The team's record was a far-from-perfect 0 and 12.

!

25c

▶
EXERCISE 3

Correct the use of exclamation points and other punctuation in these sentences.

EXAMPLE:

ORIGINAL: "Don't touch that dial!," he cried.

REVISED: "Don't touch that dial!" he cried.

1. When the cell divided, each of the daughter cells had an extra chromosome!
2. Wow. Just what I always wanted. A chocolate-brown Mercedes.
3. He stared in amazement and gasped, "That's incredible!!!!"
4. Please don't forget to leave your key in the ignition!
5. "Eureka!," cried Archimedes as he sprang from his bathtub.

▶
EXERCISE 4

Add appropriate punctuation to this paragraph.

   Dr Craig and his group of divers paused at the shore, staring respectfully at the enormous lake Who could imagine what terrors lay beneath its surface Which of them might not emerge alive from this adventure Would it be Col Cathcart Ms Wilks, the MD from the naval base Her husband, P L Fox Or would they all survive the task ahead Dr Craig decided some encouraging remarks were in order "Attention divers" he said in a loud, forceful voice "May I please have your attention The project which we are about to undertake—" "Oh, no" screamed Mr Fox suddenly "Look out It's the Loch Ness Monster" "Quick" shouted Dr Craig "Move away from the shore" But his warning came too late

26

The Comma

The **comma** is essential for clarifying relationships among words, phrases, and clauses; indicating separations between word groups; and sorting out elements in a series. Used correctly, the comma is invaluable. Used incorrectly, it confuses and even misleads your readers.

Many writers apparently believe that the best strategy for using commas is to scatter them around and hope for the best. But it is sentence structure that determines whether or not to use commas, and you must learn to make informed choices about their use.

26a Setting Off Independent Clauses

(1) Comma plus coordinating conjunction

When you form a compound sentence by linking two independent clauses with a **coordinating conjunction** (*and, but, or, nor, for, yet, so*), use a comma before the conjunction (see 7a.1).

> The year was 2081, and everybody was finally equal. (Kurt Vonnegut, Jr., "Harrison Bergeron")

> It was what I had longed for, but I can't reconstruct our reunion scene. (Geoffrey Wolfe, *The Duke of Deception*)

> Will Social Security exist by the time we retire, or will we have to rely on pensions and savings?

> The bride was not young, nor was she very pretty. (Stephen Crane, "The Bride Comes to Yellow Sky")

> He hesitated at first, for he had never encountered a princess before.

> The fires next door we extinguish without question, yet who among us would snuff out a star? (Dennis Smith, *New York Times Book Review*)

> Emily Dickinson was something of a recluse, so she did not become well known during her lifetime.

No matter how many independent clauses a compound sentence has, a comma precedes each coordinating conjunction.

> She had bonny children, yet she felt they had been thrust upon her, and she could not love them. (D. H. Lawrence, "The Rocking Horse Winner")

When correlative conjunctions link two independent clauses, use a comma after the first clause (see 7a.3).

> Just <u>as</u> it's fascinating to find out where your barber gets his hair cut or what the top chef eats, <u>so</u> it can be worthwhile to find out how top brokers invest their own money. *(Money)*

(2)   Omitting the comma

If two clauses connected by a coordinating conjunction are very short, you may omit the comma.

> Seek and ye shall find.
>
> Love it or leave it.

Some writers omit the comma when no possibility exists that the sentence will be misread without it.

> He began to feel thirsty again and he longed to be back in the hot reeking public-house. (James Joyce, "Counterparts")

In most cases, however, use a comma before any coordinating conjunction that separates two main clauses.

(3)   Substituting a semicolon

Sometimes a semicolon instead of a comma is needed to separate two clauses linked by a coordinating conjunction. For instance, you should use a semicolon for clarity when one or more of the independent clauses already contains commas (see 27b).

> The tour visited Melbourne, the capital of Australia; and then it continued on to Wellington, New Zealand.

You may also use a semicolon when one or more clauses are especially complex,

> Helena wanted to marry her sister's brother-in-law in an elaborate outdoor wedding on June 24; but her parents thought she should wait until she turned 21 in September.

or when the second clause stands in sharp contrast to the first.

> The advent of T.V. has increased the false values ascribed to read-
> ing, since T.V. provides a vulgar alternative. But this piety is silly;
> and most reading is no more cultural nor intellectual nor imagina-
> tive than shooting pool or watching *What's My Line?* (Donald Hall,
> "Four Kinds of Reading")

In these sentences you could also delete the coordinating conjunctions that follow the semicolons; however, using both makes
the separation between the clauses more emphatic.

▶
EXERCISE 1

Combine each of the following sentence pairs into one compound sentence, adding commas where necessary.

> EXAMPLE: Emergency medicine became an approved medical
>   specialty in 1979. Now pediatric emergency medicine is
>   becoming increasingly important. (and)
>
>   Emergency medicine became an approved medical
>   specialty in 1979, and now pediatric emergency medi-
>   cine is becoming increasingly important.

26b

1. Pope John Paul II did not hesitate to visit his native Poland. He did
   not hesitate to meet with Solidarity leader Lech Walesa. (nor)
2. Agents place brand name products in prominent positions in films.
   The products will be seen and recognized by large audiences. (so)
3. Unisex insurance rates may have some drawbacks for women. They
   may be very beneficial. (or)
4. Cigarette advertising no longer appears on television. It does appear
   in print media. (but)
5. Dorothy Day founded the Catholic Worker movement over fifty years
   ago. Today her followers still dispense free food, medical care, and
   legal advice to the needy. (and)

26b Setting Off Items in a Series

(1) Coordinate elements

Use commas with three or more coordinate elements (words,
phrases, or clauses).

> *Chipmunk, raccoon,* and *Mugwump* are words of Indian origin.
> (series of nouns)

> She is a child of her age, of depression, of war, of fear. (Tillie Olsen, "I Stand Here Ironing") (series of phrases)
>
> Brazilians speak Portugese, Colombians speak Spanish, and Haitians speak French and Creole. (series of clauses)

To express coordination and avoid ambiguity, always use a comma between the last two items in a series—before the coordinating conjunction if the series includes one.

> AMBIGUOUS: The party was made special by the company, the light from the hundreds of twinkling candles and the excellent hors d'oeuvres.
>
> REVISED: The party was made special by the company, the light from the hundreds of twinkling candles, and the excellent hors d'oeuvres.

Do not, however, use a comma to introduce or to close a series, unless the context requires it.

,
26b

> FAULTY: The evaluators felt the most important criteria were, fat content, presence of artificial ingredients, and taste.
>
> REVISED: The evaluators felt the most important criteria were fat content, presence of artificial ingredients, and taste.
>
> FAULTY: The French language contributed the words *garage, automobile*, and *journal*, to English.
>
> REVISED: The French language contributed the words *garage, automobile*, and *journal* to English.
>
> FAULTY: Quebec, Ontario, and Saskatchewan, are three Canadian provinces.
>
> REVISED: Quebec, Ontario, and Saskatchewan are three Canadian provinces.

NOTE: If phrases or clauses in a series already contain commas, separate the items with semicolons (see 27d).

(2) Coordinate adjectives

Two or more **coordinate adjectives**—adjectives that modify the same word or word group—take a comma between them unless they are joined by a conjunction.

> She brushed her long, shining hair.
>
> The fruit was crisp, tart, mellow—in short, good enough to eat.

If all the adjectives in the series are linked by coordinating conjunctions, commas are not used.

The baby was tired and cranky and wet.

Sometimes several adjectives will all seem to modify one noun, pronoun, or noun phrase when in fact one or more of them modifies another word or word group. In the following sentence, for instance, the adjective *red* modifies the noun *balloons,* but the adjective *ten* modifies *red balloons.*

Ten red balloons fell from the ceiling.

In this case, only one adjective modifies the noun, so no comma is needed.

One way to decide whether you need a comma in a series of adjectives is to reverse the order of the adjectives. If you can reverse the order ("She brushed her shining, long hair"), you need a comma. If you cannot ("Red ten balloons fell from the ceiling"), the adjectives are not coordinate, and you do not need a comma.

Another way to decide whether you need a comma is to insert the word *and* between the adjectives. If you can insert *and* without changing the meaning of the sentence ("She brushed her long and shining hair"), use a comma. If you cannot ("Ten and red balloons fell from the ceiling"), the adjectives are not coordinate, and you should not use a comma.

,
26b

NOTE: Numbers—such as *ten* in the example above—are not coordinate with other adjectives.

▶

EXERCISE 2

Correct the use of commas in the following sentences, adding or deleting commas where necessary. If a sentence is punctuated correctly, mark it with a C.

EXAMPLE: Neither dogs snakes bees nor dragons frighten her.

Neither dogs, snakes, bees, nor dragons frighten her.

1. Seals, whales, dogs, lions, and horses, are all mammals.
2. Mammals are warm-blooded vertebrates that bear live young, nurse them, and usually have fur.
3. Seals are mammals but lizards, and snakes, and iguanas are reptiles, and newts and salamanders are amphibians.
4. Amphibians also include frogs, and toads.
5. Eagles and geese and ostriches and turkeys chickens and ducks are classified as birds.

▶

EXERCISE 3

Add two coordinate adjectives to modify each of the following combinations, inserting commas where required.

> EXAMPLE: classical music
>
>   strong, beautiful classical music

1. distant thunder
2. silver spoon
3. New York Yankees
4. doll house
5. Rolling Stones

6. loving couple
7. computer science
8. wheat bread
9. art museum
10. new math

26c   Setting Off Introductory Elements

,
26c

Use a comma to separate introductory elements—clauses, phrases, and occasionally single words that modify a word or word group in a sentence—from the rest of the sentence.

(1)   Introductory adverb clauses

Introductory adverb clauses, including elliptical adverb clauses (see 6d.2), are generally set off from the rest of the sentence by commas.

> Although the CIA used to call undercover agents *penetration agents,* they now routinely refer to them as *moles.*
>
> When war came to Beirut and Londonderry and Saigon, the victims were the children.
>
> While working in the mines, Paul longed for a better life.

If the adverb clause is short, you may omit the comma, *provided the sentence will be clear without it.*

> When you are exercising drink plenty of water.

When an adverb clause falls at the *end* of a sentence, no comma separates it from the main clause.

> FAULTY: Jane Addams founded Hull House, because she wanted to help Chicago's poor.
>
> REVISED: Jane Addams founded Hull House because she wanted to help Chicago's poor.

NOTE: If an adverb clause at the end of a sentence is clearly non-restrictive, a comma must precede it (see 26d.1).

(2) Introductory phrases

Introductory phrases are usually set off from the rest of the sentence by commas. Such phrases include participial phrases,

> Thinking that this might be his last chance, Scott struggled toward the Pole.
>
> Overworked and underpaid, the staff did their best.

infinitive phrases,

> To succeed in a male-dominated field, women engineers must work extremely hard.
>
> To produce cancer, the carcinogen must be present in the tissue for an adequate period of time at a proper concentration.

and prepositional phrases.

> With a good deal of sarcasm and very little tact, the letter responded to his complaint.
>
> During the worst days of the Depression, movie attendance rose dramatically.

NOTE: Commas do not follow gerunds and gerund phrases that serve as subjects rather than modifiers.

> FAULTY: Laughing out loud, can release tension.
>
> REVISED: Laughing out loud can release tension.

26c

If the introductory phrase is short and no ambiguity is possible, you may omit the comma.

> For the first time Clint felt truly happy.
>
> After the exam I took a four-hour nap.

(3) Introductory transitional expressions

Conjunctive adverbs or other transitional expressions are usually set off from the rest of the sentence with commas.

> Originally, the pleats in the cummerbunds worn with tuxedos were designed to conceal theater tickets.
>
> Fortunately, Ralph got up the nerve to propose. Unfortunately, Alice turned him down.

NOTE: When a conjunction appears at the beginning of a sentence, it is not followed by a comma.

> FAULTY: Time was short. But, we managed to finish anyway.
>
> REVISED: Time was short. But we managed to finish anyway.

NOTE: Various *nonessential elements*—mild interjections, for instance—may also appear at the beginning of a sentence, and when they do, they are usually set off by commas (see 26d.d).

▶

EXERCISE 4

Add commas in this paragraph where they are needed to set off an introductory element from the rest of the sentence.

> Once upon a time European "welfare states" supported ambitious social welfare programs. However these same governments today are having economic problems that are forcing them to seriously limit their social-welfare spending. In countries like Holland, Great Britain, and Germany unexpected economic and demographic conditions have forced governments to spend less. For instance longer life expectancies have made health care and old-age pensions more costly. In addition the declining birthrate has left fewer people to support the programs with tax revenues. Finally unemployed workers are placing a strain on unemployment insurance and disability insurance funds. Burdened by the increasing costs but unwilling to abandon social programs the nations of Western Europe are unable to invest in new businesses or industry. Because the governments cannot generate sufficient revenue to support them many programs are in serious trouble. (Adapted from "The Welfare Crisis," *Newsweek*)

26d Setting Off Nonessential Elements from the Rest of the Sentence

Certain elements at the beginning, middle, or end of a sentence are considered nonessential, or parenthetical. Although these words, phrases, or clauses do contribute to the meaning of the sentence, they are not essential to its meaning.

> Designer jeans are a contradiction in terms, like educational television. (Fran Lebowitz)
>
> There is no place I know of, other than the bathtub, where people should not have to worry about manners. (Judith Martin)

Without the nonessential phrase, each of these sentences would convey a slightly different (and less effective) message, but the basic meaning of each would be the same.

> Designer jeans are a contradiction in terms.

> There is no place I know of where people should not have to worry about manners.

When a sentence includes any of the following nonessential elements, commas should mark their boundaries and keep them from blending into the rest of the sentence.

(1)   Nonrestrictive modifiers

Modifying phrases or clauses may be restrictive or nonrestrictive. **Restrictive modifiers** limit the meaning of the word or word group they modify, and they should not be separated from it by commas.

26d

> Men who were drafted when war was declared found themselves at a disadvantage.

Who were drafted when war was declared limits the noun *men* to those who were drafted, and it is therefore *restrictive*. Because the modifying clause says something essential about *men*, it is essential to the meaning of the sentence. Without the modifying clause, the meaning of the sentence would change.

Nonrestrictive modifiers do not limit or particularize the words they modify; they merely supply additional information about them.

> Men, who were drafted when war was declared, found themselves at a disadvantage.

In this sentence, the modifying clause *who were drafted when war was declared*, set off by commas, is nonrestrictive. The modifying clause in this case describes *all* the men. Without the modifying clause, the sentence would still be about all the men.

Because including or excluding commas in this situation changes the meaning of the sentence, you must use commas accurately. Commas accompany nonrestrictive modifiers *only*—never restrictive modifiers.

Here are some additional examples of restrictive and nonrestrictive modifiers.

The counterculture hero who created Zap Comix during the 1960's has also had artwork displayed at the Whitney Museum of American Art. (restrictive clause)

Robert Crumb, who created Zap Comix during the 1960's, is credited with popularizing the slogan "'Keep on Truckin.'" (nonrestrictive clause)

Environmental groups have become much more militant in recent years; now the sincere and passionate demands that such groups make are inspiring recreational campers and the logging industry to mobilize against them. (restrictive clause)

Environmental groups have become much more militant in recent years; now their sincere and passionate demands, which groups like recreational campers and the logging industry oppose, are inspiring controversy. (nonrestrictive clause)

Dr. Franklin now works in the hospital where she was born. (restrictive clause)

Dr. Franklin now works in Pennsylvania Hospital, where she was born. (nonrestrictive clause)

,
26d

NOTE: If a nonrestrictive element falls at the end of a sentence, as in the sentence above, only one comma sets it off from the rest of the sentence.

The president hoping to encourage Americans to become more physically fit was Dwight D. Eisenhower. (restrictive phrase)

President Eisenhower, hoping to encourage Americans to become more physically fit, created the President's Council on Youth Fitness. (nonrestrictive phrase)

or

Hoping to encourage Americans to become more physically fit, President Eisenhower created the President's Council on Youth Fitness. (nonrestrictive phrase)

Symptoms found in most cases of flu include fever, sore throat, and loss of appetite. (restrictive phrase)

Truffles, hunted by specially trained pigs, are extremely valuable. (nonrestrictive phrase)

During his first voyage across the Atlantic, Columbus discovered Hispaniola. (restrictive phrase)

During his first voyage, on a map-making expedition, Charles Darwin kept a journal. (nonrestrictive phrase)

To determine whether a particular modifier is restrictive or nonrestrictive, ask yourself a few questions.

1. Is the modifier essential to the meaning of the noun it modifies (*The counter culture hero who created Zap Comix*—not just any counterculture hero)? If so, it is restrictive and does not take commas. If not, commas should set off the modifier.

2. Is the modifier introduced by *that* (*the sincere and passionate demands that such groups make*)? If so, it is restrictive. *That* cannot introduce a nonrestrictive clause.

3. Can you delete the relative pronoun without causing ambiguity or confusion (*the sincere and passionate demands [that] such groups make*)? If so, the clause is restrictive and requires no commas. A relative pronoun that is not the subject of the relative clause can be deleted if the clause is restrictive. Relative pronouns that introduce nonrestrictive clauses, however, cannot be deleted.

4. Can you rearrange the sentence so that the modifying phrase or clause precedes the word or word group it modifies (*Hoping to encourage Americans to become more physically fit, President Eisenhower . . .*)? If so, the modifier is nonrestrictive and requires a comma. Restrictive phrases and clauses, on the other hand, nearly always *follow* the words they modify.

26d

▶
EXERCISE 5

Insert commas where necessary to set off nonrestrictive phrases and clauses.

> The Statue of Liberty which was dedicated in 1886 has undergone extensive renovation. The famous statue whose designer was the French engineer Alexandre Gustave Eiffel is made of copper. The Statue of Liberty created over a period of nine years by sculptor Frédéric-Auguste Bartholdi stands 151 feet tall. The people of France who were grateful for American help in the French revolution raised the money to pay the sculptor who created the statue. The people of the United States contributing over $100,000 raised the money for the pedestal on which the statue stands.

(2)   Nonrestrictive appositives

An **appositive** is a noun or noun phrase that identifies or describes a noun, pronoun, or noun phrase (see 6f.4). A *nonrestrictive* appositive, one that provides nonessential information about the word or words it modifies, is set off by commas.

Steve Howe, <u>relief pitcher for the Los Angeles Dodgers</u>, struggled with a cocaine habit. (appositive *relief pitcher for the Los Angeles Dodgers* further identifies Howe but is not essential to the meaning of *Steve Howe*)

James Watt, <u>Secretary of the Interior under President Reagan</u>, was criticized severely by environmentalists. (appositive provides information that helps to identify Watt but does not change the meaning of *James Watt*)

An appositive that is essential to the meaning of the word or word group it modifies is, however, *restrictive* and takes no commas. Normally, an appositive is restrictive if it is more specific than the noun that precedes it.

Orson Welles's film <u>*Citizen Kane*</u> has received great critical acclaim. (Without the appositive *Citizen Kane,* the sentence would imply that Welles directed only one film; therefore, the appositive is essential to the meaning of *Orson Welles's film* and to the sentence.)

The feminist author <u>Erica Jong</u> wrote *Fanny* as well as *Fear of Flying.* (Without the appositive *Erica Jong,* the sentence's meaning would change; the subject could be any feminist author, not a particular one. The appositive is therefore essential to the meaning of the sentence.)

26d

(3) Conjunctive adverbs and other transitional expressions

Conjunctive adverbs—words like *however, therefore, thus,* and *nevertheless*—and **transitional expressions** like *for example* and *on the other hand* are also nonessential. These interrupters qualify, clarify, and make connections explicit, but they are not essential to meaning. (For a complete list of such expressions, see 4c.4.)

When a conjunctive adverb or transitional expression interrupts a clause, it is set off by commas.

The House Ethics Committee recommended reprimanding two members of Congress. The House, <u>however</u>, overruled the recommendation and voted to censure them.

The Outward Bound program, <u>according to its staff</u>, is extremely safe.

No student has ever qualified for the Bamfield prize. Its standards, <u>after all</u>, are very high.

It was, <u>in short</u>, a powerful film.

A conjunctive adverb or similar expression at the *end* of a clause is still parenthetical, and it is separated from the rest of the sentence by a single comma.

> Some things were easier after school started. Other things were a lot harder, <u>however</u>.

These expressions are also usually set off by commas when they introduce a sentence (see 26c.3).

NOTE: When a conjunctive adverb or transitional expression separates two independent clauses, it must be preceded by a semicolon or a period and followed by a comma (see 27c).

> Laughter is the best medicine; <u>of course</u>, penicillin also comes in handy sometimes.

(4) Contradictory phrases

A parenthetical phrase that expresses contrast is usually set off from the rest of the sentence by commas.

> Triumphant, <u>not discouraged</u>, Sir Edmund Hillary reached the top of Mt. Everest in 1953.
>
> This medication should be taken after a meal, <u>never on an empty stomach</u>.
>
> Her reflexes were slowing down, <u>but not her mind</u>.
>
> It was Roger Maris, <u>not Mickey Mantle</u>, who broke Babe Ruth's home run record.

(5) Absolute phrases

An **absolute phrase** usually consists of a noun plus a participle. If the verb is a form of *to be*, however, the participle may be omitted (see 6f.3). An absolute phrase is always set off by commas from the sentence it modifies.

> <u>His fear increasing</u>, he waited to enter the haunted house.
>
> A number of soldiers have vanished in Southeast Asia, <u>their bodies never recovered</u>.
>
> The fish struggled on the hook, <u>its eyes bulging</u>, trying to wriggle free.

(6) Miscellaneous nonessential elements

Wherever they appear, the following nonessential elements are usually separated from the rest of the sentence by commas.

26d

Tag questions (auxiliary verb + pronoun added to a statement)

> This is your first day on the job, <u>isn't it</u>?
>
> You're not afraid, <u>are you</u>?
>
> Fido has been vaccinated against rabies, <u>hasn't he</u>?
>
> It seems possible, <u>does it not</u>, that carrots may provide some protection against cancer?

Names in direct address

> I wonder, <u>Mr. Honeywell</u>, whether Mr. Albright deserves a raise.
>
> <u>Freddie</u>, what's your opinion?
>
> What do you think, <u>Margie</u>?

Mild interjections

> <u>Well</u>, it's about time.

NOTE: Stronger interjections may be set off by dashes or exclamation points (see 30d and 25c.1).

Yes and No

> <u>Yes</u>, we have no bananas.
>
> <u>No</u>, we're all out of lemons.

26d

▶

EXERCISE 6

Set off the nonessential elements in these sentences with commas. Be sure to isolate nonrestrictive appositives, conjunctive adverbs and other transitional expressions, contradictory phrases, absolute phrases, and other nonessential elements. If a sentence is correct, mark it with a *C*.

> EXAMPLE: Piranhas like sharks will attack and eat almost anything if the opportunity arises.
>
> Piranhas, like sharks, will attack and eat almost anything if the opportunity arises.

1. Kermit the frog is a muppet a cross between a marionette and a puppet.
2. The common cold a virus is frequently spread by hand contact not by mouth.
3. The account in the Bible of Noah's Ark and the forty-day flood may be based on an actual deluge.
4. More than two-thirds of U.S. welfare recipients are people with legitimate reasons for not working such as children, the aged, the severely disabled, and mothers of children under six.
5. The submarine *Nautilus* was the first to cross under the North Pole wasn't it?
6. The 1958 Ford Edsel was advertised with the slogan "Once you've seen it you'll never forget it."

7. Superman was called Kal-El on the planet Krypton; on earth how-
    ever he was known as Clark Kent not Kal-El.
8. Its sales topping any of his previous singles Elvis Presley's "Heart-
    break Hotel" was his first million seller.
9. Two companies Nash and Hudson joined in 1954 to form American
    Motors.
10. A firefly is a beetle not a fly and a prairie dog is a rodent not a dog.

26e Using Commas in Other Conventional Contexts

Around direct quotations

In most cases, use commas to set off a direct quotation from the
identifying tag—the phrase that identifies the speaker (*he said,
she answered*).

> Emerson said to Thoreau, "I greet you at the beginning of a great
> career."
>
> "I greet you at the beginning of a great career," Emerson said to
> Thoreau.
>
> "I greet you," Emerson said to Thoreau, "at the beginning of a
> great career."

When the identifying tag interrupts one complete sentence, as it
does in the last example above, commas are used before and
after the identifying tag. When the identifying tag comes between
two complete sentences, however, the tag is introduced by a
comma but followed by a period.

> "Winning isn't everything," Vince Lombardi said. "It's the only
> thing."

If the first sentence of an interrupted quotation ends with a question mark or exclamation point, no commas are used.

> "Should we hold the front page?" she asked. "After all, nothing
> much has happened this week."
>
> "Hold the front page!" he cried. "This is the biggest story of the
> decade."

(For further information on punctuation with quotation marks,
see 29f.)

Between names and titles or degrees

Use a comma to set off a person's name from his or her title or
degree.

,
26e

Alice Vaselli, D.D.S.

Henry Kissinger, Ph.D.

Charles, Prince of Wales

Perry White, Editor-in-Chief

If the title or degree precedes the name, however, no comma is required.

Dr. Kissinger

Prince Charles

In dates and addresses

Use commas to separate items in dates and addresses.

February 17, 1971

August 9, 1975 (9 August 1975—no commas—also acceptable)

600 West End Avenue, New York, N.Y. 10024

With hundreds watching, the space shuttle Challenger was launched on August 30, 1983, from Cape Canaveral, Florida.

NOTE: Commas are not used to separate the day from the month; when only the month and year are given, no commas are used (May 1968). No comma separates the street number from the street or the state name from the zip code. When a date or address punctuated with commas appears within a sentence, another comma follows its last element.

In salutations and closings

Use commas in informal correspondence following salutations and closings

Dear John,

Dear Aunt Sophie,

and following the complimentary close in personal or business correspondence.

Sincerely,

Yours truly,

Fondly,

Love,

NOTE: Keep in mind that in business correspondence a colon, not a comma, follows the salutation (see 42a.4).

In long numbers

Use commas with long numbers.

When writing a number of four digits or more, separate the numbers by placing a comma every three digits, counting from the right.

> 1,200 (comma optional with four digits)
>
> 12,000
>
> 120,000
>
> 1,200,000

Commas are not required in long numbers used in addresses, telephone numbers, zip codes, or years. (For additional information, see Chapter 35.)

▶
EXERCISE 7

Add commas where necessary to set off quotations, names, dates, addresses, and numbers in the following sentences.

1. India became independent on August 15 1947.
2. The UAW has over 1500000 dues-paying members.
3. Nikita Krushchev, former Soviet premier, said "We will bury you!"
4. Mount St. Helens, northeast of Portland Oregon, began erupting on March 27 1980 and eventually killed at least thirty people.
5. Located at 600 Pennsylvania Avenue Washington D.C., the White House is a major tourist attraction.
6. In 1956, playing in Yankee Stadium in New York New York, Don Larsen pitched the first perfect game in World Series history before a crowd of 64519 fans.
7. Lewis Thomas M.D. was born in Flushing N.Y. and attended Harvard Medical School in Cambridge Massachusetts.
8. In 1967 2000000 people died of smallpox, but in 1977 only about twenty died.
9. "The reports of my death" Mark Twain remarked "have been greatly exaggerated."
10. The French explorer Jean Nicolet landed at Green Bay Wisconsin in 1634, and in 1848 Wisconsin became the thirtieth state; it has 10355 lakes and a population of over 4700000.

26f Using Commas to Prevent Misreading

Commas may be needed simply for clarity. Consider the following sentence.

> Those who can, sprint the final lap.

Without the comma, *can* appears to be an auxiliary verb ("Those who can sprint . . .") and the sentence seems incomplete.

Commas that tell readers to pause prevent confusion and ambiguity. To facilitate reading, commas are used frequently in two situations.

Indicating an omission

Use a comma to acknowledge the omission of a repeated word.

> Pam carried the box; Tim, the suitcase.

> Edwina went first; Marco, second.

As in these examples, the omitted word is usually a verb.

Separating repeated words

Use a comma to separate words repeated consecutively within a sentence.

> Those of you who know me well, know well that I hate to get up in the morning.

> Everything bad that could have happened, happened.

26f

▶

EXERCISE 8

Add commas where necessary to prevent misreading.

> EXAMPLE: Whatever will be will be.
>
>   Whatever will be, will be.

1. According to Bob Frank's computer has three disk drives.
2. Vasco da Gama explored Florida; Pizarro Peru.
3. By Monday evening students must begin preregistration for fall classes.
4. Whatever they built they built with care.
5. When batting practice carefully.
6. Brunch includes warm muffins topped with whipped butter and freshly brewed coffee.

▶

EXERCISE 9

Commas have been intentionally deleted from some of the following sentences by professional writers. Add commas where needed, and be prepared to explain why each is necessary. If a sentence is correct, mark it with a *C*.

1. The world is before you and you need not take it or leave it as it was when you came in. (James Baldwin, *Nobody Knows My Name*)

2. The great secret known to internists but still hidden from the general public is that most things get better by themselves. Most things in fact are better by morning. (Lewis Thomas, *Lives of a Cell*)

3. Her face was young and smooth and fresh-looking. (Katherine Ann Porter, "Rope")

4. He was wearing his cape and had his cap on and he came directly toward my machine and put his arm on my shoulder. (Ernest Hemingway, "In Another Country")

5. That she was in some way related to the girl though not of an age to be her mother was evident from their manner together. (Shirley Hazzard, *The Transit of Venus*)

6. Every family is its own country and happy families are no more alike than peaceful nations. (Frances Taliaferro, *Harper's*)

7. The downtown square is a brisk trading area its broad avenue resolving into a central square which framed by three-story buildings seems as though it is entirely walled. (Joan Chase, *During the Reign of the Queen of Persia*)

8. It had rained long and hard during the night and an early morning mist drifted over Lake Placid. Tumbling low clouds covered the tops of the mountains that ringed the lake totally obscuring Whiteface highest of the peaks. (Bernard F. Conners, *Dancehall*)

9. Dandelions crabgrass Queen Anne's lace lamb's quarters sheep sorrel and even bluegrass are but a small sample of a large constellation of alien plant species that have been assimilated into the ecology of North America. (John C. Kricher, *Natural History*)

10. Oh I know intellectually that people have been circling the earth for centuries and there's nothing to it. (Russell Baker, *New York Times Magazine*)

26g Editing to Eliminate Misuse or Overuse of Commas

Commas can easily be overused or misused. Writers who use too many commas may mislead readers by encouraging them to pause where pauses are illogical. A comma is not used in the following situations.

Between two independent clauses
Using a comma to connect two independent clauses creates a comma splice (see Chapter 12).

> FAULTY: The season was unusually cool, nevertheless the orange crop was not seriously harmed.

> REVISED: The season was unusually cool; nevertheless, the orange crop was not seriously harmed.

REVISED: The season was unusually cool. Nevertheless, the orange crop was not seriously harmed.

REVISED: The season was unusually cool, but the orange crop was not seriously harmed.

REVISED: Although the season was unusually cool, the orange crop was not seriously harmed.

Around restrictive elements

Commas are not used to set off restrictive elements (see 26d).

FAULTY: Women, who seek to be equal to men, lack ambition.

REVISED: Women who seek to be equal to men lack ambition.

FAULTY: The film, *American Graffiti,* was directed by George Lucas.

REVISED: The film *American Graffiti* was directed by George Lucas.

FAULTY: They planned a picnic, in the park.

REVISED: They planned a picnic in the park.

FAULTY: The word, *snafu,* is an acronym for "situation normal—all fouled up."

REVISED: The word *snafu* is an acronym for "situation normal—all fouled up."

Between inseparable grammatical constructions

Placing a comma between such constructions interrupts the logical flow of a sentence. A comma should not be placed between a subject and its predicate; a verb and its complement or direct object; a preposition and its object; or an adjective and the noun, pronoun, or noun phrase it modifies.

FAULTY: We think that anyone who can walk a straight line out of the office before lunch, ought to be able to travel the same route on the way back. (Advertisement, Spirits Council of the United States) (comma between subject and predicate)

REVISED: We think that anyone who can walk a straight line out of the office before lunch ought to be able to travel the same route on the way back.

FAULTY: Louis Braille developed, an alphabet of raised dots for the blind. (comma between verb and object)

REVISED: Louis Braille developed an alphabet of raised dots for the blind.

REVISED: Louis Braille, a Frenchman who was himself blind, developed an alphabet of raised dots for the blind. (note that here the comma that comes between verb and object is actually one of the pair of commas that sets off the nonrestrictive appositive)

FAULTY: They relaxed somewhat during, the last part of the obstacle course. (comma between preposition and object)

REVISED: They relaxed somewhat during the last part of the obstacle course.

FAULTY: Wind-dispersed weeds include the well-known and plentiful, dandelions, milkweed, and thistle. (comma between adjective and words it modifies)

REVISED: Wind-dispersed weeds include the well-known and plentiful dandelions, milkweed, and thistle.

Between a verb and a subordinate clause to set off indirect quotations or indirect questions

Commas are not used between verb and subordinate clause to set off indirect quotations or indirect questions.

FAULTY: Art Buchwald once said, that the problem with television news is that it has no second page.

REVISED: Art Buchwald once said that the problem with television news is that it has no second page.

FAULTY: The landlord asked, whether we would be willing to sign a two-year lease.

REVISED: The landlord asked whether we would be willing to sign a two-year lease.

26g

Between coordinate phrases that contain correlative conjunctions

FAULTY: As a rule, college students of twenty years ago had access to neither photocopiers, nor pocket calculators.

REVISED: As a rule, college students twenty years ago had access to neither photocopiers nor pocket calculators.

FAULTY: Both typewriters, and tape recorders were generally available, however.

REVISED: Both typewriters and tape recorders were generally available, however.

Between two elements of a compound subject, predicate, object, complement, or auxiliary verb

FAULTY: During the Middle Ages plagues, and pestilence were not uncommon. (comma interrupts compound subject)

REVISED: During the Middle Ages plagues and pestilence were not uncommon.

FAULTY: Women students age thirty-five and older are returning to college in large numbers, and tend to be very good students. (comma interrupts compound predicate)

REVISED: Women students age thirty-five and older are returning to college in large numbers and tend to be very good students.

FAULTY: Mattel has marketed a doctor's uniform, and an astronaut suit for its Barbie doll. (comma interrupts compound object)

REVISED: Mattel has marketed a doctor's uniform and an astronaut suit for its Barbie doll.

FAULTY: Bottled water appeals to many who believe it is pure, and fashionable. (comma interrupts compound complement)

REVISED: Bottled water appeals to many who believe it is pure and fashionable.

FAULTY: She can, and will be ready to run in the primary. (comma interrupts compound auxiliary verb)

REVISED: She can and will be ready to run in the primary.

REVISED: She can, and will, be ready to run in the primary.

,
26g

▶
EXERCISE 10

Unneeded commas have been intentionally added to some of the sentences that follow. Delete any unnecessary commas. If a sentence is correct, mark it with a *C*.

EXAMPLE: Spring fever, is a common ailment.

Spring fever is a common ailment.

1. A book is like a garden, carried in the pocket. (Arab proverb)
2. Like the iodine content of kelp, air freight, is something most Americans have never pondered. *(Time)*
3. Charles Rolls, and Frederick Royce manufactured the first Rolls Royce Silver Ghost, in 1907.
4. The hills ahead of him were rounded domes of grey granite, smooth as a bald man's pate, and completely free of vegetation. (Wilbur Smith, *Flight of the Falcon*)
5. Food here is scarce, and cafeteria food is vile, but the great advantage to Russian raw materials, when one can get hold of them, is that they are always fresh and untampered with. (Andrea Lee, *Russian Journal*)
6. At any gathering in Wincaster Row, which included children, Isabel's Jason would be the noisiest, and the roughest, and the most disobedient. (Fay Weldon, *The President's Child*)

7. London in August tends to be, hot, sticky, and very dull. (Patricia Moyes, *A Six-Letter Word for Death*)

8. *Gorky Park* is a thriller, about a triple murder, at a Moscow amusement center.

9. Willie Mays was called, the Say Hey Kid.

10. Either Felix the Cat, or Garfield, is probably the world's best-known feline.

▶

EXERCISE 11

In the following passage, punctuation errors have been deliberately made. Delete excess commas and add any necessary ones. Be prepared to justify your revisions.

> The most famous wild elephant in the world, lived in the mountain forest of Marsabit, in Kenya, and was called Ahmed. He was remarkable, for the beauty of his tusks. They descended, almost to the ground, in a graceful curve and their slender points were sharp, at the tip, and slightly raised. Ahmed was protected, from danger by special presidential decree. He was a symbol, of all the remaining animals running wild in Kenya and as such he was of some importance to both the science, and the business of supervising elephants. It would have been a very serious matter, if the president's wishes had been ignored, and Ahmed had been poached. Everywhere he went through the forest of Marsabit he was followed, by two armed forest rangers. When he left the safety of the mountain reserve, and wandered off into the surrounding desolation, his guards went, too. Because of this his position was always known, to the local authorities, and he became accustomed to people. He was very easy to photograph and every tourist, who came to Marsabit, wanted to see him. Thousands of visitors even made the uncomfortable trek, hundreds of miles away from their usual haunts, in order to view this singular beast.
>
> But one night, in 1974, Ahmed died. (Adapted from Patrick Marnham, *Harper's*)

26g ,

The Semicolon

The **semicolon** is weaker than the period and stronger than the comma. It signals a shorter pause than the former, but a longer pause than the latter. The semicolon is used only between items of equal grammatical rank: two independent clauses, two phrases, and so on. The two principal uses of the semicolon are to separate independent clauses and, in certain situations, to separate elements in a series.

27a Separating Independent Clauses

;
27a

Use a semicolon rather than a coordinating conjunction or a period between independent clauses that are closely related in meaning. Remember, using only a comma or no punctuation at all between independent clauses will produce a comma splice or a fused sentence (see Chapter 12).

> Paul Revere's *The Boston Massacre* is an early example of traditional American protest art; Edward Hicks's later "primitive" paintings are socially conscious art with a religious strain. (clauses related by contrast)

> The U.S. auto industry has been left in the dust of foreign competition; the automobile as we know it is doomed by dwindling fuel supplies; the American love affair with the automobile is dead. (Noel Grove, *National Geographic*) (clauses related by causality)

Separate sentences marked by periods would fail to convey the close relationships between the clauses.

> Paul Revere's *The Boston Massacre* is an early example of traditional American protest art. Edward Hicks's later "primitive" paintings are socially conscious art with a religious strain.

Such punctuation could also produce short, choppy sentences.

> The U.S. auto industry has been left in the dust of foreign competition. The automobile as we know it is doomed by dwindling fuel supplies. The American love affair with the automobile is dead.

Coordinating conjunctions could produce rambling sentences that lack focus.

> Paul Revere's *The Boston Massacre* is an early example of traditional American protest art, but Edward Hicks's later "primitive" paintings are socially conscious art with a religious strain.

> The U.S. auto industry has been left in the dust of foreign competition, and the automobile as we know it is doomed by dwindling fuel supplies, and the American love affair with the automobile is dead.

Semicolons economically and fluently convey the close connections between the clauses.

NOTE: In some special circumstances, a colon may separate two independent clauses (see 7a.5 and 30a).

27b Separating Complex, Internally Punctuated Clauses

;
27b

Even when two clauses are already joined by a coordinating conjunction, use a semicolon instead of a comma before the coordinating conjunction if one clause contains internal punctuation or is long or complex. Here, for instance, the semicolon signals the break between clauses.

> In October, when the fair was on, you couldn't even get into the museum without paying admission to the fairgrounds and fighting your way through the chili-dog stands and the livestock pens; and at any time of year people hesitated to go out there after dark. (Calvin Tomkins, *New Yorker*)

The semicolon in the following sentence not only distinguishes the two clauses but also emphasizes the warning at the end by isolating it.

> If such a world government is not established by a process of agreement among nations, I believe it will come anyway, and in a much more dangerous form; for war or wars can only result in one power being supreme and dominating the rest of the world by its overwhelming military supremacy. (Albert Einstein, *Einstein on Peace*)

Using a semicolon to separate clauses linked by a coordinating conjunction does more than clarify your meaning. It also conveys strong contrasts or firm distinctions between ideas.

▶
EXERCISE 1

Add semicolons, periods, or commas plus coordinating conjunctions where necessary to separate independent clauses. Reread the paragraph when you have finished to make certain no comma splices or fused sentences remain.

> EXAMPLE: *Birth of a Nation* was one of the earliest epic movies it was based on the book *The Klansman.*
>
> *Birth of a Nation* was one of the earliest epic movies; it was based on the book *The Klansman.*

During the 1950's, movie attendance died down because of the increasing popularity of television. As a result, numerous gimmicks were introduced to draw audiences into theaters. One of the first of these was Cinerama, in this technique three pictures were shot side by side and projected on a curved screen. Next came 3-D, complete with special glasses, *Bwana Devil* and *The Creature from the Black Lagoon* were two early 3-D ventures. *The Robe* was the first picture filmed in Cinemascope in this technique a shrunken image was projected on a screen twice as wide as it was tall. Smell-O-Vision (or Aroma-rama) was a short-lived gimmick that enabled audiences to smell what they were viewing problems developed when it became impossible to get one odor out of the theater in time for the next smell to be introduced. William Castle's *Thirteen Ghosts* introduced special glasses for cowardly viewers who wanted to be able to control what they saw, the red part of the glasses was the "ghost viewer" and the green part was the "ghost remover." Perhaps the ultimate in movie gimmicks accompanied the film *The Tingler* here seats in the theater were wired to generate mild electric shocks. Unfortunately, the shocks set off a chain reaction that led to hysteria in the theater. During the 1960's, such gimmicks all but disappeared, viewers were able once again to simply sit back and enjoy a movie.

▶
EXERCISE 2

Combine each of the following sentence groups into one sentence that contains only two independent clauses. Use a semicolon to join the two clauses. You will need to add, delete, relocate, or change some words; keep experimenting until you find the arrangement that best conveys the sentence's meaning.

> EXAMPLE: The Congo River Rapids is a ride at the Dark Continent in Tampa, Florida. Riders raft down the river. They glide alongside jungle plants and animals.

;
27b

The Congo River Rapids is a ride at the Dark Continent in Tampa, Florida; riders raft down the river, gliding alongside jungle plants and animals.

1. Amusement parks offer exciting rides. They are thrill packed. They flirt with danger.
2. Free Fall is located in Atlanta's Six Flags over Georgia. In this ride, riders travel up a 128-foot-tall tower. They plunge down at 55 miles per hour.
3. In the Sky Whirl riders go 115 feet up in the air and circle about 75 times. This ride is located in Great America. Great America parks are in Gurnee, Illinois, and Santa Clara, California.
4. The Kamikaze Slide can be found at the Wet 'n Wild parks in Arlington, Texas, and Orlando, Florida. This ride is a slide 300 feet long. It extends 60 feet in the air.
5. Parachuter's Perch is another exciting ride. It is found at Great Adventure in Jackson, New Jersey. Its chutes fall at 25 feet per second.
6. Astroworld in Houston, Texas, boasts Greezed Lightnin'. This ride is an 80-foot-high loop. The ride goes from 0 to 60 miles per hour in four seconds and moves forward and backward.
7. The Beast is at Kings Island near Cincinnati, Ohio. The Beast is a wooden roller coaster. It has a 7400-foot track and goes 70 miles per hour. (Adapted from *Seventeen*)

;
27c

27c Separating Clauses Containing Conjunctive Adverbs

Use a semicolon between two closely related independent clauses when the second clause is introduced by or contains a conjunctive adverb or other transitional expression. (For a complete list of such expressions, see 4c.4.)

Thomas Jefferson brought 200 vanilla beans and a recipe for vanilla ice cream back from France; <u>thus</u>, he gave America its all-time favorite ice-cream flavor.

[Washington Irving's] father was long since dead by the time his firm went bankrupt; <u>nevertheless</u>, it is not unreasonable to suppose that the humiliation his son experienced in connection with that event was identified with the puritanical merchant by whom he had always felt humiliated. (Kenneth S. Lynn, *Smithsonian*)

Because each conjunctive adverb *(thus, nevertheless)* separates two independent clauses, a semicolon is needed.

Within a clause, the position of a conjunctive adverb or other transitional expression may vary, and so will the punctuation.

He has passed the Alabama bar; <u>however</u>, he is not qualified to practice law in Louisiana.

He has passed the Alabama bar; he is not, <u>however</u>, qualified to practice law in Louisiana.

He has passed the Alabama bar; he is not qualified to practice law in Louisiana, <u>however</u>.

When the conjunctive adverb or transitional expression comes right after the semicolon, it is followed by a comma. When it comes at the end of the sentence, it is preceded by a comma. Otherwise, it is surrounded by commas (see 26d.3). (Remember that a transitional expression is least emphatic in the end-of-sentence position. See 8a.2.)

;
27c

▶

EXERCISE 3

Insert semicolons and commas where necessary in this paragraph. Add semicolons to connect any two clauses linked by conjunctive adverbs or other transitional expressions. If the conjunctive adverb or transitional expression falls within a clause, be sure to set it off with commas.

EXAMPLE: The comics have been around a long time they are losing popularity to television and video games however.

The comics have been around a long time; they are losing popularity to television and video games, however.

Comics are an important part of American culture moreover they serve a variety of purposes for Americans. Some comics are political "Pogo" for example criticized the war in Vietnam, and "Doonesbury" commented on Watergate. Other comics function as soap operas in fact "Mary Worth" is one long-running comic strip that resembles these continuing stories in many ways. "Little Orphan Annie" was one comic strip that fulfilled an emotional need specifically it helped raise America's spirits during the Depression. "Gasoline Alley," "Krazy Kat," "Mutt and Jeff," and other comics have had long lives in syndication in addition even relative newcomers like "Doonesbury" and "Peanuts" have developed loyal followings. Obviously Americans are involved with comics it is not clear how long comics can stand up to their electronic competitors however.

▶
EXERCISE 4

Combine each of the following sentence groups into one sentence that contains only two independent clauses. Use a semicolon and the conjunctive adverb or transitional phrase in parentheses to join the two clauses, adding commas within clauses where necessary. You will need to add, delete, relocate, or change some words. There is no one correct version; keep experimenting until you find the arrangement you feel is most effective.

> EXAMPLE: The Aleutian Islands are located off the west coast of Alaska. They are an extremely remote chain of islands. They are sometimes called America's Siberia. (in fact)
>
> The Aleutian Islands, located off the west coast of Alaska, are an extremely remote chain of islands; in fact, they are sometimes called America's Siberia.

1. The Aleutians lie between the North Pacific Ocean and the Bering Sea. The weather there is harsh. Dense fog, 100-mile-per-hour winds, and even tidal waves and earthquakes are not uncommon. (for example)
2. These islands constitute North America's largest network of active volcanoes. They boast some beautiful scenery. The islands are relatively unexplored. (still)
3. The Aleutians are home to a wide variety of birds. Numerous animals, such as fur seals and whales, are found there. These islands may house the largest concentration of marine animals in the world. (in fact)
4. During World War II, thousands of American soldiers were stationed on Attu Island. They were stationed on Adak Island. The Japanese eventually occupied both Attu and Kiska Islands. (however)
5. The islands' original population of native Aleuts was drastically reduced in the eighteenth century by Russian fur traders. Today the total population is only about 8500. The U.S. military and its employees comprise more than half of this. (consequently) (Adapted from Lael Morgan, *National Geographic*)

;
27d

27d Separating Items in a Series

Use semicolons between items in a series when one or more of these items are sufficiently complex to require commas. Without semicolons it may be difficult to distinguish the individual elements in the series.

Three papers are posted on the bulletin board outside the building: a description of the exams; a list of appeal procedures for students who fail; and an employment ad from an automobile factory, addressed specifically to candidates whose appeals are turned down. (Andrea Lee, *Russian Journal*)

As ballooning became established, a series of firsts ensued: the first balloonist in the United States was 13-year-old Edward Warren, in 1784; the first woman aeronaut was a Madame Thible who, depending on your source, either recited poetry or sang as she lifted off; the first airmail letter, written by Ben Franklin's grandson, was carried by balloon; and the first bird's-eye photograph of Paris was taken by a balloon. (Elaine B. Steiner, *Games*)

I saw their faces in the darkness: Daphne Gould, who had once taken me on a pony; and Mario Fischer, the millionaire's son; Dirk Schuman and Louis Peskyana and Schuyler Van Lerr, the anthropology students; Pierre Liebowitz, a rich florist who dyed his hair; two soft-voiced Negro boys I didn't know; Pamela Oates and Lily Davis, who were in love; Edmonia Lovett, who once almost suffocated to death in her orgone box; four stray soldiers—all these gave me a swift, darting glance, and turned away. (William Styron, *Lie Down in Darkness*)

;
27d

Each of the sentences above calls for strong punctuation. Even when the items in a series are brief, however, semicolons are required if any element in the series contains commas or other internal punctuation.

Laramie, Wyoming; Wyoming, Delaware; and Delaware, Ohio were the first three places they visited.

▶

EXERCISE 5

Replace commas with semicolons where necessary to separate lengthy, complex, or internally punctuated items in a series.

EXAMPLE: Luxury automobiles have some strong selling points: they are status symbols, some, such as the Corvette, appreciate in value, and they are usually comfortable and well appointed.

Luxury automobiles have some strong selling points: they are status symbols; some, such as the Corvette, appreciate in value; and they are usually comfortable and well appointed.

1. A quarter of a million Americans marched on Washington in 1983 to commemorate the twentieth anniversary of Dr. King's "I Have a Dream" speech, to remind the government that many Americans,

even those who attended the 1963 march, are still without jobs and full equality, and to demonstrate for peace.

2. Steroids, used by some athletes, can be dangerous because they can affect the pituitary gland, causing a lowered sperm count, because they have been linked to the development of liver tumors, and because they can stimulate the growth of some cancers.

3. Tennessee Williams wrote *The Glass Menagerie*, which is about a handicapped young woman and her family, *A Streetcar Named Desire*, which starred Marlon Brando, and *Vieux Carré*.

4. New expressions like *outro*, used to designate the segment of a broadcast where the announcer signs off, *heavy breather*, used to describe a popular romance novel, *commuter marriage*, a marriage in which the partners live and work in different places, and *dentophobe*, a person who is afraid of dentists, are terms which have not yet appeared in most dictionaries.

5. Carl Yastrzemski is the former Red Sox star who replaced Ted Williams in 1961, joining Boston to play left field, who was chosen an all-star eighteen times, and who hit over 450 home runs in his career and was inducted into the Hall of Fame.

;

27d

▶
EXERCISE 6

Combine each of the following sentence groups into one sentence that includes a series of items separated by semicolons. You will need to add, delete, relocate, or change words. Try several versions of each sentence until you find the most effective arrangement.

> EXAMPLE: Collecting baseball cards is a worthwhile hobby. It helps children learn how to bargain and trade. It also encourages them to assimilate, evaluate, and compare data about major league ball players. Perhaps most important, it encourages them to find role models in the athletes whose cards they collect.
>
> Collecting baseball cards is a worthwhile hobby because it helps children learn how to bargain and trade; encourages them to assimilate, evaluate, and compare data about major league ball players; and, perhaps most important, encourages them to find role models in the athletes whose cards they collect.

1. A good dictionary offers definitions of words, including some obsolete and nonstandard words. It provides information about synonyms, usage, and word origins. It also offers information on pronunciation and syllabication.

2. The flags of the Scandinavian countries all depict a cross on a solid background. Denmark's flag is red with a white cross. Norway's flag

is also red, but its cross is blue, outlined in white. Sweden's flag is blue with a yellow cross.

3. Over one hundred international collectors' clubs are thriving today. One of these associations is the Cola Clan, whose members buy, sell, and trade Coca-Cola memorabilia. Another is the Citrus Label Society. There is also a Cookie Cutter Collectors' Club.

4. Listening to the radio special, we heard "Shuffle Off to Buffalo" and "Moon Over Miami," both of which are about eastern cities. We heard "By the Time I Get to Phoenix" and "I Left My Heart in San Francisco," which mention western cities. Finally, we heard "The Star Spangled Banner," which seemed to be an appropriate finale.

5. There are three principal types of contact lenses. Hard contact lenses, also called conventional lenses, are easy to clean and handle and quite sturdy. Soft lenses, which are easily contaminated and must be cleaned and disinfected daily, are less durable. Gas-permeable lenses, sometimes advertised as semihard or semisoft lenses, look and feel like hard lenses but are more easily contaminated and less durable.

;
27e

27e Editing to Eliminate Misuse of Semicolons

Some writers use semicolons just because they feel that they are characteristic of a mature style. Others use them to break up the monotony of standard punctuation. But semicolons are only called for in the contexts outlined above. In the following situations a semicolon is not used.

Between items of unequal grammatical rank

A semicolon is not used between a dependent and an independent clause

FAULTY: She won the 5000-meter run; which was the first event she entered.

REVISED: She won the 5000-meter run, which was the first event she entered.

FAULTY: Because new drugs can now suppress the body's immune reaction; fewer organ transplants are rejected by the body.

REVISED: Because new drugs can now suppress the body's immune reaction, fewer organ transplants are rejected by the body.

or between a phrase and a clause.

FAULTY: We visited Chicago; the Windy City.

REVISED: We visited Chicago, the Windy City.

FAULTY: Increasing rapidly; computer crime poses a challenge for government, financial, and military agencies.

REVISED: Increasing rapidly, computer crime poses a challenge for government, financial, and military agencies.

FAULTY: He passed all his courses; including French.

REVISED: He passed all his courses, including French.

In introducing a list

Use a colon, not a semicolon, to introduce a list.

FAULTY: The American Cancer Society now recommends regular mammography for three groups of women; those who have already had breast cancer, those with a family history of the disease, and those over forty.

REVISED: The American Cancer Society now recommends regular mammography for three groups of women: those who have already had breast cancer, those with a family history of the disease, and those over forty.

FAULTY: The evening news is a battleground for the three major television networks; CBS, NBC, and ABC.

REVISED: The evening news is a battleground for the three major television networks: CBS, NBC, and ABC.

**;
27f**

With direct quotations

A semicolon is not used to introduce a direct quotation. (See 29a for information on punctuation with direct quotations.)

FAULTY: Marie Antoinette said; "Let them eat cake."

REVISED: Marie Antoinette said, "Let them eat cake."

FAULTY: Mr. Varady asked; "Who wants seconds?"

REVISED: Mr. Varady asked, "Who wants seconds?"

27f Editing to Eliminate Overuse of Semicolons

Semicolons must be used selectively. A string of clauses connected by semicolons can be extremely tedious. The following paragraph uses a semicolon in every possible situation.

Art deco was a reflection of the jazz age of the roaring 1920's and more sober 1930's; at that time it was the dominant style, particularly in the United States. This was an art glorifying the machine; it was inspired by the speed of the automobile and airplane. It found expression in soaring skyscrapers and luxury ocean liners; streamlined statuettes, overstuffed furniture, and jukebox designs; and radio cabinets, toasters, and other kitchen gadgetry. Art deco was motivated by the vibrant energy released at the end of World War I; it was motivated by a faith in mechanized modernity; and it was also inspired by a joy in such new materials as glass, aluminum, polished steel, and shiny chrome.

Compare the following paragraph.

Art deco was a reflection of the jazz age of the roaring 1920's and more sober 1930's when it was the dominant style, particularly in the United States. This was an art glorifying the machine and inspired by the speed of the automobile and airplane. It found expression in everything from soaring skyscrapers and luxury ocean liners to streamlined statuettes, overstuffed furniture, jukebox designs, radio cabinets, toasters, and other kitchen gadgetry. Art deco was motivated by the vibrant energy released at the end of World War I, a faith in mechanized modernity, and a joy in such new materials as glass, aluminum, polished steel, and shiny chrome. (William Fleming, *Arts & Ideas*, 6th ed.)

EXERCISE 7

Read this paragraph carefully. Then add semicolons where necessary and delete excess or incorrectly used ones, substituting other punctuations where necessary.

Barnstormers were aviators; who toured the country after World War I, giving people short airplane rides and exhibitions of stunt flying, the name *barnstormer* was derived from the use of barns as airplane hangers. Americans' interest in airplanes had all but disappeared after the war, planes had served their function in battle, but when the war ended, most people saw no future in aviation. The barnstormers helped popularize flying; especially in rural areas. Some of them were pilots who had flown in the war; others were just young men with a thirst for adventure. They gave people rides in airplanes, sometimes they charged a dollar a minute. For most passengers, this was their first ride in an airplane, in fact, sometimes it was their first sight of one. In the early 1920's, people grew bored with what the barnstormers had to offer; so groups of pilots began to stage spectacular—but often dangerous—stunt shows. Then, after Lindbergh's 1927 flight across the Atlantic; Americans suddenly needed no encouragement to embrace aviation. The barnstormers had outlived their usefulness; and an era ended. (Adapted from William Goldman, *Adventures in the Screen Trade*)

(margin) ; 27f

The Apostrophe

28a Forming the Possessive Case

The possessive case indicates ownership, specifically or generally. In English the possessive case of nouns and indefinite pronouns is indicated in two ways: either with a phrase that includes the word *of* (the hands *of* the clock) or with an **apostrophe** and, in most cases, an *-s* (the clock's hands). Special forms are used to indicate the possessive case of personal pronouns (see 28b).

With singular nouns and indefinite pronouns

To form the possessive case of singular nouns and indefinite pronouns, add *-'s*.

> "The Monk's Tale" is one of Chaucer's *Canterbury Tales.*
> When we would arrive at Dan's house was anyone's guess.
> Martha's Vineyard is an island off the coast of Massachusetts.
> One must always consider one's options carefully.
> Synonyms for many words may be found in *Roget's Thesaurus.*

With singular nouns ending in *-s*

To form the possessive case of singular nouns that end in *-s*, add *-'s* in most cases.

> Reading Henry James's *The Ambassadors* was not Maris's idea of fun.
> The class's time was changed to 8 A.M.

However, a few singular nouns that end with an *s* or *z* sound require only an apostrophe in the possessive case. This is because pronouncing the possessive ending as a separate syllable would create an awkward-sounding phrase.

> For goodness' sake—are we really required to read both Aristrophanes' *Lysistrata* and Thucydides' *History of the Peloponesian War?*

473

An apostrophe is not used to form the possessive case of a title that already contains an -'s ending; use a phrase instead.

NOT *Finnegan's Wake's* stream of consciousness style	BUT the stream of consciousness style of *Finnegan's Wake*
NOT *Logan's Run's* star	BUT the star of *Logan's Run*

With plural nouns ending in -s

To form the possessive case of regular plural nouns (those that end in -s or -es), add only an apostrophe.

The *Readers' Guide to Periodical Literature* is located in the reference section.

Religious cults' members are often young and naive.

Two weeks' severance pay and three months' medical benefits were available to some workers.

The Lopezes' three children are identical triplets.

Matthew is always ready to add his two cents' worth.

With irregular plural nouns

To form the possessive case of nouns that have irregular plurals, add -'s.

Long after they were gone, the geese's honking could still be heard.

The Children's Hour is a play by Lillian Hellman; *The Women's Room* is a novel by Marilyn French.

The two oxen's yokes were securely attached to the cart.

Note: Noun plurals that are not possessive do not use apostrophes (see 28b).

With compound nouns or groups of words

To form the possessive case of compound words or of word groups, add -'s to the last word.

The editor-in-chief's position is open.

Fran loved her father-in-law's chili.

He accepted the Secretary of State's resignation under protest.

This is someone else's responsibility.

With two or more items

To indicate individual ownership of two or more items, add -'s to each item. To indicate joint ownership, add -'s only to the last item.

INDIVIDUAL OWNERSHIP: Ernest Hemingway's and Gertrude Stein's writing styles have some similarities. (Hemingway and Stein have two separate writing styles)

JOINT OWNERSHIP: Gilbert and Sullivan's operettas include *The Pirates of Penzance* and *H.M.S. Pinafore.* (Gilbert and Sullivan collaborated on both operettas)

▶
EXERCISE 1

In these examples change the modifying phrases that follow the nouns to possessive forms that precede the nouns.

EXAMPLE: the pen belonging to my aunt

my aunt's pen

1. the songs recorded by Ray Charles
2. the red glare of the rockets
3. the idea Warren had
4. the housekeeper Leslie and Rick hired
5. the first choice of everyone
6. the dinner given by Harris
7. furniture designed by William Morris
8. the climate of Bermuda
9. the sport the Russels play
10. the role created by the French actress

28a

▶
EXERCISE 2

Wherever possible change each word or phrase in parentheses to its possessive form. In some cases you may have to use a phrase to indicate possession.

EXAMPLE: The (children) toys were scattered all over their (parents) bedroom.

The children's toys were scattered all over their parents' bedroom.

1. Jane (Addams) settlement house was called Hull House.
2. The (college library) holdings are extensive.
3. (*A Room of One's Own*) popularity increased with the rise of feminism.
4. The (chief petty officer) responsibilities are varied.
5. (Lerner and Lowe) musical *My Fair Lady* was based on George Bernard (Shaw) play *Pygmalion.*

6. (Genesis) last concert was not heavily advertised.
7. Vietnamese (restaurants) numbers have grown dramatically in ten (years) time.
8. The (goddess) smile disarmed her enemies.
9. (No one) dreams are ever fully realized.
10. (Harold Robbins) and (Jacqueline Susann) popular novels have sold millions of copies.

28b Omitting the Apostrophe

An apostrophe is not used with plural nouns that are not possessive or in the possessive case of personal pronouns.

With plural nouns

Noun plurals that are not possessive never include apostrophes.

FAULTY	REVISED
The Thompson's aren't at home.	The Thompsons aren't at home.
Chekhov's *The Three Sister's* was performed by the drama club.	Chekhov's *The Three Sisters* was performed by the drama club.
The down vest's were very warm.	The down vests were very warm.
All class's were canceled.	All classes were canceled.
The Philadelphia Seventy Sixer's played well.	The Philadelphia Seventy Sixers played well.

With personal pronouns

Personal pronouns never use apostrophes to form the possessive case. Rather, they have special possessive forms—*his, hers, its, ours, yours, theirs,* and *whose*—none of which include apostrophes.

FAULTY	REVISED
This ticket must be your's or her's.	This ticket must be yours or hers.
The next turn is their's.	The next turn is theirs.
The doll had lost it's right eye.	The doll had lost its right eye.
The next great moment in history is our's.	The next great moment in history is ours.

NOTE: Do not confuse these possessive forms of personal pronouns with contractions (see 28c.1).

▶
EXERCISE 3

In the sentences below, correct any errors in the use of apostrophes to form noun plurals or the possessive case of personal pronouns. If a sentence is correct, mark it with a *C*.

> EXAMPLE: Dr. Sampson's lecture's were more interesting than her's.
>
> Dr. Sampson's lectures were more interesting than hers.

1. The Schaefer's seats are right next to our's.
2. Most of the college's in the area offer computer courses open to outsider's as well as to their own students.
3. The network completely revamped its daytime programming.
4. Is the responsibility for the hot dog concession Cynthia's or your's?
5. Romantic poets are his favorite's.
6. Debbie returned the books to the library, forgetting they were her's.
7. Cultural revolution's do not occur very often, but when they do they bring sweeping change's.
8. Roll-top desk's are eagerly sought by antique dealer's.
9. A flexible schedule is one of their priority's, but it isn't one of our's.
10. Is yours the red house or the brown one?

28c Indicating Omissions in Contractions

Apostrophes are used to mark the omission of letters or numbers in contractions.

(1) Omitted letters

Apostrophes replace omitted letters in frequently used contractions that combine a pronoun and a verb (*he* + *will* = *he'll*) or the elements of a verb phrase (*do* + *not* = *don't*). Here are some common contractions.

it's (it is)	let's (let us)
he's (he is)	we've (we have)
who's (who is)	they're (they are)
isn't (is not)	we'll (we will)
wouldn't (would not)	I'm (I am)
couldn't (could not)	we're (we are)
don't (do not)	you'd (you would)
won't (will not)	

Although acceptable in speech and informal writing, contractions are not generally used in formal writing except to reproduce dialogue or to create an informal tone deliberately. Be especially careful not to confuse these contractions with the possessive forms of personal pronouns (see 21c and 28b). Here are some forms that are commonly mistaken.

Contractions	*Possessive Forms*
Who's on first?	Whose book is this?
They're playing our song.	Their team is winning.
It's raining.	Its paws were muddy.
You're a real pal.	Your résumé is very impressive.

Other contractions are acceptable in all situations because the contraction is the only form of the word.

will-o'-the-wisp   jack-o'-lantern   o'clock

28c

(2) Omitted numbers

In informal writing you can use an apostrophe to represent the century in a year.

Crash of '29   Class of '90   '57 Chevy

In college writing, however, write out *the Crash of 1929, the class of 1990, a 1957 Chevrolet.*

▶

EXERCISE 4

In the following sentences correct any errors in the use of standard contractions or personal pronouns. If a sentence is correct, mark it with a C.

EXAMPLE: Who's troops were sent to Korea?

Whose troops were sent to Korea?

1. Its never easy to choose a major; whatever you decide, your bound to have second thoughts.
2. Olive Oyl asked, "Whose that knocking at my door?"
3. Their watching too much television; in fact, they're eyes are glazed.
4. Whose coming along on the backpacking trip?
5. The horse had been badly treated; it's spirit was broken.
6. Your correct in assuming its a challenging course.
7. Sometimes even you're best friends won't tell you your boring.
8. They're training had not prepared them for the hardships they faced.

9.   It's too early to make a positive diagnosis.
10. Robert Frost wrote the poem that begins, "Who's woods these are, I
     think I know."

28d   Forming Plurals

The apostrophe plus -*s* is used to form plurals in some special
cases. In these cases adding an -'*s* avoids a confusing combination that might obscure the plural ending.

With plurals of letters
> The Italian language has no *j*'s or *k*'s.
>
> Mind your *p*'s and *q*'s.
>
> *Sesame Street* helps children learn their ABC's.

With plurals of numbers
> Dick Button could make outstanding figure *8*'s.
>
> Styles of the 1950's are back in fashion.

Some writers prefer to omit the apostrophe in this situation.

> The 1920s are sometimes called the roaring twenties.

With plurals of symbols
> The +'s and −'s indicate positive and negative numbers, respec-
> tively.
>
> The entire paper used &'s instead of *and*'s.

With plurals of abbreviations followed by periods
> Only two R.N.'s worked the 7-to-11 shift.
>
> Four Ph.D.'s and seven M.D.'s attended the high school reunion.

With plurals of words referred to as words
> The supervisor would accept no *if*'s, *and*'s, or *but*'s.
>
> His first sentence contained three *therefore*'s.

Letters, numerals, and words spoken of as themselves are
always set in italic type (see 32c); the plural ending is further
distinguished by being set in roman type. When you write or
type, indicate italics by underlining (see Chapter 32). If no confusion is possible, you may omit the apostrophe, but you should
still use italics where they are required.

> The word processor erased all the *4*s in the report.

28d

The Apostrophe

▶
EXERCISE 5

In the following sentences, form correct plurals for the letters, numbers, and words in parentheses. Underline to indicate italics where necessary.

> EXAMPLE: The word *bubbles* contains three (b).
>
> The word *bubbles* contains three *b*'s.

1. She closed her letter with a row of (x) and (o) to indicate kisses and hugs.
2. The three (R) are reading, writing, and 'rithmetic.
3. The report included far too many (maybe) and too few (definitely).
4. His (4) and (9) were almost identical, and his (5) looked exactly like (s).
5. Her two (M.A.) were in sociology and history.

29

Quotation Marks

A **direct quotation** is a passage borrowed word for word from another source. A pair of quotation marks (" ") establishes the boundaries of a direct quotation.

29a Setting Off Direct Quotations

When you reproduce exactly a word, phrase, or brief passage from someone else's speech or writing, you must enclose the borrowed material in a pair of quotation marks.

" "

29a

> Gloria Steinem observed, "We are becoming the men we once hoped to marry."
>
> General MacArthur promised, "I shall return."
>
> "I am not a crook," Richard Nixon insisted.

Do not use quotation marks with **indirect quotations**—that is, when you report someone else's written or spoken words without quoting them exactly.

> Gloria Steinem observed that many women are now becoming the men they once hoped to marry.
>
> General MacArthur promised he would return.
>
> Richard Nixon insisted he was not a crook.

Use single quotation marks to enclose a quotation within a quotation.

> Claire said, "It was Liberace who first said, 'I cried all the way to the bank.'"
>
> In an article about Lewis Carroll's *The Hunting of the Snark,* the critic Michael Holquist notes that "even W. H. Auden has said that the Snark is a 'pure example' of the way in which, 'if thought of as isolated in the midst of an ocean, a ship can stand for mankind and human society moving through time and struggling with its destiny.'"

481

Special punctuation problems occur when quoted material must be set off from phrases (like *he said*) that identify its source. The following guidelines cover the most common problems.

With an identifying tag in the middle of a passage

Use a pair of commas to set off the identifying phrase that interrupts a passage.

> "In the future," pop artist Andy Warhol once said, "everyone will be world-famous for 15 minutes."

NOTE: When a quotation is interrupted, a comma follows the identifying tag. The second half of the sentence is set off by quotation marks and, as part of a sentence not yet completed, is begun with a lower-case letter. However, if the identifying tag follows a completed sentence but the quoted passage continues, a period follows the tag. The new sentence, set off by quotation marks, begins with a capital letter.

> "Be careful," Erin warned. "Reptiles can be tricky."

With an introductory identifying tag

Use a comma after the tag that introduces quoted speech or writing.

> Yogi Berra said, "The game isn't over till it's over."
>
> The Raven repeated, "Nevermore."

When you quote just a word or phrase, however, you may also introduce it without any punctuation.

> The weatherman said he expected March to be "unpredictable."

A colon instead of a comma should precede a long or formal quotation.

> The Secretary of State announced: "All American citizens are asked to leave the area immediately. The instability of the military government and the acts of hostility toward Americans make this action necessary."

A colon should precede any quotation, even a brief one, if the introductory tag is an independent clause.

> She gave her final answer: "No."

With an identifying tag at the end

Use a comma to set off the end of a quotation from the identifying tag that follows.

"Be careful out there," the sergeant warned.

"'The boy stood on the burning deck,'" Celia recited.

If the quotation ends with a question mark or an exclamation point, however, that punctuation mark replaces the comma.

"Is Ankara the capital of Turkey?" she asked.

"Oh boy!" he cried.

The tag begins with a lower-case letter even though it follows end punctuation. If no identifying tag follows a quotation, use a period or other appropriate end punctuation after the quotation.

The principal said, "Education is serious business."

▶

EXERCISE 1

Add single and double quotation marks to these sentences where necessary to set off direct quotations. Then add appropriate punctuation to set off direct quotations from identifying tags. If a sentence is correct, mark it with a *C*.

> EXAMPLE: Wordsworth's phrase splendour in the grass was used as the title of a movie about young lovers.
>
> Wordsworth's phrase "splendour in the grass" was used as the title of a movie about young lovers.

1. Mr. Fox noted Few people can explain what Descartes' words I think, therefore I am actually mean.
2. Gertrude Stein said You are all a lost generation.
3. Freedom of speech does not guarantee anyone the right to yell fire in a crowded theater she explained.
4. Dorothy kept insisting there was no place quite like home.
5. If everyone will sit down the teacher announced the exam will begin.

29b Setting Off Titles

Titles of short works and titles of parts of long works are enclosed in quotation marks rather than set in italics (for more information on titles set in italics, see 32a). Use quotation marks for titles of the following.

For articles in magazines, newspapers, and professional journals

"To Live in Harlem" *(Reader's Digest)*

"A Doll for All Seasons" *(Philadelphia Inquirer)*

"The Case for Syntactic Imagery" *(College English)*

For essays
"Fenimore Cooper's Literary Offenses"

"Once More to the Lake"

For short stories
"Barn Burning"

"I Stand Here Ironing"

For short poems (those not divided into numbered sections)
"Daddy"

"The Emperor of Ice Cream"

For songs
"The Star-Spangled Banner"

"Stairway to Heaven"

For chapters or sections of books
"The Poles of Violence: Ambrose Bierce and Richard Harding Davis" (Chapter 8 of *The American 1890's*)

"Miss Sharp Begins to Make Friends" (Chapter 10 of *Vanity Fair*)

"Franklin D. Roosevelt: The Politician as Opportunist" (Chapter 12 of *The American Political Tradition*)

For unpublished speeches
"I Have a Dream" (Martin Luther King, Jr.)
"How to Tell a Story" (Mark Twain)

Descriptive titles of speeches, such as Kennedy's Inaugural Address, are not enclosed in quotation marks.

For episodes of radio or television series
"Lucy Goes to the Hospital" *(I Love Lucy)*

"Do Civil Rights Equal Affirmative Action?" *(Firing Line)*

Single quotation marks indicate a title in a quotation already enclosed in double quotation marks.

I think what she said was, "Play it, Sam. Play 'As Time Goes by.'"

29c   Setting Off Words Used in a Special Sense

Words used in a special sense are enclosed in quotation marks.

It was clear that adults approved of children who were "readers," but it was not at all clear why this was so. (Annie Dillard, *New York Times Magazine*)

It is often remarked that words are tricky—and that we are all prone to be deceived by "fast talkers," such as high-pressure sales-men, skillful propagandists, politicians or lawyers. (S. I. Hayakawa, "How Words Change Our Lives")

Coinages—that is, invented words—also take quotation marks.

After the twins were born, Martha's station wagon became a "babymobile."

When a word is referred to as a word, however, it is italicized (see 32c).

How do you pronounce *trough*?

Is their name spelled *Smith* or *Smythe*?

When you cite a dictionary definition, put it in quotation marks to indicate that the words are borrowed.

" "

29c

To infer means "to draw a conclusion"; *to imply* means "to suggest."

▶

EXERCISE 2

Add quotation marks to the following sentences where necessary to set off titles and words. If italics are incorrectly used, substitute quotation marks.

EXAMPLE: To Tim, social security means a date for Saturday night.

To Tim, "social security" means a date for Saturday night.

1. *First Fig* and *Second Fig* are two of the poems in Edna St. Vincent Millay's *Collected Poems.*
2. In the article Feminism Takes a New Turn, Betty Friedan reconsiders some of the issues first raised in her 1964 book *The Feminine Mystique.*
3. Edwin Arlington Robinson's poem Richard Cory was the basis for the song Richard Cory written by Paul Simon.
4. *Beside* means next to, but *besides* means except.
5. In an essay on *An American Tragedy* published in *The Yale Review*, Robert Penn Warren noted, Theodore Dreiser once said that his philosophy of love might be called Varietism.

29d   Editing to Eliminate Misuse or Overuse of Quotation Marks

Misusing or overusing quotation marks weakens your writing by distracting readers.

Quotation marks are not used to convey special emphasis or sarcasm

> FAULTY: William Randolph Hearst's "modest" home is a castle called San Simeon.

> REVISED: William Randolph Hearst's far-from-modest home is a castle called San Simeon.

or to set off nicknames or slang.

> FAULTY: The former "Lady Di" became the Princess of Wales when she married Prince Charles.

> REVISED: The former Lady Diana Spencer became the Princess of Wales when she married Prince Charles.

> FAULTY: Dawn is "into" running.

> REVISED: Dawn is very involved in running.

In formal writing situations, do not make the mistake of thinking that quotation marks will make nonstandard or slang terms acceptable. Avoid substituting nicknames for full names or slang for standard diction.

Quotation marks are not used to enclose titles of long works

> FAULTY: "War and Peace" is even longer than "Paradise Lost."

> REVISED: *War and Peace* is even longer than *Paradise Lost.*

or terms being defined.

> FAULTY: The word "tintinnabulation," meaning the ringing sound of bells, was used by Poe in his poem "The Bells."

> REVISED: The word *tintinnabulation,* meaning the ringing sound of bells, was used by Poe in his poem "The Bells."

NOTE: Titles of long works and words that are defined should be set off by italics (see 32a and 32c).

Quotation marks are not used to set off technical terms,

> FAULTY: "Biofeedback" is sometimes used to treat migraine headaches.

> REVISED: Biofeedback is sometimes used to treat migraine headaches.

or to set off the title on the title page of a student essay.

FAULTY: "Images of Light and Darkness in George Eliot's *Adam Bede*"

REVISED: Images of Light and Darkness in George Eliot's *Adam Bede*

Finally, quotation marks are not used to set off indirect quotations.

FAULTY: Freud wondered "What does a woman want."

REVISED: Freud wondered what a woman does want.

REVISED: Freud wondered, "What does a woman want?"

▶

EXERCISE 3

In the following paragraph, correct the use of single and double quotation marks to set off direct quotations (including dialogue), titles, and words used in a special sense. Supply the appropriate quotation marks where required, and delete those not required. Be careful not to use quotation marks where they are not necessary.

" "

29e

> In her essay 'The Obligation to Endure' from the book "Silent Spring," Rachel Carson writes: As Albert Schweitzer has said, 'Man can hardly even recognize the devils of his own creation.' Carson goes on to point out that a host of chemicals have been used to kill insects and other organisms which, she writes, are "described in the modern vernacular as pests." Carson believes such "advanced" chemicals, by contaminating our environment, do more harm than good. In addition to "Silent Spring," Carson is also the author of the book "The Sea Around Us." This work, divided into three sections (Mother Sea, The Restless Sea, and Man and the Sea About Him) was first published in 1951.

29e Setting Off Dialogue, Long Prose Passages, and Poetry

(1) Dialogue

When you record dialogue, begin a new paragraph for each new speaker. Be sure to enclose the words in quotation marks.

> "Sharp on time as usual," Davis said with his habitual guilty grin.
> "My watch is always a little fast," Castle said, apologizing for the criticism which he had not expressed. "An anxiety complex, I suppose."

"Smuggling out top secrets as usual?" Davis asked, making a playful pretense at seizing Castle's briefcase. (Graham Greene, *The Human Factor*)

Notice that the phrases identifying the speaker *(Davis said, Castle said, Davis asked)* appear in the same paragraph as the speaker's words.

In a long quotation of the words of one speaker, each new paragraph begins with quotation marks. However, closing quotation marks appear only at the end of the entire passage, not at the end of each paragraph.

▶

EXERCISE 4

Add appropriate quotation marks to the dialogue in this passage, beginning a new paragraph whenever a new speaker is introduced.

" "

29e

The next time, the priest steered me into the confession box himself and left the shutter back the way I could see him get in and sit down at the further side of the grille from me. Well, now, he said, what do they call you? Jackie, father, said I. And what's a-trouble to you, Jackie? Father, I said, feeling I might as well get it over while I had him in good humor, I had it all arranged to kill my grandmother.

He seemed a bit shaken by that, all right, because he said nothing for quite a while. My goodness, he said at last, that'd be a shocking thing to do. What put that into your head? Father, I said, feeling very sorry for myself, she's an awful woman. Is she? he asked. What way is she awful? She takes porter, father, I said, knowing well from the way Mother talked of it that this was a mortal sin, and hoping it would make the priest take a more favorable view of my case. Oh, my! he said, and I could see that he was impressed. And snuff, father, said I. That's a bad case, sure enough, Jackie, he said. (Frank O'Connor, "First Confession")

(2) Long prose passages

A prose passage of more than four lines is set off from the body of your paper. Omit quotation marks and indent the text ten spaces from the left-hand margin, with double-spacing above and below the quotation and double-spacing between lines within it. A long prose passage is generally introduced by a colon. For example, consider this excerpt from a student paper.

A portrait of Aunt Juley illustrates several of the devices Galsworthy uses throughout *The Forsyte Saga*, such as a journalistic detachment that is almost cruel in its scrutiny, a subtle sense of the grotesque, and an ironic stance:

> Aunt Juley stayed in her room, prostrated by the blow. Her face, discoloured by tears, was divided into compartments by the little ridges of pouting flesh which had swollen with emotion. . . . At fixed intervals she went to her drawer, and took from beneath the lavender bags a fresh pocket-handkerchief. Her warm heart could not bear the thought that Ann was lying there so cold. (329)

Similar characterizations appear throughout the book. . . .

NOTE: The first line is not indented when a quoted passage is a single paragraph or part of one. When quoting two or more paragraphs, indent three additional spaces to signal each new paragraph.

    If the long passage you are quoting already includes material quoted by the author, keep those words in quotation marks.

" "
29e

(3) Poetry

Three or fewer lines of poetry are treated like a short prose passage—enclosed in quotation marks and run into the text.

> One of John Donne's best-known poems begins with the line, "Go and catch a falling star."

Two or more lines of poetry should be separated by a slash (/) (see 30m).

> Alexander Pope writes, "True Ease in Writing comes from Art, not Chance, / As those move easiest who have learned to dance."

Four or more lines of poetry should be set off like a long prose passage (see 29e.2). For special emphasis, fewer lines may also be set off in this manner.

> Wilfred Owen, a poet who was killed in action in World War I, expressed the horrors of war with vivid imagery:
>
>> Bent double, like old beggars under sacks,
>> Knock-kneed, coughing like hags, we cursed through
>>> sludge,
>> Till on the haunting flares we turned our backs
>> And towards our distant rest began to trudge.

A colon precedes the passage, and the lines of poetry are aligned just as they are in the original poem. Punctuation, spelling, and indentation are also reproduced *exactly*. Two spaces are used above and below, and the whole passage is indented ten spaces from the left-hand margin. Lines of poetry are double-spaced just as lines of prose are.

29f Using Quotation Marks with Other Punctuation

Quotation marks frequently occur along with other punctuation marks. Sometimes the quotation marks are placed inside other punctuation, and sometimes they are placed outside.

“ ”
29f

With final commas or periods

Quotation marks belong *outside* the comma or period at the end of a quotation.

> Many, like Frost, think about "the road not taken," but not many really consider where it might have led them.

> Janis Joplin sang, "Freedom's just another word for nothing left to lose."

With final semicolons or colons

Quotation marks belong *inside* a semicolon or colon at the end of a quotation.

> Students who do not pass the functional-literacy test receive "certificates of completion"; those who pass are awarded diplomas.

> Taxpayers were pleased with the first of the candidate's promised "sweeping new reforms": a balanced budget.

With other end punctuation and dashes

Quotation marks may be placed inside or outside a question mark, exclamation point, or dash at the end of a quotation, depending on the sentence's meaning.

If the question mark, exclamation point, or dash is part of the quotation, place the quotation marks *outside* the punctuation.

> "Who's there?" she demanded.

> "Stop!" he cried.

> "Should we leave now, or—" Vicki paused, waiting for a sign from Joe.

If the question mark, exclamation point, or dash is not part of the quotation, place the quotation marks *inside* the punctuation.

> Did you finish reading "The Black Cat"?

> Whatever you do, don't yell "Uncle"!

> The first essay—George Orwell's "Politics and the English language"—made quite an impression on the class.

If both the quotation and the tag are questions or exclamations, place the quotation marks *inside* the punctuation.

> Who said "Is Paris Burning?"

▶
EXERCISE 5

Correct the use of quotation marks in the following sentences, making sure that the use and placement of any accompanying punctuation marks are consistent with accepted conventions. If a sentence is correct, mark it with a C.

" "

29f

> EXAMPLE: The "Watergate" incident brought many new terms into the English language.
>
> The Watergate incident brought many new terms into the English language.

1. Kilroy was here and Women and children first are two expressions *Bartlett's Familiar Quotations* attributes to "Anon."
2. Neil Armstrong said he was making a small step for man but a giant leap for mankind.
3. "The answer, my friend", Bob Dylan sang, "is blowin' in the wind".
4. The novel was a real "thriller," complete with spies and counter-spies, mysterious women, and exotic international chases.
5. The sign said, Road liable to subsidence; it meant that we should look out for potholes.
6. One of William Blake's best-known lines—To see a world in a grain of sand—opens his poem Auguries of Innocence.
7. In James Thurber's short story The Catbird Seat, Mrs. Barrows annoys Mr. Martin by asking him silly questions like Are you tearing up the pea patch? Are you scraping around the bottom of the pickle barrel? and Are you lifting the oxcart out of the ditch?
8. I'll make him an offer he can't refuse, promised "the godfather" in Mario Puzo's novel.
9. What did Timothy Leary mean by "Turn on, tune in, drop out?"
10. George, the protagonist of Bernard Malamud's short story, A Summer's Reading, is something of an "underachiever."

Other Punctuation Marks

The Colon

The colon is a strong punctuation mark that points ahead to the remainder of the sentence, linking the words that follow it to the words that precede it.

30a Using a Colon to Introduce Material

(1) Lists or series

Colons are used to set off lists or series, including those introduced by phrases like *the following* or *as follows.*

> He looked like whatever his beholder imagined him to be: a bank clerk, a high school teacher, a public employee, a librarian, a fussy custodian, an office manager. (Norman Katkov, *Blood and Orchids*)

> Like croup and whooping cough, it was treated with remedies Ida Rebecca compounded from ancient folk-medicine recipes: reeking mustard plasters, herbal broths, dosings of onion syrup mixed with sugar. (Russell Baker, *Growing Up*)

> Each camper should bring the following: a sleeping bag, a mess kit, a flashlight, and plenty of insect repellent.

NOTE: A colon introduces a list or series *only* when an independent clause precedes the colon.

> FAULTY: Each camper should bring: a sleeping bag, a mess kit, a flashlight, and plenty of insect repellent. (*Each camper should bring* is not a grammatically complete clause; colon is incorrectly used between verb and object)

> FAULTY: Each camper should be equipped with: a sleeping bag, a mess kit, a flashlight, and plenty of insect repellent. (*Each camper should be equipped with* is not a grammatically complete clause; colon is incorrectly used between preposition and object)

(2) Explanatory material

Colons often precede the introduction of material that explains, details, exemplifies, clarifies, or summarizes. They frequently introduce appositives, constructions that identify or describe nouns, pronouns, or noun phrases. In such cases, the colon substitutes for a phrase like *for example, namely,* or *that is.*

> For dancers, the call to the dance begins with the body: an accident of birth which, nurtured and sculpted through years of rigorous training, culminates in the coveted invitation to join a professional ballet company. (Diane Solway, *New York Times*)

> Her hair was the longest and strangest Mrs. Miller had ever seen: absolutely silver-white, like an albino's. (Truman Capote, "Miriam")

Sometimes a colon separates two independent clauses: one general clause and a subsequent, more specific one that illustrates or clarifies the first.

> A *U.S. News and World Report* survey has revealed a surprising fact: Americans spend more time at shopping malls than anywhere else except at home and at work.

:

30a

NOTE: When a complete sentence follows the colon, that sentence may or may not begin with a capital letter. However, if the sentence introduced by a colon is a quotation, its first word is always capitalized, unless it was not capitalized in the source.

(3) Quotations

Colons are used to set off quotations that are introduced by a complete independent clause.

> The French Declaration of the Rights of Man includes these words: "Liberty consists in being able to do anything that does not harm another person."

> With great dignity, Bartleby repeated the words once again: "I prefer not to."

A long quotation is introduced by a colon whether or not the introductory tag is a complete clause (see 29e.2).

(4) Business letters

Use a colon after the salutation to introduce the body of a business letter (see 42a.3).

Dear Dr. Evans:

Thank you for your letter of April 12, in which you commented favorably on our plan to reclassify certain controlled substances. . . .

30b Using a Colon Where Convention Requires It

Use colons in the following contexts where convention dictates their use.

To separate titles from subtitles

> *Family Installments: Memories of Growing Up Hispanic*
>
> *Tennyson: The Unquiet Heart*

To separate chapter from verse in Biblical citations

> Judges 4:14
>
> I Kings 11:8

To separate minutes from hours in numerical expressions of time

> 6:15 A.M.
>
> 3:03 P.M.

To separate place of publication from name of publisher in a list of works cited (see 38b.2).

> New York: Holt, Rinehart and Winston

30c Editing to Eliminate Misuse or Overuse of Colons

(1) After *such as, for example,* and the like

Colons are not used after expressions like *such as, namely, for example,* or *that is.* These words serve the same purpose as the colon. Remember that a colon introduces a list or series only after an independent clause.

> FAULTY: The Eye Institute treats patients with a wide variety of conditions, such as: myopia, glaucoma, cataracts, and oculomotor dysfunction.
>
> REVISED: The Eye Institute treats patients with a wide variety of conditions, such as myopia, glaucoma, cataracts, and oculomotor dysfunction.

REVISED: The Eye Institute treats patients with a wide variety of conditions: myopia, glaucoma, cataracts, and oculomotor dysfunction.

(2)   In verb and prepositional constructions

Colons should not be placed between verbs and their objects or complements or between prepositions and their object.

FAULTY: James A. Michener wrote: *Hawaii, Centennial, Space,* and *Poland.*

REVISED: James A. Michener wrote *Hawaii, Centennial, Space,* and *Poland.*

FAULTY: Hitler's armies marched through: the Netherlands, Belgium, and France.

REVISED: Hitler's armies marched through the Netherlands, Belgium, and France.

EXERCISE 1

30

Add colons where required in the following sentences. If necessary, delete superfluous colons and replace them with other marks of punctuation.

EXAMPLE: There was one thing he really hated getting up at 700 every morning.

There was one thing he really hated: getting up at 7:00 every morning.

1. Books about the late John F. Kennedy include the following *A Hero For Our Time; Johnny, We Hardly Knew Ye;* and *One Brief Shining Moment.*
2. Only one task remained to tell his boss he was quitting.
3. The story closed with a familiar phrase "And they all lived happily ever after."
4. The sergeant requested: reinforcements, medical supplies, and more ammunition.
5. She kept only four souvenirs a photograph, a matchbook, a theater program, and a daisy pressed between the pages of *William Shakespeare The Complete Works.*

The Dash

Commas are the mark of punctuation most often used to set off nonessential elements (see 26d), but dashes and parentheses also serve this function. While parentheses deemphasize the enclosed words, **dashes** tend to call attention to the material they set off.

30d Setting Off Parenthetical Material

Explanations, qualifications, or appositives are among the material that may be set off by dashes for emphasis or clarity. When you are typing, indicate a dash with two unspaced hyphens; when writing, form a dash with an unbroken line about as long as two hyphens.

Around nonessential material

Use a pair of dashes to set off nonessential material within a sentence.

> Feminists have complained for a long time that playing with dolls is one way of convincing impressionable little girls that they may only be mothers or housewives—or, as in the case of the Barbie doll, "pinup girls"—when they grow up. (Sheila Tobias, *Overcoming Math Anxiety*)

> Although we are by all odds the most social of all social animals— more interdependent, more attached to each other, more inseparable in our behavior than bees—we do not often feel our conjoined intelligence. (Lewis Thomas, *Lives of a Cell*)

Before afterthoughts

Use a single dash to set off material at the end of a sentence.

> They could not afford to jump to conclusions—any conclusions. (Michael Crichton, *The Andromeda Strain*)

> Most of the best-sellers are cookbooks and diet books—how not to eat it after you've cooked it. (Andy Rooney, *The New Yorker*)

> All the while I was writing—but for nobody in particular. (Jeremy Bernstein, *New York Times Book Review*)

30e Introducing a Summary

A dash is used to introduce a statement that summarizes a list or series before it.

> Walking to school by myself, losing my first tooth, getting my ears pierced, and starting to wear makeup—these were some of the milestones of my life.

"Study hard," "Respect your elders," "Don't talk with your mouth full"—Sharon had heard her parents say these things hundreds of times.

30f Indicating an Interruption

A dash is sometimes used in dialogue to mark a sudden interruption—for example, a correction, a hesitation, a sudden shift in tone, or an unfinished thought.

> Groucho told the steward, "I'll have three hard-boiled eggs—make that four hard-boiled eggs."

> "I think—no, I know—this is the worst day of my life," Julie sighed.

> "Don't be ridic—I mean, maybe your facts are a bit distorted," he amended.

> "The winner is—" The announcer paused dramatically as he opened the envelope.

30g

30g Editing to Eliminate Misuse and Overuse of Dashes

Dashes give a loose, casual tone to a piece of writing, but too many of them make a passage seem disorganized and out of control. Do not overuse dashes in academic writing, and do not use them carelessly in place of periods or commas or in any context that calls for other marks of punctuation (see 26d and 30h). Compare these two paragraphs.

> FAULTY: Registration was a nightmare—most of the courses I
> (overuse   wanted to take—geology and conversational Spanish,
> of   for instance—met at inconvenient times—or were
> dashes)   closed by the time I tried to sign up for them—it was
>   really depressing—even for registration.

> REVISED: Registration was a nightmare. Most of the courses I
> (moderate   wanted to take—geology and conversational Spanish,
> use of   for instance—met at inconvenient times or were
> dashes)   closed by the time I tried to sign up for them. It was
>   really depressing, even for registration.

▶

EXERCISE 2

Add dashes where needed in the following sentences. If a sentence is correct, mark it with a C.

EXAMPLE: World War I called "the war to end all wars" was, unfortunately, no such thing.

World War I—called "the war to end all wars"—was, unfortunately, no such thing.

1. Tulips, daffodils, hyacinths, lilies all these flowers grow from bulbs.
2. St. Kitts and Nevis two tiny island nations are now independent after 360 years of British rule.
3. "But it's not" She paused and reconsidered her next words.
4. He considered several different majors history, English, political science, and business before deciding on journalism.
5. The two words added to the Pledge of Allegiance in the 1950's "under God" remain part of the Pledge today.

Parentheses

Like commas and dashes, parentheses may be used to set off interruptions within a sentence.

30h Setting Off Nonessential Material

Parentheses may be used to set off nonessential material that expands, clarifies, defines, illustrates, or supplements an idea. Parentheses may enclose a single word

> A compound may be used in any grammatical function: as noun *(wishbone)*, adjective *(foolproof)*, adverb *(overhead)*, verb *(gainsay)*, or preposition *(without)*. (Thomas Pyles, *The Origin and Development of the English Language*)

or a phrase.

> It took Gilbert Fairchild two years at Harvard College (two academic years, from September, 1955, to June, 1957) to learn everything he needed to know. (Judith Martin, *Gilbert: A Comedy of Manners*)

Parentheses may also enclose a complete sentence, as in the example below. When a sentence set off by parentheses falls within another sentence, it should not begin with a capital letter or end with a period.

> Born in 1893, four years before Queen Victoria's Diamond Jubilee, at Cathedral Choir School, Oxford, where her father was headmaster, Sayers became a first-rate medievalist (she translated

Dante) and a theologian (her miracle play, *The Man Born To Be King*, outsold her mystery novels in her lifetime); she died in 1957. (Barbara Grizzuti Harrison, *Off Center*)

But if the parenthetical sentence does not interrupt another sentence, it must begin with a capital letter and end with a period, question mark, or exclamation point that falls within the closing parenthesis.

A few days later he called and asked me to come in and bring anything else I had written. (The only thing I had was a notebook full of isolated sentences like "She walked across the room wearing her wedding ring like a shield.") (Jeremy Bernstein, *New York Times Book Review*)

When a parenthetical element falls within a sentence, punctuation never precedes the opening parenthesis. Punctuation may follow the closing parenthesis, however.

( )
30i

30i In Other Conventional Situations

Parentheses are used to set off letters and numbers that identify points on a list and around dates, cross-references, and the like.

All reports must include the following components: (1) an opening summary; (2) a background statement; and (3) a list of conclusions and recommendations.

Russia was finally victorious in the Great Northern War with Sweden (1700–1721).

For detailed information on cell division, see Chapter 6 (pp. 145–72).

The teachers' contract specifies that class size be limited to thirty-three (33) children.

NOTE: The last example illustrates a convention often used in legal and technical writing.

▶
EXERCISE 3

Add parentheses where necessary in the following sentences. If a sentence is correct, mark it with a C.

EXAMPLE: The greatest battle of the War of 1812 the Battle New Orleans was fought after the war was declared over.

The greatest battle of the War of 1812 (the Battle of New Orleans) was fought after the war was declared over.

1. George Orwell's *1984* 1949 focuses on the dangers of a totalitarian society.
2. The final score 45–0 was a devasting blow for the Eagles.
3. Belize formerly British Honduras is a country in Central America.
4. The first phonics book *Phonics is Fun* has a light blue cover.
5. Some high school students have so many extracurricular activities band, sports, drama club, and school newspaper, for instance that they have little time to study.

Brackets

Brackets are used in two special situations.

30j Setting Off Comments Within Quotations

Brackets are used within quotations to tell the reader that the words enclosed are yours and not those of your source. Bracketed material might be a correction, an opinion, or a clarification.

> "Dues are being raised $1.00 per week [to $5.00]," the treasurer announced.

> "The use of caricature by Dickens is reminiscent of the satiric sketches done by [Joseph] Addison and [Richard] Steele [in *The Spectator*]."

> "Even as a student at Princeton he [F. Scott Fitzgerald] felt like an outsider."

> "The miles of excellent trails are perfect for [cross-country] skiing."

If a quotation contains an error, you may use brackets to tell the reader that the error is not yours. Follow the error with the italicized Latin word *sic* ("thus") in brackets.

> "The octopuss [*sic*] is a cephalopod mollusk with eight arms."

30k In Place of Parentheses Within Parentheses

When one set of parentheses must fall within another, substitute brackets for the inner set.

> In her narrative history of American education between 1945 and 1960 (*The Troubled Crusade* [New York: Basic Books, 1963]), Diane

Ravitch addresses issues like progressive education, race, educational reforms, and campus unrest.

The Slash

The **slash** is used as a punctuation mark in three instances: to separate options, to separate lines of poetry, and to separate elements of fractions.

30l   Separating One Option from Another

The either/or fallacy assumes that a given question has only two possible answers.

Will pass/fail courses be accepted for transfer credit?

The producer/director attracted more attention at the film festival than the actors.

In this usage, close up the space before and after the slash.

Unless you are really presenting three alternatives (Bring a pencil or pen or both to the exam), the construction *and/or* (Bring a pencil and/or a pen to the exam) should be avoided. Instead use *and* or *or*.

Bring a pencil and pen to the exam.

Bring a pencil or pen to the exam.

30m   Separating Lines of Poetry Run into the Text

The poet James Schevill writes, "I study my defects / And learn how to perfect them."

When you use the slash to separate lines of poetry, add space both before and after the slash.

30n   Separating the Numerator from the Denominator in Fractions

7/8

1 4/5

NOTE: If your typewriter or word processor has a special key for a particular fraction ($\frac{1}{2}$, $\frac{1}{4}$), use that instead of the slash.

/

30n

The Ellipsis Mark

The **ellipsis mark** (three spaced periods) indicates the omission of words from a quotation. When deleting material before inserting ellipses, always be extremely careful not to change the meaning of the original passage.

30o   Indicating an Omission in a Quotation

The ellipsis mark is used to indicate words omitted from a quotation.

> ORIGINAL: When I was a young man, being anxious to distinguish myself, I was perpetually starting new propositions. But I soon gave this over; for I found that generally what was new was false. (Samuel Johnson)

> WITH OMISSION: When I was a young man, being anxious to distinguish myself, I was perpetually starting new propositions. But I soon . . . found that generally what was new was false. (three spaced periods indicate omission)

If a punctuation mark occurs in the original text before the deleted words, include it in the quoted sentence ("If we give up now, . . . we will answer to history.").

When deleting *words at the beginning of a sentence* within a quoted passage, retain the period of the previous sentence before the ellipsis mark, leaving a space between the period and the ellipses that follow.

> ORIGINAL: And Dickens tells of long mornings when he forced himself to stay at the desk making false starts, lest by giving up he should give up forever. For all his books already in print, he might just as well have been the common schoolboy who is told to write of his visit to Aunt Julia and who honestly finds nothing to say except that he arrived on Friday and left on Sunday. (Jacques Barzun, *Writing, Editing, and Publishing*)

> WITH OMISSION: And Dickens tells of long mornings when he forced himself to stay at the desk making false starts, lest by giving up he should give up forever. . . . he might just as well have been the common schoolboy who is told to write of his visit to

> Aunt Julia and who honestly finds nothing to say
> except that he arrived on Friday and left on Sun-
> day. (period retained; three equally spaced peri-
> ods indicate omission)

In deleting *words at the end of a sentence* within a quoted passage, retain the sentence period or other end punctuation, leaving a space between it and the ellipsis mark.

ORIGINAL: We hold these truths to be self-evident, that all men are created equal, that they are endowed by their Creator with certain unalienable rights, that among these are life, liberty and the pursuit of happiness. (The Declaration of Independence)

WITH OMISSION: We hold these truths to be self-evident, that all men are created equal, that they are endowed by their Creator with certain unalienable rights. . . . (period retained; three equally spaced periods indicate omission)

In omitting *one or more complete sentences from a quoted passage*, follow any end punctuation with a space and the ellipsis mark.

ORIGINAL: Everywhere one meets the idea that reading is an activity desirable in itself. It is understandable that publishers and librarians—and even writers— should promote this assumption, but it is strange that the idea should have general currency. People surround the idea of reading with piety, and do not take into account the purpose of reading or the value of what is being read. (Donald Hall)

WITH OMISSION: Everywhere one meets the idea that reading is an activity desirable in itself. . . . People surround the idea of reading with piety, and do not take into account the purpose of reading or the value of what is being read. (period retained; three equally spaced periods indicate omission)

Note that complete sentences must precede and follow the period plus ellipsis mark.

. . .
30p

30p Indicating an Omission Within Verse

When you omit one or more lines of poetry (or a paragraph or more of prose), use a complete line of spaced periods.

ORIGINAL: Stitch! Stitch! Stitch!
> In poverty, hunger, and dirt,
> And still with a voice of dolorous pitch,
> Would that its tone could reach the Rich,
> She sang this "Song of the Shirt!" (Thomas
> Hood)

WITH OMISSION: Stitch! Stitch! Stitch!
> In poverty, hunger, and dirt,
>
> . . . .
> She sang this "Song of the Shirt!"

30q   Indicating Unfinished Statements

Like a dash (see 30f), an ellipsis mark can also be used to indicate an interrupted statement.

> "If only . . ." He sighed and turned away.

This use is generally not appropriate in academic writing.

▶
EXERCISE 4

Read this paragraph and follow the instructions below, taking care in each case not to delete essential information.

> The most important thing about research is to know when to stop. How does one recognize the moment? When I was eighteen or thereabouts, my mother told me that when out with a young man I should always leave a half-hour before I wanted to. Although I was not sure how this might be accomplished, I recognized the advice as sound, and exactly the same rule applies to research. One must stop *before* one has finished; otherwise, one will never stop and never finish. (Barbara Tuchman, *Practicing History*)

1. Delete a phrase from the middle of one sentence and mark the omission with ellipses.
2. Delete words at the beginning of any sentence and mark the omission with ellipses.
3. Delete words at the end of any sentence and mark the omission with ellipses.
4. Delete one complete sentence from the middle of the passage and mark the omission with ellipses.

▶
EXERCISE 5

Add appropriate punctuation—colons, dashes, parentheses, brackets, or slashes—to the following sentences. Be prepared to explain why you chose the punctuation marks you did. If a sentence is correct, mark it with a *C*.

> EXAMPLE: There was one thing she was sure of if she did well at the interview, the job would be hers.
>
> There was one thing she was sure of: if she did well at the interview, the job would be hers.

1. Mark Twain Samuel L. Clemens made the following statement "I can live for two months on a good compliment."
2. Liza Minnelli, the actress singer who starred in several films, is the daughter of Judy Garland.
3. Saudi Arabia, Oman, Yemen, Qatar, and the United Arab Emirates all these are located on the Arabian peninsula.
4. John Adams 1735–1826 was the second president of the United States; John Quincy Adams 1767–1848 was the sixth.
5. The sign said "No tresspassing *sic*."
6. *Checkmate* a term derived from the Persian phrase meaning "the King is dead" announces victory in chess.
7. The following people were present at the meeting the president of the board of trustees, three trustees, and twenty reporters.
8. Before the introduction of the potato in Europe, the parsnip was a major source of carbohydrates in fact, it was a dietary staple.
9. In this well-researched book (*Crime Movies* New York Norton, 1980), Carlos Clarens studies the gangster genre in film.
10. I remember reading through I can't remember where that Upton Sinclair sold plots to Jack London.

30

Student Writer at Work: Punctuation

Review Chapters 25–30; then read this student essay. Commas, semicolons, quotation marks, apostrophes, parentheses, and dashes have been intentionally deleted; only the end punctuation has been retained. When you have read the essay carefully, add all appropriate punctuation marks.

The dry pine needles crunched under our thick boots like eggshells.

Wont the noise scare them away Dad? He smiled knowingly and said No deer rely mostly on smell and sight. I thought That must be why were wearing fluorescent orange jumpsuits but I didn't feel like arguing the point.

It was a perfect day for my first hunting experience. The

biting winds were caught by the thick bushy arms of the tall
pines and I could feel a numbing redness in my face. Now I realized why Dad always grew that ugly gray beard which made
him look ten years older. A few sunbeams managed to carve
their way through the layers of branches and leaves creating
pools of white light on the dark earth.

How far have we come? I asked. Oh only a couple of
miles. We should be meeting Joe up ahead.

Joe was one of Dads hunting buddies. He always managed
to go off on his own for a few hours and come back with at least
a four-pointer. Dad was envious of Joe and liked to tell people
what he called the real story.

You know Joe paid a fortune for that buck at the checking
station hed tell his friends. Dad was sure that this would be his
lucky year.

30

We trudged up a densely wooded hill for what seemed like
hours. The sharp needled branches whipped my bare face as I
followed close behind my father occasionally I wiped my cheeks
to discover a new cut in my frozen flesh.

All this for a lousy deer I thought.

The still pine air was suddenly shattered by four rapid
gunshots echoing across the vast green valley below us.

Joes got another one. Come on! Dad yelled. It seemed as
if I were following a young kid as I watched my father take
leaping strides down the path we had just ascended. I had
never seen him so enthusiastic before.

I plodded breathlessly along trying to keep up with my father.

Suddenly out of the corner of my eye I caught sight of an
object that didn't fit in with the monotony of trunks and
branches and leaves and needles.

I froze and observed the largest most majestic buck I had
ever seen. It too stood motionless apparently grazing on some
leaves or berries. Its coloring was beautiful with alternating
patches of tan brown and snow white fur. The massive antlers
towered proudly above its head as it looked up and took notice

of me. What struck me most were the tearful brown eyes almost feminine in their gaze.

Once again the silence was smashed this time by my fathers thundering call and I watched as the huge deer scampered gracefully off through the trees. I turned and scurried down the path after my father. I decided not to mention a word of my encounter to him. I hoped the deer was far away by now.

Finally, I reached the clearing from where the shots had rung out. There stood Dad and Joe smiling over a fallen six-point buck. The purple-red blood dripped from the wounds to form a puddle in the dirt. Its sad brown eyes gleamed in the sun but no longer smiled and blinked.

Where have you been? asked Dad. Before I could answer he continued Do you believe this guy? Every year he bags the biggest deer in the whole state!

30

While they laughed and talked I sat on a tree stump to rest my aching legs. Maybe now we can go home I thought. But before long I heard Dad say Come on Bob I know theres one out there for us.

We headed right back up that same path and sure enough that same big beautiful buck was grazing in that same spot on that same berry bush. The only difference was this time Dad saw him.

This is our lucky day he whispered.

I froze as Dad lifted the barrel of his rifle and took careful aim at the silently grazing deer. I closed my eyes as he squeezed the trigger but instead of the deadly gun blast I heard only a harmless click. His rifle had jammed.

Use your rifle quick he whispered.

As I took aim through my scope the deer looked up at me. Its soulful brown eyes were magnified in my sight like two glassy bullseyes. My finger froze on the trigger.

Shoot him! Shoot him!

But instead I aimed for the clouds and fired. The deer vanished along with my fathers dreams. Dad never understood why it was the proudest moment of my life.

31

Capitalization

Familiarizing yourself with the conventions of capitalization is important. Conventions change, however, and if you are not certain whether a word should be capitalized, consult a recent dictionary.

31a Capitalizing the First Word of a Sentence or of a Line of Poetry

The first word of a sentence, including a sentence of directly quoted speech or writing, should start with a capital letter.

> The square of the hypotenuse is equal to the sum of the squares of the other two sides.
>
> Shakespeare wrote, "Who steals my purse steals trash."
>
> He asked, "Is it true pigs sleep on their right sides?"

NOTE: Do not capitalize a sentence set off within another sentence by dashes or parentheses.

> FAULTY: Finding the store closed—It was a holiday—they went home.
>
> REVISED: Finding the store closed—it was a holiday—they went home.
>
> FAULTY: The candidates are Frank Lester and Jane Lester (They are not related).
>
> REVISED: The candidates are Frank Lester and Jane Lester (they are not related).

When a complete sentence is introduced by a colon, capitalization is optional (see 30a.2).

The first word of a line of poetry is also capitalized.

> Tyger! Tyger! burning bright
> In the forests of the night,
> What immortal hand or eye
> Could frame thy fearful symmetry? (William Blake, "The Tyger")

If the poet uses a lower-case letter to begin a line, however, that style should be followed in any quotation.

> Old age is
> a flight of small
> cheeping birds
> skimming
> bare trees
> above a snowglaze. (William Carlos Williams,
>   "To Waken an Old Lady")

31b Capitalizing Proper Nouns, Titles Accompanying Them, and Adjectives Formed from Them

Proper nouns—the names of specific persons, places, or things (Diana Ross, Madras, the Enoch Pratt Free Library)—are always capitalized.

cap
31b

Specific people's names

Clark Gable	Elvis Presley
Jackie Robinson	William the Conqueror
John Beresford Tipton	Anne Frank
Joan of Arc	Ernest T. Bilko

When a title precedes a person's name, or is used instead of the name, it too is capitalized.

Dad	Princess Grace
Aunt Edna	President Taft
Count Dracula	Justice Marshall
King John	Pope John XXIII

Titles that *follow* names, or those that refer to the general position, not the particular person who holds it, are usually not capitalized. A title denoting a family relationship is never capitalized when it follows an article or a possessive pronoun.

Capitalize	*Do Not Capitalize*
Grandma	my grandmother
Private Hargrove	Mr. Hargrove, a private in the army
Queen Mother Elizabeth	a popular queen mother
Senator John Glenn; the Senator (referring to a particular senator)	John Glenn, the senator from Ohio

Capitalize	*Do Not Capitalize*
Uncle Harry	my uncle
General Patton; the General (referring to a particular general)	a four-star general

Titles or abbreviations of academic degrees are always capitalized, even when they follow a name.

Perry Mason, Attorney at Law
Benjamin Spock, M.D.

Some titles that indicate high-ranking positions may be capitalized even when they are used alone or when they follow a name.

the Secretary of Defense
the Speaker of the House
the President of the United States

cap
31b

Specific things

Capitalize names of particular structures, special events, monuments, vehicles, and so on.

Hoover Dam	the Taj Mahal
the *Titanic*	Harry's Bar
the Olympic Games	Mount Rushmore
the Brooklyn Bridge	*Challenger II*
the *Hindenburg*	the Eiffel Tower
the World Series	Independence Hall

NOTE: When a common noun such as *bridge, river,* or *lake* is part of a proper noun, it too is capitalized. Do not, however, capitalize such words when they complete the names of more than one thing (as in Kings and Queens counties).

Places, regions, and directions

Capitalize names of particular places or geographical regions.

Chicago	the Straits of Magellan
Saturn	the Western Hemisphere
Budapest	Venice
the Isthmus of Panama	the Gulf of Mexico
Walden Pond	the Fiji Islands
Lake Superior	Main Street

The points of the compass are also capitalized when they denote particular geographical regions,

The Middle West seemed like a wasteland to F. Scott Fitzgerald's Nick Carroway, so he decided to come East. (capital letters necessary because *Middle West* and *East* refer to specific regions)

but designations of directions are not capitalized.

Turn west at the corner of Broad Street and continue north until you reach Market. (no capitals needed because *west* and *north* refer to directions, not specific regions)

Days of the week, months of the year, and holidays

Saturday	Ash Wednesday
January	Rosh Hashanah
Veterans Day	Labor Day

Historical periods, events, and documents; names of legal cases and awards

World War I	the Treaty of Versailles
the Battle of Gettysburg	the Monroe Doctrine
the Industrial Revolution	the Voting Rights Act
the Reformation	*Brown* v. *Board of Education*
the Enlightenment	the Pulitzer Prize

**cap
31b**

Philosophic, literary, and artistic movements

Naturalism	Dadaism
Romanticism	Fauvism
Neoclassicism	Expressionism

NOTE: Dictionaries vary in their advice on capitalizing these nouns, but current usage tends toward capitalization.

Races, ethnic groups, nationalities, and languages

Oriental	French
Negro, Afro-American	Danish
Chicano, Chicana	Dutch
Caucasian	Turkish

NOTE: When the words *black* and *white* refer to races, they have traditionally not been capitalized. Current usage is divided on whether or not to capitalize *Black*.

Religions and their followers; sacred books and figures

Muslim	the Koran	the Virgin Mary
Jewish	God	the Messiah
Christianity	the Lord	Jehovah
Buddhism	Buddha	the Scriptures
the Bible	Allah	
the Talmud	Krishna	

NOTE: It is not necessary to capitalize pronouns referring to God unless the pronoun might also refer to another antecedent in the sentence.

> CONFUSING: Alex's grandfather taught him to trust in God and to love all his creatures.

> REVISED: Alex's grandfather taught him to trust in God and to love all His creatures.

Political, social, athletic, civic, and other groups and their members

New York Yankees
Democratic Party
Masons
International Brotherhood of Electrical Workers
National Organization for Women
National Council of Teachers of English
American Medical Association
Joffrey Ballet
Boy Scouts of America
The Who

**cap
31b**

Businesses; government agencies; and medical, educational, and other institutions

Congress
Environmental Protection Agency
Lincoln High School
Brookings Institute
University of Maryland
Children's Hospital of Philadelphia
Atari
International Harvester
Camden County Community College
Peace Corps

NOTE: When the name of a group or institution is abbreviated, the abbreviation uses capital letters in place of the capitalized words.

IBEW	EPA	USA
NOW	RCA	A & P
NCTE	IBM	

Trade names and words formed from them

Pontiac	Coke
Sanka	Pampers
Kleenex	Xerox

NOTE: Trade names that have been used so often and for so long that they have become synonymous with the product are no longer capitalized. (Consult the dictionary on whether or not to capitalize a familiar trade name.)

frisbee   victrola
jello   aspirin

Specific academic courses

Sociology 201
English 101
Zoology 305

But do not capitalize a subject area unless it is the name of a language.

Although his major was engineering, he registered for courses in sociology, English, and zoology.

Adjectives formed from proper nouns are usually capitalized.

Keynesian economics	Elizabethan era
Freudian slip	Shakespearean sonnet
Platonic ideal	Marxist ideology
Aristotelian logic	Shavian wit

cap
31c

However, when words derived from proper nouns have lost their specialized meanings, do not capitalize them.

The <u>china</u> pattern was very elaborate.

We need a 40-<u>watt</u> bulb.

They served <u>french</u>-fried onion rings.

31c Capitalizing Important Words in Titles

In general, all words in titles of books, articles, essays, films, and the like, including your own papers, are capitalized, with the exception of articles (*a*, *an*, and *the*), prepositions, conjunctions and the *to* in infinitives. If an article, preposition, or conjunction is the *first* or *last* word in the title, however, it too is capitalized.

"Dover Beach"	*On the Waterfront*
The Declaration of Independence	*The Skin of Our Teeth*
Across the River and into the Trees	*Of Human Bondage*
Two Years before the Mast	"Politics and the English Language"

31d Capitalizing the Pronoun *I* and the Interjection *O*

Even if the pronoun *I* is part of a contraction *(I'm, I'll, I've)*, it is always capitalized.

> Sam and I finally went to the Grand Canyon, and I'm glad we did.

The interjection *O* is also always capitalized.

> Give us peace in our time, O Lord.

The interjection *oh*, however, is capitalized only when it begins a sentence.

NOTE: Many other single letters are also capitalized in certain usages. Check your dictionary if you are unsure whether to use a capital letter.

U-boat	Vitamin B
D-Day	an A in history
Model T	C major

cap
31f

31e Capitalizing Salutations and Closings of Letters

In salutations of business or personal letters, always capitalize the first word.

> Dear Mr. Reynolds:
> Dear Fred,

The first word of the complimentary close is also always capitalized.

> Sincerely,   Very truly yours,

(See also 42a.3.)

31f Editing to Eliminate Misuse and Overuse of Capitals

Capital letters should not be used for emphasis or as an attention-getting device. If you are not certain whether a word should be capitalized, consult your dictionary.

Seasons

Do not capitalize the names of the seasons—summer, fall, winter, spring—unless they are strongly personified, as in Old Man Winter.

Centuries and loosely defined historical periods

Do not capitalize the names of centuries or general historical periods.

> seventeenth-century poetry
> the automobile age

Diseases and other medical terms

Do not capitalize names of diseases or medical tests or conditions unless a proper noun is part of the name.

polio	Apgar test
Reye's syndrome	mumps
Huntington's chorea	sickle-cell anemia
Tay-Sachs disease	Cooley's anemia

**cap
31f**

▶

EXERCISE

Capitalize words where necessary in these sentences.

> EXAMPLE: John F. Kennedy won the pulitzer prize for his book
> *profiles in courage.*
>
> John F. Kennedy won the Pulitzer Prize for his book
> *Profiles in Courage.*

1. The brontë sisters wrote *jane eyre* and *wuthering heights*, two nineteenth-century novels that are required reading in many english classes that study victorian literature.
2. It was a beautiful day in the spring—it was april 15, to be exact—but all Ted could think about was the check he had to write to the internal revenue service and the bills he had to pay by friday.
3. Traveling north, they hiked through british columbia, planning a leisurely return on the cruise ship *canadian princess.*
4. Alice liked her mom's apple pie better than aunt nellie's rhubarb pie; but she liked grandpa's punch best of all.
5. A new elective, political science 30, covers the vietnam war from the gulf of tonkin to the fall of saigon, including the roles of ho chi minh, the communists, and the buddhist monks; the position of presidents johnson and nixon; and the influence of groups like the student mobilization committee and vietnam veterans against the war.

6. When the central high school drama club put on a production of shaw's *pygmalion,* the director xeroxed extra copies of the parts for eliza doolittle and professor henry higgins so he could give them to the understudies.

7. Shaking all over, Bill admitted, "driving on the los angeles freeway is a frightening experience for a kid from the bronx, even in a bmw."

8. The new united federation of teachers contract guarantees teachers many paid holidays including columbus day, veterans day, and washington's birthday; a week each at christmas and easter; and two full months (july and august) in the summer.

9. The sociology syllabus included the books *beyond the best interests of the child, regulating the poor,* and *a welfare mother;* in history we were to begin by studying the stone age, the bronze age, and the iron age.

10. Winners of the nobel peace prize include lech walesa, leader of the polish trade union solidarity; the reverend dr. martin luther king, jr., founder of the southern christian leadership conference; and bishop desmond tutu of south africa.

32

Italics

In an italic typeface, the characters slant upward to the right: *The Outsiders*. The use of **italics** is indicated in written or typed text by underlining: The Outsiders. As with other punctuation marks, a number of conventions govern the use of italics.

32a Setting Off Titles and Names

Italicize the titles of books, newspapers, magazines, and journals; pamphlets; films; television and radio programs; long poems; plays; long musical works; paintings and sculpture; and names of ships, trains, aircraft, and spacecraft. All other titles are set off with quotation marks (see 29b).

NOTE: Titles of your own essays, typed at the top of the first page or on a title page, are neither italicized nor placed within quotation marks. Names of sacred books, such as the Bible, and well-known documents, such as the Constitution and the Declaration of Independence, are also neither italicized nor placed within quotation marks.

Books

David Copperfield	*The Other America*
Cujo	*A Connecticut Yankee in King Arthur's Court*

Newspapers

the *Washington Post*	*The Philadelphia Inquirer*
The New York Times	*St. Louis Post-Dispatch*

Articles and names of cities are italicized only when they are a part of a title.

Magazines

People	*Scientific American*
The Atlantic	*Psychology Today*

Journals

Columbia Journalism Review	*New England Journal of Medicine*
College English	*American Sociological Review*

Pamphlets
>Paine's *Common Sense*
>Milton's *Tetrachordon*

Films
>*Return of the Jedi*   *Psycho*
>*E.T.*   *Citizen Kane*

Punctuation is italicized when it is part of a title.

Television programs
>*Face the Nation*   *Dallas*
>*The Love Boat*   *Leave It to Beaver*

Radio programs
>*All Things Considered*   *Prairie Home Companion*
>*CBS Mystery Theater*   *Fibber McGee and Molly*

Long poems
>*Paradise Lost*   *The Faerie Queen*
>*John Brown's Body*   *Evangeline*

Plays
>*The Glass Menagerie*   *Awake and Sing*
>*Macbeth*   *A Raisin in the Sun*

Long musical works
>*Rigoletto*   *Lohengrin*
>*Eroica*   *Messiah*

Paintings and sculpture
>Rembrandt's *The Night Watch*   Wyeth's *Christina's World*
>Michelangelo's *Pietà*   Picasso's *Guernica*

Ships
>*Queen Elizabeth II*   U.S.S. *Saratoga*
>*Lusitania*   *The Delta Queen*

S.S. and U.S.S. are not italicized when they precede the name of a
ship.

Trains
>*Silver Meteor*   *The Patriot*
>*City of New Orleans*   *The Orient Express*

Aircraft
>the *Spruce Goose*   the *Hindenburg*
>*Air Force One*   *Enola Gay*

Only particular aircraft, not makes or types like Piper Cub or
Boeing 707, are italicized.

Spacecraft
>   *Sputnik*   *Apollo II*
>   *Columbia*   *Enterprise*

32b   Setting Off Foreign Words and Phrases

Thousands of foreign words and phrases are now considered
part of the English language. These words—*naive, lasso, chap-
eron,* and *catharsis,* for example—receive no special treatment.
But convention requires that foreign words and phrases not yet
fully assimilated into the language be set in italics. All such foreign words, with the exception of foreign proper nouns, must be
italicized.

ital
32c

>   The *carpe diem* theme is expressed in Andrew Marvell's poem "To
>   His Coy Mistress."
>
>   *Spirochaeta plicatilis, Treponema pallidum,* and *Spirilbum minus*
>   are all bacteria with corkscrew-like shapes.
>
>   The personnel officer asked Frank to submit a current *curriculum
>   vitae* so that she could assess his qualifications.

If you are not sure whether a foreign word has been assimilated
into English, consult a dictionary.

32c   Setting Off Elements Spoken of as Themselves and Terms Being Defined

Italicize letters, numerals, words, and phrases when they refer to
the letters, numerals, words, and phrases themselves.

>   Is that a *p* or a *g*?
>
>   I forget the exact address, but I know it has a *3* in it.
>
>   Does *through* rhyme with *cough?*
>
>   His pronunciation of the phrase *Mary was contrary* told us he was
>   from the Midwest.

Italicize to set off words and phrases that you go on to
define.

>   A *closet drama* is a play meant to be read, not performed.

32d Using Italics for Emphasis

Italics lend unusually strong weight to a word or phrase and must therefore be used in moderation. Overuse of italics interferes with the tone and even the meaning of what you write. Whenever possible, emphasis should emerge from word choice and sentence structure (see Chapter 8). These sentences illustrate acceptable use of italics for emphasis.

> As for protecting the children from exploitation, the chief and indeed only exploiters of children these days *are* schools. (John Holt, "School Is Bad for Children")

> Initially, poetry might be defined as a kind of language that says *more* and says it *more intensely* than does ordinary language. (Lawrence Perrine, *Sound and Sense*)

32e Using Italics for Clarity

Occasionally, it is necessary to italicize a word to avoid confusion or ambiguity when a sentence may have more than one meaning.

> This time Jill forgot the *key*. (last time Jill forgot something else)

> This time *Jill* forgot the key. (last time someone else forgot the key)

▶
EXERCISE

Underline to indicate italics where necessary, and delete any italics that are incorrectly used. If a sentence is correct, mark it with a C.

> EXAMPLE: However is a conjunctive adverb, not a coordinating conjunction.
>
> *However* is a conjunctive adverb, not a coordinating conjunction.

1. I said Carol, not Darryl.
2. A deus ex machina, an improbable device used to resolve the plot of a fictional work, is used in Charles Dickens's novel Oliver Twist.
3. He dotted every i and crossed every t.
4. The Metropolitan Opera's production of Carmen was a real tour de force for the principal performers.
5. *Laissez faire* is a doctrine that holds that government should not interfere with trade.
6. Antidote and anecdote are often confused because their pronunciations are similar.

7. Hawthorne's novels include Fanshawe, The House of the Seven Gables, The Blithedale Romance, and The Scarlet Letter.

8. Words like mailman, policeman, and fireman are rapidly being replaced by nonsexist terms like letter carrier, police officer, and fire fighter.

9. A classic black tuxedo was considered de rigueur at the charity ball, but Jason preferred to wear his *dashiki.*

10. Thomas Mann's novel Buddenbrooks is a Bildungsroman.

ital
32e

33

Hyphens

Hyphens have two conventional uses: to break words at the end of a typed or handwritten line and to link words in certain compounds.

33a Breaking Words at the End of a Line

Whenever possible, try to avoid breaking a word at the end of a line; if you must do so, divide words only between syllables. Consult a dictionary to determine correct syllabication. Whenever you can, divide a word between prefix and root (sus•pend) or between root and suffix (pave•ment). Divide words that contain doubled consonants between the doubled letters (let•ter) unless the doubled letters are part of the root (cross•ing) or do not break into two syllables (ex•pelled). Do not end two consecutive lines with hyphens, and never divide a word at the end of a page.

Here are additional guidelines for determining how a word should be divided.

(1) One-syllable words

Never hyphenate one-syllable words. Keep a one-syllable word intact even if it is relatively long *(thought, blocked, French, laughed)*. If you cannot fit the whole word at the end of the line, move it to the next line.

> FAULTY: Mark Twain's novel *The Prin-*
> *ce and the Pauper* considers the
> effects of environment on personality.

> REVISED: Mark Twain's novel *The Prince and the*
> *Pauper* considers the effects of environ-
> ment on personality.

(2) Short syllables

Never leave a single letter at the end of a line or carry one or two letters to the beginning of a line. One-letter prefixes (like the *a-* in

33a

522

away) or short suffixes (like *-y, -ly, -er,* and *-ed)* should not be separated from the rest of the word. The suffixes *-able* and *-ible* cannot be broken into two syllables, either.

FAULTY: Nadia walked very slowly a-
        long the balance beam.

REVISED: Nadia walked very slowly along
         the balance beam.

FAULTY: Ms. Erwin reviewed the spelling list careful-
        ly, checking for errors.

REVISED: Ms. Erwin reviewed the spelling list care-
         fully, checking for errors.

FAULTY: Amy's parents wondered whether the terrib-
        le twos would ever end.

REVISED: Amy's parents wondered whether the ter-
         rible twos would ever end.

(3) Compounds

33a

If you must hyphenate a compound word, put the hyphen be-tween the elements of the compound. (For correct use of hy-phens in compound words, see 33b.)

FAULTY: Environmentalists believe snowmo-
        biles produce air and noise pollution.

REVISED: Environmentalists believe snow-
         mobiles produce air and noise pollution.

If the compound already contains a hyphen, divide it at the exist-ing hyphen.

FAULTY: She met her ex-hus-
        band on a blind date.

REVISED: She met her ex-
         husband on a blind date.

(4) Illogical or confusing hyphenation

Some words contain letter combinations that look like other words. If a word break leaves a fragment that reads as a word not related to the divided word, the reader will be confused.

CONFUSING: The supervisor did not appreciate the face-
           tious remark.

REVISED: The supervisor did not appreciate the
facetious remark.

CONFUSING: The tiger's rampage was a cat-
astrophe for the village.

REVISED: The tiger's rampage was a catas-
trophe for the village.

(5)   Numerals, contractions, and abbreviations

Contractions, numerals, acronyms, and abbreviations should not
be divided. A hyphen is not used between a numeral and an
abbreviation.

FAULTY: Whether or not the meeting began on time was-
n't important.

REVISED: Whether or not the meeting began on time
wasn't important.

FAULTY: The special on child abuse was watched by over 23,-
000,000 Americans.

REVISED: The special on child abuse was watched by over
23,000,000 Americans.

FAULTY: During the sixties, participation in RO-
TC declined on many college campuses.

REVISED: During the sixties, participation in
ROTC declined on many college campuses.

FAULTY: The balloon was launched at precisely 8-
P.M.

REVISED: The balloon was launched at precisely
8 P.M.

33a

▶
EXERCISE 1

Divide each of these words into syllables, consulting a dictionary if necessary; then, indicate with a hyphen where you would divide each word
at the end of a line.

EXAMPLE: underground

un • der • ground

under-ground

1.	transcendentalism	6.	side-splitting
2.	calliope	7.	markedly
3.	martyr	8.	amazing
4.	longitude	9.	unlikely
5.	bookkeeper	10.	thorough

33b Dividing Compound Words

A compound word is composed of two or more words. Some familiar compound words are always hyphenated.

no-hitter	two-step
play-off	helter-skelter
run-down	topsy-turvy

Other compounds are always written as one word.

fireplace	peacetime
lighthouse	ninepin
sunset	nearsighted

Finally, some compounds are always written as two separate words.

cherry tomato	bunk bed
salt lick	labor relations
medical doctor	chocolate pudding

Your dictionary can tell you whether a particular compound requires a hyphen: *snow job*, for instance, is two unhyphenated words; *snowsuit* is one word; and *snow-white* is hyphenated. Dictionaries vary in their advice, however, and because the language changes quickly in this regard, it is important to have a dictionary that is up-to-date.

Hyphenization of compound words is not uniform, but a few reliable rules do apply.

(1) In compound adjectives

A **compound adjective** is two or more words combined into a single grammatical unit that modifies a noun. When a compound adjective *precedes* the noun it modifies, its elements must be joined by hyphens.

> He stayed tuned to his favorite listener-supported radio station, waiting for a hard-hitting editorial.
>
> The research team tried to use nineteenth-century technology to design a space-age project.

However, when a compound adjective *follows* the noun it modifies, it does not require a hyphen.

> The three government-operated programs were run smoothly, but the one that was not government operated was short of funds.

Compound adjectives that contain words ending in *-ly* are not hyphenated, even when they precede the noun.

Many <u>upwardly mobile</u> families consider items like home computers, microwave ovens, and video cassette recorders to be necessities.

Use **suspended hyphens**—hyphens followed by space or by the appropriate punctuation and space—in a series of compounds that have the same principal elements.

The seventh- and eighth-grade students were noisy.

The three-, four-, and five-year-old children were assigned to the same group.

(2) With certain prefixes or suffixes

Use a hyphen between a prefix and a proper noun or an adjective formed from a proper noun.

mid-July	trans-Siberian
non-Catholic	un-American
anti-Christ	pre-Columbian

Use a hyphen to connect the prefixes *all-, ex-, half-, quarter-, quasi-,* and *self-* and the suffixes *-elect* and *-odd* to a noun.

all-pro	quasi-serious
ex-senator	self-centered
half-pint	president-elect
quarter-moon	thirty-odd

NOTE: The words *selfhood, selfish,* and *selfless* do not include hyphens. In these cases, *self* is the root, not a prefix.

(3) For clarity

Hyphenate to prevent misreading one word for another.

co-op	coop
re-form	reform
re-creation	recreation

Hyphenate to avoid hard-to-read combinations, like two *i*'s (*semi-illiterate*) or more than two of the same consonant (*shell-less*) in a row.

Hyphenate in most cases between a capital initial and a word when the two combine to form a compound.

A-frame   T-shirt

But check your dictionary; some letter- or numeral-plus-word compounds do not require hyphens.

B flat   F major

(4)   In compound numerals and fractions

Hyphenate compounds that represent numbers below one hundred, even if they are part of a larger number.

the twenty-first century   three hundred sixty-five days

Compounds that represent numbers over ninety-nine *(two thousand, thirty million, two hundred fifty)* are not hyphenated. Therefore, in the expression *three hundred sixty-five days* the compound *sixty-five* is hyphenated because it represents a number below one hundred, but no hyphens connect *three* to *hundred.*

Hyphenate fractions when they serve as compound modifiers.

a two-thirds share of the business
a three-fourths majority

Hyphens are not required in other cases, but most writers do use them.

PREFERRED: seven-eighths of the circle

ACCEPTABLE: seven eighths of the circle

(5)   In newly created compounds

A coined compound, using a new combination of words as a unit, uses hyphens.

He looked up with a <u>who-do-you-think-you-are</u> expression on his face.

▶
EXERCISE 2

Form compound adjectives from the following word groups, inserting hyphens where necessary.

EXAMPLE: a contract for three years

a three-year contract

1. a relative who has long been lost
2. someone who is addicted to video games

33b

3. a salesperson who goes from door to door
4. a display calculated to catch the eye
5. friends who are dearly beloved
6. a household that is centered on a child
7. a line of reasoning that is hard to follow
8. the border between New York and New Jersey
9. a candidate who is thirty-two years old
10. a computer that is friendly to its users

▶
EXERCISE 3

Add hyphens to the compounds in these sentences wherever they are required. Consult a dictionary if necessary.

> EXAMPLE: Alaska was the forty ninth state to join the United States.
>
> Alaska was the forty-ninth state to join the United States.

33b

1. One of the restaurant's blue plate specials is chicken fried steak.
2. Virginia and Texas are both right to work states.
3. He stood on tiptoe to see the near perfect statue, which was well hidden by the security fence.
4. The five and ten cent store had a self service make up counter and stocked many up to the minute gadgets.
5. The so called Saturday night special is opposed by pro gun control groups.
6. He ordered two all beef patties with special sauce, lettuce, onions, cheese, and pickle on a sesame seed bun.
7. The material was extremely thought provoking, but it hardly presented any earth shattering conclusions.
8. The Dodgers Phillies game was rained out, so the long suffering fans left for home.
9. Bone marrow transplants carry the risk of what is known as a graft vs. host reaction.
10. The state funded child care program was considered a highly desirable alternative to family day care.

34

Abbreviations

Abbreviations save time and space. They also communicate your meaning quickly and efficiently, but only when they are familiar to your readers.

Many abbreviations are acceptable only in informal or technical writing and are not appropriate in college writing. If you are unsure whether to use a particular abbreviation, take the safer course and spell out the word or expression in full.

(For information on use of punctuation with abbreviations, see 25a.2; for a list of abbreviations used in footnotes and bibliographies, see 38h.)

**abbr
34a**

34a Abbreviating Titles

Titles before and after proper names are usually abbreviated.

Mr. Walter Cronkite	Dr. Helen Zweizig
Ms. Barbara Walters	Leonard Gillespie, M.D.
Mrs. Elizabeth Williams	Sammy Davis, Jr.
Henry Kissinger, Ph.D.	St. Jude

But military, religious, academic, and government titles are not abbreviated.

General George Patton
the Reverend William Gray
Professor Kenneth G. Schaefer
Senator Daniel Moynihan
the Honorable Diane Feinstein
President Lyndon Baines Johnson

In informal writing, abbreviations like Gen., Rev., Sen., and the like, are acceptable if they precede a complete name (Rep. Patricia Schroeder, for example). Abbreviated forms of these titles are not acceptable before a surname alone or when they do not precede a proper name.

FAULTY: Rep. Shroeder is a member of Congress from Colorado.

FAULTY: Patricia Shroeder is a congressional rep. from Colorado.

REVISED: Representative Patricia Shroeder is a member of Congress from Colorado.

34b Abbreviating Technical Terms and Agency Names

Certain abbreviations are frequently used in speech and in academic writing to designate groups, institutions, people, substances, and the like. Businesses and government, social, and civic organizations are commonly referred to by initials, for example. These abbreviations fall into two categories: abbreviations formed from capitalized initials (CIA) and those that are acronyms (CORE). (See 25a.2 for additional examples and explanation.)

Accepted abbreviations for terms that are not well known may also be used, but only if you have cited the abbreviation in parentheses directly after your first mention of the full term.

> Citrus farmers have been injecting ethylene dibromide (EDB), a chemical pesticide, into the soil for over twenty years. Now, however, EDB has seeped into wells and contaminated water supplies, and it is a suspected carcinogen.

Using such abbreviations is efficient, but the full term must be spelled out first so the reader knows what the abbreviation stands for.

34c Abbreviating Designations of Specific Dates, Times of Day, Temperatures, and Numbers

50 B.C. (B.C. follows the date)
A.D. 432 (A.D. precedes the date)
6 A.M.
3:03 P.M.
20° C (Centrigrade or Celsius)
180° F (Fahrenheit)

Always capitalize B.C. and A.D. You may, however, use either upper- or lower-case letters for a.m. and p.m. (A.M., a.m., P.M., p.m.). Printers conventionally set A.M., P.M., B.C., and A.D. in small capital letters (A.M., P.M., B.C., A.D.). These abbreviations are used only when they are accompanied by numbers.

> FAULTY: We will see you in the A.M.
>
> REVISED: We will see you in the morning.
>
> REVISED: We will see you at 8 A.M.

NOTE: In technical writing, you may use the abbreviation *no.* (number), but only before a specific number. This abbreviation may be written either *no.* or *No.*

> FAULTY: The no. on the label of the unidentified substance was 52.
>
> REVISED: The unidentified substance was labeled no. 52.
>
> REVISED: The number on the label of the unidentified substance was 52.

In nontechnical writing, *no.* is acceptable only in endnotes and bibliographic entries.

> CORRECT: *The Journal of the Institute for Socioeconomic Studies,* Vol. 11, No. 2, Spring 1977.
>
> FAULTY: The no. 1 consumer of electricity in many households is a frost-free refrigerator.
>
> REVISED: The number one consumer of electricity in many households is a frost-free refrigerator.

abbr
34d

34d Editing to Eliminate Misuse and Overuse of Abbreviations

Abbreviations are frequently used in technical writing, but for most college writing, abbreviations should be confined to the situations just listed. Abbreviations are not used in the following cases.

For certain familiar Latin expressions

Abbreviations of the common Latin phrases *i.e.* ("that is"), *e.g.* ("for example"), and *etc.* ("and so forth") are sometimes appropriate for informal writing, and they may occasionally be acceptable in a parenthetical note. In most college writing, however, an equivalent phrase should be written out in full.

> INFORMAL: Poe wrote "The Gold Bug," "The Masque of the Red Death," etc.

PREFERABLE: Poe wrote "The Gold Bug," "The Masque of the Red Death," and other stories.

INFORMAL: Other musicians (e.g., Bruce Springsteen) have been influenced by Dylan.

PREFERABLE: Other musicians (for example, Bruce Springsteen) have been influenced by Dylan.

The Latin abbreviations *et al.* ("and others") and *cf.* ("compare") are used only in bibliographic entries.

Davidson, Harley, et al. *You and Your Motorcycle.* New York: Ten Speed Press, 1968.

(For further information on the use of abbreviations in lists of works cited, see 38c.2.)

abbr 34d

For the names of days, months, or holidays

FAULTY: Sat., Aug. 9, was the hottest day of the year.

REVISED: Saturday, August 9, was the hottest day of the year.

FAULTY: Only twenty-three shopping days remain until Xmas.

REVISED: Only twenty-three shopping days remain until Christmas.

For units of measurement

In informal and technical writing some units of measurement are abbreviated when preceded by a numeral.

The hurricane had winds of 35 m.p.h.

The new Honda gets over 50 m.p.g.

In general academic writing, however, write out such expressions, and spell out words such as *inches, feet, years, miles, pints, quarts,* and *gallons.*

NOTE: Abbreviations for units of measurement are not used in the absence of a numeral.

FAULTY: The laboratory equipment included pt. and qt. measures and a beaker that could hold a gal. of liquid.

REVISED: The laboratory equipment included pint and quart measures and a beaker that could hold a gallon of liquid.

For names of places, streets, and the like

Abbreviations of names of streets, cities, states, countries, and geographical regions are common in informal writing. For college assignments these words should be spelled out.

FAULTY	REVISED
B'way	Broadway
Riverside Dr.	Riverside Drive
Phila.	Philadelphia
Calif. or CA	California
Catskill Mts.	Catskill Mountains

EXCEPTIONS: The abbreviations *U.S.A.*, or *USA*, and *U.S.S.R.*, or *USSR*, are often acceptable, as is *D.C.* (for District of Columbia) in the phrase *Washington, D.C.* It is also permissible to use the abbreviation *Mt.* before the name of a mountain *(Mt. Etna)* and *St.* in a place name *(St. Albans)*.

For names of academic subjects

Names of academic subjects are not abbreviated.

> FAULTY: Psych., soc., and English lit. are all required for graduation.

> REVISED: Psychology, sociology, and English literature are all required for graduation.

For parts of books

Abbreviations that designate parts of written works *(Pt. II, Ch. 3, Vol. IV, p. 6)* should not be used within the text of a paper. Such abbreviations are acceptable only in notes and bibliographic entries (see 38f).

For people's names

> FAULTY: Mr. Harris's five children were named Robt., Eliz., Jas., Chas., and Wm.

> REVISED: Mr. Harris's five children were named Robert, Elizabeth, James, Charles, and William.

In company names

The abbreviations *Inc.*, *Bros.*, *Co.*, or *Corp.* and the ampersand (&) are not used unless they are part of a firm's official name.

Company names are written exactly as the firms themselves write them.

Shearson Lehman Brothers
Holt, Rinehart and Winston
American Home Products Corporation
Western Union Telegraph Company
Santini Bros.

abbr
34d

Rohm & Haas
AT & T
TDK Electronics Corp.
Charles Schwab & Co., Inc.

Abbreviations for *company, corporation,* and the like are not used in the absence of a company name.

FAULTY: The corp. merged with a small co. in Pittsburgh.

REVISED: The corporation merged with a small company in Pittsburgh.

EXCEPTION: Shortened forms of publishers' names are preferred in bibliographic citations (see 38c.2).

The ampersand (&) is not used at all in college writing except in the name of a company that requires it.

FAULTY: "Frankie & Johnny" is a ballad about a woman who shoots her unfaithful lover.

REVISED: "Frankie and Johnny" is a ballad about a woman who shoots her unfaithful lover.

**abbr
34d**

Symbols

The symbols %, =, +, #, and ¢ are acceptable in technical and scientific writing but not in nontechnical college writing.

FAULTY: The 90¢ cost of admission represents a 50% increase over last year's price.

REVISED: The ninety-cent cost of admission represents a fifty percent increase over last year's price.

The symbol $ is acceptable in all types of writing, but only before specific numbers. It is not used as a substitute for the words *money* or *dollars.*

CORRECT: The first of her books of poetry cost $4.25 per copy.

FAULTY: The value of the $ has declined steadily in the last two decades.

REVISED: The value of the dollar has declined steadily in the last two decades.

▶

EXERCISE

Correct any incorrectly used abbreviations in the following sentences, assuming that all are intended for an academic audience. If a sentence is correct, mark it with a *C.*

EXAMPLE: *Romeo & Juliet* is a play by Wm. Shakespeare.

Romeo and Juliet is a play by William Shakespeare.

1. The committee meeting, attended by representatives from Action for Children's Television (ACT) and NOW, Sen. Putnam, & the pres. of ABC, convened at 8 A.M. on Mon. Feb. 24 at the YWCA on Germantown Ave.

2. An econ. prof. was suspended after he encouraged his students to speculate on securities issued by corps. under investigation by the SEC.

3. Benjamin Spock, the M.D. who wrote *Baby and Child Care,* is a respected dr. known throughout the USA.

4. The FDA has banned the use of Red Dye no. 2 in food, but BHT and other food additives are still in use.

5. The Rev. Dr. Martin Luther King, Jr., leader of the S.C.L.C., led the famous Selma, Ala. march.

6. Wm. Golding, a novelist from the U.K., won the Nobel Prize for lit.

7. The adult education center, financed by a major computer corp., offers courses in basic subjects like introductory bio. and tech. writing as well as teaching programming languages like COBOL and FORTRAN.

abbr

34d

8. All the bros. in the fraternity agreed to write to Pres. Dexter appealing their disciplinary probation under Ch. 4, Sec. 3 of the IFC constitution.

9. A 4 qt. (i.e., 2 gal.) container is needed to hold the salt solution.

10. According to Prof. Morrison, all those taking the MCAT's should bring two sharpened no. 2 pencils to the St. Joseph's University auditorium on Sat.

35

Numbers

Convention determines when to use a numeral (22) and when to spell out a number (twenty-two). Numerals are generally more common in scientific and technical writing, in journalism, and in informal writing, while numbers are more often spelled out in formal or literary writing. In special contexts one option is preferred over the other.

Common sense should guide your final decision. If spelling out numbers is cumbersome, use figures. Whatever your choice, usage should be consistent, and numerals and spelled-out forms should generally not be mixed in the same passage.

**num
35b**

35a Spelling Out Numbers That Begin Sentences

Never begin a sentence with a numeral. If a number begins a sentence, express it in words.

> FAULTY: 200 students are currently enrolled in freshman English.
>
> REVISED: Two hundred students are currently enrolled in freshman English.

Or reword the sentence, especially when the opening number is more than two words long.

> CORRECT: Current enrollment in freshman English is 200 students.

35b Spelling Out Numbers That Can Be Expressed in One or Two Words

Unless a number falls into one of the categories listed in 35d, spell it out if you can do so in one or two words.

> The Hawaiian alphabet has only twelve letters.
>
> Class size stabilized at twenty-eight students.

536

Approximate numbers can often be expressed in one or two words.

Guards turned away over ten thousand disappointed fans.

The subsidies are expected to total about two million dollars.

35c Using Numerals for Numbers That Cannot Be Expressed in One or Two Words

Numbers more than two words long are expressed in figures.

The pollster interviewed 3,250 voters before the election.

The dietitian prepared 125 sample menus.

When Levittown, Pennsylvania, was built in the early 1950's, the builder's purchases included 300,000 doorknobs, 153,000 faucets, 53,600 ice cube trays, and 4,000 manhole covers.

To be consistent with the spelled-out forms used in the rest of the sentence, the number 4,000 is expressed in figures even though it could be written in just two words.

num
35d

35d Using Numerals Where Convention Requires Their Use

Numerals are used for addresses; dates; exact times; exact sums of money; pages and divisions of written works; measurements accompanied by symbols or figures; numbers that include percentages, decimals, or fractions; ratios, scores, and statistics; and identification numbers.

Addresses

1600 Pennsylvania Avenue
10 Downing Street
383 Madison Avenue, New York, New York   10017

Dates

January 15, 1929   62 B.C.
November 22, 1963   1914–1919

Exact times

9:16   10 A.M. (or 10:00 A.M.)   6:50

EXCEPTIONS: Spell out times of day when they are used with *o'clock: eleven o'clock,* not *11 o'clock.* Also spell out times expressed as round numbers. (They were in bed by *ten.*)

Exact sums of money

$25.11
$6752.00 (or $6,752.00)
$25.5 million (or $25,500,000)

EXCEPTION: You may write out a round sum of money if the number can be expressed in fewer than three words.

five dollars   two thousand dollars
fifty-three cents   six hundred dollars

Pages and divisions of written works

Numerals are used for chapter numbers; volume numbers; acts, scenes, and lines of plays; books of the Bible; and line numbers of long poems.

The "Out, out brief candle" speech appears in Act 5, scene 5, of *Macbeth* (lines 17–28); in Kittredge's *Complete Works of Shakespeare* it appears on page 1142.

Measurements

When a measurement is expressed by a number accompanied by a symbol or an abbreviation, use figures.

55 mph   12″
32°   15 cc

Numbers containing percentages, decimals, or fractions

80% (or 80 percent)   6 3/4
98.6   3.14

Ratios, scores, and statistics

Children preferred Crispy Crunchies over Total Bran by a ratio of 20 to 1.

The Orioles defeated the Phillies 6 to 0.

The median age of the voters was 42; the mean age was 40.

Identification numbers

Route 66   Track 8
Channel 12   Social Security number 146–07–3846

35e Using Numerals with Spelled-out Numbers

Even when all the numbers in a particular passage are short enough to be spelled out, figures are sometimes used along with spelled-out numbers to distinguish one number from another.

**num
35e**

CONFUSING: The team was divided into twenty two-person squads.

CLEAR: The team was divided into twenty 2-person squads.

CONFUSING: They lived at 500 5th Avenue.

CLEAR: They lived at 500 Fifth Avenue.

▶

EXERCISE

Revise the use of numbers in these sentences, making sure usage is correct and consistent. If a sentence uses numbers correctly, mark it with a *C*.

EXAMPLE: The Empire State Building is one hundred and two
            stories high.

            The Empire State Building is 102 stories high.

num

35e

1. *1984*, a novel by George Orwell, is set in a totalitarian society.
2. The English placement examination included a 30-minute personal-experience essay, a 45-minute expository essay, and a 100-item objective test of grammar and usage.
3. In a control group of two hundred forty-seven patients, almost three out of four suffered serious adverse reactions to the new drug.
4. Before the thirteenth amendment to the Constitution, slaves were counted as 3/5 of a person.
5. The intensive membership drive netted 2,608 new members and additional dues of over 5 thousand dollars.
6. They had only 2 choices: either they could take the yacht at Pier Fourteen, or they could return home to the penthouse at Twenty-seven Harbor View Drive.
7. The atomic number of lithium is three.
8. Approximately 3 hundred thousand school children in District 6 were given hearing and vision examinations between May third and June 26.
9. The United States was drawn into World War II by the Japanese attack on Pearl Harbor on December seventh, 1941.
10. An upper-middle-class family can spend over two hundred fifty thousand dollars to raise each child up to age 18.

Writing with Sources

Research for Writing

We all engage in **research** from time to time. Before we make any major purchase—a car, personal computer, stereo, or television, for instance—we gather information to guide our choice. We ask friends for advice, we study ads and brochures, we look at magazines such as *Consumer Reports*. Government agencies, investment firms, advertising agencies, corporations, universities, professional organizations, political parties, and special-interest groups of all sorts also spend a lot of time—and money—doing research. In an age of proliferating information, it sometimes seems as if nothing is done without the recommendations of a research staff.

Using methods designed to locate information as quickly as possible, experienced researchers look for accurate, current, and relevant material. They do not immediately undertake an exhaustive library search. Usually they call people who can advise them, asking them which experts or which books and articles to consult. They take advantage of the computer: five minutes at a terminal can eliminate hours of poring through print indexes. In the library, they use specific research tools limited to their field of inquiry—indexes that summarize important work done in an area or that list works with bibliographies, for example. These techniques help them assemble a preliminary bibliography quickly and efficiently. Because book-length studies and even articles can be out of date by the time they appear in print, researchers often contact experts directly.

Finally, experienced researchers recognize the difference between **primary** and **secondary sources**—that is, between original documents and commentaries on those documents. Whenever they can, researchers go back to primary sources to avoid being misled by the interpretations or errors of others.

When you are preparing a college assignment, your topic and your time determine how much research you do. But knowing the techniques used by experienced researchers can streamline your task and give you more time for writing.

36a   Establishing a Research Network

Your first step in undertaking a research project should be to locate people who can suggest reliable and up-to-date sources of information. A meeting with your instructor may be all that you need to get started, or your instructor may refer you to someone else more familiar with your topic. Just one or two good contacts can help you establish a **research network**. Your first contact might suggest another, who in turn might suggest two more.

When you call on anyone for advice, be sure to observe certain courtesies. Always make an appointment to discuss your initial plans. Have ready a clear description of your topic, along with a list of specific questions. Most people will be glad to help you, but they will not have the time to determine what it is you want to know. Nor should you expect your instructors to do your work for you. Asking for a starting point is fine; asking someone else to think of a topic for you or to give you information that you could easily find yourself is not. Finally, always remember to thank the people who help you for their time. As an additional courtesy, you might offer to give them a copy of your finished paper.

**res
36b**

▶
EXERCISE 1

You are beginning to gather information for the research projects outlined below. Whom in your college or your community might you approach to establish a research network? Write five exploratory questions that you would ask each person.

1. A paper for a biology course examining new developments in DNA recombinant research
2. A short paper for a history course in which you examine the validity of slave narratives for historical research
3. A research paper for a composition course in which you explore the possibility of scientists' developing computers that can think

36b   Doing Library Research

The library is central to many research projects. To make appropriate use of the materials in your college library, you should know how the library is organized and what specialized reference tools it contains.

(1) Consulting reference books

Ordinarily you do not read a reference book from cover to cover. Instead, you look up the topic you are investigating. Some reference works—like general encyclopedias—give you overviews of a wide variety of topics. Others—like specialized dictionaries or atlases—contain detailed information about a limited number of subjects.

GENERAL ENCYCLOPEDIAS General multivolume encyclopedias such as *Encyclopedia Americana* and *Collier's Encyclopedia* contain information about many different subjects. Articles, often written by experts on the topic, are arranged alphabetically. General encyclopedias give you a good overview, but they do not replace in-depth research.

Perhaps the most respected multivolume encyclopedia is the *Encyclopaedia Britannica*, now in its fifteenth edition. The newest edition is divided into three sections: the *Propaedia*, a one-volume general subject index; the *Micropaedia*, a twelve-volume index containing brief articles; and the *Macropaedia*, a nineteen-volume detailed discussion of selected subjects listed in the *Micropaedia*. The information in the *Britannica* is invaluable, but this encyclopedia takes some getting used to. You can begin by searching the *Propaedia* for subject categories and then reading the brief articles in the *Micropaedia*. The longer discussions in the *Macropaedia* frequently contain brief bibliographies.

To get a sense of your topic in less time, use a one-volume general encyclopedia. Two of the best are *The New Columbia Encyclopedia* and *The Random House Encyclopedia*. Both contain many short entries listed in alphabetical order by subject. The cross-references and in-depth bibliographic information provided by the multivolume encyclopedias, however, do not appear in these short volumes. You may still have to consult a multivolume encyclopedia if you need more general information.

SPECIALIZED ENCYCLOPEDIAS Called either *encyclopedias* or *dictionaries*, such reference works cover one subject thoroughly. Subjects are treated in greater detail than in general encyclopedias, and articles sometimes include annotated bibliographies and cross-references. Specialized reference works are listed in Eugene P. Sheehy's *Guide to Reference Works*, available at the reference desk in most libraries. The following list of specialized encyclopedias suggests the variety of sources available.

res

36b

Art

Encyclopedia of World Art, fifteen volumes. Scholarly articles, detailed bibliographies, and many plates. Covers art of all periods and countries.

Oxford Companion to Art. A one-volume encyclopedia devoted to the visual arts.

Biology

Gray, Peter, ed. *The Encyclopedia of the Biological Sciences.* Directed at students and experts reading outside their fields. Includes bibliographies, biographical articles, and illustrations.

A Dictionary of Genetics. Comprehensive information about genetic research, including definitions of terms.

Business and Economics

The McGraw-Hill Dictionary of Modern Economics. Extended definitions of terms. Also includes bibliographies.

Heyel, Carl, ed. *The Encyclopedia of Management.* Definitions and explanations. Includes references for further reading.

Munn, Glenn Gaywaine, ed. *Encyclopedia of Banking and Finance.* Defines and explains pertinent terms.

Chemistry

Encyclopedia of Chemistry. Articles about distinguished chemists, various chemical associations, and chemicals themselves.

Chemical Technology: An Encyclopedic Treatment. Focuses on the applied uses of chemical technology.

The Merck Index of Chemicals and Drugs. Formulas, properties, and uses of drugs and chemicals. References to relevant literature.

Drama

The Oxford Companion to the Theatre. A one-volume encyclopedia of the theater.

McGraw-Hill Encyclopedia of World Drama, four volumes. Comprehensive coverage of all aspects of drama from ancient to present times.

Education

Dictionary of Education. A scholarly dictionary with extended definitions of terms.

The Encyclopedia of Education, ten volumes. Covers all aspects of the field. Emphasizes theory and history.

Engineering

Engineering Encyclopedia. A concise encyclopedia and mechanical dictionary. Includes definitions of engineering terms and some historical material.

McGraw-Hill Encyclopedia of Science and Technology, fifteen volumes. Not specifically geared to engineering, but includes articles of related interest.

History

Cambridge Ancient History. Egypt to the fall of Rome. Each chapter is written by a specialist; each volume includes a full bibliography.

Cambridge Medieval History. Reference history of the Middle Ages prepared by experts in the field.

New Cambridge Modern History. Authoritative and comprehensive general modern history, covering the Renaissance through World War II, with an emphasis on Europe.

Dictionary of American History. Brief articles on many topics on American history and life.

Oxford Companion to American History. Short articles on American history.

**res
36b**

Literature

Oxford Companion to American Literature. Short articles dealing with the literature of Canada and the United States. Entries cover a wide range of subjects: authors, specific works, historical figures.

Oxford Companion to English Literature. Concise articles on English authors and on characters and allusions encountered in English literature.

Oxford Companion to Classical Literature. Handbook of information on classical Greek and Roman literary works, authors, history, institutions, and religion.

Spiller, Robert E., et al. *Literary History of the United States,* two volumes. A detailed literary history of the United States from colonial times to the present. Volume I concentrates on specific periods; Volume II has biographical essays and a detailed index.

Cassell's Encyclopedia of World Literature, three volumes. Volume I includes brief definitions of literary terms and essays on literary history. Volumes II and III contain biographical sketches.

Princeton Encyclopedia of Poetry and Poetics. A comprehensive work dealing with history, prosody, and terminology. No biographies.

Mathematics

The Universal Encyclopedia of Mathematics. Alphabetically arranged articles on topics from arithmetic to calculus. Over 200 pages of formulas and tables.

The International Dictionary of Applied Mathematics. Defines terms and describes methods of applying mathematics to various fields of physical science and engineering.

Music

Grove's Dictionary of Music and Musicians, nine volumes. Covers the field from 1450 to the present. Includes biographies; musical history, theory, and practice; definitions of terms; analyses of songs and operas. Emphasis on English subjects.

Apel, Willi. *Harvard Dictionary of Music.* A one-volume dictionary with articles based on scholarship; numerous definitions; no biographies. Emphasizes historical point of view.

Physics

Encyclopedic Dictionary of Physics, nine volumes. A scholarly dictionary of physics. It also deals with astronomy, geophysics, biophysics, and related subjects. Articles are signed; many have biographical references.

Encyclopedia of Physics, fifty-four volumes. Covers the field comprehensively.

Political Science

The American Political Dictionary. Includes definitions and explanations of terms, laws, and cases pertaining to civil liberties, the Constitution, and the legislative process.

Dunner, Joseph, ed. *Dictionary of Political Science.* Compact encyclopedia treats important people, places, terms, and events.

Theimer, Walter. *Encyclopedia of Modern World Politics.* Brief articles on current political issues and figures of all periods and countries; also covers current political terms.

Psychology

Encyclopedia of Psychology, three volumes. Contains both short and long entries.

Encyclopedia of Human Behavior: Psychology, Psychiatry and Mental Health, two volumes. Contains long articles as well as definitions and case histories.

Contemporary Psychology. Collection of current reviews in the field.

Religion and Philosophy

Concise Encyclopedia of Living Faiths. In-depth articles on the world's religions.

Encyclopedia Judaica, sixteen volumes. Gives a comprehensive view of Jewish life, customs, religion, history, and literature.

New Catholic Encyclopedia, fifteen volumes. Examines the teachings, history, organization, and activities of the Catholic Church in detail.

Oxford Dictionary of the Christian Church. A collection of historical and biographical articles and definitions of ecclesiastical terms and customs.

Burr, Nelson R., ed. *A Critical Bibliography of Religion in America.* Bibliography of books, articles, and reviews. Includes social and cultural aspects of religion.

Edwards, Paul, ed. *The Encyclopedia of Philosophy,* eight volumes. Scholarly but accessible articles on philosophers, schools of thought, and concepts.

The Concise Encyclopedia of Western Philosophy and Philosophers. A one-volume work including brief articles on thinkers and ideas of all time periods.

**res
36b**

Sociology, Social Work, and Anthropology

Encyclopedia of Social Work. Articles on social work history, theory, practice, and policy.

Encyclopedia of Sociology. Articles by experts covering a wide variety of subjects.

International Encyclopedia of the Social Sciences. Articles to help students and professionals keep track of developments. Historical perspective and general level of information.

Winick, Charles, ed. *Dictionary of Anthropology.* Brief articles identify prominent early (pre-1900) anthropologists and their contributions.

Work, Monroe Nathan, ed. *Bibliography of the Negro in Africa and America.* Scholarly bibliography covering periodicals and books published before 1928.

Dictionary Catalog of the Schomberg Collection of Negro Literature and History. Reprints nearly 200,000 author, title, and subject catalog cards from the New York Public Library's collection.

UNABRIDGED DICTIONARIES Unabridged dictionaries list and define words in a given language (see Chapter 17).

Webster's Third New International Dictionary of the English Language (1981). Unusually clear definitions, given in historic sequence (the oldest meaning appearing first). Contains over 400,000 words and includes obsolete words and antonyms as well as synonyms. Includes biographical dictionary, abbreviations, and other supplementary lists.

The Random House Dictionary of the English Language (1980). Includes over 200,000 entries and numerous quotations. Several appendices including foreign terms, maps, and a guide to style.

Oxford English Dictionary, fifteen volumes (1884–1928; supplements 1933, 1972, 1977). The most scholarly and comprehensive English-language dictionary. Includes the history of every word used in England since 1150. Information is provided about when and how each word entered the language and about changes in spelling, meaning, and usage. Each word's history is illustrated by quotations.

SPECIAL DICTIONARIES   These dictionaries focus on particular language characteristics.

Fowler, Henry Watson. *A Dictionary of Modern English Usage*, 2d ed. Authority on problems of grammatical usage.

Nicholson, Margaret. *A Dictionary of American-English Usage.* Simplified version of Fowler, designed to meet current American needs.

Evans, Bergen, and Cornelia Evans. *Dictionary of Contemporary American Usage.* Lively treatment of questions of usage. Treats words, idioms, style, punctuation, and the like with humor.

Partridge, Eric. *Dictionary of Slang and Unconventional English*, 5th ed. Defines English slang terms and gives approximate date each word first appeared.

Webster's Dictionary of Synonyms. Lists words with similar meanings and discriminates among them.

Roget's International Thesaurus, 3d ed. Lists synonyms; groups words into categories; detailed index.

YEARBOOKS AND ALMANACS   Yearbooks and almanacs present current facts or statistics. A yearbook is an annual publication supplementing a larger publication and bringing that publication up to date. An almanac supplies lists, charts, and statistics about its subjects.

World Almanac. Includes statistics about government, population, sports, and many other subjects, as well as a chronology of events of the previous year. Published annually since 1868.

Information Please Almanac. Supplements the *World Almanac* (each work includes information unavailable in the other) and is somewhat easier to read. Published annually since 1947.

Facts on File. A news digest with index. Covering 1940 to the present, this work offers digests of important news stories from metropolitan dailies. Published weekly, *Facts on File* serves as a kind of current encyclopedia.

Editorials on File. Reprints important editorials from American and Canadian newspapers. Editorials represent both sides of controversial issues and are preceded by a summary of the principles involved.

ATLASES An atlas contains maps and charts and often includes historical, cultural, political, and economic information.
Rand McNally Cosmopolitan World Atlas. A modern and extremely legible medium-sized atlas.

Encyclopaedia Britannica World Atlas. Uses *Rand McNally Cosmopolitan* maps and includes geographical summaries and information on world population distribution.

The Times Atlas of the World, five volumes, John Bartholomew, ed. Published by *The London Times,* this is considered one of the best large world atlases. Includes inset maps for many cities. Very accurate and attractive maps throughout.

Shepherd, William Robert. *Historical Atlas,* 9th ed. Covers period from 2000 B.C. to 1955. Excellent maps showing war campaigns and development of commerce.

GENERAL BIBLIOGRAPHIES General bibliographies list books available in a number of fields.
Books in Print. A helpful index of authors and titles of every book in print in the United States. *The Subject Guide to Books in Print* indexes books according to subject area. *Paperbound Books in Print* is an index to all currently available paperbacks.

The Bibliographic Index. A tool for locating bibliographies, this index is particularly useful for researching a subject that is not well covered in other indexes. Provides references to long bibliographies in books and brief ones in periodical articles.

BIOGRAPHICAL DICTIONARIES AND INDEXES Specialized biographical reference books contain information about people's lives and sometimes about their times. Bibliographic listings are often included.

res 36b

Living Persons

Who's Who in America. Published every other year, this dictionary gives very brief biographical data and addresses of prominent living Americans.

Who's Who. Concise biographical facts about notable living English men and women.

Current Biography. Informal articles on living people of many nationalities; articles often include portraits.

Twentieth-Century Authors. Informal biographies of contemporary authors of many nationalities. Portraits and lists of authors' writings included.

Deceased Persons

Dictionary of American Biography. Considered the best of American biographical dictionaries. Offers articles on over thirteen thousand deceased Americans who have made contributions in all fields.

Dictionary of National Biography. The most important reference work for English biography.

Webster's Biographical Dictionary. Perhaps the most widely used biographical reference work. Includes people from all periods and places.

American Authors 1600–1900; European Authors 1000–1900; British Authors Before 1800. These works provide biographical data on authors who wrote before the twentieth century.

Who Was When? A Dictionary of Contemporaries. A reference source for historical biography; covers 500 B.C. through the early 1970's.

Who Was Who in America, Historical Volume, 1607–1896. Entries on deceased Americans; supplemented by *Who Was Who in America 1897–1960*. These volumes, though useful, do contain some inaccuracies.

**res
36b**

(2)   Doing a computer search

Perhaps the fastest way to locate relevant information is to do a **computer search.** Such a search enables you to scan a number of **data bases**—electronic indexes—that list thousands of bibliographic sources. All data bases contain bibliographic citations, and some contain abstracts that summarize entire books and articles. Not all data bases are equally useful. Social science and natural science data bases, for example, are currently more extensive than those in the humanities. Ask your librarian which data bases would be appropriate for your subject matter and which journals and periodicals the relevant data bases contain. If certain important journals are not included, you will also have to search the print indexes (see 36b.3).

In most college libraries the librarian carries out the computer search. However, many libraries have or will soon have equipment that enables students to do their own searches. Whatever system applies in your library, understanding the following general guidelines for carrying out a computer search should make retrieving information easier.

CHOOSING APPROPRIATE DATA BASES The first step in doing a computer search is determining which data bases include the information you need. Many colleges subscribe to information services that have access to hundreds of data bases. By reviewing the data bases available, you and your librarian can decide which ones are appropriate to your research.

NARROWING YOUR TOPIC TO KEY WORDS Before you begin a computer search, you must define your topic in one or more **key words** (sometimes called *descriptors*). These words are your entry into the data base, for they enable the computer to call up articles that contain your key words in their titles or abstracts. For this reason, the more precise your key words are, the more specific the information you get. For example, if your topic were "teaching science fiction," the key words *science* OR *teaching* would not be helpful to you, for they would yield thousands of references, most of them irrelevant. *Science fiction* would yield several hundred—still too many to be helpful. *Teaching* AND *science fiction*, however, would yield about thirty references—a manageable number.

A list of key words and phrases accompanies each data base. Some information services issue a printed book, called a **thesaurus,** that lists these words. Other data bases contain a **dictionary** that can be called up on the video terminal. By consulting the thesaurus or the dictionary, you can determine which key words best describe your topic. If the first key word or words you have chosen do not yield enough information, you will have to try different ones or different combinations to search your topic. For material about J. D. Smith, for example, you should use the key words *John D. Smith* AND *John David Smith* as well as *J. D. Smith.*

res
36b

ENTERING KEY WORDS INTO THE COMPUTER Once you have entered your key words, the computer will indicate how many citations they elicit. You can then decide if you want a printout of these citations or if you want to narrow your search. Keep in mind that you can search each key word individually, or you can examine key words in combination. By entering the combination *science fiction* AND *teaching,* for instance, you get only citations that contain *both* key words (e.g., "Teaching Children Reading Using Science Fiction"). By entering the combination *science fiction* OR *teaching,* you get citations that contain *either* key word (e.g., "Children Create Using Science Fiction" or "Science Fiction and History").

SELECTING THE FORMAT YOU WANT FOR EACH CITATION Before you print out the citations, you must select the format you prefer. You can command the computer to print just the bibliographic citation, which gives the author, title, and journal reference, or you can command the fullest format, which gives you, in addition to the above, an abstract, publishing information, reprint costs, and other key words. Between these two extremes a few other formats are usually available. Because computer time is costly, select the format that gives you only the information you need.

res
36b

MAKING A PRINTOUT You can print out all the citations, but if there are too many you may choose to print out only certain years—all entries between 1985 and 1986, for example. In the printout for a paper on teaching science fiction (see Figure 6), the student requested abstracts of all citations containing the key words *science fiction* AND *teaching.*

▶

EXERCISE 2

If you have access to computer-search facilities, answer the following questions.

1. Which data base would you use to search the topic "architectural innovations of the Brooklyn Bridge"?
2. Which key words would you use to search this topic? Use a thesaurus or dictionary to help you decide.
3. In what form would you enter the words into the computer?
4. How many citations are there under each key word or key word combination?
5. Bring to class a printout containing five useful citations or abstracts.

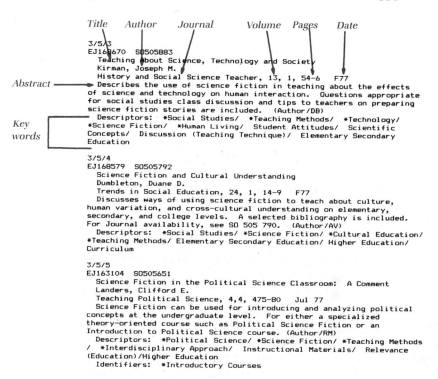

FIGURE 6

(3) Using print indexes

Many periodicals are indexed in data bases (see 36b.2), and their number is growing. But many articles in newspapers, magazines, and scholarly journals are indexed only in bound volumes or paperbound supplements kept in your library's reference section. A **periodical index** lists, by subject, articles from a selected group of magazines, newspapers, or scholarly journals. In most indexes entries are arranged according to subject. The key to the abbreviations at the front of the volume enables you to use the index and gives all the information you need to compile your documentation and list of works cited. The entry from the *Humanities Index* (see Figure 7) tells you how to find an article.

Once you have this bibliographic information, consult the special catalog that lists the journal, newspaper, and magazine holdings of your library. The card illustrated in Figure 8 is typical of those found in your library's **periodical catalog**. As this card

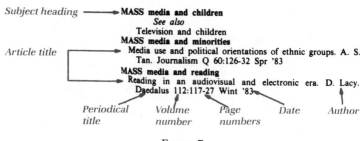

Subject heading ⟶ **MASS media and children**
See also
Television and children
MASS media and minorities
Article title — ⟶ Media use and political orientations of ethnic groups. A. S. Tan. Journalism Q 60:126-32 Spr '83
MASS media and reading
Reading in an audiovisual and electronic era. D. Lacy. Daedalus 112:117-27 Wint '83

Periodical title | *Volume number* | *Page numbers* | *Date* | *Author*

FIGURE 7

indicates, libraries house periodicals in yearly bound volumes or in current issues located in the periodical section of your library. The words *microfiche, microprint,* or *microfilm* tell you that the periodicals have been stored photographically.

GENERAL INDEXES   Various indexes list different types of periodicals—popular or semipopular magazines, scholarly journals, and so on. Here are several general indexes that many college students find useful.

Readers' Guide to Periodical Literature
The *Readers' Guide* lists articles that appear in over 150 magazines for general readers. Good for current views of history, social science, and some scientific topics, it does have limitations. Popular articles tend to oversimplify complex issues, leaving out data you might need, so you should supplement this material with information from more scholarly works. Appearing in yearly volumes and paperbound supplements, citations are listed and cross-referenced under subject headings.

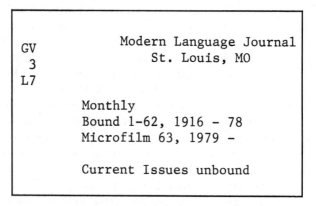

```
GV                    Modern Language Journal
 3                         St. Louis, MO
L7

                   Monthly
                   Bound 1-62, 1916 - 78
                   Microfilm 63, 1979 -

                   Current Issues unbound
```

FIGURE 8

The New York Times Index

The New York Times is an excellent and reliable record of current events. In addition to news, it contains feature-length articles on issues of general interest. *The New York Times Index* lists major articles and features of *The Times* since 1851 by year or years. To find articles on a subject, locate the volume for the appropriate year. Articles with short summaries are listed alphabetically by subject. Supplements are published every two weeks. If your library subscribes to *The New York Times* microfilm service, you have access to every issue of *The Times* back to 1851. Articles give a contemporary view of a wide variety of subjects—everything from business and politics to literature and the arts.

Book Review Digest

To determine whether a book is a reliable source, look at *Book Review Digest*. Containing selected excerpts from reviews of books when they were published, annual volumes list entries according to title and author. Look up a book in the volume with the same year of publication or the next year's volume in case the book was not reviewed in its year of publication.

Book Review Digest lets you see the initial reactions of critics to books published as far back as 1905. This gives you some insight into the critical climate of a book's times, and it also helps you judge whether a book is informative and accurate.

res
36b

Humanities Index and Social Sciences Index

Before 1974 these two indexes appeared under one title as the *Social Sciences and Humanities Index*. Now a separate publication, the *Humanities Index* lists articles from 259 scholarly journals in areas such as archeology, history, language, literary and political criticism, and religion. The *Social Sciences Index* lists articles from 265 scholarly journals that focus on economics, medicine, psychology, and sociology, for example. Both indexes follow the same format as the *Readers' Guide*. Entries are arranged alphabetically according to author and subject in the volume corresponding to the year in which the article appeared.

SPECIFIC INDEXES AND COLLECTIONS OF ABSTRACTS   For detailed information on scholarly work done in a specialized area, consult an index devoted to that field. Your instructor or your librarian will guide you in finding these. Here is a sampling of specialized indexes that illustrates the variety available.

Applied Science and Technology Index

A monthly publication that lists articles from over 300 periodicals.

Biological Abstracts
An abstract journal that summarizes selected articles in subjects
like microbiology, immunology, public health, and basic medical
sciences. BASIC *(Biological Abstracts Subjects in Context)*, a com-
putermade subject index to each issue, is also available.

Business Periodicals Index
A monthly publication covering business and related topics from
1958 to the present. Lists information under subject or company
name.

Chemical Abstracts
Includes abstracts of current periodicals and books. Excellent in-
dexing system.

Education Index
Contains listings for articles in 230 journals.

Essay and General Literature Index
Indexes essays and articles in periodicals and books by author,
subject, and sometimes title.

General Science Index
Lists articles pertaining to all scientific subjects; a basic tool for
general information on the sciences.

Historical Abstracts
Lists articles in over 2,000 periodicals and tells where to find
source material.

**MLA International Bibliography of Books and Articles on the
Modern Languages and Literature**
Lists articles and books on language and literature. Published by
the Modern Language Association.

Psychological Abstracts
Abstracts of books and articles in the field published since 1935.
Includes subject and author index.

res
36b

CITATION INDEXES   The **citation indexes** deserve special attention. Such an index lists all articles published in a given year
that mention a particular article. Seeing which articles influence
other researchers can help you to identify issues to discuss and
evaluate in your own essay. Citation indexes exist for the humanities, the sciences, and the social sciences.

    To find information in a citation index, you can look up the
author of the original article, the author of the article in which
the original article is mentioned, or the subject.

ANNUAL REVIEWS   Annual reviews summarize scholarly work done in a field. They give an overview of advances that have occurred during the year. Annual reviews are published regularly in the social sciences and the natural sciences.

BIBLIOGRAPHIC INDEX   This work lists books and articles that contain bibliographies. Entries are organized under subject headings and are easy to locate. The articles and books listed in this index can help you compile a working bibliography (see 39b.2).

This index only points you in the direction of information, however. You still have to find the book or article that contains the bibliography, evaluate the entries, and then track down the sources that seem useful.

(4)   Finding books in the card catalog

All the books in your college library are listed in the **card catalog.** Recently some libraries have installed computerized systems that allow students to call up catalog entries on video terminals. Others have transferred catalog cards to microfiche—a sheet of microfilm, containing rows of microimages of catalog cards, that you can scan on a viewing device. For the near future, however, most college libraries will continue to list their holdings in print form in the drawers of the card catalog.

Libraries have either a single catalog that interfiles author, title, and subject cards or two separate catalogs, one for author-title cards and another for subject cards. (See Figure 9 for examples of author, title, and subject cards.) Books in the author-title file are alphabetized by author or by title; books in the subject catalog are alphabetized by subject.

Generally, it is most efficient to approach the card catalog with specific authors or titles in mind. But if you have not found what you need using other resources, you might try using the subject headings to locate books about your topic.

If you have trouble thinking of subject headings or if you want to be thorough, you can consult the index volume called *Library of Congress Subject Headings*, which is kept at the reference desk. Also keep in mind that the card catalog itself contains cross-reference cards (see Figure 10) that refer you to related subject headings. By using them, you can find more material related to your subject.

res
36b

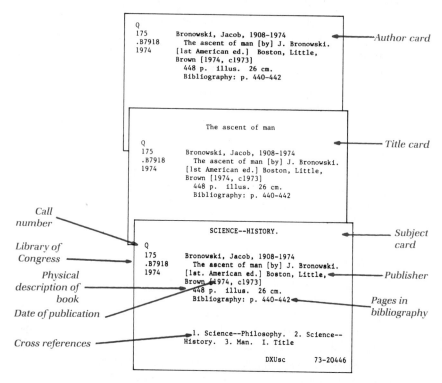

```
Q
175        Bronowski, Jacob, 1908-1974
.B7918        The ascent of man [by] J. Bronowski.
1974        [1st American ed.]  Boston, Little,
           Brown [1974, c1973]
              448 p.  illus.  26 cm.
              Bibliography: p. 440-442
```
Author card

```
              The ascent of man

Q
175        Bronowski, Jacob, 1908-1974
.B7918        The ascent of man [by] J. Bronowski.
1974        [1st American ed.] Boston, Little,
           Brown [1974, c1973]
              448 p.  illus.  26 cm.
              Bibliography: p. 440-442
```
Title card

```
              SCIENCE--HISTORY.

Q
175        Bronowski, Jacob, 1908-1974
.B7918        The ascent of man [by] J. Bronowski.
1974        [1st. American ed.] Boston, Little,
           Brown [1974, c1973]
              448 p.  illus.  26 cm.
              Bibliography: p. 440-442


           1. Science--Philosophy.  2. Science--
           History.  3. Man.  I. Title

                             DXUsc      73-20446
```
Subject card
Publisher
Pages in bibliography

Call number
Library of Congress
Physical description of book
Date of publication
Cross references

FIGURE 9

To locate a book in the stacks, you need its **call number,** which appears in the upper left of its catalog card (Figure 9). College libraries use the Dewey Decimal System, the Library of Congress System, or both to classify books. The Dewey Decimal

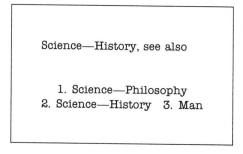

```
Science—History, see also


         1. Science—Philosophy
      2. Science—History   3. Man
```

FIGURE 10

System uses a number code to classify books according to subject. It is being replaced in most libraries, however, by the more flexible Library of Congress System, which uses a combination of numbers and letters to identify subject areas.

The call number refers you to the general area of the library that houses books on your subject. The same call number that appears on the catalog card is written on the spine of the book. When you find a book you need, look through the books shelved nearby. Browsing is not in itself an effective research technique, but as part of a focused research strategy it can sometimes yield good results.

If you cannot find a book, go to the librarian for help. The book may be out, on reserve, or held in a different section of the library. If it has been checked out, the librarian will tell you when it is due back and, in many cases, will notify the borrower that someone else needs it.

(5) Using special library services

res
36b

Your most valuable resource is your librarian, a trained professional whose business it is to know how to locate information. Before you begin any complicated research project, you should ask your librarian what relevant research sources and services the library offers.

If you need a book or article that the library does not own, you can ask your librarian to arrange an interlibrary loan. This service may, however, take more time than you have.

Your librarian can also help you locate special collections of books, manuscripts, or documents housed nearby in the community. Churches, specialized libraries, government agencies, ethnic societies, historical trusts, and museums sometimes have books and articles that you cannot find anywhere else. Your librarian may be able to get you permission to see them.

▶
EXERCISE 3

What library research sources would you consult to find the following information?

1. A book review of Maxine Hong Kingston's *China Men* (1980)
2. Biographical information about the American anthropologist Margaret Mead
3. Books about Margaret Mead and her work

4. Information about the theories of Albert Einstein
5. Whether your college library has *The Human Use of Human Beings* by Norbert Wiener
6. How many pages there are in *On Death and Dying* by Elisabeth Kübler-Ross and how long the bibliography is
7. Where you could find other books on death and dying
8. Where you could find other books by Elisabeth Kübler-Ross
9. Articles about Walt Whitman's *Leaves of Grass*
10. Whether *Leaves of Grass* is presently available in a Norton Critical Edition
11. An article describing work done in particle physics in 1985
12. Whether your library has *Yale Review* 35 (September 1945)
13. The reaction of the country to Charles Lindbergh's flight across the Atlantic Ocean
14. Information about the New York clothing industry in the late nineteenth century
15. All the articles that cited the article "A Structure for Deoxyribose Nucleic Acid" by J. D. Watson and F. H. C. Crick in 1953

36c Gathering Information Outside the Library

res
36c

By relying exclusively on the library for research materials, you may ignore important sources of more current information. Public service organizations, lobbies, and government agencies have available a wealth of current data. People who work in a field or who have a unique view of a situation are also excellent sources. Your problem as a researcher is finding these sources and obtaining information from them.

(1) Finding organizations

Several indexes can help you locate organizations that offer literature to interested parties. *Public Affairs Information Services* lists magazines, journals, and government publications that focus on public issues and public policy. The *Monthly Catalog of U.S. Government Publications* tells where to find information in many government publications. Each issue contains a subject index. The United States Government Printing Office makes available most of these reports and public service pamphlets. The *PAC Directory* lists political action committees, which often sponsor research and compile reports for distribution to anyone interested in their cause. Local businesses, chambers of commerce, and corporate public information departments are some other possible sources of information. Finally, the *Directory of Registered Lobbyists and Lobbyist Organizations*, although slightly outdated, can give you a number of leads to pursue. Remember that the information you get from political action committees, lobbies, and even some government agencies is most likely slanted, and you should balance it with further research on other points of view.

(2)   Finding people

A number of excellent guides to people who are experts in various fields are available in the reference section of your library. Most of these guides focus on people in a particular area of endeavor.

> *Who's Who Among Black Americans*
> *Who's Who and Where in Women's Studies*
> *Who's Who in American Art*
> *Who's Who in American Education*
> *Who's Who in American Politics*
> *American Men and Women of Science*
> *Biographical Directory of the American Psychological Association*
> *Contemporary Authors*
> *Directory of the Modern Language Association*

**res
36c**

Once you have identified someone who can help you, you may want to write to that person requesting the information you want. If, after consulting your instructor, you feel that to do so is appropriate, write a letter explaining why you need this person's help. (The guidelines for this type of letter appear in 42f.)

(3)   Conducting an interview

Interviews allow you to ask well-prepared questions and to follow up on the answers if necessary. You might ask for biographical information, a firsthand account of an event, or the views of an expert on a particular subject. Interviews often give you material that you cannot get by any other means.

Your interview questions must elicit detailed, useful responses, and therefore you must design them carefully. *Leading questions*, for instance, make some people defensive, and *vague questions* can confuse them. *Dead-end questions*—questions that call for yes/no answers, for example—yield limited information. As the following questions illustrate, the way you phrase a question determines the response to it.

> The city intends to spend 2 billion dollars over the next ten years to rehabilitate the port area. Do you support this? Why or why not? (good question)
>
> Are you against the city's innovative plans to rehabilitate the port area? (leading question)
>
> What are your feelings about the port area? (vague question)
>
> Do you think the port area should be developed? (dead-end question; likely to elicit a yes/no answer)

The success or failure of an interview often depends on how you prepare for it. First, learn something about your topic and about the person you are interviewing. Before interviewing the author of a new book, for example, you should have read it yourself.

Next, prepare a list of questions tailored to guide you through your interview and to fit within your time limit. It is better to have a few questions that can be answered in depth than many that can be answered only superficially.

The kinds of questions you ask depend on the kind of information you are after. **Open-ended** questions elicit general information and allow a respondent great flexibility in answering.

> How was this neighborhood's popularity different forty years ago?
>
> Do you think that students today are motivated? Why or why not?
>
> If you could change something in your life, what would it be?

Closed-ended questions elicit specific information. They enable you to zero in on a subject and flush out specific details.

> Has your family become more or less religious over the past ten years? How do you account for this?
>
> What is the most important health benefit of your findings concerning Vitamin C?
>
> How much money did the government's cost-cutting programs actually save?

Have a pencil and paper with you for the interview. Allow the person you are interviewing to complete an answer before you ask another question. Take notes, but continue to pay atten-

res
36c

tion to your respondent while you do so. If you want to use a tape recorder, get the person's permission first. The reactions of the person you are interviewing can lead you to further questions, so pay attention to them. Do not hesitate to deviate from your prepared question to follow up a particularly interesting response. Finally, after the interview, send a brief note thanking your subject for his or her time and cooperation.

▶

EXERCISE 4

Use the resources of your library to help you answer the following questions. Cite the source or sources of your answers.

1. What government publication could give you information about how to solar heat your home?
2. What government agency could you contact to find out what is being done to help the aging get proper nutrition?
3. At what address could you contact Bruce Evans, a young American artist?
4. At what university does the astronomer Carl Sagan teach?
5. What organizations could you contact to find out what is being done to prevent the killing of wolves in North America?
6. How could you get current information about the tobacco lobby?
7. What government agency could tell you what government services are available to resident aliens?
8. At what address could you contact Harold Bloom, a scholar who does work on nineteenth-century English literature?
9. Is there a government pamphlet that gives information about buying a new car?
10. How could you get current information about the Peace Corps?

res
36c

▶

EXERCISE 5

Assume you could interview the following four singers on the current status of popular music in America. Make a list of ten questions that you would ask each one, and indicate whether the questions are open or closed. Before making your list, read an article about each singer in a specialized encyclopedia of music.

1. Stevie Wonder   3. Bruce Springsteen
2. Charlie Daniels   4. Tina Turner

37

Working with Source Material

Once you have located sources of information for your paper, your next step is to read and evaluate them (see 39b.2) and to take notes on 4" × 6" cards (see 39c.2). When you write your paper, you will use these notes to support your points and to help you evaluate the work of others.

37a Taking Notes

When taking notes, experienced researchers do not simply copy a source word for word. They refine and interpret material from the very beginning. By doing so, they cut down on the amount of information that they will have to work with, thereby making the job of writing easier.

In general you can transfer source material into your notes in three ways. You can *summarize, paraphrase,* or *quote.* A good paper uses each of these techniques and blends them skillfully.

(1) Writing a summary

You summarize when you want to capture the general idea of a source. A **summary**, sometimes called a précis, is a brief restatement in your own words of the main idea of a passage, article, or entire book. Usually a summary will omit the examples, asides, and analogies that authors use to illustrate their points and to interest their readers. When you summarize, be careful not to leave out important points or to misrepresent an author's intention. You want to remain faithful to the meaning and spirit of the original. For this reason your summary should include none of your own ideas or observations.

Your summary will not be useful if you do not understand your sources. As you read, identify the topic sentence of each paragraph, and look for headings or key words that will help clarify the meaning. After you have finished reading, try to state the main idea, including all key concepts, in a sentence or two. For long passages, make an outline to clarify the progression of ideas. This approach may sound like a lot of work, but in the long run it can help you write a clear and accurate summary.

Following is an original source and a summary that appeared in a student research paper. Notice that the summary is much shorter than the original and gives just the main idea of the passage.

ORIGINAL SOURCE: Barasch, Moshe. "The City." *Dictionary of the History of Ideas*. Ed. Philip P. Wiener. 4 vols. New York: Scribner's, 1973. 1: 427.

The religious and cosmic symbolism of the city reaches back to the early stages of human culture. It seems that in none of the great archaic cultures have cities been understood simply as settlements, arbitrarily established at a certain place and in a given form; both the placing and the shape of the cities were conceived as related, in a hidden or manifested form, to the structure of the universe. The most common form of this symbolism is the belief that the cities have astral or divine prototypes, or even descended from heaven; sometimes they were believed to have a relationship to the underworld. In both cases, however, they refer to an extraterrestrial reality.

res
37a

SUMMARY: In ancient times cities had symbolic significance. They were seen, in part, as having a divine form—perhaps related to a heavenly or, less commonly, underworld counterpart.

After you have written your summary, check to make sure that it conveys the meaning and spirit of the original. Make certain that you have not missed any important points or inadvertently used any of the author's exact words. Of course you can use *some* words from a source. As a rule, you can use the same proper nouns, simple words, or technical terms as your source without documentation. Read your summary one last time to see if you can condense it further, and make sure that you have documentation to indicate the source you have summarized. If you have done a careful job, your summary will highlight the important points in a source and include no unimportant ones.

(2)   Writing a paraphrase

You **paraphrase** when you need detailed information from specific passages in a source, but not the exact words (see 37a.3 for guidelines concerning the use of quotations). A paraphrase is a detailed restatement in your own words of the content of a passage. It not only indicates its main points, but also follows its order and emphasis. Often a paraphrase will quote brief phrases from the original to convey its tone or viewpoint. Usually a paraphrase is briefer than the original, but not always. Keep in mind that when paraphrasing you convey the *author's* ideas, not your own. Keep your own analyses, interpretations, and evaluations separate.

When paraphrasing you are able to capture a fairly complete sense of an author's ideas without using the author's words. For this reason, paraphrase is especially useful for explaining technical material to a general audience. Paraphrase is also useful for conveying the essense of dialogue or for reporting complex material in easily understood terms. Moreover, the very act of putting someone else's ideas into your own words helps you to gain a better understanding of what has been said. It is therefore a good idea to develop your skill in this area by paraphrasing important material as soon as you finish reading it.

Below is a paraphrase of a passage that discusses a player's state of mind during a video game. Notice that although the paraphrase follows the order and emphasis of the original, and even includes a key phrase from the source, its wording and sentence structure are very different.

**res
37a**

ORIGINAL SOURCE: Turkle, Sherry. *The Second Self: Computers and the Human Spirit.* New York: Simon & Schuster, 1984. 83–84.

> When you play a video game you enter into the world of the programmers who made it. You have to do more than identify with a character on the screen. You must act for it. Identification through action has a special kind of hold. Like playing a sport, it puts people into a highly focused, and highly charged state of mind. For many people, what is being pursued in the video game is not just a score, but an altered state.
>
> The pilot of a race car does not dare to take . . . attention off the road. The imperative of total concentration is part of the high. Video games demand this same level of attention. They can give people the feeling of being close

to the edge because, as in a dangerous situation, there is no time for rest and the consequences of wandering attention feel dire. With pinball, a false move can be recuperated. The machine can be shaken, the ball repositioned. In a video game, the program has no tolerance for error, no margin of safety. Players experience their every movement as instantly translated into game action. The game is relentless in its demand that all other time stop and in its demand that the player take full responsibility for every act, a point that players often sum up by the phrase "One false move and you're dead."

Executives, accountants, and surgeons stand behind the junior-high-schoolers in games arcades. For people under pressure total concentration is a form of relaxation.

PARAPHRASE: The programmer controls the world of video games. Video games enable a player to merge with a character or object that is part of the game. This identification draws a player into the game. Like sports, video games put a player into an emotionally charged "altered state" that is a central part of the game.

res
37a

Because video games demand a high degree of involvement, they can simulate the thrill of participating in a dangerous activity without the risks. Unlike pinball machines, video games provide no time to rest and no opportunity to correct errors in judgment. Every move a player makes appears at once on the screen. The game forces a player to adapt to its rules and to act carefully.

Many people with high-pressure jobs use video games as a way to unwind.

After you have written your paraphrase, make certain that you have avoided the phrasing of the original and that you have put quotation marks around any terms taken from your source. Remember to document the paraphrase itself, as well any quotations (see Chapter 38). Make certain that your paraphrase contains all the important points of the original. Finally, insert any transitional words or phrases that are needed to make your paraphrase flow smoothly.

(3)   Recording quotations

You **quote** when you feel that an author's exact words will enhance your paper. When you quote, you copy an author's remarks just as they appear, word for word and punctuation mark for punctuation mark. Pay particular attention to spelling, capitalization, and punctuation. When recording quotations, do not inadvertently leave out quotation marks. You may even want to circle them to be sure that you notice them when you transfer them from your notes to your paper. If a quotation continues onto another note card, clearly mark where it begins and ends so that you do not confuse it with your own words later.

37b   Integrating Source Material into Your Writing

res 37b

As a rule, avoid including numerous direct quotations in your papers. When used indiscriminately, they break the flow of your discussion and give the impression that your paper is nothing more than a collection of other people's words. Quote only when something vital would be lost otherwise, and use only those quotations that support your points and provide a perspective that contributes to the effectiveness of your presentation. Before you include any quotation, ask yourself if your purpose would be better served by using your own words.

These three guidelines will help you determine whether you should use a quotation.

> Quote when a source's wording or phrasing is so distinctive that to summarize or paraphrase would diminish its impact. In such cases it is best to let the source speak for itself.
> Quote when a source's words lend authority to your presentation. If an author is a recognized expert on your subject, his or her words are as convincing as expert testimony at a trial.
> Quote when an author's words are so concise that a paraphrase would create a long, clumsy, or incoherent phrase or would change the meaning of the original.

(1)   Integrating quotations

Like every other element, quotations must be smoothly woven into the fabric of your discussion—introduced by identifying phrases, embedded into sentences, and commented upon afterward. In other words, they must be placed in context. Consider this passage.

> For the Amish, the public school system represents a problem. "A serious problem confronting Amish society from the viewpoint of the Amish themselves is the threat of absorption into mass society through the values promoted in the public school system" (Hostetler 193).

The direct quotation is awkwardly dropped into the passage. It could be worked into the sentence this way.

> For the Amish the public school system represents "the threat of absorption into mass society" (Hostetler 193).

Or you could use a **running acknowledgment,** where you introduce the source of the quotation into the text.

> John A. Hostetler points out that the Amish feel that the public school system threatens them with "absorption into the mass society. . ." (193).

You could also combine quotation and paraphrase, quoting only a significant word or two and paraphrasing the rest.

**res
37b**

> According to John A. Hostetler one of the most serious problems that the Amish face is a "threat of absorption" posed by the public schools (193).

Just as you should vary your use of quotation, paraphrase, and summary, you should also experiment with different methods of integrating quoted material into your paper. As a rule, the running acknowledgment is most effective when you want to call attention to the author's name because his or her expertise in the area you are researching strengthens your paper's credibility. You should vary the verbs you use for attribution; for example, you can use *suggests, observes, notes, concludes, believes,* or any of several other more precise alternatives to *says.* You can also vary the placement of the identifying phrase, putting it at the beginning or at the end of the quoted material, or even in the middle.

> "A serious problem confronting Amish society from the viewpoint of the Amish themselves," observes Hostetler, "is the threat of absorption into mass society through the values promoted in the public school system" (193).

If the verb tense of the quotation is not consistent with the tense of your sentence, you may need to change it somewhat. If you alter words, *you must acknowledge your changes* by enclosing them in brackets.

AWKWARD: The Amish were traditionally opposed to the modern industrialized society around them. "They are a slow-changing, distinctive cultural group who place a premium on cultural stability rather than change" (Hostetler vii).

REVISED: The Amish were traditionally opposed to the modern industrialized society around them and tended toward "cultural stability rather than change" (Hostetler vii). (words omitted from the original quotation)

REVISED: The Amish were traditionally opposed to the modern industrialized society around them: "They [were] a slow-changing, distinctive cultural group who [placed] a premium on cultural stability rather than change" (Hostetler vii). (verb tense changed to match the paper's tense)

**res
37b**

You can reduce the length of quotations by substituting an ellipsis mark for the deleted words (see 30o).

ORIGINAL: "Not only have the Amish built and staffed their own elementary and vocational schools, but they have gradually organized on local, state, and national levels to cope with the task of educating their children" (Hostetler 206).

REVISED: "Not only have the Amish built and staffed their own elementary and vocational schools, but they have gradually organized . . . to cope with the task of educating their children" (Hostetler 206).

Occasionally, you may want to use a quotation consisting of more than four lines of text. Set off this quotation from the text by indenting it ten spaces from the margin. Double-space, and do not use quotation marks. You usually introduce a long quotation with a colon, but sometimes the context may call for different punctuation. If you are quoting a single paragraph, do not indent the first line (see 29e.2).

According to Hostetler, the Amish were not always hostile to public education:

> The one-room rural elementary school served the
> Amish community well in a number of ways. As long

as it was a public school, it stood midway between the
Amish community and the world. Its influence was tol-
erable, depending upon the degree of influence the
Amish were able to bring to the situation. As long as it
was small, rural, and near the community, a reasonable influence could be maintained over its worldly
character (196).

Use long quotations when you want to convey a sense of an
author's style or thought process. Keep in mind, however, that
long quotations can be extremely distracting. They interrupt
your argument and, when used excessively, give the impression
that you have relied far too heavily on the words of others.

▶

EXERCISE 1

Assume that in preparation for a paper on the topic "The effects of the
rise of suburbia," you read the following passage from the book *Great
Expectations: America and the Baby Boom Generation* by Landon Y.
Jones. In your notes write a one-paragraph summary of the passage.
Then, paraphrase one paragraph. Finally, make a note that combines
paraphrase with quotation, making certain to quote only when appropriate.

res
37b

>   As an internal migration, the settling of the suburbs was
> phenomenal. In the twenty years from 1950 to 1970, the popula-
> tion of the suburbs doubled from 36 million to 72 million. No less
> than 83 percent of the total population growth in the United States
> during the 1950's was in the suburbs, which were growing fifteen
> times faster than any other segment of the country. As people
> packed and moved, the national mobility rate leaped by 50 per-
> cent. The only other comparable influx was the wave of European
> immigrants to the United States around the turn of the century.
> But as *Fortune* pointed out, more people moved to the suburbs
> every year than had ever arrived on Ellis Island.
>   By now, bulldozers were churning up dust storms as they
> cleared the land for housing developments. More than a million
> acres of farmland were plowed under every year during the 1950's.
> Millions of apartment-dwelling parents with two children were
> suddenly realizing that two children could be doubled up in a
> spare bedroom, but a third child cried loudly for something more.
> The proportion of new houses with three or more bedrooms, in
> fact, rose from one-third in 1947 to three-quarters in 1954. The
> necessary *Lebensraum* could only be found in the suburbs. There
> was a housing shortage, but young couples armed with VA and

FHA loans built their dream homes with easy credit and free spending habits that were unthinkable to the baby-boom grand-parents, who shook their heads with the Depression still fresh in their memories. Of the 13 million homes built in the decade before 1958, 11 million of them—or 85 percent—were built in the sub-urbs. Home ownership rose 50 percent between 1940 and 1950, and another 50 percent by 1960. By then, one-fourth of *all* housing in the United States had been built in the fifties. For the first time, more Americans owned homes than rented them.

We were becoming a land of gigantic nurseries. The biggest were built by Abraham Levitt, the son of poor Russian-Jewish immigrants, who had originally built houses for the Navy during the war. The first of three East Coast Levittowns went up on the potato fields of Long Island. Exactly $7900—or $60 a month and no money down—bought you a Monopoly-board bungalow with four rooms, attic, washing machine, outdoor barbecue, and a tele-vision set built into the wall. The 17,447 units eventually became home to 82,000 people, many of whom were pregnant or wanted to be. In a typical story on the suburban explosion, one magazine breathlessly described a volleyball game of nine couples in which no less than five of the women were expecting.

(2)   Interpreting source material

A research paper usually does more than present summaries and paraphrases of your sources. It also contains passages of interpretation in which you present your conclusions and sup-port them with your own ideas and with the ideas of others, recorded in your notes (see 39f.2).

An **interpretation**, sometimes called a critique, is a system-atic evaluation of a source. When interpreting source material, you put it into perspective, comment on its usefulness, or ex-plain what it means. An interpretation involves more than saying that an article is "interesting" or that a discussion "sheds light on a subject"; to be effective, it must clearly present the standards by which you judge your material. When they read your interpreta-tion, your readers must be able to understand the thought proc-esses that led you to your conclusions.

Sometimes you are able to make critical judgments based on personal knowledge of a subject. Often, however, your re-search yields the information on which you base your interpreta-tion. As you read, you begin to develop basic assumptions about your subject. Perhaps several of the authors whose works you read share a set of ideas. Or perhaps several authors disagree.

You will find, however, that there are no ready-made criteria by which you can judge your sources. Writing a good interpretation takes time and practice, and it also involves taking some risks. After all, it requires you to judge other people's ideas. To do so you must read widely and consider varying points of view; you must then isolate specific points in your source and decide how valid you think they are. Having arrived at your conclusions, you must support your judgments with references to the author's words, with personal insights, or with material that others have written about your subject.

Following is an interpretation of a short passage about the movie director John Ford. In it the student isolates important points from his source and counters them with his own judgments.

ORIGINAL SOURCE: Bogdanovich, Peter. "The Cowboy and the American West . . . as Directed by John Ford." *Esquire* Dec. 1983: 423.

In his later years, nevertheless, Ford came to be considered close to a reactionary, because throughout the Sixties, while the chic American cultural fashion became increasingly . . . antimilitarist, antipolice, and antifamily, Ford continued to make pictures with men in uniform, fighting the chivalrous fight, honoring the women and the way of life they protected and cherished.

res 37b

INTERPRETATION: In a recent article in *Esquire* Peter Bogdanovich evaluates the career of the famous director, John Ford. Although Bogdanovich is correct in saying that Ford was seen by some in the 1960's as reactionary, he simplifies the situation by ignoring the fact that Ford has always enjoyed great popularity, and in recent years has become something of a cult figure. Bogdanovich seems to accept the critical position that Ford glorifies the military and uses violence as a ready solution to complex problems. But when these themes occur in Ford's films—and they do not occur in all of them—they are usually in service of a much larger theme: the ability of the individual to affect events. Films like *The Informer* (1935), *The Grapes of Wrath* (1940), *The Quiet Man* (1952), and *Mister Roberts* (1962) demonstrate the versatility of Ford's vision and his ability to move beyond the narrow limits that Bogdanovich discusses.

The student who wrote the preceding interpretation evaluated his source using his own knowledge. But as already indicated, often you will have to use research to help you analyze and evaluate the ideas of others—when you are writing about works of literature or controversial subjects, for example. If you do use the ideas of others, remember to clearly identify ideas that are not your own (see 37c).

Below is an interpretation of the novel *Huckleberry Finn* by Mark Twain. The student who wrote this interpretation begins by establishing the context of her discussion and then goes on to define her subject. Notice how she uses her research and several references to the novel to bolster her argument.

> When we consider the novel *Huckleberry Finn*, one question should be asked. Does *Huckleberry Finn* reflect the social attitudes prevalent at the time Twain wrote it? Apparently a number of schools think so because they have removed the book from their reading lists.

**res
37b**

> Although well meaning, these detractors focus on only one part of *Huckleberry Finn*. When the character of Jim is considered in the context of the whole novel, another picture emerges. On the raft, Jim and Huck achieve understanding and, eventually, mutual respect. Perhaps no other sequence in the book more accurately and clearly reflects Twain's feelings about the subject of slavery. To Twain, the raft floating in the river is a symbol of freedom. It is cut loose from the land and, by implication, from the land's constraints and prejudices (Fiedler 72). On the raft, Huck comes to see Jim not as a slave but as a human being, a friend, and eventually as a person who wants to return to his wife and children. According to Daniel Hoffman, when Jim emerges from slavery, he is transformed into a man. This view, says Hoffman, coincides with Twain's own growth as a novelist (433).

> Twain also characterizes as cruel and without honor the society that upholds the values of slavery. The Grangerford-Shepherdson feud is shown by Twain to be a senseless waste of life. The Duke and the King are shown to be two confidence men who degrade Huck and Jim and treat them as if they were objects (Fetterley 447). Tom Sawyer, who enters the book near the end, is shown to be a self-righteous and hypocritical representative of the larger society. By the end of the book Huck, as well as the reader, is brought to the realization that any society that can accept the buying and selling of human beings like Jim is hopelessly corrupt (Fetterley 450).

> In this light *Huckleberry Finn* can be seen as a story about Huck's spiritual maturation. Those who claim that the novel is

unsuitable for students can be criticized on two grounds: (1) that they oversimplify the book; and (2) that by removing it from schools, they take away from students the opportunity to read one of America's great literary works.

Remember that interpretations are as varied as the people who write them. Different people might have opposing opinions on the same topic or focus on entirely different issues. No matter what your point of view, however, your interpretation should clearly distinguish between your ideas and the ideas of the author you are interpreting.

▶

EXERCISE 2

Look back at Exercise 1 and write an interpretation of the passage, discussing what you believe to be the author's attitude toward his subject. Use material from the source to support your assertions, and document all material that is not your own.

37c Avoiding Plagiarism

Plagiarism is presenting another person's words or ideas as if they were your own. By not acknowledging a source, you mislead readers into thinking that the material you are presenting is yours when, in fact, it is the result of someone else's time and effort.

Some writers plagiarize deliberately, copying passages word for word or even going as far as presenting another person's entire work as their own. Students who do so are doing themselves and their classmates a great disservice. They are undercutting the learning process, thereby sacrificing the education that they are in college to obtain. If found out, they are usually punished severely. Some students have failed courses and even had degrees withheld because of plagiarism.

Most plagiarism, however, is accidental. It results when students are not aware of what constitutes plagiarism, or when they forget that a note they jotted down is really a direct quotation or that an idea they are using is really someone else's. Sometimes students just forget to document a paraphrase or summary, or forget to include quotation marks when they write their paper. Even so, accidental plagiarism is often dealt with just as harshly as intentional plagiarism. Plagiarism is not taken lightly in education, business, or anyplace else. Plagiarism is theft.

In general, you must document the following information (see Chapter 38 for a discussion of documentation).

Direct quotations

Opinion, judgments, and insights of others that you summarize or paraphrase

Facts that are open to dispute or that are not common knowledge

Tables, graphs, charts, and statistics taken from any source

Common knowledge, information that you would expect most educated readers to know, need not be documented. You can safely use facts that are widely available in encyclopedias, textbooks, newspapers, and magazines without citing their source. Even if the information is new to you, if it is generally known you need not indicate a source. You can usually assume that information which appears in several of your sources is generally known. Information that is in dispute, however, or that a particular person has discovered or theorized about, must be acknowledged. You need not, for example, document the fact that John F. Kennedy graduated from Harvard in 1940 or that he was elected president in 1960. You must, however, document a historian's analysis of Kennedy's performance as president or a researcher's recent discoveries about his private life.

When you write your paper, give credit to the authors whose works you use. The following examples contrast the correct and incorrect crediting of sources.

plag

37c

ORIGINAL:
Friedman, Meyer, and R. H. Rosenman, *Type A Behavior and Your Heart*. New York: Knopf, 1974. 87.

The person with Type B Behavior Pattern is the exact opposite of the Type A subject. He, unlike the Type A person, is rarely harried by desires to obtain a wildly increasing number of things or participate in an endlessly growing series of events in an ever-decreasing amount of time. His intelligence may be as good as or even better than that of the Type A subject. <u>Similarly, his ambition may be as great as or even greater than that of his Type A counterpart.</u> He may also have a considerable amount of "drive," but its character is such that it seems to steady him, give confidence and security to him, rather than to goad, irritate, and infuriate, as with the Type A man.

PLAGIARISM:
The Type B person is not the same as the Type A person. Unlike the Type A, the Type B is not bothered by a need to acquire things or to participate in a great number of activities. The

> Type B may be as bright as the Type A, and <u>his
> ambition may be as great as or greater than
> that of his Type A counterpart</u>. He may also be
> just as motivated, but his motivation gives him
> balance and confidence and does not drive
> him the way a Type A person's does (Friedman
> and Rosenman 87).

The student who wrote this passage is guilty of plagiarism. Even though he documents the entire paragraph, he neglects to acknowledge that he borrows a specific phrase. To correct this problem, the student should reword the questionable phrase or use quotation marks to indicate his borrowing.

CORRECT: The Type B person is not the same as the Type A person. Unlike the Type A, the Type B is not bothered by a need to acquire things or to participate in a great number of activities. The Type B may be as bright as the Type A, and <u>be just as ambitious</u>. He may also be just as motivated, but his motivation gives him balance and confidence and does not drive him the way a Type A person's does (Friedman and Rosenman 87). (with phrase reworded)

CORRECT: The Type B person is not the same as the Type A person. Unlike the Type A, the Type B is not bothered by a need to acquire things or to participate in a great number of activities. The Type B may be as bright as the Type A, and, according to Friedman and Rosenman, "<u>his ambition may be as great as or greater than that of his Type A counterpart</u>." (87). He may also be just as motivated, but his motivation gives him balance and confidence and does not drive him the way a Type A person's does (Friedman and Rosenman 87). (with phrase in quotation marks)

**plag
37c**

Here is another example of plagiarism.

ORIGINAL:
Sheils, Merrill, et al. "And Man Created the Chip." *Newsweek* 30 June 1980: 92.

Another advantage of transistors is that they lose none of their capacity as they shrink in size. The next giant step in the small-is-beautiful revolution was the simultaneous announcement in 1959 by Texas Instruments Company and Fairchild Semiconductor that both had successfully produced integrated circuits—single semiconductor chips containing several complete electronic circuits. Once again, the breakthrough enabled manufacturers to pack more computing power into less space.

PLAGIARISM: One additional characteristic of the transistor
is that it retains its power no matter how small
it is. After transistors came semiconductors,
pioneered by Texas Instruments Company
and Fairchild Semiconductor. This advance-
ment enabled companies to build smaller and
more powerful computers.

Although this student does not use the exact words of her
source, she does incorporate the author's main points, order,
and emphasis. Without documentation this paraphrase constitutes plagiarism. The student could have easily avoided this plagiarism by inserting the appropriate documentation at the end of
her paragraph.

One additional characteristic of the transistor
is that it retains its power no matter how small
it is. After transistors came semiconductors,
pioneered by Texas Instruments Company
and Fairchild Semiconductor. This advance-
ment enabled companies to build smaller and
more powerful computers (Sheils et al., 92).

If you have any doubt about whether something should or
should not be documented, cite your source. It is better to err on
the side of thoroughness.

Student Writer at Work: Working with Source Material

This student paragraph uses material from three sources, but its
author has neglected to cite them. After reading the paragraph
and the three sources that follow it, identify material that has
been quoted directly from one of the sources. Compare the
wording against the original for accuracy, and insert quotation
marks where necessary, making sure that the quoted passages fit
smoothly into the text. Next, paraphrase passages that the student did not need to quote, and after consulting Chapter 38,
document each piece of information that requires it.

Student Paragraph: Oral History

Oral history became a legitimate field of study in 1948, when
the Oral History Research Office was established by Allan Nevins. Like recordings of presidents' fireside chats and declara-

tions of war, oral history is both oral and historical. But it is
more: oral history is the creation of new historical documentation, not the recording or preserving of documentation that already exists. Oral history also tends to be more spontaneous
and personal and less formal than ordinary tape recordings.
Nevins's purpose was to collect and prepare materials to help
future historians to better understand the past. Oral history
has enormous potential to do just this, for it draws on people's
memories of their own lives and deeds and of their associations
with particular people, periods, or events. The result, when it is
recorded and transcribed, is a valuable new source.

Source 1

. . . when Allan Nevins set up the Oral History Research Office
in 1948, he looked upon it as an organization that in a systematic way could obtain from the lips and papers of living Americans who had led significant lives a full record of their participation in the political, economic, and cultural affairs of the
nation. His purpose was to prepare such material for the use of
future historians. It was his conviction that the individual
played an important role in history and that an individual's autobiography might in the future serve as a key to an understanding of contemporary historical movements. (Excerpted
from Benison, Saul. "Reflections on Oral History." *The American Archivist* 28.1 [January 1965]: 71.)

res
37

Source 2

Typically, an oral history project comprises an organized series
of interviews with selected individuals or groups in order to
create new source materials from the reminiscences of their
own life and acts or from their association with a particular
person, period, or event. These recollections are recorded on
tape and transcribed on a typewriter into sheets of tran-
script. . . . Such oral history may be distinguished from more
conventional tape recordings of speeches, lectures, symposia,
etc., by the fact that the former creates new sources through the

more spontaneous, personal, multitopical, extended narrative, while the latter utilizes sources in a more formal mode for a specific occasion. (Excerpted from Rumics, Elizabeth. "Oral History: Defining the Term." *Wilson Library Bulletin* 40 [1966]: 602.)

Source 3

. . . oral history, as the term came to be used, is the creation of new historical documentation, not the recording or preserving of documentation—even oral documentation—that already exists. Its purpose is not, like that of the National Voice Library at Michigan State University, to preserve the recordings of fireside chats or presidential declarations of war or James Whitcomb Riley reciting "Little Orphan Annie." These are surely oral and just as surely the stuff of history; but they are not oral history. For this there must be the creation of a new historical document by means of a personal interview. (Excerpted from Hoyle, Norman. "Oral History." *Library Trends* July 1972: 61.)

res
37

38

Documentation

Documentation allows you to identify your sources for your readers. They are then able to judge the quality and originality of your work and to determine how authoritative and relevant the work you cite is.

38a Knowing What to Document

Documentation is the formal acknowledgment of the sources you use for your paper. In addition to printed material, sources may include interviews, conversations, films, records, or radio or television programs. In general, you should document any information that is not yours, except for information that is common knowledge (see 37c).

You must place notes after all quotations and at the end of paraphrase and summary passages. As a beginning researcher, you should document any material you think might need it to avoid any possibility of plagiarism (see 37c). Your notes should clearly indicate the sources of all your information. Readers should not have to guess what passages you attribute to your sources and what statements you claim as your own. For this reason you should avoid "blanket" notes—single notes meant to cover several unrelated borrowings throughout a passage.

You can also use notes to provide explanations or additional information that does not fit into your text.

38b Using Documentary Forms

Different fields of study use different forms of documentation. The most widely used formats are those recommended by the Modern Language Association (MLA) and the American Psychological Association (APA). Instructors in the humanities usually prefer the MLA style, which uses parentheses around references within the text to refer to sources listed at the end of the paper.

doc
38b

583

Instructors in the social sciences and in education prefer the APA style, which varies slightly from MLA style. Other disciplines—the physical and biological sciences and medicine, for example—prefer a number-reference format, which uses numbers in parentheses in the text to refer to a list of works at the end of the paper.

Find out what form your instructor requires before you begin any paper. Then consult the appropriate guide and follow it to the letter (see 38g for a list of style manuals).

38c Using MLA Format*

MLA format is recommended by the Modern Language Association of America, a professional organization of more than 25,000 teachers of English and other languages. It is required by teachers in the humanities at colleges throughout the United States and Canada. This method of documentation has three parts: parenthetical references in the text, a list of works cited, and explanatory notes.

doc
38c

(1) Providing parenthetical references in the text

MLA documentation uses references inserted in parentheses within the text and keyed to a list of works cited at the end of the paper. A typical reference consists of the author's last name and a page number.

> The colony's religious and political freedom appealed to many ideal-
> ists in Europe (Ripley 132).

If you use more than one source by the same author, shorten the title of the work to one or two key words and include it in the parenthetical reference.

> Penn emphasized his religious motivation (Kelley, William Penn
> 116).

If any of these elements is stated in the text, omit it in the parenthetical reference.

---

*MLA documentation format follows the guidelines set in the *MLA Handbook for Writers of Research Papers*. 2d ed. New York: MLA, 1984.

Penn's political motivation is discussed by Joseph P. Kelley in <u>Pennsylvania, The Colonial Years, 1681–1776</u> (44).

NOTE: Because the author's name is mentioned in the text, only a page reference is necessary.

Keep in mind that you punctuate differently for indirect references, direct quotations in the text, and quotations that are set off from the text and indented.

Parenthetical documentation for *indirect references* should appear *before* all punctuation marks.

Penn's writings epitomize seventeenth-century religious thought (Degler and Curtis 72).

Parenthetical documentation for *direct quotations* used in the text should appear *after* the quotation marks but *before* the punctuation.

As Ross says, "Penn followed his conscience in all matters" (127).

Parenthetical documentation for quotations that are set off from the text should appear two spaces after the final punctuation.

. . . a commonwealth in which all individuals can follow God's truth and develop according to God's will. (Smith 314)

**doc
38c**

Sample References

Parenthetical references are a straightforward and easy way to provide documentation. Here are the forms specified for more complicated citations.

Works by more than one author

One group of physicists questioned many of the assumptions of relativity (Harbeck and Johnson 31).

With the advent of behaviorism psychology began a new phase of inquiry (Cowen, Barbo, and Crum 31–34).

NOTE: For books with three authors, list the authors in the order in which they appear on the title page, with *and* before the last name.

A number of important discoveries were made off the coast of Crete in 1960 (Dugan et al., 63).

NOTE: For books with more than three authors, list the first author followed by *et al. (and others)* in place of the rest.

Works with a volume and page number

> In 1912 Virginia Stephen married Leonard Woolf, with whom she
>
> founded the Hogarth Press (Woolf 1: 17).

NOTE: The number before the colon is the volume number; the number after the colon is the page number.

Works without a listed author

> Television ratings wars have escalated during the past ten years
>
> ("Leaving the Cellar" 102).

NOTE: For works without a listed author, use a shortened version of the title in the parenthetical reference.

> It is a curious fact that the introduction of Christianity at the end of
>
> the Roman Empire "had no effect on the abolition of slavery" ("Slav-
>
> ery").

NOTE: Omit the page reference if you are citing a one-page article.

Indirect sources

> Wagner said that myth and history stood before him "with opposing
>
> claims" (qtd. in Winkler 10).

NOTE: You should always try to get material from the original source, but sometimes you will have to use an indirect source. Indicate the material is from an indirect source by using the abbreviation *qtd. in (quoted in)* as part of the parenthetical reference.

(2)   Listing works cited

The *Works Cited* section appears at the end of your paper and lists all the research materials that you have used. If your instructor tells you to list all the sources you read, whether you actually cite them or not, use the title *Works Consulted.*

If you have no explanatory notes, the list of works cited begins on a new page after the last page of text. Number the page on which the list of works cited begins as the next page of text—for example, if your paper ends on page 8, the *Works Cited* section begins on page 9. The items should appear in alphabetical order according to the authors' last names. If one of your sources

doc
38c

is unsigned, as is the case with many magazine and newspaper articles, alphabetize by the first main word of the title.

The first line of each entry should be flush with the left-hand margin, and subsequent lines of the entry should be indented five spaces from the left. The list of works cited is double-spaced within and between items.

An item in a list of works cited usually has three divisions, each separated by a period and two spaces.

Works Cited Format

Name: *last name first*   *The three sections end with periods (double-spaced between each section)*

Dyson, Freeman. Disturbing the Universe. New York:

Harper, 1979.

Citations for Books

A book by one author

> Bettelheim, Bruno. The Uses of Enchantment: The Meaning and Importance of Fairy Tales. New York: Knopf, 1976.

NOTE: Enter the full title of the book. To conserve space use a short form of the publisher's name; do not include *Incorporated, Publishers,* or *Company* after the name of the publisher. *Alfred A. Knopf, Inc.,* for example, is shortened to *Knopf,* and *Oxford University Press* becomes *Oxford UP.*

A book by two or more authors

> Davidson, James West, and Mark Hamilton Lytle. After the Fact: The Art of Historical Detection. New York: Knopf, 1982.

NOTE: Only the first author's name is reversed, with last name first. Authors' names should be listed in the order in which they appear on the book's title page.

> Spiller, Robert E., et al., Literary History of the United States. New York: Macmillan, 1974.

NOTE: For more than three authors, list the first author followed by *et al. (and others).*

Two or more books by the same author

> Thomas, Lewis. The Lives of a Cell: Notes of a Biology Watcher. New York: Viking, 1974.

doc
38c

---. The Medusa and the Snail: More Notes of a Biology Watcher. New York: Viking, 1979.

NOTE: Books by the same author are listed in alphabetical order by title. Three hyphens followed by a period takes the place of the author's name after the first entry.

An edited book

Bartram, William. The Travels of William Bartram. Ed. Mark Van Doren. New York: Dover, 1955.

An essay appearing in a book

Lloyd, G. E. R. "Science and Mathematics." The Legacy of Greece. Ed. M. I. Finley. New York: Oxford UP, 1981. 256–300.

NOTE: After skipping two spaces, include the *full* span of pages on which the whole essay appears, even though you may cite only one page in your paper. If you use several essays from one volume in your paper, list the book itself, not the individual essays, in the *Works Cited* section.

Finley, M. I., ed. The Legacy of Greece. New York: Oxford UP, 1981.

doc
38c

A multivolume work

Raine, Kathleen. Vol. 1 of Blake and Tradition. 2 vols. Princeton: Princeton UP, 1968.

The foreword, preface, or afterword of a book

Taylor, Telford. Preface. Less Than Slaves. By Benjamin B. Ferencz. Cambridge: Harvard UP, 1979. xiii–xxii.

An encyclopedia article

"Cubism." Encyclopaedia Britannica: Macropaedia. 1974 ed.

NOTE: Enter the title of an unsigned article just as it is listed in the encyclopedia. For a signed article, enter the author's name, last name first, and then cite the title of the article using normal word order. Because entries appear in alphabetical order, no volume number is needed.

Monro, D. H. "Humor." The Encyclopedia of Philosophy. 1974 ed.

A reprint of an older edition

Wharton, Edith. The House of Mirth. 1905. New York: Scribner's, 1975.

A pamphlet or bulletin

> United States. President's Commission for the Study of Ethical Prob-
>
> lems in Medicine and Biomedical and Behavioral Research. De-
>
> ciding to Forego Life-Sustaining Treatment: Ethical, Medical, and
>
> Legal Issues in Treatment Decisions. Washington: GPO, 1983.

NOTE: Government publications come from many sources and thus present problems in citation. If the publication has no author, state the name of the government first, followed by the name of the agency and then the title of the pamphlet or bulletin.

A translation

> García Márquez, Gabriel. One Hundred Years of Solitude. Trans.
>
> Gregory Rabassa. New York: Avon, 1971.

Citations for Articles

An article in a scholarly journal with continuous pagination through an annual volume

> Huntington, John. "Science Fiction and the Future." College English
>
> 37 (1975): 340–58.

doc
38c

NOTE: Article citations give the pages on which the full article appears. The abbreviations *p.* and *pp.* are not included.

An article in a scholarly journal that has separate pagination in each issue

> Sipes, R. G. "War, Sports, and Aggression: An Empirical Test of Two
>
> Rival Theories." American Anthropologist 4.2 (1973): 65–84.

NOTE: For a journal with separate pagination in each issue, add a period and the issue number after the volume number.

An article in a weekly magazine

> Begley, Sharon. "Redefining Intelligence." Newsweek 14 Nov. 1983:
>
> 123–24.

NOTE: The date is in parentheses only when a volume number is mentioned. Notice that dates for articles follow military format, with the day preceding the month.

An unsigned article in a weekly magazine

> "Solzhenitsyn: A Candle in the Wind." Time 23 March 1970: 70+.

NOTE: When an article does not appear on consecutive pages—
that is, it begins on page 70, continues on page 71, and skips to
page 74—include only the first page and a plus sign (+).

An article in a monthly magazine

> Roll, Lori. "Careers in Engineering." Working Woman Nov. 1982: 62.
>
> Hoffman, Donald D. "The Interpretation of Visual Illusions." Scien-
> tific American Dec. 1983: 154–62.

An article in a daily newspaper

> Stipp, David. "Japanese Firms Find Little Success in the U.S. Small
> Computer Market." Wall Street Journal 11 Sept. 1983, late ed.:
> B6.

An editorial

> "We Hear You, Mr. President." Editorial. New York Times 11 Sept.
> 1983, late ed.: C11.

A review

> Prescott, Peter S. "A Movable Feast of Fiction." Rev. of The Assassina-
> tion of Jessie James by the Coward Robert Ford, by Ron Hansen.
> Newsweek 14 Nov. 1983: 112.

**doc
38c**

NOTE: The citation begins with the reviewer's name and is followed by the name of the review (if any), the title and author of
the book reviewed, and when the review appeared. An unsigned
review begins with the name of the review, if any, or the title of
the book being reviewed.

Citations for Nonprint Sources

Computer software

> Atkinson, Bill. Macpaint. Computer software. Apple, 1983.

NOTE: This citation includes the writer of the program, the title of
the program, a descriptive label (*Computer software*), the distributor, and the date of publication.

Material from a computer service

> Baer, Walter S. "Telecommunications Technology in the 1980's." Com-
> puter Science June 1984: 137+. DIALOG file 102, item 0346142.

NOTE: Enter material from a computer service—BRS or DIALOG, for example—just as you would other printed material. Mention the information service and the identification numbers of the material at the end of the entry.

A lecture

> Sandman, Peter. "Communicating Scientific Information." Communi-
>> cations Seminar, Dept. of Humanities and Communications.
>> Drexel U, 26 Oct. 1984.

An interview

> Cavett, Dick. Personal interview. 28 Dec. 1983.
> Sagan, Carl. Telephone interview. 8 June 1984.

A personal letter

> Kingston, Maxine Hong. Letter to author. 7 April 1982.

A film

> The Big Chill. Dir. Lawrence Kasdan. With Kevin Kline, William Hurt,
>> Jeff Goldblum, Tom Berenger, Glenn Close, Mary Kay Place, Jo-
>> beth Williams, and Meg Tilly. Columbia Pictures, 1983.

**doc
38c**

NOTE: The citation includes the title of the film (underlined), the distributor, and the date. You may also include other information such as the performers, the director, and the writer if this information would be of use to a reader. If you are focusing on the contribution of a particular person, begin with that person's name (Kasdan, Lawrence, dir. The Big Chill . . .).

A television or radio program

> Kennedy. Writ. Reg Gadney. With Martin Sheen, John Shea, and Blair
>> Brown. NBC. KYW, Philadelphia. 20 Nov. 1983.

(3)   Using explanatory notes

Explanatory notes—commentary on sources or additional information on content that does not fit tightly into the text—may be used along with parenthetical documentation and are indicated by a raised number in the text. The full text of these notes appears on the first full numbered page, entitled *Notes,* following the last page of the paper and before the list of works cited.

For more than one source

Use explanatory notes to cite multiple sources in a single reference. Multiple references in a single pair of parentheses distract readers.

In the paper

Many researchers emphasize the necessity of having dying patients share their experiences.[1]

In the note

[1]Kübler-Ross 27; Stinnette 43; Poston 70; Cohen and Cohen 31–34; Burke 1: 91–95.

For explanations

Use notes to provide comments or explanations that are needed to clarify a point in the text.

In the paper

The massacre of the Armenians by the Turks during World War I is an event that the survivors cannot forget.[2]

In the note

[2]For a first-hand account of these events, see Bedoukian 17–81.

doc 38d

38d Using APA Format

APA format, which is used extensively in the social sciences, also relies on short references—consisting of the last name of the author and the year of publication—inserted within the sentence. As with MLA style, you do not include information that appears in the text in the parenthetical reference.

(1) Providing parenthetical references in the text

One author

One study of stress in the workplace (Weisberg, 1983) shows a correlation between. . . .

NOTE: APA style calls for a comma between the name and the date, whereas MLA style does not.

Author's name in text

In his study Weisberg (1983) shows a correlation. . . .

Author's name and date in text

> In Weisberg's 1983 study of stress in the workplace. . . .

Two publications by same author(s), same year

> When he completed his next study of stress (Weisberg, 1983b). . . .

NOTE: If you use two or more publications by the same author that appeared the same year, the first is designated *a*, the second *b* (e.g., Weisberg 1983a and Weisberg 1983b), and so on. These letter designations also appear in the reference list that follows the text of your paper.

Two authors

> There is a current and growing concern over the use of psychological
>
> testing in elementary schools (Albright & Glennon, 1982).

NOTE: With two authors, both names are cited. If a work has more than two authors but fewer than six authors, mention all names in the first reference, and in subsequent references cite the first author followed by *et al.* and the year (Sparks et al., 1984.). When a work has six or more authors, cite the name of the first author followed by *et al.* and the year.

doc
38d

Specific parts of a source

> These theories have an interesting history (Lee, 1966, p. 53).

NOTE: When citing a specific part of a source, you should indicate the appropriate point in the text. APA documentation includes an abbreviation for the word *page*, whereas MLA format does not.

(2)   Listing the references

The list of all the sources cited in your paper falls at the end on a new page with the heading *References*.

Items are arranged in alphabetical order, with the author's last name spelled out in full and initials only for the author's first and second names. Next comes the date of publication, title, and, for journal entries, volume number and pages. For books, the date of publication, city of publication, and publisher are included.

Capitalize only the first word of the title and subtitle of books. Be sure to underline the title and to enclose in parentheses the date, volume number, and edition number.

A book with one author

> Maslow, A. H. (1974). <u>Toward a psychology of being</u>. Princeton: Van
> Nostrand.

A book with more than one author

> Blood, R. O., & Wolf, D. M. (1960). <u>Husbands and wives: The dynamics
> of married living</u>. Glencoe: Free Press.

NOTE: Both authors are cited last name first.

An edited book

> Lewin, K., Lippitt, R., & White, R. K. (Eds.). (1985). <u>Social learning and
> imitation</u>. New York: Basic Books.

Capitalize only the first word of the title and subtitle of articles. Do not underline the article or enclose it in quotation marks. Give the journal title in full; underline the title and capitalize all major words. Underline the volume number and include the issue number in parentheses. Give inclusive page numbers.

doc
38d

An article in a scholarly journal with continuous pagination through an annual volume

> Miller, W. (1969). Violent crimes in city gangs. <u>Journal of Social Is-
> sues, 27</u>, 581–593.

An article in a scholarly journal that has separate pagination in each issue

> Williams, S., & Cohen. L. R. (1984). Child stress in early learning situ-
> ations. <u>American Psychologist, 21</u> (10), 1–28.

A magazine article

> McCurdy, H. G. (1983, June). Brain mechanisms and intelligence.
> <u>Psychology Today</u>, pp. 61–63.

NOTE: Use *pp.* when referring to page numbers in magazines but not when referring to page numbers in journals.

A newspaper article, no author

> Study finds many street people mentally ill. (1984, June). <u>New York
> Times</u>, p. 7.

A newspaper article, author

> James, W. R. (1985, January 3). The unemployed and the flat tax. <u>Wall</u>
>
> <u>Street Journal</u>, pp. 1, 12.

NOTE: This article appears on two separate pages.

38e   Using Number-Reference Format

The **number-reference format** is used in several of the sciences. Instead of parenthetical name and year citations, numbers in the text refer to a numbered reference list of works cited at the end of the paper. Works cited appear either in alphabetical order or in the order in which they are cited in the paper.

Reference within text

> While most women belong to a specialty organization or local or state
>
> medical society, only four in ten are members of the American Medi-
>
> cal Society (1). Few hold offices. . . .

Reference list following the paper

> 1. Bensley, L. (1983, April) Profiling the woman physician. <u>Medica</u>,
>
> 1, 40–45.

**doc
38f**

38f   Using Endnotes and Footnotes

Some instructors, regardless of discipline, prefer footnotes or endnotes to parenthetical references for documentation. This system consists of a footnote or endnote number in the text, a footnote at the bottom of the page or list of endnotes at the end of the paper, and a bibliography. If you employ this method of documentation for research papers, use endnotes rather than footnotes unless you are told otherwise.

(1)   Numbering the endnote

Endnote (or footnote) numbers replace documentation in parentheses and draw a reader's attention to citations. The endnote number in the text that refers to the note itself directly follows the material you are documenting and is typed slightly above the line. Notes are numbered consecutively throughout the paper and placed *after* all punctuation.

". . . encountered in these disciplines."⁵

(2) MLA style of endnotes for books*

These endnotes, which refer to the same entries as the sample entries in "Listing Works Cited" (38c.2), illustrate many of the situations you will encounter. Endnotes for first references to a book contain the following information.

1. A number that matches the number in the text
2. Author's name (as it appears on the title page: first name, middle name or initial, and last name
3. Book title (underlined)
4. City of publication ⎫
5. Publisher ⎬ Enclosed in parentheses
6. Year of publication ⎭
7. Page reference

doc 38f

The first line of each note is indented five spaces. It begins with a number, typed slightly above the line, that corresponds to the number of the note in the text. Type all the lines that follow flush with the left margin.

Endnotes are double-spaced within notes as well as between notes. Footnotes are single-spaced within notes and double-spaced between notes.

Sample endnote

¹Colin M. Turnbull, <u>The Mountain People</u> (New York: Simon, 1972) 151.

Sample footnote

¹Peter Laslett, <u>The World We Have Lost</u> (New York: Scribner's, 1971) 268.

Punctuate exactly as shown in these sample references for both endnotes and footnotes.

A book by one author

Bruno Bettelheim, <u>The Uses of Enchantment: The Meaning and Importance of Fairy Tales</u> (New York: Knopf, 1976) 137.

*Endnote and footnote forms follow the guidelines set in the *MLA Handbook for Writers of Research Papers.* 2d ed. New York: MLA, 1984.

A book by two or more authors

> [2]James West Davidson and Mark Hamilton Lytle, <u>After the Fact:
> The Art of Historical Detection</u> (New York: Knopf, 1982) 171.

> [3]Robert E. Spiller, et al., <u>Literary History of the United States</u>
> (New York: Macmillan, 1974) 321.

An edited book

> [4]William Bartram, <u>The Travels of William Bartram</u>, ed. Mark Van
> Doren (New York: Dover, 1955) 223.

An essay appearing in a book

> [5]G. E. R. Lloyd, "Science and Mathematics," <u>The Legacy of Greece</u>,
> ed. M. I. Finley (New York: Oxford UP, 1981) 267.

A multivolume work

> [6]Kathleen Raine, <u>Blake and Tradition</u>, 2 vols. (Princeton:
> Princeton UP, 1968) 1: 115.

The foreword, preface, or afterword of a book

> [7]Telford Taylor, preface, <u>Less than Slaves</u>, by Benjamin B.
> Ferencz (Cambridge: Harvard UP, 1979) xxi.

An article in an encyclopedia

> [8]"Cubism," <u>New Encyclopaedia Britannica: Macropaedia</u>, 1974
> ed.

> [9]D. H. Monro, "Humor," <u>The Encyclopedia of Philosophy</u>, 1974 ed.

A reprint of an older edition

> [10]Edith Wharton, <u>The House of Mirth</u> (1905; New York: Scrib-
> ner's, 1975) 196.

A pamphlet or bulletin

> [11]United States, President's Commission for the Study of Ethical
> Problems in Medicine and Biomedical and Behavioral Research, <u>De-
> ciding to Forego Life-Sustaining Treatment: Ethical, Medical and
> Legal Issues in Treatment Decisions</u> (Washington: GPO, 1983) 81.

A translation

> [12]Gabriel García Márquez, <u>One Hundred Years of Solitude</u>,
> trans. Gregory Rabassa (New York: Avon, 1971) 127.

**doc
38f**

(3)   MLA style of endnotes for articles

Endnotes for articles are similar to those for books; the differences have to do with the serial nature of publication. An endnote that makes a first reference to an article includes the following.

1. A number that matches the number in the text
2. Author's name as it appears in the article: first name, middle name or initial, and last name
3. Article title (full title in quotation marks)
4. Title of journal or magazine (underlined)
5. Volume number (in Arabic numbers)
6. Date of publication
7. Page reference

Like endnotes for books, endnotes for articles are double-spaced throughout. (Footnotes are single-spaced.)

An article in a scholarly journal with continuous pagination through an annual volume

[1] John Huntington, "Science Fiction and the Future," College English 37 (1975): 345.

An article in a scholarly journal that has separate pagination in each issue

[2] R. G. Sipes, "War, Sports, and Aggression: An Empirical Test of Two Rival Theories," American Anthropologist 4.2 (1973): 68.

An article in a weekly magazine

[3] Sharon Begley, "Redefining Intelligence," Newsweek 14 Nov. 1983: 123.

An unsigned article in a weekly magazine

[4] "Solzhenitsyn: A Candle in the Wind," Time 23 March 1970: 71.

An article in a monthly magazine

[5] Lori Roll, "Careers in Engineering," Working Woman Nov. 1982: 62.

[6] Donald D. Hoffman, "The Interpretation of Visual Illusions," Scientific American Dec. 1983: 154–56.

An article in a daily newspaper

[7] David Stipp, "Japanese Firms Find Little Success in the U.S.

Small Computer Market," <u>Wall Street Journal</u> 11 Sept. 1983, late ed.: B6.

An editorial

[8]"We Hear You, Mr. President," editorial, <u>New York Times</u> 11 Sept. 1983, late ed.: C11.

A review

[9]Peter S. Prescott, "A Movable Feast of Fiction," rev. of <u>The Assassination of Jesse James by the Coward Robert Ford</u>, by Ron Hansen, <u>Newsweek</u> 14 Nov. 1983: 112.

(4)   Style of endnotes for nonprint sources

Computer software

[1]Bill Atkinson, <u>Macpaint</u>, computer software, Apple, 1983.

Material from a computer service

[2]Walter S. Baer, "Telecommunications in the 1980's," <u>Computer Science</u> June 1984: 137+ (DIALOG file 102, item 0346142).

A lecture

[3]Peter Sandman, "Communicating Scientific Information," Communications Seminar, Dept. of Humanities and Communications, Drexel U, 26 Oct. 1984.

An interview

[4]Dick Cavett, personal interview, 28 Dec. 1983.

[5]Carl Sagan, telephone interview, 8 June 1985.

A personal letter

[6]Maxine Hong Kingston, letter to the author, 7 April 1982.

A film

[7]<u>The Big Chill</u>, dir. Lawrence Kasdan, with Kevin Kline, William Hurt, Jeff Goldblum, Tom Berenger, Glenn Close, Mary Kay Place, Jobeth Williams, and Meg Tilly, Columbia Pictures, 1983.

A television or radio program

[8]<u>Kennedy</u>, writ. Reg Gadney, with Martin Sheen, John Shea, and Blair Brown, NBC, KYW, Philadelphia, 20 Nov. 1983.

(5)   MLA style for subsequent references

After the first full reference to a book, you should use a shortened
form. The author's last name and the page reference for the citation are sufficient.

First reference to a book

> [1]Jonathan Schell, The Fate of the Earth (New York: Knopf,
> 1982) 83.

Subsequent reference to a book

> [2]Schell 116.

If you refer to two or more books by the same author, subsequent references to each book include a shortened form of the
title, or the full title if it is already short.

Subsequent reference to more than one book by the same author

> [7]Schell, The Fate of the Earth, 147.

> [8]Schell, The Time of Illusion, 24.

**doc
38f**

Subsequent references for *articles* follow the same format.
Here, too, if you use two or more articles by the same author,
include titles in your references.

First reference to an article

> [12]Mark L. Greenberg, "Shared Struggles, Shared Triumphs:
> Watching Writers Write," The CEA Critic 3.1 (1980): 3.

Subsequent reference to an article

> [13]Greenberg 7.

The once-popular abbreviations Ibid. ("in the same place"),
op. cit. ("in the work cited") and loc. cit. ("in the place cited") are
now seldom used. (See 38h for a list of other abbreviations you
may encounter.)

When you use a work extensively in a paper—when you
cite a particular novel many times, for example—you may indicate in the first reference that all future references will be included parenthetically within the paper.

First reference

> [4]Samuel L. Clemens, Adventures of Huckleberry Finn (New
> York: Lancer Books, 1967) 65. All further references to this work
> appear in the text.

Subsequent reference in the text

> Reflecting the folk wisdom that characterizes his thinking, Huck says, "If I never learnt nothing else out of pap, I learnt the best way to get along with his kind of people is to let them have their own way" (196).

When a quotation is documented parenthetically, the end-of-sentence period follows the closing parenthesis and the quotation marks. After a long quotation (more than four lines) set off from the text, however, the punctuation comes at the end of the sentence, and the parenthetical reference follows the punctuation with no end punctuation of its own.

(6)   Endnotes versus bibliographic entries

The list of sources at the end of a paper, called the bibliography, follows the same format as the list of works cited (see 38c.2).

Endnotes and bibliographic entries provide the same information, but they differ slightly in form.

doc 38f

Endnote form

Endnotes have four divisions: the author's name in normal order, the title, the publication information, and the page reference.

Name: Normal order

Number   *Comma*   *Title*

¹Barbara W. Tuchman, The Guns of August (New York: Macmillan, 1962) 8.

Page reference   *Parentheses*   *Publication information*

Bibliographic form

Bibliographic entries have three divisions: the author's name in inverted order, the title, and the publication information.

Name: last name first   *The three sections of the entry end with periods.*

Tuchman, Barbara W. The Guns of August. New York: Macmillan, 1962.

No parentheses

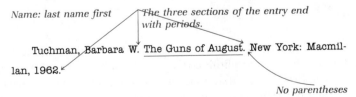

38g   Using Other Documentary Forms

Here are some style manuals that describe documentation formats different from the ones mentioned above. When the need arises, consult them in your college library.

Biology

> Council of Biology Editors. Style Manual Committee. <u>CBE Style Manual: A Guide for Authors, Editors, and Publishers in the Biological Sciences</u>. 5th ed. Bethesda: Council of Biology Editors, 1983.

Chemistry

> American Chemical Society. <u>Handbook for Authors of Papers in American Chemical Society Publications</u>. Washington: American Chemical Soc., 1978.

Linguistics

> Linguistic Society of America. <u>LSA Bulletin</u>, Dec. issue, annually.

doc
38h

Mathematics

> American Mathematical Society. <u>A Manual for Authors of Mathematical Papers</u>. 7th ed. Providence: American Mathematical Soc., 1980.

Physics

> American Institute of Physics. Publications Board. <u>Style Manual for Guidance in the Preparation of Papers</u>. 3rd ed. New York: American Inst. of Physics, 1978.

See John Bruce Howell, *Style Manuals for the English-Speaking World* (Phoenix: Oryx, 1983) for other guides to style.

38h   Using Abbreviations

Although many of the abbreviations that made documentation so tedious have been eliminated, you should be familiar with certain abbreviations that you may encounter in your research. Remember that your audience determines whether or not you abbreviate. If you suspect that an abbreviation will confuse your readers, write out the word in full.

anon.	anonymous
bk., bks	book(s)
c., ca.	*circa* ("about"), as in c. 1920 (approximately 1920)
cf	*confer* ("compare")
ch., chs.	chapter(s)
col., cols.	column(s)
comp., comps.	compiled by, compiler(s)
diss.	dissertation
ed., eds.	edition(s), editor(s)
et al.	*et alia* ("and others")
ff.	and the following pages, as in pp. 88 ff.
illus.	illustrated by, illustration(s)
l., ll.	line(s)
ms, mss	manuscript(s)
n., nn.	note(s), as in p. 12, n. 1
n.d.	no date (of publication)
n.p.	no place (of publication), no publisher
n. pag.	no pagination
p., pp.	page(s)
passim	throughout
q.v.	*quod vide* ("which see")
rev.	revision, revised by
rpt.	reprint, reprinted
sec.	section
supp., supps.	supplement(s)
trans.	translated by

doc
38h

►
EXERCISE

The following are the notes for a paper on approaches to teaching composition. Put them in the proper format for MLA parenthetical documentation and then arrange them in the proper format for the list of works cited. (If your instructor requires a different method of documentation, use it instead.)

1. Page 2 in a book called Teaching Expository Writing by William F. Irmscher. The book has 188 pages and was published by Holt, Rinehart and Winston, who have offices in New York, in 1979. (author's name mentioned in the text of your paper)
2. Something Erika Lindemann said in a lecture on November 9, 1982. She called the talk Some Approaches to Teaching. (no name mentioned in text)

3. Irmscher's book again, this time pages 34, 35, and 36. (author's name mentioned in the text)

4. The Search for Intelligible Structure, an essay written by Frank J. D'Angelo in a book by Gary Tate and Edward P. J. Corbett that is a collection of essays. Oxford University Press in New York published the book, and its copyright date is 1981. Your quotation is from the first page of the essay, which runs from page 80 to page 88. The book is called The Writing Teacher's Sourcebook. (no name mentioned in the text)

5. Page vii of the introduction to a book called Teaching Composition: 10 Bibliographical Essays, which Texas Christian University Press published in 1976 in Fort Worth. It was edited by Gary Tate. (no name mentioned in the text)

6. An article in *Time* on October 25, 1980, called Teaching Johnny to Write. You paraphrased a paragraph on page 73. The article ran from page 72 to page 79, and the last page was signed M. Hardy Jones. (no name mentioned in the text)

7. Page 61 in Teaching Expository Writing. (author's name mentioned in the text)

doc
38h

8. Using a Newspaper in the Classroom, which appeared in the Durham Morning Herald on page 1 of section D in the Sunday paper on November 14, 1982. It was written by Kim Best. (no name mentioned in the text)

9. Lee Odell's article in the February 1979 issue of College Composition and Communication. The article, called Teachers of Composition and Needed Research in Discourse Theory, ran from page 39 to page 45, and you got your information from page 41. That was volume 30 of the journal. (author's name mentioned in the text)

10. You found a book written by Erika Lindemann that you want to quote. You use material on pages 236 and 237 of the book, titled A Rhetoric for Writing Teachers, which was published in 1982 by the New York office of Oxford University Press. (no name mentioned in the text)

11. You decide you need to talk to someone with some experience at the University of North Carolina, so you interview English professor Robert Bain. You talked to him on November 5 and now you are quoting something he said. (no name mentioned in the text)

12. This material is from page 78 of that *Time* article. (no name mentioned in the text)

13. You summarize pages 179–185 of Irmscher. (author's name mentioned in the text)

14. You find the perfect conclusion on page 635 of volume 33 of College English in Richard Larson's article Problem-Solving, Composing and Liberal Education. This is the March 1972 issue and the article begins on page 628 and ends on page 635. (no name mentioned in the text)

39

Writing a Research Paper

Doing research involves more than absorbing the ideas of others; it requires you to evaluate and interpret the ideas presented in your sources and to develop ideas of your own. As you prepare your paper, you decide which materials to keep and which to discard as you come to see the connections among the ideas in your sources. You also decide whether you have enough material or whether you need to do more research. These decisions lead you to the conclusions that give shape and direction to your paper.

Searching out resources involves considerably more than looking in the card catalog and consulting a few indexes (see Chapter 36). Conducting research requires planning, as do arriving at a thesis, finding an effective arrangement of your material, and writing several drafts of your paper. As you plan your paper, leave enough time to formulate and reformulate ideas. The final shape of your paper emerges gradually as your ideas and your understanding of your subject become clearer.

Planning

39a Forming a Hypothesis

A **hypothesis** is a tentative thesis, an educated guess about your topic that your research will lead you to accept, modify, or reject. Your hypothesis enables you to formulate questions about your material as you go through the preliminary phases of the research process. The sooner you arrive at a hypothesis about a specific topic, the more productive your research will be.

(1) Choosing a topic

Usually your research begins with an assignment from your instructor that may or may not specify a topic. If your instructor does not assign a specific topic, you must find one yourself. You do this in much the same way you formulate a topic for a short essay: you brainstorm, ask questions, talk to people, and read widely. With a research paper, however, you set out to investigate some aspect of your topic *by examining other people's ideas about it.*

The topic you choose must be manageable enough to enable you to do productive research. For instance, the subjects on the list below are too general for research. The narrowed topics are more suitable starting points.

Subject	*Topic*
Computers	The possible negative effects of computer games on adolescents
Feminism	The relationship between the feminist movement and the use of sexist language
Mood-altering drugs	The use of mood-altering drugs in state mental hospitals

res

39a

A topic must fit within the boundaries of your assignment; it can be neither too broad nor too narrow. "Julius and Ethel Rosenberg: Atomic Spies or FBI Scapegoats?" is far too broad for a ten-page—or even a hundred-page—treatment. But how one newspaper reported the Rosenbergs' trial or how college students reacted at the time to the couple's 1953 execution for espionage might work. On the other hand, "One piece of evidence that played a decisive role in establishing the Rosenbergs' guilt" would probably be too narrow for a ten-page research paper—even if you could gain access to significant information.

The topic you choose must also be suitable for research. Topics based exclusively on personal experience or on value judgments are thus ruled out. "How attending an integrated high school has made me a more tolerant person" is a topic that can be supported only by self-analysis. "The immorality of the Vietnam War" or "The superiority of J. R. R. Tolkein's work to that of Frank Herbert" are issues that might interest you, but neither research nor expert testimony can ever resolve them.

(2) Moving from topic to hypothesis

A **hypothesis** is a tentative statement about what you think your research will prove. This preliminary statement, which you will eventually refine into a thesis, develops as you think about your topic. It guides your exploratory research and your assembly of a working bibliography. By suggesting ideas to skim for, it helps you decide which sources to collect, which sources to examine first, and which sources to skip.

A hypothesis is *not* a topic reworded as a question. Rather, it is a statement that contains a tentative conclusion, one that suggests a specific direction for your research.

Subject	*Topic*	*Hypothesis*
Computers	The possible negative effects of computer games on adolescents	Computer games interfere with adolescents' ability to learn.
Feminism	The relationship between the feminist movement and the use of sexist language	The feminist movement is largely responsible for the decline of sexist language.
Mood-altering drugs	The use of mood-altering drugs in state mental hospitals	The use of mood-altering drugs has changed the population of state mental hospitals.

**res
39a**

Your hypothesis must be debatable. (Research papers do not simply report information or rehash issues.) "The standard elementary school mathematics curriculum in the United States has remained virtually unchanged for years" is not debatable, but "The standard elementary school mathematics curriculum in the United States, unlike the curricula in Western European countries, does not adequately prepare students for higher mathematics" is. And you can locate data to support this hypothesis, consider a variety of opinions, and then draw your conclusion.

As you move through the research process, your hypothesis and even your topic may change considerably. A line of inquiry may lead to a dead end, a key source may not be available, or a lead you uncover in your research may cause you to branch out in a new direction. But whether or not you make major adjustments to your hypothesis, it should grow increasingly more precise, eventually leading you to a thesis your research can support.

A Student Does Research: Forming a Hypothesis

Michael Schrader, a student in a freshman composition class, was given this research assignment: "Write a ten- to twelve-page research paper on some aspect of the immigrant experience in America, choosing *one* ethnic group and exploring *one* issue." This was a full-semester project, so Michael had fourteen weeks to research and write the paper.

Michael's mother's family was Italian, so he decided to do his paper on Italian-Americans. His maternal grandparents lived in an Italian neighborhood and subscribed to ethnic newspapers and magazines. They had many friends among political, religious, and social leaders of the community who could be of great assistance to him. Narrowing down the subject to one aspect of the Italian immigrant experience took more time. After brainstorming, Michael eventually decided to research family life. Exploring this area would be interesting and fruitful, and his own family, with whom he was very close, could be of help. With these decisions, Michael had moved from subject to topic.

res

39a

Subject	*Topic*
One aspect of one ethnic group's immigrant experience	Family life of Italian immigrants

Now he needed a hypothesis to guide his exploratory research. After talking with his mother and his grandmother, he formed this hypothesis.

In the United States, as in Italy, the family is the Italian immigrant's most important resource.

▶

EXERCISE 1

Narrow five of the following ten general subjects to a more specific topic and then to a hypothesis for a ten-page research paper. Be sure that each hypothesis is suitable for research.

1. The death penalty
2. Artificial intelligence
3. The Bay of Pigs (1962)
4. Textbook censorship

5. Willa Cather
6. Primal scream therapy
7. *Peter Pan*
8. Marcus Garvey's black nationalist movement
9. The Boston Massacre
10. Tay-Sachs disease

▶
EXERCISE 2

Using your own instructor's guidelines for selecting a research topic, form a hypothesis for a research paper of your own.

39b Doing Exploratory Research and Assembling a Working Bibliography

Research is a process of questioning, and the key to successful research lies in finding out what questions to ask. Do your exploratory research with an open mind, allowing the results to determine your conclusions. Look at a wide range of material. Accidents, wrong turns, and unconventional sources sometimes yield the most exciting results. As you explore possible sources, be alert for material that will shed light on your topic and help you refine your hypothesis.

**res
39b**

(1) Doing exploratory research

At this early stage, you want to explore the boundaries of your topic, checking to make sure that you can find enough information to support your hypothesis. Read quickly and note bibliographic information. Your notes should record potential sources and their locations, not the specific information each contains. Evaluate each briefly, perhaps rating its importance or highlighting promising areas.

The most productive approach to research is to begin with those sources that are likely to yield the most helpful material—in the library and outside it. How do you know which sources are the most pertinent? Sometimes you will have to rely on trial and error or on wading through the card catalogs. But often you can simplify your task by establishing a research network and setting priorities for your research (see 36a).

A Student Does Research:
Doing Exploratory Research

Establishing a Research Network

Michael Schrader began his work on the topic "Family life of Italian immigrants" by conferring with his instructor. She suggested that he start by consulting the *Harvard Encyclopedia of American Ethnic Groups*, which has listings for each ethnic group, and perhaps a general encyclopedia, which would provide an overview of his topic. Then she referred him to a colleague in the sociology department, Dr. Harold Kramer, who had recently done some research on Italians in America. To prepare for a meeting with Dr. Kramer, Michael visited the library. There he looked at the *Harvard Encyclopedia of American Ethnic Groups*, photocopying the helpful bibliography that followed the entry on Italians, and read the entry on Migration in the *Encyclopedia Brittanica*.

**res
39b**

Consulting an Expert

Michael then met with Dr. Kramer and spent about twenty minutes with him reviewing potential sources. Dr. Kramer directed Michael to two classic works: Herbert Gans's *The Urban Villagers*, a 1962 study of Italian immigrants in Boston, and Nathan Glazer and Daniel F. Moynihan's *Beyond the Melting Pot*, a 1963 study of ethnic groups in New York City. Dr. Kramer strongly suggested that Michael look at the relevant sections of the most recent edition of each. Then he suggested two specialized indexes, *Public Affairs Information Services* and *Sociological Abstracts*, pointing out that the library subscribed to information services whose data bases included these two publications. Next he thought Michael should proceed to the *Social Sciences Index*, a print index that was not included in his college library's data base. This indexes (among other periodicals) two specialized journals, the *American Sociological Review* and the *American Journal of Sociology*. Thus, Michael could first do a computer search and then supplement his search if necessary by consulting the *Social Sciences Index*. Dr. Kramer also suggested that Michael check a 1983 *New York Times* article about a major conference on Italian-Americans that Kramer had attended.

Dr. Kramer also strongly recommended that Michael do some field work. Specifically, Michael should interview members of his own family, his grandparents' parish priest, and his grandfather's barber (the barber shop is the center of social life in Italian communities in Italy). He might observe his grandparents' neighborhood firsthand, and he might also ask the Sons of Italy, the largest Italian fraternal order, for material that could help him.

Dr. Kramer had many other suggestions. For instance, he thought Michael could try examining church records, census data, and other primary sources. Michael listened politely and took careful notes, but privately he knew that he did not have time to do everything Dr. Kramer suggested. As Michael took notes, he asked Dr. Kramer to spell unfamiliar names and to clarify his instructions. He listened especially carefully to Dr. Kramer's advice about what his priorities should be. When he got home, he sent a note to Dr. Kramer thanking him for his time.

Establishing Research Priorities

During the next few days, Michael planned his research. He checked the Gans and the Glazer and Moynihan books out of the library, noting other books on his topic in the stacks nearby. He found the listing for the article Dr. Kramer had suggested—"Scholars Find Bad Image Still Plagues U.S. Italians," by Walter Goodman—in the *New York Times Index* and noted the date it appeared. But he decided not to read the article yet, or to look for any other specific information, until he knew exactly what he wanted.

He did call his grandparents, asking them for their help in setting up interviews with the parish priest and the neighborhood barber. In a brief letter to the local Sons of Italy chapter, he explained the purpose of his paper and asked these questions: What activities does your group offer? What services do you provide, and how have they changed in the last fifty years? Do you collect statistics on family situations? Has your membership increased or decreased in the past fifty years? Finally, he asked for permission to attend an upcoming Sons of Italy meeting, and he promised to send a copy of his finished paper to the organization for its files.

Next Michael went back to the library to ask the librarian's assistance with the computer search. The librarian consulted the **thesaurus,** a printed index listing key words (see

res

39b

36b.2) and advised him to begin by requesting all citations that included the words *Italy, Italian,* or *Italians* and *family* or *families.*

Michael had a few ideas of his own, too. He remembered seeing a film on educational television of director Martin Scorcese interviewing his Italian immigrant parents. He thought he might try to locate a copy of it, and perhaps look at some back issues of *Attenzione,* a popular magazine for Italian-Americans to which his grandfather subscribed. Perhaps, too, informal telephone surveys of his Italian friends and relatives might yield information. He kept all these ideas in mind as he moved on to the next stage of his research, the assembly of his working bibliography.

(2)   Assembling a working bibliography

res
39b

Whenever you encounter a promising source, jot down its complete bibliographic information on a 3″ × 5″ card. Once you are reasonably sure that you have access to enough good sources to support your hypothesis, you can begin to construct a **working bibliography.** Your index cards represent all the sources (print and nonprint) that you will examine later when you do your concentrated research and take notes. This preliminary bibliography is neither permanent nor complete: you may eventually discard some of the sources, and you may add others. Even so, record full and accurate bibliographical data for each source so that you can find it if you do need it.

You want to evaluate the potential usefulness of a source quickly so you will not waste time on irrelevant reading. One efficient way to do this is to consult an expert, in person or in print. But even if a book is highly recommended, it may not suit your particular needs. You will have to evaluate most sources on your own.

Print Sources

To measure the usefulness of a print source, look at its *scope.* How comprehensively does it treat your subject? Skim a book's table of contents and index for references to your topic; if a long passage looks helpful, skim it to make sure. To be of any real help, a book should devote a section or chapter to your topic, not simply a footnote or a brief mention. For articles, read the entire abstract, or skim the entire article for key facts, looking closely at section headings, boldface type, and topic sentences. An article should have your topic as its central subject.

The *date of publication* tells you whether the information in a book or article is current. A discussion of computer languages written in 1966, for instance, is probably obsolete. Scientific and technological subjects usually demand state-of-the-art treatment. Even in the humanities new discoveries and new ways of thinking lead scholars to reevaluate and modify their ideas over time.

Some classic works, however, never lose their usefulness. Although Edward Gibbon wrote *The History of the Decline and Fall of the Roman Empire* in the eighteenth century, the book still offers a valuable overview of the events it describes. Contemporary historians may interpret events differently, but Gibbon's information is sound, and the book is required reading for anyone studying Roman history. If a number of your sources cite certain earlier works, you should consult those works, regardless of their publication dates. Do, however, check such sources for information that may be obsolete.

Another factor to consider is the *reliability* of your source. Is a piece of writing intended to inform or to persuade? Does the author have an ulterior motive? One way to judge the objectivity of a source is to find out something about its author. The source itself may contain biographical information, sometimes in a separate section, or you can consult a biographical dictionary. Skim the preface to see what the author says about his or her purpose. What do other sources say about the author: Is he or she well known and respected, or unknown? reliable or unreliable? fair or biased? Compare a few statements with another source—a textbook, for instance—to see whether an author is slanting facts.

res 39b

Be sure to examine periodical articles very carefully for reliability. You may consult popular sources for background or for leads. But remember that such sources are commercial. Because their aim is to sell copies to many people, their treatments may be biased, superficial, or sensational, and you should *not* base research on such material.

Finally, your sources must represent a reasonably wide *variety of viewpoints.* Your research paper cannot depend on one or two sources or lean heavily on the work of one or two authorities. Therefore, tracking down sources that you come across during your reading is usually worth the trouble. The bibliographies, footnotes, and references that you find in one source may be excellent leads to other sources.

Nonprint Sources

Nonprint sources—interviews, telephone calls, films, and so on—must also be evaluated. Here too you must consider the *scope* of the source—the extent to which it covers your topic. An interview with an expert on family planning who knows little about sex education may be an excellent source if your paper will focus on changing trends in birth control methods, but such an interview may not be worth your while if your paper is about teenage pregnancy.

The *currency* of a nonprint source is also a factor. A 1970 television documentary on the topography of a Pacific island may still be accurate, but a documentary on the lives of its people may not reflect today's conditions at all.

Reliability is important, too. Is a radio feature on energy conservation part of a balanced news program or a thinly veiled commercial sponsored by a public utility? Is the material presented by experts in the field or by actors? You must consider the source carefully.

You must also determine whether a nonprint source represents a *variety of viewpoints.* Does a film or a television or radio program present a balanced picture of an issue? Check the credits and acknowledgments and read reviews to see which sources were consulted. Do the participants in a panel discussion on nuclear weapons all agree on how they should be deployed, or do they represent different points of view? Find out who they are and try to check their credentials. Is a person you plan to interview fair and impartial or biased on some issues? No single source has to represent all sides of an issue, but you should know how to evaluate each source so that you can put together a balanced paper.

A Student Does Research: Assembling a Working Bibliography

During his exploratory research, Michael Schrader recorded evaluations of his sources as well as bibliographical data on his 3″ × 5″ cards. Michael's first advisors had directed him to many of his most important sources and had given him good information about them. He knew, for instance, that the books by Gans and by Glazer and Moynihan, although not recently published, were still considered important works. The participants in the conference on Italian-Americans described in the *New York Times* article represented a variety of viewpoints that, if pursued, would lead to a balanced picture. After consulting with his grandparents, Michael was reassured that his personal interviews with the elderly barber and the parish priest would give him a comprehensive view of changes in various aspects of Italian family life, at least in one community. He also decided that information from his grandparents, though limited to their own experience, would dramatize many points in his paper. He was able to evaluate the usefulness of print sources he found on his own by reading abstracts of articles or skimming the preface or index of books. One 1948 article in the *American Journal of Sociology* still seemed worth reading because, he noticed, it was included in bibliographies in Gans's book and in the *Harvard Encyclopedia of American Ethnic Groups*. By the time he had completed his exploratory research, Michael had a good idea what help his sources would give him, and he had a good start on his working bibliography.

res
39b

▶
EXERCISE 3

Read the following paragraphs, paying close attention to the information provided about their sources and authors as well as to their content. Decide which sources would be most useful and reliable in supporting the hypothesis "Winning the right to vote has (or has not) significantly changed the role of women in national politics." Which sources, if any, should be disregarded? Which would you examine first? Be prepared to discuss your decisions.

1. Almost forty years after the adoption of the Nineteenth Amendment, a number of promised or threatened events have failed to materialize. The millennium has not arrived, but neither has the country's social fabric been destroyed. Nor have women organized a political party to elect only women candidates to public office. . . . Instead, women have shown the same tendency to divide along orthodox party lines as male voters. (Eleanor Flexner, *Century of Struggle*, Atheneum 1968. A scholarly treatment of women's role in America since the Mayflower, this book was well reviewed by historians.)

2. In Kentucky a woman breezed to victory in the state's gubernatorial election. San Francisco's Mayor Dianne Feinstein won re-election with an overwhelming 80 percent of the vote—then grew irritable at questions about whether she is available for the vice presidency.

Houston's Mayor Kathy Whitmire fought off an oilman's spirited challenge and won re-election with more than 63 percent of the vote. ("Lessons from the Off-Off Year Vote," *Newsweek,* 1984)

3. Woman has been the great unpaid laborer of the world, and although within the last two decades a vast number of new employments have been opened to her, statistics prove that in the great majority of these, she is not paid according to the value of the work done, but according to sex. The opening of all industries to women, and the wage question as connected with her, are the most subtle and profound questions of political economy, closely interwoven with the rights of self-government. (Susan B. Anthony; first appeared in Vol. I of *The History of Woman Suffrage;* reprinted in *Voices from Women's Liberation,* ed. Leslie B. Tanner, NAL 1970. An important figure in the battle for women's suffrage, Susan B. Anthony [1820–1906] also lectured and wrote on abolition and temperance.)

4. Women . . . have never been prepared to assume responsibility; we have never been prepared to make demands upon ourselves; we have never been taught to expect the development of what is best in ourselves because no one has ever expected *anything* of us—or for us. Because no one has ever had any intention of turning over any serious work to us. (Vivian Gornick, "The Next Great Moment in History is Ours," *Village Voice* 1969. The *Voice* is a liberal New York City weekly.)

5. With women as half the country's elected representatives, and a woman President once in a while, the country's *machismo* problems would be greatly reduced. The old-fashioned idea that manhood depends on violence and victory is, after all, an important part of our troubles. . . . I'm not saying that women leaders would eliminate violence. We are not more moral than men; we are only uncorrupted by power so far. When we do acquire power, we might turn out to have an equal impulse toward aggression. (Gloria Steinem, "What It Would Be Like If Women Win," *Time* 1970. Steinem, a well-known feminist and journalist, was one of the founders of *Ms.* magazine.)

6. 1982 was the year that time ran out for the proposed equal rights amendment. Eleanor Smeal, president of the National Organization for Women, the group that headed the intense, 10-year struggle for the ERA, conceded defeat on June 24. Only 24 words in all, the ERA read simply: "Equality of rights under the law shall not be denied or abridged by the United States or by any state on account of sex." Two major opinion polls had reported just weeks before the ERA's defeat that a majority of Americans continued to favor the amendment. (June Foley, "Women 1982: The Year that Time Ran Out," *The World Almanac & Book of Facts,* 1983)

(3)   Making bibliography cards

When you make up a 3″ × 5″ card for a source that looks promising, include the following information.

Book	*Article*
Author(s)	Author(s)
Title (underlined)	Title of article (in quotation marks)
Call number (for future reference)	Title of journal (underlined)
City of publication	Volume
Publisher	Date
Date of publication	Inclusive page numbers
Brief evaluation	Brief evaluation

You should also make up cards for interviews (including telephone interviews), meetings, lectures, films, and any other less traditional sources of information. Here too you should include all essential information.

These cards need not follow the format of your final bibliography, but bibliographic information must be *full and accurate.* If it is not, you may be unable to find sources later. Include a brief evaluation of each source as you prepare each card: kind of information, how much information there is, its relevance to your topic, and its limitations—whether it is biased or outdated, for instance.

res
39b

When you have compiled your bibliography cards, look them over. You may want to adjust your hypothesis on the basis of the content of the sources. Once you have confirmed your hypothesis, look over your cards once again to reevaluate the usefulness of your sources. Select the cards that seem essential, and make them the basis of your working bibliography. Retain *all* the cards you have made, however, even those for sources that do not seem very promising. You may decide to use a rejected source later on when you have refined your hypothesis further.

Once your exploratory research is finished, recheck your cards for completeness. Then look at your hypothesis one last time to see that your sources support it sufficiently. If you still have questions, or if you notice gaps, note where further research is needed.

A Student Does Research: Making Bibliography Cards

Two of Michael Schrader's working bibliography cards are illustrated in Figures 11 and 12.

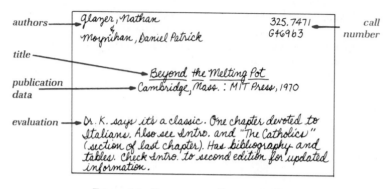

authors
title
publication
data
evaluation

call
number

Glazer, Nathan
Moynihan, Daniel Patrick

325.7471
G46963

Beyond the Melting Pot
Cambridge, Mass. : MIT Press, 1970

Dr. K. says it's a classic. One chapter devoted to Italians. Also see Intro. and "The Catholics" (section of last chapter). Has bibliography and tables. Check Intro. to second edition for updated information.

FIGURE 11   BIBLIOGRAPHY CARD FOR A BOOK

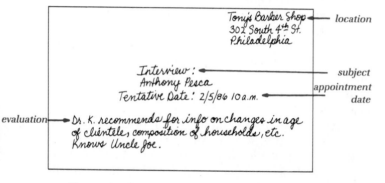

location
subject
appointment
date

evaluation

Tony's Barber Shop
302 South 4th St.
Philadelphia

Interview :
Anthony Pesca
Tentative Date: 2/5/86 10 a.m.

Dr. K. recommends for info on changes in age of clientele, composition of households, etc. Knows Uncle Joe.

FIGURE 12   BIBLIOGRAPHY CARD FOR AN INTERVIEW

res
39b

During this phase of his work, Michael noticed that many of his most promising sources suggested that Italian family life, while still strong, had deteriorated somewhat in this country. On this basis, he decided to modify his hypothesis.

Family life, while still the Italian immigrant's most important resource, is not as important in America as it was in Italy.

Still narrow enough to be explored in ten to twelve pages, this hypothesis had more focus and interest than his original one.

▶
EXERCISE 4

Do exploratory research to support the hypothesis you selected in Exercise 2, evaluating the relevance and usefulness of each source carefully.

Make a bibliography card for each source, and compile a working bibliography for your research paper in progress. When you have finished, reevaluate your hypothesis to make sure that your sources can support it, and adjust it as you think necessary.

39c   Doing Focused Research and Taking Notes

Good research requires careful reading, listening, and observation as well as taking comprehensive, accurate notes, recorded on cards according to a clear, consistent format.

(1)   Doing focused research

Once you have located your print sources and mapped out a plan for acquiring firsthand information from other sources, you are ready to begin your focused research and note taking. Your time limit makes it impossible for you to read all your print sources thoroughly, so you must read only those sections of a work that pertain to your topic. Before you begin, survey the work carefully, checking a book's index, and also the headings and subheadings in the table of contents, to determine which pages to read thoroughly and which to skim. Look carefully at abstracts and headings of articles. As you read, take notes on index cards: you will use this information as you plan and write your paper.

By focusing on sources that are directly relevant to your hypothesis, you narrow your topic further. As you begin to grasp your subject and to develop ideas about it, continue taking careful notes. This whole process is what moves you toward your thesis.

(2)   Making note cards

The advantages of using index cards become obvious when you start arranging and rearranging your material. You seldom know where a particular piece of information belongs at first—or even whether you will use it. You will rearrange your ideas many times, and index cards make it easy for you to add and delete information and to experiment with different sequences. You cannot do that with notes on a tablet or on loose sheets.

As you do library research, take notes on 4″ × 6″ index cards. Transfer the information you have acquired from nonprint sources—interviews, lectures, films, observation, and so on—onto cards, too. Do not get carried away at the copying machine. Duplicating every source is expensive and inefficient. If you encounter a promising new source while you are taking notes, make up a bibliography card for the new source immediately.

At the top of each card, *include a short heading* that links the information on your card to some aspect of your topic. This heading will help you make your outline and organize your notes.

Each card should accurately *identify the source* of the information you are recording. You need not include the complete citation, but you must include enough information to identify your source. "Gallo, p. 53" would be enough to send you back to the bibliography card carrying the complete documentation for Patrick Gallo's *Old Bread, New Wine*. For a book with more than one author or one of two books by the same author, you need a more complete reference. "Glazer and Moynihan, p. 16" would suffice for Nathan Glazer and Daniel Moynihan's *Beyond the Melting Pot*. "Gallo, *Old Bread*, p. 53" would be necessary if you were using more than one book by Patrick Gallo. Be sure to identify each nonprint source with a brief descriptive heading. The rest of the card should carry the information you may include in your paper.

Taking certain precautions at this stage will make the actual writing of your paper easier.

Put only one note on each card. If you do not do this, you lose the flexibility that is the whole point of this method of note taking.

Include everything now that you will need later to understand your note. After a few weeks you will not remember the meaning of any but the most explicit notes.

Indicate what kind of information appears on your note card. If you copy a source's words, use quotation marks. If you use a source's ideas but not its words, do not use quotation marks. If you write down your own ideas, enclose them in brackets. This system will help you to avoid mixups—and plagiarism (see 37c).

Put an author's comments into your own words whenever possible. Word-for-word copying is probably the most inefficient way to take notes. You may use quotations in your final paper, but for the most part you will summarize and paraphrase your source material (see 37a), adding your own observations and

**res
39c**

judgments. Putting information into your own words initially prevents you from producing a paper that is a patchwork of other people's words. If you do need to use an author's words, be sure to copy them accurately, transferring the author's exact words, spelling, punctuation marks, and capitalization to your note card. Figure 13 illustrates two good note-card formats, the first for a print source, the second for a nonprint source.

Author, page

short heading —— *Emigration to Italy*   —*Gans*, p. 205

note (summary, —— *Italian immigrants brought their social structure to*
paraphrase, or   *America. In the cities, they usually "settled in*
quotation)   *Italian neighborhoods, where relatives often lived*
                      side by side, and in the midst of people from the same
                      Italian town. Under these conditions, the family
                      circle was maintained much as it had existed in
                      Southern Italy."

your comment —— *[Gans bases his comments on immigrants in this*
(opinions, reactions, *section not on the Boston neighborhood he studied*
etc.)   *but on a study of New York's East Harlem area*
                       by Leonard Covello - see my bibliography card
                       on Covello.]

Family responsibilities   *Sons of Italy*
                                                  meeting

    One man responded angrily to Congressman
Flavio's suggestion that the 4ᵗʰ ward welcome
federal scatter-site housing, insisting the
family and the community -- not the federal
government-- should be responsible for its
poor. His statement was applauded.

res
39c

FIGURE 13

A Student Does Research: Doing Focused Research and Taking Notes

Library Work

At the library, Michael started by tracking down the most promising of the articles whose abstracts appeared on his computer printout. He also found an additional journal article in the *Social Sciences Index*. He took careful notes on most of the articles (periodicals do not circulate), but he duplicated two especially useful pieces so that he would have them at home for reference.

In the card catalog he found the call numbers of several books he had seen mentioned in other sources and then went to the stacks to find these and other books in his working bibliography. He skimmed each source and decided which to check out and what to photocopy. When he could not find a book, he tried to determine whether or not it had been checked out. If it had, he put a hold on it. When the librarian told him that the one book on his list that the library did not have could be acquired through an interlibrary loan—but that this would take several weeks—Michael decided to look in another library, but he asked her to request the book anyway.

Field Work

With his library research well underway, Michael set out for his grandparents' neighborhood to begin his field work.

Walking Tour. He started by making observations during a walk around the neighborhood. He noticed, for instance, an unusual number of elderly people in the community and a good many more children than in his own suburban neighborhood. He also saw four men in the barber shop, only one of whom was getting a haircut. He made notes on everything he saw and planned to follow up by asking his grandparents for their observations.

Interviews. Michael did not want a formal interview with his grandparents, but rather a discussion. He told his grandparents at the outset that he needed to find out the differences between family life in Italy and in America. He did not ask prepared questions because he knew from experience that his gregarious subjects would willingly describe their vivid memories. The trick would be to keep them focused on his topic. Michael's primary role as interviewer, then, would be to guide them tactfully back to the topic whenever they digressed. As he expected, his grandparents were extremely generous with their reminiscences. In fact, his grandmother even produced a letter his uncle had written to her in 1980 while he was in the army. Michael thought he might quote a section of it in his paper.

Before Michael set out to interview the barber and the priest, he first learned something about them from his grandfather. His grandfather's introductions lent a positive tone to the interviews. Michael assured both men of confidentiality, asking their permission for him to take notes and use a tape recorder. He had also prepared in advance several questions arising from his reading. Michael asked Father D'Ancona about changes in the parish's marriage and divorce rates, in family size, in church attendance, and in sources of family tension. He also asked about general differences between family life in Italy and in the United States and about where the children of the parish settle when they marry, and why.

Michael was able to get a good deal of valuable information from Father D'Ancona, and he planned to transfer his notes to note cards quickly. His interview with Anthony Pesca, the barber, did not go as smoothly. People kept poking their heads into the barber shop to say hello and trade bits of news and gossip, so Michael finally arranged to continue the interview by telephone. When he reached Mr. Pesca, he had time to ask only a few general questions about the differences between Pesca's American-born and Italian-born customers and about the most obvious value conflicts between parents and children. Mr. Pesca did recommend, however, that Michael look at the community newspaper and the church bulletin board if he wanted to know what was going on in the neighborhood.

res
39c

Follow-up. Michael felt he had accumulated some significant firsthand information to supplement his reading. He reviewed his notes, transferred portions of them onto $4'' \times 6''$ index cards, and made notes of follow-up questions he wanted to ask and inconsistencies he needed to check. He wrote thank-you notes to Mr. Pesca and Father D'Ancona, taking the opportunity to ask Father D'Ancona another question: whether those who move out of the neighborhood bring their children back to be christened.

Observation. The Sons of Italy had answered Michael's letter and invited him to attend the next meeting. At the meeting, Michael took notes on the proceedings. He noticed that the average age of the members was about fifty and that the questions they asked the speaker revealed a conservative approach to social issues like welfare, taxes, and public housing. Toward the end of the meeting, Michael got some useful information: one particularly vocal person drew applause when he said that family and community—not public tax revenues—should be responsible for supporting and housing indigent persons. Michael jotted down these remarks and the audience reaction. When he got home, he put this one note on an index card (see p. 621) and also made an accurate bibliography card for the meeting, listing date, time, location, and the speaker's name and organizational affiliation. Then he wrote a brief note thanking the chapter president.

▶
EXERCISE 5

Begin focused research for your paper, taking notes from your sources on 4″ × 6″ cards. Remember that your notes should include paraphrase, summary, and your own observations and reactions as well as direct quotations.

Shaping Your Material

res
39d

39d Deciding on a Thesis

Even after finishing your focused research and note taking, you may not have settled on a definite thesis for your paper. Your hypothesis has been narrowed and modified, but it remains tentative. Now you must refine it into a **thesis,** a carefully worded statement that takes a stand about your topic and draws a conclusion that your research can support. This thesis will give your paper a clear focus and direction and will help you shape your material.

To decide on a thesis you must add to or change the hypothesis so that it is consistent with the ideas you have formed and the source material you have explored. Your thesis should be considerably more focused and detailed than your hypothesis, presenting an overview of the main points your paper will make.

Hypothesis	*Thesis*
Computer games interfere with adolescents' ability to learn.	Because they interfere with concentration and teach players to expect immediate gratification, computer games interfere with adolescents' ability to learn.

The feminist movement is responsible for the decline of sexist language.	By raising public awareness of careless language habits and changing the image of women, the feminist movement has helped to bring about a decline of sexist language.
The development of mood-altering drugs has changed the population of state mental hospitals.	It is the development of psychotropic (mood-altering) drugs, not advances in psychotherapy, that has made possible the release of large numbers of mental patients from state hospitals into the community.

If your thesis still does not seem quite right to you, or if it does not convey the point you want to make, you may need to do more than revise or reword it. Sometimes rereading your note cards and grouping ideas in different ways will help you to arrive at an accurate thesis. Sometimes making a scratch outline will help you see what it is your notes can demonstrate (see 39e). Or you may try other techniques—for instance, brainstorming or freewriting with your hypothesis as a starting point, or asking questions about your topic. Most often, however, you reconsider the different hypotheses you developed as you did your research and took notes. The thesis you decide on depends on the kind and amount of source material you have collected and the ideas you have developed in response to that material.

res
39d

A Student Does Research: Deciding on a Thesis

As Michael Schrader did his research, he revised his hypothesis several times. He had begun with "In the United States as in Italy, the family is the Italian immigrant's most important resource" because this was what he had expected his research to support. As he read, however, he found that, in fact, family ties eroded to some extent after emigration from Italy. He therefore modified his hypothesis to reflect this realization: "Family life, while still the Italian immigrant's most important resource, is not as important in America as it was in Italy."

Throughout his research, Michael vacillated between these two statements. He had to decide which stand to take, but he had to take the stand his research would support, not the one he preferred. When he reread his note cards, he understood the reason for his indecision: to some extent his notes supported both hypotheses. His final thesis was a compromise between the two.

Although emigration from Italy led to assimilation, which weakened the family system to some extent, the Italian family in the United States remains unusually close and stable.

This thesis combines the idea of the erosion of family ties with the idea of continued strength in the family unit. It also indicates that Michael considers the latter more significant and that this is the point his paper will make.

▶
EXERCISE 6

Read these three passages from various sources. Imagine that you are writing a research paper on the influences that shaped young writers in the 1920's. What possible thesis statements could be supported by the information in these passages?

1. Yet in spite of their opportunities and their achievements the generation deserved for a long time the adjective that Gertrude Stein had applied to it. The reasons aren't hard to find. It was lost, first of all, because it was uprooted, schooled away and almost wrenched away from its attachment to any region or tradition. It was lost because its training had prepared it for another world that existed after the war (and because the war prepared it only for travel and excitement). It was lost because it tried to live in exile. It was lost because it accepted no older guides to conduct and because it formed a false picture of society and the writer's place in it. The generation belonged to a period of transition from values already fixed to values that had to be created. (Malcolm Cowley, *Exile's Return*)

2. The 1920's were a time least likely to produce substantial support among intellectuals for any sound, rational, and logical program. Prewar stability and convention were condemned because all evidences of stability seemed illusory and artificial. The very lively and active interest in science was perhaps the decade's most substantial contribution to modern civilization. Yet in this case as well, achievement became a symbol of disorder and a source for disenchantment. (Frederick J. Hoffman, *The 20's*)

3. Societies do not give up old ideals and attitudes easily; the conflicts between the representatives of the older elements of traditional American culture and the prophets of the new day were at times as bitter as they were extensive. Such matters as religion, marriage, and moral standards, as well as the issues over race, prohibition, and immigration were at the heart of the conflict. (Introduction to *The Twenties*, ed. George E. Mowry)

▶
EXERCISE 7

Carefully read over all the notes you have collected during your concentrated research, and develop a thesis for your paper.

39e Making an Outline

Once you have a thesis, you can plan a more definite structure for your paper. Making an outline helps you to put your research into focus. Once you see how different aspects of your research are connected, you can isolate gaps or inconsistencies in your material.

res
39e

At some stage of your focused research, you should draw up a **scratch outline,** a list of the major points you will present in the order in which you think you will present them. This informal outline serves as a general guide, and its divisions enable you to sort and categorize your note cards. Before you arrange your cards, however, check each card carefully to make sure it contains only one general idea or one brief related group of facts. If it does not, distribute the information among two or more cards. If the information on two cards overlaps, combine it on one card. Then make sure the headings on all your cards are accurate.

Lay out your note cards on a big table—or on the floor—and sort them into piles, one for each division of your scratch outline. (Keep a miscellaneous pile for notes that do not seem to fit anyplace. You may discard these notes later, or you may find—or make—a place for them in your paper when you construct your formal outline.) With your piles assembled, you can see how well your categories are balanced. What if, for example, most of your notes support only three divisions of a four-division outline? You have two options: (1) do more research to fill out the fourth point; or (2) drop it, narrow the scope of your paper, and revise your thesis. A review of your notes should tell you which course to take.

Guided by the headings in the upper left-hand corner of each card, sort and organize the cards *within* each group. Put together related information within each category in an order that highlights the most important ideas and subordinates lesser ones. Once again, do some discarding, setting aside notes that do not fit into your emerging scheme. (And remember to retain these cards. They may fit a new line of inquiry as you experiment with different arrangements.) When you have organized the notes in each pile, review the order of the major divisions of your scratch outline to make sure the sequence is right.

When you are satisfied with the arrangement, make a **formal outline**, with subdivisions corresponding to those of your note cards. This outline can be either a **topic outline**, which uses short phrases or single words, or a **sentence outline**, which uses complete sentences. Reviewing your completed outline reveals whether you are short of supporting information in a particular area or placing too much emphasis on a relatively unimportant idea. Because an outline is a skeleton version of your note cards, it can also tell you at a glance if ideas are illogically or ineffectively placed, or if similar concepts turn up in different parts of your plan.

**res
39e**

A Student Does Research: Making an Outline

Michael's scratch outline reflected the four major divisions that emerged as he did his focused research.

Thesis: Although emigration from Italy led to assimilation, which weakened the family system to some extent, the Italian family in the United States remains unusually close and stable.

  I. Situation in Italy
 II. Changes resulting from emigration
III. Current status of Italian family
 IV. Projections for future of Italian family

Following this outline, Michael sorted his note cards into four groups. When he was satisfied with his arrangement, he went on to organize the cards *within* each group, making changes in his outline as he went along. This process forced him to consider the relevance of each piece of information carefully and to discard material that seemed irrelevant to his paper. For example, Michael found that the interview with his grandparents seemed too personal, and that much of their conversation was not relevant to his thesis. As he tried different arrangements of his note cards, he found himself changing his outline somewhat so that it accurately reflected his material. When he had finished sorting his note cards, he constructed the topic outline that follows. (A sentence outline appears with his paper on pp. 640–643.)

Thesis: Although emigration from Italy led to assimilation, which weakened the family system to some extent, the Italian family in the United States remains unusually close and stable.

res
39e

I. Characteristics of southern Italian villages
   A. Self-contained
      1. Villagers within sound of bell
      2. Strangers beyond sound of bell
   B. Unique
      1. Separate customs maintained in Italy
      2. Villages created in America
         a. Identification in Italy
         b. Identification in America
II. Italian villagers' reliance on family
   A. Rigid hierarchy of relationships
      1. *La famiglia*
      2. *Comparaggio*
      3. Casual acquaintances
      4. *Stranieri*
   B. Patriarchal structure
      1. Mother's responsibilities
      2. Father's responsibilities
   C. Children's roles
      1. Sons
      2. Daughters

III. Italians' insulation from outside world
   A. Family as refuge
   B. Distrust of outsiders
IV. Italian-Americans' aloofness
   A. "Little Italys"
      1. Remain in northeastern United States
      2. Improve neighborhoods
      3. Often make two-generational moves
      4. Live near parents and siblings
   B. Family-oriented society
V. Changes experienced in United States
   A. Employment for women
   B. Parent-child conflicts
   C. Changes in family system
      1. Family less patriarchal
      2. Sex roles less rigid
      3. Friends preferred over relatives

res
39f

VI. Family closeness and stability
   A. Family closeness
      1. Extended family more important
      2. Elderly relatives welcomed
      3. Emotional and social support provided
   B. Family stability
      1. Low divorce, separation, and desertion rates
      2. Low intermarriage rate

▶
EXERCISE 8

Review your notes and your thesis carefully. If you have not already
done so, make a scratch outline for your paper. Sort and group your
note cards accordingly, and construct an outline for your paper.

Writing and Revising

39f Writing Your First Draft

When you are ready to write your first draft, lay out your note
cards in the order in which you intend to use them. Follow your

outline as you write, moving from one entry to the next and using your note cards as you need them. It is important to keep referring to the outline because it reminds you of the hierarchy of your ideas and the connections among them.

Your paragraphs will probably correspond to subdivisions of your outline, at least in this draft. As you write, make an effort to supply transitions between sentences and paragraphs. These transitions need not be polished; you will refine them in subsequent drafts. But if you leave them out entirely at this stage, you may forget what they are, which will make revising much more difficult.

The purpose of the first draft is to get ideas down on paper. You will not be able to write the whole draft in a single sitting, but do plan to write in segments that you can complete without interruption. One major heading from your outline, for instance, is a realistic goal for a morning or afternoon of writing. Once you get started, you will find it surprisingly easy to write. The time you spent taking careful, accurate notes and preparing a formal outline will now pay off. If you do have trouble, freewriting for a short period can get you started. Sometimes leaving your paper for only five or ten minutes gives you a fresh view of your material. Just do not give up. You will begin to move eventually.

As you write, concentrate on getting out your ideas. You should *expect* to revise (see 3b), so postpone precise word choices and refinements of style. As you write, jot down questions to yourself or points that need further checking, leave space for material you plan to add, and bracket phrases or whole sections that you may move or delete—in other words, lay the groundwork for a major revision. You are working from an outline and note cards, but you are not bound to follow their content or sequence exactly. In the process of getting your words on paper quickly, new ideas or new connections between ideas will occur to you. Jot them down as they come to mind, and plan to incorporate them in your next draft. If you find yourself deviating from your thesis or outline, reexamine them to see whether the departure is justified. (For information about drafting your essay on a word processor, see Appendix A.)

**res
39f**

(1) The parts of the paper

Like most essays the research paper has an introduction, a body, and a conclusion. Here, however, each of these elements is expanded.

Introduction

You open the introduction by identifying your overall topic and establishing those aspects of it that you will discuss. You can, for example, survey previous research in a field or provide background for a problem. Next, state your thesis—the position you will support in the rest of the paper. You might then go on to summarize briefly your major supporting points (the major divisions of your outline) in the order in which you will present them. This overview of your thesis and support provides a smooth transition into the body of your paper.

You should not spend much time crafting an introduction for a rough draft. Your ideas will take shape as you write, and you will want to refine your introduction later to reflect these revisions. For now, a paragraph or two is all you need.

Body

Follow your formal outline as you draft the body of your paper, indicating the direction of your paper by using strong topic sentences that correspond to the divisions of your outline.

res
39f

The immigrants maintained their Old World family system in the United States.

You can also use section headings if your instructor requires them.

Family Solidarity

Family solidarity gave the southern Italian family its essential unity and cohesiveness.

Even in your first draft, descriptive headings and topic sentences will help you keep your discussion under control.

Use the patterns of development discussed in 4e to construct the individual sections of your paper, and be sure to connect ideas with transitional words and phrases. The same principles that apply to writing good paragraphs and essays also apply to writing research papers.

Conclusion

Restate your thesis in your conclusion. This is especially important in a long paper because by the time your readers get to the end, they may have lost sight of your thesis. After this restatement, you can end your paper with a summary of your major points, a call for action, or perhaps an apt quotation. Just remember that your conclusion must be based on your data and that it should help persuade your reader to accept your thesis.

(2) Working source material into your paper

One of the biggest problems students have is taking control of their source material. A good research paper evaluates and interprets its sources, comparing different ideas and synthesizing conflicting points of view. As a writer, your job is to consolidate information from various sources into a paper that presents a coherent view of your topic to your readers. To this end, as you draft your paper you must make certain to use your sources effectively, paraphrasing and summarizing accurately, smoothly blending your direct quotations into your text, and drawing your own conclusions to create an original paper (see Chapter 37).

Your source material must be truly integrated to create a new whole. Blend the opinions of one source with those of another so that the relationship between them is apparent. This is easy to do when one source supports another. If, however, two sources present conflicting interpretations, use precise language and accurate transitions to make the contrast readily apparent. You will then have a context for making your own comments and drawing conclusions. If your sources present partial pictures of a subject, blend details from each source *carefully*, providing an accurate account of which details come from which source, to reveal the complete picture.

As you write your rough draft, *be sure to keep track of your sources.* You will find it very difficult to fill in source information later, so if you are not sure that a piece of information needs documentation, supply the source anyway and make a final decision when you revise. For now, *include every source and page number in the text*, as Michael Schrader does in the paragraphs from his draft on pages 635 and 636.

res
39f

▶
EXERCISE 9

Write a draft of your paper, being careful to incorporate source material smoothly and to record source information accurately.

39g   Revising Your Drafts

A good way to start revising is to make sure that your thesis still suits your paper. The research paper you have actually drafted may not exactly match the paper you planned. Make an outline of your draft, and compare it with the outline you made before you began the draft. If you find significant differences, you will have to refine your thesis or rewrite sections of your paper. Valuable new ideas do occur to you as you write, so changes are to be expected. Make sure, though, that the rest of your paper and your thesis are consistent with any revisions you make.

When reconsidering your draft, follow the revision procedures that apply to any paper. Make sure that your introduction and conclusion are effective, and read the body of your paper paragraph by paragraph, asking yourself if thesis and topic sentences are supported with enough material. Should you do more research to find support for certain points? Do you need to reorder the major divisions of your discussion? Should you rearrange the order in which you present your points within those divisions? Do you need section headings? Clearer topic sentences or transitions? Stylistic changes in sentences or individual words?

Next, look at how you have integrated your sources into your paper. Are direct quotations blended with paraphrase, summary, and your own observations and reactions? Are they woven seamlessly into the text? Do you introduce your sources smoothly and draw original conclusions from your research?

If your instructor allows peer criticism, take advantage of it. The first draft is primarily for you. As you move toward a final draft, however, you must think more and more about your readers' reactions. Testing out your draft at this point can be extremely helpful.

A Student Does Research:
Writing and Revising

When Michael Schrader revised his first draft, he made changes in structure and style. Using his note cards as a guide, Michael drafted the paragraphs illustrated in Figure 14.

Italian-Americans, even gangsters, typically maintain very close and highly stable family relationships. [Glazer and Moynihan, p. 196]

In addition, Italians are more likely to have relatives over 60 living with them. [Goodman, New York Times 10/15/83] *In a walking tour of a typical Italian-American neighborhood, I noticed a large proportion of elderly residents, often accompanied by children and grandchildren as they conducted routine errands and shopping. This convinced me that generations remain close.* [2/10/86]

Even though households may not include members of the extended family, the family relationships are close; the family provides close emotional support and serves as a social network. [Gans, p. 46]

FIGURE 14

When Michael reviewed this section of his first draft, he saw that he had simply copied material from his note cards without introducing it, adding proper transitions, or drawing his own conclusions. In his next draft (see Figure 15) he tried to incorporate his source material more smoothly, reworking three skimpy paragraphs into one unified whole that blended material from three sources with his own observations and conclusions. Simply by reworking his material, Michael gave it new shape and eliminated the impression that he was parroting other people's ideas.

res
39g

You will probably take your paper through several drafts, changing different parts of it each time or working on one part over and over again. After editing your original draft thoroughly, you should probably type out a corrected version and make additional corrections on that draft before typing your final version. Or you may prefer to recopy revised sections by hand and then type the final draft from the legible revision.

To facilitate the revision process, be sure to follow the guidelines recommended in 3b: double-space, write on only one side of your paper, and so on. Be very careful to recopy your source information accurately *on each draft*, placing the exact information as close as possible to the material it identifies. (For information on revising with a word processor, see Appendix A.)

Clear topic sentence
reflects main idea

> *After they emigrated from Italy to America, the Italian-American family continued to be extremely close. Today Italians remain more likely than most other ethnic groups to have relatives over 60 living with them. [Goodman, New York Times, 10/15/83] A walking tour of a typical urban Italian-American neighborhood confirmed this, revealing a large proportion of elderly residents, often accompanied by children and grandchildren as they conducted routine errands and shopping. (2/10/86) Even when members of the extended family are not actually part of the household, the relationships among family members are close; the family provides close emotional support and also serves as a social network. [Gans, p. 46] In fact, even Italian-American gangsters typically maintain very close and highly stable family relationships. [Glazer and Moynihan, p. 196]*

Support: examples from
reading and firsthand
observation

FIGURE 15

**res
39h**

▶

EXERCISE 10

Following the guidelines in 39g and in 3d and e, revise your research paper until you feel you are ready to prepare your final draft.

39h   Preparing Your Final Draft

With your revision complete, you can see what sources need to be acknowledged. At this point you can prepare your documentation and your list of works cited (see 38c) and go on to choose a title.

Your title must be descriptive enough to tell your readers what your paper is about, but it need not be dull. Consider how these authors have tried to find titles with some appeal.

> "How to Make Mulligan Stew: Process and Product Again." Robert M. Gorrell, *College Composition and Communication*

> "Is the Welfare State Replacing the Family?" Mary Jo Bane, *The Public Interest*

> "The Limited American, the Great Loneliness, and the Singing Fire: Carl Sandburg's 'Chicago Poems.'" William Alexander, *American Literature*

Of course, you would hardly want a witty title for a paper about the death penalty or world hunger. Still, your titles can be engaging and to the point and sometimes even provocative. Often a quotation from one of your sources suggests a likely title. Michael Schrader used "The Italian Family" as the working title for his paper, but "The Italian Family: 'Stronghold in a Hostile Land,'" which included a quotation from one of his sources, conveyed his paper's thesis more dramatically.

When you have chosen a title, you can proceed to type your final draft—and your outline, if your instructor requires one. (See Appendix B for full information on manuscript preparation.) Before you hand in your manuscript, read it through one last time to look for grammar, spelling, or typing errors you may have missed. Pay particular attention to notes and bibliographic references. Remember that every error takes away from the credibility of your whole paper. If your instructor gives you permission, you may make *minor* corrections on your final draft with correction fluid or by neatly crossing out a word or two and writing or typing the correct word or phrase above the line. If you find a mistake that you cannot correct neatly, however, retype the page. Once you are satisfied that your manuscript is as accurate as you can make it, you are ready to hand it in.

res
39h

▶
EXERCISE 11

Type your research paper, including notes and list of works cited, according to the format your instructor requires.

A Student Does Research: The Completed Paper

Michael Schrader's completed research paper, "The Italian Family: 'Stronghold in a Hostile Land,'" appears on the pages that follow. The paper uses MLA documentation. It is accompanied by a sentence outline, explanatory notes, and a list of works cited. Annotations opposite each page of the manuscript comment on stylistic and structural aspects of the paper; explain the format for proper documentation; illustrate various methods of incorporating source material into the paper; and highlight some of the choices Michael made as he moved from note cards to first draft to completed paper.

If your instructor does not require a title page, include all identifying information—your name, the name of the course, your instructor's name, and the date—in the upper left-hand corner of your paper's first page, one inch from the top and flush with the left-hand margin. The title should be centered two spaces below the last line of this heading.

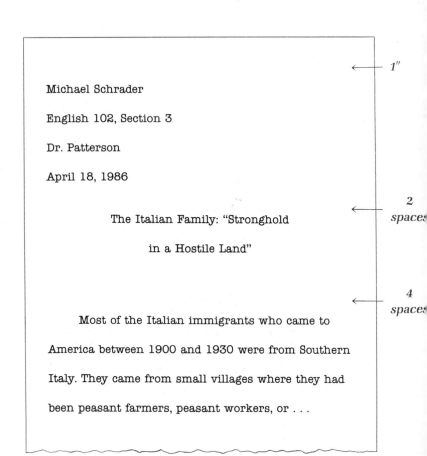

Michael Schrader

English 102, Section 3

Dr. Patterson

April 18, 1986

                    The Italian Family: "Stronghold

                         in a Hostile Land"

    Most of the Italian immigrants who came to America between 1900 and 1930 were from Southern Italy. They came from small villages where they had been peasant farmers, peasant workers, or . . .

1″

2 spaces

4 spaces

About ⅓ down page

Double-space The Italian Family: "Stronghold   *Title*
                in a Hostile Land"

                                                            2″

                          by
                   Michael Schrader   *Name*

                                                            2″

              English 102, Section 3   *Course*
Double-space   Dr. Patterson   *Instructor*
                   April 18, 1986   *Date submitted*

center   Outline
double space

Thesis: Although emigration from Italy led to assimilation,

which weakened the family system to some extent,

the Italian family in the United States remains

unusually close and stable.

I. Most Italian immigrants came from the Mezzogiorno,

where each village was separate and unique.

A. Each village was self-contained.

1. All villagers recognized the sound of their church

bell.

2. Those beyond the bell's range were considered

strangers.

B. Each village was unique.

1. Each village in Italy had its own customs.

2. Italians in America sought out their paisani and

re-created their Italian villages.

a. In Italy, Italians identified with family and vil-

lage.

b. In America, Italians began to identify with

other Italians.

II. Most Italians from the Mezzogiorno were of the contadino class, which relied solely on the family.

A. A rigid hierarchy defined family relationships and responsibilities.

   1. La famiglia included blood relatives.

   2. Comparaggio included the godparents.

   3. A third group consisted of casual acquaintances and respected families.

   4. Stranieri included all others.

B. The contadino family was usually patriarchal.

   1. The mother maintained the home and managed the finances.

   2. The father earned the money and made all major decisions.

C. Children's roles mirrored adult roles.

   1. Parents taught their sons to be patient, controlled, and respectful.

   2. Parents taught their daughters household skills and qualities that would make them good wives and mothers.

III. Family solidarity insulated the contadino family from the hostile outside world.

    A. Barzini sees the family as a "stronghold" and a "refuge."

    B. Italians did not trust outsiders.

IV. Italians in America have remained somewhat aloof.

    A. Immigrants often joined fellow villagers in urban "Little Italys."

        1. Most Italians remain in northeastern United States.

        2. Italians are more likely to improve old neighborhoods than to relocate.

        3. Two generations often move to suburbs together.

        4. Italians are more likely to live near parents and siblings than are other ethnic groups.

    B. Immigrants maintain a family-oriented society in America.

V. The Italian family in America has undergone many changes.

    A. Some women have sought employment.

    B. Conflicts have occurred between parents and children.

    C. The family system has changed.

1. The family has become less patriarchal and more democratic.

2. Third-generation Italian-Americans have relaxed the rigid sex roles of Old World society to some extent.

3. Third-generation Italian-Americans often prefer to associate with friends rather than relatives.

VI. Despite changes, the family remains close and stable.

A. The Italian family remains close.

1. The extended family has become more important.

2. Italians are more likely than other ethnic groups to open their homes to elderly relatives.

3. The family provides emotional and social support.

B. The Italian family remains stable.

1. Italians have low rates of divorce, separation, and desertion.

2. Italians have a low intermarriage rate.

Title typed 2" from top of page

Four spaces between title and first line of paper

¶1: Introduction, presenting background information

<u>*Cordasco and Bucchioni 312*</u> *indicates that the
    first two sentences paraphrase ideas in a
    source.*

Thesis

The Italian Family:
"Stronghold in a Hostile Land"

¶1   Most of the Italian immigrants who came to America between 1900 and 1930 were from Southern Italy. They came from small villages where they had been peasant farmers, peasant workers, or artisans (Cordasco and Buchioni 312). When they emigrated to America, these southern Italians brought with them their close family system and their enormous respect for the family unit. Even with all of the demands and pressures of adjusting to life in a foreign country, the family remained the number-one priority for the Italians. Today, this is still true among Italian-Americans. Some assimilation did occur after migration, but it did not take place to the same degree as it did with other ethnic groups. Although emigration from Italy led to assimilation, which weakened the family system to some extent, the Italian family in the United States remains unusually close and stable.

From page 2 on, type your last name and the page number one-half inch from the top in the upper right-hand corner. Do not punctuate the page number. Leave one-inch margins.

¶2: Introduces discussion of outline point IA [Each village was self-contained.]

Femminella and Quadagno 63–64 *summarizes two pages of a source.*

Femminella and Quadagno 63 *indicates that the preceding direct quotation is taken from a source.*

¶3: Outline point IB [Each village was unique.]

¶2   The southern peasant Italians came to America from a

region known as the Mezzogiorno, which consisted of six

provinces south and east of Rome. Here each village was

self-contained, and each was different from the others.

Every village in Southern Italy had a local church with a

bell tower (Femminella and Quadagno 63-64). In each vil-

lage, the bell's sound was "unique and familiar to each and

every person . . . and over the centuries the attachment the

villagers felt for the bell metamorphosed into a sense of

loyalty to the village itself and to one's neighbors"

(Femminella and Quadagno 63). The sound of the church

bell drew the imaginary boundary lines of the village.

Those people who lived beyond the sound were considered

outsiders or strangers, and they were not to be trusted

(Femminella and Quadagno 63).

¶3   Each village in Italy was unique. The language, man-

ners, and mores differed from village to village. When the

Italian villagers migrated to America, they usually sought

out their paisani, their fellow villagers, who had already

come to the United States. There they tried to establish

<u>*Femminella and Quadagno 61–64*</u> *refers to four pages of source material, summarized here to convey general ideas rather than specific detail.*

¶4: Outline point IIA [A rigid hierarchy defined family relationships and responsibilities.]

Schrader 3

customs and living conditions similar to those they had

left behind. In Italy, the people did not see themselves as

Italians; they identified with their families, villages, and

towns. In fact, Italian immigrants did not really take on an

Italian ethnic identity until after they arrived in America

(Femminella and Quadagno 61-64).

¶4 Most Italians who emigrated from the Mezzogiorno

area were of the peasant class of farmers and day laborers

called the contadino class (Femminella and Quadagno 64).

Because their lives were difficult and they were exploited

by landowners, they rejected the social institutions of the

rest of the country and came to rely almost exclusively on

the family. A hierarchy defined relationships among indi-

viduals and their responsibilities to one another. The first

category in this hierarchy, la famiglia, included blood rela-

tives, those who deserved all one's loyalty. The second

group, comparaggio, included the godparents, and the third

was made up of casual acquaintances and those people

who were respected because of their family status. The

last group, which included all other people, was called

¶5: *Outline point IIB [The <u>contadino</u> family was usually patriarchal.]*

<u>Femminella and Quadagno 65–66</u> *indicates that preceding material summarizes two pages in the source.*

Quotation woven into last sentence of paragraph.

¶6: *Outline point IIC [Children's roles mirrored adult roles.]*

Schrader   4

stranieri; members of this category were viewed with sus-

picion and kept at a distance (Femminella and Quadagno

65).

¶5 For the southern Italian, family meant not only hus-

band, wife, and children, but also grandparents, uncles,

aunts, and cousins—in fact, all blood relatives—and even

godparents. This contadino family is usually seen as patri-

archal, but although the father was the head of the family,

the mother had a great deal of power. For example, the

mother was responsible for maintaining the home, the

true center of the family; for arranging her children's mar-

riages; and for managing financial affairs. The father

made all major decisions that involved the family's rela-

tionship with the world at large and, of course, was re-

sponsible for earning a living (Femminella and Quadagno

65-66). In short, the Italian family was "father-dominated

but mother-centered" (Yans-McLaughlin 84).

¶6 Children were a very important part of the family, and

the roles defined for them by their parents mirrored tradi-

tional adult roles. The contadino parents wanted their

<u>Gallo, Old Bread 152</u> *indicates that information is a paraphrase of source material. A short title is included because two books by Gallo are used in this paper.*

¶7: Outline point IIIA [Barzini sees the family as a "stronghold" and a "refuge."]

Both references in ¶ 7 cite the same source; two separate references are needed because a direct quotation requires its own reference.

Long quotation is introduced by a running acknowledgment.

Over four lines long, this quotation is typed as a block, indented ten spaces from the left margin, double-spaced, with two spaces above and below. No quotation marks are used. Because the quotation is a single paragraph, no further paragraph indentation is needed. Note that in a block quotation, final punctuation is placed before the parenthetical reference.

children to be well educated in proper behavior, but their
expectations were very different for their sons and their
daughters. Male children were taught to be patient, to
have inner control over their emotions, and to show respect for their elders and acknowledge their wisdom. The
females were taught household skills and encouraged to
develop qualities that would enable them to take their
place as the center of the family (Gallo, Old Bread 152).

¶7 Family solidarity gave the southern Italians a sense of
unity and cohesiveness (Gallo, Old Bread 152). Within the
family, a strong value system protected each individual
from a hostile environment. Luigi Barzini describes the
role of the family in Italian society in this way:

> The Italian family is a stronghold in a hostile
> land; within its walls and among its members,
> the individual finds consolation, help, advice, pro-
> vision, loans, weapons, allies, and accomplices to
> aid in his pursuits. No Italian who has a family
> is ever alone. He finds in it a refuge in which to
> lick his wounds after a defeat, or an arsenal and

*Gallo, Old Bread 152 indicates that the Barzini
quotation was cited in Gallo's Old Bread, New
Wine. Notice that the reference is placed in
the right-hand margin of the block quotation.*

*¶8: Outline point IIIB [Italians did not trust out-
siders.]*

*Quotation is blended into last sentence of para-
graph. Direct quotation is used here because
wording of original is distinctive and hard to
paraphrase.*

*¶9: Transitional paragraph. Introduces outline
point IV [Italians in America have remained
somewhat aloof.]*

Schrader   6

a staff for his victorious drives. (qtd. in Gallo,

Old Bread 152)

The Italian family was so strongly bonded that it became

the most powerful single unit to the individual. Since

Southern Italy was perceived as threatening and lawless,

the family was the only unit the individual could rely on.

¶8   The southern Italian family rarely became entangled

in conflicts outside its own close-knit unit. If individuals

placed any type of trust outside the family, they were con-

sidered by members of their own family to be taking risks

that in the end could cause them to lose everything. To go

outside the family for help was just not done since by so

doing Italians would be placing themselves in a situation

where "the form was alien, the access unequal, the rules

unknown, and the justice pernicious" (Gallo, Old Bread

156).

¶9   The Italians came to America with a culture that was

in many ways different from a rapidly developing indus-

trial society, a society that needed their labor but rejected

their "unusual" customs. The extent to which they were

Two references indicate that the paragraph's information comes from two different sources.

¶10: *Outline point IVA [Immigrants often joined fellow villagers in urban "Little Italys."]*

Paragraph 10 uses paraphrase, summary, and direct quotation from four sources. Here is Michael's note card for Gans 205 (his own comments appear in brackets):

Emigration to Italy   —Gans, p. 205

Italian immigrants brought their social structure to America. In the cities, they usually "settled in Italian neighborhoods, where relatives often lived side by side, and in the midst of people from the same Italian town. Under these conditions, the family circle was maintained much as it had existed in Southern Italy."

[Gans bases his comments on immigrants in this section not on the Boston neighborhood he studied but on a study of New York's East Harlem area by Leonard Covello - see my bibliography card on Covello.]

successful in staying apart from the larger society can be
seen through an examination of the characteristics of
Italian-Americans today. Although assimilation has occurred, cultural traditions, maintained by strong family
ties, have affected the relationship of the Italians to American society (Yans-McLaughlin 79). In addition, the Italians have become increasingly aware that their ethnic
identity has been maintained by the stability and isolation
of their communities and by their reliance on the services
and institutions offered by their communities (Yancy,
Ericksen, and Juliani 399).

¶10   Many Italian families migrated to America to join relatives or friends from their villages. At the beginning of
the immigration, many Italians settled into areas known
as "Little Italys," urban neighborhoods "where relatives
often lived side by side, and in the midst of people from the
same Italian town. Under these conditions, the family circle was maintained much as it had existed in Southern
Italy" (Gans 205). To a great extent, these "Little Italys"
have been maintained, becoming extended families for their

Three references indicate paraphrase of source material.

Original source for Femminella and Quadagno 77: "According to the 1960 census, nearly 70 percent of Italian-Americans are concentrated in the northeastern portion of America."

Original source for Glazer and Moynihan 187: "Even the trek to the suburbs, when it does occur among Italians, is very often a trek of families of two generations, rather than simply of the young. And it is striking how the old neighborhoods have been artfully adapted to a higher standard of living rather than simply deserted, as they would have been by other groups, in more American style."

Original source for Femminella and Quadagno 77: ". . . of all the ethnic groups, Italians most often live in the same neighborhood as their parents and siblings and visit them every week."

See page 621 for Michael's note card for the Sons of Italy meeting.

The last sentence of paragraph 10 sums up main idea of paragraph and clarifies connections among sources' ideas.
¶11: Outline point IVB [Immigrants maintain a family-oriented society in America.]

residents. The 1960 census showed that almost 70 percent of Italian-Americans were still clustered in the northeastern region of the United States (Femminella and Quadagno 77). Glazer and Moynihan note that second- and third-generation Italian-Americans are more likely to work to improve old neighborhoods than to move. When they do leave the old neighborhoods, children and parents often move together (187). National Opinion Research Center surveys have found that Italians are more likely than other ethnic groups to live in the same neighborhood as their closest family members and to visit them regularly (Femminella and Quadagno 77). Italian-Americans also exhibit a strong sense of loyalty to and responsibility for their paisani, insisting, for instance, that family and community should house and support their own indigents rather than relying on government agencies (Sons of Italy). It is clear that many Italian-Americans value their ethnic solidarity and their independence from the larger society.

¶11   Italian immigrants have by and large maintained

Yans-McLaughlin 61 indicates paraphrase of a
source. The original reads: "The society
which these peasants left behind is frequently
termed 'familistic' because the nuclear and
extended family, rather than the individual or
the community, dominated social life to such
an extent that an individual's primary social
role was his or her role in the family."

¶12: Outline points VA and B [Some women have
sought employment. Conflicts have occurred
between parents and children.]

Paragraph 12 opens with a transitional phrase
("Despite this cohesiveness. . . .") introducing
a discussion of the changes the family experienced in America and relating them to the
preceding discussion. The paragraph combines paraphrase, summary, and direct quotation from two print sources and two interviews.

their Old World family system in the United States. The

type of society they left behind is frequently referred to as

"familistic" because the individual's social role was defined

primarily by the family (Yans-McLaughlin 61). In the

United States as in Italy, the importance of the family over

the community or the individual was maintained, and this

too kept Italians somewhat aloof from outsiders.

¶12   Despite this cohesiveness, the first-generation Italian

family in America was in transition. It was torn between

the Italian culture transmitted by the family and the

American culture transmitted by American institutions.

Many changes occurred when the family came to America.

When the Italian immigrants arrived in America, many

were faced with difficulties in finding work. It was often

necessary for the mother to go out and find a job. In

Southern Italy, the mother rarely left the house to go out

and work, but in America her employment was often nec-

essary for the family's survival. Some researchers view

this as a breakdown of the Italian-American family, but

others disagree, believing women took only those jobs that

Femminella and Quadagno 71 indicates a paraphrase of a source.

Comments of interview subjects, summarized,
are introduced by running acknowledgments.
Interview subjects are listed in the Works
Cited section at the end of the paper.

Source for *Gallo, Old Bread 159* uses present
tense. To tailor the quotation to the sentence,
the verb are was dropped.

Notice the reference to the explanatory note at
the end of paragraph 12. Michael includes
material in this note that would distract readers if it were included in the text. The note
itself does not present information that is
necessary to the discussion, but it does shed
light on Michael's research.

¶13: Outline point VC [The family system has
changed.]

Schrader   10

they felt were in line with the family value system—for

instance, work in a factory that employed other Italian-

American women (Femminella and Quadagno 71). Father

Vincent P. D'Ancona, a parish priest in the heavily Italian

South Philadelphia area, reports that even today a wife's or

mother's need to seek employment remains one of the pri-

mary sources of family tension, whether the need is eco-

nomic or emotional. Conflicts also occurred among par-

ents and their children—even though many children

agreed that their parents were "too good to fight with"

(Gallo, Old Bread 159). Both Father D'Ancona and barber

Anthony Pesca, long-time residents of South Philadelphia,

observe that today parents and children (despite their love

and respect for each other) regularly engage in heated

quarrels over issues like dating and curfews, use of drugs

and alcohol, and church attendance. The most sensitive

issue, Father D'Ancona believes, is the desire of a child to

live outside the community or to marry a non-Italian.[1]

¶13   Although some patterns did remain the same, the Old

World family system changed as time went on. Paul J.

Paragraph 13 opens with a transitional phrase ("Although some patterns did remain the same. . . .") to signal movement from discussion of adherence to Old World family system to focus on changes within the family. The topic sentence is supported by information from two sources.

Summary of main points of Campisi article is introduced by a running acknowledgment citing author, date, and title of this important study.

<u>443–49</u> *cites the entire article, indicating that the material represents a summary of the article. Because the author's name appears in the text, only the page numbers are noted parenthetically.*

Three references are made to Herbert Gans's book-length study, which is the source of the paraphrase and quotation in this paragraph. Running acknowledgments clearly distinguish information in Gans's original 1962 study from material added in the second edition (1982) and points made by Gans himself from conclusions drawn by Crispino and only cited by Gans.

Schrader   11

Campisi's often-cited 1948 study, "Ethnic Family Patterns:
The Italian Family in the United States," examines the
changes between the southern Italians and first- and
second-generation Italian-Americans. One of the major
changes this study found was that although the peasant
family was primarily ruled by the father, by the second
generation the family had become democratic, with the father's position more equal to that of the mother and children. Campisi also found that the influence of Italian culture was growing weaker, with more and more cultural
values shaped by the larger society rather than by the family (443-49). As recently as 1962, however, Herbert Gans
noted that the husband was still the breadwinner and the
wife's primary responsibilities were still her home and
children. In fact, in Gans's working-class population, the
roles of husband and wife were clearly differentiated (50-
52). But in the 1982 update of his study, when he considers the third generation of Italian-Americans, Gans finds
that even in Italian urban neighborhoods, "the traditional
social segregation of husbands and wives has been reduced

Michael's discussion of the Crispino study cited by Gans blends a direct quotation smoothly into the sentence. Because it is clear that Crispino is quoted by Gans, there is no need to include the abbreviation qtd. in *as part of the citation. Ellipses indicate the omission of an unnecessary word. The original source reads: "Increasingly, friends replaced family members as preferred associates, however, and many were not Italian-American or peers they had known since childhood." The last sentence sums up the paragraph's main point and ends with a reference to an explanatory note. Again, the information in this note would have interrupted the flow of the discussion, so the decision to put it in a note was a sensible one.*

¶14: Outline point VIA [The Italian family remains close.]

Paragraph 14 begins with a transitional phrase ("Despite these changes. . . ."), which introduces information directly supporting the paper's thesis.

The paragraph includes summary, paraphrase, and direct quotation from five different sources—four print sources and Michael's own observations. See page 636 for an earlier draft of part of this paragraph.

Schrader   12

considerably, although some men remain reluctant to help

with childrearing and housework" (231). In his study,

Gans cites an unpublished study of Bridgeport, Connecticut,

by James Crispino. As Gans notes, Crispino reports that

while his third-generation Italian-Americans felt very close

to their relatives, more and more often "friends replaced

family members as preferred associates . . . and many

were not Italian-American or peers they had known since

childhood" (230). It is clear, then, that some aspects of

the traditional family systems are changing.[2]

¶14   Despite these changes, however, the Italian-American

family has remained close-knit and stable. After coming to

America, the Italian-American family continued to be ex-

tremely close. In fact, in one study, which involved fifty

first-generation and ninety second-generation Italian-

American adults from an ethnic neighborhood in New

York City, researchers found that the extended family was

more important to second-generation than to first-genera-

tion Italian-Americans. Although the second-generation

family had generally become larger, relatives tended to live

Palisi 49–50 indicates that the preceding sentences summarize information from two
pages of a source.

*Goodman's article is one page long; therefore,
no page number is included in the citation.*

¶15: Outline point VIB [The Italian family remains stable.]

*Paragraph 15 combines paraphrase, summary,
and direct quotation from three sources.*

in closer physical proximity and to have closer and more

extensive social ties with one another (Palisi 49-50).

Today, Italians remain more likely than members of most

other ethnic groups to have relatives over sixty living with

them (Goodman). A walking tour of a typical urban Ital-

ian-American neighborhood supports this, showing a large

proportion of elderly residents, often accompanied by chil-

dren and grandchildren as they go about routine errands

and shopping. Even when members of the extended family

are not actually part of the household, the relationships

among family members are close; the family provides emo-

tional support and also serves as a social network (Gans

46). In fact, even Italian-American gangsters typically

maintain very close and highly stable family relationships

(Glazer and Moynihan 196).

¶15 The stability of the Italian family is reflected in the

low rates of divorce and intermarriage. The 1970 census

showed that only about 3 percent of all Italian-Americans

were divorced and that the divorce rate was not signifi-

cantly higher for younger Italians. Alfred J. Tella, special

*Ellipsis mark indicates that nonessential mate-
rial has been deleted from the end of a sentence.*

¶16: Conclusion

*Topic sentence of paragraph 16 indicates para-
graph will draw paper's ideas together.*

*Direct quotations from a personal letter and a
scholarly source both stress the continuing
importance of family to Italian-Americans,
reinforcing the paper's thesis.*

adviser to the Director of the Census Bureau, notes that despite increasing affluence, Italian-Americans retain closer family ties than other groups. Tella sees the fact that Italians as a group get fewer divorces as one indication of this continued closeness (Goodman). Glazer and Moynihan support this view. They say: "That the family is 'strong' is clear. Divorce, separation, and desertion are relatively rare. Family life is considered the norm for everyone . . ." (197). Moreover, two separate studies show Italians to have one of the lowest intermarriage rates; thus it can be concluded that they retain a high degree of ethnic identity (Femminella and Quadagno 74).

¶16 Several conclusions may be drawn about the Italian-American family today. Assimilation has occurred, but the notion of the importance of family has been passed down from generation to generation and has remained an important characteristic of the Italian-American family. As Frank Mucci, a third-generation Italian-American says, "You can't do without your family, and they can't do without you. Your family has to stay your first responsibility,

no matter what happens." So far, the stable Italian family

system has survived through the years, and it seems likely

to continue to do so. As Patrick Gallo notes, "The family

for the southern Italian remains the supreme societal or-

ganization" (<u>Ethnic</u> 87).

This page receives a number.

*Notes 1 and 2 are explanatory notes that provide
supplementary information to the reader.*

1″

center   Notes
double space

[1]Because of the many interruptions in the interview

with Mr. Pesca, I was unable to determine which issue he

views as most likely to produce serious conflict between

parents and children.

[2]The nomination of Congresswoman Geraldine Ferraro,

an Italian-American wife and mother, as the Democratic

vice-presidential candidate in 1984 seems to support the

fact that the role of women in the Italian family is chang-

ing.

Every page of the Works Cited section receives a number.

The first entry illustrates the correct form for a signed journal article by a single author. Note that it provides inclusive pagination.

Use alphabetical order

Indent 5 spaces

Double-space between and within entries

Entry illustrates form for a book with more than one author.

Entry identifies the subject of a personal interview.

Entry refers to an article by Femminella and Quadagno in a book edited by Mindel and Habenstein.

The List of Works Cited contains two works by Patrick Gallo. Note that the author's name is not repeated; instead, three unspaced hyphens, followed by a period, are used.

Entry identifies a book with a single author.

1″   Schrader   17

center   **Works Cited**
double space
Campisi, Paul J. "Ethnic Family Patterns: The Italian

  Family in the United States." American Journal of

  Sociology 53 (1948): 443-49.

Cordasco, Francesco, and Eugene Bucchioni. The Italians,

  Social Backgrounds of an American Group. New York:

  Sentry, 1974.

D'Ancona, Father Vincent P. Personal interview. 10 Feb.

  1986.

Femminella, Francis X., and Jill S. Quadagno. "The Italian

  American Family." Ethnic Families in America. Ed.

  Charles H. Mindel and Robert W. Habenstein. New

  York: Elsevier Scientific, 1976. 61-88.

Gallo, Patrick J. Ethnic Alienation. Cranbury, N.J.: Fair-

  leigh Dickinson UP, 1974.

---. Old Bread, New Wine. Chicago: Nelson-Hall, 1981.

Gans, Herbert J. The Urban Villagers. New York: Free,

  1982.

Glazer, Nathan, and Daniel Patrick Moynihan. Beyond the

  Melting Pot. 2nd ed. Cambridge, Mass.: MIT P, 1970.

Entry refers to a signed newspaper article, giving section and page number of the article.

Entry refers to a personal letter.

Entry identifies the subject of a telephone interview.

Entry refers to a meeting the author attended.

Entry refers to a neighborhood walking tour taken by the author.

Entry refers to a signed journal article with more than one author.

Schrader   18

Goodman, Walter. "Scholars Find Bad Image Still Plagues

U.S. Italians." New York Times 15 Oct. 1983, late ed.:

B25.

Mucci, Frank. Letter to author's grandmother. 17 Nov.

1980.

Palisi, Bartolomeo S. "Ethnic Generation and Family Struc-

ture." Journal of Marriage and Family 28 (1966):

49-50.

Pesca, Anthony. Telephone interview. 10 Feb. 1986.

Sons of Italy Meeting. Philadelphia, PA. 30 March 1986.

Walking Tour. South Philadelphia. 10 Feb. 1986.

Yancy, William L., Eugene Ericksen, and Richard N. Juliani.

"Emergent Ethnicity: A Review and Reformulation."

American Sociological Review 41.3 (1976): 391-403.

Yans-McLaughlin, Virginia. Family and Community: Ital-

ian Immigrants in Buffalo. Ithaca: Cornell UP, 1977.

VIII

Writing Special Assignments

Writing Essay Examinations

Taking examinations is a skill, one you have been practicing throughout your life as a student. Although both short-answer and essay examinations require you to study, to recall what you know, and to budget your time carefully as you write your answers, only essay questions ask you to synthesize information and to arrange ideas in a series of clear, logically connected sentences. To write an essay examination, you must do more than memorize facts; you must master those facts. You must see the relationships among many facts and be able to infer from them a meaning that is greater than the sum of its parts.

40a Planning an Essay Examination

Because you write quickly and under pressure during an examination, you may be tempted to skip the planning and revision stages. But writing in a frenzy and handing in your examination without a second glance can result in a disorganized or even incoherent answer. With advance planning and sensible editing, you can produce a more organized, coherent answer that gets a higher mark—provided the answer is correct. You should therefore use the same strategies you use to write any essay even though you are writing for a different purpose.

(1) Review your material

Be sure you know beforehand the scope and format of the examination. How much of your text and class notes will the examination cover—the entire semester's work or just the material covered since the last test? Will you have to answer every question, or will you be able to choose among alternatives? Will the examination be composed entirely of short-answer questions, or will it include one-sentence, one-paragraph, or essay-length answers as well? Will the examination emphasize your recall of specific facts or your ability to demonstrate your understanding of the course material by drawing conclusions?

Examinations challenge you to recall and express in writing what you already know—what you have read, what you have heard in class, what you have reviewed in your notes. Before you even begin your examination, then, you will have studied for it: rereading your text and class notes, underlining key points, and perhaps outlining key sections of your notes. If you are preparing for a short-answer examination, you may memorize facts—the definition of pointillism, the date of Queen Victoria's death, the formula for a quadratic equation, three reasons for the fall of Rome, two examples of conditioned reflexes, four features of a feudal economy, six steps in the process of synthesizing vitamin C—without analyzing their relationship to one another or to a body of knowledge as a whole. When preparing for an essay examination, however, you must do more than remember information; you must also make connections among ideas and relate them to the question you are considering.

When you are certain that you know what to expect, you can prepare by carefully reviewing the appropriate material. You should also try to anticipate the essay questions your instructor might ask. As you study, mentally note key concepts and the connections among them, and answer likely essay questions in your mind or even in writing. Try out potential questions on classmates, and see whether you can brainstorm together on a few of them.

**exam
40a**

(2)   Consider your audience and purpose

The *audience* for any examination is almost always the instructor who prepared it. He or she already knows the answers to the questions and a great deal more about the subject. As you read the questions, think about what your instructor has emphasized in class. Although you want to respond to your instructor's question, you may certainly arrange material in a new way or use it to make your own point. Do keep in mind, however, that your *purpose* is to demonstrate that you understand the material, not to make clever remarks or bring up irrelevant information. Your instructor reads a lot of examinations, and anything you can do to ease this task will be appreciated.

(3) Read through the entire examination

Your time is usually limited when you take an examination, so you must plan carefully. How long should a "short-answer" or "one-paragraph" or "essay-length" answer be? How much time should you devote to answering each question? The question itself may specify the length of your answer, so look for that information. More often the point value of each question or the number of questions on the examination will determine how much time to spend on each answer. If an essay question is worth 50 out of 100 points, for example, you will probably have to spend at least half and perhaps more of your time planning, writing, and proofreading your answer.

Before you begin to write, read the entire examination carefully to determine your priorities and your strategy. First, make sure that your copy of the test is complete and that you understand the format each question requires. Ask your instructor or proctor if you need clarification. Then decide where to start. Responding first to short answers (or to essay questions whose answers you are sure of) is usually a good strategy because it ensures that you will not get bogged down in a question that baffles you, leaving too little time to write a strong answer to a question you understand well. Moreover, answering first the questions you are sure of can help build confidence.

exam
40a

(4) Read each question very carefully

To answer correctly, you need to know exactly what the question asks. As you read any essay question, you may find it helpful to underline key words.

> SOCIOLOGY: <u>Distinguish</u> among <u>Social Darwinism</u>, <u>instinct theory</u>, and <u>sociobiology</u>, giving <u>examples</u> of each.

> MUSIC: <u>Explain how</u> Milton <u>Babbitt</u> used the <u>computer</u> to expand <u>Schoenberg's</u> <u>twelve-tone</u> method.

> PHILOSOPHY: <u>Define existentialism</u> and name <u>three</u> influential existentialist <u>works</u>, explaining <u>why</u> they are important.

Look at the verbs contained in the instructions: explain, compare, contrast, trace, evaluate, discuss, interpret, analyze, summarize, describe, classify, or give examples. Then look at the other words. If the question calls for a *comparison and contrast* of *two* styles of management, a *description* or *analysis* of *one* style, no matter how well done, will not be acceptable. If the question asks for causes *and* effects, a comprehensive discussion of causes alone will not do. The wording of the question suggests what you should emphasize. For instance, an American history instructor would expect very different answers to these two examination questions.

1. Give a detailed explanation of the major *causes* of the Great Depression, noting briefly some of the effects of the economic collapse on the United States. (1 hour)
2. Give a detailed summary of the *effects* of the Great Depression on the United States, briefly discussing the major causes of the economic collapse. (1 hour)

Although these questions look somewhat alike, the first calls for an essay that focuses on *causes*, whereas the second asks you to stress the *effects*.

(5)   Brainstorm to find ideas

Once you understand the question, begin brainstorming. The brainstorming process will help reveal the scope of your knowledge. If you know your material well, you may be able to brainstorm mentally. Otherwise, write down your ideas. Quickly list all the relevant points you can remember; then select key points and delete less promising ones. You might even tentatively arrange the key points you have arrived at. A quick review of your ideas should lead you toward a workable thesis for your essay answer.

40b   Shaping an Examination Answer

(1)   Finding a thesis

Often you can expand the examination question into a thesis statement. For example, the second American history examination question above suggests this idea.

> EFFECTIVE THESIS: The Great Depression, caused by the American government's economic policies, had major political, economic, and social effects on the United States.

A good thesis addresses all aspects of the question but

highlights only relevant concerns. The following thesis statements are not effective.

> VAGUE: The Great Depression, caused largely by profligate spending patterns, had a number of very important results.

> INCOMPLETE: The Great Depression caused major upheaval in the United States.

> IRRELEVANT: The Great Depression, caused largely by America's poor response to the 1929 crash, had more important consequences than World War II.

(2) Making a scratch outline

Because time is limited, it is all the more important that you plan your answer before you write it. Therefore, once you have a suitable thesis, you should make a scratch outline of your major points.

Write on the inside cover of your exam book or its last sheet. Use the pattern of development suggested by the question—process, classification, or cause and effect, for instance—to shape your outline, and list your supporting points in their approximate order. Once you have a plan, check it against the question to make certain it covers everything the question requires and only what the question requires.

exam
40b

A scratch outline for an answer to the American history question might look like this.

> QUESTION: Give a detailed summary of the effects of the Great Depression on the United States, briefly discussing the major causes of the economic collapse.

> THESIS: The Great Depression, caused by the American government's economic policies, had major political, economic, and social effects on the United States.

> SUPPORTING
> POINTS: *Causes.* American economic policies: income poorly distributed, factories expanded too much, more goods produced than could be purchased.
>
> *Results*
> 1. Economic situation worsened—farmers, businesses, workers, and stock market all affected.
> 2. Roosevelt elected—closed banks, worked with Congress to enact emergency measures.

3. Reform—TVA, AAA, NIRA, etc.

4. Social Security Act, W.P.A., P.W.A.

An answer based on this outline will correctly follow a *cause-and-effect* pattern (see 4e.5), with an emphasis on effects, not causes.

40c Writing and Revising an Examination Answer

Referring to both thesis and outline, you can now write your answer. A simple statement of your thesis that summarizes your answer is your best introduction, for it shows the reader that you are addressing the question directly. Do not reach for stylistic effects; your time is precious, and so is your reader's.

Follow your outline point by point, using clear topic sentences and transitions to indicate your progression and to help the reader see that you are answering the question in full. Such signals, along with parallel sentence structure and repeated key words, make your answer easy to follow.

Essay answers must be complete and detailed, but they must not contain irrelevant material. Every unnecessary fact or opinion only increases your chance of error. Do not repeat yourself or volunteer unrequested information. Padding is instantly recognized. Do not express your own feelings or opinions or make unsupported generalizations. Use objective evidence, and be sure to support all your general statements with specific facts or examples.

Finally, leave enough time to reread and revise what you have written. Try to view your answer from a fresh perspective. Have you left out words or written illegibly? Is your thesis clearly worded? Does your answer support your thesis and answer the question? Are your facts right, and are your ideas presented in some logical order? Look at your topic sentences and transitions. Check sentence structure and word choice, spelling and punctuation. If a sentence—or even a whole paragraph—seems irrelevant, cross it out. If you suddenly remember something you want to add, you can insert a few additional words using a caret (∧). Neatly insert a longer addition at the end of your answer, box it, and write a brief note telling your instructor where it belongs.

exam
40c

In the following essay answer, notice how the student re-states the question in her thesis and keeps the question in focus by using words like *cause, effect, result, response,* and *impact*.

¶1 *Introduction—*
Thesis

Rephrases
exam
question

The Great Depression, caused by the American government's economic policies, had major political, economic, and social effects on the United States.

¶2 *Summarizes*
policies
leading to
Depression
(causes)

The Depression was precipitated by the stock market crash of October 1929. But its actual causes were more subtle; they lay in the U.S. government's economic policies. First, personal income was not well distributed. Although production rose during the 1920's, the farmers and other workers got too little of the profits; instead, a disproportionate amount of income went to the richest 5 percent of the population. The tax policies at this time made inequalities in income even worse. A good deal of income also went into development of new manufacturing plants. This expansion stimulated the economy but encouraged the production of more goods than consumers could purchase. Finally, during the economic boom of the 1920's the government did not attempt to limit speculation or impose regulations on the securities market; it also did little to help build up farmers' buying power. Even after the crash began, the government made mistakes: instead of trying to counter the country's deflationary economy, the government focused on keeping the budget balanced and making sure the United States adhered to the gold standard.

exam
40c

¶3 *Transition
from
causes to
effects*

The Depression, devastating to millions of individuals, had a tremendous impact on the nation as a whole. Its political, economic, and social consequences were great.

¶4 *Early
effects*

*Paragraphs
4–8
summarize
important
results in
chronological
order*

Between October 1929 and Roosevelt's inauguration on March 4, 1932, the economic situation grew worse and worse. Businesses were going bankrupt, banks were failing, and stock prices were falling. Farm prices fell drastically, and hungry farmers were forced to burn their corn to heat their homes. There was massive unemployment, with millions of workers jobless and humiliated, losing skills and self-respect. President Hoover's Reconstruction Finance Corporation made loans available to banks, railroads, and businesses, but he felt state and local funds (not the federal government) should finance public works programs and relief. Confidence in the president declined as the country's economic situation worsened.

**exam
40c**

¶5 *More
effects:
Roosevelt's
emergency
measures*

One result of the Depression, then, was the election of Franklin Delano Roosevelt. By the time of his inauguration, most American banks had closed, 13 million workers were unemployed, and millions of farmers were threatened by foreclosure. Roosevelt's response was immediate: two days after he took office, he closed all banks and took steps to support the stronger ones with loans and prevent weak ones from reopening. During the first hundred days of his administration, he kept Congress in special session. Under his leadership, Congress enacted emergency measures designed to provide "Relief, Recovery, and Reform."

¶6 *More effects: Roosevelt's reform measures*
In response to the problems caused by the Depression, Roosevelt set up agencies to reform some of the conditions that had helped to cause the Depression in the first place. The Tennessee Valley Authority, created in May of 1933, was one of these. Its purposes were to control floods by building new dams and improving old ones and to provide cheap, plentiful electricity. The TVA improved the standard of living of area farmers and drove down the price of power all over the country. The Agricultural Adjustment Administration, created the same month as the TVA, provided for taxes on basic commodities, with the tax revenues used to subsidize farmers to produce less. This caused prices to rise.

¶7 *More effects: NIRA, etc.*
Another important act passed in response to the problems of the Depression was the National Industrial Recovery Act. This act established the National Recovery Administration, an agency that set minimum wages and maximum hours for workers and set limits on production and prices. Other laws passed by Congress between 1935 and 1940 strengthened federal regulation of power, interstate commerce, and air traffic. Roosevelt also changed the federal tax structure to redistribute American income.

exam 40c

¶8 *More effects: Social Security, etc.*
One of the most important results of the Depression was the Social Security Act of 1935, which established unemployment insurance and provided financial aid for the blind and disabled

and for dependent children and their mothers.
The Works Progress Administration (W.P.A.)
gave jobs to over 2 million workers, who built
public buildings, roads, streets, bridges, and
sewers. The W.P.A. also employed artists,
musicians, actors, and writers. The Public
Works Administration (P.W.A.) cleared slums
and created public housing. In the National
Labor Relations Act (1935), workers received a
guarantee of government protection for their
unions against unfair labor practices by
management.

¶9   *Conclusion*   As a result of the economic collapse
known as the Great Depression, Americans saw
their government take responsibility for
providing immediate relief, for helping the
economy recover, and for taking steps to ensure
that the situation would not be repeated. The
economic, political, and social impact of the
laws passed during the 30's are still with us
today, helping to keep our government and our
economy stable.

exam
40c

Notice that this student does *not* describe the conditions of people's lives in detail, blame anyone in particular, discuss the president's friends and enemies, or consider parallel events in other
countries. She covers only what the question asks for. Notice, too,
how topic sentences—like "One result of the Depression. . . . ";
"In response to the problems caused by the Depression. . . . ";
and "One of the most important results of the Depression. . . ."
—keep the primary purpose of the essay in focus and serve as a
guide for the reader.

   A well-planned essay like this one is not easy to write. Consider this answer to the same question.

¶1   The Great Depression is generally
considered to have begun with the Stock

No clear thesis
Vague,
subjective
impressions of
the Depression

Market Crash of October 1929 and to have lasted until the defense build-up for World War II. It was a terrible time for millions of Americans, who were not used to being hungry or out of work. Perhaps the worst economic disaster in our history, the Depression left its scars on millions of once-proud workers and farmers who found themselves reduced to poverty. We have all heard stories of businessmen committing suicide when their investments failed, of people selling apples on the street, and of farmers and their families leaving the dust bowl in desperate search of work. My own grandfather, laid off from his job, had to support my grandmother and their four children on what he could make from odd carpentry jobs. This was the Depression at its worst.

¶2

What else did the Depression produce? One result of the Depression was the election of Franklin Delano Roosevelt. Roosevelt immediately closed all banks. Then Congress set up the Federal Emergency Relief Administration, the Civilian Conservation Corps, the Farm Credit Administration, and the Home Owners' Loan Corporation. The Reconstruction Finance Corporation and the Civil Works Administration were two other agencies designed to provide Relief, Recovery, and Reform. All these agencies helped Roosevelt in his efforts to lead the nation to recovery while providing relief and reform.

Gratuitous
summary

¶3

Along with these emergency measures, Roosevelt set out to reform some of the conditions he felt were responsible for the economic collapse. Accordingly, he created the Tennessee Valley Authority (TVA) to control floods and provide electricity in the Tennessee Valley. The Agricultural Adjustment Agency levied taxes and got the farmers to grow less, causing prices to rise.

Unsupported generalization

Thus these two agencies, the TVA and the AAA, helped to ease things for the farmers.

¶4

The National Industrial Recovery Act established the National Recovery Administration, which was designed to help workers. It established minimum wages and maximum hours, both of which made conditions better for workers. Other important agencies included the Federal Power Commission, the Interstate Commerce Commission, the Maritime Commission, and the Civil Aeronautics Authority. Changes in the tax structure at about this time made the tax system fairer and eliminated some inequities. Roosevelt, working smoothly with his cabinet and with Congress, took many important steps to ease the nation's economic burden.

Why were these agencies important? What did they do?

**exam
40c**

¶5

Roosevelt, despite the fact that he was handicapped by polio, was a dynamic president. His fireside chats, which millions of Americans heard on the radio every week, helped to reassure Americans that things would be fine. This increased his popularity. But he had problems, too. Not everyone agreed with him. Private electric companies

Discussion of Roosevelt irrelevant to topic

opposed the TVA, big business disagreed with his support of labor unions, the rich did not like the way he restructured the tax system, and many people saw him as dangerously radical. Still, he was one of our most popular presidents ever, and he was elected to four terms.

¶6   Social Security Act—unemployment insurance, aid to blind and disabled and children

Undeveloped information   WPA—built public projects

PWA—public housing

National Labor Relations Act—strengthened labor unions

This essay only partly answers the examination question. It devotes too much space to unnecessary elements—an emotional introduction, repetition of words and phrases, gratuitous summaries, and unsupported generalizations. With no thesis, the writer easily slips into a discussion that considers only the immediate impact of the Depression and never discusses its causes or long-term effects. Although the body paragraphs do provide the names of many agencies created by the Roosevelt administration, they do not explain the purpose of most of them. It appears that the student considers the mere formation of the agencies, not their contributions, to be the Depressions's most significant result.

Because the student took a time-consuming detour, she ends up having to list points at the end of the essay without discussing them fully. Although it is better to include undeveloped information than to skip it altogether, an undeveloped list has shortcomings. Essay answers are by definition made up of full paragraphs, and many teachers subtract credit if you do not write out your answer in full. More important, you cannot effectively show sequential or causal relationships in a list. The worst result of this student's digression, however, is that she saved no time to sum up her main points, even in a one-sentence conclusion.

exam
40c

40d Writing Paragraph-length Examination Answers

Some essay questions ask for a paragraph-length answer, not a full essay. A paragraph should be just that: not one or two sentences, not a list of points, not more than one paragraph.

A paragraph-length answer should be *unified* by a clear topic sentence. Just as an essay answer begins with a thesis statement, a paragraph answer opens with a topic sentence that summarizes what the paragraph says. You should generally phrase this sentence to echo the examination question. The paragraph should also be *coherent*—that is, its statements should be linked by transitions that move the reader along. And the paragraph should be as *complete* as possible, with enough relevant detail to convince your reader that you know what you are talking about. (See Chapter 4 for a full discussion of paragraphs.)

A typical paragraph-length answer to a question on a business examination might look like this.

QUESTION: In one paragraph, define the term *management by objectives*, give an example of how it works, and briefly discuss an advantage of this approach.

ANSWER:

**exam
40d**

Definition   As defined by Horngren, <u>management by</u> <u>objectives</u> is an approach whereby a manager and his or her superior together formulate goals, and plans by which they can achieve these goals, for a forthcoming period. For

Example   example, a manager and a superior can formulate a responsibility accounting budget, and the manager's performance can then be measured according to how well he or she meets the objectives defined by the budget. The

Advantage   advantage of this approach is that the goals set are attainable because they are not formulated in a vacuum. Rather, the objectives are based on what the entire team, with knowledge of the constraints on its task, reasonably expects to accomplish. As a result, the burden of responsibility is shifted from the superior to the team: the goal itself defines all the steps needed for its completion.

In this answer, key phrases ("As *defined* by. . . ."; "For *example*. . . ."; "The *advantage* of this approach. . . .") point to the various aspects of the question being covered. The writer volunteers no more than the question asks for, and his use of the wording of the question helps make the paragraph orderly, coherent, and emphatic.

The following paragraph is less successful.

Sketchy, casual definition	Management by objectives is when managers and their bosses get together to formulate their goals. This is a good system of management because it cuts down on hard feelings between the managers and their superiors. Since they set the goals together, they can make sure they're attainable by considering all possible influences, constraints, etc., that might occur. This way neither the manager nor the superior gets all the blame when things go wrong.
No example given	
Vague	

exam 40d

This student may know what *management by objectives* is, but his paragraph sounds more like a casual explanation to a friend than an answer to an examination question. Just as with an essay-length answer, a paragraph answer will not be effective unless you take the time to read the question carefully, plan your response, and outline your answer before you begin to write. It is always a good idea to echo the wording of the question early in your answer and to reread your answer to make sure it explicitly addresses the question.

Student Writer at Work:
Writing Essay Examinations

The long student paragraph below was written in response to a
question on an American literature examination.

> QUESTION: In one paragraph, explain the thematic relationship
> between the vignettes and the short stories in Heming-
> way's *In Our Time*, giving a few brief examples to illus-
> trate the parallels.

Edit this rambling answer to eliminate irrelevancies, redundancies, and superfluous information. You should end up with a
tightly organized paragraph under a topic sentence that explicitly addresses the question.

> ANSWER:

Hemingway's short-story collection In Our Time consists of
fifteen short stories and sixteen brief vignettes. The vignettes
originally appeared as a separate collection, published in 1924
as in our time. Later they were interspersed with short stories
to form In Our Time (1925). In both the stories and the vignettes there is an undercurrent of brutality and emptiness and
tragedy. In "On the Quai at Smyrna," the introduction, the narrator talks about women and their dead babies, and about mules
with broken legs being pushed off the dock into the water. In
the first short story, "Indian Camp," a boy, Nick Adams (who
appears in several of the stories and vignettes), accompanies his
father, a physician, to an Indian camp to deliver a baby. There
he not only sees the woman's suffering but also the Indian father who has slashed his own throat. A thread of senseless violence runs through the vignettes. Some depict women suffering
through childbirth and people in pain. Many treat the senseless
brutality of war in grim, matter-of-fact accounts of bombings
and shootings, descriptions of dead bodies lying about, and even
a sketch of Nick himself wounded and paralyzed. Five vignettes
are about bullfighting, with vivid images of dead and wounded
bulls and matadors. The short stories, some of which are about
Nick Adams, deal with unpleasant things like lies, bitter arguments, lack of communication, and drinking. One depicts de-

serted land where a thriving lumber mill once stood; another describes an encounter with a washed-up former champion fighter. "My Old Man" is about a jockey who is killed in an accident; his son witnesses his death and hears his horse being shot. In "Big Two-Hearted River" Nick Adams, apparently recovering from terrible war experiences, takes refuge in a deserted, burned-out setting and takes comfort in the rituals of setting up camp. The collection takes its title from a prayer: "Give us peace in our time, O Lord."

exam
40

41

Writing About Literature

When you write a critical essay about a creative work, your primary task is to state an attitude and then to give reasons and explanations that support it. But before you begin to write, you must first analyze the text to discover its meaning or meanings, which are conveyed *indirectly*, suggested rather than explicitly stated.

When you write a critical essay, you analyze, interpret, and sometimes evaluate a work.

When you *analyze*, you systematically consider the different elements of a work—the plot (what happens?), the characters (what are they like?), and so on—and examine the writer's techniques. You look closely at the text itself, studying words and phrases.

When you *interpret*, you use your analysis to determine what the work means.

When you *evaluate*, you consider whether a work succeeds or not, building on your analysis and interpretation to help you make your judgments. Thus, you cannot evaluate a work until you have analyzed and interpreted it.

41a Taking a Critical Stance

What is critical writing, and how is it different from other writing? Consider these two paragraphs about James Joyce's short story "Counterparts." A student in an introductory survey of literature course wrote the first in answer to the examination question "Briefly explain how Joyce illustrates the building frustration of Farrington, the main character in 'Counterparts.'"

Throughout the day described in "Counterparts," Joyce shows Farrington's frustration building. Trapped in a monotonous, dead-end job, ruled by the clock, Farrington cannot escape the constant criticism of his boss, Mr. Alleyne. Farrington is angry when Alleyne humiliates him in front of Miss Delacour, but the ultimate humiliation comes when Farrington is forced to apologize to Alleyne. He is further frustrated by his defeat in the arm-wrestling match, a defeat that leads to public humiliation. Farrington's failure at everything he attempts causes his frustration to build to unbearable limits.

Because the question called for facts, not analysis or interpretation or evaluation, the student provided plot summary. In a critical essay, he would have to do more.

Another student wrote this paragraph in answer to the question, "Why does Farrington beat his son?"

> Farrington is a victim. He is humiliated by his boss, ignored by the woman in the bar, and defeated by a younger man in an arm-wrestling contest. Powerless in all those areas of his life, he returns home at the end of the day to take out his frustrations on the only one weaker than he is: his son.

In her answer, this student goes on to analyze how and why the victim becomes the oppressor. Because the question requires a critical judgment, the student conveys her attitude toward the characters and analyzes their relationships. Before she could do so, she had to understand the story fully.

lit
41a

Literature is not the only subject of critical writing. Television shows, performances, films, paintings, songs, and architectural structures are all good subjects for the amateur or professional critic. In fact, you can take a critical approach to any aspect of life: to government policies or social programs, college curricula or employee performance. And, of course, here the word *critical* does not suggest negative judgments, although you might be used to thinking of it that way. When you criticize a work, you share your attitudes—favorable or unfavorable—with your reader.

You most often encounter critical writing in newspaper and magazine reviews—of restaurants, books, plays and films, even record albums, computer software, and music videos. But many of the critical essays you write in college will be about literature. You use the same systematic writing process with which you are already familiar: you plan your essay, shape your material, and write and revise your drafts. But when the subject matter is literature, there are special considerations.

41b   Planning the Critical Essay

First, of course, you must know what work or works you will
discuss. Your instructor may give you the option of choosing for
yourself, or the choice may be made for you. In either case, you
must decide on an attitude toward the work, the point you want
to make. You start by *reading your material*—reading it several
times, in fact—carefully, thoroughly, and critically. If the subject
is a poem, read it aloud and—line by line—try to paraphrase it.
After your first reading, reread your material, underlining lines or
passages that seem pertinent to your assignment.

As you read, *keep your assignment in mind.* Make sure you
understand exactly what it is you are to do. Your assignment may
be as general as "Write a critical essay about any work or works
we studied this semester," or it may suggest that you focus on a
particular area—for instance, that you analyze a character in a
story or consider the rhyme and meter of a poem. It may ask you
to compare two works, two writing styles, or two characters. It
may even specify the work and the way you are to approach it
("Why does Farrington beat his son?"). Such specific assignments
are particularly common on examinations. These assignments
narrow the subject for you. But if the assignment is open, allowing you to select the work and the point of view, then you have to
narrow the subject yourself.

Once you know your assignment, consider your audience
and purpose. Your *audience*—your instructor in most cases—is
familiar with the work, so keep plot summaries to a minimum,
unless a summary is explicitly asked for, and refer to the author's
technique without too many definitions. Your assignment may
specify *purpose*—that is, your instructor may ask you to analyze,
clarify, enlighten, argue, interpret, compare, or evaluate. A critical
essay can have one or many of these purposes. And always, your
general purpose is to shed light on a work of literature.

Other considerations also come into play. For instance, the
occasion for your writing helps determine your content. In an
examination, the limited time and the limited scope of the questions curtails your exploration of such considerations as comparisons with other works or biographical details. For a long
paper done at home, however, such explorations may be entirely
appropriate. In class you probably can't include any but the
briefest quotations, even if your teacher allows you to refer to

your text. At home, however, you have the time to look up quotations that illustrate your points.

The *length* of your paper also imposes certain limitations. In a long paper, naturally, you can explore areas that a brief essay can only touch on. A five-hundred-word essay about a short story might let you examine a character, the setting, or some aspect of language, but in it you could not do justice to all three. A longer paper might let you treat all these elements, and others: the author's other works, his or her life, major influences, or critical responses to the work, for example.

Assessing your own *knowledge* also helps you choose a subject. How much you now know and how much you can get to know quickly should give you a direction for your essay.

Finally, as you decide how you will approach your subject, you consider, one by one, the several elements in terms of which we analyze literature.

(1)   Plot

With a novel or short story or play, begin by considering the plot—what happens in the work. Examine how the events relate to one another and how single events relate to the work as a whole. You might look at how the writer has arranged events in time and compare that with the order in which they actually happened. You could also identify the *conflicts* that occur in the story and consider how they move the plot along. These conflicts usually occur between the main character, called a *protagonist*, and another character who opposes him or her, called the *antagonist*. (The antagonist may also be society in general, or a force within the protagonist's own mind.) There is always more to a plot than "boy meets girl" or "whodunit" or "rags to riches." If you can speak about the juxtaposition of individual events and what they mean, you are on your way to a successful analysis of plot.

lit
41b

(2)   Character

Analyzing **characters** and their motivations helps you understand the plot, but this analysis isn't always easy. A character's traits and feelings and values may be communicated directly, or they may have to be inferred from his or her actions or relationships to other characters or from what he or she *doesn't* say or do. What are the characters like? The protagonist need not be strong or brave or beautiful or even likable—he or she may be weak or greedy or foolish or indecisive. Characters may be complex and fully developed or barely delineated. Some characters may even be easily recognizable stereotypes, characters so often encountered by readers of fiction that they are completely predictable—the wicked stepmother, the straying husband, or the helpless, lovely damsel in distress, for instance. These *stock characters* may efficiently convey an impression, but major characters—ones who engage our interest—must be more fully developed. Do the major characters remain essentially unchanged by events or do they grow and develop and undergo significant changes in response to these events? What do they learn? How does this knowledge affect the other characters? The plot? What role do the minor characters play? These and other questions can lead you to material for a paper about character.

(3) Setting

Setting—where and when the action takes place—gives you the context in which to interpret what happens. *Setting* refers not just to a specific physical place—the dining room, for example—but also to the larger geographical location and historical period of the action. Is the setting so central to the action that the story could not take place anywhere else? Or is it almost incidental to the work? Is the *absence* of setting striking? Authors choose settings carefully, and their reasons for doing so should be considered just as carefully.

(4) Point of view

Point of view is another element you must consider. In a work of fiction, a narrator, or speaker, usually tells the story to readers from his or her point of view, or perspective. Do not confuse this narrator with the work's author: the narrator has a role to play, just as the other characters do. As one of the story's characters, a narrator may speak and think in the *first person* ("I"); this first-person narrator may be a major character who is actively involved in the story's events or a minor character who only observes much of the story's action.

Of course, when a story is told entirely in the *third person* (referring to characters as "he," "she," and "they"), you cannot identify the narrator as a particular character. But the narrator still conveys an attitude and reveals his or her feelings toward the people and events in the story. When a story is told in the third person, the narrator may be *omniscient* (all-knowing), seeing into the characters' minds, or *objective*, reporting events from the outside and seeing into no character's mind but leaving you to draw your own conclusions about the feelings and opinions of the characters. (In most plays, of course, there is no narrator, but a play still has a point of view: the author always tries to communicate some attitude through the use of sympathetic or unappealing characters.)

Understanding point of view can be challenging, but the writer's point of view controls how you grasp a work's meaning: it determines how much you know about the characters and events and how you perceive them.

(5) Tone and style

Tone varies significantly from author to author and work to work: it can be light or serious, straightforward or ironic, bitter or enthusiastic (see 1a.3). A narrator's tone reveals approval or disapproval of characters and action—and the whole range of attitudes in between. If you sense a discrepancy between the narrator's stated feeling and the attitudes the author conveys more subtly through word choice and arrangement, this too helps you unlock a writer's meaning. Or the narrator may take a certain tone toward the audience, becoming closely involved with the reader or maintaining some distance, for instance. Or a work's tone can be ironic. *Irony* is the use of language to suggest a discrepancy or incongruity between what a narrator says and what he or she actually means; between what a character says and what the reader actually knows; between what appears to be true and what actually is true; or between what does happen and what probably should have happened. Recognizing a note of irony in a writer's tone adds to our understanding of a writer's intentions.

Analysis of a writer's **style** also deepens your understanding of a work. Tone, diction, and sentence structure all work to shape style in an essay. This is even more true of creative writing. Style in a work of literature can be terse and understated or elaborately detailed, stiff and formal or loose and conversational. Writers often use *imagery* and *symbolism* to enrich style and reinforce meaning, so it is essential that you recognize these elements and understand why an author has chosen to use them—or not to use them. *Imagery*—that is, figurative language—and *symbolism* are effective because they carry a complex message in relatively few words. A well-crafted metaphor or symbol suggests meaning without explicit statement or cumbersome explanation (see 16d). Examining tone and style can be a rewarding way to analyze a work of literature.

(6) Theme

When we refer to the **theme** of a novel or short story or play, we mean the point or points the author sets out to make—the "message" or central concept of the work. To understand this theme, you must consider the author's purpose in writing, what truth he or she is trying to convey. The theme is often subtle, yet many of the story's elements will point to it.

As you consider all these elements, you will discover that certain aspects of the work seem more promising than others for development into a strong critical essay. This should help you decide on a topic. If after reviewing these elements you still can't find a workable topic, try something else: look for parallels between plot, character, and so on, in the work you are studying and those same elements in another work with which you are familiar—or between the work and "real life." If you still cannot find a topic, brainstorm, keeping in mind the individual elements of literary criticism as you write down ideas. If the subject of your critical essay is a poem, different considerations apply. In addition to tone and style, point of view, and theme (and, in a narrative poem, plot and character), you must also look at rhyme and other sound patterns, meter, and the form of the whole poem.

Being a good critic requires a thorough knowledge and understanding of your subject. This helps you to determine what elements to focus on—and later, what kind of critical language to use as you write.

When you have a topic, brainstorm to find something to say about it. You now have a literary work to consider as well as a topic, so your brainstorming list will include more material than a similar list for an essay on what you did last summer. But recalling your narrowed subject as you brainstorm should keep your list specific.

In addition to brainstorming, you may do some research,

talk with friends or with your instructor, or review your class notes. When you have sharpened the focus for your essay, you are ready to work on a thesis.

▶
EXERCISE 1

Choose a short story to use as the subject of a critical essay. Read the story carefully, and then reread it, several times if necessary. When you are sure you understand the story, complete the following tasks.

1. Consider plot, character, setting, point of view, tone, style, and theme, one by one. Which two elements seem to suggest the most promising topics for a critical essay? Try to find a good topic for a critical essay about the story by examining these two elements in detail.
2. Brainstorm to find material for a critical essay.

41c Shaping Your Material

If the wording of your assignment or the topic you have decided on is specific, your thesis may be taken directly from it. For instance, if your assignment asks, "Why does Farrington beat his son?" your thesis might be, "Farrington beats his son because after a day of being victimized, he needs a victim on whom to vent his frustrations." Or your thesis may emerge as you brainstorm.

lit
41c

　　　The purpose of your paper always determines your thesis. If the purpose is to compare—or defend or analyze—then your thesis should indicate this. In addition, you can state that a work is good (or not so good), that it resembles another work, that its theme is not the one that first meets the eye, that its characters are not individuals but types—there are many possibilities. Remember, though, that your thesis must be a *specific, arguable statement*—not, for instance, "Farrington victimizes his son" but "Farrington beats his son because after a day of being victimized, he needs a victim on whom to vent his frustrations." Once your work-in-progress has a tentative thesis, you can begin deciding on an effective arrangement for your ideas and gathering supporting examples and quotations. You can then make a working plan (see 2c) or outline (see 2d) to guide you as you begin drafting your critical essay.

▶
EXERCISE 2

Look over the brainstorming list you prepared in Exercise 1. Arrange the points on your list in a logical scheme, and decide on a tentative thesis for your paper. Then, prepare a working plan for the paper.

41d Writing and Revising

With the shape of your essay in mind, you can write your first draft. Write this draft quickly, without paying much attention to style, following your working plan or outline.

As you proceed, use *present tense* verbs. They indicate that the literary work has an existence outside your paper— "Lessing's short stories *focus* on different themes at different stages of her career . . ."; "Both Lady Gregory and Chekhov *arrange* their one-act plays to highlight the pattern of separation and reconciliation between the main characters." But when you refer to biographical data, use the *past tense*—"Plath's unresolved conflicts with her father *led* her to portray him as a Nazi."

As you write, you should cast yourself as an *objective narrator*. Avoid feeble phrases like *in my opinion* and *I feel*. If your evidence demonstrates that a judgment is valid, why suggest that it is true only because you say so? Keep your point of view professional and your paper will be more credible.

Guided by your tentative thesis and by your working plan or outline as well, you should be able to give your first draft focus with a thesis-and-support structure. Make sure your tentative thesis is strong and that the facts and examples in your draft support it; arrange your material so that your essay has an introduction that expresses your attitude toward the work you are evaluating, a body that gives reasons and explanations for your attitude, and a conclusion that reaffirms your position. Here is one possible essay structure.

1. Begin with a one- or two-paragraph *introduction*. If you are responding to a specific question, be sure to echo its wording. Here, too, you want to present some background on your subject—information about the author, perhaps, or about comparable works that have relevance to the work you are discussing. You might describe the work, review its most striking features, *briefly* summarize its plot, or place it in its historical context. Your beginning paragraphs exist simply to

lit
41d

give your readers an overview of the work and a clear idea of your thesis.

2. The *body* of your essay moves on to elaborate your specific points. It may be necessary to analyze in detail some or all of the elements—plot, character, theme—that apply to the work you are discussing. Here you support your critical judgments with specific references to the work. Be sure to use enough evidence to support your assertions; when you make a judgment, back it up with pertinent examples from the text itself. You may recount events, quote dialogue, describe character or setting, or paraphrase ideas, but you must supply a sufficient number—and a sufficiently wide range—of examples if your readers are to accept your conclusions. You cannot just assert that a story's theme depends on a Biblical allusion or that a pattern of imagery exists; you must explain the allusion or list the related images that contribute to the pattern.

Use a direct quotation if you must—when a writer says something important or unusual in a special way. Don't overdo it, however, or your essay will be no more than a string of quotations. And be sure that your quotations actually illustrate your points. Before using a quotation, ask yourself whether the author's exact words are really crucial to your point. Could a paraphrase be equally effective? If so, then paraphrase. (For more on summary, paraphrase, and quotation, see 37a.)

Your familiarity with different patterns of development should guide you as you shape your essay. You can give your critical paper an underlying structure by using comparison and contrast ("Compare the plot structures of Lady Gregory's *The Workhouse Ward* and Chekhov's *The Marriage Proposal*); cause and effect ("Trace the influence of Zen on the later works of J. D. Salinger"); classification ("Discuss the feminist, leftist, and apocalyptic themes that dominate Doris Lessing's short stories"); or any other pattern or combination of patterns (see 4e).

3. In the *conclusion* of your paper, review your main points, perhaps reaffirm and clarify your thesis, and close your essay gracefully yet emphatically. The last paragraph may include comparisons with other works, a particularly apt quotation from the work, a statement by the author or a literary critic, or simply a summary of the work's significance to its literary genre, to its historical era—or to you as a reader.

Once your first draft is completed, you should begin to focus on revision. Reconsider the soundness of your ideas, the phrasing of your thesis, the number and suitability of your supporting examples, and the logic of your organizing pattern. Consider too your tone and your style, your sentence construction, and your choice of words.

lit
41d

You may use any of the revision strategies discussed in 3d—peer criticism, outlining, or checklists—to help you revise your critical essay. When you are satisfied with your essay's basic content, logic, structure, and style, it is time to review your mechanics and do some editing and checking. Are spelling and punctuation correct? Have you quoted your sources accurately? Have you remembered to include the page number (for fiction), line number (for poetry), or act and scene number (for drama) parenthetically after each quotation, and to give credit for each idea that is not your own? Is the paper arranged, presented, and typed neatly, and according to the format required by your instructor?

Here is a critical essay written by a student to fulfill an English composition assignment. The assignment was, "Write a two-page critical essay comparing any two stories we studied this semester."

Meeting the Challenge

Both "A & P" by John Updike and "A Woman on a Roof" by Doris Lessing focus on young working men. Each of these young men is infatuated with a woman he does not really know. While these two stories have many obvious similarities in character and situation, they differ in how the central characters meet the challenge they face.

The basic situations and characters of the stories are similar up to a point. Both Sammy and Tom are young, innocent men who spend a good deal of time fantasizing. Both stories take place in the summertime, and both involve aloof, scantily clad women, and men who watch them and disapprove. In each story the young man's infatuation leads him to imagine a potential relationship with the woman, whom he sets on a pedestal. When, in each story, an older man insults the woman, the young man imagines himself as her protector, her savior. Despite these basic similarities, however, the stories develop quite differently.

Setting is one element that leads the two stories to their different resolutions. The supermarket in "A & P" is a society in miniature, complete with people and products, traffic and noise.

When Sammy realizes how much he despises this society, he is
pressured to take some action. The roof in Lessing's story, however, stands apart from society and its rules and conventions;
no other characters are up on the roof besides the workmen and
the woman across the way. Without an audience, Tom is not
pressured into making a grand gesture. The extreme heat of the
roof is also a factor missing in the artificial climate of the supermarket. This brutal heat is an important element in the
story. Not only does it partially explain the men's anger and
frustration, but it also encourages Tom's elaborate fantasies to
build to a point where disappointment is inevitable. Moreover,
it hypnotizes Tom and paralyzes him, preventing him from making the decision to act in the woman's defense.

Sammy, unlike Tom, actually carries out his fantasy and
acts as Queenie's savior. Although Tom's rich fantasies convince
him that the woman in the bikini is worthy of his respect and
even his love, he is still unable to protect her from another
man's rude remarks. Tom's defense of the woman takes place
only in his mind, but Sammy acts. Whatever his motives are,
Sammy actually takes a stand against his boss's treatment of
Queenie and her friends when he says, "I quit."

lit
41d

The contrast between Tom's failure to act and Sammy's gal-
lant (though useless) gesture illustrates the fundamental differences between the two characters. Although Sammy never con-
fronts Queenie, he does confront Lengel, taking a strong stand
for what he believes. Tom does finally speak with the woman of
his dreams, but his long-awaited meeting falls flat when she reveals her lack of interest in him. Neither Sammy nor Tom is
able to attract the object of his fantasy, but Sammy has the satisfaction of knowing he has spoken out, and Tom must live with
the knowledge that he has remained a passive voyeur.

Tom never gains any insight into himself. After he is rejected, he gets drunk to soothe his anger and hatred; he is disil-
lusioned about women and disgusted with himself. He has accomplished nothing, neither rescued the lady in distress nor
gained her admiration or affection. As "A & P" ends, however,

Sammy is a stronger person. He knows the world is going to be a hard place to live in from now on, but he also knows that he has broken out of the conformity that the supermarket society tries to enforce. He has reason to be proud of himself.

This assignment specifically asked for a comparison of two works, so the student's first step was to review the stories the class had read and select two to compare. Next she reread those stories carefully and identified the similarities and differences she could best discuss.

In the essay itself, the student begins by introducing the stories she will discuss, making it clear that she will be comparing them. She states her thesis at the end of paragraph 1. In the body of the essay, she analyzes plot, character, and setting, giving specific examples to support her assertions. In paragraph 2 she summarizes the main similarities between the two stories, presenting these first and in little detail because she considers them less important than the differences developed in paragraphs 3, 4, and 5. In her conclusion she reinforces her essay's main point: given similar challenges Sammy and Tom react quite differently. Throughout her essay, the student uses present tense to discuss the two works of literature. She avoids extensive plot summary and basic explanations and identifications, confident that her audience will be thoroughly familiar with both stories.

lit
41d

▶

EXERCISE 3

Write a first draft for the paper you planned in Exercises 1 and 2. Then revise until you are satisfied with your critical essay.

Writing Business Letters and Memos

Everyone writes business letters from time to time—to request information, to order a product, to complain about something, or to make an application. Many of the principles of college writing also apply to this kind of writing.

42a Composing Business Letters

(1) Planning your letter

Before you sit down to write a business letter, you should think carefully about your purpose. You should decide in advance why you are writing your letter and keep that objective in mind as you write. Furthermore, you should evaluate your audience. Are you writing to a single person? Will a group of people see your letter and act on it? What information and what approach must you use to influence this audience? When you have answered these questions to your own satisfaction, do some brainstorming or some research to gather the information that you will need to write your letter.

(2) Organizing your material

Once you have the information that you want to convey, you should organize it into large categories and put those categories into order. This arrangement becomes the structure for your letter. For example, a student in a work-study program who had to write a letter to a potential customer explaining the advantages of the Apple IIe as a word processor over manual typing did some research and brainstorming and assembled this list of information.

> The Apple IIe has a text editor.
> The Apple IIe system costs $3700.
> Temporary typists cost $5700 per year.

Deadlines disturb routines.
Employee morale is down.
Rental typewriters cost $873 per year.
The Apple IIe does not make errors.
Floppy disks are $14.95 a box.
The Apple IIe is four times faster than manual typing.
Floppy disks make storage easier and cheaper.

Reviewing her list, the student realized that she could group her information under two topics: cost and efficiency. As she did this, she discarded some points and added others.

Cost
The Apple IIe system costs $3700.
Floppy disks are $14.95 a box.
Temporary typists cost $5700 per year.
Rental typewriters cost $873 per year.
Total savings first year: $3373.

Efficiency
The Apple IIe is four times faster than manual typing.
The Apple IIe has a text editor.
The Apple IIe does not make errors.
The Apple IIe makes deadlines easier to meet.
Floppy disks make storage easier and cheaper.

**bus
42a**

After putting her subpoints in logical order, she was ready to write her first draft.

(3)   Writing and revising your letter

Most businesses receive hundreds of letters each day, so your letter should be brief and to the point. Important information should appear early in the letter, and you should not digress. Be concise and try to sound as natural as possible. Stilted or flowery language is out of place, and so is legalistic terminology *(in re: your letter)* and business jargon *(in regards to, herewith enclosed)*, which get in the way of clear communication.

The first paragraph of your letter should introduce your subject and mention any relevant previous correspondence. The rest of your letter should present your reader with the facts needed to understand what you are saying. If the matter is complicated, you may want to list information in numbered points. Your conclusion should reinforce your message, and the whole letter should communicate your good will.

Type your business letter on good-quality 8½″ × 11″ paper. Leave wide margins, at least an inch all around, and balance your letter on the page. Type your letter single-spaced and use block format (see below). The **block format** letter begins every line at the left-hand margin and separates paragraphs with a double space. Double-space between the inside address and the salutation, between the salutation and the text, and between the text and the complimentary close.

After you proofread your letter, you may have to retype it. The appearance of your letter affects your reader's response to it. A neatly typed letter, free of smudges and errors, makes a favorable impression. A sloppy letter or one with misspellings or corrections made by hand presents you and your case badly. (See 42a.4 for more information on the format of business letters.)

Sample Letter—Block Format

Heading 6732 Wyncote Avenue
    Houston, Texas 77004
    May 3, 1986

Inside William S. Price, Jr., Director
address Division of Archives and History
    Department of Cultural Resources
    109 East Jones Street
    Raleigh, North Carolina 27611

Salutation Dear Mr. Price:

    Thank you for sending me the material I requested
    about the pirates in colonial North Carolina.

Body Both the pamphlets and the bibliography were
    extremely useful for my research. My instructor said
    that I had presented information in my paper that he
    had never seen before. Without your help, I am sure
    my paper would not have been so well received.

    I have enclosed a copy of my paper, and I would
    appreciate any comments you may have. Again, thank
    you for your time and trouble.

bus

42a

Complimentary close	Sincerely yours,

| *Written Signature* | |

| *Typed signature* | Kevin Wolk |

| *Additional data* | Enclosure |

(4) Understanding the conventions of a business letter

The format of a business letter may seem arbitrary and prescriptive, but remember that this format has evolved in response to the special needs of the business audience. Using an inside address, for example, seems pointless until you consider that business letters often circulate to people other than the recipient, and to these readers knowing the original recipient is often important. Dates are also important. Letters frequently become part of a permanent record, filed for some future use. These letters can have an importance weeks, months, and even years later that no one could have originally predicted.

By conforming to the following conventions when writing business letters, you will be less likely to forget an important bit of information—and of course your readers will know where to look for it in your letter.

The Heading

The **heading** of a business letter consists of the sender's return address, but not his or her name, and the date the letter is written. If you use letterhead stationary, supply only the date, typing it two spaces below the letterhead. Each line of the heading falls under the one above it, flush to the left.

Spell out words like *Street, Avenue, Road, Place, East,* and *West* in full. You may, however, abbreviate the names of the states using the postal list of abbreviations found in many college dictionaries. Be sure to punctuate the heading correctly. Commas separate the name of the city from that of the state and the day from the year. Do not, however, use punctuation before the zip code or at the ends of lines.

The Inside Address

The **inside address** cites the *recipient's* name and address. It begins at the left margin four to six lines below the heading, depending on the need to use space for a balanced page. Include an appropriate title (Mr., Mrs., Miss, Ms., Dr.) with the recipient's name and the recipient's full address. Previous correspondence should be your guide to your recipient's correct name and title.

The Salutation

The **salutation** ("Dear So and So") appears two spaces below the inside address, flush to the left margin. In business letters the salutation almost always ends with a colon, not a comma. It includes the person's title followed by the last name as it appears on the inside address.

If you do not know how to address a person in a specific profession—a judge, for instance—consult the index of a college dictionary such as *Webster's Ninth New Collegiate Dictionary* for a list of proper forms of address.

**bus
42a**

Addressee	Form of Address	Salutation
Federal judge	The Honorable John Smith, United States District Judge	Dear Judge Smith:

If you are on a first-name basis with someone, you should still use his or her *full name* and title in the inside address. You may, however, use the first name, followed by a *comma*, in the salutation.

If you are writing to a woman, refer to previous correspondence and use the title that she uses. If you do not know her preference, use Ms. If you know someone's initials but do not know whether the person is a man or a woman, you might call the company switchboard and ask. You can also use a neutral form of address—*Dear Editor* or *Dear Supervisor*, for example.

If you are writing to someone you do not know—the Director of Personnel, for example—you can avoid the awkward phrase *To whom it may concern* by routing your letter to a specific department or by referring to a particular subject.

College Department
Holt, Rinehart and Winston
383 Madison Avenue
New York, NY 10017

Attention: Director of Personnel

                    or

Subject: Sales Position

Keep in mind that salutations such as *Gentlemen* and *Dear Sirs* are considered antiquated (to say nothing of sexist) by many people and are fading from standard usage.

The Body
The **body** of your letter contains your message. Begin this section two spaces below the salutation, and single-space the text. In a short letter of two or three sentences, you may double-space throughout. In a block format letter you do not use paragraph indentations; in some other formats you indent paragraphs five spaces from the left-hand margin.

If your letter takes more than one page, the addressee's name, the date, and the page number should be placed in the upper left-hand corner of the second page.

The Complimentary Close
The **complimentary close** appears two spaces below the body of the letter and flush to the left.

The most common complimentary closes are *Sincerely yours*, *Yours truly*, and *Yours very truly*. If you are on friendly terms with the recipient, *Best wishes* or *Cordially* is appropriate. More formal letters to high government officials, members of the clergy, or diplomats might call for *Respectfully yours*. Note that only the first word of the complimentary close is capitalized.

The Signature
Leave four spaces below the complimentary close, and type your name and title in full. Sign your name, without a title, above the typewritten line.

Additional Data

Indicate additional information below the signature, to the left.

Enclosures

cc: Eric Brody *(Copy sent to the person mentioned)*

SJL/lew *(The initials of the writer/the initials of the typist)*

42b Writing Letters Requesting Employment

When requesting employment, your primary objective is to interest a prospective employer enough so that he or she will schedule an interview with you. Before you write, collect all the information you need for your letter—previous employment, employers, dates, and relevant courses, for example. Then consider why you want the job and what about you might interest a prospective employer. You will want to make a scratch outline before you begin your rough draft (see 39e).

Begin your letter by stating which job you are applying for and where you heard about it—in a newspaper, in a journal, from a professor, or from the school job placement service. Be sure to include the date of the advertisement and the exact title of the position. End your introduction with your thesis: a statement of your ability to do the job.

The body of your letter provides the information that will convince your reader of your qualifications. Mention any relevant courses you have taken and any pertinent job experiences. Take care to address any specific concerns mentioned in the advertisement. Above all, emphasize your strengths. If you are applying for a sales job, for example, stress your ability to communicate effectively, not your limited experience. If you have special training, such as word processing skills, be sure to mention it.

Conclude by referring to your résumé. Say that you are available for an interview, listing any dates that you cannot be available. You may offer to call the person, but do not say that you will drop in. The prospective employer will make the appointment.

As always, your letter should be smooth, natural, and free of errors.

bus
42b

Sample Letter of Employment

246 Hillside Drive
Urbana, Illinois 61801
October 20, 1986

Maurice Snyder, Personnel Director
Guilford, Fox, and Morris
Eckerd Building
22 Hamilton Street
Urbana, Illinois 61822

Dear Mr. Snyder:

My adviser, Dr. Raymond Walsh, has told me that you are
interested in hiring a part-time accounting assistant. I feel that
my academic background and my work experience qualify me
for this position.

I am presently a junior accounting major at the University of
Illinois. During the past year, I have taken courses in taxation,
trusts, and business law. I have worked with a microcomputer
and have developed my own tax program. Last spring, I worked
in the department's tax clinic and gained much practical
accounting experience.

**bus
42b**

After I graduate, I hope to get a Master's degree in taxation and
then return to the Urbana area. I feel that my experience in
taxation as well as my familiarity with the local business
community would enable me to contribute much to your firm.

I have enclosed a résumé for your examination, and I will be
available for an interview any time after mid-term
examinations, which end October 25. I look forward to hearing
from you.

Sincerely yours,

Sandra Kraft

Sandra Kraft

Enclosure

▶
EXERCISE 1

Look at the employment ads in your local paper or your college placement service. Choose one and write a letter of application in which you
outline your qualifications and achievements and discuss why you want
the job.

42c Writing Résumés

The letter of application presents your qualifications and interest
in a specific job that you would like to get. The résumé that
accompanies it provides an overview of what you have already
done. It focuses on your education and your work experience. A
résumé should create one dominant impression—that you are a
motivated person who has the ability and maturity to do a job
well.

　　Before you compose your résumé, make a list of all the facts
that you can think of about your education, your job experience,
your goals, and your personal interests. Then select the information that is appropriate for the job you want, emphasizing the
accomplishments that differentiate you from other candidates. If
you have received academic honors or awards, or if you have
financed your own education, include this information as well.

**bus
42c**

　　There is no single correct format for a résumé. Whatever its
arrangement, however, it should be brief—one page is sufficient
for an undergraduate—easy to read, and well organized. An
employer should be able to see at a glance what your qualifications are. All résumés usually contain the following sections.

　　The *heading* includes your name, school address, home
address, and phone number.

　　The *education section* includes the schools you have attended, starting with the most recent one and working back in
time. After graduation from college, do not list your high schools
unless you have a compelling reason to do so.

　　The *summary of work experience* starts with your most recent job and works back.

　　The *background section* lists special interests and community service. (Just a few examples will suffice.)

　　The *references section* lists the full name and address of at
least three references. If you already have a full-page résumé, a

line saying that your references will be sent upon request is sufficient. You may also want to include an *honors section* in which you list academic achievements and awards. You may also include at the top of the page a statement of your *career objective.*

Remember that federal law prohibits employers from discriminating on the basis of age, sex, or race, and you should not include this information in your résumé.

Sample Résumé

Michael D. Fuller

Address	**Home**	**Campus**
	1203 Hampton Road	27 College Avenue
	Joppa, MD 21085	College Park, MD 20742
	Telephone:	Telephone:
	(301) 877-1437	(301) 357-0732

Education
1983–1985

University of Maryland, College Park, MD (sophomore). Biology major. Expected date of graduation: June 1987. Presently maintain a 3.3 average on a 4.0 scale.

1979–1983

Forrest Park High School, Baltimore, MD. Basketball team, track team, debating society, class president, and mathematics tutor. Graduated in the top fifth of the class.

Experience
1984–1985

University of Maryland Library, College Park, MD. Assistant to the reference librarian. Filed, sorted, typed, shelved, and catalogued. Earnings offset college expenses.

1983–1984

University of Maryland Cafeteria, College Park, MD. Busboy. Cleaned tables, set up cafeteria, and prepared hot trays.

1982
Summer

McDonald's Restaurant, Pikesville, MD. Cook. Prepared hamburgers. Acted as assistant manager for two weeks when manager was on vacation.

Background

Member of University Debating Society. Tutor in University Program for Disadvantaged Students.

References   Ms. Stephanie Young, Librarian
                      Library
                      University of Maryland
                      College Park, MD 20742

                      Mr. William Czernick, Manager
                      Cafeteria
                      University of Maryland
                      College Park, MD 20742

                      Mr. Arthur Sanducci, Manager
                      McDonald's Restaurant
                      5712 Avery Road
                      Pikesville, MD 22513

▶
EXERCISE 2

Prepare a résumé to include with the letter of employment you wrote for
Exercise 1.

42d Writing Follow-up Letters

It is a good idea to send a brief follow-up letter a week or two
after an interview. Thank the people whom you met for their
courtesy, and restate your interest in the job. Such letters show
both courtesy and professionalism.

**bus
42d**

Sample Follow-up Letter

17 West Third Street
New York, New York 10003
April 7, 1985

Mr. Thomas Crawford, Manager
FDS Capital Corporation
Two World Trade Center
New York, New York 10015

Dear Mr. Crawford:

Thank you so much for interviewing me for the work-study
position and showing me your offices on March 25th. Your

computer department was very interesting, and the information I received will help me be more specific in my career goals.

I especially enjoyed seeing how you use computer-generated graphics in your investment division. I now feel certain that I want to enter this field after I graduate in 1986. Any work I could do for you this summer would help me prepare for this rapidly developing field.

Again, thank you very much.

Sincerely,

Sara Katz

▶
EXERCISE 3

Assume that you were interviewed for the job you applied for in Exercise 1. A week has passed. Write a follow-up letter thanking the person you saw.

42e Writing Letters to Graduate or Professional Schools

Graduate and professional schools routinely ask applicants for statements explaining why they have applied. These personal statements reveal a great deal about you, including your goals, your maturity, and your ability to communicate. They are read carefully, and they often are important in determining whether or not you will be accepted.

Do some soul searching before you begin planning a personal statement. Write down your reasons for wanting to enter your intended profession, and do some freewriting on the subject. Think too about the qualities that suit you for this profession. Study this material, and organize it into an outline. Next, write a rough draft quickly, without worrying about how it looks or sounds. Keep in mind that personal statements are difficult to write, and you may have to do a number of drafts.

As you revise, concentrate on what distinguishes you from others who are applying to the school. Be specific, offering examples from your experience to illustrate the points you make. Everything in your statement should underscore your thesis: that you are committed to the field and should be admitted to a program.

Sample Personal Statement

During my sophomore and junior years in college, I worked part-time for a law firm in Cincinnati. I began as a file clerk and eventually was promoted to the research department of the firm. This experience was a turning point in my life. It helped me to decide to become a lawyer and to take courses that would prepare me for this goal.

The firm in which I worked does general practice and also a good deal of community legal work. After being there for eight months I was given the responsibility of screening legal-aid clients and assigning them to one of three lawyers. I consulted attorneys and, at times, discussed specific cases with them. Eventually they allowed me to be present when depositions were taken.

I learned a great deal about the legal profession from my job. One case stands out in my mind. An elderly man had been run down by a bus and was partially disabled. He had no hospitalization and no income other than Social Security. The firm took his case and arranged for the bus company to pay all medical bills and for the man to begin physical therapy. As a result, our client is now able to live at home with the help of a visiting nurse. While doing research for the attorney who handled this case, I saw how much good a lawyer can do and how important it is for those in the legal profession to help those who cannot help themselves.

bus
42e

My experiences with a law firm have given me a realistic picture of what the practice of law is and have enabled me to make a mature, informed decision to become a lawyer. I am certain that as a result, I will be an understanding and compassionate attorney, one who puts her clients' interests before her own.

To prepare for my legal career, I have majored in political science and minored in business. My grade point average has been good: 3.65 on a 4.0 scale. I have taken courses in political theory, government, accounting, and constitutional law. I have also taken a number of courses in sociology, psychology, and business writing. In addition, I am a member of the school's pre-law society, and I won honorable mention in a regional moot-court competition held last spring.

This past year I was the student representative on a search committee for a new dean of the College of Liberal Arts. I worked closely with the former dean and with faculty members from various departments. I have found that this experience has increased my confidence and has made me an effective negotiator. I have learned to state a position clearly and forcefully and not to be intimidated by the arguments of others.

My background has made me realize my responsibility to the legal profession and to society. My exposure to the legal profession has provided me with the motivation to pursue a career in law. My academic record and my experience with legal work make me certain that a career in law is a realistic goal for me.

▶

EXERCISE 4

Assume that you are applying to one of the following graduate programs.

> Law school
> Medical school
> Library school
> Business school
> Journalism school
> Social work school
> A graduate program in an academic field

bus 42f

Write a personal statement in which you tell the admissions officer what led you to choose your field. Be specific in describing your motivation, your experience, and your aspirations.

42f Writing Letters Requesting Information

Students often have to send letters requesting information from a person or a business. For instance, you might ask an instructor for a recommendation or write to an expert in a field to gather information for a research project.

Before you write such a letter you should decide just what information you need. Make a list if necessary, and eliminate questions that you can answer yourself. Think about what you need the information for and how much time you have to get it. Usually you can limit your request to a few questions that can be answered quickly and easily.

Write a courteous and concise letter. Introduce yourself, and say clearly what information you want and why you want it. Be specific; your reader will be doing you a favor by responding, and you should not waste his or her time. If you have several requests, number them—and keep them simple.

Sample Letter Requesting Information

17 Maple Drive
Clinton, Mississippi 39058
December 2, 1985

Dr. Norman Murphy
English Department
Louisiana State University
    at Shreveport
Shreveport, Louisiana 75115

Dear Dr. Murphy:

I am a third-year English major at Clinton College, and I am interested in pursuing a career in scientific and technical writing. Dr. Stewart Lage, my adviser, thought that you could give me advice about schools that have graduate programs in this field.

bus 42f

Although I prefer to stay in the South, I am willing to go to school in any part of the country. I am particularly interested in schools that have internship programs that would allow me to gain practical experience in industry. I have already written to Stanford University and Drexel University and am waiting for their catalogues.

I am currently at home and will be back at school on January 6th. I would appreciate any information you could mail to me or to Dr. Lage.

I hope to hear from you soon.

Yours truly,

Daniel Howell, Jr.

Daniel Howell, Jr.

It is always a good idea to thank the person who responds to your letter. An example of such a letter appears at the beginning of this chapter (pp. 715–716).

▶
EXERCISE 5

For a research paper on television situation comedies, write a letter requesting information from Alan Friedman (38 University Place, New York University, New York, NY 10003), a noted authority on this subject. Ask him four questions you would like him to answer. Remember that Dr. Friedman is very busy, but he will probably answer a sensible, interesting short letter.

▶
EXERCISE 6

Three weeks have passed, and Dr. Friedman has not answered. Write a follow-up letter in which you gently remind him of your request and of your deadline.

42g Writing Letters of Complaint

bus

42g

Often the only way you can solve a problem or rectify a mistake is to complain in writing. Many companies realize that it takes some effort to write a letter of complaint, and when they receive one, they respond. If you feel that you have been treated unfairly or incorrectly, a letter may help you to remedy the situation.

Before you write a letter of complaint, you should list the facts that are important to your case. Exact names and dates are extremely important; so are serial numbers and warranty provisions. Reconstruct the facts of your case, keeping events in chronological order. As you look over your list, eliminate details that are not central to your purpose. The fact that a salesperson was rude, for instance, may be less important than his or her misrepresentation of a product.

The purpose of writing your letter is to get satisfaction or redress. To achieve this, your letter should maintain a rational tone. Present yourself as a reasonable person who sees both sides of the issue and who expects to be taken seriously. Anger or sarcasm undercuts your cause, and neither has a place in an effective letter of complaint. Your logic is what will lead a company to act in your favor.

Revise your first draft with your reader in mind. If your reader is unfamiliar with your case, your letter should begin with an overview, not an involved discussion of your problem. Make sure that you explain the facts clearly. Put events in logical order, with transitions that make their sequence apparent, and tell your story without editorial comment.

Make certain that your tone is firm but reasonable and your request for action is appropriate to the problem. Finally, try to end on a positive note—at least by asserting your belief in the good will of the company.

Sample Letter of Complaint

2133 Northridge Avenue
Los Angeles, CA 90024
May 8, 1986

Time, Inc.
Subscription Department
Rockefeller Center
New York, NY 10020

**bus
42g**

Subject: Canceled subscription

On November 5th I sent a letter to you canceling my subscription. Since then, I have continued getting magazines despite my efforts to stop them.

On March 2nd I sent you a second letter, this time by certified mail; I enclose a copy of my receipt. On April 11th I got a letter (copy enclosed) from the Eastern Collection Agency telling me to pay your bill or risk legal action. I called Eastern (at a cost to me of $3.65) and was told by their manager, Mr. Wolfson, that there was nothing he could do until I paid the bill or until you told him the bill was canceled.

I am disturbed for two reasons. First, should not one letter be enough to cancel my subscription? Must I write three letters if I want you to take action? Second, surely you do not expect me to pay for magazines that you sent after I canceled my subscription. As far as I am concerned I did not order these magazines so I should not be responsible for them.

I am certain that Time, Inc., values its good reputation and will want to settle this matter promptly.

Yours truly,

Suzanne Cozmo

Suzanne Cozmo

▶

EXERCISE 7

Your college or university owes you a $250 refund from your tuition. Apparently they charged you twice for a student activities fee. After discovering the error you went to the registrar, who told you that as a matter of policy all refunds are credited to the next semester's tuition. After a day and a half of hearing the same story at one office after another, you decide to write a letter to the president of the school. In this letter tell the president why you think the school should reimburse you. Make a strong case, and present the facts clearly and logically.

---

bus
42h

42h Composing Memos

The process of composing memos is much the same as the process of composing business letters. Unlike letters, however, memos communicate information *within* a business organization. They can communicate brief messages of a paragraph or two, or short reports or proposals. Their function is generally to convey information or to persuade.

Whatever their function, most memos have the same general structure. The opening component—*to, from, subject,* and the *date*—replaces the heading and inside address of a letter (see sample, p. 731). This section establishes at a glance the audience and subject of your communication. Because a memo often circulates beyond its original audience, the names and titles of both parties should be stated in full. The *subject* line exists to give your reader a clear idea what your memo is about and should include more than one word. "Housing" means very little to readers unfamiliar with your subject. "Changes in Student Housing Policy" states the subject more precisely.

Your memo should begin with a purpose statement containing key words that immediately convey your message.

This Memo	evaluates	reports
	proposes	describes
	questions	presents

Your first paragraph summarizes your conclusions; the rest of your memo tells readers how you arrived at your conclusions, backing them up with facts and figures. Often each paragraph of a memo has a heading, indicating its subject. The headings guide readers through the body of your memo.

Your memo should end with a detailed restatement of your conclusions. If its purpose is to persuade your readers of something, you should include a list of recommendations. Because readers remember best what comes last, you should end your memo with a summary of the action that should be taken or the conclusions that should be drawn.

In the following memo from the editor of a college newspaper to the dean of freshmen, the writer states his reason for writing the memo in the first sentence and then goes on to explain how the editorial board reached its decision. The short memo reports information but does not make recommendations.

bus
42h

TO: Donald Abrams, Dean of Freshmen
FROM: Alex McCullough, Editor, the *Triangle*
SUBJECT: Printing the Freshmen Orientation Schedule
DATE: April 23, 1985

As editor of the *Triangle* I would like to report the decision the editorial board made concerning your request to print the Freshman Orientation Schedule in our August 5th issue.

During our conversation on April 3rd, you asked if the *Triangle* would print a four-page pull-out of the Freshmen Orientation Schedule. As you suggested, I brought up this matter with the editorial board and our faculty adviser. The editorial board agreed to print the schedule, but asked that the university pay the cost of printing and that the pull-out not be counted in the eight-page limit the university placed on the *Triangle* last year.

I hope you find our decisions satisfactory. I will be glad to answer any questions you may have about this matter.

The following memo deals with a more complicated subject. The student who wrote this memo uses headings to underscore the major divisions of her discussion and emphasizes her recommendations by putting them in list form. Her purpose is to persuade her audience; therefore, she discusses her reader's major concerns—cost, ease of construction, and projected benefits—and she ends with a list of recommendations.

TO: Ina Ellen, Senior Counselor
FROM: Kim Williams, Student Tutor Supervisor
SUBJECT: Construction of a Tutoring Center
DATE: November 10, 1986

The purpose of this memo is to propose constructing a tutoring center in the Office of Student Affairs.

BACKGROUND

Under the present system, student tutors must work with students in a number of facilities scattered across the university campus. This situation causes a number of problems, including a lack of contact among tutors and the inability of tutors to get immediate help with problems if they need it. As a result, tutors waste a lot of time running from one facility to another—and often miss appointments. Most tutors agree that the present system is unwieldy and ineffective.

NEW FACILITY

I propose that we build a tutoring room adjacent to the Office of Student Affairs. The two empty classrooms adjacent to the office, presently used for storage of office furniture, would be ideal for this use. Incurring a minimum of expense and using maintenance workers, the university could convert these rooms into ten small offices. We could furnish these offices with the desks and file cabinets already stored in these rooms.

BENEFITS

The benefits of this facility would be the centralizing of the tutoring service and the proximity of the facility to the Office of Student Affairs. The tutoring facility could also use the secretarial services of the Office of Student Affairs, ensuring that student tutors get messages from the students with whom they work.

bus
42h

RECOMMENDATIONS

To implement this project we would need to do the following:

1. Clean up and paint rooms 331 and 333 and connect them to the Office of Student Affairs
2. Use folding partitions to divide each room into five single-desk offices
3. Use stored office equipment to furnish the center

I am certain that these changes will do much to improve the tutoring service that the Office of Student Affairs now offers, and I look forward to discussing this matter with you in more detail.

▶

EXERCISE 8

Your duties at your summer job with a public utility in your area include reading correspondence that goes from your division to the public. While reading a pamphlet that discusses energy conservation, you come across the following words and sentences: "Each consumer must do *his* part," "*repairman*," and "*Mothers* should teach their children about energy conservation." With the approval of your supervisor, you decide to write a memo to John Durand, Public Relations Manager, explaining to him that these words could offend some readers. In your memo explain to Mr. Durand why the words should be changed and what words he could use in their place. Mr. Durand is your superior, so maintain a reasonable tone.

**bus
42h**

Appendix A

Composing on a Word Processor

The word processor gives you the flexibility that writing requires. Once you are accustomed to your equipment and your software, the speed with which you can draft your thoughts lets you do more work in less time. Some of the following suggestions will be of immediate help. Others will help you develop your own ideas for using the word processor creatively to plan, shape, and write and revise your essays.

A1 Using the Word Processor to Plan Your Papers

Because of its ability to record and store information, the word processor can help you plan your writing. In addition, the word processor keeps a neat record of all your preliminary notes so you are able to sort through this material easily when it comes time to write a draft.

**wp
A1**

(1) Freewriting

Freewriting (see 1b.2) on the word processor enables you to get down ideas more quickly and with less fatigue than if you used pen and paper. The computer keyboard lets your fingers keep up with your mind. If you pause to correct typing errors, however, you will lose this advantage, so try to ignore the screen. If you are unable to do so, turn down the brightness. When you cannot see the words, they cannot distract you. Free from such distractions, you may capture some important ideas.

If your freewriting yields an interesting idea for a paper, you can move this idea to the beginning of a new page, rephrase it as a sentence, and freewrite on it for another set period of time. If the sentence moves off the screen, move it back to the top. Keeping it constantly on the screen helps you stay focused as you generate ideas.

(2) Questioning

With a word processor you can also save the questions you use to find something to say. You might, for example, type

> Who am I writing to?
> Do I want to entertain, convey information, convey my attitude, convince readers to do something?
> What is my purpose?
> How much can I write?

Each time you begin a new paper, you can call up these questions, review and answer them, and save both the questions and the answers for future reference. You can easily refer to the questions you have saved as you prepare to write any new assignment.

Any thought-provoking questions that your instructor recommends—the journalistic questions, for example (see 1b.4)—can go into your question file for recall when you need them.

wp
A2

A2 Using the Word Processor to Shape Your Material

Because of its flexibility, the word processor can help you organize your ideas. Its ability to move text easily enables you to arrange and rearrange ideas as you shape your essay.

(1) Outlining

Some instructors may ask for a formal or informal outline (see 2d) of your ideas. If you use the word processor to construct an outline, you can easily insert new ideas and rearrange ideas that you have already typed in. For preparing outlines, working on the word processor is especially efficient because you can make major changes while leaving the unchanged parts clean and legible.

(2) Using paper

Writing out ideas on paper is still useful, of course. As you begin to shape your essay, you may not want to view your preliminary notes on the video monitor. Instead, you may find it easier to print out the notes you have prepared and refer to them as you start to put your ideas in order.

If new ideas come to you as you work, jot them down on the printout sheets rather than going back to the computer. This technique saves time and lets you stay on track.

A3 Using the Word Processor to Write Your Rough Draft

When writing a rough draft you should try to get your ideas down as quickly as possible. Using a word processor does not automatically eliminate the problems that can occur at this stage of your writing, but it can offer you some unique ways of surmounting them.

(1) Overcoming writer's block

wp
A3

If you find yourself staring far too long at a blank screen, just as you would at a blank sheet of paper, try turning down the screen's brightness. This strategy gives you a chance to concentrate on ideas rather than on the "look" of your sentences. Many people find this "invisible writing" a useful way to overcome writer's block.

Another technique that may help you to overcome writer's block is to make two or three starts. Begin your paper and label it "paper 1." Do as much as you think would make a good beginning, then stop and read through what you have written. Now start over again, labeling your new work "paper 2." Continue starting over until you have captured the idea you want to convey. If after several revisions you find that your first version was best, go back to "paper 1" and continue writing from there. Or you may find a good sentence in "paper 1," two good sentences in "paper 2," and a good transition in "paper 3." Select the best elements in each and transfer them to a new version, "paper 4," and then proceed.

(2) Getting clean copy

One clear advantage of using a word processor is that you always have clean copy. The push of a button lets you erase, transpose, replace, and rewrite single words or whole sections of text. The very ease with which you can perform these operations may encourage you to revise a great deal as you write, but keep one caution in mind. You may reject an idea now, but if you erase it, it is lost forever, and you have no way to review it should you want to. Take out anything you like, but never discard anything until your paper is finished.

When using a word processor, try writing without erasing—at least on your first few drafts. Something wrong for an introduction may fit perfectly into the conclusion you have not yet written. Saving your progressive versions is, then, the safest and most useful way to compose.

A4 Using the Word Processor to Revise Your Papers

wp
A4

Revising a paper involves reconsidering many of the decisions that you made when you wrote your first draft. Revision involves adding, substituting, and deleting material. (For detailed information on revision, see 3c–3e.) Although these operations can be tedious when carried out with pen and paper, they are relatively simple when you use a word processor.

(1) Adding

When you reread your writing after a day or two, you may find that certain paragraphs do not have enough supporting evidence or detail, that your introduction lacks a clear thesis, or that your conclusion proceeds from unproven assumptions. In short, you may need to *add* material.

Word processors make adding easy. If you print out your draft with a wide margin, you can use the margin for notes about the additions you need. You can then type in your additions when you return to the word processor.

For most students, university writing will

now include more than pen, paper, and typewriter. As computers become common and inexpensive, more students will prepare academic papers on a word processor linked to a university's mainframe computer system or on a personal computer at home. In addition to easing the drudgery of preparing typed papers, word processors can be valuable writing aids.

Only academic papers?

Do I need a better transition?

(2) Substituting

The "find" and "replace" commands help when you substitute one word or phrase for another. But suppose you want to replace one example with another, stronger one. Rather than deleting and replacing, you should insert the new example, read the whole paragraph, and then move the rejected example, if it is rejected, to the end of your paper. You can delete it later if you decide not to use it anywhere. If you do find a place for it, however, you will still have it.

(3) Deleting

Use the end of your paper as temporary storage space as you revise. If you keep moving unwanted sentences and paragraphs to the end, you can delete them when the paper becomes more polished. Remember that hasty deletion does mean loss of material, so keep even the material you have rejected until you are ready to hand in your paper.

(4) Checking organization

The computer cannot organize your essay for you, but it can help you see whether or not you have stayed on your topic.

   After you complete a draft, copy the topic sentences of each paragraph. Move these sentences, which form a rough outline of the paper, to the beginning of your paper, keeping them separated by blank lines so that you know where the paragraph

wp
A4

breaks are. You can then check this outline for logic, completeness, and flow of ideas.

If you have digressed from your thesis anywhere in the paper, the outline will show you exactly where. You can then revise either the thesis or those paragraphs that have wandered from the point. After you have checked the organization of your paper, you can erase your outline from the revised version of the paper.

(5) Checking paragraphs

If you suspect that certain paragraphs of an essay are less fully developed than others or are not coherent, you can use the computer to help you chart paragraph structure as you did in Chapter 4. You need not follow this procedure for every paragraph, but you can certainly use the word processor to help you with your weakest sections.

To analyze paragraph structure, first move each sentence so that it begins on a new line and so that the paragraph will not automatically reformat when you insert characters. (With most word processors, you will have to include a blank line or some special character next to the sentence.) Then pick out the most general sentence in your paragraph, put a numeral 1 beside it, and move it toward the left margin. Put a 1 beside each thought that is equally general and align them all at the left margin. Mark more detailed sentences 2 and move them to the left, indented five spaces. Mark the most detailed sentences 3 and align them to the left, indenting another five spaces.

Once you have formatted a paragraph in this way, you can restructure it either by adding or deleting material or by rearranging sentences.

wp
A4

(6) Revising from checklists

You can also use your computer to make a revision checklist that includes questions about audience, purpose, thesis statement and topic sentences, details, transitional elements, and any other points your instructor suggests (see 3d.3 for a sample revision checklist).

You might also add to your list notes about the grammatical or stylistic problems that your instructor identifies on your papers. Copying specific sentences or phrases from earlier papers into this list might help you in revising later papers. The computer's memory thus serves as an active notebook that reminds you of your most common problems.

(7) Revising for style and mechanics

As you revise for style and mechanics, the "find" and "replace" commands are especially useful. If you tend to overuse certain words—*very* or *really*, for example—you can search for their every appearance and delete empty usages. Or you can call up every comma in a graded and returned paper and review those you misused.

The computer is especially helpful to you when you study punctuation because unlike the human eye, it skips nothing. Although you may tire of checking punctuation, the computer does not.

(8) Revising on a printout

Many writers find it hard to make revisions that affect the whole paper while they are sitting at the computer terminal. For one thing, most screens show only twenty-one lines of single-spaced text at a time. Paragraph length, an important indication of paragraph development, is difficult to judge when text moves off the top of the screen. Furthermore, it is hard for most of us to remember what preceded and what follows when we can see only twenty-one lines at a time. We are more accustomed to leafing through the pages to recall what we have written. When we cannot do this, many aspects of the paper, particularly connections, are bound to become fuzzy.

wp
A4

Therefore, you should always read and revise your essays on paper. Many printers are able to print a draft-quality copy at very high speed, and this copy can be used for revising and editing. (Use only a letter-quality or a high-quality dot matrix printer for a draft that you intend to submit.)

(9) Proofreading

When you have completed your final draft, be sure to proofread carefully. Always proofread on the screen, even though doing so is comparatively difficult, *and* on paper before you submit a final draft.

A5 Revising and Editing Aids

(1) Spelling checkers

Computers are particularly good at identifying patterns, and they can quickly locate words that violate expected patterns—that is, words that are misspelled or mistyped. Some word-processing programs include dictionaries that check spelling, but more often you must purchase such programs separately.

Spelling checkers have limited words lists, and they do not identify words that are not in their programs. Most programs let you add to your computer's dictionary, and the user's manual should tell you how. Keep in mind that spelling checkers will not identify a word that is spelled correctly but used incorrectly (*there* used instead of *their*, for example). For this reason, you still need to read for spelling errors even if you use a spelling checker.

Before you even think about using a spelling checker for your college work, be sure to get explicit approval from your instructor. Learning to spell and punctuate correctly *on your own* is more important than submitting a mechanically perfect paper that has been corrected without your participation.

(2) Text-analysis programs

**wp
A5**

Text-analysis programs, which scan for other errors, are also on the market. Most of these are proofreading and style checkers that look for simple punctuation placement errors.

> INCORRECT: "John", he said painfully, "I've been shot".
>
> CORRECT: "John," he said painfully, "I've been shot."

Almost all identify overused or misused words—and some look for wordy or vague expressions. A program might highlight wordy phrases, or it might give you this message.

> Check line 10 for *due to the fact that;* consider using *because* to reduce wordiness.

Other text-analysis programs do more elaborate stylistic checking and analysis. If you are interested in trying text-analysis programs, be sure to ask your instructor for permission.

Appendix B

Preparing Your Papers

A clean, neatly typed or handwritten paper is a courtesy that you owe your readers. Sloppily typed or smudged papers not only make reading difficult but also detract from your ideas. Some of your instructors will undoubtedly give you specific guidelines for preparing a paper—and of course you should follow them. But others will expect you to be familiar with the conventions for preparing a paper suitable for submission. The following instructions are standard and, in general, are consistent with those found in the MLA style sheet (2nd ed).

B1 Typed Papers

Submit typed papers whenever possible. Because typewritten papers are easier to read and to correct, they are worth the extra effort—even if you are a slow typist. Before you type, make sure that your keys are clean and that you have a fresh black ribbon. Do not use "fancy" type, such as script, that could distract your readers. Be sure to make a carbon or photocopy for your files in case your instructor mislays your paper.

Use white, twenty-pound weight 8½″ × 11″ bond paper. Avoid both erasable paper and "onionskin." Not only do they smudge, but they are also difficult to read. In addition, it is hard to make corrections in ink on coated paper. If you feel that you must use erasable paper, make a copy of your finished paper on uncoated paper and submit the photocopy. Remember, never use paper that is not white or that is smaller than 8½″ × 11″.

Double-space your paper throughout. Single spacing does not leave enough room for instructors' comments or corrections (see B6 for further instructions).

B2   Handwritten Papers

If you have permission to submit a handwritten paper, use 8½″ × 11″ wide-lined paper. Do not use narrow-lined paper, un-lined paper, or paper larger or smaller than 8½″ × 11″. Your best choice is paper that you can easily and neatly detach from a tablet. Do not use paper that leaves a ragged edge when torn from a spiral-bound notebook. Leave wide margins, write on every other line, and be sure to use only one side of each page. Use black or dark blue ink, never colored ink or pencil.

Make certain that you write clearly and that you form each letter carefully. If your handwriting is sloppy, try printing. Keep in mind that your instructor has many papers to mark and does not appreciate having to struggle with handwriting that is diffi-cult to read.

B3   Format

Leave a one-inch margin on the top and bottom and on both sides of your paper. Indent five spaces for each new paragraph.

Many instructors do not require a separate title page. If yours does not, type your name, your instructor's name, the course number, and the date one inch from the top of the first page of the paper, flush with the left-hand margin. Double-space again and center the title. If the title is longer than a single line, double-space and center the second line below the first. Capital-ize all important words in the title, but not prepositions, con-junctions, articles, or the *to* in infinitives, unless they begin or end the title. Do not underline the title or enclose it in quotation marks. Underline words in the title if they are underlined in your paper (e.g., book titles). Never put a period after a title, even if it is a sentence. Double-space twice between the last line of the title and the first line of text.

Number all subsequent pages of your paper consecutively in the upper right-hand corner one-half inch from the top. Do not put periods or any other punctuation after the page num-bers. To ensure that your instructor will be able to replace sepa-rated pages, put your name next to the page number of all pages other than the first.

ms
B3

First Page of Manuscript Without a Title Page

1"

Mark Williamson

R 101   1"

Dr. Stevens

March 20, 1985

Two spaces ⎯⎯⎯→

Big Brother in George Orwell's <u>1984</u>

Four spaces ⎯⎯⎯→

Indent five
spaces ⎯⎯⎯⎯→ Although the year 1984 has just

passed, Orwell's novel by the same

name. . . .

Subsequent Page of a Paper

½"

Williamson 2

1"

1"   The language, manners, and mores of Orwell's

world are determined by the state. When the

characters in <u>1984</u> are faced with a decision,

they usually . . . .

ms
B3

Some instructors, however, prefer a separate title page, like the one appearing with the paper at the end of Chapter 39 (page 639). It carries the title; your name, course, and section number; your instructor's name; and the date you submitted your paper. When you use a title page, repeat your title on the first page of your manuscript. Subsequent pages follow the format for a paper with a title page.

First Page of a Manuscript with a Title Page

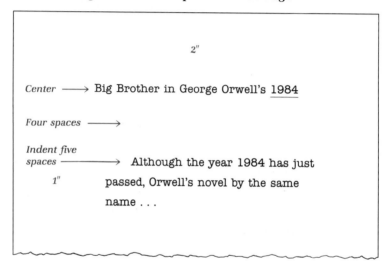

Center ⟶ Big Brother in George Orwell's <u>1984</u>

Four spaces ⟶

Indent five spaces ⟶ Although the year 1984 has just

1″   passed, Orwell's novel by the same

name . . .

B4 Editing Your Final Draft

After finishing the final draft of your paper, proofread it carefully and correct any errors. If a page is messy or if you have to make extensive corrections, retype the entire page. Make minor corrections with correction fluid. Never make corrections in the margin or below the line. If your instructor gives you permission, you may make some corrections in black ink.

You can correct an inaccurate word by drawing a line through it, inserting a caret (∧) underneath it, and writing the correct word neatly above the line.

Orwell's society is a ∧ ~~representation~~ *microcosm* of the larger world.

You can add words by putting a caret where you want to insert the missing term and writing the new word above the line.

Fortunately for ∧ *us* Orwell's predictions have not occurred.

You can delete a letter by drawing a line through it and indicating that the space should be closed up.

The year 1984 has always been thr̂ought of . . .

You can delete a word by drawing a line through it.

Orwell relied ~~wholly~~ upon the technology of his day for his novel.

You can transpose letters within a word by means of a curved line (∾).

Although he was a literary critic Orwell dis̆t̆r̆usted intellectuals.

You can indicate a space between words by drawing a vertical line where the space should be.

Although some parts of 1984 seem dated, most of̸ it has withstood the passage of time.

You can indicate a new paragraph by putting the sign ¶ in the proper place.

. . . his use of language. ¶ Not only was language a concern of Orwell's. . . .

You can indicate that you do not want to begin a paragraph by drawing a line to connect the two sentences.

George Orwell's real name was Eric Blair.⌐
 ⌐He was born in India and eventually moved to. . . .

B5 Submitting Your Paper

When you are ready to submit your paper, fasten the pages together with a paper clip or a single staple in the upper left-hand corner. Do not staple the paper together like a book or use a binder that cannot easily be removed. Remember that your instructor cannot write comments on your paper if he or she cannot separate the pages.

B6 Typing Punctuation

The following table illustrates the conventions that determine the spacing of typed punctuation. Be sure to follow them consistently throughout your paper.

Type of Punctuation	Typing Conventions	Examples
1. apostrophes	Leave no spaces before or after the apostrophe unless the apostrophe ends a word.	Turner's landscapes The writers' local color novels
2. commas and semicolons	Leave no spaces before commas or semicolons; leave one space after commas and semicolons.	In fact, the story. . . . her son; in England. . . .
3. colons, question marks, and exclamation points	Leave no spaces before these punctuation marks; leave one space after a colon and two spaces after a question mark or exclamation point.	. . . the following: plot, character, and theme. Was he correct? The debate. . . . Never! Tyranny can never. . . .
4. quotation marks	Leave no spaces between quotation marks and the words or punctuation marks they enclose.	The short story "The Gold Bug" is by Poe. "I come to bury Caesar," said Mark Antony, "not to praise him."
5. periods	Leave no space before a period at the end of a sentence. Leave two spaces after the period.	. . . since 1938. The fight for intellectual freedom. . . .
6. hyphens or dashes	A hyphen is one stroke; a dash is two unbroken strokes.	quick-witted Ford was born poor–not rich–on a farm . . .

ms
B6

Type of Punctuation	Typing Conventions	Examples
7. ellipsis marks	Separate all periods of an ellipsis mark by one space. Do not leave a space before the period at the end of a sentence that is followed by an ellipsis mark.	It was . . . a bitter satire of the motion picture industry. The report examines many classes of people. . . .
8. italics	Underline words to indicate italics. You can use a single line or underline each word separately.	The Sun Also Rises The Sun Also Rises
9. parentheses, brackets	Leave one space before opening a parenthesis and after closing a parenthesis. Do not space between the enclosed words and the parentheses. If the parentheses contain an entire sentence, leave two spaces before and after the parentheses. Brackets follow the same conventions as parentheses.	Charles Lindbergh attended the University of Wisconsin (1920–22) but left to learn how to fly. In 1907, Luther Burbank wrote *Training of the Human Plant.* (The pamphlet dealt with environment and human development.) In 1909. . . .
10. slashes	Leave no space before or after a slash except if the slash separates lines of poetry. In this case leave one space before and after the slash.	The object travels at 800 m/sec in a parallel direction. "Nature's first green is gold / Her hardest hue to hold." (Robert Frost)

ms
B6

Glossary of Usage

This glossary of usage provides you with a list of words and phrases that often give trouble to writers. As you use it, remember that this glossary is intended as a guide and that nothing in it is absolute. Language is constantly changing, so throughout this glossary an effort has been made to reflect current usage in college, business, and technical writing. When a usage is in dispute or in flux, the alternatives are discussed along with the advantages and disadvantages of each. In addition to the advice you receive from this glossary, your own sense of the language, as well as your assessment of your audience and purpose, should help you decide if a particular usage is appropriate. Remember, however, that this glossary is not a dictionary; whenever you need more information about a word, you should consult one of the general-purpose or specialized dictionaries described in Chapter 17.

a, an   Use *a* before words that begin with consonants or words that have initial vowels that sound like consonants.

a primitive artifact   *a* one-horse carriage

Use *an* before words that begin with vowels and words that begin with a silent *h*.

an aqueous solution   *an* honest person

accept, except   *Accept* is a verb that means "to receive." *Except* is a preposition or conjunction that means "other than." As a verb *except* means "to leave out."

The auditors will *accept* all your claims *except* the last two.

Aliens who have lived in the United States for more than five years are *excepted* from the regulation.

advice, advise   *Advice* is a noun meaning "opinion or information offered." *Advise* is a verb that means "to offer advice to."

The king sent a messenger to the oracle to ask for *advice*.

The broker *advised* her client to stay away from speculative stocks.

affect, effect   *Affect* is a verb meaning "to influence." *Effect* can be a verb or a noun. As a verb it means "to bring about," and as a noun it means "result."

A severe cutback in federal funds for student loans could *affect* his plans for graduate school.

The arbitrator tried to *effect* a settlement that would satisfy both the teachers and the school board.

The most notable *effect* of the German bombing of London was to strengthen the resolve of the British.

usage

afraid, frightened   See **frightened, afraid**.

all ready, already   *All ready* means "wholly prepared." *Already* means "by or before this or that time."

> During the thirties President Roosevelt made the country feel that it was *all ready* for any challenge that might confront it.

> By the time Horatius decided to call for help, it was *already* too late.

all right, alright   Although there is a tendency in the direction of *alright*, current usage accepts only *all right*.

allusion, illusion   An *allusion* is a reference or hint. In literature it is a brief reference to a person, place, historical event, or other literary work with which a reader is expected to be familiar. An *illusion* is something that is not what it seems.

> In *The Catcher in the Rye*, the main character makes an *allusion* to *The Return of the Native*, a book by Thomas Hardy.

> The Viking landing proved that the canals of Mars are an *illusion* caused by atmospheric and topographical conditions.

among, between   *Among* is used to refer to groups of more than two things. *Between* refers to just two things. The distinction between these terms seems to be fading, and it is becoming increasingly acceptable when speaking to use *between* for three or more things when *among* would sound awkward. In formal writing situations, however, you should maintain the distinction.

> The three parties agreed *among* themselves to settle the question out of court.

> By the time of his death in 323 B.C., Alexander's empire encompassed all the territory *between* Macedon and India.

amount, number   *Amount* refers to a quantity that cannot be counted. *Number* refers to things that can be counted. Always use *number* when referring to people.

> Because he had missed several payments, the bank called in the full *amount* of the loan.

> Seeing their commander fall, a large *number* of troops ran to his aid.

an, a. See **a, an**.

ante-, anti-   Many students confuse these prefixes. *Ante-* means "before" or "in front of," and *anti-* means "against" or "opposed to."

> *ante*bellum   *anti*aircraft

apt to   See **likely to, liable to**.

as ...as ...   In such constructions, *as* signals a comparison. To avoid awkwardness, you must use the second *as*.

usage

AWKWARD   John Steinbeck's *East of Eden* is as long if not longer than *The Grapes of Wrath*.

CLEAR   John Steinbecks' *East of Eden* is almost as long as *The Grapes of Wrath*.

Traditionally *as . . . as* was used for a positive comparison and *so . . . as* for a negative one. Current usage, however, accepts *as . . . as* for both.

The winters in England are not *as* harsh *as* those in many parts of the United States.

as, like   Current usage accepts *as* as a conjunction or a preposition. *Like*, however, should be used as a preposition only. If a full clause is introduced, *as* is preferred.

In his novel *The Scarlet Letter* Hawthorne uses imagery *as* he does in his other works.

In its use of imagery *The Scarlet Letter* is *like The House of the Seven Gables*.

When you use *as* as a preposition, it indicates equivalency or identity.

After classes he works *as* a manager of a fast-food restaurant.

Like, however, indicates resemblance but never identity.

Writers *like* Carl Sandburg appear once in a generation.

as, than   When making comparisons, either objective or subjective case pronouns can follow *as* or *than*. To determine case, you must know whether the things being compared are subjects or objects of verbs. A simple way to test this is to add the missing verb.

Nassim was as tall *as he* (is tall).

I have walked farther *than he* (has walked).

I like Jim more *than* (I like) *him*. ("Him" is the object of the missing verb "like.")

assure, ensure, insure   *Assure* means "to tell confidently or to promise." *Ensure* and *insure* can be used interchangeably to mean "to make certain." *Insure*, however, is almost always reserved for "the protection of people or property against loss."

Caesar wished to *assure* the people that if they surrendered, he would not plunder their city.

To *ensure* (or *insure*) the smooth operation of the mechanism, you should oil it every six months.

It is extremely expensive for physicians to *insure* themselves against malpractice suits.

at, to   Many people use the prepositions *at* and *to* after *where* in conversation. This colloquialism is redundant and should not be used in college writing.

COLLOQUIAL   *Where* are you working *at?*
   Where are you going *to?*

STANDARD   Where are you working?
   Where are you going?

awhile, a while   *Awhile* is an adverb. *A while* consists of an article and a noun that you can use as an object of a preposition.

Before we continue we will rest *awhile.* (Modifies the verb *rest.*)

Before we continue we will rest for *a while.* (Object of the preposition *for.*)

bad, badly   *Bad* is an adjective and *badly* is an adverb. So used, they should cause you no problems.

The school board decided that *The Tin Drum* by Günter Grass was a *bad* book and deleted it from the high school reading list.

For the past five years, American automobile makers have been doing *badly.*

After verbs that refer to any of the senses or any other linking verb, use the adjective form.

He looked *bad;* he felt *bad;* it tasted *bad.*

Bad meaning "very much" is colloquial and should be avoided in academic writing.

COLLOQUIAL   Jake Barnes felt that he needed a vacation in Spain *bad.*

STANDARD   Jake Barnes felt that he needed a vacation in Spain *very much.*

being as, being that   Colloquial for *because.* These awkward phrases add unnecessary words and weaken your sentences.

Because (not *being that*) the climate was getting colder, a great number of animals migrated southward.

beside, besides   *Beside* is a preposition meaning "next to" and occasionally "apart from." *Besides* can be either a preposition or an adverb. As a preposition, *besides* means "except" or "other than." As an adverb it means "in addition to."

Beside the tower was a wall that ran the length of the old section of the city.

The judge pointed out to the lawyer that his argument was *beside* the point.

Besides its peaceful uses, laser technology has many wartime applications.

Edison not only invented the light bulb and the ticker tape, but the phonograph *besides.*

between, among   See **among, between.**

usage

bi-, semi-   *Bi-* is a prefix meaning "two" or "having two" (*bi*valve, *bi*carbonate, *bi*lingual). *Semi-* is a prefix meaning "half of" or "divided by two." The use of these prefixes, however, is not regular. Thus, *biennial* means "happening every two years" and *biannual* means "happening twice in one year." To avoid confusion, consult a dictionary. Or avoid the situation altogether and say "happening every two years," or "happening twice in one year."

bring, take   *Bring* means to transport from a farther place to a nearer place. *Take* means to carry or convey from a nearer place to a farther one.

> In the late nineteenth century many Russian Jewish immigrants were able to *bring* to this country only the clothes they wore.

> *Take* this message to the general and wait for a reply.

can, may   *Can* denotes ability and *may* indicates permission.

> *Can* (are they *able* to?) freshmen participate in the work-study program if they have not completed composition?

> *May* (do they have permission?) registered aliens collect unemployment benefits?

censor, censure   To *censor* is to label as undesirable passages of books, plays, films, news, essays, etc. To *censure* is to condemn or criticize harshly.

> Recently Studs Terkel's book *Working* was *censored* by a school district in Pennsylvania.

> In 1633 Galileo was *censured* by the Inquisition for holding that the sun was the center of the universe.

center around   This common colloquialism is acceptable in speech but not in writing. You may write *revolve around* or *center on* but never *center around* (which is not accurate).

> The report *centers on* (not *around*) the effects of cigarette smoking on the circulatory system.

cite, sight, site   *Cite* means "to quote or mention as an example." *Sight* means "spectacle or view," and *site* means "location or place." Because these words sound exactly alike, they can be confusing.

> Ordinarily the Supreme Court allows one-half-hour to an hour for lawyers to *cite* cases that will support their arguments.

> Several days before their first *sight* of land Columbus's crew attempted a mutiny.

> The engineers surveyed the *site* before they began the plans for the new office complex.

compare, contrast   *Contrast* means to show differences. *Compare* means to show both similarities *and* differences.

Ernest Jones wrote a book in which he *compared* Hamlet and Oedipus. (He discussed their similarities and differences.)

The company's earnings this year *contrast* sharply with its earnings last year. (The earnings are different.)

compare to, compare with   Formal usage calls for *compare to* when you want to stress similarities, and *compare with* when you want to analyze similarities *and* differences. Many instructors do not insist on this distinction, but you should be aware of it for formal writing situations.

In one of Shakespeare's sonnets, the speaker *compares* his beloved *to* a summer's day.

This study *compares* Nat Turner's revolt *with* other slave revolts that occurred in the eighteenth and nineteenth centuries.

complement, compliment   *Complement* means "to complete or add to." *Compliment* means "to give praise."

A double-blind study would *complement* their preliminary work on this anticancer drug.

Before accepting the 1949 Nobel Prize for literature, William Faulkner *complimented* the people of Sweden for their courtesy and kindness.

conscious, conscience   *Conscious* means "having one's mental faculties awake." *Conscience* is the moral sense of right and wrong.

With a local anesthetic a patient remains *conscious* during this procedure.

During the American Civl War, the Copperheads followed the dictates of *conscience* and refused to fight.

consensus   "Consensus of opinion" is redundant because *consensus* means an "agreement of the majority." Never write "they reached a consensus of opinion." Using "they agreed" or "the majority view was" eliminates any possibility of misunderstanding.

continual, continuous   These words are frequently confused. *Continual* means "recurring at intervals" *Continuous* refers to an action that occurs without interruption.

usage

A pulsar is a star that emits a *continual* stream of electromagnetic radiation. (It emits radiation at regular intervals.)

A small battery allows the watch to run *continuously* for five years. (It runs without stopping.)

could of, would of   In speech, the contractions *could've* and *would've* sound like these constructions, but *could of* and *would of* are nonstandard. Spell out *could have* and *would have* in academic writing.

Macbeth *would have* (not *would of*) defied his wife if he *could have* (not *could of*).

council, counsel, consul   Because of their similar pronunciation and spelling, these words are commonly confused. A *council* is a noun meaning "a body of persons that passes laws or gives advice." *Counsel* is a verb meaning "to give advice." Thus, a counselor is a person who gives advice. *Consul* is a noun meaning "a representative of a country who lives in a foreign city."

couple of   *Couple* means "a pair," but *couple of* may mean loosely "several" or "a few." When you designate quantities, avoid ambiguity. Write "four points," "three reasons," or "two examples" rather than "a couple of" or "several."

criterion, criteria   Although many people use these singular and plural words interchangeably, *criteria,* from the Greek, is the plural of *criterion,* meaning "standard for judgment," and you should use each term correctly.

Of all the *criteria* for hiring graduating seniors, class rank is the most important *criterion*.

curriculum   *Curriculum,* from the Latin, is a noun meaning "a course of study." The correct plural form is *curricula*.

The premedical *curriculum* at this university is extremely demanding.

There are three *curricula* you can take in the college of business.

data   *Data* is the plural of the Latin *datum,* meaning "fact." In everyday speech and writing *data* is used for both singular and plural. In college writing preserve the distinction.

The *data* discussed in this section *are* summarized in the graph in Appendix A.

You can avoid the problem by using *facts* or *results* instead of *data*.

device, devise   *Device* is a noun meaning "a thing adapted for a particular function." *Devise* is a verb meaning "to invent."

Simple *devices* like the zipper or the safety pin can make their inventors rich.

A common theme in folklore and fairy tales is young lovers *devising* a plan to outwit an evil parent or guardian.

usage

different from, different than   *Different than* is used extensively in American speech. Stylists, who point out that *different than* indicates a comparison where none is intended, prefer *different from*. In college writing, use *different from*.

His test scores were not much *different from* (not *than*) mine.

discreet, discrete   *Discreet* means "careful or prudent." *Discrete* means "separate or individually distinct."

Because Madame Bovary was not *discreet* with her lover, her reputation suffered.

Current research has demonstrated that atoms can be broken into hundreds of *discrete* particles.

disinterested, uninterested   *Disinterested* means "objective or capable of making an impartial judgment." *Uninterested* means "indifferent or unconcerned."

The narrator of Ernest Hemingway's "A Clean, Well-Lighted Place" is a *disinterested* observer of the action.

Finding no treasure after leading an expedition from Florida to Oklahoma, Hernando de Soto was *uninterested* in going farther.

economic, economical   *Economic* refers to "things maintained for profit or for business." It can also refer to the science of economics. *Economical* means "thrifty and avoiding waste."

A depression is a period of *economic* crisis characterized by falling prices, tightening of credit, lowering of production, and increased unemployment.

Silas Marner was *economical* to the point of being a miser.

effect, affect   See **affect, effect**.

elicit, illicit   *Elicit* means "to draw out" or "evoke." *Illicit* means "unlawful" or "forbidden."

Some psychiatrists will hypnotize patients to *elicit* responses from them.

Mata Hari was a German agent who obtained *illicit* information from French officials by seducing them.

emigrate from, immigrate to   *To emigrate* is "to leave one's country and settle in another." *To immigrate* is "to come to another country and reside there." The noun forms of these words are *emigrant* and *immigrant*.

In 1887 my great-grandfather *emigrated from* the Russian city of Minsk and traveled by ship to Boston. During that year many other *emigrants* made the same trip.

The potato famine of 1846–1847 caused many Irish to *immigrate to* the United States . These *immigrants* became builders, politicians, and storekeepers.

ensure, assure, insure   See **assure, ensure, insure**.

enthused   *Enthused* is a colloquial form of *enthusiastic* and should never be used.

President John F. Kennedy was *enthusiastic* (not *enthused*) about the United States space program.

equally as good   A redundant blend of the two phrases "equally good" and "as good as." Use one or the other, but not *equally as good*.

etc.   *Etc.*, the abbreviation of *et cetera*, means "and the rest." The construction *and etc.*, therefore, is redundant. Although *etc.* is common in popular writing and speech, do not use it in your academic writing. Say "and so on" or, better, specify exactly what *etc.* stands for.

> UNCLEAR Before beginning a research paper you should have paper and pencil, *etc.*

> REVISED Before beginning a research paper you should have a pencil, bond paper, and a clean typewriter ribbon.

everyday, every day *Everyday* means "ordinary" or "commonplace." *Every day* means "occurring daily."

> In the Gettysburg Address, Lincoln used *everyday* words to create a model of clarity and conciseness.

> In *The Canterbury Tales* Chaucer depicts a group of pilgrims who tell stories *every day* as they ride from London to Canterbury.

except, accept See **accept, except**.

farther, further The distinction between these words as adjectives has all but disappeared. In formal writing, however, some stylists prefer *farther* to designate distance and *further* to designate degree.

> The Pioneer 10 Space Probe has traveled *farther* in space than any other man-made object.

> Critics of the welfare system charge that government subsidies to the poor encourage *further* dependence.

Two uses of *further* are still very much with us. As a conjunctive adverb *further* means "besides." As a transitive verb, *to further* means "to promote" or "to advance."

> Napoleon I was one of the greatest generals in history; *further*, he promoted liberalism through widespread legal reforms.

> Tom Jones, the hero of Fielding's novel, was a poor boy who was able to *further* himself with luck and good looks.

fewer, less Use *fewer* with nouns that can be counted: *fewer* books, *fewer* people, *fewer* dollars. Use *less* with quantities that cannot be counted: *less* pain, *less* power, *less* enthusiasm.

> *Fewer* young families than ever can afford the high interest rates on home mortgages.

> Sufferers of arthritis often take large quantities of aspirin so they will have *less* pain.

figuratively, literally See **literally, figuratively**.

firstly (secondly, thirdly, . . .) Archaic forms meaning "in the first . . . second . . . third place." Use *first, second, third.*

former, formerly, formally *Former* as an adjective means "preceding" or "previous." As a noun it means "the first of two things mentioned previously." It is often used in conjunction with *latter.*

> The *former* residents of this area, the Delaware Indians, were forced to cede their land in 1795.

usage

Two books mark the extremes of Herman Melville's career: *Typee* and *Moby Dick*. The *former* was a best seller; the *latter* was generally ignored by the public.

Formerly means "just before" or "in a time past."

Formerly, tonality, as it evolved in the seventeenth century, was considered the natural law in music.

Formally means "ceremonially" or "in a manner required by convention."

Before assuming their duties, ambassadors have their credentials *formally* accepted by the president.

freshman, freshmen *Freshman* is singular and *freshmen* is plural. Even so, only *freshman* is used as the adjective form: *freshman* composition, *freshman* registration, *freshman* dormitories.

frightened, afraid Much confusion surrounds the prepositions that follow these words. *Frightened* should be accompanied by *at* or *by*; *afraid* by *of*.

Dolley Madison, wife of President James Madison, was *frightened at* the thought of the British burning Washington.

In Charles Dickens's *A Christmas Carol*, Scrooge is *frightened by* three ghosts.

Young children are often *afraid of* the dark.

further, farther See **farther, further**.

good, well *Good* is an adjective, never an adverb.

The townspeople thought the proposal for a new municipal water plant was a *good* one.

Well can function as an adverb or an adjective. As an adverb it means "in a good manner." In slang expressions, such as "He did *good* on the test" or "She swam *good* in the meet," *good* is wrong. Correct usage requires "He did *well* on the test" and "She swam *well* in the meet."

Well is used as an adjective with verbs that denote a state of being or feeling. Here *well* can mean "in good health": "I feel *well*." If you mean that your sense of feeling is acute, however, "my feeling is good" leaves no ambiguity.

good and This colloquial phrase meaning "very" is not appropriate in academic writing.

After escaping from the Iroquois, Natty Bumppo was *very* [not *good and*] tired.

got to *Got to* is slang and not suitable in academic writing. To indicate obligation use *have to, has to,* or *must.*

INAPPROPRIATE Anyone who takes a literature course has *got to* get a copy of *A Glossary of Literary Terms* by M. H. Abrams.

REVISED Anyone who takes a literature course *has* to get a copy of *A Glossary of Literary Terms* by M. H. Abrams.

usage

hanged, hung   Both *hanged* and *hung* are past participles of *hang*. *Hanged* is used to refer to executions. *Hung* is used in all other senses meaning "suspended" or "held up."

Billy Budd was *hanged* from the mainyard of the ship for killing the master-at-arms.

The pictures in the National Gallery were *hung* to take advantage of the natural lighting in the various rooms.

he, she   Traditionally *he* has been used in the generic sense to refer to both males and females.

Before registering, each student should be sure *he* has received *his* student number.

You can acknowledge equality of both sexes by avoiding the generic *he*. Efforts in the direction of a new neutral pronoun have not caught on. And constructions such as *he or she* or *he/she* are cumbersome, especially when used a number of times in a paragraph. To avoid problems, use the second person singular or first and third person plural pronouns when possible.

TRADITIONAL   Before registering, *each student* should be sure *he* has received *his* student number.

REVISION   Before registering, *you* should receive *your* student number.

REVISION   Before registering, *we* should receive *our* student numbers.

REVISION   Before registering, *students* should receive *their* student numbers.

hopefully   The adverb *hopefully* should modify a verb, an adjective, or another adverb. Increasingly, however, *hopefully* is being used as a sentence modifier meaning "it is hoped." At present, some stylists object to this use, so to be safe and unambiguous, use *hopefully* in its traditional sense.

AMBIGUOUS   *Hopefully*, scientists will find an alternative energy source by the end of the century. (Who is hopeful? Scientists or the writer?)

REVISED   Scientists *hope* they will find an alternative energy source by the end of the century.

Here is an acceptable use of *hopefully*.

During the 1930's many of the nation's jobless looked *hopefully* to the federal government for relief. (*Hopefully* modifies *looked*.)

illicit, elicit   See **elicit, illicit**.
illusion, allusion   See **allusion, illusion**.
immigrate, emigrate   See **emigrate, immigrate**.
imply, infer   *Imply* means "to hint" or "to suggest." *Infer* means "to conclude from." When you *imply*, you *send out* a suggestion; when

usage

you *infer*, you *receive* or draw a conclusion. You should maintain this distinction in your writing.

> Mark Antony *implied* that Brutus and the other conspirators had wrongfully killed Julius Caesar.

> The crowd *inferred* his meaning and called for the punishment of the conspirators.

in, into Use *in* when you want to indicate position. Use *into* when you want to indicate "motion to a point within a thing."

> As he stood *in* the main burial vault of the tomb of Tutankhamen, Howard Carter saw a wealth of artifacts.

> Before he walked *into* the cave, Tom Sawyer grasped Becky Thatcher's hand.

> In 1828 Russia and Persia entered *into* the Treaty of Turkmanchai.

infer, imply See **imply, infer**.

ingenious, ingenuous *Ingenious* means "clever at inventing or organizing." *Ingenuous* means "open" or "artless."

> Ludwig van Beethoven is recognized as one of the most *ingenious* composers who ever lived.

> For a politician the mayor was surprisingly *ingenuous*.

insure, ensure, assure See **assure, ensure, insure**.

irregardless, regardless See **regardless, irregardless**.

its, it's *Its* is a possessive pronoun. *It's* is a contraction of *it is*. Remember this distinction, and do not use these words interchangeably.

> The most obvious characteristic of a modern corporation is the separation of *its* management from *its* ownership.

> *It's* not often that you can see a collection of rare books such as the one housed in the Library of Congress.

-ize, -wise The suffix *-ize* is used to change nouns and adjectives into verbs: *civilize, industrialize, Westernize, immunize*. The suffix *-wise* is used to change a noun or adjective into an adverb: "likewise," "otherwise." Unfortunately, business, advertising, and government people, along with professional educators, use these suffixes carelessly, making up words as they please: *finalize, prioritize, taste-wise, weather-wise*, and *policy-wise*, for example. Be sure to look up suspect *-ize* and *-wise* words in the dictionary to make sure that they are accepted usages.

judgment, judgement Both are acceptable spellings, although the American *judgment* is preferred over the British spelling *judgement*.

kind of, sort of *Kind of* and *sort of* to mean "rather" or "somewhat" are colloquial and should not appear in college writing.

> COLLOQUIAL   The countess was surprised to see that Napoleon was *kind of* short.

usage

REVISED   The countess was surprised to see that Napoleon was *rather* short.

Reserve *kind of* and *sort of* for occasions when you categorize.

Willie Stark, a character in Robert Penn Warren's *All the King's Men*, is the *kind of* man who begins by meaning well and ends by being corrupted by his success.

latter   See **former, formerly, formally**.

lay, lie   See **lie, lay**.

lead, led   The verb *lead* (rhymes with *feed*) means "to guide or direct." As a noun, *lead* (rhymes with *bed*) denotes a metal.

You can *lead* a horse to water, but you can't make him drink.

For centuries alchemists searched for the formula that would enable them to change *lead* into gold.

Led (also rhymes with *bed*) is the past tense and the past participle form of the verb *lead*.

The remarkable Indian woman Sacajawea *led* the Lewis and Clark expedition across the high Rocky Mountains.

leave, let   *Leave* means "to go away from" or "to let remain." *Let* means "to allow" or "to permit."

Many missionaries were forced to *leave* China after the Communist revolution in 1948.

As the liquid boils away, it will *leave* a dark brown precipitate at the bottom of the flask.

In London it is illegal to *let* dogs foul the footpath.

led, lead   See **lead, led**.

lend, loan   See **loan, lend**.

less, fewer   See **fewer, less**.

let, leave   See **leave, let**.

liable to   See **likely to, liable to, apt to**.

lie, lay   *Lie* is an intransitive verb (one that does not take an object) that means "to recline." *Lay* is a transitive verb meaning "to put" or "to place."

Base Form	Past	Past Participle	Present Participle
lie	lay	lain	lying

Each afternoon she would *lie* in the sun and listen to the surf.

As I Lay Dying is a book by William Faulkner.

In 1871 Heinrich Schliemann unearthed the city of Troy that had *lain* undisturbed for two thousand years.

The painting *Odalisque* by Eugène Delacroix shows a nude *lying* on a couch.

Base Form	Past	Past Participle	Present Participle
lay	laid	laid	laying

The Federalist Papers *lay* the foundation for the American conservative movement.

In October of 1781 the British *laid* down their arms and surrendered to George Washington at Yorktown.

After he had *laid* his money on the counter, he walked out of the restaurant.

We watched the Amish stone masons *laying* a wall without using mortar.

like, as   See **as, like**.

likely to, liable to, apt to   *Likely to* implies a strong chance something might happen. *Liable to* implies that something undesirable is about to occur. *Apt to* implies having a natural tendency.

Medical researchers feel that in fifty years human beings are *likely to* have a life span of over a hundred years.

If we do not do something to correct the poor drainage in this area, we are *liable to* repeat last year's flooding.

Old books are *apt to* increase in value if you protect them from heat and moisture.

literally, figuratively   *Literally* means "following the letter" or "in a strict sense." *Figuratively* is its opposite and means "metaphorically" or "not literally." Don't use *literally* when you don't mean it.

Literally, the Declaration of Independence is a list of grievances that the English colonists had against their king.

Figuratively, the Declaration of Independence is a document that elevates the rights of the common man above the divine right of kings.

loan, lend   American usage prefers *lend* as a verb and *loan* as a noun. "He offered to *lend* me his car." "I negotiated a *loan* with the bank."

loose, lose   *Loose* is an adjective meaning "not rigidly fastened or securely attached." *Lose* is a verb meaning "to misplace."

usage

The barons turned King John *loose* after he agreed to sign the Magna Carta.

The marble facing of the building became *loose* and fell to the sidewalk.

After only two drinks, most people *lose* their ability to judge distance.

mad, angry   In American colloquial usage, *mad* has become a synonym for *angry*. In writing, however, you should maintain the distinction between these words. *Angry* means "annoyed" or "irritated" and *mad* means "insane."

COLLOQUIAL   The librarian was *mad* when they returned the books six months late.

REVISED   The librarian was *angry* when they returned the books six months late.

The term 'lunacy" derives from the ancient belief that the light of the moon can drive people *mad*.

majority, plurality   These words are often confused. *Majority* denotes more than half. *Plurality* means a larger number but not necessarily a majority. A candidate with a *majority* has over 50 percent of the votes cast. A candidate with a *plurality* has more votes than any of the other candidates, but not over 50 percent of the total. Use *most* rather than *majority* when you do not know the exact numbers.

INCORRECT   The soprano got the *majority* of the applause.

CORRECT   The soprano got *most* of the applause.

man   Like the generic pronoun *he, man* has been used in English to denote members of both sexes. Certain words, especially those describing occupations, disturb those concerned with the status of women: *policeman, chairman, postman,* and *fireman,* for example. In recent years, neutral terms that refer to *both* men and women have emerged: *police officer, chairperson, letter carrier,* and *fire fighter.* Other terms, such as *police person* and *statesperson,* seem awkward and are not widely used. When you write, be sure to consider your audience and use words that will not offend.

may, can   See **can, may**.

media, medium   *Medium,* meaning a "means of conveying or broadcasting something," is singular. *Media* is the plural form.

Television has replaced print and film as the *medium* of communication that has the most profound effect on our lives.

A good business presentation uses a number of *media* to make its point.

might have, might of   *Might of* is not the written form for the contraction of *might have.* Do not use it in your writing.

John F. Kennedy *might have* (not *might of*) been a great president had he not been assassinated.

number, amount   See **amount, number**.

on account of   Use *because of.*

The Ford Motor Company had to recall over a million Pintos *because of* (not *on account of*) their faulty gasoline tanks.

passed, past   *Passed* means "left behind," "threw," or "attained a certain standard."

Even though we were going sixty miles an hour, another car *passed* us as though we were standing still.

usage

Last season the Dallas Cowboys' quarterback *passed* for over a thousand yards.

After trying for nearly four months, my brother finally *passed* his driver's test.

Past has several meanings. As a noun, *past* means "a time gone by."

Recent discoveries of fossils in Africa tell us a great deal about our *past*.

As an adjective, *past* refers to a previous time.

In Stephen Crane's novel *Maggie: A Girl of the Streets*, the main character, Maggie, pays dearly for her *past* mistakes.

As a preposition, *past* means "beyond in time or place."

The space shuttle has been designed to operate *past* the upper level of the earth's atmosphere.

per Acceptable for technical and business writing, *per* is considered colloquial in academic writing.

The minimum wage was raised to $3.10 *an* (not *per*) hour.

percent, percentage *Percent* indicates a part of a hundred when a specific number is referred to: "10 *percent* of his weekly salary"; "5 *percent* of the monthly rent." *Percentage* is used when no specific number is referred to: "a *percentage* of the people"; "a *percentage* of next year's receipts." In technical and business writing it is permissible to use the % sign after percentages you are comparing. Write out *percent* in academic writing. But note that the number before *percent* is given in figures.

persecute, prosecute *Persecute* means "to harass or worry, especially for political or religious beliefs." *Prosecute* means "to institute legal proceedings against."

Quakers were *persecuted* in England until the passage of the Toleration Act of 1689.

Because of the suspect's age, the district attorney decided not to *prosecute*.

personal, personnel *Personal* means "one's own" or "private." *Personnel* means "people who are employed in a business firm or in the military."

Years ago many people kept journals in which they recorded their *personal* experiences.

The first person I met when I arrived at the plant for my interview was the *personnel* manager.

The military transported the troops to battle in armored *personnel* carriers.

usage

phenomenon, phenomena A *phenomenon* is a single observable fact or event. It can also refer to a rare or significant thing. *Phenomena* is the plural form.

Metamorphosis is a *phenomenon* that occurs in many insects, mollusks, amphibians, and fish.

John Stuart Mill was a *phenomenon.* He could read classical Greek at the age of five.

Comets are celestial *phenomena* that have been regarded with awe and terror and were once taken as omens of unfavorable events.

plurality, majority See **majority, plurality**.

precede, proceed *Precede* means "to go or come before." *Proceed* means "to go forward in an orderly way."

Robert Frost's *North of Boston* was *preceded* by another volume of poetry, *A Boy's Will.*

In 1532 Francisco Pizarro landed at Tumbes and *proceeded* south until he encountered the Incas.

principal, principle As a noun, *principal* means "a sum of money (minus interest) invested or lent" or "a person in the leading position." As an adjective it means "most important."

If you cash the bond before maturity, a penalty can be subtracted from the *principal* as well as the interest.

The *principal* of the high school is a talented administrator who has instituted a number of changes.

Women are the *principal* wage earners in over 20 percent of American households.

A *principle* is a rule of conduct or a basic truth.

The Constitution embodies the fundamental *principles* upon which the American republic is founded.

quote, quotation *Quote* is a verb meaning "to speak or write a passage from another." *Quotation* is a noun meaning "something that is quoted."

Be sure to use a footnote when you *quote* one of your sources.

In "Politics and the English Language," George Orwell offers several *quotations* (not *quotes*) as examples of bad prose.

raise, rise *Raise* is a transitive verb and *rise* is an intransitive verb. Thus, *raise* takes an object and *rise* does not.

A famous photograph taken during World War II shows American Marines *raising* the flag on Iwo Jima.

As Babe Ruth ran the bases after hitting a home run, he would *raise* his cap to the crowd.

usage

The planet Venus is called the morning star because when it *rises,* it is brighter than any light in the sky except the sun or moon.

It was only sixty-six years from the time the Wright Brothers' plane first *rose* into the air until the first moon landing.

real, really   *Real* means "genuine" or "authentic." *Really* means "actually." In your college writing, do not use *real* as an adjective meaning "very."

With its ducklike bill, flat tail, and webbed feet, the platypus hardly looks *real*.

When news of the bombing of Pearl Harbor was first broadcast, many people did not believe that it had *really* happened.

COLLOQUIAL   The planaria is a *real* flat worm that we studied in biology class.

REVISED   The planaria is a *very* flat worm that we studied in biology class.

reason is that, reason is because   Most authorities still insist that *reason* be used with *that* and not *because*. *Because* is redundant here and should be avoided.

The *reason* he moved out of the city *is that* (not *because*) property taxes rose sharply.

regardless, irregardless   *Irregardless* is a nonstandard version of *regardless*. The suffix "-less" means "without" or "free from," so the prefix "ir-" is unnecessary.

SLANG   *Irregardless* of what some people might think, drunk drivers kill more than twenty-five thousand people a year.

REVISED   *Regardless* of what some people might think, drunk drivers kill more than twenty-five thousand people a year.

respectively, respectfully, respectably   *Respectively* means "in the order given." *Respectfully* means "giving honor or deference." *Respectably* means "worthy of respect."

In this paper I will discuss "The Sisters" and "The Dead," which are, *respectively,* the first and last stories in James Joyce's collection *Dubliners*.

When being presented to Queen Elizabeth of England, foreigners are asked to bow *respectfully*.

Even though Abraham Lincoln ran a *respectable* campaign for the United States Senate, he was defeated by Stephen Douglas in 1858.

rise, raise   See **raise, rise**.
semi-, bi-   See **bi-, semi-**.
set, sit   *To set* means "to put" or "to lay." *To sit* means "to assume a sitting position."

usage

Base Form	Past	Past Participle	Present Participle
set	set	set	setting
sit	sat	sat	sitting

After rocking the baby, he *set* it down carefully in its crib.

Research has shown that many children *sit* in front of the television five to six hours a day.

shall, will   *Will* is swiftly replacing *shall* to express all future action.

should of   See **could of, would of**.

sight, cite, site   See **cite, site, sight**.

sit, set   See **set, sit**.

site, sight, cite   See **cite, sight, site**.

sometime, sometimes, some time   *Sometime* means "at some time in the future." *Sometimes* means "now and then." *Some time* means "a period of time."

In his essay "The Case Against Man," Isaac Asimov says that *sometime,* far in the future, human beings will not be able to produce enough food to sustain themselves.

All automobiles, no matter how well constructed, *sometimes* need repairs.

At the battle of Gettysburg, General Meade's failure to counterattack gave Lee *some time* to regroup his troops.

sort of, kind of   See **kind of, sort of**.

stationary, stationery   *Stationary* means "staying in one place." *Stationery* means "materials for writing" or "letter paper."

When viewed from the earth, a communications satellite traveling at the same speed as the earth appears to be *stationary* in the sky.

The secretaries are responsible for keeping departmental offices supplied with *stationery.*

take, bring   See **bring, take**.

than, then   *Than* is a conjunction used to indicate a comparison, and *then* is an adverb indicating time.

The new shopping center is bigger *than* the old one.

He did his research; *then* he wrote a report.

than, as   See **as, than**.

that, which, who   Use *that* or *which* when referring to a thing. Use *who* when referring to a person.

In *How the Other Half Lives,* Jacob Riis described the conditions *that* existed in working-class slums in nineteenth-century America.

The Wonderful Wizard of Oz, which was published in 1900, was originally entitled *From Kansas to Fairyland.*

usage

Anyone *who* (not *that*) has every visited Maine cannot help being impressed by the beauty of the scenery and the ruggedness of the landscape.

themselves, theirselves, theirself   *Theirselves* and *theirself* are nonstandard variants of *themselves*.

Pioneer families had to build their shelter and clear their land by *themselves* (not *theirself* or *theirselves*).

then, than   See **than, then**.

there, their, they're   Use *there* to indicate place and in the expressions *there is* and *there are*.

I have always wanted to visit the Marine Biological Laboratory in Woods Hole, Massachusetts, but I have never gotten *there*.

There is nothing that we can do to resurrect a species once it becomes extinct.

Their is a possessive pronoun.

James Watson and Francis Crick did *their* work on the molecular structure of DNA at the Cavendish Laboratory at Cambridge University.

They're is a contraction of *they are*.

White sharks and Mako sharks are dangerous to human beings because *they're* good swimmers and especially sensitive to the scent of blood.

thus, therefore   *Thus* means "in this way," not "therefore" or "so."

In Joseph Conrad's *Heart of Darkness*, Kurtz becomes a man-god to the natives. *Thus*, he is able to collect a fortune in ivory.

INCORRECT   Throughout the past year interest rates have dropped dramatically. Thus, businesses are able to buy the equipment they need to modernize their operations.

REVISED   Throughout the past year interest rates have risen dramatically, so businesses are unable to buy the equipment they need to modernize their operations.

to, at   See **at, to**.

to, too, two   *To* is a preposition that indicates direction.

Last year we flew from New York *to* California.

Too is an adverb that means "also" or "more than is needed."

"Tippecanoe and Tyler *too*" was William Henry Harrison's campaign slogan during the 1840 presidential election.

The plot was *too* complicated.

Two expresses the number "2."

Just north of *Two* Rivers, Wisconsin, is a petrified forest.

usage

try to, try and   *Try and* is the colloquial equivalent of the more formal *try to*, which more clearly indicates the sense of purpose.

COLLOQUIAL   Throughout most of his career E. R. Rutherford was determined to *try and* discover the structure of the atom.

REVISED   Throughout most of his career E. R. Rutherford *tried to* discover the structure of the atom.

-type   Newspaper and television reporters insist upon adding *-type* to adjectives. Deleting this empty suffix eliminates clutter and clarifies meaning.

COLLOQUIAL   Found in the wreckage of the house was an *incendiary-type* device.

REVISED   Found in the wreckage of the house was an *incendiary* device.

COLLOQUIAL   It was a *cancer-type* tumor.

REVISED   The tumor was *cancerous.*

uninterested, disinterested   See **disinterested, uninterested**.

unique   *Unique* means "the only one," not "remarkable" or "unusual."

COLLOQUIAL   Its undershot lower jaw makes the English bulldog *unique* among dogs.

REVISED   Its undershot lower jaw makes the English bulldog unusual among dogs.

CORRECT USAGE   In their scope and unity, Michelangelo's paintings are *unique.*

Because *unique* means "the only one," it can take no intensifiers. Never use constructions like "the most unique" or "very unique."

used to, use to   *Used to* is the standard form; *use to* is not.

Before factories many women *used to* (not *use to*) be limited to work they could do at home.

wait for, wait on   *To wait for* means "to defer action until something occurs." *To wait on* means "to act as a waiter."

COLLOQUIAL   I am *waiting on* dinner.

REVISED   I am *waiting for* dinner.

CORRECT   The captain *waited on* the head table himself.

(a) wake, (a) waken   Like *lie* and *lay,* these two verbs are easily confused. As a transitive verb, *wake* means "to arouse from sleep," and as an intransitive verb it means "to cease sleeping." *Waken* is usually used as a transitive verb that means "to arouse from sleep."

Base Form	Past	Past Participle	Present Participle
(a) wake	woke	waked	waking
(a) waken	wakened	wakened	wakening

usage

The alarm clock *wakes* Jim up at 6:30 every morning.

Jane Pauley of the *Today Show* says that she *wakes* up at 3:30 every morning.

After entering the castle, the prince *awakened* Sleeping Beauty with a kiss.

weather, whether   *Weather* refers to atmospheric conditions such as rain, snow, wind, or hail. *Whether* can introduce an indirect question or mean "in either case."

Space shots are often postponed because of unfavorable *weather* conditions at the launch site.

Whether or not the country will have a tax increase is up to Congress.

well, good   See **good, well**.

were, we're   Some people pronounce these words alike and so they confuse them when they write. *Were* is a verb; *we're* is the contraction of *we are*.

The Trojans *were* asleep when the Greeks climbed out of the wooden horse and took the city.

We Americans are affected by the advertising we see. *We're* motivated by the ads we see to buy billions of dollars worth of products each year.

which, who, that   See **that, which, who**.

who's, whose   Use *who's* when you mean *who is*.

Who's going to take calculus?

Use *whose* when you want to indicate possession.

The writer *whose* book was in the window was autographing copies in the store.

will, shall   See **shall, will**.

-wise, -ize   See **-ize, -wise**.

would of, could of   See **could of, would of**.

your, you're   Because these words are pronounced alike, they are often confused. *Your* indicates possession and *you're* is the contraction of *you are*.

usage

You can improve *your* stamina by jogging two miles a day.

You're certain to be impressed the first time you see the Golden Gate Bridge spanning San Francisco Bay.

Glossary of Grammatical Terms

absolute phrase See phrase.

abstract noun See noun.

acronym A word formed from the first letters or initial sounds of a group of words: NATO = North Atlantic Treaty Organization.

active voice See voice.

adjectival A word or word group used as an adjective to modify a noun: *dancing bear*. **24d**

adjective A word that describes, limits, qualifies, or in any other way modifies nouns or pronouns. A **descriptive adjective** names a quality of the noun or pronoun it modifies: *jet plane; junior year*. A **proper adjective** is formed from a proper noun: *Russian cosmonaut; Hegelian philosophy*. Other kinds of words may be used to limit or qualify nouns, and are then considered adjectives: **articles** (*a, an, the*): *the book; a peanut;* **possessive adjectives** (*my, your, his,* and so on): *their apartment, my house;* **demonstrative adjectives** (*this, these, that, those*): *that table, these chairs;* **interrogative adjectives** (*what, which, whose,* and so on): *Which card is mine?;* **indefinite adjectives** (*another, each, both, many,* and so on): *any minute, some day;* **relative adjectives** (*what, whatever, which, whichever, whose, whoever*): *Bed rest was what the doctor ordered.;* **numerical adjectives** (*one, two, first, second,* and so on): *The first day of spring Claire saw two robins.* **20d**

adjective clause See clause.

adverb A word that describes the action of verbs or modifies adjectives, other adverbs, or complete phrases, clauses, or sentences. Adverbs answer the questions "How?" "Why?" "Where?" "When?" "To what extent?" and "To what degree?" Adverbs are formed from adjectives, many by adding *-ly* to the adjective form (*dark/darkly, solemn/solemnly*), and may also be derived from prepositions (*Joe carried on.*). Other adverbs that indicate time, place, condition, cause, or degree do not derive from other parts of speech: *then, never, very,* and *often,* for example. The words *how, why, where,* and *when* are classified as **interrogative adverbs** when they ask questions (*How did we get into this mess?*). See also conjunctive adverb. **20e**

adverb clause See clause.

adverbial A word or word group that is used as an adverb to modify a verb, adjective, other adverbs, or complete phrases, clauses, or sentences: *The sun rises in the east.; Our vacation begins Saturday.*

adverbial conjunction See conjunctive adverb.

agreement The correspondence between words in number, person, and gender. Subjects and verbs must agree in number (singular

terms

or plural) and person (first, second, or third): *Soccer is a popular European sport.; I play soccer too.* **23a** Pronouns and their antecedents must agree in number, person, and gender (masculine, feminine, neuter): *Lucy loaned Charlie her car.* **23b**

allusion   A form of figurative language in which the writer describes a subject by referring to a famous historical or literary person or event. **16d.5**

analogy   A form of figurative language in which the writer explains an unfamiliar idea or object by comparing it to a more familiar one: *Sensory pathways of the central nervous system are bundles of nerves rather like telephone cables that feed information about the outside world into your brain for processing.* **16d.3**

antecedent   The word or group of words to which a pronoun refers: *Brian finally bought the stereo he had always wanted.* (*Brian* is the antecedent of the pronoun *he*)

appositive   A noun or noun phrase that identifies, in different words, the noun or pronoun it follows: *Columbus, the capital of Ohio, is in the central part of the state.* Appositives may be used without special introductory phrases, as in this example, or they may be introduced by *such as, or, that is, for example,* or *in other words: Japanese cars, such as Hondas, now have a large share of the U.S. automobile market.* In an inverted appositive, the appositive precedes the noun or pronoun it modifies: *The singing cowboy, Gene Autry, became owner of the California Angels.* **6f.4**

article   See adjective.

auxiliary verb   See verb.

balanced sentence   A sentence neatly divided between two parallel structures. Balanced sentences are typically **compound sentences** made up of two parallel clauses (*The telephone rang, and I answered.*), but the parallel clauses of a **complex sentence** can also be balanced. **8c**

cardinal number   A number that expresses quantity—*seven, thirty, one-hundred.* (Contrast **ordinal**.)

case   The form a noun or pronoun takes to indicate how it functions in a sentence. English has three cases: **subjective** (or **nominative**) case: A pronoun takes the subjective case when it acts as the subject of a sentence or a clause: *I am an American.* **21a**; **objective case:** A pronoun takes the objective case when it acts as the object of a verb or a preposition: *Fran gave me her dog.* **21b**; **possessive** (or **genitive**) case: Both nouns and pronouns take the possessive case when they indicate ownership: *My house is brick; Brandon's T-shirt is red.* This is the only case in which nouns change form. **21c**

clause   A group of related words that includes a subject and a predicate. An **independent** (main) **clause** may stand alone as a sentence (*Yellowstone is a national park in the West.*), but a **dependent** (subordinate) **clause** must always be accompanied by an independent clause

terms

(*Yellowstone is a national park in the West that is known for its geysers.*).
Subordinate clauses are classified according to their function in a sentence. An **adjective clause** (sometimes called a **relative clause**) modifies nouns or pronouns: *That philodendron, which grew to be twelve feet tall, finally died.* (the clause modifies *philodendron*). An **adverb clause** modifies single words (verbs, adjectives, or adverbs) or an entire phrase or clause: *The film was exposed when Bill opened the camera.* (the clause modifies *exposed*). A **noun clause** acts as a noun (as subject, direct object, indirect object, or complement) in a sentence: *Whoever arrives first wins the prize.* (the clause is the subject of the sentence). An **elliptical clause** is grammatically incomplete—that is, part or all of the subject or predicate is missing. If the missing part can be easily inferred from the context of the sentence, such a construction is acceptable: *When (they are) pressed, the committee will act.* **6d**

   climactic word order   The writing strategy of moving from the least important to the most important point in a sentence and ending with the key idea. **8a.2**

   collective noun   See noun.

   comma splice   A run-on sentence that occurs when two independent clauses are incorrectly joined by a comma. **12a–12e**

COMMA SPLICE:	The Mississippi River flows south, the Red River flows north.
REVISED:	The Mississippi River flows south. The Red River flows north.
REVISED:	The Mississippi River flows south; the Red River flows north.
REVISED:	The Mississippi River flows south, and the Red River flows north.

   common noun   See noun.

   comparison   The form taken by an adjective or an adverb to indicate degree. The **positive degree** describes a quality without indicating comparison (*Frank is tall.*) The **comparative degree** indicates comparison between two persons or things (*Frank is taller than John.*) The **superlative degree** indicates comparison between one person or thing and two or more others (*Frank is the tallest boy in his scout troop.*). **24c**

   comparative degree   See comparison.

   complement   A word or words that describes or renames a subject, an object, or a verb. A **subject complement** is a word or phrase that follows a **linking verb** and renames the subject. It can be an adjective (called a **predicate adjective**) or a noun (called a **predicate nominative**): *Clark Gable was a movie star.* An **object complement** is a word or phrase that describes or renames a direct object. Object complements can be either adjectives or nouns: *We built the treehouse out of wood.*

terms

complete predicate See predicate.

complete subject See subject.

complex sentence See sentence.

compound Two or more words that function as a unit, such as compound nouns: *attorney at law; boardwalk;* compound adjectives: *hard-hitting editorial;* compound prepositions: *by way of, in addition to;* compound subjects: *April and May are spring months.;* compound predicates: *Many have tried and failed to change his mind.*

compound adjective See compound.

compound noun See compound.

compound predicate See compound.

compound preposition See compound.

compound sentence See sentence.

compound subject See compound.

compound-complex sentence See sentence.

conjunction A word or words used to connect single words, phrases, clauses, and sentences. Coordinating conjunctions (*and, or, but, nor, for, so, yet*) connect words, phrases, or clauses of equal weight: *crime and punishment* (coordinating conjunction *and* connects two words). Correlative conjunctions (*both . . . and, either . . . or, neither . . . nor*), always used in pairs, also link items of equal weight: *Neither Texas nor Florida crosses the Tropic of Cancer.* (correlative conjunction *neither . . . nor* connects two words). Subordinating conjunctions (*since, because, although, if, after,* and so on) introduce adverbial clauses: *You will have to pay for the tickets now because I will not be here later.* (subordinating conjunction *because* introduces the adverbial clause). **20g**

conjunctive adverb An adverb that joins and relates independent clauses in a sentence (*also, anyway, besides, hence, however, nevertheless, still,* and so on): *Howard tried out for the Yankees; however, he didn't make the team.* **20e**

connotation The emotional associations that surround a word. (Contrast denotation.) **16b.1**

contraction The combination of two words with an apostrophe replacing the missing letters: *we + will = we'll; was + not = wasn't.*

coordinate adjective One of a series of adjectives that modify the same word or word group: *The glen was quiet, shady, and cool.*

coordinating conjunction See conjunction.

coordination The pairing of similar elements (words, phrases, or clauses) to give equal weight to each. Coordination is used in simple sentences to link similar elements to form compound subjects, predicates, complements, or modifiers. It can also link two independent clauses to form a compound sentence: *The sky was cloudy, and it looked like rain.* (Contrast subordination.) **7a**

correlative conjunction See conjunction.

terms

cumulative sentence A sentence that begins with a main clause followed by additional words, phrases, or clauses that expand or develop it: *On the hill stood a schoolhouse, paint peeling, windows boarded, playground overgrown with weeds.*

dangling modifier A modifier for which no true headword appears in the sentence. To correct dangling modifiers, either change the subject of the sentence's main clause, creating a subject that can logically serve as the headword of the dangling modifier, or add words that transform the dangling modifier into a subordinate clause. **13e–13g**

DANGLING: Pumping up the tire, the trip continued.

REVISED: After pumping up the tire, they continued the trip.

dead metaphor A metaphor so overused that it has become a pat, meaningless cliché. **16e.1**

declarative sentence See sentence.

demonstrative adjective See adjective.

demonstrative pronoun See pronoun.

denotation The dictionary meaning of a word. (Contrast connotation.) **16b.1**

dependent clause See clause.

descriptive adjective See adjective.

direct address A word or phrase within a sentence that indicates the person, group, or thing spoken to: *Remember, scouts, to do a good deed today. Drivers, start your engines.*

direct object See object.

direct quotation See quotation.

double negative The use of two negative words within a single sentence: *She didn't have no time.* Such constructions are nonstandard English. Revised: *She had no time* or *She did not have time.*

ellipsis mark Three spaced periods used to indicate the omission of a word or words from a quotation: *"The time has come . . . and we must part."* **30o–30q**

elliptical clause See clause.

embedding A strategy for varying sentence structure that involves changing some sentences into modifying phrases and working them into other sentences. **10b.3**

expletive A construction in which *there* or *it* is used with a form of the verb *be: There is no one here by that name.*

faulty parallelism See parallelism.

figurative language Imaginative comparisons between different ideas or objects using common figures of speech—simile, metaphor, analogy, personification, and allusion. **16d**

figure of speech See figurative language.

finite verb A verb that can stand as the main verb of a sentence. Unlike **participles, gerunds,** and **infinitives** (see **verbal**), finite verbs do

terms

not require an auxiliary in order to function as the main verb: *The rooster crowed.*

fragment See sentence fragment.

function word An article, preposition, conjunction, or auxiliary verb that indicates the function of and the grammatical relationship among the nouns, verbs, and modifiers in a sentence.

fused sentence A run-on sentence that occurs when two independent clauses are joined either without suitable punctuation or without a coordinating conjunction. Fused sentences can be corrected by separating the independent clauses with a period, a semicolon, or a comma and a **coordinating conjunction;** or by using **subordination. 12f–12i**

FUSED SENTENCE:	Protein is needed for good nutrition lipids and carbohydrates are too.
REVISED:	Protein is needed for good nutrition. Lipids and carbohydrates are too.
REVISED:	Protein is needed for good nutrition; lipids and carbohydrates are too.
REVISED:	Protein is needed for good nutrition, but lipids and carbohydrates are too.
REVISED:	Although protein is needed for good nutrition, lipids and carbohydrates are too.

gender The classification of nouns and pronouns as masculine (*mailman, butler, lad, he*), feminine (*chambermaid, hostess, girl, she*), or neuter (*letter carrier, radio, kitten, them*).

genitive case See case.

gerund A special form of verb ending in *-ing* that is always used as a noun. *Fishing is relaxing.* (gerund *fishing* serves as subject; gerund *relaxing* serves as subject complement) Note: When the *-ing* form of a verb is used as a modifier, it is considered a **present participle.** (See also **verbal.**)

gerund phrase See phrase.

headword The word or phrase in a sentence that is described, defined, or limited by a modifier.

helping verb See auxiliary verb.

idiom An expression that is characteristic of a particular language and whose meaning is not predictable from the meaning of its individual words: *lend a hand.*

imperative mood See mood.

indefinite adjective See adjective.

indefinite pronoun See pronoun.

independent clause See clause.

indicative mood See mood.

terms

indirect object See object.

indirect question A question that tells what has been asked but, because it does not use the speaker's exact words, does not take a question mark: *He asked for permission to use the family car.*

indirect quotation See quotation.

infinitive The base form of the verb preceded by *to,* an infinitive can serve as an adjective (*He is the man to watch.*), an adverb (*Chris hoped to break the record.*), or a noun (*To err is human.*). See also **verbal**.

infinitive phrase See phrase.

intensifier A word that adds emphasis but not additional meaning to words it modifies: *much, really, too, very,* and *so* are typical intensifiers.

intensive pronoun See pronoun.

interjection A grammatically independent word, which expresses emotion, that is used as an exclamation. Interjections can be set off by a comma, or, for greater emphasis, they can be punctuated as independent units, set off by an exclamation point: *Ouch! That hurt.* 20h

interrogative adjective See adjective.

interrogative adverb See adverb.

interrogative pronoun See pronoun.

intransitive verb See verb.

inverted appositive See appositive.

irregular verb A verb that does not form both its past tense and past participle by the addition of *-d* or *-ed* to the base form of the verb. 22a–22b

isolate Any word, including **interjections,** that can be used in isolation: *Yes. No. Hello. Good-bye. Please. Thank you.*

linking verb A verb that connects a subject to its complement: *The crowd became quiet.* Words that can be used as linking verbs include *seem, appear, believe, become, grow, turn, remain, prove, look, sound, smell, taste, feel,* and forms of the verb *be.*

main clause See clause.

main verb See verb.

mass noun See noun.

metaphor A form of figurative language in which the writer makes an implied comparison between two unlike items, equating them in an unexpected way: *He rode the subway, coursing through the arteries of the city.* 16d.2

misplaced modifier A modifier that has no clear relationship with its headword, usually because it is placed too far from it. 13a–d

MISPLACED: By changing his diapers, Dan learned much about the new baby.

REVISED: Dan learned much about the new baby by changing his diapers.

terms

mixed construction A sentence made up of two or more parts that do not fit together grammatically, causing readers to have trouble determining meaning. 15b

MIXED: The Great Chicago Fire caused terrible destruction was what prompted changes in the fire code. (independent clause used as a subject)

REVISED: The terrible destruction of the Great Chicago Fire prompted changes in the fire code.

REVISED: Because of the terrible destruction of the Great Chicago Fire, the fire code was changed.

mixed metaphor The combination of two or more incompatible images in a single figure of speech: *During the race John kept a stiff upper lip as he ran like the wind.* 16e.2

modal auxiliary See verb.

modifier A word that adds information to a sentence and shows connections between ideas.

mood The verb form that indicates the writer's basic attitude. There are three moods in English. The **indicative mood** is used for statements and questions: *Nebraska became a state in 1867.* 22g The **imperative mood** specifies commands or requests and is often used without a subject: *(You) Pay the rent.* 22h The **subjunctive mood** expresses wishes or hypothetical conditions: *I wish the sun were shining.* 22i

nominal A word, phrase, or clause that functions as a noun.

nominative case See case.

nonfinite verb See verbal.

nonrestrictive modifier A modifying phrase or clause that does not limit or particularize the words it modifies, but rather supplies additional information about them. Nonrestrictive modifiers are set off by commas: *Oregano, also known as marjoram and suganda, is a member of the mint family.* 26d.1 (Contrast **restrictive modifier.**)

noun A word that names people, places, things, ideas, actions, or qualities. A **common noun** names any of a class of people, places, or things: *lawyer, town, bicycle.* A **proper noun,** always capitalized, refers to a particular person, place, or thing: *F. Lee Bailey, Chicago, Schwinn.* A **mass noun** names a quantity that is not countable: *sand, time, work.* An **abstract noun** refers to an intangible idea or quality: *bravery, equality, hunger.* A **collective noun** designates a group of people, places, or things thought of as a unit: *Congress, police, family.* 20a

noun clause See clause.

noun phrase See phrase.

number The form taken by a noun, pronoun, demonstrative adjective, or verb to indicate one (**singular**): *car, he, this book, boasts;* or many (**plural**): *cars, they, those books, boast.* 15a.4

numerical adjective See adjective.

terms

object A noun, pronoun, or other noun substitute that is influenced by a transitive verb, verbal, or preposition. A direct object indicates where the verb's action is directed and who or what is affected by it: *John caught a butterfly.* An indirect object tells to or for whom the verb's action was done: *John gave Nancy his butterfly.* An object of a preposition is a word or word group introduced by a preposition: *John gave Nancy his butterfly for an hour.*

object complement See complement.

object of a preposition See object.

objective case See case.

ordinal number A number that indicates position in a series: *seventh, thirtieth, one-hundredth.*

parallelism The use of similar grammatical elements in sentences or parts of sentences: *We serve beer, wine, and soft drinks.* Words, phrases, clauses, or complete sentences may be parallel, and parallel items may be paired or presented in a series. When elements that have the same function in a sentence are not presented in the same terms, the sentence is flawed by **faulty parallelism. 8c**

participial phrase See phrase.

participle A verb form that functions in a sentence as an adjective. Virtually every verb has a **present participle,** which ends in *-ing* (*breaking, leaking, taking*), and a **past participle,** which usually ends in *-d* or *-ed* (*agreed, walked, taken*). Note: When the *-ing* form of a verb is used as a noun, it is considered a gerund. (See also verbal.) Present participle: *The heaving seas swamped the dinghy.* (present participle *heaving* modifies noun *seas*); past participle: *The aged deserve respect.* (past participle *aged* is the subject of the sentence)

parts of speech The eight basic building blocks for all English sentences: *nouns, pronouns, verbs, adjectives, adverbs, prepositions, conjunctions,* and *interjections.*

passive voice See voice.

past participle See participle.

periodic sentence A sentence that moves from a number of specific examples to a conclusion. A strategy for achieving **subordination** through a gradual building of intensity until a climax is reached in the main clause: *Wan and pale and looking ready to crumble, the marathoner headed into the last mile of the race.*

person The form a pronoun or verb takes to indicate the speaker (first person): *I am/we are;* those spoken to (second person): *you are;* and those spoken about (third person): *he, she, it is; they are.* **15a.4**

personal pronoun See pronoun.

personification A form of figurative language in which the writer describes an idea or inanimate object in terms that imply human attributes, feelings, or powers: *The big feather bed beckoned to my tired body.* **16d.4**

terms

phrase   A grammatically ordered group of related words that lacks a subject or a predicate or both and functions as a single part of speech. A **verb phrase** consists of the word or words that denote the subject's action or state of being: *The wind was blowing hard.* A **noun phrase** includes a noun or pronoun plus all related modifiers: *She broke the track record.* A **prepositional phrase** consists of a preposition, its object, and any modifiers of that object: *The errant ball sailed over the fence.* A **verbal phrase** consists of a verbal and its related objects, modifiers, or complements. A verbal phrase may be a **participial phrase** (*Undaunted by the sheer cliff, the climber scaled the rock.*), a **gerund phrase** (*Swinging from trees is a monkey's favorite way to travel.*), or an **infinitive phrase** (*Wednesday is Bill's night to cook spaghetti.*) An **absolute phrase** usually consists of a noun or pronoun and a participle, accompanied by modifiers: *His heart racing, he dialed her number.* 6d

positive degree   See comparison.

possessive adjective   See adjective.

possessive case   See case.

predicate   A verb or verb phrase that tells or asks something about the subject of a sentence is called a **simple predicate**: *Well-tended lawns grow green and thick.* (*grow* is the simple predicate) A **complete predicate** includes all the words associated with the predicate: *Well-tended lawns grow green and thick.* (*grow green and thick* is the complete predicate) 6a

predicate adjective   See complement.

prefix   A letter or group of letters put before a root or word that adds to, changes, or modifies it. 18e.2

preposition   A part of speech that introduces a word or word group consisting of one or more nouns or pronouns or of a phrase or clause functioning in the sentence as a noun: *Jeremy crawled under the bed.* 20f

prepositional phrase   See phrase

present participle   See participle

principal parts   The forms of a verb from which all other forms can be derived. The principal parts are the **base form** (*give*), the **present particle** (*giving*), the **past tense** (*gave*), and the **past participle** (*given*).

pronoun   A word that may be used in place of a noun in a sentence. The noun for which a pronoun stands is called its **antecedent**. There are eight different types of pronouns. Some have the same form but are distinguished by their function in the sentence. A **personal pronoun** stands for a person or thing: *I, me, we, us, my,* and so on. (*They broke his window.*) A **reflexive pronoun** ends in *-self* or *-selves* and refers to the subject of the sentence or clause: *myself, yourself, himself,* and so on. (*They painted the house themselves.*) An **intensive pronoun** ends in *-self* or *-selves* and emphasizes a noun or pronoun. (*Custer himself died in the battle.*) A **relative pronoun** introduces an adjective or noun clause

terms

in a sentence: *which, who, whom,* and so on. (*Sitting Bull was the Sioux chief who defeated Custer.*) An **interrogative pronoun** introduces a question: *who, which, what, whom,* and so on. (*Who won the lottery?*) A **demonstrative pronoun** points to a particular thing or group of things: *this, that, these, those.* (*Who was that masked man?*) A **reciprocal pronoun** denotes a mutual relationship: *each other, one another.* (*We still have each other.*) An **indefinite pronoun** refers to persons or things in general, not to specific individuals. Most indefinite pronouns are singular: *anyone, everyone, one, each,* but some are always plural: *both, many, several.* (*Many are called, but few are chosen.*) **20b**

 proper adjective See adjective

 proper noun See noun.

 quotation The use of the written or spoken words of others. A direct quotation occurs when a passage is borrowed word for word from another source. Quotation marks (" ") establish the boundaries of a direct quotation: *"These tortillas taste like cardboard," complained Beth.* **29a** An indirect quotation reports someone else's written or spoken words without quoting that person directly. Quotation marks are not used: *Beth complained that the tortillas tasted like cardboard.*

 reciprocal pronoun See pronoun

 reflexive pronoun See pronoun.

 regular verb A verb that forms both its past tense and past participle by the addition of *-d* or *-ed* to the base form of the verb. **22**

 relative adverb See adverb.

 relative clause See clause.

 relative pronoun See pronoun.

 restrictive modifier A modifying phrase or clause that limits the meaning of the word or word group it modifies. Restrictive modifiers are not set off by commas: *The Ferrari that ran over the fireplug was red.* **26d.1** (Contrast nonrestrictive modifier.)

 root A word from which other words are formed. An understanding of a root word increases understanding of other unfamiliar words that incorporate the root. **18e.2**

 run-on sentence An incorrect construction that results when the proper connective or punctuation does not appear between independent clauses. A run-on occurs either as a **comma splice** or as a **fused sentence.**

 sentence An independent grammatical unit that contains a subject and a predicate and expresses a complete thought: *Carolyn sold her car.* **6a** Sentences can be classified in any one of four ways: A **simple sentence** consists of one subject and one predicate: The season ended. **6e**; a compound sentence is formed when two or more simple sentences are connected with coordinating conjunctions, conjunctive adverbs, semicolons, or colons: *The rain stopped, and the sun began to shine.* **7a**; a complex sentence consists of one simple sentence, which functions as

terms

an independent clause in the complex sentence, and at least one dependent clause, which is introduced by a subordinating conjunction or a relative pronoun: *When he had sold three boxes* (dependent clause), *he was halfway to his goal.* (independent clause) **7b**; and a **compound-complex sentence** consists of two or more independent clauses and at least one dependent clause: *After he prepared a shopping list* (dependent clause), *he went to the store* (independent clause), *but it was closed.* (independent clause) **7c**

sentence fragment An incomplete sentence, phrase, or clause that is punctuated as if it were a complete sentence. **11**

shift A change of *tense, voice, mood, person, number,* or *type of discourse* within or between sentences. Some shifts are necessary, but problems occur with unnecessary or illogical shifts. **15a**

simile A form of figurative language in which the writer makes a comparison, introduced by *like* or *as*, between two unlike items on the basis of a shared quality: *Like sands through the hourglass, so are the days of our lives.; The wind was as biting as his neighbor's doberman.* **16d.1**

simple predicate See predicate.

simple sentence See sentence.

simple subject See subject.

split infinitive An infinitive whose parts are separated by a modifier. **13d**

SPLIT: She expected *to* ultimately *swim* the channel.

REVISED: She expected ultimately *to swim* the channel.

squinting modifier A modifier that seems to modify either a word before it or one after it and conveys a different meaning in each case. **13a**

SQUINTING: The task completed simply delighted him.

REVISED: He was delighted to have the task completed simply.

REVISED: He was simply delighted to have the task completed.

subject A noun or noun substitute that tells who or what a sentence is about is called a **simple subject**: *Healthy thoroughbred horses run like the wind.* (*horses* is the simple subject) The **complete subject** of a sentence includes all the words associated with the subject: *Healthy thoroughbred horses run like the wind.* (*healthy thoroughbred horses* is the complete subject) **6a**

subject complement See complement.

subjective case See case.

subjunctive mood See mood.

subordinate clause See clause.

subordination Making one or more clauses of a sentence gram-

terms

matically dependent upon another element in a sentence: *Preston was only eighteen when he joined the firm.* (Contrast **coordination**.) **7b**

    subordinating conjunction See conjunction.

    suffix A syllable added at the end of a word or root that changes its part of speech. **18e.2**

    superlative degree See comparison.

    suspended hyphen A hyphen followed by a space or by the appropriate punctuation and a space: *The wagon was pulled by a two-, four-, or six-horse team.*

    tag question A question, consisting of an auxiliary verb plus a pronoun, that is added to a statement and set off by a comma: *You know it's going to rain, don't you?*

    tense The form of a verb that indicates when an action has occurred or when a condition existed. **22c–22f**

    transitive verb See verb.

    verb A word or phrase that expresses action (*He painted the fence.*) or a state of being (*Henry believes in equality.*) A **main verb** carries most of the meaning in the sentence or clause in which it appears: *Winston Churchill smoked long, thick cigars.* A main verb is a **linking verb** when it is followed by a subject complement: *Dogs are good pets.* An **auxiliary verb** (sometimes called a **helping verb**) combines with the main verb to form a **verb phrase**: *Graduation day has arrived.* The auxiliaries *be* and *have* are used to indicate the tense and voice of the main verb. The auxiliary *do* is used for asking questions and forming negative statements. Other auxiliary verbs, known as **modal auxiliaries** (*must, will, can, could, may, might, ought (to), should,* and *would*), indicate necessity, possibility, willingness, obligation, and ability. *It might rain next Tuesday.* A **transitive verb** requires an object to complete its meaning in the sentence: *Pete drank all the wine.* (*wine* is the direct object) An **intransitive verb** has no direct object: *The candle glowed.* **20c**

    verb phrase See phrase.

    verbal (nonfinite verb) Verb forms—**participles, infinitives,** and **gerunds**—that are used as nouns, adjectives, or adverbs. Verbals do not behave like verbs. Only when used with an auxiliary can such a verb form serve as the main verb of a sentence. *The wall painted* is not a sentence; *The wall was painted* is. **20c**

    verbal phrase See phrase.

    voice The form that determines whether the subject of a verb is acting or is acted upon. When the subject of a verb performs the action, the verb is in the **active voice**: *Palmer sank a thirty-foot putt.* When the subject of a verb receives the action—that is, is acted upon—the verb is in the **passive voice**: *A thirty-foot putt was sunk by Palmer.* **8e**

terms

Acknowledgments

p. 6   Copyright © 1983 by the New York Times Company. Reprinted by permission.

pp. 15–17   From *Born on the Fourth of July* by Ron Kovic, pp. 37–39, © 1976 McGraw-Hill Book Company. Reprinted by permission.

pp. 63–64   Reprinted from *Seventeen* Magazine. Copyright © 1972 by Triangle Communications, Inc. All rights reserved.

pp. 118–119   From *Science and Human Values* by J. Bronowski. Copyright © 1956, 1965 by J. Bronowski. Reprinted by permission of Julian Messner, a division of Simon & Schuster, Inc.

pp. 202–203   Adapted from *How Would Your Life Be Different If You'de Been Born a Boy?* by Carol Tavres with Alice I. Baumgartner.

pp. 277–278   From *World of Our Fathers* by Irving Howe. Reprinted by permission of Harcourt Brace Jovanovich, Inc.

p. 555   Courtesy of *ERIC*, Current Index to Journals in Education.

p. 556   From *The Humanities Index.*

pp. 568–569   From *The Second Self.* Copyright © 1984 by Sherry Turkle. Reprinted by permission of Simon & Schuster, Inc.

pp. 573–574   Reprinted by permission of the Putnam Publishing Group from *Great Expectations: America and the Baby Boom Generation* by Landon Y. Jones. Copyright © 1980 by Landon Y. Jones.

p. 626   From *Exile's Return* by Malcolm Cowley. Copyright © 1976, 1978, 1980 by Malcolm Cowley. Reprinted by permission of Viking Penguin, Inc.

Index

Numbers in **boldface** refer to sections of the handbook; other numbers refer to pages.

Guide to the Plan of the Book

The detailed table of contents on the following pages highlights key elements of the table of contents on pages ix to xix and gives an overview of the entire book. Use this guide when you are looking for a specific subject or a discussion that you know is part of a specific chapter. Your instructor may also use this guide to direct you to a particular topic within a chapter.